N F T ™

Not For Tourists™ Guide to **BOSTON**

Get more on
notfortourists.com

Keep connected with:

Twitter:
twitter//notfortourists

D1332029

Cardiff Libraries
www.cardiff.gov.uk/libraries

Llyfrgelloedd Caer
www.ca...f.gov.uk/llyfrg

2010

Published and designed by:
Not For Tourists, Inc.
NFT.—Not For Tourists. Guide to BOSTON 2010
www.notfortourists.com

Publisher
Jane Pirone

Information Design
Jane Pirone
Rob Tallia
Scot Covey

Managing Editors
Craig Nelson
Rob Tallia

Design Production Manager
Aaron Schielke

Database Manager
Michael Dale

City Editor
Patrick Hellen

Writing and Editing
Patrick Hellen
Emily Doutre

Research
Deborah Blumenthal
Michael Dale
Melanie Grave

Contributors
Brian Colby
Stuart Spina

Graphic Design/Production
Suzan Choy
Ching Hsieh
Aaron Schielke

Sales & Marketing
Lea Garrett
Sarah Hocevar
Michael Salerno

Web Guru
Juan Molinari

Printed in China
ISBN# 978-0-9795339-1-4 $16.99
Copyright © 2009 by Not For Tourists, Inc.

Every effort has been made to ensure that the information in this book is as up-to-date as possible at press time. However, many details are liable to change—as we have learned. The publishers cannot accept responsibility for any consequences arising from the use of this book.

Not For Tourists does not solicit individuals, organizations, or businesses for listings inclusion in our guides, nor do we accept payment for inclusion into the editorial portion of our book; the advertising sections, however, are exempt from this policy. We always welcome communications from anyone regarding ANYTHING having to do with our books; please visit us on our website at www.notfortourists.com for appropriate contact information.

Dear Non-Tourist,

Welcome to your 2010 NFT Guide to the Hub of the Universe, Boston, Massachusetts. Within these black bound and pocket sized pages, our crack team of Writer/Editor Gods and Goddesses present to you all the information you need for this great city. We've barely slept in the last year as we've doggedly hunted down every single item that a non-tourist needs to know. As you turn these pages, you'll find hundreds of places to eat, drink, dance, go "Hmmmmm" at artwork, shop, catch a live show, and maybe even catch a foul ball.

Of course, none of this incredible guide could have been possible without our fellow Boston contributors that we call out on the facing page. They are the front line troops, investigating every new food joint to make sure it's up to snuff, and sampling every drop of booze in that new bar before recommending it your way. In short, if it's worth knowing about, we at NFT have done our damnedest to present it to you here. In fact, we're so sure that this guide will prove indispensable, we'll wait here while you go up and purchase it. Go on. It's worth it.

Now, don't think that we only look internally for information on our fair city. We rely on the feedback and suggestions that you, our readers, send our way. If we missed something or if there's anything you'd like to see in the next edition of NFT Boston, please hit us up on the web at www.notfortourists.com and let us know. This is a Guide-ocracy, not a Guide-tatorship, so we value your contributions mightily.

While you're there, take a look at the daily "On Our Radar," for up to the minute tips on restaurants, events, new products (maybe you've heard of this thing called an iPhone app?) sign up for the weekly newsletter, and feel free to become a member and submit a review or listing yourself.

Here's hoping you find what you need,

Jane, Rob, Craig, and Patrick

Central Boston

Map 1 • Beacon Hill / West End.....................6
Map 2 • North End / Faneuil Hall 12
Map 3 • Downtown Crossing / Park Square /
    Bay Village 18
Map 4 • Financial District / Chinatown............24
Map 5 • Back Bay (West) / Fenway (East)...........30
Map 6 • Back Bay (East) / South End (Upper)......36
Map 7 • South End (Lower)..........................42

Waterfront Boston

Map 8 • Charlestown 48
Map 9 • East Boston 54
Map 10 • South Boston (West) / Fort Point........60
Map 11 • South Boston (East) 66

JP, Fenway & Roxbury

Map 12 • Newmarket / Andrew Square...........72
Map 13 • Roxbury 78
Map 14 • Jamaica Plain 84
Map 15 • Fenway (West) / Mission Hill.............90

Brookline & Allston/Brighton

Map 16 • Kenmore Square / Brookline (East)......96
Map 17 • Coolidge Corner / Brookline Hills 102
Map 18 • Brighton..................................108
Map 19 • Allston (South) / Brookline (North).....114

Cambridge & Somerville

Map 20 • Harvard Square / Allston (North).......120
Map 21 • West Cambridge 126
Map 22 • North Cambridge / West Somerville ...132
Map 23 • Central Somerville / Porter Square 138
Map 24 • Winter Hill / Union Square.............144
Map 25 • East Somerville / Sullivan Square 150
Map 26 • East Cambridge / Kendall Square / MIT 156
Map 27 • Central Square / Cambridgeport.......162
Map 28 • Inman Square.........................168

Dorchester & Southwest

Map 29 • West Roxbury 174
Map 30 • Roslindale...........................176
Map 31 • Mattapan / Dorchester (West).........178
Map 32 • Dorchester (East) 180
Map 33 • Hyde Park...........................182

Parks & Places

Copley Square 184
BPL Central Library...........................185
Cambridge Common...........................186
Charlestown Navy Yard........................187
Boston Common..............................188
Freedom Trail & Black Heritage Trail............189
Emerald Necklace.............................192
Faneuil Hall Marketplace......................194
Long Wharf & Rowes Wharf....................196
Prudential Center.............................198
Newbury Street...............................200
Boston Convention & Exhibition Center.........204
Hynes Convention Center......................206
Bayside Expo & Conference Center..............208
JFK Library & Museum.........................210
Cape Cod....................................211

Colleges & Universities

Berklee College of Music 214
Boston College...............................216
Boston University.............................218
Emerson College..............................220
UMass Boston................................221
Harvard University............................222
MIT..224
Northeastern University.......................226
Tufts University..............................228
Continuing Education.........................230

Sports

Boating / Sailing / Rowing.....................231
Biking 232
Skating......................................234
Tennis.......................................235
Golf / Bowling................................236
Yoga / Billiards...............................237
Hiking.......................................238
Swimming....................................240
Fenway Park..................................241

Gillette Stadium..............................242
TD Garden....................................243

Transit

Logan Airport................................244
The Big Dig...................................246
Bridges and Tunnels..........................247
Driving......................................248
Parking......................................249
MBTA Subway................................250
MBTA Buses / Cambridge EZ Ride..............252
Regional Buses...............................253
MBTA Commuter Rail.........................254
North and South Stations / Amtrak.............256
MBTA Ferries / Water Taxis....................258
Car Rental...................................260
Zipcar.......................................261

General Information

Landmarks...................................262
Hospitals....................................266
Post Offices & Zip Codes......................268
Police.......................................269
FedEx.......................................270
For the Kids..................................272
Libraries.....................................275
LGBT..276
Hotels.......................................278
Practical Information.........................282
Calendar of Events...........................284
Media.......................................286
WiFi & Internet...............................287
Self-Storage / Van & Truck Rental..............288
24-Hour Services.............................289

Arts & Entertainment

Restaurants..................................290
Nightlife.....................................304
Shopping....................................311
Movie Theaters...............................319
Art Galleries 320
Bookstores...................................322
Museums....................................326
Institute of Contemporary Art.................327
Museum of Fine Arts..........................328
Children's Museum of Boston..................330
Theaters.....................................331
Symphony Hall...............................332
Orpheum Theater............................333
Shubert Theater..............................334
Wang Theater................................335

Street Index 343

Boston Area Driving Map
and Downtown Boston Map
foldout, last page

Beacon Hill is still home to some of the most expensive real estate in America. Charming brick row houses reflect a long and storied history; where the State House stands, John Hancock once grazed cows. Full gentrification has yet to reach the West End, where government buildings, hospitals, and tucked-away burrito joints mingle fairly harmoniously.

Banks

- **Bank of America** • 104 Canal St [Valenti]
- **Bank of America** • 161 Cambridge St [Joy St]
- **Bank of America** • 3 Center Plz [Cambridge St]
- **Bank of America (ATM)** • 125 Nashua St [Storrow]
- **Bank of America (ATM)** • 200 Portland St [Valenti]
- **Bank of America (ATM)** • 243 Charles St [Fruit]
- **Bank of America (ATM)** • 45 Charles St [Chestnut St]
- **Banknorth Massachusetts (ATM)** •
  126 Causeway St [Canal St]
- **Cambridge Trust** • 65 Beacon St [Charles St]
- **Citizens Bank** • 1 Center Plz [Cambridge St]
- **Citizens Bank (ATM)** • 122 Cambridge St [Temple St]
- **Citizens Bank (ATM)** • 250 Cambridge St [Garden St]
- **Citizens Bank (ATM)** • 55 Fruit St [N Grove]
- **Citizens Bank (ATM)** • Boston Museum of Science •
  Science Park [Monsignor O'Brien Hwy]
- **Sovereign Bank** • 1 Beacon St [Tremont St]
- **Sovereign Bank** • 125 Causeway St [Canal St]
- **Sovereign Bank** • 67 Beacon St [Charles St]
- **Sovereign Bank (ATM)** • 1 Ashburton Pl [Somerset St]
- **Sovereign Bank (ATM)** • CVS/Pharmacy •
  191 Cambridge St [S Russell]
- **Sovereign Bank (ATM)** • CVS/Pharmacy •
  2 Center Plz [Somerset St]
- **Sovereign Bank (ATM)** • 27 Beacon St [Park St]

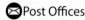 Donuts

- **Dunkin' Donuts** • 106 Cambridge St [Bowdoin]
- **Dunkin' Donuts** • 111 Causeway St [Friend]
- **Dunkin' Donuts** • 125 Nashua St [Storrow]
- **Dunkin' Donuts** • 16 Tremont St [Court]
- **Dunkin' Donuts** • 180 Canal St [Causeway]
- **Dunkin' Donuts** • 22 Beacon St [Bowdoin]
- **Dunkin' Donuts** • 59 Causeway St [Lancaster St]

Emergency Rooms

- **Massachusetts Eye and Ear Infirmary** •
  243 Charles St [Fruit]
- **Massachusetts General Hospital** •
  55 Fruit St [N Grove]

Landmarks

- **Abiel Smith School** • 46 Joy St [Smith Ct]
- **Acorn Street** • b/w West Cedar St & Willow St, running
  parallel to Chestnut St
- **Boston Athenaeum** • 10 1/2 Beacon St [Somerset St]
- **Longfellow Bridge** • Cambridge St & Charles St
- **Louisburg Square** • b/w Mt Vernon St & Pinckney St
- **Make Way for Ducklings** • Beacon St & Charles St
- **Massachusetts General Hospital** • 55 Fruit St [N Grove]
- **TD Garden** • 150 Causeway St [Beverly]
- **Vilna Shul** • 18 Phillips St [Garden St]

Libraries

- **West End** • 151 Cambridge St [Lynde]

Pharmacies

- **Rite Aid** • 100 Cambridge St [Bowdoin]
- **CVS** • 155 Charles St [Silver Pl]
- **CVS** • 191 Cambridge St [S Russell]
- **CVS** • 2 Center Plz [Cambridge St]
- **Gary Drug** • 59 Charles St [Mount Vernon St]

Police

- **District A-1**
  (Temorariy relocated to 152 North End St) •
  40 New Sudbury St [Bulfinch]

Post Offices

- **Charles Street Station** • 136 Charles St [Revere St]
- **John F Kennedy Station** • 25 New Chardon St [Bulfinch]
- **State House Station** • 24 Beacon St [Park St]

Schools

- **Advent School** • 15 Brimmer St [Pinckney]
- **Boston Children's School** • 8 Whittier Pl [Martha]
- **Park Street School** • 67 Brimmer St [Chestnut St]
- **Suffolk University** • 8 Ashburton Pl [Somerset St]

Supermarkets

- **Whole Foods Market** • 181 Cambridge St [Joy St]

Map 1 · Beacon Hill / West End

N

Land Blvd

O'Brien Hwy

▶26

Museum of Science

Charles River

8▼

Leverett Connector

Charles/Charlestown

Nashua St.

Science Park

Leverett Cir

Whittier Pl.   Martha Rd.   Amy Ct.

Emerson Pl.

Merrimac St.

B&M Railroad

West St.

93

PAGE 243
TD Garden/
North Station

PAGE 256

North Station

Haverhill St.

Canal St.

Causeway St.

O'Neill Federal Building

Lomasney Way

A

Charles St.

Blossom St.

Hawkins St.
Hancock Pl.

Massachusetts General Hospital

William Cardinal O'Connell Way

Stanford St.

Longfellow Pl.

Merrimac St.

Courthouse

New Chardon St.

Bowker St.

2▶

State Service Center

Hawkins St.

Fruit St.

Parkman St.

Bridge Ct.
Adams Pl.

Cambridge St. Ave.

Grove St.

Charles/MGH

Longfellow Bridge

Lindall Pl.

Anderson St.

Garden Arch

3

Russell St.

Cambridge St.

Smith Ct.

Temple St.

North Russell St.

Bowdoin

Bulfinch Pl.

New Sudbury St.

Somerset St.

Storrow Dr.

Irving St.

Phillips St.

Chambers St.

Goffin

Garden St.

Joy St.

Hancock St.

Derne St.

Bowdoin St.

State Office Buildings

Center Plaza

Storrow Dr.

W Hill Pl.

Silver Pl.

Putnam Ave.

Myrtle St.

Ashburton Pl.

County Courthouse

Charles River Esplanade

Charles St.

Revere St.

Pinckney St.

W Cedar St.

Brimmer St.

Mt. Vernon Sq.

Louisburg Sq.

Mt. Vernon Pl.

Mass. State House

Pemberton Sq.

Tremont St.

B

Acorn St.

Mt. Vernon Pl.

Joy Pl.

Park Pl.

Bowdoin St.

Mugar Way

Lime St.

Chestnut St.

Walnut St.

Beacon St.

Park St.

Bosworth St.

Wesleyan Pl. Bromfield

Spruce St.

Spruce Pl.

Branch St.

Beaver Pl.

Byron St.

Beacon St.

Park St.

Hamilton Pl.

Temple Pl.

Winter St.

West St.

Storrow Dr.

Embankment Rd.

3▼

PAGE 188

Frog Pond

Downtown Crossing

Public Garden

Charles St.

The

Boston Common

1/4 mile   .25 km

Sundries / Entertainment

Map 1

Locals praise the community feel of the square mile that constitutes Beacon Hill. Pubs like Seven's and The Four's cater to sports fans, and the crispy pizza at Upper Crust causes mini sidewalk traffic jams. The Public Garden and Boston Common function as the neighborhood's backyard.

Coffee

- **Bagels Etc** • 70 Staniford St [Longfellow Pl]
- **Capital Coffee House** • 122 Bowdoin St [Ashburton]
- **Starbucks** • 1 Charles St [Beacon St]
- **Starbucks** • 222 Cambridge St [Irving St]
- **Starbucks** • 97 Charles St [Pinckney]
- **Tammy's Place** • 25 New Sudbury St [Bulfinch]

Copy Shops

- **Copy Clone** • 31 Mt Vernon St [Hancock St]
- **FedEx Kinko's** • 2 Center Plz [Cambridge St] ♿
- **Johnson's Printing** • 15 Tremont Pl [Beacon St]
- **The UPS Store** • 139 Charles St [Revere St]

Gyms

- **Beacon Hill Athletic Club** • 261 Friend St [Causeway]
- **Beacon Hill Athletic Club** • 3 Hancock St [Cambridge St]
- **Boston Sports Club** • 1 Bulfinch Pl [Bowdoin]
- **Fitcorp** • 1 Beacon St [Tremont St]

Hardware Stores

- **Charles Street Supply** • 54 Charles St [Mount Vernon St]

Liquor Stores

- **Beacon Capitol Market** • 32 Myrtle St [Joy St]
- **Beacon Hill Wine & Spirits** • 63 Charles St [Mount Vernon St]
- **Charles Street Liquors** • 143 Charles St [Silver Pl]
- **DeLuca's Market** • 11 Charles St [Branch]
- **Demetri Brothers Liquor & Gifts** • 53 Revere St [Grove St]
- **Jobi's Liquors** • 170 Cambridge St [Joy St]
- **Mccormack's Liquors** • 82 Hancock St [Mount Vernon St]
- **Simmons Liquor Store** • 210 Cambridge St [S Russell]
- **Swetts Liquors** • 3 Somerset St [Beacon St]

Movie Theaters

- **Mugar Omni Theatre** • 1 Science Park [Monsignor O'Brien Hwy]

Nightlife

- **21st Amendment** • 150 Bowdoin St [Mount Vernon St]
- **6B** • 6 Beacon St #B [Tremont Pl]
- **Alibi Lounge** • 215 Charles St [Cambridge St]
- **Beacon Hill Pub** • 149 Charles St [Silver Pl]
- **Cheers** • 84 Beacon St [Brimmer]
- **The Four's** • 166 Canal St [Causeway]
- **Greatest Bar** • 262 Friend St [Causeway]
- **The Harp** • 85 Causeway St [Portland]
- **Hill Tavern** • 228 Cambridge St [Irving St]
- **Seven's** • 77 Charles St [Mount Vernon St]
- **Sullivan's Tap** • 168 Canal St [Causeway]

Restaurants

- **75 Chestnut** • 75 Chestnut St [River St]
- **Artu** • 89 Charles St [Pinckney]
- **Beacon Hill Bistro** • 25 Charles St [Chestnut St]
- **BoYo** • 175 Cambridge St [Chestnut St]
- **Clink.** • 215 Charles St [Fruit St]
- **The Federal** • 204 Cambridge St [S Russell St]
- **The Federalist** • XV Beacon Hotel • 15 Beacon St [Somerset St]
- **Figs** • 42 Charles St [Chestnut St]
- **Grotto** • 37 Bowdoin St [Cambridge St]
- **Harvard Gardens** • 316 Cambridge St [Grove St]
- **Hungry I** • 71 1/2 Charles St [Mount Vernon St]
- **King & I** • 145 Charles St [Silver Pl]
- **Lala Rokh** • 97 Mt Vernon St [W Cedar]
- **Ma Soba** • 156 Cambridge St [Hancock St]
- **Panificio** • 144 Charles St [Silver Pl]
- **The Paramount** • 44 Charles St [Chestnut St]
- **Phoenicia** • 240 Cambridge St [Garden St]
- **Pierrot** • 272 Cambridge St [Anderson St]
- **Pierrot** • 272 Cambridge St [Anderson St]
- **Tory Row** • 3 Brattle Wy [Cambridge St]
- **Upper Crust** • 49 Brattle Wy [Blfinch Pl]
- **Villa Mexico Cafe** • 296 Cambridge St [Grove St]

Shopping

- **Black Ink** • 101 Charles St [Pinckney]
- **DeLuca's Market** • 11 Charles St [Branch]
- **Eugene Galleries** • 76 Charles St [Mount Vernon St]
- **The Flat of the Hill** • 60 Charles St [Mount Vernon St]
- **Good** • 88 Charles St [Pinckney]
- **Hilton's Tent City** • 272 Friend St [Causeway]
- **Moxie** • 51 Charles St [Mount Vernon St]
- **The Red Wagon** • 69 Charles St [Mount Vernon St]
- **Savenor's Market** • 160 Charles St [Cambridge St]
- **Wish** • 49 Charles St [Mount Vernon St]

Video Rental

- **Mike's Movies** • 250 Cambridge St [Garden St]

Map 1 • **Beacon Hill / West End**

Ⓝ

1 **2**

Land Blvd

O'Brien Hwy

26

Museum of Science

Charles River

Nashua St

Science Park

Leverett Connector

Elevated Railroad

8

93

PAGE 243

TD Garden/ North Station

Leverett Cir

Whittier Pl

Martha Rd

Amy Ct

West End

Red Auerbach Way

PAGE 256

North Station

O'Neill Federal Building

A

Emerson Pl

Blossom St

Blossom Ct

Hawthorne Pl

Lomasney Way

Causeway St

Lancaster St

Portland St

Friend St

Merrimac St

4

Longfellow Pl

Massachusetts General Hospital

William Cardinal O'Connell Way

Stanford St

Courthouse

State Service Center

New Chardon St

Beverly St

Valenti Way

Canal St

Haverhill St

2

Charles St

Fruit St

Parkman St

N Bridge Ct

N Anderson St

Adams St

Blossom St

Cambridge St Ave

N Grove St

Cambridge St

Bowker St

Hawkins St

Bulfinch Pl

New Sudbury St

Bowdoin

Charles/MGH

Longfellow Bridge

Cardinal

Lindall Pl

Stong Ct

Anderson Garden Arch

S Russell St

S Anderson St

Irving St

Smith Ct

Temple St

Joy St

Bowdoin St

Somerset St

State Office Buildings

Courthouse

Storrow Dr

Silver Pl

W Hill Pl

Charles River Sq

Revere St

Putnam Ave

Branch Ln

Sentry Hill Pl

Grove Ct

Ridgeway Ln

Phillips St

Garden St

Ridgeway St

Garden Ct St

Chauncy

Anderson St

Myrtle St

Derne St

Ashburton Pl

Pemberton Sq

B

Charles River Esplanade

Storrow Dr

Pinckney St

Brimmer St

Mt Vernon Sq

Charles St

W Cedar St

Cedar Lane Way

Willow St

Louisburg Sq

Acorn St

Wadsworth St

Mt Vernon St

Walnut St

Mt Vernon Pl

Joy Pl

Mass State House

Beacon St

Park St

Tremont St

Bosworth St

Province St

Park St

Brimmer St

Otis Pl

Lime St

Chestnut St

Beaver Pl

Byron St

Spruce Pl

Spruce Ct

Spruce St

Branch St

43 **55**

Beacon St

Park St

Charles St

3

PAGE 188

Frog Pond

Winter St

Temple Pl

Wesleyan Pl

Bromfield

Downtown Crossing

Murray Way

Beaver St

Beacon St

Charles St

Public Garden   The

Boston Common

West St

| 1/4 mile | .25 km |

Public transit (or your own two feet) remains the best way to travel in this parking-scarce neighborhood. A walk down Charles Street from the Charles/MGH Red Line T station to the Boston Common is an especially stress-free way to experience the area. If you simply must drive, be prepared for the havoc wreaked by never-ending construction.

Subway

- Bowdoin
- Charles/MGH
- Downtown Crossing
- North Station
- Park Street
- Science Park

Bus Lines

- **4** · North Station—World Trade Center via Federal Courthouse
- **43** · Ruggles Station—Park & Tremont Streets
- **55** · Jersey & Queensberry Streets—Copley Square or Park & Tremont Streets

Car Rental

- **Avis** · 3 Center Plz [Cambridge St] · 617-534-1400
- **Dollar** · Government Ctr · 209 Cambridge St [S Russell] · 617-723-8312

Car Washes

- **Professional Auto Detailers** · 1 Center Plz [Cambridge St]

Gas Stations

- **Arthur's Sunoco** · 70 River St [Mount Vernon St]
- **Exxon** · 239 Cambridge St [Blossom St] ⏰
- **Gulf** · 296 Cambridge St [Strong]
- **Mobil** · 150 Friend St [Valenti]
- **Sunoco** · 70 River St [Mt Vernon St]

Parking

Boston's version of Little Italy, the North End is a maze of narrow streets and brick buildings with a decidedly European air. With the Rose Kennedy Greenway fully finished, the connection from the North End is once again green, only this time it's grass instead of steel.

Banks

- **Bank of America** · 260 Hanover St [Parmenter]
- **Bank of America** · 60 State St [Kilby St]
- **Bank of America (ATM)** · 2 Atlantic Ave [High St]
- **Bank of America (ATM)** · 283 Causeway St [Endicott St]
- **Bank of America (ATM)** · 4 Commercial St [State]
- **Bank of America (ATM)** · 48-50 Salem St [Morton St]
- **Century Bank** · 136 State St [India St]
- **Century Bank** · 275 Hanover St [Richmond St]
- **Citizens Bank** · 28 State St [Congress]
- **Citizens Bank** · 315 Hanover St [Prince]
- **Citizens Bank** · 53 State St [Congress]
- **Citizens Bank (ATM)** · 1 Boston Pl [Court]
- **Citizens Bank (ATM)** · 1 Cambridge St [Sudbury]
- **Citizens Bank (ATM)** · 1 State St [Washington St]
- **Citizens Bank (ATM)** · 100 City Hall Plz [Cambridge St]
- **Citizens Bank (ATM)** · 177 State St [McKinley]
- **Citizens Bank (ATM)** · 342 Hanover St [N Bennet St]
- **Citizens Bank (ATM)** · 92 State St [Broad]
- **First National Bank of Ipswich** · 33 State St [Congress]
- **Sovereign Bank** · 287 Hanover St [Richmond St]
- **Sovereign Bank** · 75 State St [Kilby St]
- **Sovereign Bank (ATM)** · 1 Union St [North St]
- **Sovereign Bank (ATM)** · Central Wharf [Central St]
- **Sovereign Bank (ATM)** · CVS · 218 Hanover St [Cross St]

Donuts

- **Dunkin' Donuts** · 1 Congress St [North St]
- **Dunkin' Donuts** · 1 TD Banknorth Garden [Hanover St]
- **Dunkin' Donuts** · 100 City Hall Plz [Cambridge St]
- **Dunkin' Donuts** · 111 State St [Broad]
- **Dunkin' Donuts** · 2 City Hall Sq [Cambridge St]
- **Dunkin' Donuts** · 20 North St [Scott Aly]

Landmarks

- **All Saints Way** · Battery St & Hanover St
- **Boston Sailing Center** · 54 Lewis Wharf [Atlantic Ave]
- **The Boston Stone** · Marshall St [Hanover St]
- **Boston Tea Kettle** · 63 Court St [Cambridge St]
- **The Brink's Job** · 165 Prince St [Causeway]
- **Christopher Columbus Park** · Atlantic Ave at Richmond St
- **City Hall** · 1 City Hall Plz [Cambridge St]
- **Faneuil Hall** · Congress St & North St
- **Holocaust Memorial** · Congress St & Union St
- **Leonard P Zakim Bunker Hill Bridge** · 100 Beverly St
- **New England Aquarium** · Central Wharf [Central St]
- **North End Playground** · Commercial St & Foster St
- **Old North Church** · 193 Salem St [Hull St]
- **Paul Revere House** · 19 North Sq [Garden Ct St]
- **Union Oyster House** · 41 Union St [Marshall St]

Libraries

- **North End** · 25 Parmenter St [Hanover St]

Pharmacies

- **CVS** · 218 Hanover St [Cross St]
- **Green Cross Pharmacy** · 393 Hanover St [Clark St]

Post Offices

- **Hanover Street Station** · 217 Hanover St [Cross St]
- **Post Offices** · Faneuil Hall Retail Unit · 1 Faneuil Hall Sq [S Market]

Schools

- **Eliot Elementary** · 16 Charter St [Unity St]
- **St John** · 9 Moon St [Lewis St]

Sundries / Entertainment

While Boston has begun to be much more foodie centric, the North End has been keeping it real for decades. Good luck finding a bad meal. By night, young professionals reemerge from Faneuil Hall and hit the clubs—hard. Night owls stop by Modern Pastry for the best cannoli in the city.

Map 2

☕ Coffee

- **Anne-Marie's Place** •
  251 Causeway St [Medford St]
- **Boston Bean Stock Coffee** •
  97 Salem St [Wiget]
- **Caffe Paradiso** •
  255 Hanover St [Richmond St]
- **Caffe Victoria** • 296 Hanover St [Prince]
- **Causeway Café** •
  239 Causeway St [Medford St]
- **Contrata's** • 396 Hanover St [Salutation]
- **Polcari's Coffee Shop** •
  105 Salem St [Parmenter]
- **Red Barn Coffee Roasters** •
  1 Faneuil Hall Sq [S Market]
- **Starbucks** • 2 Atlantic Ave [High St]
- **Starbucks** •
  Faneuil Hall Marketplace [Commercial St]
- **Starbucks** • Boston Long Wharf Marriott
  • 296 State St [Atlantic Ave]
- **Starbucks** • 63 Court St [Cambridge St]
- **Starbucks** • 84 State St [Kilby St]

📋 Copy Shops

- **AlphaGraphics** • 74 Canal St [Valenti]
- **FedEx Kinko's** • 60 State St [Kilby St]
- **Sir Speedy Printing Center** •
  123 N Washington St [Medford St]
- **Staples** • 25 Court St [Tremont St]
- **The UPS Store** • 71 Commercial St [Cross]

🌾 Farmers Markets

- **City Hall Plaza**
  (May–Nov, Mon 11–6, Wed 11–6) •
  19 Cambridge St [Tremont St]

💪 Gyms

- **Beacon Hill Athletic Club** •
  85 Atlantic Ave [High St]
- **Fitness Together** •
  145 Hanover St [Blackstone]

🔧 Hardware Stores

- **Boston Hardware** •
  16 Fleet St [Garden Ct St]
- **Salem Street True Value** •
  89 Salem St [Wiget]

🍸 Liquor Stores

- **Cirace's Liquor** • 173 North St [Moon]
- **Federal Wine & Spirits** •
  29 State St [Devonshire]
- **Hanover Liquors** •
  363 Hanover St [N Bennet St]
- **Martignetti Liquors** •
  64 Cross St [Morton St]

- **Wine Bottega (wine only)** •
  341 Hanover St [Prince]
- **Wine Cave** • 33 Union St [Marshall St]

🎬 Movie Theaters

- **Simons IMAX Theatre** •
  Central Wharf [Central St]

🌃 Nightlife

- **Bell in Hand Tavern** •
  45 Union St [Marshall St]
- **Black Rose** • 160 State St [Commercial St]
- **Boston Beer Works** •
  112 Canal St [Valenti]
- **Boston Rocks** • 245 Quincy Market
- **Boston Sail Loft** •
  80 Atlantic Ave [High St]
- **Green Dragon Tavern** •
  11 Marshall St [Hanover St]
- **The Hong Kong** •
  65 Chatham St [Chatham Row]
- **McFadden's** • 148 State St [India St]
- **Paddy O's** • 33 Union St [Marshall St]
- **Parris** • Quincy Market [S Market]
- **Purple Shamrock** • 1 Union St [North St]
- **Sanctuary** • 189 State St [McKinley]
- **Tia's on the Waterfront** •
  200 Atlantic Ave [State]
- **Vertigo** • 126 State St [Broad]

🍴 Restaurants

- **Abruzzo Restaurant** •
  289 Causeway St [Prince]
- **Al's State Street Café** •
  110 State St [Broad]
- **Antico Forno** • 93 Salem St [Wiget]
- **Billy Tse** • 240 Commercial St [Atlantic]
- **Boston Sail Loft** • 80 Atlantic Ave [High St]
- **Bova's Bakery** • 134 Salem St [Prince] 🕐
- **Bricco** • 241 Hanover St [Cross St]
- **Caffe Paradiso** •
  255 Hanover St [Richmond St]
- **The Daily Catch** •
  323 Hanover St [Prince]
- **Ernesto's** • 69 Salem St [Morton]
- **Galleria Umberto** •
  289 Hanover St [Richmond St]
- **Green Dragon Tavern** •
  11 Marshall St [Hanover St]
- **Haymarket Pizza** •
  106 Blackstone St [Hanover St]
- **Il Panino Express** •
  11 Parameter St [Hanover St]
- **L'Osteria** • 104 Salem St [Bartlett Pl]
- **La Famiglia Giorgio's** •
  112 Salem St [Cooper]
- **La Summa** • 30 Fleet St [McClellan Hwy]
- **Lucca** • 226 Hanover St [Cross St]
- **Lulu's Bake Shoppe** •
  227 Hanover St [N Hanover]

- **Mamma Maria** • 3 North Sq [Garden Ct St]
- **Massimino's Cucina Italiana** •
  207 Endicott St [Lafayette]
- **Maurizio's** • 364 Hanover St [N Bennet St]
- **McCormick & Schmick's** •
  1 Faneuil Hall Marketplace [S Market]
- **Nebo Pizzeria** •
  90 N Washington St [Medford St]
- **Neptune Oyster** • 63 Salem St [Morton St]
- **Pizzeria Regina** •
  11 1/2 Thacher St [N Margin]
- **Prezza** • 24 Fleet St [Garden Ct St]
- **Sel de la Terre** • 255 State St [Atlantic]
- **Sensing** • 5 Battery St [Hanover]
- **Taranta** • 210 Hanover St [Cross St]
- **Theo's Cozy Corner** •
  162 Salem St [Tileston St]
- **Trani** • 111 Salem St [Cooper]
- **Trattoria Il Panino** •
  11 Parmenter St [Hanover St]
- **Union Oyster House** •
  41 Union St [Marshall St]
- **Wagamama Faneuil Hall** •
  Quincy Market Building

🛍️ Shopping

- **Boston Halal Meat Market** •
  114 Blackstone St [Hanover St]
- **Bova's Bakery** • 134 Salem St [Prince] 🕐
- **Brooks Brothers** • 75 State St [Kilby St]
- **Dairy Fresh Candies** •
  57 Salem St [Morton St]
- **DePasquale Homemade Pasta**
  Shoppe • 66 Cross St [Endicott St]
- **Fresh Cheese** • 81 Endicott St [Stillman St]
- **Green Cross Pharmacy** •
  393 Hanover St [Clark St]
- **Holbrows Flowers** •
  100 City Hall Plz [Cambridge St]
- **Karma** • 26 Prince St [Hanover St]
- **Maria's Pastry Shop** •
  46 Cross St [Morton St]
- **Mike's Pastry** • 300 Hanover St [Prince]
- **Modern Pastry** •
  257 Hanover St [Richmond St]
- **Monica's Salumeria** •
  130 Salem St [Prince]
- **Newbury Comics** •
  1 Washington Mall [Court]
- **Salumeria Italiana** •
  151 Richmond St [North St]
- **Salumeria Toscana** •
  272 Hanover St [Parmenter]
- **Stanza dei Sigari** •
  292 Hanover St [Prince]
- **Staples** • 25 Court St [Tremont St]
- **Twilight** • 12 Fleet St [Hanover St]

📹 Video Rental

- **North End Video** •
  292 North St [Moon]

Map 2 · **North End / Faneuil Hall**

Charles River

Langone Park

US Coast Guard

1

2

Charlestown Bridge

Commercial St.

Battery Wharf

Sumner Tunnel

Callahan Tunnel

Lincoln Wharf

Union Wharf

Sargents Wharf

Lewis Wharf

Prince St.

Charter St

Jackson Ave

Commercial St.

Hanover St.

Constitution Wharf

Snow Hill St

N Hudson St

Hull St

Sheafe St

Foster St

Greenough Ln

Foster St

Vernon Pl

Holden Ct

Battery Wharf

Battery St

Powers Ct

Salem St

Cleveland Pl

Salem St

Unity St

Webster Ave

Tileston St

Charter St

Fountain Pl

Salutation St

Hanover Ave

Lincoln Wharf

Murphy Ct

Lafayette Ave

N Margin St

Endicott St

Butler

Endicott Ct

Thatcher St

Lombard

Prince St.

Wiget St

N Bennet St

Sheafe St

Morton St

Baldric Pl

Walsh Pl

Harris St

Clark St

Union Wharf

Douglas Ct

Pond St

Noyes Pl

Baldwin Pl

Richmond St

Parmenter St

Fleet St

North St

Eastern Ave

Morton St

Bartlett Pl

Cooper St

Stillman St

Anthony

N Hanover Ct

Board Aly

Wesley Pl

Lathrop Pl

North Bennet Court

Lewis St

Garden Ct

Bakers Aly

Quincy Ct

Clark St

Sargents Wharf

Cross St.

Haymarket

Hanover St.

Richmond St

Fulton St

Lewis Wharf

Blackstone St.

North St

Felton St

Commercial St.

Commercial Wharf N

New Sudbury St.

Creek Sq

Marsh Ln

Salt Ln

Scott Aly

Ferry St.

Atlantic Ave

Commercial Wharf

Commercial Wharf

JFK Fed Bldg

Marshall St

Union St.

Clinton St

Surface Rd

Christopher Columbus Park

City Hall

Congress St.

North St

Faneuil Hall Marketplace

Chatham St

Faneuil Hall

Butler Row

Chatham Row

Commercial St.

Aquarium

Atlantic Ave

New England Aquarium

Government Center

Washington Mall

Court St

State St

Broad St

Central St

Central St

Long Wharf

Long Wharf

Commercial Wharf

A

B

1/4 mile

.25 km

Take the T. Just take the T. Honestly. If you're one of those people who can afford to valet, or doesn't mind parking at one of the garages along Atlantic, so be it. Most of the charm of the North End involves walking around and eating and looking for parking for 45 minutes tends to kill the mood, and the planet.

Subway

- ■ · **Aquarium**
- ■ · **Haymarket**
- ■ · **State**

Bus Lines

- **4** · North Station—World Trade Center via Federal Courthouse
- **92** · Assembly Square Mall—Downtown via Sullivan Square Station, Main Street
- **93** · Sullivan Square Station—Downtown via Bunker Hill Street & Haymarket Station
- **111** · Woodlawn or Broadway & Park Ave—Haymarket Station via Mystic River/Tobin Bridge

🚗Car Rental

· **Enterprise** · 1 Congress St [North St] · 617-723-8077

🌢Car Washes

· **Bradford Auto Park & Wax** · 75 State St [Kilby St]

🅿Gas Stations

· **Mobil** · 420 Commercial St [Holden Ct]

🅿Parking

Downtown Crossing is abuzz with pedestrians from all walks of life. You'll find a lively mixture of financial types, shoppers, New England Medical Center doctors, and the down-and-out. High-end development continues, but remnants of the old Combat Zone remain. Bay Village, a tiny 19th-Century enclave, is pleasantly serene after a snowstorm.

$ Banks

- **Bank of America** • 157 Stuart St [Warrenton St]
- **Bank of America** • 315 Washington St [Milk St]
- **Bank of America** • 6 Tremont St [Court]
- **Bank of America** • 710 Washington St [Kneeland]
- **Bank of America (ATM)** • 11 Winter St [Winter Pl]
- **Bank of America (ATM)** • 175 Tremont St [Avery St]
- **Bank of America (ATM)** • 58 Winter St [Tremont St]
- **Bank of America (ATM)** • 630 Washington St [Essex]
- **Bank of America (ATM)** • 80 Boylston St [Tremont St]
- **Cathay Bank** • 621 Washington St [Hayward Pl]
- **Citizens Bank** • 73 Tremont St [Beacon St]
- **Citizens Bank (ATM)** • 1 Milk St [Washington St]
- **Citizens Bank (ATM)** • 750 Washington St [Kneeland]
- **Sovereign Bank** • 30 Winter St [Winter Pl]
- **Sovereign Bank** • 61 Arlington St [St James Ave]
- **Sovereign Bank (ATM)** • 600 Washington St [Hayward Pl]
- **Sovereign Bank (ATM)** • 769 Washington St [Kneeland]

Donuts

- **Dunkin' Donuts** • 1 Summer St [Washington St]
- **Dunkin' Donuts** • 127 Tremont St [Park St]
- **Dunkin' Donuts** • 130 Broadway [Melrose St]
- **Dunkin' Donuts** • 235 Washington St [Devonshire Pl]
- **Dunkin' Donuts** • 357 Tremont St [Church St]
- **Dunkin' Donuts** • 363 Tremont St [Marginal Rd]
- **Dunkin' Donuts** • 417 Washington St [Winter St]
- **Dunkin' Donuts** • 426 Washington St [Winter St]
- **Dunkin' Donuts** • 630 Washington St [Essex]
- **Dunkin' Donuts** • 750 Washington St [Kneeland]
- **Dunkin' Donuts** • 8 Park Plz [Boylston St]
- **Dunkin' Donuts** • 80 Boylston St [Tremont St]

Emergency Rooms

- **Tufts-New England Medical Center** • 750 Washington St [Kneeland]

Landmarks

- **Arlington Street Church** • 351 Boylston St [Arlington St]
- **Boston Irish Famine Memorial** • School St & Washington St
- **Boston Opera House** • 539 Washington St [Ave de Lafayette]
- **Colonial Theatre** • 106 Boylston St [Tremont St]
- **Four Seasons Hotel** • 200 Boylston St [Charles St]
- **Frog Pond** • Boston Common
- **Granary Burying Ground** • Tremont St & Park St
- **Hub of the Universe Bronze Marker** • Washington St & Summer St
- **John Hancock's Phallic Gravestone** • Tremont St & Park St
- **Old South Meeting House** • 310 Washington St [Milk St]
- **Old State House** • 206 Washington St [Court]
- **Omni Parker House** • 60 School St [Chapman]
- **Opera House** • 539 Washington St [Ave de Lafayette]
- **State House** • Beacon St & Park St
- **Swan Boats** • Arlington St & Boylston St
- **Wang Theatre** • 270 Tremont St [Hollis St]

Libraries

- **Kirstein Business** • 20 City Hall Ave [Pl]

Pharmacies

- **CVS** • 631 Washington St [Essex]

Schools

- **Boston Renaissance Charter** • 250 Stuart St [Church St]
- **Emerson College** • 120 Boylston St [Boylston Pl]
- **Josiah Quincy Elementary** • 885 Washington St [Oak St W]
- **Josiah Quincy Upper School** • 900 Washington St [Pine St]
- **New England School of Law** • 154 Stuart St [Warrenton St]
- **Quincy Upper** • 152 Arlington St [Melrose]
- **Suffolk University Law School** • 120 Tremont St [Hamilton Pl]
- **Transportation Children's Center** • 10 Park Plz [Providence]

Supermarkets

- **C-Mart** • 692 Washington St [Kneeland]

Map 3 • **Downtown Crossing/Park Square/Bay Village**

Map 1

Locals still mourn the loss of Jordan Marsh. It's hard to get excited about TJ Maxx and Marshall's. The best way to finish a weekday shopping excursion here is with a scrumptious Chilean sandwich from Chacarero, or the amazing Mike & Patty's. For a top-end meal, try Aujourd'hui or No. 9 Park across the Common.

Coffee

- **Café** • 1 City Hall Plaza [Court]
- **Starbucks** • 12 Winter St [Washington St]
- **Starbucks** • 143 Stuart St [Warrenton St]
- **Starbucks** • 240 Washington St [Water]
- **Starbucks** • 27 School St [Province St]
- **Starbucks** • 62 Boylston St [Tremont St]
- **Tremont Tea Room** (tea only) • 48 Winter St [Tremont St]

Copy Shops

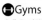

- **BFS Business Printing** • 10 Park Plz [Providence]
- **Copy Cop** • 260 Washington St [Water]
- **Emerson College Print Copy Center** • 80 Boylston St [Tremont St]
- **FedEx Kinko's** • 125 Tremont St [Park St]
- **Mail Boxes Etc** • 276 Washington St [Spring Ln]
- **Staples** • 25 Winter St [Winter Pl]
- **The UPS Store** • 198 Tremont St [Boylston St]

Gyms

- **Bally Total Fitness** • 17 Winter St [Winter Pl]
- **Sports Club LA** • 4 Avery St [Washington St]
- **Wang YMCA of Chinatown** • 8 Oak St W [Tremont St]
- **Women's Fitness of Boston** • 27 School St [Province St]

Liquor Stores

- **Boston Liquor Depot** • 861 Washington St [Oak St W]
- **Wine Cellar** • 497 Washington St [Temple Pl]

Movie Theaters

- **AMC Loews Boston Common** • 175 Tremont St [Avery St]

Nightlife

- **Aria** • 246 Tremont St [Stuart]
- **Felt** • 533 Washington St [Ave de Lafayette]
- **Jacque's** • 79 Broadway [Winchester St]
- **Limelight Stage and Studios** • 204 Tremont St [Lagrange]
- **Matrix** • 275 Tremont St [Hollis St]
- **MJ O'Connor's** • 27 Columbus Ave [Park Sq]
- **Mojitos Lounge** • 48 Winter St [Tremont St]
- **Parker's Bar** • 60 School St [Chapman]
- **Roxy** • 279 Tremont St [Common]
- **Rumor** • 100 Warrenton St [Stuart]
- **The Tam** • 222 Tremont St [Stuart]
- **Venu** • 100 Warrenton St [Stuart]
- **Whiskey Park** • 64 Arlington St [Providence]

Restaurants

- **Bonfire** • Park Plaza Hotel • 50 Park Plz [Providence St]
- **Buddha's Delight** • 5 Beach St [Washington St]
- **Chacarero** • 101 Arch St [Winter St]
- **Dedo** • 69 Church St [Piedmont]
- **Emperor's Garden** • 690 Washington St [Lagrange]
- **Herrera's Mexican Grille** • 11 Temple Pl [Tremont St]
- **Intermission Tavern** • 228 Tremont St [Stuart]
- **Ivy** • 49 Temple Pl [Washington St]
- **Jacob Wirth** • 31 Stuart St [Dartmouth St]
- **Know Fat!** • 530 Washington St [Ave de Lafayette]
- **Legal Sea Foods** • 26 Park Plz [Hadassah]
- **Locke-Ober** • 3 Winter Pl [Winter St]
- **Lu's Sandwich Shop** • 2 Knapp St [Monsignor Shea Rd]
- **Mantra** • 52 Temple Pl [Tremont St]
- **Marliave** • 10 Bosworth St [Chapman Pl]
- **McCormick & Schmick's** • 34 Columbus Ave [Park Sq]
- **Mike and Patty's** • 12 Church St [Fayette St]
- **Montien** • 63 Stuart St [Tremont St]·
- **New Saigon Sandwich** • 696 Washington St [Kneeland]
- **New York Pizza** • 224 Tremont St [Lagrange]
- **No. 9 Park** • 9 Park St [Beacon St]
- **Penang** • 685 Washington St [Lagrange]
- **Pigalle** • 75 Charles St S [Stuart]
- **Sam LaGrassa's** • 44 Province St [Bosworth]
- **Silvertone Bar & Grill** • 69 Bromfield St [Tremont St]
- **Smith & Wollensky** • 101 Arlington St [Stuart]
- **Teatro** • 177 Tremont St [Head]
- **Tequila Mexican Grill** • 55 Bromfield St [Tremont St]
- **Via Matta** • 79 Park Plz [Hadassah]
- **Viga** • 304 Stuart St [Arlington St]

Shopping

- **Beacon Hill Skate Shop** • 135 Charles St S [Fayette St]
- **Borders** • 10 School St [Washington St]
- **Bromfield Camera & Video** • 10 Bromfield St [Washington St]
- **City Antiques** • 362 Tremont St [Jefferson St]
- **City Sports** • 11 Bromfield St [Washington St]
- **DSW** • 385 Washington St [Bromfield]
- **Eddie Bauer Outlet** • 500 Washington St [West St]
- **H&M** • 350 Washington St [Franklin St]
- **Lambert's** • Washington St & Summer St
- **LJ Peretti** • 2 1/2 Park Sq
- **Macy's** • 450 Washington St [Temple Pl]
- **Marshall's** • 350 Washington St [Franklin St]
- **Roche-Bobois** • 2 Avery St [Washington St]
- **Staples** • 25 Winter St [Winter Pl]
- **TJ Maxx** • 350 Washington St [Franklin St]
- **Windsor Buttons** • 35 Temple Pl [Tremont St]

Video Rental

- **Kung Fu Video** • 365 Washington St [Bromfield]

Map 3

This area is well served by the T and buses, and there's little reason to drive around here. Note that Tremont Street runs in only one direction until it intersects with, uh, Tremont Street, and that Washington Street north of Temple Place in Downtown Crossing is a pedestrian mall closed to traffic.

Subway

- **Arlington**
- **Boylston**
- **Chinatown**
- **Downtown Crossing**
- **Government Center**
- **NE Medical Center**
- **Park Street**

Bus Lines

9 · City Point—Copley Square via Broadway Station

11 · City Point—Downtown, Bayview Route

43 · Ruggles Station—Park & Tremont Streets

55 · Jersey & Queensberry Streets—Copley Square or Park & Tremont Streets

Car Rental

- **Budget** · Motor Mart Garage · 28 Park Plz · 617-497-3669
- **Hertz** · 30 Park Plz · 617-338-1500

Gas Stations

- **Getty** · 825 Washington St [Oak St W]

Parking

Map 4 • **Financial District / Chinatown**

Essentials

Map 4

The center of the Financial District has changed from The Big Dig to the Rose Kennedy Greenway, and as it's getting very little use, it's just as controversial as its predecessor. Sit on the very pristine grass and then hit up the always bustling Chinatown. For an introduction, stroll and window-shop along Beach Street and its cross-streets.

Banks

- **Asian American Bank & Trust ·** 68 Harrison Ave [Beach St]
- **Bank of America ·** 100 Federal St [Franklin St]
- **Bank of America ·** 125 High St [Pearl St]
- **Bank of America ·** 175 Federal St [High St]
- **Bank of America ·** 65 Franklin St [Arch St]
- **Bank of America (ATM) ·** Post Office Sq [Congress]
- **Bank of America (ATM) ·** 1 Financial Ctr [Summer]
- **Bank of America (ATM) ·** 1 Post Office Sq [Water]
- **Bank of America (ATM) ·** 175 Federal St [High St]
- **Bank of America (ATM) ·** 30 Rowes Wharf [High St]
- **Bank of America (ATM) ·** 730 Atlantic Ave [Beach St]
- **Bank of America (ATM) ·** 79 Summer St [Otis St]
- **Banknorth Massachusetts ·** 15 Broad St [Doane]
- **Banknorth Massachusetts ·** 75 Federal St [Franklin St]
- **Boston Private Bank & Trust ·** 10 Post Office Sq [Water]
- **Century Bank ·** 24 Federal St [Milk St]
- **Century Bank ·** 280 Atlantic Ave [Central St]
- **Citizens Bank ·** 1 Financial Ctr [Summer]
- **Citizens Bank ·** 40 Summer St [Arch St]
- **Citizens Bank ·** 6 Ave de Lafayette [Chauncy St]
- **Citizens Bank ·** 77 Franklin St [Arch St]
- **Citizens Bank (ATM) ·** 2 Delafayette Ave [Harrison Ave]
- **Citizens Bank (ATM) ·** 650 Atlantic Ave [Essex]
- **Citizens Bank (ATM) ·** 700 Atlantic Ave [East St]
- **Eastern Bank ·** 101 Federal St [Matthews]
- **Eastern Bank ·** 265 Franklin St [Oliver]
- **One United Bank ·** 133 Federal St [Milton Pl]
- **Sovereign Bank ·** 1 Federal St [Milk St]
- **Sovereign Bank ·** 100 Oliver St [High St]
- **Sovereign Bank ·** 125 Summer St [Bedford]
- **Sovereign Bank ·** South Station [Essex]
- **Sovereign Bank ·** 43 Kneeland [Harrison Ave]
- **Sovereign Bank ·** 61 Harrison Ave [Beach St]
- **Sovereign Bank (ATM) ·** 160 Federal St [Milton Pl]
- **Sovereign Bank (ATM) ·** CVS/Pharmacy · 55 Summer St [Arch St]
- **Sovereign Bank (ATM) ·** CVS/Pharmacy · 81 Milk St [Congress]
- **Wainwright Bank & Trust ·** 63 Franklin St [Arch St]

Donuts

- **Dunkin' Donuts ·** 10 Winthrop Sq [Devonshire]
- **Dunkin' Donuts ·** 101 Summer St [Lincoln St]
- **Dunkin' Donuts ·** 16 Kneeland St [Shea]
- **Dunkin' Donuts ·** 176 Federal St [High St]
- **Dunkin' Donuts ·** 265 Franklin St [Oliver]
- **Dunkin' Donuts ·** 3 Post Office Sq [Water]
- **Dunkin' Donuts ·** 70 E India Row [Atlantic Ave]
- **Honey Dew Donuts ·** South Station · 700 Atlantic Ave [East St]

Landmarks

- **Boston Harbor Hotel ·** 70 Rowes Wharf [High St]
- **Chinatown Gate ·** Beach St & Hudson St
- **Custom House Tower ·** 3 McKinley Sq [Central St]
- **Federal Reserve ·** 600 Atlantic Ave [Summer]
- **South Station ·** Atlantic Ave & Summer St

Pharmacies

- **CVS ·** 340 Washington St [Bromfield]
- **CVS ·** 55 Summer St [Chauncy St]
- **PharmaCare Specialty Pharmacy ·** 35 Kneeland St [Harrison Ave]
- **Tai Tung Pharmacy ·** 256 Harrison Ave [Johnny]

Post Offices

- **Fort Point Station ·** 25 Dorchester Ave [Summer]
- **Lafayette Station ·** 7 Ave de Lafayette [Chauncy St]
- **Milk Street ·** 31 Milk St [Arch St]

Schools

- **Tufts University School of Medicine ·** 136 Harrison Ave [Harvard St]

Supermarkets

- **C-Mart ·** 109 Lincoln St [Tufts]
- **Super 88 ·** 73 Essex St [Oxford St]

Map 4 • **Financial District / Chinatown**

Chinatown = Chau Chow City for dim sum, Taiwan Café for the real deal, Ocean Wealth for seafood, or Shabu-Zen for Japanese hot pot. For late-night bites, remember that the South Street Diner serves well into the night. Some of Boston's top restaurants, including Radius, Julien, and Meritage, call the Financial District home.

Coffee

- **Bean & Leaf Company** • 20 Custom House St [India St]
- **Peet's Coffee & Tea** • 176 Federal St [High St]
- **Starbucks** • 1 Federal St [Milk St]
- **Starbucks** • 1 Financial Ctr [Summer]
- **Starbucks** • 1 International Pl [High St]
- **Starbucks** • 101 Federal St [Matthews]
- **Starbucks** • 211 Congress St [High St]
- **Starbucks** • 125 Summer St [High St]

Copy Shops

- **Air Graphics** • 89 Broad St [Franklin St]
- **BFS Business Printing** • 76 South St [Tufts]
- **Boston Business Printing** • 115 Broad St [Wendell St]
- **Copy Cop** • 125 High St [Pearl St]
- **Copy Cop** • 85 Franklin St [Devonshire]
- **FedEx Kinko's** • 10 Post Office Sq [Water]
- **FedEx Kinko's** • 211 Congress St [High St]
- **Litigation Document Productions** • 61 Batterymarch St Fl 4 [Wendell St]
- **News Clips Etc Inc** • 42 Chauncy St [Bedford]
- **Sir Speedy Printing** • 1 Milk St [Washington St]

Farmers Markets

- **Dewey Square (May–Nov; M,W,Th; 11:30 am–6:30 pm)** • Summer St & Atlantic Ave

Gyms

- **Boston Sports Club** • 10 Franklin St [Washington St]
- **Boston Sports Club** • 695 Atlantic Ave [East St]
- **Boston Racquet Club** • 100 Summer St [Bedford]
- **Fitcorp** • 125 Summer St [Bedford]
- **Fitness International** • 1 International Pl [High St]
- **Langham Hotel Health Club** • 250 Franklin St [Oliver]
- **Rowes Wharf Health Club & Spa** • 70 Rowes Wharf [High St]

Nightlife

- **An Tain** • 31 India St [Milk St]
- **Aqua** • 120 Water St [Kilby St]
- **Bond** • 250 Franklin St [Oliver St]
- **Elephant & Castle** • 161 Devonshire St [Milk St]
- **Good Life** • 28 Kingston St [Bedford]
- **The International** • 184 High St [Batterymarch St]
- **JJ Foley's** • 21 Kingston St [Summer]
- **Jose McIntyre's** • 160 Milk St [India St]
- **Les Zygomates** • 129 South St [Tufts]
- **Mr Dooley's Boston Tavern** • 77 Broad St [Custom]
- **News** • 150 Kneeland St [Utica St]

- **Revolution Rock Bar** • 200 High St [Batterymarch St]
- **Rowes Wharf Bar** • Boston Harbor Hotel • 70 Rowes Wharf [High St]
- **Times Restaurant and Bar** • 112 Broad St [Wendell St]
- **Umbria** • 295 Franklin St [Batterymarch St]

Pet Shops

- **Aqua World (fish only)** • 20 Tyler St [Kneeland]

Restaurants

- **Chau Chow City** • 83 Essex St [Ping]
- **China Pearl** • 9 Tyler St [Beach St]
- **Ginza** • 16 Hudson St [Kneeland]
- **Hei La Moon** • 88 Beach St [Lincoln St]
- **The Hong Kong Eatery** • 79 Harrison Ave [Knapp]
- **J Pace & Son** • 1 Federal St [Milk St]
- **Julien** • Langham Hotel • 250 Franklin St [Oliver]
- **King Fung Garden** • 74 Kneeland St [Hudson St]
- **Les Zygomates** • 129 South St [Tufts]
- **Mei Sum Inc** • 40 Beach St [Harrison Av]
- **Meritage** • 70 Rowes Wharf [High St]
- **Milk Street Cafe** • 50 Milk St [Devonshire]
- **New Shanghai** • 21 Hudson St [Kneeland]
- **Noodle Alcove** • 10 Tyler St [Beach St]
- **Ocean Wealth** • 8 Tyler St [Beach St]
- **Osushi** • 101 Arch St [Snow Pl]
- **Peach Farm** • 4 Tyler St [Beach St]
- **Pho Hoa** • 17 Beach St [Shea]
- **Pizza Oggi** • 131 Broad St [Wendell St]
- **Pressed Sandwiches** • 2 Oliver St [Milk St]
- **Radius** • 8 High St [Summer]
- **Rowes Wharf Sea Grille** • 70 Rowes Wharf [Atlantic Ave]
- **Sakurabana** • 57 Broad St [Broad]
- **Shabu-Zen** • 16 Tyler St [Beach St]
- **Sophia's Green Cafe** • 14 Dorchester Ave [Summer St]
- **South Street Diner** • 178 Kneeland St [South St] ⏱
- **Sultan's Kitchen** • 116 State St [Broad]
- **Taiwan Café** • 34 Oxford St [Oxford Pl]
- **Umbria** • 295 Franklin St [Batterymarch St]
- **Upper Crust** • 245 Summer St [Dorchester St]
- **Xinh Xinh** • 7 Beach St [Monsignor Shea Rd]

Shopping

- **Anna's Dessert House** • 66 Harrison Ave [Beach St]

Video Rental

- **Top Ten Video Music (Chinese)** • 219 Harrison Ave [Oak St]

Map 4 • **Financial District / Chinatown**

Transportation

Map 4

The Dig may be over, and all of the lanes in O'Neill Tunnel may finally be open, but there's still some surface road construction in the Financial District. If you don't need to drive here, don't, especially during rush hour. There is street parking on weeknights/weekend nights if you look hard enough.

Subway

- **Chinatown**
- **Downtown Crossing**
- **Park Street**
- **South Station**
- **State**

Bus Lines

- **4** • North Station—World Trade Center via Federal Courthouse
- **7** • City Point—Otis & Summer Streets via Northern Avenue & South Station
- **92** • Assembly Square Mall—Downtown via Sullivan Square Station, Main Street
- **93** • Sullivan Square Station—Downtown via Bunker Hill Street & Haymarket Station
- **448** • Marblehead—Haymarket, Downtown Crossing, or Wonderland
- **449** • Marblehead—Haymarket, Downtown Crossing, or Wonderland
- **459** • Marblehead—Haymarket, Downtown Crossing, or Wonderland

Car Rental

- **Alamo** • 270 Atlantic Ave [Central St] • 617-557-7179
- **Dollar** • Boston Harbor Hotel • 30 Rowes Wharf [High St] • 617-367-2654
- **Hertz** • 2 International Pl [Purchase] • 617-204-1165
- **Hertz** • South Station Amtrak • Summer St & Atlantic Ave • 617-338-1503
- **National** • 270 Atlantic Ave [E India] • 617-557-7179

Car Washes

- **Executive Car Care** • 125 High St [Pearl St]

Parking

Map 5 • Back Bay (West) / Fenway (East)

Traffic on Mass Ave! MassPIRG on Newbury Street! Berklee students between classes! This area is fraught with minor perils, but that's because there's a lot going on here. The striking group of buildings that comprises the Christian Science Center, together with the Pru and 111 Huntington (the "Daily Planet"), looks great at night.

$ Banks

- **Bank of America** ·
  133 Massachusetts Ave [Boylston St]
- **Bank of America** ·
  285 Huntington Ave [Gainsborough]
- **Bank of America** · 855 Boylston St [Gloucester]
- **Bank of America** ·
  133 Massachusetts Ave [Boylston St]
- **Bank of America (ATM)** ·
  161 Massachusetts Ave [Belvidere St]
- **Bank of America (ATM)** ·
  221 Massachusetts Ave [Clearway]
- **Bank of America (ATM)** ·
  285 Huntington Ave [Gainsborough]
- **Bank of America (ATM)** ·
  393 Massachusetts Ave [St Botolph St]
- **Bank of America (ATM)** ·
  346 Huntington Ave [Opera]
- **Bank of America (ATM)** ·
  800 Boylston St [Fairfield St]
- **Bank of America (ATM)** ·
  90 Massachusetts Ave [Comm Ave]
- **Citizens Bank (ATM)** ·
  141 Massachusetts Ave [Boylston St]
- **Citizens Bank (ATM)** · 800 Boylston St [Fairfield St]
- **Citizens Bank (ATM)** · 900 Boylston St [Gloucester]
- **Sovereign Bank** · 279 Massachusetts Ave [Westland]
- **Sovereign Bank** · 800 Boylston St [Fairfield St]
- **Sovereign Bank (ATM)** · CVS/Pharmacy ·
  240 Newbury St [Fairfield St]
- **Sovereign Bank (ATM)** · 799 Boylston St [Fairfield St]

Community Gardens

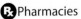 Donuts

- **Dunkin' Donuts** · 1108 Boylston St [Hemenway St]
- **Dunkin' Donuts** ·
  153 Massachusetts Ave [Belvidere St]
- **Dunkin' Donuts** · 283 Huntington Ave [Gainsborough]
- **Dunkin' Donuts** · 333 Newbury St [Hereford]
- **Dunkin' Donuts** · 434 Massachusetts Ave [Columbus]

O Landmarks

- **Burrage House** · 314 Commonwealth Ave [Hereford]
- **Christian Science Center** ·
  175 Huntington Ave [W Newton]
- **Hynes Convention Center** ·
  900 Boylston St [Gloucester]
- **Jordan Hall** · 30 Gainsborough St [Huntington]
- **Prudential Tower** · 800 Boylston St [Fairfield St]
- **Symphony Hall** ·
  301 Massachusetts Ave [Huntington]

Libraries

- **The Mary Baker Eddy Library** ·
  200 Massachusetts Ave [Clearway]

Rx Pharmacies

- **CVS** · 231 Massachusetts Ave [Clearway]
- **CVS** · 240 Newbury St [Fairfield St]
- **Walgreens** · 841 Boylston St [Fairfield St] ⊕

Post Offices

- **Astor Station** · 207 Massachusetts Ave [Clearway]
- **Prudential Center Post Office** ·
  800 Boylston St [Fairfield St]

Schools

- **Berklee College of Music** ·
  1140 Boylston St [Hemenway St]
- **Boston Conservatory** · 8 The Fenway [Boylston St]
- **City on a Hill Charter** · 320 Huntington Ave [Opera]
- **Kingsley Montessori** · 30 Fairfield St [Comm Ave]
- **New England Conservatory** ·
  290 Huntington Ave [Gainsborough]
- **Newman Preparatory** · 247 Marlborough St [Exeter St]

Supermarkets

- **Trader Joe's** · 899 Boylston St [Gloucester]
- **Whole Foods Market** · 15 Westland Ave [Edgerly Rd]

Sundries / Entertainment

Trident Booksellers and Café is a terrific spot for brunching and browsing. Get earthy (or just drink) at Other Side Cosmic Café. Beer drinkers who can handle Tunnel-level stereo volume and a touch of attitude should try Bukowski's. Berklee students often sit in at Wally's, joining more established musicians to play live jazz most nights of the week.

Coffee

- **Café Golden Horn** • 334 Massachusetts Ave [St Botolph]
- **Espresso Royale** • 286 Newbury St [Gloucester]
- **Espresso Royale** • 44 Gainsborough St [Huntington]
- **Natural Bean** • 250 Newbury St [Fairfield St]
- **Starbucks** • 151 Massachusetts Ave [Haviland St]
- **Starbucks** • 273 Huntington Ave [Gainsborough]
- **Starbucks** • 346 Huntington Ave [Opera Pl]
- **Starbucks** • 350 Newbury St [Mass Ave]
- **Starbucks** • Sheraton Hotel • 39 Dalton St [Scotia]
- **Trident Booksellers & Café** • 338 Newbury St [Hereford]

Copy Shops

- **FedEx Kinko's** • 900 Boylston St [Gloucester]
- **Gnomon Copy** • 325 Huntington Ave [Opera]
- **Sir Speedy Printing Center** • 827 Boylston St [Fairfield St]
- **The UPS Store** • 263 Huntington Ave [Gainsborough]
- **The UPS Store** • 304 Newbury St [Hereford]

Gyms

- **Atlantis Sports Club** • 39 Dalton St [Scotia St]
- **Boston Sports Club** • 361 Newbury St [Mass Ave]
- **Central YMCA** • 316 Huntington Ave [Gainsborough]
- **Tennis & Racquet Club** • 939 Boylston St [Hereford]

Hardware Stores

- **Economy Hardware** • 219 Massachusetts Ave [Clearway]

Liquor Stores

- **Bauer Wine & Spirits** • 330 Newbury St [Hereford]
- **Choice Mart** • 181 Massachusetts Ave [St Germain]
- **DeLuca's Market** • 239 Newbury St [Fairfield St]
- **Huntington Wine & Spirits** • 301 Huntington Ave [Gainsborough]

Nightlife

- **Bukowski's** • 50 Dalton St [Scotia]
- **Crossroads** • 495 Beacon St [Mass Ave]
- **Dillon's** • 955 Boylston St [Hereford]
- **Kings** • 10 Scotia St [Dalton St]
- **The Last Drop** • 421 Marlborough St [Mass Ave]
- **Lir** • 903 Boylston St [Gloucester]
- **Match** • 94 Massachusetts Ave [Newbury St]
- **McGreevey'** • 911 Boylston St [Gloucester St]
- **Our House East** • 52 Gainsborough St [St Stephen]
- **Pour House** • 907 Boylston St [Gloucester]
- **Sonsie** • 327 Newbury St [Hereford]
- **TC's Lounge** • 1 Haviland St [Mass Ave]

- **Top of the Hub** • 800 Boylston St [Fairfield St]
- **Wally's Café** • 427 Massachusetts Ave [Columbus]

Restaurants

- **Bangkok City** • 167 Massachusetts Ave [Belvidere St]
- **Bhindi Bazaar** • 95 Massachusetts Ave [Newbury St]
- **Bukowski's** • 50 Dalton St [Scotia]
- **Café Jaffa** • 48 Gloucester St [Boylston St]
- **Capital Grille** • 359 Newbury St [Mass Ave]
- **Casa Romero** • 30 Gloucester St [Newbury St]
- **Chilli Duck** • 829 Boylston St [Fairfield St]
- **Clio** • 370A Commonwealth Ave [Mass Ave]
- **India Samraat Restaurant** • 51 Massachusetts Ave [Marlborough St]
- **Island Hopper** • 91 Massachusetts Ave [Newbury St]
- **Kashmir** • 279 Newbury St [Gloucester]
- **Other Side Cosmic Café** • 407 Newbury St [Mass Ave]
- **Pour House** • 907 Boylston St [Gloucester]
- **Sonsie** • 327 Newbury St [Hereford]
- **Spike's Junkyard Dogs** • 1076 Boylston St [Mass Ave]
- **Tapeo** • 266 Newbury St [Gloucester]
- **Top of the Hub** • 800 Boylston St [Fairfield St]
- **Trident Booksellers & Café** • 338 Newbury St [Hereford]

Shopping

- **Army Barracks** • 328 Newbury St [Hereford]
- **Back Bay Bicycle** • 366 Commonwealth Ave [Mass Ave]
- **Bôn Bön** • 197 Massachusetts Ave [Clearway St]
- **The Compleat Strategist** • 201 Massachusetts Ave [Clearway St]
- **Daddy's Junky Music** • 159 Massachusetts Ave [Belvidere St]
- **DeLuca's Market** • 239 Newbury St [Fairfield St]
- **Economy Hardware** • 219 Massachusetts Ave [Clearway]
- **Emack & Bolio's** • 290 Newbury St [Gloucester]
- **Firefly Jewelry & Gifts** • 270 Newbury St [Gloucester]
- **John Fluevog** • 302 Newbury St [Hereford]
- **Johnny Cupcakes** • 279 Newbury St [Gloucester]
- **Johnson Artist Materials** • 355 Newbury St [Mass Ave]
- **J.P. Licks** • 352 Newbury St [Mass Ave]
- **Luna Boston** • 286 Newbury St [Gloucester]
- **Matsu** • 259 Newbury St [Fairfield St]
- **Orpheus** • 362 Commonwealth Ave [Mass Ave]
- **Sephora** • 800 Boylston St [Fairfield St]
- **Sweet-N-Nasty** • 90 Massachusetts Ave [Comm Ave]
- **Trident Booksellers & Café** • 338 Newbury St [Hereford]
- **Urban Outfitters** • 361 Newbury St [Mass Ave]
- **Utrecht Art Supply Center** • 333 Massachusetts Ave [St Botolph]

Video Rental

- **Blockbuster** • 235 Massachusetts Ave [Clearway]
- **Hollywood Video** • 899 Boylston Ave [Gloucester]

33

Traffic is always nasty on Mass Ave during the week. On weekends it becomes a parking lot, so avoid driving around here on Saturdays and Sundays if at all possible. And remember: there's no left turn from inbound Boylston Street onto Mass Ave. Few spots in Boston make it so easy for traffic cops to fill their quotas.

Map 5

Subway

- **Massachusetts Avenue**
- **Hynes Convention Center (B,C,D)**
- **Prudential (E)**
- **Symphony (E)**

Bus Lines

- **CT1** • Central Square, Cambridge—BU Medical Center/BU Medical Campus
- **1** • Harvard/Holyoke Gate—Dudley Station via Massachusetts Avenue & BU Medical Center
- **9** • City Point—Copley Square via Broadway Station
- **39** • Forest Hills Station—Back Bay Station via Huntington Avenue
- **55** • Jersey & Queensberry Streets—Copley Square or Park & Tremont Streets

Car Rental

- **Enterprise** • 800 Boylston St [Fairfield St] • 617-262-8222
- **Select Car Rental** • 39 Dalton St [Scotia] • 617-236-6088

Gas Stations

- **Shell** • 584 Columbus Ave [Mass Ave] ♿
- **Sunoco** • 266 Massachusetts Ave [Westland Ave]

Parking

Map 6 • **Back Bay (East) / South End (Upper)**

26

Charles River

Hatch Shell

Charles River Esplanade

PAGE 220

Emerson College

Beaver Pl

Old Pl

Byron St

Beacon St

Boston Commo.

PAGE 188

Storrow Dr

French Library and Cultural Center

Berkeley St

Commonwealth Ave

Arlington St

The Lagoon

Public Garden

Charles St

Beacon St

Back St

Clarendon St

First Church in Boston

Church of the Covenant

Arlington

Boylston St

A

1

Marlborough St

Commonwealth Ave

New England Historic Genealogical Library

Hadassah Way

Park Pl

Park Sq

Columbus Ave

PAGE 200

5

Commonwealth Ave

2 $

Providence St

$

Stuart St

Piedmont St

Exeter St

Fairfield St

Newbury St

Old South Church

Copley

$ $

PAGE 184

Trinity Church

St James Ave

$

Arlington St

Isabella St

PAGE 185

Boylston St

2 $

Copley Sq

John Hancock Tower

Stuart St

Cortes St

3

Tremont St

Gloucester St

Boston Public Library

Blagden St

Dartmouth St

Trinity Pl

Stuart St

Chandler St

R

Ring Rd

Stuart St

Massachusetts Tpk Ra

Chambers Pl

Charlesgate

Herald St

2 $

Back Bay

Buckingham St

Clarendon St

Gray St

Prudential Center

PAGE 198

3 $

2 $

Blagden St

Harcourt St

Harriet Tubman St

2 $

7

Lawrence St

Appleton St

Dartmouth St

E Berkeley St

Belvidere St

$

Prudential

W Canton St

Columbus Ave

Warren Ave

Montgomery St

Union Park

Huntington Ave

Symphony

2 ✳

Braddock Park

Columbus Sq

Harriet Tubman Square

W Newton St

Massachusetts Avenue

$

✳ ✳ ✳

W Rutland Sq

Rutland St

✳

✳

✳ ✳

Wellington

Greenwich Park

$

1/4 mile   .25 km

Map 6

The eastern end of Back Bay features the "top" of Newbury Street, with its mix of locals, tourists, and international students keeping its mainly highbrow merchants busy. The upper regions of the South End—especially Columbus Avenue—are now home to excellent restaurant upon excellent restaurant, with a culturally-correct number of galleries thrown in as well.

$ Banks

- **Bank of America** • 210 Berkeley St [St James Ave]
- **Bank of America** • 699 Boylston St [Exeter St]
- **Bank of America (ATM)** •
  101 Huntington Ave [Garrison St]
- **Bank of America (ATM)** •
  110 Huntington Ave [Harcourt]
- **Bank of America (ATM)** •
  130 Dartmouth St [Columbus]
- **Bank of America (ATM)** • 145 Dartmouth St [Stuart]
- **Bank of America (ATM)** • 31 St James Ave [Arlington St]
- **Bank of America (ATM)** •
  465 Columbus Ave [W Newton]
- **Bank of America (ATM)** •
  557 Boylston St [Clarendon St]
- **Bank of America (ATM)** • 745 Boylston St [Exeter St]
- **Banknorth Massachusetts** •
  579 Boylston St [Dartmouth St]
- **Boston Private Bank & Trust** •
  500 Boylston St [Clarendon St]
- **Citizens Bank** • 426 Boylston St [Berkeley St]
- **Citizens Bank** • 535 Boylston St [Clarendon St]
- **Citizens Bank** • 607 Boylston St [Dartmouth St]
- **Citizens Bank (ATM)** • 101 Huntington Ave [Garrison St]
- **Citizens Bank (ATM)** • 111 Huntington Ave [Garrison St]
- **Citizens Bank (ATM)** • 145 Dartmouth St [Stuart]
- **Citizens Bank (ATM)** • 200 Clarendon St [St James Ave]
- **Citizens Bank (ATM)** • 717 Boylston St [Exeter St]
- **Sovereign Bank** • 575 Boylston St [Dartmouth St]
- **Sovereign Bank (ATM)** •
  100 Huntington Ave [Harcourt]
- **Sovereign Bank (ATM)** •
  Prudential Center Shoppe •
  111 Huntington Ave [W Newton St]
- **Sovereign Bank (ATM)** •
  200 Clarendon St [St James Ave]
- **Sovereign Bank (ATM)** •
  United Settlement House •
  566 Columbus Ave [Wellington St]
- **Sovereign Bank (ATM)** • CVS/Pharmacy •
  587 Boylston St [Dartmouth St]
- **Wainwright Bank & Trust** •
  155 Dartmouth St [Stuart]

✿ Community Gardens

◉ Donuts

- **Dunkin' Donuts** • 145 Dartmouth St [Stuart]
- **Dunkin' Donuts** • 2 Copley Pl [Dartmouth St]
- **Dunkin' Donuts** • 430 Stuart St [Trinity]
- **Dunkin' Donuts** • 715 Boylston St [Exeter St]

◉ Landmarks

- **Boston Public Library** • 700 Boylston St [Exeter St]
- **Charles River Esplanade** • Storrow Drive
- **Church of the Covenant** • 67 Newbury St [Berkeley St]
- **Commonwealth Ave** • Arlington to Mass Ave
- **Copley Square** • Boylston St & Dartmouth St
- **First Church in Boston** •
  66 Marlborough St [Berkeley St]
- **French Library and Cultural Center** •
  53 Marlborough St [Berkeley St]
- **Harriet Tubman Square** • Columbus Sq
- **Hatch Shell** • Esplanade [Congress]
- **John Hancock Tower** • 200 Clarendon St [St James Ave]
- **New England Historic Genealogical Library** •
  101 Newbury St [Clarendon St]
- **Old South Church** • 645 Boylston St [Dartmouth St]
- **Trinity Church** • 206 Clarendon St [St James Ave]

📖 Libraries

- **Boston Public Library** • 700 Boylston St [Exeter St]

℞ Pharmacies

- **Bioscrip Pharmacy** • 21 Stanhope St [Berkeley St]
- **CVS** • 587 Boylston St [Dartmouth St] ⓐ

✉ Post Offices

- **Back Bay Annex Station** •
  31 St James Ave [Arlington St]
- **Post Offices** • Back Bay Retail Unit •
  31 St James Ave [Arlington St]

🎓 Schools

- **Commonwealth** •
  151 Commonwealth Ave [Dartmouth St]
- **Fisher College** • 118 Beacon St [Berkeley St]
- **Learning Project Elementary** •
  107 Marlborough St [Clarendon St]
- **Snowden International High** •
  150 Newbury St [Dartmouth St]

🛒 Supermarkets

- **Shaw's** • 53 Huntington Ave [Exeter St]
- **South End Food Emporium** •
  469 Columbus Ave [W Newton]

Map 6 • **Back Bay (East) / South End (Upper)**

Sundries / Entertainment

Map 6

Grab a great sandwich at Parish Café, a curry at House of Siam, or, if you're operating on an expense account, a steak at Grill 23. If you're just thirsty, you can hit the roof-deck at Rattlesnake, or if you need to be seen while seeing, stop off at Saint.

Coffee

- **L'Aroma Café** •
  85 Newbury St [Clarendon St]
- **Starbucks** • Westin Hotel •
  10 Huntington Ave [Dartmouth St]
- **Starbucks** • Copley Place •
  110 Huntington Ave [Harcourt]
- **Starbucks** •
  165 Newbury St [Dartmouth St]
- **Starbucks** • 441 Stuart St [Trinity]
- **Starbucks** • 443 Boylston St [Berkeley St]
- **Starbucks** • 755 Boylston St [Fairfield St]
- **Tealuxe** • 108 Newbury St [Clarendon St]
- **Uptown Espresso Caffe** •
  563 Columbus Ave [W Springfield]

Copy Shops

- **BFS Printers** • 320 Stuart St [Columbus]
- **Copy Cop** •
  601 Boylston St [Fairfield St]
- **FedEx Kinko's** •
  187 Dartmouth St [St James Ave]
- **FedEx Kinko's** •
  575 Boylston St [Dartmouth St]
- **Printing Plus** •
  31 St James Ave [Arlington St]
- **Pro Print** • 410 Boylston St [Berkeley St]
- **The UPS Store** •
  110 Huntington Ave [Harcourt]
- **The UPS Store** •
  398 Columbus Ave [W Canton]

Farmers Markets

- **Copley Square** •
  (May–Nov; Tues 11 am–6 pm.
  Fri 11 am–6 pm) • 139 St James Ave

Gyms

- **Body Evolver Health Fitness Center** •
  364 Boylston St [Arlington St]
- **Boston Sports Club** •
  505 Boylston St [Clarendon St]
- **Fitcorp** •
  111 Huntington Ave [Garrison St]
- **Fitcorp** • 197 Clarendon St [St James Ave]
- **Fitcorp** • 800 Boylston St [Fairfield St]
- **Fitness Together** •
  36 Newbury St [Berkeley St]
- **HealthWorks Fitness Center**
  (Women Only) • 441 Stuart St [Trinity]
- **Revolution Fitness** •
  209 Columbus Ave [Berkeley St]

Hardware Stores

- **Park True Value Hardware** •
  233 Newbury St [Fairfield St]

Liquor Stores

- **Best Cellars (Wine Only)** •
  745 Boylston St [Exeter St]
- **Clarendon Wine** •
  563 Boylston St [Clarendon St]
- **The Wine Emporium** •
  474 Columbus Ave [W Newton]

Nightlife

- **Anchovies** • 433 Columbus Ave [Braddock]
- **Champions** • Marriott •
  110 Huntington Ave [Harcourt]
- **City Bar** • Lenox Hotel •
  61 Exeter St [Boylston St]
- **Clery's** • 113 Dartmouth St [Columbus]
- **Club Café** •
  209 Columbus Ave [Berkeley St]
- **Flash's** • 310 Stuart St [Arlington]
- **Rattlesnake** • 384 Boylston St [Berkeley St]
- **Rise** • 306 Stuart St [Columbus]
- **Saint** • 90 Exeter St [Blagden]
- **Vox Populi** • 755 Boylston St [Fairfield St]

Restaurants

- **33** • 33 Stanhope St [Clarendon St]
- **Abe & Louie's** •
  793 Boylston St [Fairfield St]
- **b.good** • 131 Dartmouth St [Columbus]
- **Bouchee** • 159 Newbury St [Dartmouth St]
- **Brasserie Jo** •
  120 Huntington Ave [W Newton]
- **Charlie's Sandwich Shoppe** •
  429 Columbus Ave [Holyoke St]
- **Claremont Café** •
  535 Columbus Ave [Claremont Pk]
- **Coda** • 329 Columbus Ave [Dartmouth]
- **Davio's** • 75 Arlington St [Stuart]
- **Domani** • 51 Huntington Ave [Exeter St]
- **Flash's** • 310 Stuart St [Arlington]
- **Grill 23 & Bar** • 161 Berkeley St [Stuart]
- **House of Siam** •
  542 Columbus Ave [Worcester St]
- **L'Aroma Café** •
  85 Newbury St [Clarendon St]
- **Laurel** • 142 Berkeley St [Columbus]
- **Legal Sea Foods** •
  800 Boylston St [Fairfield St]
- **Mistral** • 223 Columbus Ave [Cahners]
- **The Oak Room** •
  138 Saint James Ave [Trinity]
- **Osushi** • 10 Huntington Ave [Dartmouth St]
- **Parish Café** • 361 Boylston St [Arlington St]
- **Petsi Pies** • 285 Beacon St [Exeter St]
- **Shino Express Sushi** •
  144 Newbury St [Dartmouth St]
- **Upper Crust** • 222 Newbury St [Exeter St]

Shopping

- **All Things Chocolate** •
  31 St James Ave [Arlington St]
- **Amazing Express** •
  57 Stuart St [Huntington]
- **Anthropologie** •
  799 Boylston St [Fairfield St]
- **Barneys New York** •
  100 Newbury Ave [Exeter St]
- **Best of Scotland** •
  115 Newbury St, Ste 202 [Clarendon St]
- **Brooks Brothers** •
  46 Newbury St [Berkeley St]
- **City Sports** •
  480 Boylston St [Clarendon St]
- **Crate & Barrel** •
  777 Boylston St [Fairfield St]
- **First Act Guitar Studio** •
  745 Boylston St [Exeter St]
- **Hempest** • 207 Newbury St [Exeter St]
- **International Poster Gallery** •
  205 Newbury St [Exeter St]
- **Kitchen Arts** •
  161 Newbury St [Dartmouth St]
- **Lindt Master Chocolatier** •
  704 Boylston St [Exeter St]
- **Lord & Taylor** •
  760 Boylston St [Fairfield St]
- **Louis Boston** •
  234 Berkeley St [Newbury St]
- **Luna Boston** •
  166 Newbury St [Dartmouth St]
- **Marc Jacobs** •
  81 Newbury St [Clarendon St]
- **Marshall's** •
  500 Boylston St [Clarendon St]
- **Neiman Marcus** •
  5 Copley Pl [Dartmouth St]
- **O & Co.** • 161 Newbury St [Dartmouth St]
- **Paper Source** •
  338 Newbury St [Arlington St]
- **Saks Fifth Avenue** • 1 Ring Rd [Waltham]
- **Second Time Around** •
  176 Newbury St [Exeter St]
- **Shreve, Crump & Low** •
  440 Boylston St [Berkeley St]
- **Stil** • 170 Newbury St [Dartmouth St]
- **Teuscher Chocolates** •
  230 Newbury St [Fairfield St]

Map 6 • **Back Bay (East) / South End (Upper)**

Map 6

In Boston, jaywalking is a time-honored pastime, especially around the Pru and along Boylston and Newbury Streets. Back Bay is generally well-served by public transportation, even though (somewhat unusually) no buses actually run down Commonwealth Ave. Street parking? Good luck.

Subway

- **Arlington**
- **Copley**
- **Back Bay**

Bus Lines

- **9** • City Point—Copley Square via Broadway Station
- **10** • City Point—Copley Square via Andrew Station & BU Medical Area
- **39** • Forest Hills Station—Back Bay Station via Huntington Avenue
- **43** • Ruggles Station—Park & Tremont Streets
- **55** • Jersey & Queensberry Streets—Copley Square or Park & Tremont Streets

Car Rental

- **Avis** • 100 Clarendon St [Stanhope] • 617-534-1404
- **Dollar** • Marriott Copley Place • 110 Huntington Ave [Harcourt] • 617-578-0025
- **Hertz** • 10 Huntington Ave [Dartmouth St] • 617-338-1506
- **Hertz** • Back Bay Station Amtrak • 145 Dartmouth St [Stuart] • 617-338-1500

Car Washes

- **Magic Touch** • 131 Dartmouth St [Columbus]

Parking

Map 7 • South End (Lower)

Ⓝ

Boylston St
Boylston St
Boylston
Chinatown

Commonwealth Ave
Copley
Arlington

Clarendon St
Stuart St

Boylston St
Berkeley St
Dartmouth St
Columbus Ave
Charles St
Stuart St
Oak St W

Ring Rd
Massachusetts Tpk Rd
90
Tremont St
Corning St
NE Med Ctr

Framingham Worcester Line
Back Bay
Chandler St
Herald St
Paul Pl

A Prudential
Huntington St
Needham Line

Buckingham St

6
Lawrence St
Appleton St
Dartmouth Pl
Gray St

Warren Ave
Milford St
E Berkeley St

2 $

Montgomery St
Union Park

R
Union Park St

W Newton St
Tremont St

Shawmut Ave

4
E Berkeley St

Fort Point Channel

W 4th St

Paul Sullivan Way
Albany St

SoWa Building

Cathedral of the Holy Cross

Randolph St
Malden St

13
Massachusetts Ave

Washington St
Newton St
E Newton St

12
Worcester Sq

Mass Ave
Harrison Ave

Lenox St

Boston University Medical Center
Albany St

Melnea Cass

Harrison Ave
Gen Pulaski Skwy

Melnea Cass Blvd
Southampton St

Southampton St

1/4 mile   .25 km

Map 7

The South End is America's largest Victorian neighborhood, has the city's largest gay population, and, after years of gentrification, is now a "destination" spot. All this hipness, of course, makes the South End more expensive than it was a decade ago. Ultra-trendy boutiques rub shoulders with family-friendly brasseries (especially on happening Tremont Street).

$ Banks

- **Bank of America** · 557 Tremont St [Waltham]
- **Century Bank (ATM)** · BU Dental School · 100 E Newton St [Harrison Ave]
- **Century Bank (ATM)** · BU Parking Garage · 710 Albany St [E Concord]
- **Century Bank (ATM)** · BU Med School · 715 Albany St [E Concord]
- **Citizens Bank** · 1355 Washington St [Waltham]
- **Citizens Bank (ATM)** · 840 Harrison Ave [E Springfield]
- **Mercantile Bank** · 1320 Washington St [Rollins St]
- **Sovereign Bank** · 521 Tremont St [Dwight]
- **Sovereign Bank (ATM)** · CVS · 400 Tremont St [Herald]
- **Sovereign Bank (ATM)** · Boston Center for the Arts · 539 Tremont St [Hanson St]
- **Sovereign Bank (ATM)** · 818 Harrison Ave [Worcester St]

❀ Community Gardens

◎ Donuts

- **Dunkin' Donuts** · 1138 Washington St [E Berkeley]
- **Dunkin' Donuts** · 616 Massachusetts Ave [Shawmut Ave]

✚ Emergency Rooms

- **Boston Medical Center** · 1 Boston Medical Ctr Pl [Mass Ave]

O Landmarks

- **Cathedral of the Holy Cross** · 1400 Washington St [Union Pk St]
- **SoWa Building** · 450 Harrison Ave [Thayer St]

📖 Libraries

- **South End** · 685 Tremont St [W Newton]

℞ Pharmacies

- **Boston Medical Outpatient Pharmacy** · 720 Harrison Ave [E Brookline]
- **CVS** · 400 Tremont St [Herald]
- **Tremont Drug** · 610 Tremont St [W Dedham]
- **Walgreens** · 1603 Washington St [Rutland]

🕊 Police

- **District D-4** · 650 Harrison Ave [E Dedham]

✉ Post Offices

- **Cathedral Station** · 59 W Dedham St [Shawmut Ave]

🎓 Schools

- **Cathedral Grammar** · 595 Harrison Ave [Malden]
- **Cathedral High** · 74 Union Park St [Harrison Ave]
- **Joseph J Hurley Elementary** · 70 Worcester St [Tremont St]
- **William Blackstone Elementary** · 380 Shawmut Ave [W Dedham]
- **William McKinley** · 90 Warren Ave [Columbus]

🛒 Supermarkets

- **Foodie's Urban Market** · 1421 Washington St [Upton]
- **Ming's Supermarket** · 1102 Washington St [E Berkeley]
- **Super 88** · 50 Herald St [Washington St]

Start your night at Delux, a beloved neighborhood bar complete with Elvis shrine. Then head to Joe V's for Italian, or Aquitaine for French. After a few bottles of wine, hit up Pho Republique. The morning after, treat your stomach to Mike's City Diner or the pajama brunch at Tremont 647. If you're still alive after all that, call us.

Coffee

- Francesca's • 564 Tremont St [Union Pk St]
- Haley House Bakery & Café • 23 Dartmouth St [Montgomery St]
- Starbucks • 627 Tremont St [W Canton]

Copy Shops

- FedEx Kinko's • 715 Albany St [E Concord]
- Stratografix • 1200 Washington St [Perry St]

Farmers Markets

- South End at the Open Market (May 23—Oct; Sun 10am—4pm) • 540 Harrison Ave [Savoy St]

Gyms

- Boston Sports Club • 560 Harrison Ave [Rollins St]

Hardware Stores

- Warren Hardware • 470 Tremont St [E Berkeley]

Liquor Stores

- Brix Wine Shop • 1284 Washington St [Savoy St]
- The Wine Emporium • 607 Tremont St [Dartmouth St]

Nightlife

- Beehive • 541 Tremont St [Hanson St]
- Delux Café • 100 Chandler St [Clarendon St]
- Eagle • 520 Tremont St [Dwight]
- Franklin Café • 278 Shawmut Ave [Hanson]
- Pho Republique • 1415 Washington St [Union Pk St]

Pet Shops

- The Pet Shop Girls • 12 Union Park St [Shawmut Ave]
- Polka Dog Bakery • 256 Shawmut Ave [Milford]
- s'Poochies Spa & Boutique • 400 Tremont St [Herald]

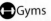 Restaurants

- Addis Red Sea • 544 Tremont St [Waltham]
- Appleton Bakery & Café • 123 Appleton St [Appleton St]
- Aquitaine • 569 Tremont St [Union Pk St]
- B&G Oysters • 550 Tremont St [Waltham]
- BanQ • 1375 Washington St [Union Park St]
- DaVinci Ristorante • 162 Columbus Ave [Arlington St]
- Delux Café • 100 Chandler St [Clarendon St]
- El Triunfo • 147 E Berkeley St [Harrison Ave]
- flour bakery + café • 1595 Washington St [Rutland]
- Franklin Café • 278 Shawmut Ave [Hanson]
- Garden of Eden • 571 Tremont St [Union Pk St]
- Gaslight 560 • 560 Harrison Ave [Waltham St]
- Hamersley's Bistro • 553 Tremont St [Waltham]
- Joe V's • 315 Shawmut Ave [Waltham]
- L'Espalier • 774 Boylston St [Newbury St]
- Masa • 439 Tremont St [Appleton St]
- Mela • 578 Tremont St [Upton St]
- Metropolis Café • 584 Tremont St [Upton]
- Mike's City Diner • 1714 Washington St [W Springfield]
- Morse Fish • 1401 Washington St [Union Pk St]
- Myers + Chang • 1145 Washington St [E Berkeley]
- Oishii • 1166 Washington St [E Berkeley]
- Orinoco • 477 Shawmut Ave [W Concord St]
- Pho Republique • 1415 Washington St [Union Pk St]
- Picco • 513 Tremont St [E Berkeley]
- Red Fez • 1222 Washington St [Perry St]
- Rocca • 500 Harrison Ave [Perry St]
- Sage • 1395 Washington St [Union Pk St]
- Sibling Rivalry • 525 Tremont St [Dwight]
- South End Pita • 473 Albany St [Union Park St]
- Stella • 1525 Washington St [E Brookline]
- Tremont 647 • 647 Tremont St [W Brookline]
- Union Bar and Grille • 1357 Washington St [Waltham]
- Upper Crust • 683 Tremont St [W Newton]

Shopping

- Aunt Sadie's • 18 Union Park St [Shawmut Ave]
- Bobby from Boston • 19 Thayer St [Harrison Ave]
- Brix Wine Shop • 1284 Washington St [Savoy St]
- The Butcher Shop • 552 Tremont St [Waltham]
- Community Bicycle Supply • 496 Tremont St [E Berkeley]
- Ilex • 73 Berkeley St [Chandler St]
- Lekker • 1317 Washington St [Rollins St]
- Lionette's • 577 Tremont St [Union Pk St]
- Motley • 623 Tremont St [W Canton St]
- Picco • 513 Tremont St [E Berkeley]
- Posh • 557 Tremont St [Waltham]
- South End Buttery • 314 Shawmut Ave [Union Pk St]
- South End Formaggio • 268 Shawmut Ave [Milford]
- Uniform • 511 Tremont St [E Berkeley]
- Urban Living Studio • 58 Clarendon St [Chandler St]

Video Rental

- Mike's Movies • 630 Tremont St [W Canton]

Street parking north of Washington Street is a disaster, a situation compounded by the paucity of parking lots and garages. Visitors should strongly consider using the Silver Line, particularly to go to any spot on or near Washington Street. Check Gaslight 560 for the food and the huge parking lot for diners.

Subway

- NE Medical Center
- Herald St
- E Berkeley St
- Union Park St
- Newton St
- Worcester Sq
- Massachussetts Ave
- Lenox St
- Melnea Cass Blvd

Bus Lines

- **CT1** · Central Square, Cambridge—BU Medical Center/BU Medical Campus
- **CT3** · Beth Israel Deaconess Medical Center—Andrew Station via BU Medical Center
- **1** · Harvard/Holyoke Gate—Dudley Station via Mass Ave & BU Medical Center
- **8** · Harbor Point/UMass—Kenmore Station via South End Medical Area
- **9** · City Point—Copley Square via Broadway Station
- **10** · City Point—Copley Square via Andrew Station & BU Medical Area
- **43** · Ruggles Station—Park & Tremont Streets
- **47** · Central Square, Cambridge—Broadway Station via South End Medical Area

Gas Stations

- **Mobil** · 273 E Berkeley St [Albany St] ♿
- **Stop N Gas** · 970 Washington St [Herald]
- **Sunoco** · 976 Washington St [Herald]

Ⓟ Parking

Map 8

Looking at Charlestown now, it's hard to believe that this small (one square mile) neighborhood was once the stolen car capital of the entire country (and home to many of Boston's infamous Irish gangsters). Despite the public housing blocks that still sit along the edge of town, Charlestown is now an upscale, quaint community.

$ Banks

- **Citizens Bank** · 5 Austin St [Warren St]
- **Citizens Bank (ATM)** · 140 Main St [Church Ct]
- **Co-Operative Bank** · 201 Main St [Hathon]

✳ Community Gardens

⊙ Donuts

- **Dunkin' Donuts** · 11 Austin St [Warren St]

O Landmarks

- **Bunker Hill Monument** · Monument Ave [High St]
- **Charlestown Navy Yard** ·
  Constitution Rd & Warren St
- **Tobin Memorial Bridge** · US-1
- **Warren Tavern** · 2 Pleasant St [Main]

📖 Libraries

- **Charlestown** · 179 Main St [Wood St]

℞ Pharmacies

- **CVS** · Bunker Hill Mall · 5 Austin St [Warren St]
- **High Pharmacy** · 54 High St [Green St]

✉ Post Offices

- **Charlestown** · 23 Austin St [Lawrence St]

🎓 Schools

- **Charlestown High** · 240 Medford St [Polk]
- **Clarence R Edwards Middle** · 28 Walker St [High St]
- **Harvard-Kent Elementary** ·
  50 Bunker Hill St [Moulton St]
- **The Holden School** · 8 Pearl St [Wesley St]
- **Warren Prescott Elementary** ·
  50 School St [Bartlett St]

Map Grid

	1	2

Mystic River

A

Choate St
St Martin St
Medford St
Woods
Pl
Mead St
Grants
Webster
Ct
Pearl St
Mystic St
Terminal St
Tobin Memorial Bridge
Mead St
Clapen
Bunker Hill St
Bremont St
Sackley St
Cook St
Elm St
Casey Ct
Old Landing Way
Old Ironsides Way
Medford St
Russell St
Wall St
Russell St
Mason St
Avon St
Walford Way
Mishawm Ct
O'Brien Ct
Chelsea St
Decatur St
Walker St
Perry Pl
Bartlett St
Hancock
O'Reilly Way
Tufts St
Mount Vernon Ave
Government Center
16th St
15th St
13th St
Exchange Ct
Main St
School St
Soley St
Linwood
Cordis Ave
Jefferson Ave
Monument Ct
Concord Ave
Lexington St
Mount Vernon St
Vine St
1st Ave
3rd Ave
4th Ave
O'Brien Ct
B'way
Dunstable Ct
Sullivan St
Belmont
High St
Tremont St
Corey St
Adams St
Lowney Way
Chelsea St
2nd Ave
Baxter Rd
Shexby St
Jamaica St
Church St
Baldwin
Mount Vernon Ave
Prospect St
Winthrop St
Chestnut St
9
W School St
Pleasant St
Harvard St
Adams St
Water St
1st Ave
25
Austin St
Rutherford Ave
Union St
Washington St
Soley
Henley St
Constitution Rd
PAGE 187
Charlestown Navy Yard
New Rutherford Ave
Lynde St
Hugh Pl
Foss St
Harvard Pl
Mason St
Harvard St
Champney St
Boston National Historic Park
2
3

B

Leverett Connector
Rankin Bunker Hill Br
Charlestown Bridge

1

Charles River

1/4 mile	.25 km

Two notable restaurants along Charlestown's City Square are Olives and Tangierino. On Flagship Wharf, views of the city can't be beat while eating oysters at the recently upscaled Tavern on the Water. For history buffs, nothing's better than the Warren Tavern, one of the oldest bars in the country.

Coffee

- **Coffee Shop** · 1 Thompson Square [Austin]
- **Sorelle** · 100 City Sq [Park St]

Farmers Markets

- **Charlestown (July—Oct; Wed 2 pm—7 pm)** ·
  Main St & Austin St

Gyms

- **Boston Young Men's Christian Union** ·
  48 Boyle St [Pleasant St]

Liquor Stores

- **Bunker Hill Liquors** · 200 Bunker Hill St [Green St]
- **Charlestown Liquors** · 10 Thompson Sq [Austin]
- **McCarthy Brothers Liquors** ·
  9 Moulton St [Bunker Hill St]

Nightlife

- **Goody Glovers** · 50 Salem St [High St]
- **Sullivan's Pub** · 85 Main St [Monument Ave]
- **Tavern on the Water** · 1 Pier 6 at E 8th St
- **Warren Tavern** · 2 Pleasant St [Main]

Restaurants

- **Figs** · 67 Main St [Monument Ave]
- **Ironside Grill** · 25 Park St [Warren St]
- **Jenny's Pizza** · 320 Medford St [Allston St]
- **Navy Yard Bistro & Wine Bar** · 1 1st Ave [3rd St]
- **Ninety Nine** · 29 Austin St [Lawrence St]
- **Olives** · 10 City Sq [Main]
- **Paolo's Trattoria** · 251 Main St [Lawnwood]
- **Sorelle** · 1 Monument Ave [Main]
- **Sorelle** · 100 City Sq [Park St]
- **Tangierino** · 83 Main St [Monument Ave]
- **Warren Tavern** · 2 Pleasant St [Main]

Shopping

- **A Wild Flower** · 73 Main St [Monument Ave]
- **Bunker Hill Florist** · 1 Thompson Sq [Austin]
- **Doherty's Flowers** · 223 Main St [School St]
- **The Joy of Old** · 85A Warren St [Pleasant St]
- **Serenade Chocolates** · 5 Harvard Sq [Andem Pl]

Map 8 · **Charlestown**

Map 3

In the middle of winter, it's a long, bitter hike into Charlestown from the Orange Line at Community College or Sullivan Square. Driving is ill-advised, but cabs are a quick hop from downtown. Warmer options are buses 92 or 93. A great summer alternative is the City Water Taxi from Long Wharf.

Bus Lines

92 • Assembly Square Mall—Downtown via
  Sullivan Square Station, Main St

93 • Sullivan Square Station—Downtown via
  Bunker Hill Street & Haymarket Station

111 • Woodlawn or Broadway & Park Ave—
  Haymarket Station via Mystic River/Tobin Bridge

Gas Stations

• **Shell** • 1 Rutherford Ave [N Washington] ♿

Parking

Map 9

Isolated from the city by water and the airport, Eastie's tree-lined streets and copious three-deckers are home to a diverse and vibrant Latin American community. Maverick Square is busy, but you'll want to make the walk up to Day Square to get a better sense of the turf.

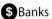 Banks

- **Bank of America (ATM)** • 3-11 Porter St [Central Sq]
- **Bank of America (ATM)** • 47 Maverick Sq [Sumner St]
- **Citizens Bank** • 26 Central Sq [Bennington]
- **Citizens Bank (ATM)** • 49 White St [Monmouth]
- **East Boston Savings Bank** •
  1 Bennington St [Porter St]
- **East Boston Savings Bank** •
  10 Meridian St [Maverick St]
- **East Boston Savings Bank (ATM)** •
  294 Bennington St [Chelsea St]
- **Eastern Bank (ATM)** • 246 Border St [Lexington St]
- **Sovereign Bank** • 2 Meridian St [Maverick St]
- **Sovereign Bank (ATM)** • 1 Porter St [Bennington St]
- **Sovereign Bank (ATM)** • CVS/Pharmacy •
  210 Border St [Saratoga St]

✴ Community Gardens

◉ Donuts

- **Dunkin' Donuts** • 13 Maverick Sq [Sumner St]
- **Honey Dew Donuts** • 12 Maverick Sq [Sumner St]
- **Honey Dew Donuts** • 470 Meridian St [Condor]

O Landmarks

- **LoPresti Park** • Summer St

📖 Libraries

- **East Boston** • 276 Meridian St [Princeton St]

℞ Pharmacies

- **CVS** • 210 Border St [Saratoga St] ♿
- **Walgreens** • 1 Central Sq [Meridian St] ♿

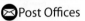 Police

- **District A-7** • 69 Paris St [Emmons St]

✉ Post Offices

- **East Boston Station** • 50 Meridian St [Paris St]

Schools

- **Dante Alighieri Elementary** • 37 Gove St [Paris St]
- **Donald McKay Elementary/Middle** •
  122 Cottage St [Maverick St]
- **East Boston Central Catholic** •
  69 London St [McClellan Hwy]
- **East Boston High** • 86 White St [Eutaw]
- **Hugh Roe O'Donnell Elementary** •
  33 Trenton St [Marion St]
- **James Otis Elementary** • 218 Marion St [Morris]
- **Patrick J Kennedy Elementary** •
  343 Saratoga St [Putnam St]
- **Samuel Adams Elementary** • 165 Webster St [Ruth]
- **St Mary Star of the Sea Elementary** •
  58 Moore St [London St]
- **Umana/Barnes Middle** • 312 Border St [Eutaw]

Supermarkets

- **Shaw's** • 246 Border St [Lexington St]

Santarpio's Pizza is one of the best in the country, and worth the trip alone, but it's the pañerias, rotisseries, and taquerias that dominate the dining scene. Try the Peruvian chicken at the Rincon Limeno in Day Square, or the refined Salvadoran fare at El Buen Gusto. Small Latin American shops abound, selling piñatas, saint votives, and soccer kits.

Coffee

- **Café Zing** · 25 White St [Marion St]
- **La Sultana** · 40 Maverick Sq [Winthrop St]
- **Peaches & Cream** · 73 Bennington St [London St]
- **Spinelli's** · 282 Bennington St [Prescott St]

Copy Shops

- **The UPS Store** · 2 Neptune Rd [Bennington]

Liquor Stores

- **Castillo Liquors** · 228 Meridian St [Saratoga St]
- **Clipper Ship Wine & Spirits** · 17 Maverick Sq [Sumner St]
- **Day Square Liquor** · 288 Bennington St [Chelsea St]
- **Neptune Liquors** · 1 Neptune Rd [Bennington]

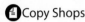Nightlife

- **Kelly Square Pub** · 84 Bennington St [Marion St]
- **Trainor's Café** · 127 Maverick St [Paris St]

Restaurants

- **Angela's Café** · 131 Lexington St [Brooks St]
- **Café Belo** · 254 Bennington St [Prescott St]
- **Café Italia** · 150 Meridian St [London St]
- **Café Meridian** · 271 Meridian St [Princeton St]
- **El Buen Gusto** · 295 Bennington St [Chelsea St]
- **El Chalan** · 405 Chelsea St [Shelby St]
- **Jeveli's** · 387 Chelsea St [Bennington]
- **La Frontera** · 290 Bennington St [Chelsea St]
- **La Terraza** · 19 Bennington St [Porter St]
- **Rincon Limeno** · 409 Chelsea St [Shelby]
- **Santarpio's Pizza** · 111 Chelsea St [Porter St]
- **TacoMex** · 65 Maverick Sq [Sumner St]
- **Taqueria Cancun** · 192 Sumner St [Maverick Sq]

Shopping

- **Brazilian Soccer House** · 110 Meridian St [London St]
- **Globos y Fiesta** · 52A Bennington St [London St]
- **Lilly's Flower Shop** · 512 Saratoga St [Chelsea St]
- **Lolly's Bakery** · 158 Bennington St [Brooks]
- **Studium Spanish Bookstore** · 268 Bennington St [Prescott St]

Video Rental

- **Blockbuster** · 184 Border St [Central Sq]
- **Maverick Audio & Video** · 25 Maverick Sq [Sumner St]

Driving means the Callahan Tunnel—stay in the right lane as you exit the tunnel. When leaving, keep a map handy, as there are about 30 roads in, and only 4 out, so it's very easy to get turned around. Also, keep a few dollars handy, as the airport toll will hit you on the way back. For public transportation, take the Blue line to the Maverick or Wood Island stops.

Subbway

- ■ · **Maverick**
- ■ · **Airport**
- ■ · **Wood Island**

Bus Lines

- ⑫ · Wellington Station—Wood Island Station via Central Ave, Mystic Mall & Admiral's Hill
- ⑯ · Wonderland Station—Maverick Station via Revere St
- ⑰ · Wonderland Station—Maverick Station via Revere St
- ⑳ · Orient Heights Station—Maverick Station via Bennington St
- ㉑ · Wood Island Station—Maverick Station via Lexington

⚿Car Rental

- **Affordable Auto Rental** · 84 Condor St [Brooks] · 617-561-7000
- **Alamo** · 2 Tomahawk Dr [Lamson St] · 617-561-4100

⬤Car Washes

- **Squikee Clean** · 452 Bremen St [Bennington]

⛽Gas Stations

- **Citgo** · 110 Service Rd [Mass Tpke]
- **Getty** · 331 Bennington St [Bremen St]
- **Mobil** · 396 Chelsea St [Shelby]
- **Mobil** · 470 Meridian St [Condor] ✪
- **Shell** · 52 Meridian St [Paris St] ✪

ⓅParking

Map 10 · **South Boston (West) / Fort Point** Ⓝ

Map 1

Southie seems to be in its renaissance. The formerly locals-only neighborhood has attracted yuppies, artists, and college students with a flurry of new condos, restaurants, and a short commute downtown. For proof of this, take a look at the Fan Pier by the ICA, which will soon be Boston's hippest address.

$ Banks

- **Bank of America** · 460 W Broadway [Dorchester St]
- **Bank of America (ATM)** · 332 Congress St [Sleeper]
- **Boston Private Bank & Trust** · 157 Seaport Blvd [B]
- **Citizens Bank** · 441 W Broadway [F]
- **Citizens Bank (ATM)** · 405 W Broadway [F]
- **Citizens Bank (ATM)** · 415 Summer St [D]
- **Citizens Bank (ATM)** · 482 W Broadway [Dorchester St]
- **Citizens Bank (ATM)** · 555 E Broadway [H]
- **Eastern Bank** · 470 W Broadway [Dorchester St]
- **Mt Washington Bank** · 430 W Broadway [F]
- **Mt Washington Bank** · 455 W Broadway [Dorchester]
- **Sovereign Bank** · 474 W Broadway [Dorchester St]
- **Sovereign Bank (ATM)** · 200 Seaport Blvd [WTC]
- **Sovereign Bank (ATM)** · 300 Congress St [Dorchester]
- **Sovereign Bank (ATM)** · 330 Congress St [Sleeper]
- **Sovereign Bank (ATM)** · CVS/Pharmacy · 423 W Broadway [F]

✳ Community Gardens

◉ Donuts

- **Dunkin' Donuts** · 268 Summer St [A St]
- **Dunkin' Donuts** · 330 Congress St [Sleeper]
- **Dunkin' Donuts** · 415 Summer St [WTC]
- **Dunkin' Donuts** · 482 W Broadway [Dorchester St]
- **Dunkin' Donuts** · 75 Old Colony Ave [C]

○ Landmarks

- **Boston Children's Museum** · 300 Congress St [Sleeper]
- **Boston Convention & Exhibition Center** · 415 Summer St [D]
- **Institute of Contemporary Art** · 100 Northern Ave [E Service]
- **South Boston Liquor Mart** · 295 Old Colony Ave [Jenkins]

📖 Libraries

- **Washington Village** · 1226 Columbia Rd [Mercer St]

Ⓡ Pharmacies

- **CVS** · 423 W Broadway [F]
- **Prescription Shoppe** · 378 W Broadway [E]

○ Police

- **District C-6** · 101 W Broadway [A St]

✉ Post Offices

- **South Boston Station** · 444 E 3rd St [Emerson St]

🏫 Schools

- **Excel High** · 95 G St [E 6th]
- **James Condon Elementary** · 200 D St [W 5th]
- **Michael J Perkins Elementary** · 50 Burke St [Pilsudski]
- **Monument High** · 95 G St [E 6th]
- **Odyssey High** · 95 G St [E 6th]
- **Patrick F Gavin Middle** · 215 Dorchester St [W 5th]
- **St Augustine's** · 209 E St [Baxter]

For after work drinks in the Summer, nothing beats Barking Crab. Drinkin' establishments are great here—especially Lucky's and Shenanigans. Finish your new pad with retro pieces from Machine Age. To get a dose of culture, catch a flick at the new ICA.

☕ Coffee

- **Café Arpeggio** · 398 W Broadway [F]
- **Yada Yada Café** · 34 Farnsworth St [Congress St]

📋 Copy Shops

- **FedEx Kinko's** · 415 Summer St [D]
- **Sir Speedy Printing Centers** · 266 Summer St [A St]

🍎 Farmers Markets

- **Children's Museum (July–Oct; Tues 4 pm–7 pm)** · 300 Congress St [Sleeper]
- **South Boston (July–Oct; Mon 12 pm–6 pm)** · 444 W Broadway [F]

💪 Gyms

- **Focus Fitness** · 303 Congress St [Dot Ave]
- **Regan's Motivated Fitness** · 315 W Broadway [D]

🔧 Hardware Stores

- **Seaport Hardware** · 369 Congress St [Stillings]

🍷 Liquor Stores

- **Al's Liquors** · 226 W Broadway [C]
- **Leonid Wine Company** · 341 W Broadway [E]
- **New Bay View Liquors** · 108 Dorchester St [W 2nd]
- **O'Donoghue's Liquor Store** · 341 West Broadway [D]
- **Old Colony Wine** · 259 Dorchester Ave [W 5th]

🎦 Movie Theaters

- **Institute of Contemporary Art** · 100 Northern Ave [B]

🍸 Nightlife

- **Atlantic Beer Garden** · 146 Seaport Blvd [Service St]
- **Blackthorn Pub** · 471 W Broadway [Dorchester St]
- **The Cornerstone** · 16 W Broadway [Dot Ave]
- **The Junction** · 110 Dorchester St [W 2nd]
- **Lucky's** · 355 Congress St [A St]
- **The Quiet Man** · 11 W Broadway [Dot Ave]
- **Shenanigans** · 332 W Broadway [D]
- **Stadium** · 232 Old Colony Ave [Mitchell]

🍴 Restaurants

- **Amrheins** · 80 W Broadway [A St]
- **Anthony's Pier 4** · 140 Northern Ave [Seaport Blvd]
- **Barking Crab** · 88 Sleeper St [Northern Ave]
- **The Daily Catch** · 2 Northern Ave [Sleeper]
- **Fresh Tortillas** · 475 W Broadway [Dorchester St]
- **Kingston Station** · 25 Kingston St [Bedford St]
- **Lucky's** · 355 Congress St [A St]
- **Mul's Diner** · 80 W Broadway [A St]
- **R&L Delicatessen** · 313 Old Colony Ave [Jenkins]
- **Salsa's Mexican Grill** · 118 Dorchester St [W B'way]
- **Slainte** · 28 W Broadway [Dot Ave]
- **Stadium** · 232 Old Colony Ave [Mitchell]
- **Teriyaki House** · 32 W Broadway [Dot Ave]

🛍 Shopping

- **Bob's Your Uncle** · 25 Channel Center St [Midway St]
- **Machine Age** · 645 Summer St [Fargo]
- **Scooters Go Green** · 220 Old Colony Ave [Damrell St]

📀 Video Rental

- **Blockbuster** · 267 Old Colony Ave [Patterson]

Parking here is hard to find and mostly residential. The Red Line and the Silver Line graze this area, and don't get you very close to Broadway, so to get to Broadway from Back Bay or the South End, consider taking the 9 bus.

Map

Subway

- **South Station**
- **Broadway**
- **Andrew**
- **Courthouse**
- **World Trade Center**
- **Silver Line Way**
- **BCEC**

Bus Lines

- **CT3** • Beth Israel Deaconess Medical Center—Andrew Station via BU Medical Center
- **4** • North Station—World Trade Center via Federal Courthouse
- **5** • City Point—McCormack Housing via Andrew Station
- **9** • City Point—Copley Square via Broadway Station
- **10** • City Point—Copley Square via Andrew Station & BU Medical Area
- **11** • City Point—Downtown, Bayview Route
- **47** • Central Square, Cambridge—Broadway Station via South End Medical Area

Car Rental

- **Select Car Rental** • Seaport Hotel • 1 Seaport Ln [Northern Ave] • 617-345-0203

Car Washes

- **Super Shine Auto Wash** • 39 Old Colony Ave [C]

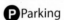

Gas Stations

- **Exxon** • 79 W Broadway [A St]
- **Shell** • 302 W Broadway [D]

Parking

Well-known as a working class Irish 'hood in a very Irish city, Southie's ethnic and socioeconomic makeup is slowly changing. Many young professionals, swayed by Southie's charm and priced out of other neighborhoods, are renovating triple-deckers.

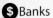 Banks

- **Bank of America** • 636 E Broadway [Emerson St]
- **Citizens Bank (ATM)** • 713 E Broadway [K St]
- **First Trade Union Bank** • 1 Harbor St [Dry]
- **First Trade Union Bank** •
  10 Drydock Ave [Design Ctr Pl]
- **First Trade Union Bank** • 753 E Broadway [L]
- **Mt Washington Bank** • 708 E Broadway [K St]
- **Sovereign Bank (ATM)** • 1 Seaport Ln [Northern Ave]
- **Sovereign Bank (ATM)** • 2 Seaport Ln [Northern Ave]

Donuts

- **Dunkin' Donuts** • 1 Fish Pier [Northern Ave]
- **Dunkin' Donuts** • 200 Seaport Blvd [WTC]
- **Joseph's Bakery** • 258 K St [E 4th St]

Landmarks

- **Bank of America Pavilion** •
  290 Northern Ave [Mass Tpke]
- **Black Falcon Terminal** •
  1 Black Falcon Ave [Design Ctr Pl]
- **Boston Design Center** •
  1 Design Center Pl [Black]
- **Boston Fish Pier** • 212 Northern Ave [D]
- **Giant Unholy Rat of Disease** • P St [E 4th St]
- **Harpoon Brewery** • 306 Northern Ave [Harbor St]
- **L Street Bathhouse** • William J Day Blvd & L St
- **L Street Tavern** • 658 E 8th St [L]
- **World Trade Center Boston** •
  200 Seaport Blvd [WTC]

Libraries

- **South Boston** • 646 E Broadway [Emerson St]

Pharmacies

- **Rite Aid** • 710 E Broadway [K St]

Schools

- **Gate of Heaven** • 609 E 4th St [I St]
- **Joseph P Tynan Elementary** • 640 E 4th St [I St]
- **Oliver Hazard Perry Elementary** • 745 E 7th St [N]
- **St Brigid's** • 866 E Broadway [O St]
- **St Peter's** • 518 E 6th St [I St]
- **Uphams Corner Charter** • 7 Elkins St [Summer]

Supermarkets

- **Stop & Shop** • 713 E Broadway [K St]

Map 1

During the summer, sea-bathers gather at the beaches along Dorchester Bay, or "The Irish Riviera." Good beer spots abound—take a tour of Harpoon Brewery for the samples of the freshest possible ale—and you can count on No Name Restaurant for reliable seafood.

Coffee

- **Cranberry Cafe** · 704 E Broadway [K St]
- **Java House** · 566 E Broadway [H]
- **Margaret's Coffee Shop** · 11 Elkins St [Summer]
- **Sidewalk Café** · 764 E 4th St [M St]
- **Starbucks** · 601 Congress St [D]

Copy Shops

- **Copy Cop** · 12 Channel St [Harbor]

Gyms

- **Boston Athletic Club** · 653 Summer St [W 1st]

Hardware Stores

- **Backstage True Value** · 21 Drydock Ave [Tide]

Liquor Stores

- **East Side Market** · 474 E 8th St [Winfield]
- **Jimmy's Korner** · 143 P St [E 6th]

Nightlife

- **Boston Beer Garden** · 732 E Broadway [L]
- **Corner Tavern** · 645 E 2nd St [K St]
- **L Street Tavern** · 658 E 8th St [L]
- **Murphy's Law** · 837 Summer St [E 1st]
- **Playwright** · 658 E Broadway [K St]

Restaurants

- **Aura** · Seaport Hotel · 1 Seaport Ln [Northern Ave]
- **Boston Beer Garden** · 732 E Broadway [L]
- **Café Porto Bello** · 672 E Broadway [K St]
- **Kelly's Landing** · 81 L St [E 4th]
- **KuDeTa** · 663 E Broadway [K St]
- **L Street Diner** · 108 L St [E 5th]
- **LTK (Legal Test Kitchen)** · 225 Northern Ave [D]
- **No Name Restaurant** · 15 Fish Pier St E [Northern Ave]
- **Playwright** · 658 E Broadway [K St]
- **Summer Street Grille** · 653 Summer St [W 1st]
- **Terrie's Place** · 676 E Broadway [K St]

Shopping

- **EP Levine** · 23 Drydock Ave [Tide]
- **Ku De Ta** · 663 E Broadway [K St]
- **Miller's Market** · 336 K St [E 7th]
- **Stapleton Floral** · 635 E Broadway [Emerson St]

Video Rental

- **Hub Video** · 604 E Broadway [Emerson St]

The addition of Silver Line stops in the neighborhood has made Southie much more accessible. If you drive, you'll have to find visitor parking, as the majority of the neighborhood is now resident only. Move a cone from a shoveled out parking spot, and be prepared to lose tires/windshield/wipers.

Subway

- Silver Line Way
- Northern Ave - Harbor St
- Northern Ave - Tide St
- Dry Dock Ave - Design Center Pl
- Summer St - Power House St
- E 1st St - M St
- City Point

Bus Lines

- **5** · City Point—McCormack Housing via Andrew Station
- **7** · City Point—Otis & Summer Streets via Northern Avenue & South Station
- **9** · City Point—Copley Square via Broadway Station
- **10** · City Point—Copley Square via Andrew Station & BU Medical Area
- **11** · City Point—Downtown, Bayview Route

Car Washes

· **Mr Perfection** · 1 Seaport Ln [Northern Ave]

Gas Stations

· **Exxon** · 57 L St [E 3rd]

Parking

Map 12 • Newmarket / Andrew Square

Food distributors, u-store warehouses, and the big box chains at South Bay Shopping Center are the heart of this commercial and industrial area. Unless you've got a trip to Target, Home Depot, or are visiting family at the Suffolk County House of Correction, you'll find only the fraying edges of Southie, Dorchester, and Roxbury worth a deeper look.

$ Banks

- **Bank of America** ·
  1104 Massachusetts Ave [Newmarket]
- **Bank of America (ATM)** ·
  150 Mt Vernon St [Morrissey]
- **Citizens Bank** · 60 Newmarket Sq [Mass Ave]
- **Citizens Bank (ATM)** · 863 Columbia Rd [Buttonwood]
- **Mt Washington Bank** · 501 Southampton St [Ellery St]

Community Gardens

- **Leyland St Community Garden and Tot Lot** ·
  6 Leyland St [E Cottage St]

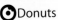 Donuts

- **Doughboy Deli** · 220 Dorchester Ave [W 5th]
- **Dunkin' Donuts** ·
  1100 Massachusetts Ave [Newmarket]
- **Dunkin' Donuts** · 22 W Broadway [Dot Ave]
- **Dunkin' Donuts** · 256 Boston St [Roseclair]
- **Dunkin' Donuts** · 510 Southampton St [Ellery St]
- **Dunkin' Donuts** · 847 Dorchester Ave [Mount Vernon St]

O Landmarks

- **Suffolk County House of Correction** ·
  20 Bradston St [Southampton]

Pharmacies

- **Stop & Shop** · 1100 Massachusetts Ave [Newmarket]
- **Target** · 7 Allstate Rd [Mass Ave]

Schools

- **Boston Collegiate Charter** ·
  11 Mayhew St [Boston St]
- **Community Academy Middle** ·
  76 Shirley St [Roswell]
- **Roger Clap Elementary** · 35 Harvest St [Boston St]
- **Samuel W Mason Elementary** ·
  150 Norfolk Ave [Proctor]
- **St Mary's Elementary** · 52 Boston St [Father Songin]
- **William E Russell Elementary** ·
  750 Columbia Rd [Pond St]

Supermarkets

- **Super 88** · 101 Allstate Rd [Mass Ave]

Map 12 • **Newmarket / Andrew Square**

Map 12

Treat your date at an out-of-the-way den of romance. Cozy 224 Boston Street fits that bill, with reasonable prices to boot. For a southern fried meal, try the Hen House for wings and waffles. It would be a shame to overlook the authentic Polish cuisine of tiny Café Polonia.

Coffee

- **Starbucks** • Target • 7 Allstate Rd [Mass Ave]
- **Sugar Bowl** • 837 Dorchester Ave [Mount Vernon St]

Gyms

- **Gold's Gym** • 323 Dorchester Ave [W 7th]

Hardware Stores

- **Home Depot** • 5 Allstate Rd [Mass Ave]
- **PJ O'Donnell & Co** • 115 Boston St [Washburn St]

Liquor Stores

- **Andrew Square Liquors** • 605 Dorchester Ave [Boston St]
- **Cape Verdean Liquors** • 690 Columbia Rd [Elder]

Nightlife

- **Aces High** • 551 Dorchester Ave [Dexter St]
- **Dot Tavern** • 840 Dorchester Ave [Harvest St]
- **Sports Connection Bar** • 560 Dorchester Ave [Leeds]

Pet Shops

- **Skipton Kennel & Pet Center** • 70 Southampton St [Bradston]

Restaurants

- **224 Boston Street** • 224 Boston St [St Margaret]
- **Alex's Pizza** • 580 Dorchester Ave [Leeds]
- **Avenue Grille** • 856 Dorchester Ave [Mount Vernon St]
- **Baltic Deli & Café** • 632 Dorchester Ave [Father Songin]
- **Café Polonia** • 611 Dorchester Ave [Boston St]
- **Franklin Cafe** • 152 Dorchester Ave [W 4th St]
- **The Hen House** • 1033 Massachusetts Ave [Proctor]
- **Restaurante Laura** • 688 Columbia Rd [Elder]
- **Singh's Roti Shop** • 692 Columbia Rd [Elder]
- **Taqueria Casa Real** • 860A Dorchester Ave [Mount Vernon St]
- **Venetian Garden** • 1269 Massachusetts Ave [Columbia Rd]
- **Victoria's Diner** • 1024 Massachusetts Ave [Newmarket]
- **World Seafood Restaurant** • 400 Dorchester Ave [D]

Shopping

- **Home Depot** • 5 Allstate Rd [Mass Ave]
- **Marshall's** • 8D Allstate Rd [Mass Ave]

Video Rental

- **North End Video** • 292 Boston St [Roseclair St]

This largely commercial and industrial area isn't well served by public transportation. If you need to get to the South Bay Shopping Center without driving, take the 10 bus from Andrew Square or Copley. If you're out for a stroll, make sure to leave the JFK/UMass T stop to the north onto Columbia Road.

Map 1

Subway

- **Broadway**
- **Andrew**
- **JFK/UMass**

Bus Lines

- **CT3** • Beth Israel Deaconess Medical Center—Andrew Station via BU Medical Center
- **5** • City Point—McCormack Housing via Andrew Station
- **8** • Harbor Point/UMass—Kenmore Station via South End Medical Area
- **9** • City Point—Copley Square via Broadway Station
- **10** • City Point—Copley Square via Andrew Station & BU Medical Area
- **11** • City Point—Downtown, Bayview Route
- **16** • Forest Hills Station—Andrew Station or UMass via Columbia Road
- **17** • Fields Corner Station—Andrew Station via Uphams Corner & Edward Everett Square
- **18** • Ashmont Station—Andrew Station via Fields Corner Station
- **47** • Central Square, Cambridge—Broadway Station via South End Medical Area
- **171** • Dudley Station—Logan Airport via Andrew Station

Car Rental

- **Enterprise** • 230 Dorchester Ave [W 5th] • 617-268-1411

Car Washes

- **Bubbles Car Wash** • 90 Southampton St [Mass Ave]
- **Scrubadub** • 25 W Howell St [Boston St]

Gas Stations

- **Gulf** • 888 Dorchester Ave [Columbia Rd] ⊘
- **Independent** • 150 Southampton St [Topeka] ⊘
- **Mobil** • 85 Southampton St [Bradston]
- **Sunoco** • 895 Massachusetts Ave [Island]

There's a beauty to Roxbury, despite its roughness. Dudley Square is Roxbury's commercial center, but businesses are also finding opportunity closer to the busy Orange Line and along Blue Hill Avenue. Highlights include The National Center of Afro-American Art, the largest mosque in New England, and the view from Fort Hill.

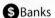 Banks

- **Bank of America** • 114 Dudley St [Washington St]
- **Bank of America (ATM)** • 1762 Washington St [Mass Ave]
- **Bank of America (ATM)** • 39 Warren St [Ziegler]
- **Citizens Bank** • 2343 Washington St [Marvin St]
- **Sovereign Bank** • 3060 Washington St [Walnut Pk]
- **Sovereign Bank** • 330 Martin Luther King Blvd [Washington St]
- **Sovereign Bank (ATM)** • 1010 Harrison Ave [Melnea]
- **Sovereign Bank (ATM)** • Boston Medical Center • 850 Harrison Ave [Mass Ave]

Community Gardens

- **The Food Project Lot #2** • Brook Ave & Cottage St]
- **James E Small, Sr Garden** • 15 Kearsarge Ave
- **Phyllis Wheatley School Garden** • 20 Kearsarge
- **Winthrop St Garden** • 25 Winthrop St [Kearsarge Ave]

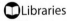 Donuts

- **Dunkin' Donuts** • 1131 Tremont St [Ruggles St]
- **Dunkin' Donuts** • 1350 Tremont St [Prentiss]
- **Dunkin' Donuts** • 17 Melnea Cass Blvd [Hampden]
- **Dunkin' Donuts** • 2360 Washington St [Roxbury]

O Landmarks

- **Highland Park** • Fort Ave & Beech Glen St
- **Islamic Cultural Center** • 1 Malcolm X Blvd [Roxbury]
- **Malcolm X and Ella Little-Collins House** • 72 Dale St [Wakullah]
- **National Center for Afro-American Artists** • 300 Walnut Ave [Cobden]
- **Roxbury Center for Arts** • 182 Dudley St [Harrison Ave]
- **Shirley-Eustis House** • 33 Shirley St [Clifton St]

Libraries

- **Dudley** • 65 Warren St [Dudley St]

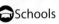 Pharmacies

- **Kornfield Drug** • 2121 Washington St [Williams St]
- **Ruggles Square Pharmacy** • 1123 Tremont St [Ruggles St]
- **Walgreens** • 2275 Washington St [Vernon]
- **Walgreens** • 416 Warren St [Townsend]

Police

- **District B-2** • 135 Dudley St [Warren St]

Post Offices

- **Roxbury Station** • 55 Roxbury St [Shawmut Ave]

Schools

- **826 Boston** • 3035 Washington St [W Walnut Park]
- **Boston Adult Academy** • 55 New Dudley St [King St]
- **Boston Day and Evening Academy** • 20 Kearsarge Ave [Warren St]
- **Boston Latin Academy** • 205 Townsend St [Humboldt Ave]
- **Carter Development Center** • 396 Northampton St [Columbus]
- **David A Ellis Elementary** • 302 Walnut Ave [Cobden]
- **Eliot Educational Center** • 56 Dale St [Walnut Ave]
- **George Lewis Middle** • 131 Walnut Ave [Dale]
- **Haynes Early Education Center** • 263 Blue Hill Ave [Dove St]
- **Henry Dearborn Middle** • 35 Greenville St [Dudley St]
- **Henry L Higginson Elementary** • 160 Harrishof St [Haley]
- **James P Timilty Middle** • 205 Roxbury St [Centre St]
- **John Winthrop Elementary** • 35 Brookford St [Dromey]
- **Madison Park Technical Vocational High School** • 75 Malcolm X Blvd [Roxbury]
- **Nathan Hale Elementary** • 51 Cedar St [Hawthorne St]
- **O'Bryant School of Math & Science** • 55 Malcolm X Blvd [Roxbury]
- **Orchard Gardens K-8** • 906 Albany St [Webber]
- **Paige Academy** • 40 Highland Ave [Centre St]
- **Ralph Waldo Emerson Elementary** • 6 Shirley St [Roxbury]
- **Roland Hayes School of Music** • 55 Malcolm X Blvd [Roxbury]
- **Roxbury Community College** • 1234 Columbus Ave [Cedar St]
- **St Joseph School** • 18 Hulbert St [Regent St]
- **St Patrick Elementary** • 131 Mt Pleasant Ave [Blue Hill]
- **William Monroe Trotter Elementary** • 135 Humboldt Ave [Wyoming]

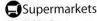 Supermarkets

- **Tropical Foods** • 2101 Washington St [Williams St]

Map 13

Lunch counters here serve soul food, jerk, and Latin American delicacies. Hankering for Dominican food? It doesn't get better than Merengue. Pepper Pot will hook you up Jamaican style. Grab a drink at local joints C&S or El Mondonguito.

Coffee

- **Blue Hill Coffee Shop** · 170 Blue Hill Ave [Clifford]

Farmers Markets

- **Dudley Town Common**
  (Jun—Oct; Tues & Thurs 4 pm—7 pm) ·
  Dudley St & Blue Hill Ave

Gyms

- **Body by Brandy Fitness Center** ·
  2181 Washington St [Ruggles St]
- **Roxbury Family YMCA** ·
  285 Martin Luther King Blvd [Walnut Ave]

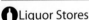Liquor Stores

- **Brothers Liquors** · 616 Shawmut Ave [Lenox]
- **Caribbean Liquors** · 527 Dudley St [North Ave]
- **Folgers Liquors** · 2665 Washington St [Cedar St]
- **Garden Liquors** · 276 Warren St [Waverly St]
- **Giant** · 2371 Washington St [Roxbury]
- **Hollywood Liquors** · 950 Tremont St [Davenport]
- **Liquor Land** · 874 Harrison Ave [Northampton St]
- **Simon's Liquor** · 2169 Washington St [Ruggles St]
- **Warren Liquors** · 368 Warren St [Maywood St]

Nightlife

- **C&S Tavern** · 380 Warren St [Maywood St]
- **El Mondonguito** · 221 Dudley St [Greenville St]
- **Slade's** · 958 Tremont St [Davenport]

Restaurants

- **Breezeway Bar and Grill** · 153 Blue Hill Ave [Julian]
- **Ideal Sub Shop** · 522 Dudley St [Burrell St]
- **Merengue** · 156 Blue Hill Ave [Julian]
- **Pepper Pot** · 208 Dudley St [Winslow St]
- **Stash's Grille** · 150 Dudley St [Warren St]

Shopping

- **Bikes Not Bombs** · 18 Bartlett St [Washington St]

Potholed and neglected, Roxbury's streets are fiendishly difficult to travel. Considering how many people call the neighborhood home, the public transportation is woefully inadequate. Unless you skirt the perimeter on the Orange Line or the pleasant Southwest Corridor bike trail, you'll likely head through Dudley Station, the busy bus hub packed with loiterers.

Subway

- Massachusetts Ave
- Ruggles
- Roxbury Crossing
- Jackson Square
- Northeastern (E)
- Museum (E)
- Ruggles (E)
- Mass Ave
- Lenox St
- Melnea Cass Blvd
- Dudley Square

Bus Lines

- **CT1** · Central Square, Cambridge—BU Medical Center/BU Medical Campus
- **CT3** · Beth Israel Deaconess Medical Center—Andrew Station via BU Medical Center
- **1** · Harvard/Holyoke Gate—Dudley Station via Massachusetts Ave & BU Medical Center
- **8** · Harbor Point/UMass—Kenmore Station via South End Medical Area
- **14** · Roslindale Square—Heath Street via Dudley Station, Grove Hall & American Legion Hwy
- **15** · Kane Square or Fields Corner Station—Ruggles Station via Uphams Corner
- **19** · Fields Corner Station—Ruggles Station via Grove Hall & Dudley Streets
- **22** · Ashmont Station—Ruggles Station via Talbot Ave & Jackson Square
- **23** · Ashmont Station—Ruggles Station via Washington Street
- **28** · Mattapan Station—Ruggles Station via Dudley Station
- **41** · Centre & Eliot Streets—JFK/Umass Station via Dudley Station, Centre Street & Jackson Square Station
- **44** · Jackson Square Station—Ruggles Station via Seaver Street & Humboldt Avenue

Car Rental

- **Enterprise** ·
  17 Melnea Cass Blvd [Hampden] · 617-442-7500

Gas Stations

- **Citgo** · 294 Blue Hill Ave [Quincy St]
- **Ho Gas** · 57 Blue Hill Ave [Winthrop St]
- **Independent** · 67 Blue Hill Ave [Moreland]
- **Sunoco** · 785 Tremont St [Northampton St] ⏰

P Parking

Map 14 · **Jamaica Plain**

N

1   2

Leverett Pond

Heath Street

▲ 15

PAGE 192

Olmstead Park

New Heath St

Jackson Square

13 ▶

A

28

Spontaneous Celebrations

Stony Brook

Jamaica Pond

17 ◀

Samuel Adams Brewery

The Footlight Club

First Church, Unitarian Universalist

3 $
R
3 $

The Loring-Greenough House

Green Street

Washington St

Glen Rd

B

Franklin Park

2

Doyle's Cafe

30 ▼

Arnold Arboretum

Forest Hills

Msgr William Casey Hwy South St

| 1/4 mile | .25 km |

Map 14

Despite the ongoing gentrification, Jamaica Plain is still home to a diverse population of artists, yuppies, students, lesbians, and immigrants. Stunning Jamaica Pond, the Arnold Arboretum, and the Franklin Park Zoo are all great reasons to head outside. Colorful festivals are a highlight of the summer months in Boston funkiest 'hood.

$ Banks

- **Bank of America** • 315 Centre St [Walden St]
- **Bank of America** • 677 Centre St [Seaverns]
- **Boston Private Bank & Trust (ATM)** •
  403 Centre St [Barbara]
- **Citizens Bank** • 696 Centre St [Burroughs St]
- **Citizens Bank (ATM)** • 301 Centre St [Walden St]
- **Citizens Bank (ATM)** • 684 Centre St [Seaverns]
- **Hyde Park Cooperative Bank** •
  733 Centre St [Harris Ave]
- **People's Federal Savings Bank** •
  725 Centre St [Harris Ave]
- **Roxbury Highland Bank** •
  515 Centre St [Spring Pk Ave]
- **Sovereign Bank (ATM)** • CVS/Pharmacy •
  467 Centre St [Roseway]
- **Wainwright Bank & Trust** • 687 Centre St [Seaverns]

Community Gardens

O Donuts

- **Dunkin' Donuts** • 1926 Columbus Ave [Walnut Pk]
- **Dunkin' Donuts** • 315 Centre St [Walden St]
- **Dunkin' Donuts** • 684 Centre St [Seaverns]
- **Dunkin' Donuts** • 757 Centre St [Thomas St]

O Landmarks

- **Arnold Arboretum** • 125 Arborway [Centre St]
- **Doyle's Café** • 3484 Washington St [Williams St]
- **First Church, Unitarian Universalist** •
  6 Eliot St [Centre St]
- **The Footlight Club** • 7A Eliot St [Centre St]
- **The Loring-Greenough House** •
  12 South St [Centre St]
- **Samuel Adams Brewery** • 30 Germania St [Brookside]
- **Spontaneous Celebrations** •
  75 Danforth St [Boylston St]

Libraries

- **Connolly** • 433 Centre St [Paul Gore St]
- **Jamaica Plain** • 12 Sedgwick St [South St]

Rx Pharmacies

- **CVS** • 467 Centre St [Boylston St]
- **CVS** • 704 Centre St [Burroughs St]
- **Egleston Square Pharmacy** •
  3090 Washington St [Beethoven]
- **Samuels Pharmacy** •
  46 Woodside Ave [Washington St]
- **Stop & Shop Pharmacy** • 301 Centre St [Johnson]
- **Walgreens** • 1890 Columbus Ave [Bray]

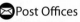 Police

- **District E-13** • 3345 Washington St [Green St]

✉ Post Offices

- **Jamaica Plain Station** • 655 Centre St [Myrtle St]

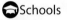 Schools

- **Blessed Sacrament Elementary** •
  30 Sunnyside St [Westerly]
- **Compass** • 26 Sunnyside St [Westerly]
- **Egleston High** • 3134 Washington St [School St]
- **Ellis Mendell Elementary** • 164 School St [Copley]
- **English High** • 144 McBride St [Call]
- **Greater Egleston Community High** •
  80 School St [Weld]
- **James Curley Elementary** •
  40 Pershing Rd [Centre St]
- **John F Kennedy Elementary** •
  7 Bolster St [Wyman St]
- **Louis Agassiz Elementary** • 20 Child St [South St]
- **Mary E Curley Middle** • 493 Centre St [Pershing]
- **Nativity Prep** • 39 Lamartine St [Roys]
- **Our Lady of Lourdes Elementary** •
  54 Brookside Ave [Minton]

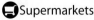 Supermarkets

- **Harvest Co-op Market** • 57 South St [Custer]
- **Hi-Lo** • 415 Centre St [Moraine]
- **Stop & Shop** • 301 Centre St [Walden St]

Centre Street functions as the main artery in JP, lined with restaurants and shops of all kinds. NFT picks = Brendan Behan Pub. La Pupusa Guanaca, Zon's, Midway Café, and James's Gate. Jackson Square and Washington Street offer the flavors of its Puerto Rican, Dominican, and Cape Verdean communities.

Coffee

- **Canto 6** • 3346 Washington St [Green St]
- **Cha Fahn** • 763 Centre St [Greenough Ave]
- **Fiore's Bakery** • 55 South St [Carolina Ave]
- **June Bug Café** • 403A Centre St [Barbara]
- **Sweet Christophers Desserts** • 601 Centre St [Pond St]
- **Sweet Finnish** • 761 Centre St [Eliot St]
- **ULA Café** • 284 Amory St [New Minton]

Copy Shops

- **Fresh Copy** • 64 South St [Carolina Ave]
- **Schell Printing** • 3399 Washington St [Green St]

Farmers Markets

- **Jamaica Plain**
  (July—Oct; Tues 12 pm—5 pm, Sat 12 pm—3 pm) •
  677 Centre St [Seaverns]

Gyms

- **Mike's Fitness** • 284 Amory St [Porter St]
- **YMCA Egleston Square Youth Center** •
  3134 Washington St [School St]

Hardware Stores

- **Hardware City** • 656 Centre St [Myrtle St]
- **Yumont True Value Hardware** •
  702 Centre St [Burroughs St]

Liquor Stores

- **Blanchard Liquors** • 741 Centre St [Harris Ave]
- **Chauncy Liquor Mart** • 3100 Washington St [Beethoven]
- **Egleston Liquors** • 3086 Washington St [Beethoven]
- **Fine Wine Cellars** • 7 Boylston St [Centre St]
- **Foerster's Market & Liquors** • 78 Boylston St [Danforth St]
- **Hyde Square Wine & Liquor** • 391 Centre St [Sheridan St]

Nightlife

- **Alchemist Lounge** • 435 S Huntington Ave [Centre St]
- **Brendan Behan Pub** • 378 Centre St [Sheridan St]
- **Costello's Tavern** • 723 Centre St [Harris Ave]
- **Doyle's Café** • 3484 Washington St [Williams St]
- **Drinking Fountain** • 3520 Washington St [Rossmore]
- **James's Gate** • 5 McBride St [South St]
- **Jeanie Johnston Pub** • 144 South St [Hall St]

- **Midway Café** • 3496 Washington St [Williams St]
- **The Milky Way** • 284 Amory St [Lamartine St Ext]
- **Samuel Adams Brewery** • 30 Germania St [Brookside]

Restaurants

- **Alex's Chimis** • 358 Centre St [Forbes]
- **Bukhara** • 701 Centre St [Burroughs St]
- **Café D** • 711 Centre St [Burroughs St]
- **Centre Street Café** • 699 Centre St [Burroughs St]
- **Cha Fahn** • 763 Centre St [Greenough Ave]
- **Dogwood Café** • 3712 Washington St [Arborway]
- **Doyle's Café** • 3484 Washington St [Williams St]
- **El Oriental de Cuba** • 416 Centre St [Paul Gore St]
- **Fredy's Pastelito** • 3381 Washington St [Green St]
- **The Galway House** • 720 Centre St [Burroughs St]
- **Great Wall** • 779 Centre St [Eliot St]
- **James's Gate** • 5 McBride St [South St]
- **JP Seafood Café** • 730 Centre St [Harris Ave]
- **La Pupusa Guanaca** • 378 Centre St [Sheridan St]
- **Miami Restaurant** • 381 Centre St [Sheridan St]
- **Sorella's** • 388 Centre St [Sheridan St]
- **Tacos El Charro** • 349 Centre St [Westerly]
- **Ten Tables** • 597 Centre St [Pond St]
- **Vee Vee** • 763 Centre St [Eliot St]
- **Wonder Spice Café** • 697 Centre St [Burroughs St]
- **Yely's Coffee Shop** • 284 Centre St [Chestnut Ave]
- **Zon's** • 2 Perkins St [Perkins Sq]

Shopping

- **Boing! JP's Toy Shop** • 729 Centre St [Harris Ave]
- **Boomerangs** • 716 Centre St [Burroughs St]
- **Canto 6** • 3346 Washington St [Green St]
- **City Feed and Supply** • 66 Boylston St [Chestnut Ave]
- **Eye Q Optical** • 7 Pond St [Centre St]
- **Fat Ram's Pumpkin Tattoo** • 380 Centre St [Sheridan St]
- **Ferris Wheels Bicycle Shop** • 66 South St [Carolina Ave]
- **Fire Opal** • 683 Centre St [Seaverns]
- **Gadgets** • 671 Centre St [Seaverns]
- **Hatched Boston** • 5 Green St [Centre St]
- **Honeyspot** • 48 South St [Essex St]
- **J.P. Licks** • 659 Centre St [Starr Ln]
- **Petal & Leaf** • 48 South St [Boylston St]
- **Salmagundi** • 765 Centre St [Eliot St]

Video Rental

- **Columbus Video** • 1967 Columbus Ave [Washington St]
- **Video Underground** • 385 Centre St [Sheridan St]

Map 1

Driving is fairly convenient in JP, thanks to the quick flow of traffic on the Riverway and the abundance of free parking. Locals use the 39 bus as often as the Orange Line. Make Al Gore proud—take the bike trail in Southwest Corridor Park alongside the Orange Line all the way downtown.

Subway

- Jackson Square
- Stony Brook
- Green St
- Forest Hills
- Heath St (E)

Bus Lines

16 · Forest Hills Station—Andrew Station or UMass via Columbia Road

21 · Ashmont Station—Forest Hills Station via Morton Street

38 · Wren Street—Forest Hills Station via Centre & South Streets

39 · Forest Hills Station—Back Bay Station via Huntington Avenue

42 · Forest Hills Station—Ruggles Station via Washington Station & Dudley Square

48 · Jamaica Plain Loop Monument—Jackson Square Station via Green Street

Car Washes

· **Jamaica Plain Car Wash** · 3530 Washington St [Rossmore]

Gas Stations

· **Citgo** · 3055 Washington St [Walnut Pk]
· **Hatoff's** · 3440 Washington St [Union Ave]
· **Independent** · 581 Centre St [Goodrich]

Parking

Map 1

Ah, Mission Thrill. The place where culture, education, and sports meet, you can wander among fine art museums, green parks, eclectic colleges, top medical centers, and historic Fenway Park. While high-rise condos are changing the face of Fenway, Mission Hill is still a funky mix of students, families, and young professionals.

💲 Banks

- **Bank of America** • 1614 Tremont St [Wigglesworth]
- **Bank of America** • 333 Longwood Ave [Binney St]
- **Bank of America (ATM)** • 1643 Tremont St [Wigglesworth]
- **Bank of America (ATM)** • Ruggles St MBTA • 249 Ruggles St [Leon]
- **Bank of America (ATM)** • 300 The Fenway [Palace]
- **Bank of America (ATM)** • 360 Huntington Ave [Opera]
- **Bank of America (ATM)** • 550 Huntington Ave [Ruggles St]
- **Bank of America (ATM)** • 610 Huntington Ave [St Alphonsus]
- **Bank of America (ATM)** • 621 Huntington Ave [Tetlow]
- **Bank of America (ATM)** • MBTA Roxbury Crossing • Tremont St & Columbus Ave
- **Citizens Bank** • 1628 Tremont St [Wigglesworth]
- **Citizens Bank (ATM)** • 1 Francis St [Kent St]
- **Citizens Bank (ATM)** • 1620 Tremont St [Wigglesworth]
- **Citizens Bank (ATM)** • Boston Children's Hospital • 300 Longwood Ave [Blackfan]
- **Citizens Bank (ATM)** • 33 Kilmarnock St [Boylston St]
- **Citizens Bank (ATM)** • 75 Francis St [Vining]
- **Sovereign Bank** • 6 Francis St [Huntington]
- **Sovereign Bank (ATM)** • 350 Longwood Ave [Brookline Ave]
- **Sovereign Bank (ATM)** • 58 Forsyth St [Greenleaf]

✳️ Community Gardens

⦿ Donuts

- **Dunkin' Donuts** • 115 Forsyth St [Greenleaf]
- **Dunkin' Donuts** • 1420 Boylston St [Kilmarnock]
- **Dunkin' Donuts** • 1620 Tremont St [Wigglesworth]
- **Dunkin' Donuts** • 1631 Tremont St [Wigglesworth]
- **Dunkin' Donuts** • 350 Longwood Ave [Brookline Ave]
- **Dunkin' Donuts** • 360 Huntington Ave [Opera]
- **Mike's Donuts** • 1524 Tremont St [Carmel]

➕ Emergency Rooms

- **Brigham and Women's Hospital** • 75 Francis St [Vining]
- **Children's Hospital** • 300 Longwood Ave [Blackfan]

⭘ Landmarks

- **Isabella Stewart Gardner Museum** • 280 The Fenway [Palace]
- **Mission Church Basilica** • 1545 Tremont St [Pontiac]
- **Museum of Fine Arts** • 465 Huntington Ave [Museum Rd]
- **Warren Anatomical Museum** • 10 Shattuck St [Binney St]

📖 Libraries

- **Parker Hill** • 1497 Tremont St [Burney]

℞ Pharmacies

- **Rite Aid** • 1295 Boylston St [Yawkey]
- **CVS** • 300 Longwood Ave [Blackfan]
- **CVS** • 350 Longwood Ave [Brookline Ave]
- **Walgreens** • 1630 Tremont St [Wigglesworth]

✉️ Post Offices

- **Mission Hill Station** • 1575 Tremont St [S Whitney]

🎓 Schools

- **Boston Latin School** • 78 Ave Louis Pasteur [Longwood]
- **David Farragut Elementary** • 10 Fenwood Rd [Huntington]
- **ELC - West Zone** • 200 Heath St [Schiller]
- **Emmanuel College** • 400 The Fenway [Ave Louis Pasteur]
- **Harvard Medical** • 25 Shattuck St [Binney St]
- **Harvard School of Dental Medicine** • 188 Longwood Ave [Palace]
- **Harvard School of Public Health** • 677 Huntington Ave [Washington St]
- **Health Careers Academy** • 360 Huntington Ave [Opera]
- **James Hennigan Elementary** • 200 Heath St [Schiller]
- **Manville School** • 3 Blackfan Cir [Longwood]
- **Massachusetts College of Art** • 621 Huntington Ave [Tetlow]
- **Massachusetts College of Pharmacy and Health Sciences** • 179 Longwood Ave [Palace]
- **Mission Hill** • 67 Alleghany St [Parker St]
- **New Mission High School** • 67 Alleghany St [Parker St]
- **Northeastern University** • 360 Huntington Ave [Opera]
- **Roxbury Preparatory Charter** • 120 Fisher Ave [Hayden St]
- **School of the Museum of Fine Arts** • 230 The Fenway [Evans Rd]
- **Simmons College** • 300 The Fenway [Palace]
- **Wentworth Institute of Technology** • 550 Huntington Ave [Ruggles St]

🛒 Supermarkets

- **Shaw's** • 33 Kilmarnock St [Boylston St]
- **Stop & Shop** • 1620 Tremont St [Wigglesworth]

The New Fenway developments continue to bring upscale shops and restaurants, but head out of the fray to neighborhood favorites like El Pelon Taqueria and Rod Dee II. In Mission Hill, Penguin Cafe makes delicious pizzas with creative toppings, and the best pints flow at Flann O'Briens.

Coffee

- **Brigham Circle Diner** ·
  737 Huntington Ave [Francis St]
- **Red Bean Coffee Roasters** ·
  350 Longwood Ave [Brookline Ave]
- **Starbucks** · Children's Hospital ·
  283 Longwood Ave [Blackfan]

Copy Shops

- **FedEx Kinko's** · 1373 Boylston St [Kilmarnock St]
- **The Print House** · 660 Huntington Ave [Washington St]
- **The Print House** · 75 Francis St [Vining]
- **USP** · 360 Huntington Ave [Opera]

Farmers Markets

- **Mission Hill (June—Oct; Thurs 11:30 am—6 pm)** ·
  · Huntington Ave & Tremont St

Gyms

- **Custom Fitness** · 75 St Alphonsus St [Smith St]
- **Fitcorp** · 77 Ave Louis Pasteur [Longwood]

Hardware Stores

- **AC Hardware** · 1562 Tremont St [St Alphonsus]

Liquor Stores

- **Bradley Liquors** · 1383 Boylston St [Kilmarnock]
- **Brigham Liquors** · 732 Huntington Ave [Calumet]
- **Dara's Wine & Spirits** ·
  750 Huntington Ave [Fenwood]
- **Fuentes Market and Liquor Store** ·
  680 Parker St [Gurney]
- **Jersey Street Liquors** · 48 Queensberry St [Jersey]
- **Mission Hill Liquors** · 1623 Tremont St [Wigglesworth]

Movie Theaters

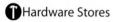

- **Museum of Fine Arts** ·
  465 Huntington Ave [Museum Rd]

Nightlife

- **Baseball Tavern** · 1270 Boylston St [Jersey]
- **Flann O'Brien's** · 1619 Tremont St [Wigglesworth]
- **Machine** · 1256 Boylston St [Yawkey]
- **Punter's Pub** · 450 Huntington Ave [Parker St]
- **Ramrod** · 1254 Bolyston St [Yawkey]

Restaurants

- **Bravo** · 465 Huntington Ave [Museum Rd]
- **Brigham Circle Chinese Food** ·
  737 Huntington Ave [Francis St]
- **Brigham Circle Diner** ·
  728 Huntington Ave [Francis St]
- **Brown Sugar Café** · 129 Jersey St [Queensberry]
- **Chacho's** · 1502 Tremont St [Burney]
- **Church** · 69 Kilmarnock St [Queensberry]
- **Halal Indian Cuisine** ·
  736 Huntington Ave [Fenwood Rd]
- **Huntington Pizza & Café** ·
  764 Huntington Ave [Wait]
- **Longwood Grille & Bar** ·
  342 Longwood Ave [Brookline Ave]
- **Mississippi's** · 103 Terrace St [Cedar St]
- **Penguin Café** · 735 Huntington Ave [Francis St]
- **Solstice Café** · 1625 Tremont St [Wigglesworth]
- **Squealing Pig** · 134 Smith St [Washington St]
- **Upper Crust** · 1330 Boylston St [Kilmarnock]

Video Rental

- **Blockbuster** · 171 Centre St [Nathanial Askia Way]

Avoid driving around Fenway during Sox games, Huntington Avenue during rush hour, and Longwood at any time. Street parking is never easy. Fenway and Longwood have garages (beware of game day price hikes), but are also served by the Green Line D train. The Green Line E tram runs up Huntington.

Subway

- · **Northeastern (E)**
- · **Museum of Fine Arts (E)**
- · **Longwood Medical Area (E)**
- · **Brigham Circle (E)**
- · **Fenwood Rd (E)**
- · **Mission Park (E)**
- · **Riverway (E)**
- · **Back of the Hill (E)**
- · **Heath (E)**
- · **Roxbury Crossing**

Bus Lines

- CT2 · Sullivan Station—Ruggles Station via Kendall/MIT
- CT3 · Beth Israel Deaconess Medical Center—Andrew Station via BU Medical Center
- 8 · Harbor Point/UMass—Kenmore Station via South End Medical Area
- 8 · Roslindale Square—Heath Street via Dudley Station, Grove Hall & American Legion Hwy
- 22 · Ashmont Station—Ruggles Station via Talbot Avenue & Jackson Square
- 39 · Forest Hills Station—Back Bay Station via Huntington Avenue
- 41 · Centre & Eliot Streets—JFK/UMass Station via Dudley Station, Centre Street & Jackson Square Station
- 47 · Central Square, Cambridge—Broadway Station via South End Medical Area
- 60 · Chestnut Hill—Kenmore Station via Brookline Village & Cypress Street
- 65 · Brighton Center—Kenmore Station via Washington Street, Brookline Village
- 66 · Harvard Square—Dudley Station via Allston & Brookline

🅖 Gas Stations

- · **Citgo** · 914 Huntington Ave [S Huntington]
- · **Exxon** · 1420 Boylston St [Kilmarnock] 🕐
- · **Getty** · 1600 Tremont St [Wigglesworth]
- · **Mobil** · 1301 Boylston St [Yawkey] 🕐
- · **Shell** · 1241 Boylston St [Yawkey] 🕐

🅟 Parking

Under the watchful triangular eye of the revamped Citgo sign, the Kenmore Square area is notable for sprawling Boston University, the nightclub scene on Lansdowne Street, and, of course, Fenway Park. Beyond Fenway and the core of Kenmore Square, urban bustle gives way to the more serene residential neighborhoods of affluent Brookline.

$ Banks

- **Bank of America** · 410 Brookline Ave [Longwood]
- **Bank of America** ·
  540 Commonwealth Ave [Kenmore]
- **Bank of America** ·
  771 Commonwealth Ave [St Mary's St]
- **Bank of America (ATM)** ·
  1024A Beacon St [St Mary's St]
- **Bank of America (ATM)** · 201 Brookline Ave [Park Dr]
- **Bank of America (ATM)** · 4 Brookline Pl [Brookline Ave]
- **Bank of America (ATM)** ·
  540 Commonwealth Ave [Brookline Ave]
- **Bank of America (ATM)** · 660 Beacon St [Comm Ave]
- **Bank of America (ATM)** · BU - Warren Towers · 700 Commonwealth Ave [Cummington]
- **Bank of America (ATM)** ·
  BU - George Sherman Union ·
  775 Commonwealth Ave [University Rd]
- **Brookline Savings Bank** · 1016 Beacon St [St Mary's St]
- **Brookline Savings Bank** ·
  160 Washington St [White Pl]
- **Century Bank** · 512 Commonwealth Ave [Kenmore]
- **Century Bank** · 771 Commonwealth Ave [St Mary's St]
- **Century Bank (ATM)** · Barnes & Noble ·
  660 Beacon St [Comm Ave]
- **Century Bank (ATM)** ·
  770 Commonwealth Ave [St Mary's St]
- **Citizens Bank** · 435 Brookline Ave [Longwood]
- **Citizens Bank** · 560 Commonwealth Ave [Beacon St]
- **Citizens Bank (ATM)** · 1 Deaconess Rd [Pilgrim Rd]
- **Citizens Bank (ATM)** · 49 Lansdowne St [Ipswich St]
- **Citizens Bank (ATM)** ·
  542 Commonwealth Ave [Brookline Ave]
- **Citizens Bank (ATM)** · Barnes & Noble ·
  660 Beacon St [Commonwealth Ave]
- **Mercantile Bank** · 61 Brookline Ave [Lansdowne]
- **People's Federal Savings Bank** ·
  160 Washington St [White Pl]
- **Sovereign Bank** ·
  552 Commonwealth Ave [Brookline Ave]
- **Sovereign Bank (ATM)** · CVS ·
  1249 Boylston St [Ipswich St]
- **Sovereign Bank (ATM)** · CVS ·
  730 Commonwealth Ave [St Mary's St]

Donuts

- **Dunkin' Donuts** · 1008 Beacon St [St Mary's St]
- **Dunkin' Donuts** · 1108 Beacon St [Hawes St]
- **Dunkin' Donuts** · 330 Brookline Ave [Short St]
- **Dunkin' Donuts** · 457 Brookline Ave [Longwood]
- **Dunkin' Donuts** ·
  530 Commonwealth Ave [Brookline Ave]

+ Emergency Rooms

- **Beth Israel Deaconess Medical Center** ·
  330 Brookline Ave [Short St]

O Landmarks

- **BU Bridge** · Essex St & Mountfort St
- **Citgo Sign** · Commonwealth Ave & Beacon St
- **Fenway Park** · 4 Yawkey Wy [Brookline Ave]

Rx Pharmacies

- **CVS** · 730 Commonwealth Ave [St Mary's St]
- **PharmaCare Specialty Pharmacy** ·
  350 Longwood Ave [Brookline Ave]
- **Pierce Apothecary** · 1180 Beacon St [Kent St]
- **Village Pharmacy** · 1 Brookline Pl [Brookline Ave]

Post Offices

- **Boston University** ·
  775 Commonwealth Ave [Mountfort]
- **Kenmore Station** · 11 Deerfield St [Comm Ave]

Schools

- **Amos A Lawrence** · 27 Francis St [St Albans]
- **Ansin Religious School of Ohabei Shalom** ·
  1187 Beacon St [Marshall St]
- **Boston Arts Academy** · 174 Ipswich St [Lansdowne]
- **Boston University** · 1 Sherborn St [Comm Ave]
- **Boston University Academy** ·
  1 University Rd [Comm Ave]
- **Fenway High** · 174 Ipswich St [Lansdowne]
- **Ivy Street** · 200 Ivy St [Essex]
- **Kids Are People Elementary** ·
  656 Beacon St [Comm Ave]
- **Neha/Lubavitch School for Girls** ·
  9 Prescott St [Lenox]
- **New England Hebrew Academy** ·
  9 Prescott St [Lenox]
- **New England School of Photography** ·
  537 Commonwealth Ave [Brookline Ave]
- **Wheelock College** · 200 Riverway [Short St]
- **The Winsor School** · 103 Pilgrim Rd [Short St]

Map 16 • **Kenmore Square / Brookline (East)**

Map 16

With the addition of the gigantic House of Blues, some of the former club options have lessened in quantity, but not in quality. For non-clubbers, Elephant Walk or Taberno de Haro are excellent dining options. For those lucky enough to score tickets, the best entertainment in the world is at Fenway Park.

Coffee

- **Cafe Fixe** • Beacon St [St Mary's St]
- **Espresso Royale** • 736 Commonwealth Ave [St Mary's St]
- **Java Stop** • 4 Brookline Pl [Brookline Ave]
- **Kookoo** • 7 Station St [Washington St]
- **Starbucks** • Beth Israel Hospital • 364 Brookline Ave [Short St]
- **Starbucks** • 148 Brookline Ave [Kilmamock St]
- **Starbucks** • 595 Commonwealth Ave [Sherborn St]
- **Starbucks** • 775 Commonwealth Ave [Mountfort]
- **Starbucks** • 874 Commonwealth Ave [Armory]

Copy Shops

- **FedEx Kinko's** • 115 Cummington St [Babbitt]
- **Minuteman Press** • 870 Commonwealth Ave [Amory St]
- **Staples** • 401 Park Dr [Brookline Ave]
- **The UPS Store** • 423 Brookline Ave [Longwood]

Gyms

- **Boston Sports Club** • 201 Brookline Ave [Park Dr]
- **Boston University Nutrition & Fitness Center** • 635 Commonwealth Ave [Hinsdale]
- **Gold's Gym** • 71 Lansdowne St [Brookline Ave]

Hardware Stores

- **Economy Hardware** • 1012 Beacon St [St Mary's St]

Liquor Stores

- **Wine Gallery** • 516 Commonwealth Ave [Kenmore]
- **Wine Press** • 1024 Beacon St [St Mary's St]

Movie Theaters

- **Regal Fenway Stadium 13** • 201 Brookline Ave [Park Dr]

Nightlife

- **An Tua Nua** • 835 Beacon St [Munson]
- **Audubon Circle** • 838 Beacon St [Munson]
- **Bill's Bar and Lounge** • 5 1/2 Lansdowne St [Ipswich St]
- **Cask 'n' Flagon** • 62 Brookline Ave [Lansdowne]
- **The Dugout** • 722 Commonwealth Ave [St Mary's St]
- **Embassy** • 36 Lansdowne St [Ipswich St]
- **Foundation Lounge** • 500 Commonwealth Ave [Kenmore]
- **Game On!** • 82 Lansdowne St [Brookline Ave]
- **House of Blues** • 36 Lansdowne St [Ipswich]
- **Lucky Strike Lanes** • 145 Ipswich St [Lansdowne]
- **The Modern** • 36 Lansdowne St [Ipswich St]
- **PJ Kilroy's Pub** • 822 Beacon St [Munson St]
- **Tequila Rain** • 3 Lansdowne St [Ipswich St]
- **Who's on First?** • 19 Yawkey Wy [Brookline Ave]

Restaurants

- **Ankara Café** • 472 Commonwealth Ave [Kenmore]
- **Audubon Circle** • 838 Beacon St [Munson]
- **Boston Beer Works** • 61 Brookline Ave [Lansdowne]
- **Café Belo** • 636 Beacon St [Raleigh]
- **Cornwall's** • 654 Beacon St [Comm Ave]
- **Eastern Standard** • 528 Commonwealth Ave [Kenmore]
- **Elephant Walk** • 900 Beacon St [Park Dr]
- **Ginza** • 1002 Beacon St [St Mary's St]
- **India Quality** • 484 Commonwealth Ave [Kenmore]
- **La Verdad** • 1 Lansdowne St [Ipswich]
- **New England Soup Factory** • 2 Brookline Pl [Brookline Ave]
- **Noodle Street** • 627 Commonwealth Ave [Sherborn St]
- **O'Leary's Pub** • 1010 Beacon St [St Mary's St]
- **Petit Robert Bistro** • 468 Commonwealth Ave [Kenmore]
- **Taberno de Haro** • 999 Beacon St [St Mary's St]
- **Uburger** • 636 Beacon St [Raleigh]

Shopping

- **Bed Bath & Beyond** • 401 Park Dr [Brookline Ave]
- **Best Buy** • 401 Park Dr [Brookline Ave]
- **Blick Art Materials** • 401 Park Dr [Brookline Ave]
- **Boston Bicycle** • 842 Beacon St [Arundel]
- **Economy Hardware** • 1012 Beacon St [St Mary's St]
- **Guitar Center** • 750 Commonwealth Ave [St Mary's St]
- **Hunt's Photo and Video** • 520 Commonwealth Ave [Kenmore]
- **Japonaise Bakery** • 1020 Beacon St [St Marys St]
- **Jean Therapy** • 524 Commonwealth Ave [Brookline Ave]
- **Nantucket Natural Oils** • 508 Commonwealth Ave [Kenmore]
- **Nuggets** • 486 Commonwealth Ave [Kenmore]
- **REI** • 401 Park Dr [Brookline Ave]
- **Ski Market** • 860 Commonwealth Ave [Armory]
- **University Computers** • 533 Commonwealth Ave [Brookline Ave]

The Green Line T stops around Kenmore Square and BU are frequently overrun by students and baseball fans, so B train riders might prefer the 57 bus during peak school and game hours. For parking, trawl Bay State Road and Cummington Street or head further west on Commowealth Ave.

Subway

- **Kenmore**
- **Blandford St** (B)
- **BU East** (B)
- **BU Central** (B)
- **BU West** (B)
- **St Paul St** (B)
- **St Mary's St** (C)
- **Hawes St** (C)
- **Kent St** (C)
- **St Paul St** (C)
- **Fenway** (D)
- **Longwood** (D)
- **Brookline Village** (D)

Bus Lines

- **CT2** · Sullivan Station—Ruggles Station via Kendall/MIT
- **55** · Jersey & Queensberry Streets—Copley Square or Park & Tremont Streets
- **57** · Watertown Yard—Kenmore Station via Newton Corner & Brighton Center
- **65** · Brighton Center—Kenmore Station via Washington Street, Brookline Village

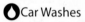

Car Rental

- **Select Car Rental** · 500 Commonwealth Ave
  [Kenmore] · 617-532-5060

Car Washes

- **Advance Auto Detailing** · 401 Park Dr [Brookline Ave]

Gas Stations

- **Gulf** · 25 Washington St [Brooklin Pl] ⏰
- **Sunoco** · 850 Commonwealth Ave [Amory St]

Parking

(101)

Map 17 • Coolidge Corner / Brookline Hills

This neighborhood is a vibrant mix of old and new, urban and suburban, old-fashioned and eclectic. Long-time residents in stately Victorian homes share quiet neighborhood parks, diverse restaurants and shops, and a buzzing nightlife with transient college students and well-paid young professionals.

Banks

- **Bank of America** • 1319 Beacon St [Harvard St]
- **Bank of America (ATM)** •
  1624 Beacon St [Washington St]
- **Bank of America (ATM)** • 225 Washington St [Snow]
- **Banknorth Massachusetts** •
  1641 Beacon St [University Rd]
- **Brookline Cooperative Bank** •
  264 Washington St [Davis Ave]
- **Brookline Savings Bank** •
  1340 Beacon St [Harvard St]
- **Brookline Savings Bank** •
  1661 Beacon St [Winthrop Rd]
- **People's Federal Savings Bank** •
  254 Washington St [Harvard St]
- **Sovereign Bank** • 1 Harvard St [Kent St]
- **Sovereign Bank** • 1341 Beacon St [Harvard St]

Donuts

- **Dunkin' Donuts** • 1316 Beacon St [Harvard St]
- **Dunkin' Donuts** • 20 Boylston St [High St]
- **Dunkin' Donuts** • 265 Boylston St [Cameron St]
- **Dunkin' Donuts** • 8 Harvard St [Kent St]

Landmarks

- **Frederick Olmstead Home** • 99 Warren St [Welch]

Libraries

- **Brookline Main Library** •
  361 Washington St [Goodwin Pl]

Pharmacies

- **CVS** • 1322 Beacon St [Harvard St]
- **CVS** • 294 Harvard St [Green St]
- **CVS** • 400 Washington St [Cypress St]
- **Walgreens** • 1324 Beacon St [Harvard St]
- **Walgreens** • 99 Harvard St [School St]

Police

- **Brookline Police Department** •
  350 Washington St [Thayer St]

Post Offices

- **Brookline Branch** • 1295 Beacon St [Pleasant St]
- **Brookline Village Branch** •
  207 Washington St [Station]

Schools

- **Boston Graduate School of Psychoanalysis** •
  1581 Beacon St [Washington St]
- **Brookline High** • 115 Greenough St [Davis Ave]
- **Israeli Complementary School** •
  50 Sewall Ave [Charles St]
- **John D Runkle** • 50 Druce St [Buckminster]
- **Maimonides** • 34 Philbrick Rd [Boylston St]
- **Pierce** • 50 School St [Washington St]
- **St Mary of the Assumption** • 67 Harvard St [Kent St]
- **William H Lincoln** • 19 Kennard Rd [Boylston St]

Supermarkets

- **Star Market** • 1717 Beacon St [Tappan]
- **Stop & Shop** • 155 Harvard St [Harris St]
- **Trader Joe's** • 1317 Beacon St [Harvard St]

Map 17 • **Coolidge Corner / Brookline Hills**

1/4 mile   .25 km

Sundries / Entertainment

Map 17

Brookline is a place where specialty shops mingle with chain stores, and an ethnic array of food spans from the inexpensive Rani Indian Bistro and Boca Grande to the upscale Fireplace and Fugakyu. The popular Art Deco Coolidge Corner Theater shows first-run, repertory, midnight movies, and occasional burlesque.

Coffee

- **Athan's Bakery** • 1621 Beacon St [Washington St]
- **Heney's Resa** • 220 Washington St [Davis St]
- **Starbucks** • 15 Harvard St [Webster Pl]
- **Starbucks** • 1655 Beacon St [Winthrop Rd]

Copy Shops

- **FedEx Kinko's** • 1370 Beacon St [Centre St]
- **Mail Boxes Etc** • 258 Harvard St [Beacon St]
- **The UPS Store** • 288 Washington St [Holden St]

Farmers Markets

- **Brookline (June–Oct; Thurs 1:30 pm–dusk)** •
  Centre St at Beacon St [Beacon St]

Gyms

- **Beacon Hill Athletic Club** • 279 Washington St [Holden St]
- **Fitness Together** • 1404 Beacon St [Winchester St]
- **Fitness Unlimited** • 62 Harvard St [Kent St]

Hardware Stores

- **Connelly's Hardware** • 706 Washington St [Beacon St]

Liquor Stores

- **Best Cellars (wine only)** • 1327 Beacon St [Harvard St]
- **Foley's Liquor Store** • 228 Cypress St [Rice St]
- **Food Center Liquors** • 10 Harvard Sq [Andem]
- **Gimbel's Liquors** • 1637 Beacon St [University Rd]
- **Wine Gallery** • 375 Boylston St [Brington]

Movie Theaters

- **Coolidge Corner Theatre** • 290 Harvard St [Green St]

Nightlife

- **Matt Murphy's Pub** • 14 Harvard St [Webster Pl]
- **The Publick House** • 1648 Beacon St [Washington St]
- **Washington Square Tavern** •
  714 Washington St [Beacon St]

Pet Shops

- **Brookline Grooming & Pet Supplies** •
  148 Harvard St [Harris St]

Restaurants

- **Boca Grande** • 1294 Beacon St [Pleasant St]
- **Bottega Fiorentina** • 41 Harvard St [Andem]
- **Brookline Family Restaurant** •
  305 Washington St [Holden St]
- **Chef Chow's House** • 230 Harvard St [Webster St]
- **Dok Bua** • 411 Harvard St [Fuller St]
- **Fireplace** • 1634 Beacon St [Washington St]
- **Fugakyu** • 1280 Beacon St [Pleasant St]
- **Gourmet India** • 1335 Beacon St [Harvard St]
- **Khao Sarn** • 250 Harvard St [Longwood]
- **La Morra** • 48 Boylston St [High St]
- **Matt Murphy's Pub** • 14 Harvard St [Webster Pl]
- **Martin's Coffee Shop** • 35 Harvard St [Linden St]
- **Michael's Deli** • 256 Harvard St [Longwood]
- **Orinoco** • 22 Harvard St [Pierce St]
- **Pho Lemongrass** • 239 Harvard St [Webster St]
- **Rani Indian Bistro** • 1353 Beacon St [Webster St]
- **Rod Dee** • 1430 Beacon St [Summit Ave]
- **Shawarma King** • 1383 Beacon St [Park St]
- **Village Fish** • 22 Harvard St [Webster Pl]
- **Virginia's Fine Foods** • 8 Cypress St [Washington St]
- **Washington Square Tavern** •
  714 Washington St [Beacon St]

Shopping

- **Athan's Bakery** • 1621 Beacon St [Washington St]
- **EC Florist & Gifts** • 224 Washington St [Davis Ct]
- **Emack & Bolio's** • 1663 Beacon St [Winthrop Rd]
- **Eureka Puzzles** • 1349 Beacon St [Centre St]
- **Madras Masala** • 191 Harvard St [Marion St]
- **Marathon Sports** • 1638 Beacon St [University Rd]
- **Paper Source** • 1361 Beacon St [Webster St]
- **Party Favors** • 1356 Beacon St [Webster St]
- **Petropol** • 1428 Beacon St [Summit Ave]
- **Pier 1 Imports** • 1351 Beacon St [Webster St]
- **Russian Village** • 1659 Beacon St [Winthrop Rd]
- **Ten Thousand Villages** • 226 Harvard St [Sewall Ave]
- **Wild Goose Chase** • 1431 Beacon St [Summit Ave]

Video Rental

- **Hollywood Video** • 111 Harvard St [Harvard Ct]
- **Movieworks** • 1658 Beacon St [Winthrop Rd]

Map 19 • **Coolidge Corner / Brookline Hills**

Transportation

Map 17

Brookline welcomes visitors, but as with any house guest, you aren't expected to stay too long. A two-hour parking limit is strictly enforced, and overnight street parking is forbidden. The alternative? The maddeningly slow and crowded Green Line C train and 66 bus. The D train serves Brookline Hills.

Subway

- **Kent St (C)**
- **St Paul St (C)**
- **Coolidge Corner (C)**
- **Summit Ave (C)**
- **Brandon Hall (C)**
- **Fairbanks St (C)**
- **Washington Sq (C)**
- **Tappan St (C)**
- **Dean Rd (C)**
- **Brookline Village (D)**
- **Brookline Hills (D)**
- **Beaconsfield (D)**

Bus Lines

- **60** · Chestnut Hill—Kenmore Station via Brookline Village & Cypress Street
- **65** · Brighton Center—Kenmore Station via Washington Street, Brookline Village
- **66** · Harvard Square—Dudley Station via Allston & Brookline

Car Washes

- **Effective Car Detail** · 40 Aspinwall Ave [Harvard St]
- **Scrubadub** · 143 Harvard St [Harris St]

Gas Stations

- **Mobil** · 198 Harvard St [Marion St]
- **Mobil** · 345 Boylston St [Cypress St] ♨

Map 18 • **Brighton**

1 2

Arsenal St

N Beacon St

Charles River

Soldiers Field Rd

Western

Richardson St
Waverly St
Lothrop St
School St
Centola Rd
Ricardson St
Lincoln St

Charles River Rd

Soldiers Field Rd

Soldiers Field Pl

Birmingham Pkwy

90

Nonantum Rd

A

N Beacon St

Vineland St

Guest St

19

Faneuil St

Lawrence Pl

Cambridge St

Warren St

Washington St

Arlington St

Bennett St

Faneuil St

Washington St

Kenrick St

Chandler Pond

B

Boston College

South St

Commonwealth Ave

Chestnut Hill Ave

Chiswick Rd

Commonwealth Ave

Sutherland Rd

Washington St

Chestnut Hill Ave

Beacon St

Englewood Ave

Cleveland Circle

Boston College

PAGE 216

Chestnut Hill Reservoir

1/2 mile   .5 km

Brighton is the more sedate half of the Allston-Brighton duo but, like its rowdier neighbor, it attracts plenty of college students and young folk. Narrow, tangled, residential streets surround the cluster of shops and restaurants on Washington Street in Brighton Center.

Map

$ Banks

- **Bank of America** • 350 Chestnut Hill Ave [Englewood]
- **Bank of America** • 5 Chestnut Hill Ave [Washington St]
- **Bank of America (ATM)** • 1650 Soldiers Field Rd [Soldiers Field Pl]
- **Bank of America (ATM)** • 175 Market St [N Beacon]
- **Bank of America (ATM)** • 401 Washington St [Dighton]
- **Cambridge Trust (ATM)** • 2 Soldiers Field Rd [Soldiers Field Pl]
- **Citizens Bank** • 2000 Beacon St [Sutherland]
- **Citizens Bank** • 35 Washington St [Monastery]
- **Citizens Bank** • 414 Washington St [Parsons]
- **Citizens Bank (ATM)** • 1912 Beacon St [Ayr]
- **Citizens Bank (ATM)** • 241 Market St [Cypress Rd]
- **Mercantile Bank** • 423 Washington St [Parsons]
- **People's Federal Savings Bank** • 435 Market St [Surrey]
- **People's Federal Savings Bank (ATM)** • 236 Faneuil St [Arlington St]
- **Sovereign Bank** • 30 Birmingham Pkwy [Waverly St]
- **Sovereign Bank** • 415 Market St [Henshaw]
- **Sovereign Bank** • CVS/Pharmacy • 1927 Beacon St [Ayr]
- **Sovereign Bank (ATM)** • 250 Washington St [Shepard St]
- **Sovereign Bank (ATM)** • CVS/Pharmacy • 427 Washington St [Eastburn St]

✳ Community Gardens

◎ Donuts

- **Dunkin' Donuts** • 1955 Beacon St [Ayr]
- **Dunkin' Donuts** • 214 N Beacon St [Market St]
- **Dunkin' Donuts** • 350 Washington St [Academy Hill]

📖 Libraries

- **Brighton** • 40 Academy Hill Rd [Peaceable]
- **Faneuil** • 419 Faneuil St [Bigelow St]

℞ Pharmacies

- **CVS** • 1927 Beacon St [Ayr]
- **CVS** • 427 Washington St [Eastburn St]
- **Rite Aid** • 399 Market St [Henshaw]
- **Sutherland Pharmacy** • 1690 Commonwealth Ave [Wilson Pk]

🚓 Police

- **District D-14** • 301 Washington St [Wirt]

✉ Post Offices

- **Brighton** • 424 Washington St [Parsons]

🏫 Schools

- **Alexander Hamilton Elementary** • 198 Strathmore Rd [Lothian]
- **Another Course to College** • 20 Warren St [Nevins]
- **Boston Community Leadership Academy** • 20 Warren St [Nevins]
- **Brighton High** • 25 Warren St [Monastery]
- **Conservatory Lab Charter** • 25 Arlington St [Leicester]
- **James Garfield Elementary** • 95 Beechcroft St [Hester]
- **Kennedy Day School Program** • 30 Warren St [Monastery]
- **Mary Lyon Elementary/Middle** • 50 Beechcroft St [Hester]
- **Mesivta High School of Greater** • 34 Sparhawk St [Bentley]
- **Mount St Joseph Academy** • 617 Cambridge St [Eleanor]
- **Shaloh House Hebrew Day** • 29 Chestnut Hill Ave [Dighton]
- **St. Columbkille Elementary** • 25 Arlington St [Leicester]
- **Thomas A Edison Junior High** • 60 Glenmont Rd [Willoughby St]
- **William H Taft Middle** • 20 Warren St [Nevins]
- **Winship Elementary** • 54 Dighton St [Chestnut Hill Ave]

Map 18

Meet a BC student at Mary Ann's or watch a soccer match at Roggie's. Want frills? Try Soho, a modern, two-level club that tries to emulate Manhattan chic. Hungry? Grab some tapas and, of course, sangria at Tasca. Late night, head to IHOP on Soldiers Field Road for boisterous times and reliable breakfast fare.

Coffee

- **Starbucks** • 1660 Soldiers Field Rd [Soldiers Field Pl]
- **Starbucks** • 470 Washington St [Allen St]

Copy Shops

- **FedEx Kinko's** • 252 Washington St [Shepard St]
- **Staples** • 1660 Soldiers Field Rd [Soldiers Field Pl]
- **The UPS Store** • 2193 Commonwealth Ave [Lake St]

Farmers Markets

- **Brighton (July–Oct; Sat 12–4:30)** •
  5 Chestnut Hill Ave [Washington St]

Gyms

- **Bally Total Fitness** • 25 Guest St [Life]
- **Beacon Hill Athletic Club** •
  1686 Commonwealth Ave [Colborne Ave]
- **Beacon Hill Athletic Club** •
  470 Washington St [Allen Rd]
- **Oak Square YMCA** • 615 Washington St [Breck]

Hardware Stores

- **Cleveland Circle Hardware** • 1920 Beacon St [Ayr]

Liquor Stores

- **Dorr's Liquor Mart** •
  354 Washington St [Chestnut Hill Ave]
- **Martignetti Liquors** •
  1650 Soldiers Field Rd [Soldiers Field Pl]
- **Oak Square Liquors** • 610 Washington St [Breck]
- **Reservoir Wines & Spirits** • 1922 Beacon St [Ayr]
- **Walsh Wine & Spirits** • 313 Washington St [Waldo Ter]

Movie Theaters

- **National Amusements Circle Cinemas** •
  399 Chestnut Hill Ave [Beacon St]

Nightlife

- **Cityside Bar & Grill** • 1960 Beacon St [Sutherland]
- **Green Briar** • 304 Washington St [Wirt]
- **Irish Village** • 224 Market St [Saybrook St]
- **Joey's** • 416 Market St [Henshaw]
- **The Last Drop** • 596 Washington St [Griggs Rd]
- **Mary Ann's** • 1937 Beacon St [Ayr]
- **Roggie's** • 356 Chestnut Hill Ave [Englewood]
- **Soho** • 386 Market St [Henshaw]

Pet Shops

- **No Bones About It** • 1786 Beacon St [Warwick Rd]
- **Toureen Kennels & Grooming Salon** •
  505 Western Ave [Mackin]

Restaurants

- **Bamboo** • 1616 Commonwealth Ave [Washington St]
- **Bangkok Bistro** • 1952 Beacon St [Sutherland]
- **Bluestone Bistro** •
  1799 Commonwealth Ave [Chiswick Rd]
- **Café Mirror** • 362 Washington St [Goodwin Pl]
- **Cityside Bar & Grill** • 1960 Beacon St [Sutherland]
- **Devlin's** • 332 Washington St [Waldo Ter]
- **Green Briar** • 304 Washington St [Wirt]
- **IHOP** • 1850 Soldiers Field Rd [N Beacon] ⑤
- **Jasmine Bistro** • 412 Market St [Henshaw]
- **Moogy's** • 154 Chestnut Hill Ave [Embassy]
- **Roggie's** • 356 Chestnut Hill Ave [Englewood]
- **Soho** • 386 Market St [Henshaw]
- **Tasca** • 1612 Commonwealth Ave [Washington St]

Shopping

- **Amanda's Flowers** • 347 Washington St [Academy Hill]
- **CompUSA** • 205 Market St [Lawrence St]
- **New Balance Factory Store** • 40 Life St [Guest]
- **Staples** • 1660 Soldiers Field Rd [Soldiers Field Pl]

Video Rental

- **Blockbuster** • 358 Chestnut Hill Ave [Englewood]
- **Brighton Video** • 572 Washington St [Brackett]
- **Hollywood Video** • 103 N Beacon St [Arthur]

The bus dominates public transportation in Brighton—the 57 bus brings riders into Kenmore Square, and the 64 and 86 buses lead into Cambridge and Somerville. The Green Line's C train creeps along the southern edge of Brighton to Cleveland Circle.

Subway

- **Warren St (B)**
- **Washington St (B)**
- **Sutherland Rd (B)**
- **Chiswick Rd (B)**
- **Chestnut Hill Ave (B)**
- **South St (B)**
- **Boston College (B)**
- **Englewood Ave (C)**
- **Cleveland Circle (C)**

Bus Lines

- **57** • Watertown Yard—Kenmore Station via Newton Corner & Brighton Center
- **64** • Oak Square—Central Square, Cambridge, or Kendall/MIT
- **65** • Brighton Center—Kenmore Station via Washington Street, Brookline Village
- **70** • Cedarwood, N Waltham, or Watertown Square—University Park via Central Square
- **70A** • Cedarwood, N Waltham, or Watertown Square—University Park via Central Square
- **86** • Sullivan Square Station—Cleveland Circle via Harvard/Johnson Gate

 ## Car Rental

• **Rent A Wreck** •
  2022 Commonwealth Ave [Gerald] • 617-254-9540

 ## Car Washes

• **Scrubadub** • 235 Market St [Faneuil]

 ## Gas Stations

- **Econogas** • 1550 Commonwealth Ave [Melvin Ave] ♿
- **Gulf** • 1650 Commonwealth Ave [Mt Hood]
- **Gulf** • 195 Market St [N Beacon]
- **Mobil** • 500 Western Ave [Mackin]
- **Shell** • 332 Chestnut Hill Ave [Englewood]
- **Sunoco** • 602 Washington St [Breck]

Map 19 • Allston (South) / Brookline (North)

For most Bostonians, crowded living and rowdy students define Allston. There's no place in the city where so many cheap eats, dive bars, and used goods are crammed into so few blocks. It's a dirty mashup and the city is better for it.

Banks

- **Bank of America** •
1237 Commonwealth Ave [Harvard Ave]
- **Bank of America (ATM)** •
1236A Commonwealth Ave [Harvard Ave]
- **Bank of America (ATM)** • 186 Brighton Ave [Quint]
- **Bank of America (ATM)** • 400 Western Ave [Litchfield St]
- **Bank of America (ATM)** • 881 Commonwealth Ave [Buick]
- **Bank of America (ATM)** •
957 Commonwealth Ave [Harry Agganis]
- **Century Bank** • 300 Western Ave [Everett St]
- **Citizens Bank** • 315 Harvard St [Babcock]
- **Citizens Bank** • 429 Western Ave [Coolidge St]
- **Citizens Bank** • 60 Everett St [Harvester]
- **Citizens Bank (ATM)** • 1065 Commonwealth Ave [Alcorn]
- **Citizens Bank (ATM)** •
1219 Commonwealth Ave [Harvard Ave]
- **Citizens Bank (ATM)** • 157 Brighton Ave [Harvard Ave]
- **Citizens Bank (ATM)** • 370 Western Ave [Telford]
- **Citizens Bank (ATM)** • 509 Cambridge St [Barrows]
- **People's Federal Savings Bank** •
229 N Harvard St [Franklin St]
- **Sovereign Bank** • 487 Harvard St [Lawton]
- **Sovereign Bank (ATM)** • CVS/Pharmacy •
1266 Commonwealth Ave [Gorham St]
- **Sovereign Bank (ATM)** • CVS/Pharmacy •
900 Commonwealth Ave [St Paul]
- **UCB** • 230 Harvard Ave [Brainerd]
- **Wainwright Bank & Trust** • 301 Harvard St [Babcock]

✴ Community Gardens

⦿ Donuts

- **Dunkin' Donuts** • 100 Cambridge St [Soldiers Field Rd]
- **Dunkin' Donuts** • 179 Brighton Ave [Parkvale]
- **Dunkin' Donuts** • 209 N Harvard St [Western]
- **Dunkin' Donuts** • 210 Harvard Ave [Comm Ave]
- **Dunkin' Donuts** • 60 Everett St [Harvester]
- **Twin Do-Nuts** • 501 Cambridge St [Barrows]

⦾ Landmarks

- **JFK National Historic Site** • 83 Beals St [Harvard St]
- **The Publick Theatre** • 1400 Soldiers Field Rd [Western]

📖 Libraries

- **Coolidge Corner** • 31 Pleasant St [John St]
- **Honan-Allston** • 300 N Harvard St [Eatonia]

℞ Pharmacies

- **CVS** • 1266 Commonwealth Ave [Gorham St]
- **CVS** • 900 Commonwealth Ave [St Paul]
- **Osco • Shaw's** 1065 Commonwealth Ave [Alcorn]
- **Osco** • 370 Western Ave [Telford]
- **Pelham Healthcare Services** • 280 Lincoln St [Eric]
- **Rite Aid** • 181 Brighton Ave [Parkvale]
- **Stop & Shop** • 60 Everett St [Harvester]

✉ Post Offices

- **Allston Station** • 47 Harvard Ave [Farrington]
- **Soldiers Field Station** • 117 Western Ave [Hague]

🎓 Schools

- **Bay Cove Academy** • 156 Lawton St [Abbottsford]
- **Beacon High** • 74 Green St [Dwight]
- **Congregation Kehillath Israel Religious School** •
384 Harvard St [Beals]
- **Edward Devotion** • 345 Harvard St [Shailer]
- **Harriet Baldwin Elementary** • 121 Corey Rd [Washington St]
- **Horace Mann School for the Deaf and Hard of
Hearing** • 40 Armington St [Webley]
- **Jackson Mann Elementary** • 40 Armington St [Webley]
- **Media and Technology Charter High** •
1001 Commonwealth Ave [Babcock]
- **Michael Driscoll** • 64 Westbourne Ter [Bartlett St]
- **St Herman of Alaska Christian School** •
62 Harvard Ave [Farrington]
- **Thomas Gardner Elementary** • 30 Athol St [Brentwood]
- **Torah Academy** • 11 Williston Rd [Salisbury]

🛒 Supermarkets

- **Bazaar** • 424 Cambridge St [Rugg]
- **The Butcherie** • 428 Harvard St [Coolidge St]
- **Osco • Shaw's** • 1065 Commonwealth Ave [Alcorn]
- **Shaw's** • 370 Western Ave [Telford]
- **Stop & Shop** • 60 Everett St [Harvester]
- **Super 88** • 1 Brighton Ave [Malvern St]
- **Whole Foods Market** • 15 Washington St [Corey Rd]

Map 19 · **Allston (South) / Brookline (North)**

Allston Rock City! Clubs drive the scene here, with live music and DJs every night of the week. Check Paradise, Harper's Ferry, Great Scott, and even the velvet rope at Wonder Bar. Taps dominate Sunset Grill and Big City. As for food, we've been known to fantasize about Lebanese at Reef Café, Chinese at Gitlo's, and Bánh Mi at Super 88.

Coffee

- **Caffe LaScala** · 318 Harvard St [Babcock]
- **Peet's Coffee & Tea** · 285 Harvard St [Green St]
- **Starbucks** · 277 Harvard St [Green St]
- **Starbucks** · 473 Harvard St [Lawton]

Copy Shops

- **Prinstant Press Inc** · 15 North Beacon St [Cambridge St]
- **Signal Graphics** · 450 Cambridge St [Emery]
- **Staples** · 214 Harvard St [Comm Ave]
- **The UPS Store** · 1085 Commonwealth Ave [Malvern St]

Gyms

- **Boston Sports Club** · 15 Gorham St [Comm Ave]
- **Commonwealth Health** · 1079 Commonwealth Ave [Malvern St]
- **Coolidge Corner Gym** · 310 Harvard St [Babcock]
- **HealthWorks Fitness Center (Women Only)** · 920 Commonwealth Ave [St Paul]

Hardware Stores

- **Aborn True Value** · 438 Harvard St [Coolidge St]
- **Economy Hardware** · 144 Harvard Ave [Glenville Ter]
- **Model Hardware** · 22 Harvard Ave [Cambridge St]

Liquor Stores

- **Allston Food and Spirits** · 223 Cambridge St [N Harvard]
- **Blanchard Liquors** · 103 Harvard Ave [Brighton Ave]
- **Brookline Liquor Mart** · 1354 Commonwealth Ave [Walbridge]
- **Hurley's** · 1441 Comm Ave [Warren St]
- **Mall Discount Liquors & Wines** · 525 Harvard St [Verndale]
- **Marty's Liquors** · 193 Harvard Ave [Comm Ave]
- **Wine Shop** · 370 Western Ave [Telford]

Nightlife

- **Avenue Bar & Grille** · 1249 Commonwealth Ave [Royce Rd]
- **Big City** · 138 Brighton Ave [Harvard Ave]
- **Bus Stop Pub** · 252 Western Ave [N Harvard]
- **Common Ground** · 85 Harvard Ave [Gardner St]
- **District Restaurant & Lounge** · 180 Lincoln St [Everett St]
- **Great Scott** · 1222 Commonwealth Ave [Harvard]
- **Harper's Ferry** · 156 Brighton Ave [Harvard Ave]
- **Harry's Bar & Grill** · 1430 Commonwealth Ave [Kelton]
- **Joshua Tree** · 1316 Commonwealth Ave [Redford]
- **The Kells** · 161 Brighton Ave [Harvard Ave]
- **Model Café** · 7 N Beacon St [Cambridge St]
- **O'Brien's** · 3 Harvard Ave [Cambridge St]
- **Our House** · 1277 Comm Ave [Spofford]
- **Paradise Rock Club & Lounge** · 967 Commonwealth Ave [Harry Agganis]
- **Scullers Jazz Club** - Doubletree Hotel · 400 Soldiers Field Rd [Cambridge St]
- **Silhouette Lounge** · 200 Brighton Ave [Allston St]
- **Sports Depot** · 353 Cambridge St [Highgate]
- **Sunset Grill & Tap** · 130 Brighton Ave [Linden St]
- **T's Pub** · 973 Commonwealth Ave [Crowninshield Rd]
- **White Horse Tavern** · 116 Brighton Ave [Linden St]
- **Wonder Bar** · 186 Harvard Ave [Glenville Ter]

Pet Shops

- **The Pet Shop** · 165 Harvard Ave [Glenville Ave]
- **Petco** · 304 Western Ave [Everett St]

Restaurants

- **Aneka Rasa** · 122 Harvard Ave [Brighton Ave]
- **Angora Café** · 1024 Commonwealth Ave [Babcock]
- **Anna's Taqueria** · 446 Harvard St [Thorndike]
- **Bagel Rising** · 1243 Comm Ave [Harvard]
- **Big City** · 138 Brighton Ave [Harvard Ave]
- **Bottega Fiorentina** · 313B Harvard St [Babcock]
- **Breakfast Club Diner** · 270 Western Ave [McDonald]
- **Buk Kyung II** · 151 Brighton Ave [Harvard]
- **Café Brazil** · 421 Cambridge St [Denby]
- **Camino Real** · 48 Harvard Ave [Farrington]
- **Charlie's Pizza & Café** · 177 Allston St [Kelton]
- **Coolidge Corner Clubhouse** · 307 Harvard St [Babcock]
- **El Cafétal** · 479 Cambridge St [Islington St]
- **Gitlo's** · 138 Brighton Ave [Parkvale Ave]
- **Grasshopper** · 1 N Beacon St [Cambridge St]
- **Grecian Yearning** · 174 Harvard Ave [Glenville Ave]
- **Habanero Mexican Grill** · 166 Brighton Ave [Parkvale Ave]
- **Indian Dhaba Roadside Diner** · 180 Brighton Ave [Harvard Ave]
- **La Mama Pizza** · 190 Brighton Ave [Quint]
- **Mr Sushi Japanese Restaurant** · 329 Harvard St [Babcock]
- **Nori Sushi** · 398 Harvard St [Naples]
- **Paradise Rock Club & Lounge** · 967 Commonwealth Ave [Harry Agganis]
- **Paris Creperie** · 278 Harvard St [Green St]
- **Pho Viets** · 1095 Commonwealth Ave [Brighton Ave]
- **Quan's Kitchen** · 1026 Commonwealth Ave [Winslow Rd]
- **Rangoli** · 129 Brighton Ave [Linden St]
- **Redneck's Roast Beef** · 140 Brighton Ave [Harvard Ave]
- **Reef Café** · 170 Brighton Ave [Parkvale]
- **Saigon** · 431 Cambridge St [Denby]
- **Saray** · 1098 Commonwealth Ave [Brighton Ave]
- **Spike's Junkyard Dogs** · 108 Brighton Ave [Linden St]
- **Steve's Kitchen** · 120 Harvard Ave [Brighton Ave]
- **Sumi** · 182 Brighton Ave [Parkvale]
- **Sunset Grill & Tap** · 130 Brighton Ave [Linden St]
- **Super 88 Food Court** · 1095 Commonwealth Ave [Malvern St]
- **Upper Crust** · 286 Harvard St [Green St]
- **Victoria Seafood** · 1029 Comm Ave [Winslow]
- **Wisteria** · 1095 Comm Ave [Brighton Ave]
- **YoMa** · 5 N Beacon St [Cambridge St]
- **Zaftigs Delicatessen** · 335 Harvard St [Shailer]

Shopping

- **Berezka International Food Store** · 1215 Commonwealth Ave [Linden St]
- **Bicycle Bill's** · 253 N Harvard St [Easton]
- **Bob Smith's Wilderness House** · 1048 Commonwealth Ave [Winslow Rd]
- **Brookline News and Gifts** · 313 Harvard St [Babcock]
- **Catering by Andrew** · 402 Harvard St [Naples]
- **City Housewares** · 434 Harvard St [Coolidge]
- **City Sports** · 1035 Comm Ave [Winslow Rd]
- **Clear Flour** · 178 Thorndike St [Lawton]
- **Coco Cosmetics** · 192 Harvard Ave [Comm Ave]
- **Eastern Mountain Sports** · 1041 Commonwealth Ave [Winslow Rd]
- **Economy Hardware** · 144 Harvard Ave [Glenville Ter]
- **Herrell's Ice Cream** · 155 Harvard Ave [Harvard Ave]
- **In Your Ear** · 957 Comm Ave [Harry Agganis]
- **International Bicycle Center** · 89 Brighton Ave [Reedsdale]
- **Israel Bookshop** · 410 Harvard St [Fuller St]
- **J.P. Licks** · 311 Harvard St [Babcock]
- **Kolbo Fine Judaica** · 437 Harvard St [Coolidge St]
- **Kupel's Bake & Bagel** · 421 Harvard St [Fuller St]
- **New England Comics** · 131 Harvard Ave [Brighton Ave]
- **Re:Generation Records and Tattoo** · 155 Harvard Ave [Glenville Ave]
- **Richman's Zipper Hospital** · 318 Harvard St [Babcock]
- **Stingray Body Art** · 1 Harvard Ave [Cambridge St]
- **TJ Maxx** · 525 Harvard St [Verndale]
- **Urban Renewals** · 122 Brighton Ave [Linden]
- **Vespa Boston** · 22 Brighton Ave [St Lukes]
- **Wulf's Fish Market** · 407 Harvard St [Fuller St]

Video Rental

- **Blockbuster** · 473 Harvard St [Lawton]
- **Cinemasmith** · 279 Harvard St [Green St]
- **Korean Book & Video (Korean & Japanese)** · 156 Harvard Ave [Glenville]

Map
17 15
16
14

The Green Line doesn't get more crowded and unbearable than the B train to BC. Parking is notoriously difficult in Allston. Clubbing and busing go like this: 66 bus to Harvard, 64 bus to Central Square, and if you think it's faster than the T, 54 bus to Kenmore Square.

Subway

- **St Paul St** (B)
- **Pleasant St** (B)
- **Babcock St** (B)
- **Packard's Corner** (B)
- **Harvard Ave** (B)
- **Griggs St** (B)
- **Allston St** (B)
- **Warren St** (B)
- **Washington St** (B)

Bus Lines

57 · Watertown Yard—Kenmore Station via Newton Corner & Brighton Center

64 · Oak Square—Central Square, Cambridge, or Kendall/MIT

65 · Brighton Center—Kenmore Station via Washington Street, Brookline Village

66 · Harvard Square—Dudley Station via Allston & Brookline

70 · Cedarwood, N Waltham, or Watertown Square—University Park via Central Square

70A · Cedarwood, N Waltham, or Watertown Square—University Park via Central Square

86 · Sullivan Square Station—Cleveland Circle via Harvard/Johnson Gate

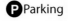Car Rental

- **Adventure Vehicle Rental** · 226 Harvard Ave [Brainerd] · 617-566-1018
- **Adventure Vehicle Rental** · 27 Harvard Ave [Cambridge St] · 617-783-3825
- **Budget** · 95 Brighton Ave [Linden St] · 617-497-3608
- **Enterprise** · 292 Western Ave [Everett St] · 617-783-2240
- **Enterprise** · 996 Commonwealth Ave [Babcock] · 617-738-6003
- **Hertz** · 414 Cambridge St [Denby] · 617-787-2894
- **U-Save Auto & Truck Rental** · 25 Harvard Ave [Cambridge St] · 617-254-1000

Car Washes

- **Allston Car Wash** · 434 Cambridge St [Rugg]
- **Shield System Cloth Car Wash** · 365 Western Ave [Telford]

Gas Stations

- **Citgo** · 180 Western Ave [Hague]
- **Exxon** · 198 Western Ave [N Harvard] ✆
- **Gulf** · 226 Harvard Ave [Brainerd]
- **Independent** · 445 Harvard St [Thorndike]
- **Mobil** · 434 Cambridge St [Rugg]
- **Sunoco** · 454 Harvard St [Thorndike]

Parking

Map 20 • **Harvard Square / Allston (North)**

Map 2

Despite an onslaught of retail chain stores, Harvard Square still retains some of its eccentric charm, with speed chess players, quirky stores, and eclectic eateries. Stroll up Brattle Street to admire the magnificent houses or step into Harvard Yard to escape into another world.

Banks

- **Bank of America** • 1414 Massachusetts Ave [JFK]
- **Bank of America (ATM)** • 1 Mifflin Pl [Mt Auburn]
- **Bank of America (ATM)** •
  1663 Massachusetts Ave [Hudson St]
- **Bank of America (ATM)** • 28 Eliot St [Winthrop St]
- **Bank of America (ATM)** • 45 Quincy St [Kirkland St]
- **Bank of America (ATM)** • 47 Oxford St [Everett St]
- **Bank of America (ATM)** • 67 Mt Auburn St [Linden St]
- **Bank of America (ATM)** • Spangler Ctr [Hague]
- **Boston Private Bank & Trust (ATM)** •
  104 Mt Auburn St [Brattle St]
- **Cambridge Savings Bank** •
  1374 Massachusetts Ave [Holyoke St]
- **Cambridge Savings Bank (ATM)** •
  36 JFK St [Mt Auburn]
- **Cambridge Trust** •
  1336 Massachusetts Ave [Holyoke St]
- **Cambridge Trust** •
  1720 Massachusetts Ave [Garfield St]
- **Cambridge Trust (ATM)** •
  124 Mt Auburn St [University Rd]
- **Citizens Bank** • 6 JFK St [Brattle Sq]
- **Citizens Bank (ATM)** • 1 Bennett St [Eliot St]
- **Sovereign Bank** • 1420 Massachusetts Ave [Church St]
- **Sovereign Bank (ATM)** •
  125 Mt Auburn St [University Rd]
- **Wainwright Bank & Trust** • 1 Brattle St [Story]

Community Gardens

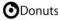 Donuts

- **Dunkin' Donuts** • 1 Bow St [Mass Ave]
- **Dunkin' Donuts** • 65 JFK St [Eliot St]
- **Dunkin' Donuts** • Harvard MBTA •
  Massachusetts Ave & Brattle St
- **Nornie B's Sandwich & Donut Shop** •
  61 Church St [Palmer St]

O Landmarks

- **Brattle Theatre** • 40 Brattle St [Church St]
- **Fogg Art Museum** • 32 Quincy St [B'way]
- **Harvard Museum of Natural History** •
  26 Oxford St [Kirkland St]
- **Harvard Stadium** •
  N Harvard St & Soldiers Field Rd
- **Harvard Yard** • 2 Kirkland St b/w Broadway,
  Quincy St, Peabody St, & Massachusetts Ave
- **John Harvard Statue** • Mass Ave [Quincy St]
- **Memorial Hall** • 45 Quincy St [Cambridge St]
- **Out of Town News** • Harvard Sq [JFK]
- **The Pit** • Harvard Sq [JFK]
- **Weeks Footbridge** • Memorial Dr & DeWolfe St

Pharmacies

- **CVS** • 1426 Massachusetts Ave [Church St] ☺
- **Rite Aid** • 1740 Massachusetts Ave [Prentiss]

Post Offices

- **Harvard Square Station** •
  125 Mt Auburn St [University Rd]

☺ Schools

- **Boston Archdiocesan Choir School** •
  29 Mt Auburn St [Athens St]
- **Graham and Parks** • 44 Linnaean St [Avon St]
- **Harvard Business** • Soldiers Field Rd [Soldiers Field Rd]
- **Harvard Law** • 1563 Massachusetts Ave [Waterhouse]
- **Harvard University** •
  1350 Massachusetts Ave [Holyoke St]
- **Lesley University** • 29 Everett St [Mass Ave]
- **Maria L Baldwin** • 28 Sacramento St [Sacramento Pl]
- **St Peter's** • 96 Concord Ave [Buckingham St]

Map 20 · **Harvard Square / Allston (North)**

If the people watching isn't enough, browse the Harvard Bookstore, grab a beer at Grendel's, or indulge in LA Burdick's justly celebrated hot chocolate. For meaty grub, nothing beats Bartley's Burger Cottage. If you want to dress up a little, try Chez Henri, then hit up Regattabar.

☕ Coffee

- **Algiers** • 40 Brattle St [Story]
- **Au Bon Pain** •
  1360 Massachusetts Ave [Holyoke St]
- **Boston Tea Stop** • 54 JFK St [Winthrop]
- **Crema Cafe** • 27 Brattle St [Peabody]
- **Dado Tea (tea only)** •
  50 Church St [Palmer St]
- **LA Burdick** • 52 Brattle St [Farwell]
- **Peet's Coffee & Tea** •
  100 Mt Auburn St [JFK]
- **Simon's Coffee House** •
  1736 Massachusetts Ave [Prentiss]
- **Starbucks** •
  1662 Massachusetts Ave [Shepard St]
- **Starbucks** • 31 Church St [Palmer St]
- **Starbucks** • 36 JFK St [Mt Auburn]
- **Tealuxe** • 9 Brattle St [Hague]

📋 Copy Shops

- **FedEx Kinko's** • 1 Mifflin Pl [Mt Auburn] ⏱
- **Flash Print** • 99 Mt Auburn St [JFK]
- **Gnomon Copy** •
  1308 Massachusetts Ave [Hollow Ln]
- **Staples** •
  57 John F Kennedy St [Winthrop St]

🥕 Farmers Markets

- **Cambridge/Charles Square**
  (May–Nov; Fri 1 pm–6 pm,
  Sun 10 am–3 pm) •
  1 Bennett St [Eliot St]

🏋 Gyms

- **Wellbridge Health and Fitness Center** •
  5 Bennett St [Eliot St]

🔨 Hardware Stores

- **Dickinson Brothers True Value** •
  26 Brattle St [Church St]

🍾 Liquor Stores

- **Harvard Wine** •
  1664 Massachusetts Ave [Shepard St]
- **University Wine Shop** •
  1739 Massachusetts Ave [Prentiss]

🎬 Movie Theaters

- **AMC Loews Harvard Square** •
  10 Church St [Mass Ave]
- **Brattle Theatre** • 40 Brattle St [Church St]
- **Harvard Film Archive** •
  24 Quincy St [B'way]

🍸 Nightlife

- **Cambridge Common** •
  1667 Massachusetts Ave [Hudson St]
- **Charlie's Kitchen** • 10 Eliot St [Winthrop St]
- **Club Passim** • 47 Palmer St [Church St]
- **The Comedy Studio** •
  1238 Massachusetts Ave [Plympton]
- **Grendel's Den** • 89 Winthrop St [JFK]
- **Hong Kong Lounge** • 1238 Mass Ave
- **John Harvard's Brew House** •
  33 Dunster St [Mt Auburn]
- **Lizard Lounge** •
  1667 Massachusetts Ave [Hudson St]
- **Noir** • Charles Hotel • 1 Bennett St [Eliot St]
- **Redline** • 59 JFK St [Winthrop St]
- **Regattabar** • Charles Hotel •
  1 Bennett St [Eliot St]
- **Shay's Lounge** • 58 JFK St [South St]
- **Temple Bar** • 1688 Massachusetts Ave
  [Sacramento St]
- **Tommy Doyle's** •
  96 Winthrop St [Winthrop St]
- **West Side Lounge** •
  1680 Massachusetts Ave [Sacramento St]

🐾 Pet Shops

- **Cambridge Pet Care Center** •
  1724 Massachusetts Ave [Garfield St]

🍴 Restaurants

- **Algiers** • 40 Brattle St [Story]
- **b. good** • 24 Dunster St [Mass Ave]
- **Border Café** • 32 Church St [Palmer St]
- **Café Pamplona** • 12 Bow St [Arrow]
- **Caffe Paradiso** • 1 Eliot Sq [Mt Auburn]
- **Cambridge, 1** • 27 Church St [Palmer St]
- **Casablanca** • 40 Brattle St [Story St]
- **Charlie's Kitchen** • 10 Eliot St [Winthrop St]
- **Chez Henri** • 1 Shepard St [Mass Ave]
- **Crazy Doughs** • 36 JFK St [Mt Auburn]
- **Darwin's Ltd** • 148 Mt Auburn St [Brewer]
- **Felipe's Taqueria** • 83 Mt Auburn St [JFK St]
- **Flat Patties** • 81 Mt Auburn St [Summer]
- **Grafton Street** •
  1230 Massachusetts Ave [Bow St]
- **Grendel's Den** • 89 Winthrop St [JFK]
- **Harvest** • 44 Brattle St [Story]
- **John Harvard's Brew House** •
  33 Dunster St [Mt Auburn]
- **Mr & Mrs Bartley's Burger Cottage** •
  1246 Massachusetts Ave [Plympton]
- **My Thai Vegetarian Café** •
  404 Harvard St [Prescott St]
- **OM** • 92 Winthrop St [JFK]
- **Pho Pasteur** • 35 Dunster St [Mt Auburn]
- **The Red House** • 98 Winthrop St [JFK]
- **Rialto** • 1 Bennett St [Eliot St]
- **Sabra Grill** • 20 Eliot St [JFK]
- **Sandrine's** • 8 Holyoke St [Mass Ave]
- **Shilla** • 57 JFK St [Winthrop St]
- **Takemura** • 18 Eliot St [JFK St]
- **Tamarind Bay** • 75 Winthrop St [Dunster St]
- **UpStairs on the Square** •
  91 Winthrop St [JFK]

- **Veggie Planet** • 47 Palmer St [Church St]
- **Wagamama** • 57 JFK St [Winthrop St]

🛍 Shopping

- **Abodeon** • 1731 Massachusetts Ave [Prentiss]
- **Alpha Omega** •
  1380 Massachusetts Ave [Holyoke St]
- **Berk's Shoes** • 50 JFK St [Winthrop St]
- **Black Ink** • 5 Brattle St [Brattle Sq]
- **Bob Slate** •
  1288 Massachusetts Ave [Linden St]
- **Brattle Square Florist** •
  31 Brattle St [Eliot St]
- **Cardullo's Gourmet Shoppe** •
  6 Brattle St [Brattle Sq]
- **City Sports** • 44 Brattle St [Story]
- **Colonial Drug** • 49 Brattle St [Farwell Pl]
- **Crate & Barrel** • 48 Brattle St [Story]
- **Harvard Bookstore** •
  1256 Massachusetts Ave [Plympton]
- **Harvard Coop** •
  1400 Massachusetts Ave [Dunster St]
- **Herrell's Ice Cream** •
  15 Dunster St [Mass Ave]
- **Hidden Sweets** • 25 Brattle St [Church St]
- **In Your Ear** • 75 Mt Auburn St [Bow St]
- **LA Burdick Homemade Chocolates** •
  52D Brattle St [Story]
- **Leavitt & Pierce** •
  1316 Massachusetts Ave [Holyoke St]
- **Little Tibet** •
  1174 Massachusetts Ave [DeWolfe St]
- **Lizzy's Ice Cream** • 29 Church St [Palmer St]
- **Lush** • 30 John F Kennedy St [Winthrop St]
- **Mint Julep** • 6 Church St [Mass Ave]
- **Museum of Useful Things** •
  49 Brattle St [Farwell]
- **Newbury Comics** • 36 JFK St [Mt Auburn]
- **Nomad** • 1741 Massachusetts Ave [Prentiss]
- **On Church Street** • 54 Church St [Palmer St]
- **Oona's** • 1210 Massachusetts Ave [Bow St]
- **Out of Town News** • Harvard Sq [JFK]
- **Planet Records** • 54B JFK St [Winthrop St]
- **Proletariat** • 36 JFK St [Mt Auburn]
- **Staples** •
  57 JFK St [Winthrop St]
- **Stereo Jack's** •
  1686 Massachusetts Ave [Sacramento St]
- **Tannery** • 11A Brattle St [Brattle Sq]
- **Tealuxe** • 9 Brattle St [Hague]
- **Tennis and Squash Shop** •
  67 Mt Auburn St [Linden St]
- **Tess and Carlos** • 20 Brattle St [Church St]
- **Twisted Village** • 12B Eliot St [Winthrop St]
- **Urban Outfitters** • 11 JFK St [Brattle Sq]
- **ZIPA Jewelry** •
  1316 Massachusetts Ave [Holyoke St]

📼 Video Rental

- **Hollywood Express** •
  1740 Massachusetts Ave [Prentiss]
- **Quick Flix** • 8 Bow St [Mass Ave]

Map 20 Harvard Square / Allston (North)

All roads, or at least many bus routes and the Red Line, lead to Harvard Square. Throngs of pedestrians are sure to slow down those brave enough to drive, and parking is hard to find, though diligent circling—and a little bit of luck—usually yields results.

Subway

■ · **Harvard**

Bus Lines

1 · Harvard/Holyoke Gate—Dudley Station via Massachusetts Avenue & BU Medical Center

66 · Harvard Square—Dudley Station via Allston & Brookline

68 · Harvard/Holyoke Gate—Kendall/MIT via Broadway

69 · Harvard/Holyoke Gate—Lechmere Station via Cambridge Street

71 · Watertown Square—Harvard Station via Mt Auburn Street

72 · Huron Avenue—Harvard Station via Concord Avenue

73 · Waverley Square—Harvard Station via Trapelo Road

74 · Belmont Center—Harvard Station via Concord Avenue

75 · Belmont Center—Harvard Station via Concord Avenue

77 · Arlington Heights—Harvard Station via Massachusetts Ave

77A · North Cambridge—Harvard Station, Local

78 · Arlmont Village—Harvard Station via Park Circle

86 · Sullivan Square Station—Cleveland Circle via Harvard/Johnston Gate

96 · Medford Square—Harvard Station via George Street & Davis Square

 Car Rental

· **Alamo** ·
  1663 Massachusetts Ave [Hudson St] · 617-661-8747
· **Avis** · 1 Bennett St [Eliot St] · 617-534-1430
· **Hertz** · 24 Eliot St [Winthrop St] · 617-338-1520
· **National** ·
  1663 Massachusetts Ave [Hudson St] · 617-661-8747
· **Thrifty** · Harvard Square Hotel ·
  110 Mt Auburn St [Eliot St] · 617-876-2758

P Gas Stations

· **Gulf** · 1725 Massachusetts Ave [Garfield St]

P Parking

Map 21 • West Cambridge
N

Tucked behind bustling Harvard Square, this hushed suburban community is nice for a pleasant, house-viewing stroll, but little else. Beautiful Mt. Auburn Cemetery is certainly a neighborhood highlight. Stop by and pay your respects to such long-ago dignitaries as Winslow Homer and Henry Cabot Lodge.

Banks

· **Cambridge Savings Bank (ATM)** ·
  168 Huron Ave [Manassas]
· **Cambridge Trust** · 353 Huron Ave [Chilton]

Community Gardens

Donuts

· **Dunkin' Donuts** · 201 Alewife Brook Pkwy [Terminal]
· **Dunkin' Donuts** · 517 Concord Ave [Concord Ln]

Emergency Rooms

· **Mount Auburn** · 330 Mt Auburn St [Longfellow Rd]

Libraries

· **Boudreau Public Library** ·
  245 Concord Ave [Donnell]

Pharmacies

· **CVS** · 211 Alewife Brook Pkwy [Concord Ave] ☼

Schools

· **Buckingham Browne & Nichols** ·
  80 Gerrys Landing Rd [Greenough Blvd]
· **Cambridge Montessori** · 161 Garden St [Walden St]
· **John M Tobin** · 197 Vassal Ln [Standish]

Supermarkets

· **Whole Foods Market** ·
  200 Alewife Brook Pkwy [Concord Ave]

If you're a gourmand—and particularly if you're a cheese enthusiast—make the trip to Formaggio Kitchen. For a quick bite along Huron Avenue, grab a slice at Armando's. And for pastries galore, stop by Hi-Rise Bread Company, on the ever-engaging corner of Concord Avenue.

Coffee

- **Starbucks** · 220 Alewife Brook Pkwy [Concord Ave]

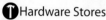Hardware Stores

- **Masse's True Value Hardware** ·
  249 Walden St [Sherman St]

Liquor Stores

- **Kappy's Liquors** ·
  215 Alewife Brook Pkwy [Concord Ave]
- **Mall Discount Liquors & Wines** ·
  202 Alewife Brook Pkwy [Concord Ave]

Pet Shops

- **Jeana's Dirty Dog Salon** ·
  298 Concord Ave [Walden St]
- **Pet Supply Outlet Store** ·
  211 Alewife Brook Pkwy [Concord Ave]
- **Raining Cats and Dogs** · 368 Huron Ave [Standish]

Restaurants

- **Armando's** · 163 Huron Ave [Concord Ave]
- **Cheddars** · 201 Alewife Brook Pkwy [Concord Ln]
- **Full Moon** · 344 Huron Ave [Chilton]
- **Hi-Rise Bread Company** · 208 Concord Ave [Huron]
- **Il Buongustaio** · 369 Huron Ave [Standish]
- **Trattoria Pulcinella** · 147 Huron Ave [Concord Ave]

Shopping

- **Formaggio Kitchen** · 244 Huron Ave [Appleton St]
- **Henry Bear's Park** · 361 Huron Ave [Standish]
- **Newbury Comics** ·
  211 Alewife Brook Pkwy [Concord Ave]

Unless you live here, you're not going to have an easy time parking. You might snag a space on Huron Avenue, but that's about it. Red Line stops are also far away; to get here by public transportation, take one of the buses that originate at Harvard Square.

Bus Lines

- **71** • Watertown Square—Harvard Station via Mt Auburn Street
- **72** • Huron Avenue—Harvard Station via Concord Avenue
- **73** • Waverley Square—Harvard Station via Trapelo Road
- **74** • Belmont Center—Harvard Station via Concord Avenue
- **75** • Belmont Center—Harvard Station via Concord Avenue
- **78** • Arlmont Village—Harvard Station via Park Circle

🅿 Gas Stations

- **Citgo** • 199 Concord Ave [Huron]
- **Mobil** • 343 Fresh Pond Pkwy [Lake View Ave] 🕐
- **Shell** • 603 Concord Ave [Wheeler]
- **Sunoco** • 515 Concord Ave [Concord Ln] 🕐

Map 22 • North Cambridge / West Somerville

Essentials

Map 22

Over the years, the Cambridge contingent has pushed working-class Somerville back into Medford, and claimed Davis Square as its capital. Blending NPR culture with town-center appeal, there is a virtual Benetton ad of businesses, bars, restaurants, and bodegas---not to mention a diner and an ice cream shop.

Banks

- **Bank of America** • 406 Highland Ave [Grove St]
- **Bank of America (ATM)** • 1116 Broadway [Holland St]
- **Bank of America (ATM)** •
  2168 Massachusetts Ave [Rindge Ave]
- **Bank of America (ATM)** •
  2502 Massachusetts Ave [Cottage Pk]
- **Bank of America (ATM)** • 253 Elm St [Chester St]
- **Century Bank** • 2309 Massachusetts Ave [Meacham Rd]
- **Citizens Bank** • 212 Elm St [Bowers]
- **Citizens Bank (ATM)** • 1 Holland St [College]
- **Citizens Bank (ATM)** • 4 College Ave [Winter St]
- **East Cambridge Savings Bank** •
  2067 Massachusetts Ave [Walden St]
- **First National Bank of Ipswich** •
  2067 Massachusetts Ave [Walden St]
- **Middlesex Federal Savings** •
  1 College Ave [Highland Ave]
- **Middlesex Federal Savings** • 1196 Broadway [Hill]
- **Wainwright Bank & Trust** •
  176 Alewife Brook Pkwy [Terminal]
- **Wainwright Bank & Trust** • 250 Elm St [Chester St]

Community Gardens

Donuts

- **Dunkin' Donuts** • 244 Elm St [Chester St]
- **Dunkin' Donuts** •
  2480 Massachusetts Ave [Washburn Ave]
- **Verna's Donut Shop** •
  2344 Massachusetts Ave [Norris]

Landmarks

- **Somerville Theatre** • 55 Davis Sq [Highland Ave]

Libraries

- **O'Neill Public Library** • 70 Rindge Ave [Rindgefield]
- **Somerville West** • 40 College Ave [Morrison Ave]

Pharmacies

- **Rite Aid** • 393 Highland Ave [Grove St]

Post Offices

- **West Somerville** • 58 Day St [Herbert]

Schools

- **Benjamin Banneker Charter** •
  21 Notre Dame Ave [Middlesex St]
- **Cambridge Friends** • 5 Cadbury Rd [Wood St]
- **Ecole Bilingue, The French American International School** •
  45 Matignon Rd [Murray Hill Rd]
- **Matignon High** • 1 Matignon Rd [Churchill Ave]
- **North Cambridge Catholic High** •
  40 Norris St [Cedar St]
- **Peabody** • 70 Rindge Ave [Rindgefield]
- **Powder House Community** •
  1060 Broadway [Packard]
- **SCALE** • 167 Holland St [Cameron Ave]
- **St John the Evangelist** • 122 Rindge Ave [Rice St]
- **Tufts University** • 169 Holland St [Cameron Ave]

Supermarkets

- **Sessa's Cold Cuts & Italian Specialties** •
  414 Highland Ave [Grove St]

Map 22 • **North Cambridge / West Somerville**

Whatever your taste in food and entertainment, you'll satisfy it here. Try Out of the Blue's delicious and inexpensive seafood, Redbones' barbecue, or belly-warming momo from House of Tibet. Live Music=Somerville Theatre or Johnny D's. Somerville Shuffle=Sligo Pub. The perfect Guinness=The Burren.

🖥️ Coffee

- **Diesel Café** • 257 Elm St [Chester St]
- **Starbucks** • 260 Elm St [Chester St]

📄 Copy Shops

- **Budget Copy** • 2449 Massachusetts Ave [Gold Star Rd]
- **Princeton Printing** • 260 Elm St [Chester St]
- **Staples** • 186 Alewife Brook Pkwy [Terminal]
- **The UPS Store** • 411 Highland Ave [Grove St]

🍎 Farmers Markets

- **Somerville (May—Nov; Wed 12 pm—6 pm)** •
  Day St & Herbert St

🔧 Hardware Stores

- **City Paint & Supply** •
  2564 Massachusetts Ave [Newman St]

🧴 Liquor Stores

- **Downtown Wine & Spirits** • 225 Elm St [Grove St]
- **Norton Beverage** • 2451 Massachusetts Ave [Gold Star Rd]
- **Pemberton Fruit Market** •
  2225 Massachusetts Ave [Rindge Ave]
- **Teele Square Liquor** • 1119 Broadway [Westminster St]

🎭 Movie Theaters

- **Entertainment Cinemas Fresh Pond** •
  168 Alewife Brook Pkwy [Terminal]
- **Somerville Theatre** • 55 Davis Sq [Highland Ave]

🍸 Nightlife

- **The Burren** • 247 Elm St [Chester St]
- **Diva Lounge** • 246 Elm St [Chester St]
- **Johnny D's Uptown** • 17 Holland St [Winter St]
- **PJ Ryan's** • 239 Holland St [Broadway]
- **Redbones** • 55 Chester St [Herbert]
- **Sligo Pub** • 237A Elm St [Grove St]
- **Somerville Theatre** • 55 Davis Sq [Highland Ave]

🐾 Pet Shops

- **Animal Spirit** • 2348 Massachusetts Ave [Norris]

🍴 Restaurants

- **Anna's Taqueria** • 236 Elm St [Chester St]
- **Antonia's Italian Bistro** • 37 Davis Sq [Highland Ave]
- **Blue Shirt Café** • 424 Highland Ave [Elm St]
- **Café Barada** • 2269 Massachusetts Ave [Dover]
- **Dave's Fresh Pasta** • 81 Holland St [Irving St]
- **Diesel Café** • 257 Elm St [Chester St]
- **Diva Indian Bistro** • 246 Elm St [Chester St]
- **Elephant Walk** • 2067 Massachusetts Ave [Walden St]
- **Gargoyles on the Square** • 219 Elm St [Grove St]
- **House of Tibet** • 235 Holland St [B'way]
- **Jasper White's Summer Shack** •
  149 Alewife Brook Pkwy [Rindge Ave]
- **Jose's** • 131 Sherman St [Bellis Cir]
- **Joshua Tree** • 256 Elm St [Chester St]
- **Martsa on Elm** • 233A Elm St [Grove St]
- **Namaskar** • 236 Elm St [Chester St]
- **Orleans** • 65 Holland St [Buena Vista Rd]
- **Out of the Blue** • 215 Elm St [Grove St]
- **Qingdao Garden** • 2382 Massachusetts Ave [Alberta]
- **Redbones** • 55 Chester St [Herbert]
- **Renee's Cafe** • 198 Holland st [Claremon St]
- **Richardson's Ice Cream** • 55 Davis Sq
- **Rosebud Diner** • 381 Summer St [Cutler Ave]
- **Rudy's Café** • 248 Holland St [Newbury St]
- **Sabur** • 212 Holland St [Moore]
- **Snappy Sushi** • 420 Holland St [Elm St]
- **Spike's Junkyard Dogs** • 217 Elm St [Grove St]
- **Teele Square Café** • 1153 Broadway [Clarendon Ave]
- **Tip Top Noodle Shop** • 1153 Broadway [Clarendon Ave]

🛍️ Shopping

- **Bicycle Exchange** • 2067 Massachusetts Ave [Walden St]
- **Black & Blues** • 89 Holland St [Simpson Ave]
- **CD Spins** • 235 Elm St [Grove St]
- **China Fair** • 2100 Massachusetts Ave [Walden St]
- **Chinook Outdoor Adventure** •
  93 Holland St [Simpson Ave]
- **Cibeline** • 85 Holland St [Irving St]
- **Magpie** • 416 Highland Ave [Grove St]
- **McKinnon's Choice Meat Market** • 239A Elm St [Grove St]
- **Modern Brewer** • 2304 Massachusetts Ave [Rice St]
- **Nellie's Wildflowers** • 72 Holland St [Buena Vista Rd]
- **Poor Little Rich Girl** • 255 Elm St [Chester St]
- **Staples** • 186 Alewife Brook Pkwy [Terminal]

📀 Video Rental

- **Blockbuster** • 180 Alewife Brook Pkwy [Terminal]
- **Hollywood Express** • 238 Elm St [Chester St]
- **Palmer Video** • 2368 Massachusetts Ave [Nickerson Rd]

Driving is no fun in Davis Square; parking is painful. Ditto for the area around Alewife. The Red Line serves both areas, but if you must drive, look for parking along Holland Avenue, a bit outside the Square. For North Cambridge haunts along Mass Ave and its side streets, get to know the 77 bus.

Subway

- **Davis**
- **Alewife**

Bus Lines

- **74** • Belmont Center—Harvard Station via Concord Avenue
- **75** • Belmont Center—Harvard Station via Concord Avenue
- **77** • Arlington Heights—Harvard Station via Massachusetts Avenue
- **77A** • North Cambridge—Harvard Station Local
- **78** • Arlmont Village—Harvard Station via Park Circle
- **79** • Arlington Heights—Alewife Station via Massachusetts Avenue
- **83** • Rindge Ave—Central Square, Cambridge via Porter Square Station
- **87** • Arlington Center or Clarendon Hill—Lechmere Station
- **88** • Clarendon Hill—Lechmere Station via Highland Avenue
- **89** • Clarendon Hill—Sullivan Square Station via Broadway
- **90** • Davis Square—Wellington Station via Sullivan Square Station
- **96** • Medford Square—Harvard Station via George Street & Davis Square
- **350** • North Burlington—Alewife Station via Burlington

 Car Washes

- **Cambridge Car Wash** •
  2013 Massachusetts Ave [Regent St]

 Gas Stations

- **Independent** • 2535 Massachusetts Ave [Rindge Ave]
- **Mobil** • 2615 Massachusetts Ave [Alewife Brook]

 Parking

Porter Square feels less polished than Harvard and Davis, and living space here and in neighboring Somerville is slightly more affordable. Shops and restaurants are concentrated on Mass Ave, and a mix of young people, families, and townies populates the residential neighborhoods.

$ Banks

- **Bank of America** · 1847 Massachusetts Ave [Upland]
- **Bank of America (ATM)** ·
  1815 Massachusetts Ave [Roseland]
- **Cambridge Savings Bank** · 53 White St [Elm St]
- **Cambridge Savings Bank (ATM)** ·
  36 White St [White St Pl]
- **Cambridge Savings Bank (ATM)** ·
  711 Somerville Ave [Elm St]
- **Central Bank** · 399 Highland Ave [Grove St]
- **Century Bank (ATM)** · 110 Medford St [Dexter St]
- **Citizens Bank (ATM)** ·
  Somerville Ave & Massachusetts Ave
- **East Cambridge Savings Bank** ·
  285 Highland Ave [Cedar St]
- **Sovereign Bank** · 403 Highland Ave [Grove St]
- **Sovereign Bank (ATM)** · CVS/Pharmacy ·
  36 White St [Somerville Ave]
- **Winter Hill Bank** · 5 Cutter Ave [Elm St]
- **Winter Hill Bank** · 691 Broadway [Boston Ave]

Community Gardens

Donuts

- **Dunkin' Donuts** · 1 White St [Somerville Ave]
- **Dunkin' Donuts** · 154 Highland Ave [Central St]
- **Dunkin' Donuts** · 504 Broadway [Hinckley]
- **Dunkin' Donuts** · 519 Somerville Ave [Park St]
- **Russ' Donuts** · 2 Highland Rd [Morrison Ave]

Emergency Rooms

- **Somerville Hospital** · 230 Highland Ave [Tower St]

Landmarks

- **Art at Porter Square** ·
  Somerville Ave & Massachusetts Ave
- **Milk Row Cemetery** · 439 Somerville Ave [School St]
- **Powderhouse** · College Ave & Broadway
- **Random British Soldier Grave** · 145 Elm St
- **The Round House** · 36 Atherton St [Beech St]
- **Somerville Museum** · 1 Westwood Rd [Central St]

Pharmacies

- **CVS** · 36 White St Pl [White St] ♻
- **CVS** · 532 Medford St [Lowell St]
- **Rite Aid** · 530 Somerville Ave [Park St]

Post Offices

- **Porter Square** · 1953 Massachusetts Ave [Allen St]

Schools

- **Benjamin G Brown** · 201 Willow Ave [Kidder]
- **John F Kennedy** · 5 Cherry St [Elm St]
- **St Anthony Elementary** ·
  480 Somerville Ave [Loring]
- **St Catherine's of Genoa** ·
  192 Summer St [Belmont St]
- **St Clement's Elementary** · 589 Boston Ave [Warner]
- **St Clement's High** · 579 Boston Ave [Warner]

Supermarkets

- **Star Market** · 275 Beacon St [Sacramento St]
- **Star Market** · 49 White St [White St Pl]

The best bet for nearby entertainment is to hop on the Red Line and head one stop in either direction (toward Davis or Harvard). If you do stay local, enjoy a low-key meal at Christopher's, or hit Toad, where there's live music almost every night. Also don't pass up a fresh, homemade taco at Anna's Taqueria.

Coffee

- **Café Rustica** • 356 Beacon St [Roseland]
- **Caffé Rossini** • 278 Highland Ave [Cedar St]
- **Starbucks** • 711 Somerville Ave [Elm St]
- **True Grounds** • 717 Broadway [Willow Ave]

Copy Shops

- **The UPS Store** • 1770 Massachusetts Ave [Lancaster St]
- **The UPS Store** • 519 Somerville Ave [Park St]

Gyms

- **Bally Total Fitness** • 1815 Mass Ave [Roseland]
- **Curves For Women** • 622 Somerville Ave [Kent St]
- **HealthWorks Fitness Center (Women Only)** • 35 White St [White St Pl]

Hardware Stores

- **City Paint & Supply** • 729 Broadway [Bristol Rd]
- **Tags Hardware** • 29 White St [White St Pl]

Liquor Stores

- **Ball Square Fine Wines & Liquors** • 716 Broadway [Willow Ave]
- **Crowley's Liquors** • 152 Boston Ave [Highland Rd]
- **Liquor World** • 13 White St [Somerville Ave]
- **Seven Hills Wine & Spirits** • 288 Beacon St [Sacramento St]
- **Somerville Wine & Spirits** • 235 Highland Ave [Crocker]
- **Woody's Liquor** • 594 Somerville Ave [Garden Ct]
- **Woody's Liquors** • 523 Broadway [William St]

Nightlife

- **Christopher's** • 1920 Massachusetts Ave [Porter Rd]
- **Newtowne Grille** • 1945 Mass Ave [Davenport]
- **Olde Magoun Saloon** • 518 Medford St [Lowell St]
- **On the Hill Tavern** • 499 Broadway [Medford St]
- **Samba Bar & Grill** • 608 Somerville Ave [Kent St]
- **Toad** • 1912 Massachusetts Ave [Porter Rd]

Pet Shops

- **Big Fish, Little Fish** • 55 Elm St [Cedar St]
- **Stinky's Kittens & Doggies Too** • 110 Bristol Rd [B'way]

Restaurants

- **Anna's Taqueria** • 822 Somerville Ave [Acadia Pk]
- **Blue Fin** • 1815 Massachusetts Ave [Roseland]
- **Broken Yolk** • 136 College Ave [B'way]
- **Café Mami** • Porter Exchange • 1815 Massachusetts Ave [Roseland St]
- **Café Rustica** • 356 Beacon St [Roseland]
- **Caffé Rossini** • 278 Highland Ave [Cedar St]
- **Christopher's** • 1920 Massachusetts Ave [Porter Rd]
- **Kelly's Diner** • 674 Broadway [Boston Ave]
- **Lemon Thai** • 215 Highland Ave [Lowell St]
- **Lil Vinny's** • 525 Medford St [Lowell St]
- **Lyndell's Bakery** • 720 Broadway [Willow Ave]
- **Passage to India** • 1900 Massachusetts Ave [Porter Rd]
- **RF O'Sullivan's** • 282 Beacon St [Sacramento St]
- **Sound Bites** • 708 Broadway [Willow Ave]
- **Stone Hearth Pizza Co.** • 1782 Mass Ave [Lancaster]
- **Sugar & Spice** • 1933 Massachusetts Ave [Davenport]
- **Tacos Lupita** • 13 Elm St [Porter St]
- **True Grounds** • 717 Broadway [Willow Ave]
- **Tu y Yo** • 858 Broadway [Walker St]
- **Wang's Fast Food** • 509 Broadway [Hinckley]

Shopping

- **Ace Wheelworks** • 145 Elm St [Willow Ave]
- **Big Fish, Little Fish** • 55 Elm St [Cedar St]
- **Bob Slate** • 1975 Massachusetts Ave [Beech St]
- **Cambridge Music Center** • 1906 Massachusetts Ave [Porter Rd]
- **Cambridge Naturals** • 23 White St [Somerville Ave]
- **City Sports** • 1815 Massachusetts Ave [Roseland]
- **Greenward** • 1776 Massachusetts Ave [Lancaster St]
- **Joie de Vivre** • 1792 Massachusetts Ave [Arlington St]
- **Lyndell's Bakery** • 720 Broadway [Willow Ave]
- **Paper Source** • 1810 Massachusetts Ave [Arlington St]
- **Porter Square Books** • 25 White St [Somerville Ave]
- **Roach's Sporting Goods** • 1957 Mass Ave [Allen St]

Video Rental

- **Blockbuster** • 1 Porter Sq [White St]

Guarded by a 46-foot steel kinetic sculpture (painted red to match the subway line), centrally located Porter Square T stop makes it easy to get from Porter to other corners of Cambridge or all the way into Boston. Street parking is generally plentiful.

Subway

 · Porter

Bus Lines

77 · Arlington Heights—Harvard Station via Massachusetts Avenue

77A · North Cambridge—Harvard Station Local

80 · Arlington Center—Lechmere Station via Medford Hills

83 · Rindge Avenue—Central Square, Cambridge via Porter Square Station

85 · Spring Hill—Kendall/MIT Station via Summer Street & Union Square

86 · Sullivan Square Station—Cleveland Circle via Harvard/Johnson Gate

88 · Clarendon Hill—Lechmere Station via Highland Avenue

90 · Davis Square—Wellington Station via Sullivan Square Station

94 · Medford Square—Davis Square Station via W Medford & Medford Streets

96 · Medford Square—Harvard Station via George St & Davis Square

101 · Malden Center Station— Sullivan Square Station

 Car Rental

· **Hertz** · 646 Somerville Ave [Lowell St] · 617-625-7958

Car Washes

· **Somerville Car Wash** · 680 Somerville Ave [Craigie St]

Gas Stations

· **Fortini's Service Station** · 225 Beacon St [Kent St]
· **Gulf** · 367 Highland Ave [West St]
· **Gulf** · 583 Broadway [Alfred St]
· **Gulf** · 701 Somerville Ave [Elm St]
· **Sunoco** · 541 Broadway [William St]

Here you'll find remnants of Somerville's working-class neighborhoods, City Hall, and the 93-year-old library. Bypass residential Winter Hill for the livelier Union Square, and don't miss the view of Boston (and July 4 fireworks) from Prospect Hill, where America's first flag was raised in 1776.

$ Banks

- **Bank of America (ATM)** • 5 Middlesex Ave [Main]
- **Bank of America (ATM)** • 68 Union Sq [Stone Ave]
- **Century Bank** • 102 Fellsway W [Shore]
- **Citizens Bank** • 338 Broadway [School St]
- **Citizens Bank** • 40 Union Sq [Warren Ave]
- **Citizens Bank** • 779 McGrath Hwy [Mystic Ave]
- **Citizens Bank (ATM)** • 321 Broadway [Temple St]
- **Sovereign Bank** • 125 Broadway [Wisconsin]
- **Sovereign Bank (ATM)** •
  77 Middlesex Ave [Kensington Ave]
- **Winter Hill Bank** • 342 Broadway [School St]

✳ Community Gardens

◎ Donuts

- **Dunkin' Donuts** • 220 Broadway [McGrath Hwy]
- **Dunkin' Donuts** • 498 Mystic Ave [Butler Dr]
- **Dunkin' Donuts** • 709 McGrath Hwy [Blakeley Ave]
- **Dunkin' Donuts** • 76 Middlesex Ave [Kensington Ave]
- **Dunkin' Donuts** • 90 Washington St [Franklin St]

○ Landmarks

- **Prospect Hill Monument** •
  Munroe St b/w Prospect Hill Ave & Walnut St
- **Somerville City Hall** • 93 Highland Ave [School St]

◫ Libraries

- **Somerville East** • 115 Broadway [Michigan]
- **Somerville Main Library** •
  79 Highland Ave [Prescott St]

℞ Pharmacies

- **Rite Aid** • 299 Broadway [Marshall St]
- **Stop & Shop** • 779 McGrath Hwy [Mystic Ave]
- **Walgreens** • 343 Broadway [Dartmouth St]

⬡ Police

- **Somerville Police Department** •
  220 Washington St [Merriam St]

✉ Post Offices

- **Somerville Branch** • 237 Washington St [Bonner Ave]
- **Winter Hill Branch** • 320 Broadway [Marshall St]

◉ Schools

- **Arthur D Healey** • 5 Meacham St [Ash Ave]
- **Capuano Ecc** • 150 Glen St [Dell]
- **Cummings** • 42 Prescott St [Summer]
- **East Somerville Community** • 115 Pearl St [Rush]
- **Full Circle High** • 8 Bonair St [Royce Pl]
- **Lincoln Park Community** •
  290 Washington St [Parker St]
- **Lincoln Park Community Edgerly** •
  8 Bonair St [Royce Pl]
- **Lincoln Park Community Thurston** •
  50 Thurston St [Evergreen Ave]
- **Little Flower Elementary** •
  17 Franklin St [Arlington St]
- **Next Wave Middle** • 8 Bonair St [Royce Pl]
- **Somerville High** • 81 Highland Ave [School St]
- **St Ann's** • 50 Thurston St [Evergreen Ave]
- **Winter Hill Community** •
  115 Sycamore St [Evergreen Ave]

⬒ Supermarkets

- **Star Market** • 299 Broadway [Marshall St]
- **Stop & Shop** • 779 McGrath Hwy [Mystic Ave]

Map 24 • **Winter Hill / Union Square**

Sundries / Entertainment

Perpetually up-and-coming, Union Square has a thriving dining and drinking scene, outdoor arts festivals, and a weekend farmers market. Free bands at PA's Lounge and Sally O'Brien's, Peruvian food at Machu Picchu, and the huge breakfasts at Neighborhood Restaurant can't be beat. If you want to go out, try the Independent.

Map 24

Coffee

- **Block 11 Café** • 11 Bow St [Walnut St]
- **Sherman Café** • 257 Washington St [Webster Ave]

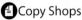Copy Shops

- **Staples** • 165 Middlesex Ave [Cummings St]

Farmers Markets

- **Union Square (June—Oct; Sat 9 am—1 pm)** • Somerville St

Gyms

- **Planet Fitness** • 5 Middlesex Ave [Mystic Ave]
- **YMCA** • 101 Highland Ave [School St]

Hardware Stores

- **Robi Tool Sales** • 168 Broadway [Cross St]

Liquor Stores

- **Jerry's Liquor** • 329 Somerville Ave [Hawkins]
- **Joe's Liquors** • 166 Broadway [Rush]
- **Paul Revere Beverage** • 10 Main St [Edgar Ave]
- **Trans Liquor Mart** • 545 McGrath Hwy [Pearl St]
- **Winter Hill Liquor Mart** • 313 Broadway [Temple St]

Nightlife

- **11th Chapter Saloon** • 366 Somerville Ave [Carlton]
- **The Independent** • 75 Union Sq [Stone Ave]
- **Khoury's State Spa** • 118 Broadway [Glen St]
- **PA's Lounge** • 345 Somerville Ave [Hawkins]
- **Sally O'Brien's** • 335 Somerville Ave [Hawkins]
- **Toast** • 70 Union Sq [Stone Ave]

Restaurants

- **Café Belo** • 120 Washington St [New Washington]
- **Fasika Ethiopian Restaurant** • 145 Broadway [Rush]
- **Great Thai Chef** • 255 Washington St [Bonner Ave]
- **Leone's** • 292 Broadway [Marshall St]
- **Machu Picchu** • 25 Union Sq [Webster Ave]
- **Neighborhood Restaurant & Bakery** • 25 Bow St [Walnut St]
- **Sherman Café** • 257 Washington St [Webster Ave]
- **Ronnarong Thai Tapas Bar** • 255 Washington St [Bonner Ave]
- **Sweet Ginger** • 22 Bow St [Walnut St]
- **Taqueria la Mexicana** • 247 Washington St [Bonner Ave]

Shopping

- **Bombay Market** • 359 Somerville Ave [Kilby St]
- **Bostonian Florist** • 92 Highland Ave [School St]
- **Christmas Tree Shops** • 177 Middlesex Ave [Cummings St]
- **Mudflat Studio** • 149 Broadway [Minnesota]
- **Reliable Market** • 45 Union Sq [Warren Ave]
- **Ricky's Flower Market** • 9 Union Sq [Stone Ave]

Video Rental

- **Palmer Video** • 345 Broadway [Dartmouth St]

Map 24 · **Winter Hill / Union Square**

A pinwheel of converging roads, including the city's oldest, Washington Street, Union Square has preserved its ethnic diversity by remaining inaccessible by subway. Served by the 86, 87, and 91 buses, we hope a long-proposed T extension that could spoil the neighborhood flavor never sees the light of day.

Bus Lines

- **CT2** · Sullivan Station—Ruggles Station via Kendall/MIT
- **85** · Spring Hill—Kendall/MIT Station via Summer Street & Union Square
- **86** · Sullivan Sq Station—Cleveland Circle via Harvard/Johnson Gate
- **87** · Arlington Center or Clarendon Hill—Lechmere Station
- **89** · Clarendon Hill—Sullivan Square Station via Broadway
- **90** · Davis Square—Wellington Station via Sullivan Square Station
- **91** · Sullivan Square Station—Central Square, Cambridge via Washington
- **92** · Assembly Square Mall—Downtown via Sullivan Square Station, Main Street
- **95** · West Medford—Sullivan Square Station via Mystic Avenue
- **101** · Malden Center Station—Sullivan Square Station

Car Rental

- **Americar Auto Rental** ·
  90 Highland Ave [School St] · 617-776-4640

Gas Stations

- **Gulf** · 212 Broadway [McGrath Hwy]
- **Gulf** · 231 Washington St [Columbus]
- **Hess** · 709 McGrath Hwy [Blakeley] ☉
- **Mobil** · 360 Medford St [School St]
- **Sunoco** · 258 Broadway [Walnut St]
- **Sunoco** · 434 McGrath Hwy [Greenville St]
- **Vincente Brothers** · 345 Medford St [Pearl St]

People go to Sullivan Square for the Orange Line or if they have a package at UPS. The historic Schrafft's Building, formerly the country's largest candy factory, looms over this throughway of a neighborhood from Cambridge/Somerville to Charlestown, Everett, and Malden.

Banks

- **Bank of America (ATM)** ·
  22 McGrath Hwy [Fitchburg]
- **Citizens Bank (ATM)** ·
  250 New Rutherford Ave [W School St]
- **East Cambridge Savings Bank (ATM)** ·
  534 Medford St [Short St]
- **Sovereign Bank** · 437 Rutherford Ave [Essex]

Community Gardens

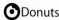 Donuts

- **Dunkin' Donuts** · Sullivan Sq Station ·
  1 Broadway [Mystic Ave]
- **Dunkin' Donuts** · 14 McGrath Hwy [Fitchburg]
- **Dunkin' Donuts** · 99 Cambridge St [Carter St]

O Landmarks

- **Schrafft's Building** · 529 Main St [Mishawum]

Pharmacies

- **Melrose Drug Center** · 462 Main St [Charbonnier]
- **Rite Aid** · 14 McGrath Hwy [Fitchburg] ♿
- **Teamsters Care Pharmacy** · 552 Main St [Mishawum]

Schools

- **Bunker Hill Community College** ·
  250 New Rutherford Ave [W School St]

Supermarkets

- **Shaw Market** · 14 McGrath Hwy [Fitchburg]

Map 25 • **East Somerville / Sullivan Square**

Vinny's at Night is the best reason to visit this part of town. Don't be fooled by the convenience store frontage: in back lies a treasure trove of unreal Sicilian food. Good Time Emporium is the ideal place for ping pong, free darts, or a good batting cage heart-to-heart à la Good Will Hunting.

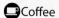 Coffee

· **Ro-Lin's Breakfast & Lunch** ·
78 Arlington Ave [Dorrance]

📄 Copy Shops

· **Go Ape** · 21 McGrath Hwy [Rufo]

Gyms

· **Fitcorp** · 529 Main St [Mishawum]
· **Gold's Gym** · 14 McGrath Hwy [Fitchburg]

🔨 Hardware Stores

· **Everett Supply & True Value Hardware** ·
403 Main St [Auburn St]
· **Home Depot** · 75 Mystic Ave [N Union]

🍾 Liquor Stores

· **Bairos Liquors** · 78 Broadway [Hathorn]
· **Blue Label Liquors** · 2 Carter St [Richerd St]
· **Middlesex Beverages** ·
30 Broadway [Mount Vernon St]
· **Sav-Mor Discount Liquors** · 15 McGrath Hwy [Rufo]

🍸 Nightlife

· **Good Time Emporium** ·
30 Assembly Square Dr [Foley]
· **Night Games** · 30 Washington St [Florence St]

🍴 Restaurants

· **Beijing Taste** · 99A Cambridge St [Brighton St]
· **Mount Vernon** · 14 Broadway [Mt Pleasant St]
· **Vinny's at Night** · 76 Broadway [Hathorn]

🛍️ Shopping

· **Home Depot** · 75 Mystic Ave [N Union]
· **Vinny's Superette** · 76 Broadway [Hathorn]

Map 25 • **East Somerville / Sullivan Square**

Sullivan Square Station is a major stop on the T's Orange Line and several bus routes. If driving, beware of the other drivers (true in all of Boston but must be highlighted here), confusing signage (ditto), multiple rotaries (ditto), and annoying traffic (you guessed it).

Bus Lines

- **CT2** • Sullivan Station—Ruggles Station via Kendall/MIT
- **80** • Arlington Center—Lechmere Station via Medford Hills
- **86** • Sullivan Square Station—Cleveland Circle via Harvard/Johnson Gate
- **87** • Arlington Center or Clarendon Hill—Lechmere Station
- **88** • Clarendon Hill—Lechmere Station via Highland Avenue
- **89** • Clarendon Hill—Sullivan Square Station via Broadway
- **90** • Davis Square—Wellington Station via Sullivan Square Station
- **91** • Sullivan Square Station—Central Square, Cambridge via Washington Street
- **92** • Assembly Square Mall—Downtown via Sullivan Square Station, Main Street
- **93** • Sullivan Square Station—Downtown via Bunker Hill Street & Haymarket Station
- **95** • West Medford—Sullivan Square Station via Mystic Avenue
- **101** • Malden Center Station—Sullivan Square Station
- **104** • Malden Center Station—Sullivan Square Station
- **105** • Malden Center Station—Sullivan Square Station
- **109** • Linden Square—Sullivan Square Station via Glendale Square

Car Rental

- **Enterprise** • 37 Mystic Ave [N Union] • 617-625-1766

Gas Stations

- **Hess** • 123 Cambridge St [Parker St] ♿
- **Independent** • 339 Main St [Eden]
- **Mobil** • 386 Main St [Lyndeboro St]

Once dominated by countless factories producing candy and candles, East Cambridge is now dominated by MIT and countless labs and tech companies. These eager beavers have a sweet tooth for sleek architecture; the most striking example being the Stata Center.

Map 2

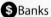 ## $ Banks

- **Bank of America** · 100 Cambridgeside Pl [Land]
- **Bank of America** · 226 Main St [Wadsworth St]
- **Bank of America** · 84 Massachusetts Ave [Vassar]
- **Bank of America (ATM)** ·
  150 Cambridge Park [Land]
- **Bank of America (ATM)** · 2 Canal Park [Land]
- **Bank of America (ATM)** · 4 Cambridge Ctr [Dock]
- **Bank of America (ATM)** · 600 Technology Sq [B'way]
- **Bank of America (ATM)** ·
  77 Massachusetts Ave [Amherst]
- **Boston Private Bank & Trust** ·
  1 Cambridge Ctr [Hayward St]
- **Cambridge Trust** · 326 Main St [Dock]
- **Citizens Bank** · 225 Cambridge St [3rd St]
- **East Cambridge Savings Bank** · 1 Canal Park [Land]
- **East Cambridge Savings Bank** ·
  292 Cambridge St [Sciarappa]
- **Sovereign Bank (ATM)** · 3 Cambridge Ctr [Dock]
- **Wainwright Bank & Trust** · 1 Broadway [Main]

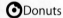 ## ⊙ Donuts

- **Dunkin' Donuts** · Sullivan Sq Station ·
  1 Broadway [Main]
- **Dunkin' Donuts** · 100 Cambridgeside Pl [Land]
- **Dunkin' Donuts** · 5 Third St [Monsignor O'Brien Hwy]

⚪ Landmarks

- **Harvard Bridge** · Massachusetts Ave [Memorial Dr]
- **Kendall/MIT T Station** · Main St [B'way]
- **Stata Center** · 32 Vassar St [Main]

 ## 📖 Libraries

- **O'Connell Public Library** · 48 Sixth St [Thorndike]

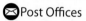 ## ℞ Pharmacies

- **Ciampa Apothecary** · 425 Cambridge St [5th St]

 ## ✉ Post Offices

- **East Cambridge Station** ·
  303 Cambridge St [Sciarappa]
- **Kendall Square Station** · 250 Main St [Hayward St]
- **MIT** · 84 Massachusetts Ave [Vassar]

🏫 Schools

- **Community Charter School of Cambridge** ·
  245 Bent St [5th St]
- **Kennedy-Longfellow** · 158 Spring St [7th St]
- **Massachusetts Institute of Technology** ·
  77 Massachusetts Ave [Amherst]

Map 20 • **East Cambridge/Kendall Square/MIT**

Sundries / Entertainment

East Cambridge is home to the tasty Helmand Restaurant and the indie-chain Kendall Square Cinema. Grab a beer at Cambridge Brewing Company after a film (or before, if called for). The Apple Store at Cambridgeside Galleria is a chain store we can easily live with.

Coffee

- **Beantowne Coffee House** · One Kendall Sq [Hampshire St]
- **Starbucks** · 100 Cambridgeside Pl [Land]
- **Starbucks** · Marriott Hotel · 2 Cambridge Ctr [Hayward St]
- **Starbucks** · 6 Cambridge Ctr [Dock]
- **Sweet Touch** · 241 Cambridge St [3rd St]

Copy Shops

- **Dmr Print** · 5 Cambridge Ctr [Dock]
- **FedEx Kinko's** · 600 Technology Sq [B'way]
- **Kendall Press** · 1 Main St [1st St]
- **The UPS Store** · One Kendall Sq [Hampshire St]

Gyms

- **Cambridge Racquet & Fitness Club** · 215 First St [Linskey]
- **Fitcorp** · 600 Technology Sq [B'way]

Hardware Stores

- **Sears** · 100 Cambridgeside Pl [Land]

Liquor Stores

- **660 Liquors** · 660 Cambridge St [Max]

Movie Theaters

- **Landmark Kendall Square Cinema** · One Kendall Sq [Hampshire St]

Nightlife

- **Cambridge Brewing Company** · One Kendall Sq, Bldg 100 [Hampshire St]
- **Flat Top Johnny's** · One Kendall Sq, Bldg 200 [Hampshire St]
- **Pugliese's** · 635 Cambridge St [Lambert St]

Pet Shops

- **Petco** · 119 First St [Charles St]

Restaurants

- **Aceituna** · 605 W Kendall St [Athenaeum]
- **Bambara** · 25 Land Blvd [Cambridgeside]
- **Black Sheep Café** · 350 Main St [Dock]
- **The Blue Room** · One Kendall Sq [Hampshire St]
- **Court House Seafood** · 498 Cambridge St [6th St]
- **Desfina** · 202 Third St [Charles St]
- **Helmand Restaurant** · 143 First St [Land]
- **Legal Sea Foods** · 5 Cambridge Ctr [Dock]
- **Second Street Café** · 89 Second St [Spring]
- **Technique** · 215 1st St [Athanaeum St]

Shopping

- **Apple Store** · 100 Cambridgeside Pl [Land]
- **Best Buy** · 100 Cambridgeside Pl [Land]
- **Calumet Photographic** · 65 Bent St [2nd St]
- **Cambridge Antique Market** · 201 Monsignor O'Brien Hwy [Water]
- **Mayflower Poultry** · 621 Cambridge St [8th St]

Video Rental

- **Hollywood Video** · 25 Massachusetts Ave [Memorial Dr]

Map 26

Map 26 • **East Cambridge/Kendall Square/MIT**

Parking at the Galleria is reasonably priced and handy if street parking is difficult to locate. Perennially confusing is the One Kendall Square complex not being located at Kendall Square—it's actually a few blocks up Broadway toward Cardinal Medeiros Avenue.

Subway

- Lechmere
- Kendall/MIT

Bus Lines

- **CT2** · Sullivan Square Station—Ruggles Station via Kendall/MIT
- **68** · Harvard/Holyoke Gate—Kendall/MIT via Broadway
- **69** · Harvard/Holyoke Gate—Lechmere Station via Cambridge Street
- **80** · Arlington Center—Lechmere Station via Medford Hills
- **85** · Spring Hill—Kendall/MIT Station via Summer Street & Union Square
- **87** · Arlington Center or Clarendon Hill—Lechmere Station
- **88** · Clarendon Hill—Lechmere Station via Highland Avenue

Car Rental

· **Enterprise** · 1 Broadway [Main] · 617-577-0404

Car Washes

· **Lechmere Auto Wash Centers** · 262 Monsignor O'Brien Hwy [Sciarappa]

Gas Stations

· **Shell** · 239 Monsignor O'Brien Hwy [Sciarappa]

Parking

Map 2

Central Square is a mix of MIT residences, biotech companies, rock clubs, and angry cab drivers. Sadly, the old Necco candy factory is now a Novartis research facility. However, the gorgeous Cambridge City Hall has not been converted to a biotech lab…yet. Find all your grocery needs (and tasty organic food supplies) at Harvest Co-op.

$ Banks

- **Bank of America** ·
  727 Massachusetts Ave [Pleasant St]
- **Bank of America (ATM)** ·
  1000 Massachusetts Ave [Ellery St]
- **Bank of America (ATM)** ·
  139 Massachusetts Ave [Vassar]
- **Bank of America (ATM)** · 235 Main St [Hayward St]
- **Bank of America (ATM)** ·
  622 Massachusetts Ave [Essex]
- **Bank of America (ATM)** · 820 Memorial Dr [River St]
- **Cambridge Savings Bank** ·
  630 Massachusetts Ave [Essex]
- **Cambridge Trust** · 350 Massachusetts Ave [Blanche]
- **Citizens Bank** · 689 Massachusetts Ave [Temple St]
- **Sovereign Bank** · 515 Massachusetts Ave [Norfolk St]
- **Wainwright Bank & Trust** ·
  647 Massachusetts Ave [Prospect St]

✹ Community Gardens

◉ Donuts

- **Dunkin' Donuts** · 84 Massachusetts Ave [Vassar]

O Landmarks

- **Cambridge City Hall** ·
  795 Massachusetts Ave [Bigelow St]
- **Edgerton Center & Strobe Alley** ·
  77 Massachussetts Ave [Vassar]
- **Necco Building/Novartis** ·
  250 Massachusetts Ave [Landsdowne]
- **Polaroid Building** · 784 Memorial Dr [Pleasant St]
- **Shell Oil Sign** · 187 Magazine St [Granite]
- **Simmons Hall** · 229 Vassar St [Concord Ave]
- **University Park** · Massachusetts Ave & Sidney St

Libraries

- **Central Square Public Library** ·
  45 Pearl St [Franklin St]

℞ Pharmacies

- **CVS** · 624 Massachusetts Ave [Essex]
- **Rite Aid** · 330 River St [Blackstone]
- **Walgreens** · 625 Massachusetts Ave [Essex]

Police

- **Cambridge Police Department** ·
  5 Western Ave [Magazine St]

✉ Post Offices

- **Cambridge** · 770 Massachusetts Ave [Inman St]

Schools

- **Amigos Elementary** · 100 Putnam Ave [Magee]
- **Henry Buckner** ·
  85 Bishop Richard Allen Dr [Norfolk St]
- **James F Farr Academy** · 71 Pearl St [Auburn St]
- **Martin Luther King Jr** · 100 Putnam Ave [Magee]
- **Morse School** · 40 Granite St [Pearl St]

🛒 Supermarkets

- **Harvest Co-op Market** ·
  581 Massachusetts Ave [Essex]
- **Star Market** · 20 Sidney St [Green St]
- **Trader Joe's** · 748 Memorial Dr [Pleasant St]
- **Whole Foods Market** · 340 River St [Blackstone]

Map 27 • Central Square / Cambridgeport N

Not the obvious place to frolic the day away, Central's full of funk-venture by night. Seeing a rock show at The Middle East earns you instant cool. The Field pours a perfect pint. River Gods is a sacrilegiously charming place to chill. Do Phoenix Landing for dancing on the weekends and Great Eastern Trading Company for vintage duds.

Map 2

☕ Coffee

- **1369 Coffee House** •
  757 Massachusetts Ave [Inman St]
- **Carberry's Bakery & Coffee House** •
  74 Prospect St [St Paul]
- **Clear Conscience Café** •
  581 Massachusetts Ave [Essex St]
- **Dado Tea (tea only)** •
  955 Massachusetts Ave [Bay St]
- **Mariposa Bakery** •
  424 Massachusetts Ave [Main]
- **Starbucks** •
  655 Massachusetts Ave [Prospect St]

🖨 Copy Shops

- **Classic Copy & Printing** •
  678 Massachusetts Ave [Western]
- **Reproman Reprographics** •
  675 Massachusetts Ave [Temple St]
- **The UPS Store** •
  955 Massachusetts Ave [Bay St]

🌽 Farmers Markets

- **Cambridgeport**
  (June—Oct; Sat 10:30–3:30) •
  Magazine St & Memorial Dr
- **Central Square**
  (May—Nov; Mon 11:30am—6 pm) •
  - Bishop Richard Allen Dr at Norfolk St

🏋 Gyms

- **Boston Sports Club** •
  625 Massachusetts Ave [Essex]
- **Cambridge Family YMCA** •
  820 Massachusetts Ave [Bigelow St]
- **Athens Sports Club** •
  350 Massachusetts Ave [Blanche]
- **Curves** • 614 Massachusetts Ave [Essex]

🔧 Hardware Stores

- **Economy Hardware** •
  438 Massachusetts Ave [Main]
- **Pill Hardware** •
  743 Massachusetts Ave [Pleasant St]

🍾 Liquor Stores

- **Dana Hill Liquors** •
  910 Massachusetts Ave [Lee]
- **Libby's Liquors** •
  575 Massachusetts Ave [Essex]
- **Whole Foods Market** •
  340 River St [Blackstone]

🍸 Nightlife

- **All Asia** •
  334 Massachusetts Ave [Blanche]
- **Cantab Lounge** •
  738 Massachusetts Ave [Pleasant St]
- **The Cellar** •
  991 Massachusetts Ave [Dana St]
- **Enormous Room** •
  567 Massachusetts Ave [Pearl St]
- **The Field** • 20 Prospect St [Mass Ave]
- **The Middle East** •
  472 Massachusetts Ave [Douglas St]
- **Middlesex** •
  315 Massachusetts Ave [State]
- **Miracle of Science** •
  321 Massachusetts Ave [State]
- **People's Republik** •
  880 Massachusetts Ave [Lee]
- **Phoenix Landing** •
  512 Massachusetts Ave [Brookline St]
- **Plough & Stars** •
  912 Massachusetts Ave [Hancock St]
- **River Gods** • 125 River St [Kinnaird]
- **TT the Bear's Place** •
  10 Brookline St [Green St]
- **Western Front** •
  343 Western Ave [Putnam Ave]

🍴 Restaurants

- **Asgard** •
  350 Massachusetts Ave [Blanche]
- **Asmara** •
  739 Massachusetts Ave [Pleasant St]
- **Brookline Lunch** •
  9 Brookline St [Mass Ave]
- **Café Baraka** • 80 1/2 Pearl St [William St]
- **Carberry's Bakery & Coffee House** •
  74 Prospect St [St Paul]
- **Central Kitchen** •
  567 Massachusetts Ave [Norfolk St]
- **Coast Cafe** • 233 River St [Rockwell]
- **Cuchi Cuchi** • 795 Main St [Cherry St]
- **Dolphin Seafood** •
  1105 Massachusetts Ave [Remington]
- **Four Burgers** •
  704 Massachusetts Ave [Prospect]
- **Green Street Grill** •
  280 Green St [Magazine St]
- **Hi-Fi Pizza & Subs** •
  496 Massachusetts Ave [Brookline St]
- **India Pavilion** •
  17 Central Sq [Pleasant St]
- **Mary Chung** •
  464 Massachusetts Ave [Douglas St]
- **The Middle East** •
  472 Massachusetts Ave [Douglas St]
- **Miracle of Science** •
  321 Massachusetts Ave [State]
- **Moody's Falafel Palace** •
  25 Central Sq [Pleasant St]
- **Olive Tree Cafe** •
  245 Massachusetts Ave [Landsdowne]
- **Picante Mexican Grill** •
  735 Massachusetts Ave [Pleasant St]
- **Pu Pu Hot Pot** •
  907 Main St [Columbia St]
- **Rangzen Tibetan Restaurant** •
  24 Pearl St [Green St]
- **Rendezvous** •
  502 Massachusetts Ave [Brookline St]
- **Salts** • 798 Main St [Windsor St]
- **Zoe's** •
  1105 Massachusetts Ave [Remington]
- **ZuZu!** •
  474 Massachusetts Ave [Douglas St]

🛍 Shopping

- **Buckaroo's Mercantile** •
  5 Brookline St [Mass Ave]
- **Cambridge Bicycle** •
  259 Massachusetts Ave [Front]
- **Cheapo Records** •
  538 Massachusetts Ave [Norfolk St]
- **Cremaldi's** • 31 Putnam Ave [Green St]
- **Economy Hardware** •
  438 Massachusetts Ave [Main]
- **Great Eastern Trading Company** •
  49 River St [Auburn St]
- **Hubba Hubba** •
  534 Massachusetts Ave [Norfolk St]
- **Looney Tunes** •
  1001 Massachusetts Ave [Ellery St]
- **Micro Center** •
  730 Memorial Dr [Riverside Rd]
- **Pandemonium Books** •
  4 Pleasant St [Mass Ave]
- **Pearl Art & Craft Supplies** •
  579 Massachusetts Ave [Pearl St]
- **Shalimar** •
  571 Massachusetts Ave [Pearl St]
- **Ten Thousand Villages** •
  694 Massachusetts Ave [Western]
- **Toscanini's** • 899 Main St [Columbia St]
- **University Stationery** •
  311 Massachusetts Ave [State]
- **Weirdo Records** •
  844 Massachusetts Ave [Sellers St]

📀 Video Rental

- **Blockbuster** •
  541 Massachusetts Ave [Norfolk St]
- **Hollywood Express** •
  765 Massachusetts Ave [Inman St]

Parking around Central Square is not easy, but with a little persistence, you can find a spot on a side street, or you can drop a couple of bucks in the garages at University Park. The Cambridge Department of Public Works has a phone number you can call to "report a street or sidewalk" defect, tempting us to call them once a day to report "all of Mass Ave."

Subway

- **Central**

Bus Lines

- **CT1** • Central Square, Cambridge—BU Medical Center/BU Medical Campus
- **CT2** • Sullivan Station—Ruggles Station via Kendall/MIT
- **1** • Harvard/Holyoke Gate—Dudley Station via Massachusetts Avenue & BU Medical Center
- **47** • Central Square, Cambridge—Broadway Station via South End Medical Area
- **64** • Oak Square—Central Square, Cambridge, or Kendall/MIT
- **68** • Harvard/Holyoke Gate—Kendall/MIT via Broadway
- **69** • Harvard/Holyoke—Lechmere Station via Cambridge Street
- **70** • Cedarwood, N Waltham, or Watertown Square—University Park via Central Square
- **70A** • Cedarwood, N Waltham, or Watertown Square—University Park via Central Square
- **83** • Rindge Avenue—Central Square, Cambridge via Porter Square Station
- **85** • Spring Hill—Kendall/MIT Station via Summer Street & Union Square
- **91** • Sullivan Square Station—Central Square, Cambridge via Washington

Car Rental

- **Budget** • Hotel at MIT • 20 Sidney St [Green St] • 617-577-7606
- **Enterprise** • 25 River St [Franklin St] • 617-547-7400

Gas Stations

- **Mobil** • 816 Memorial Dr [River St] ⊕
- **Shell** • 207 Magazine St [Riverside Rd] ⊕
- **Shell** • 820 Memorial Dr [River St] ⊕
- **Sunoco** • 808 Memorial Dr [River St]

Parking

Inman Square is an almost-hidden treasure at the center of the Cambridge/ Somerville vortex. Folks from the rest of Boston are increasingly finding their way to Inman, particularly when they're hungry. We still miss seeing Julia Child walking around her old neighborhood.

Banks

- **Bank of America (ATM)** •
  120 Beacon St [Washington St]
- **Bank of America (ATM)** •
  1400 Cambridge St [Antrim]
- **Cambridge Savings Bank** •
  1378 Cambridge St [Hampshire St]
- **Cambridge Trust (ATM)** • 468 Broadway [Ware]
- **Citizens Bank** • 141 Portland St [B'way]
- **East Cambridge Savings Bank** •
  1310 Cambridge St [Oak St]

Community Gardens

Donuts

- **Cambridge Coffee Shop** •
  847 Cambridge St [Harding St]
- **Dunkin' Donuts** • Shell •
  1001 Cambridge St [Windsor St]
- **Dunkin' Donuts** • 222 Broadway [Moore]
- **Dunkin' Donuts** • 282 Somerville Ave [Prospect St]

Emergency Rooms

- **The Cambridge Hospital** •
  1493 Cambridge St [Highland Ave]

Landmarks

- **Julia Child's Home** • 103 Irving St [Bryant]

Libraries

- **Cambridge Main Library** • 359 Broadway [B'way Ter]
- **Valente Public Library** •
  826 Cambridge St [Harding St]

Pharmacies

- **Inman Pharmacy** • 1414 Cambridge St [Antrim]
- **Skenderian Apothecary** •
  1613 Cambridge St [Roberts Rd]
- **Target** • 180 Somerville Ave [Mansfield]
- **Walgreens** • 16 Beacon St [Concord Ave]

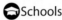 Post Offices

- **Inman Square Station** • 1311 Cambridge St [Oak St]

Schools

- **Cambridge Rindge & Latin High** •
  459 Broadway [Ware]
- **Cambridgeport** • 89 Elm St [Market St]
- **Castle** • 298 Harvard St [Lee]
- **Fletcher/Manyard Academy** •
  225 Windsor St [Broadway]
- **King Open School** • 850 Cambridge St [Harding St]
- **Prospect Hill Academy Charter** •
  15 Webster Ave [Everett St]
- **Rindge School of Technical Arts** •
  459 Broadway [Ware]

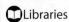 Supermarkets

- **Farmer's Bounty** • 234 Elm St [Chester St]
- **Whole Foods Market** • 115 Prospect St [Harvard St]

Map 28 • Inman Square

Eats and treats. Choose one of over a hundred beers at Bukowski's. Sample Dali's to-die-for tapas or Ole Grill's amazing Mexican dishes. All-Star Sandwich Bar is a must for gourmet sandwiches. Curious shoppers will not be disappointed by Boutique Fabulous or The Garment District, a thrift megastore whose basement sells clothes at $1 per pound.

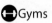 Coffee

- **1369 Coffee House** · 1369 Cambridge St [Springfield]
- **Cambridge Coffee Shop** ·
  847 Cambridge St [Harding St]
- **Peet's Coffee & Tea** · Whole Foods ·
  115 Prospect St [Harvard St]
- **Starbucks** · 468 Broadway [Ware]

Gyms

- **Fitness Together** · 143 Hampshire St [Norfolk St]

Hardware Stores

- **City Paint & Supply** · 1149 Cambridge St [Norfolk St]
- **Inman Square Ace Hardware** ·
  1337 Cambridge St [Springfield]

Liquor Stores

- **Prospect Liquor** · 1226 Cambridge St [Prospect St]
- **Wine Cask** · 407 Washington St [Beacon St]

Nightlife

- **Abbey Lounge** · 3 Beacon St [Dickinson St]
- **Atwood's Tavern** · 877 Cambridge St [Hunting]
- **Bukowski's** · 1281 Cambridge St [Oakland St]
- **The Druid** · 1357 Cambridge St [Springfield]
- **Ryles Jazz Club** · 212 Hampshire St [Inman St]
- **Thirsty Scholar Pub** · 70 Beacon St [Cooney]

Pet Shops

- **Boston Dogs** · 70 Beacon St [Cooney]

Restaurants

- **All-Star Sandwich Bar** ·
  1245 Cambridge St [Prospect St]
- **Amelia's Trattoria** · 111 Harvard St [Davis St]
- **Atasca** · 50 Hampshire St [Webster Ave]
- **Café Kiraz** · 119 Hampshire St [Columbia St]
- **City Girl Café** · 204 Hampshire St [Inman St]
- **Dali** · 415 Washington St [Beacon St]
- **East Coast Grill & Raw Bar** ·
  1271 Cambridge St [Oakland St]
- **Emma's Pizzeria** · 40 Hampshire St [Webster Ave]
- **EVOO** · 118 Beacon St [Washington St]
- **The Friendly Toast** · 1 Kendall Sq
- **Hungry Mother** · 233 Cardinal Medeiros Ave
- **Koreana** · 154 Prospect St [B'way]
- **Midwest Grill** · 1124 Cambridge St [Norfolk St]
- **Montien** · 1287 Cambridge St [Oakland St]
- **Muqueca** · 1093 Cambridge St [Elm St]
- **O Cantinho** · 1128 Cambridge St [Norfolk St]
- **Ole Mexican Grill** · 11 Springfield St [Cambridge St]
- **Oleana** · 134 Hampshire St [Elm St]
- **Pho Lemon** · 228 Broadway [Clark St]
- **Punjabi Dhaba** · 225 Hampshire St [Cambridge St]
- **S&S Restaurant** · 1334 Cambridge St [Oak St]
- **Toscanini and Sons** · 406 Washington St [Beacon St]
- **Tupelo** · 1193 Cambridge St [Tremont St]

Shopping

- **Boston Costume Company** ·
  200 Broadway [Davis St]
- **Boutique Fabulous** · 1309 Cambridge St [Oak St]
- **Bowl & Board** · 255 Elm St St [Webster St]
- **Central Bakery** · 732 Cambridge St [Marion St]
- **Christina's Homemade Ice Cream** ·
  1255 Cambridge St [Prospect St]
- **The Garment District** · 200 Broadway [Davis St]
- **Inman Square Market** ·
  1343 Cambridge St [Springfield]
- **Royal Pastry** · 738 Cambridge St [Marion St]
- **Sadye & Company** · 121 Hampshire St [Columbia St]
- **Target** · 180 Somerville Ave [Mansfield]
- **Urban Oasis** · 243 Hampshire St [Dickinson St]
- **Wine Cask** · 407 Washington St [Beacon St]

Can't get there by T, but it's easy enough to hop a bus or take a short walk from the Central or Kendall Square T stops. Parking is for the adventurous, though there are a couple of public lots. The neighborhood is a cyclists' mecca—drivers, take heed.

Bus Lines

- **CT1** · Central Square, Cambridge—BU Medical Center/BU Medical Campus
- **CT2** · Sullivan Station—Ruggles Station via Kendall/MIT
- **1** · Harvard/Holyoke Gate—Dudley Station via Massachusetts Avenue & BU Medical Center
- **47** · Central Square, Cambridge—Broadway Station via South End Medical Area
- **64** · Oak Square—Central Square, Cambridge, or Kendall/MIT
- **68** · Harvard/Holyoke Gate—Kendall/MIT via Broadway
- **69** · Harvard/Holyoke Gate—Lechmere Station via Cambridge Street
- **70** · Cedarwood, N Waltham, or Watertown Square—University Park via Central Square
- **70A** · Cedarwood, N Waltham, or Watertown Square—University Park via Central Square
- **80** · Arlington Center—Lechmere Station via Medford Hills
- **83** · Rindge Avenue—Central Square, Cambridge via Porter Square Station
- **85** · Spring Hill—Kendall/MIT Station via Summer Street & Union Square
- **86** · Sullivan Square Station—Cleveland Circle via Harvard/Johnson Gate
- **87** · Arlington Center or Clarendon Hill—Lechmere Station
- **88** · Clarendon Hill—Lechmere Station via Highland Avenue
- **90** · Davis Square—Wellington Station via Sullivan Square Station
- **91** · Sullivan Square Station—Central Square, Cambridge via Washington

Car Rental

- **U-Save Auto & Truck Rental** · 70 Prospect St [Webster Ave] · 617-628-8800

Gas Stations

- **Citgo** · 277 Broadway [Elm St]
- **Exxon** · 209 Broadway [Moore]
- **Hess** · 287 Prospect St [Hampshire St] ⌚
- **Mobil** · 320 Broadway [Prospect St]
- **Shell** · 1001 Cambridge St [Windsor St]

1 2

Roxbury Pkwy Roxbury... Walnut Hills
Cemetery

30▶ VFW

3 1

▶Belgrade

1. Park Lane Dr
2. Ellswood St
3. Amesbury St
4. Long Ter
5. Oenwell St
6. Jennett Ave
7. Pleasant Ave
8. Henshaw Ter
9. Francesca St
10. Porter Ter
11. Ancarer Ln
12. Maple Ter
13. Theodore Parker Rd
14. Paulman Cir
15. Belgrade Ter
16. Anawan Ter
17. New Park Ave
18. Ardmore Rd
19. Cubhert Rd
20. Pine Lodge Rd
21. Rockingham Ave
22. Westmoor Cir
23. Camp Rd
24. Maple Rd
25. Bartlett Ave

26. Billings St
27. March Way
28. March Ter
29. Cypress St
30. Spring Valley Rd
31. Moloney St
32. Miami Ter
33. Miami Ave
34. Autumn St
35. Atta Crest Rd
36. Ashland Ave
37. Running Brook Rd
38. Trevore Diedord St
39. Peacock Ln
40. Stimson Rd

**Millennium
Park**

Cow Island Pond

Cutler
Park

33▶

Stony Brook
State Reserva

Turtle Pond

Emskong Pkwy

Stony Brook
State Reservation

Charles River

Dedham Mall

Draper
Playground

Grove Street
Cemetery

Map 29 • West Roxbury

Essentials

West Roxbury is a suburb-within-the-city community, with selective shopping and some good food. Millennium Park has fields, paths, and playgrounds, and a drive along VFW can be nice when the construction isn't bad and the trees are in bloom. The area exists as a middle ground between suburban Newton and city communities like Roslindale. With supermarkets and places to park, West Roxbury is a good place to settle if you want to stay in the city and own an affordable house.

O Landmarks

· **Millennium Park** · VFW Pkwy & Gardner St

Sundries/Entertainment

For a tasty lunch, try a sandwich from Real Deal or a kabob from Samia Bakery. For a great Euro-South American take on dinner, try MaSoNa by the commuter rail on Corey Street.

Restaurants

· **Himalayan Bistro** · 1735 Centre St [Manthorne Rd]
· **MaSoNa Grill** · 4 Corey St [Park St]
· **Real Deal** · 1882 Centre St [Hastings St]
· **Samia Bakery** · 1894 Centre St [Hastings St]
· **Skara Grill** · 1985 Centre St [Mt Vernon St]
· **Upper Crust** · 1727 Centre St [Manthorne Rd]
· **Vintage** · 1430 VFW Pkwy [Caledonian Ave]
· **West on Centre** · 1732 Centre St [Manthorne Rd]

Shopping

· **Irish Cottage** · 1898 Centre St [Park St]
· **Jack Davis Florist** · 2097 Centre St [Temple St]

Transportation

The subway doesn't extend into West Roxbury, but you can use the Needham commuter rail line. Pick it up at the Forest Hills stop (on the T's Orange Line) and get off at either the Highland stop or the West Roxbury stop

Essentials

Over the last few decades, Roslindale Square (also known as Roslindale Village) has received awards for turning a virtual ghost town into a nice place to live through local shops and some great restaurants. The city subsidies didn't hurt either. Walking through the village area, one gets the sense of a community proud of itself. As a bonus, Roslindale Village is within walking distance of the Arnold Arboretum, the best park in Boston and possibly the best urban park in America.

O Landmarks

- **Forest Hills Cemetery** • 95 Forest Hills Ave [Morton St]
- **Roslindale Square** • Washington St [Belgrade Ave]

Sundries/Entertainment

What Rozzie lacks in hip bars, it makes up for in restaurants like Delfino, shopping like Joanne Rossman and Pazzo, and a surprisingly large amount of bakeries like Fornax Bread Baking Company. If you wanna get your drink on, you'll have to hightail it for JP. Or do what the locals do—spend an evening at Pleasant Café.

 Nightlife

- **JJ Foley's Fireside Tavern** •
  30 Hyde Park Ave [Weld Hill St]

 Restaurants

- **Birch Street Bistro** • 14 Birch St [Corinth St]
- **Delfino** • 754 South St [Taft Ct]
- **Diane's Bakery** • 9 Poplar St [South St]
- **Geoffrey's Café** • 4257 Washington St [Corinth St]
- **John's Bakery** • 31 Poplar St [Washington St]
- **Pleasant Café** • 4515 Washington St [Cedrus Ave]
- **Primavera** • 289 Walk Hill St [Canterbury St]
- **Romanos Pizzeria & Taqueria** •
  4249 Washington St [Corinth St]
- **Roslindale House of Pizza** •
  4168 Washington St [Bexley Rd]
- **Sophia's Grotto** • 22 Birch St [Corinth St]
- **Village Sushi & Grill** • 14 Corinth St [Birch St]
- **Yucatan Tacos** • 1417 Centre St [Knoll St]

 Shopping

- **Atlas Liquors** • 591 Hyde Park Ave [Cummins Hwy]
- **Boston Cheese Cellar** • 18 Birch St [Corinth St]
- **Droubi Bakery** • 748 South St [Cohasset St]
- **Emack & Bolio's** • 2 Belgrade Ave [Birch St]
- **Exotic Flowers** •
  609 American Legion Hwy [Canterbury St]
- **Fornax Bread Baking Company** •
  27 Corinth St [Washington St]
- **Joanne Rossman: Purveyor of the Unnecessary & The Irresistible** • 6 Birch St [Corinth St]
- **Pazzo Books** • 4268 Washington St [Corinth St]
- **Roslindale Fish Market** •
  389 Poplar St [Washington St]
- **Solera** • 12 Corinth St [Birch St]
- **Thrift Shop of Boston** • 17 Corinth St [Birch St]
- **Village Books** • 751 South St [Taft Ct]

Transportation

To get to Roslindale without driving, you can either take the T's Orange Line to the Forest Hills stop and from there take an MBTA bus, or you can ride the commuter rail to Roslindale Village or Bellevue.

Map 31

Essentials

Mattapan is mostly residential and home to about 40,000 people. It has a growing Haitian-American community (the largest in Massachusetts), and has smaller communities whose roots are in many of the nations of the Caribbean. This is reflected in the wealth of Caribbean restaurants located on Blue Hill Avenue.

O Landmarks

- **Franklin Park Zoo Bear Cages** · 1 Franklin Park Rd [Blue Hill Ave]
- **United House of Prayer** · 206 Seaver St [Elm Hill Ave]

Sundries/Entertainment

Commercial activity in Mattapan clusters around Mattapan Square. Here you can argue with your friends about whether Haitian patties are tastier than Jamaican patties. Then, as you head towards Morton Street, you can stop arguing to stuff your mouths with roti at Ali's. Pit Stop Bar-B-Q, with its great ribs, represents.

Restaurants

- **Ali's Roti** · 1188 Blue Hill Ave [Morton St]
- **Bon Appetit** · 1138 Blue Hill Ave [Livingstone St]
- **Brothers** · 1638 Blue Hill Ave [Fairway St]
- **Flames** · 461 Blue Hill Ave [Georgia St]
- **Flames** · 663 Morton St [Rhoades Ave]
- **Lenny's Tropical Bakery** · 1195 Blue Hill Ave [Deering Rd]
- **P&R Ice Cream** · 1284 Blue Hill Ave [Evelyn St]
- **Picasso Creole Cuisine** · 1296 Blue Hill Ave [Fessenden St]
- **Pit Stop Bar-B-Q** · 888A Morton St [Cemetery Rd]
- **R&S Jamaican Restaurant** · 770 Blue Hill Ave [Wales St]
- **Simco's on the Bridge** · 1509 Blue Hill Ave [Regis Rd]
- **Tastee Jamaican Restaurant** · 522 River St [Cummins Hwy]
- **United House of Prayer** · 206 Seaver St [Elm Hill]

Shopping

- **Dark Horse** · 2297 Dorchester Ave [Adams St]
- **Le Foyer Bakery** · 132 Babson St [Fremont St]
- **Taurus Records** · 1282 Blue Hill Ave [Evelyn St]

Transportation

To get to the Mattapan T stop, choose an Ashmont-bound train. At the Ashmont station, the "it's not retro, it's old" Mattapan trolley will take you as far as Mattapan Square. The MBTA commuter rail's Fairmount line makes a stop at Morton Street.

Map 32 · Dorchester (East)

N

1

2

12

113

A

31

B

Columbus
Park

Dorchester
Bay

James
Blake
House

Dorchester North
Burying Ground

Strand
Theatre

JFK/
UMass

Mount Vernon St

**PAGE
208**

JFK Library
and Museum

**PAGE
210**

Commonwealth
Museum

Savin Hill Ave

**PAGE
221**

Savin
Hill

Dorchester
Bay

Ronan
Park

Fields Corner

Shawmut

Ericson St

All Saints
Church

Ashmont

1. Cawfield St
2. Quincefield St
3. Wendover St
4. Dudley St
5. Humphreys St
6. Belden Sq
7. Dawes Ter
8. Sumner St
9. Bakersfield St
10. Annapolis St
11. Altair Ter
12. Sumner Park
13. Stoughton Ter
14. Kevin Rd
15. Sumner Sq
16. Chase St
17. Dawes St
18. Uphams Ct
19. Whittemore ter
20. Mount Cushing Ter
21. Wheelock Ave
22. Higham Ave
23. Wilbur St
24. Whitney St
25. Hesston Ter
26. Greenmount Ave

27. Island View Pl
28. Harbor Point Blvd
29. Westwind Rd
30. Ocean View
31. Oyster Bay Rd

32. Caspian Way
33. Rockshire St
34. Playstead Rd
35. Genny St
36. Southview St
37. Wilkinson Park
38. Melwinside Ter
39. Treadway Rd
40. Dunn St
41. Ritchie Ter
42. Tovar St
43. Wilder St
44. Martin Way
45. Duncan Pl
46. Clayton St
47. Dartervale Park
48. Levant St
49. Tabor St
50. Eunice St
51. Westview Ter
52. Dayton St
53. Ronsington St
54. Endicott Ter
55. Elmdale St
56. Popes Hill St
57. Saint Clare Rd
58. Southwick St
59. Rosmington
60. Lorenzo St
61. Berry St
62. Woodworth St
63. Walnut St
64. Taylor St
65. Ashmont Ct
66. Burgoyne St
67. Beaumont St
68. Westmoreland
69. Radford Ln
70. Northam Park
71. Argyle St
72. Argyle Ter
73. Denton St
74. Joseph St
75. Tilman St
76. Greenfield St

Essentials

(In)famous for protecting turf, Dorchester is a collection of distinct neighborhoods and ethnicities. Uphams Corner, Savin Hill, Fields Corner, Ashmont, Codman Square, and Grove Hall are but a few of the areas that comprise Boston's largest district. Sure, there's crime, but let's hope the gentrification creeping down Dot Ave doesn't entirely rob Dorchester of its cred.

O Landmarks

- **All Saints' Church** • 209 Ashmont St[Bushnell St]
- **Commonwealth Museum** • 220 Morrissey Blvd [Dominic J Bianculli]
- **Dorchester North Burying Ground** • Columbia Rd & Stoughton St [Stoughton St]
- **The James Blake House** • 735 Columbia Rd [Pond St]
- **John F Kennedy Library and Museum** • Morrissey Blvd & Columbia Pt
- **Strand Theatre** • 543 Columbia Rd [Dudley St]

Sundries/Entertainment

Irish bars line Dot Ave; they lack tourists and charge three bucks for Guinness. If you're looking for a trendier night spot, check out dBar. Mixed in are the city's best pho houses. You'll find excellent Caribbean cuisine along Blue Hill Avenue. Go to Grove Hall and Uphams Corner for soul food.

Nightlife

- **Banshee** • 934 Dorchester Ave [Edison Grn]
- **Boston Bowl** • 820 Morrissey Blvd [Tenean St]
- **dBar** • 1236 Dorchester Ave [Hoyt St]
- **Eire Pub** • 795 Adams St [Washington St]
- **Harp & Bard** • 1099 Dorchester Ave [Savin Hill Ave]

Restaurants

- **Antojitos y Panaderia Chapinas** • 299 Hancock St [Dorchester]
- **Ashmont Grill** • 555 Talbot Ave [Ashmont]
- **Ba-Le Restaurant** • 1052 Dorchester Ave [William St]
- **Blarney Stone** • 1505 Dorchester Ave [Park St]
- **Blasi's Café and Fat Belly Deli** • 762 Adams St [Minot St]
- **CF Donovan's** • 112 Savin Hill Ave [Sydney]
- **Charlie's Place** • 1740 Dorchester Ave [Semont Rd]
- **Chef Lee's II** • 554 Columbia Rd [Dudley St]
- **dBar** • 1236 Dorchester Ave [Hancock St]

- **Irie Jamaican Style Restaurant** • 310 Bowdoin St [Quincy St]
- **Ka' Carlos** • 33 Hancock St [Bird St]
- **Lucky Café** • 1107 Dorchester Ave [Saving Hill Ave]
- **O Ya** • 9 East St [South St]
- **Osaka Shabu** • 203 Adams St [Arcadia St]
- **Phillips Old Colony House** • 780 Morrissey Blvd [Freeport St]
- **Pho 2000** • 198 Adams St [Arcadia St]
- **Pho Hoa** • 1356 Dorchester Ave [Kimball St]
- **Restaurante Cesaria** • 266 Bowdoin St [Draper St]
- **Shanti: Taste of India** • 1111 Dorchester Ave [Savin Hill Ave]
- **Sunrise** • 1157 Dorchester Ave [Dunn St]

Shopping

- **Asian Bookstore** • 1392 Dorchester Ave [Greenwich St]
- **Boston Winery** • 26 Ericsson St [Lawley St]
- **Coleen's Flowershop** • 912 Dorchester Ave [Grafton St]
- **Greenhill's Irish Bakery** • 780 Adams St [Henderson Rd]
- **Open Boxes** • 1080 Dorchester Ave [Elton St]

Transportation

In a word: Underserved! The Red Line tracks along the eastern side of Dorchester, roughly parallel to Dot Ave. From Ashmont, a trolley line wraps around to Mattapan Square. Buses run along Blue Hill Avenue; unfortunately, none of these buses directly connects Dorchester to Central Boston. The commuter rail's Fairmount line makes a stop at Uphams Corner and Morton Street.

Map 33 • **Hyde Park**

Map 33

Essentials

Almost as large as Franklin Park, Stony Brook Reservation covers 475 acres and includes low hills, dense woods, rock outcroppings, and marshland. The park's largest feature is Turtle Pond, where you can fish for perch and sunfish. There are also several miles of bicycle paths and the most extensive hiking opportunities within the city limits. Among the park's many recreational facilities is the John F. Thompson Center, New England's first recreational facility designed specifically to accommodate handicapped visitors.

O Landmarks

• **Stony Brook Reservation** • Washington St [Turtle Pond Pkwy]

Sundries/Entertainment

If you're hungry, check out the food at African Cuisine. If you're looking for entertainment, enjoy some bowling at Ron's. If you're not into bowling but you have pimped your ride, then you're at least able to cruise Hyde Park Avenue for hotties and doughnuts.

Nightlife

• **Townsend's Restaurant** • 81 Fairmount Ave [Pierce St]

Restaurants

• **African Cuisine** • 1248 Hyde Park Ave [River St]
• **Dottie's Deli** • 5 Fairmount Ave [River St]
• **Rincon Caribeno** • 18 Fairmount Ave [River St]
• **Townsend's Restaurant** • 81 Fairmount Ave [Pierce St]

Shopping

• **Capone Foods** • 14 Bow St [Garfield Ave]
• **Marascio's Market** • 1758 River St [Neponset Valley Pkwy]
• **Ron's Gourmet Ice Cream** • 1231 Hyde Park Ave [Everett St]
• **Tutto Italiano** • 1893 River St [Solaris Rd]

Transportation

To get to Hyde Park, Take the MBTA commuter rail's, Franklin, Fairmount or Providence line. The Providence line stops at Forest Hills, where you can transfer from the T's Orange Line. The Franklin line usually stops at Readville, but also does have a stop in Hyde Park at certain times. You can pick up the Franklin at South Station, which is served by the T's Red Line. The Fairmount branch serves Uphams Corner, Morton Street, Fairmount Ave. and Readville via the Dorchester/Midland branch.

Overview

Copley Square is named after Boston-born portrait painter John Singleton Copley (1738–1815), America's first great artist. His portraits of America's founding fathers are on display at the Massachusetts Historical Society, across the street from the square, and at the Museum of Fine Arts. The Boston Marathon, held annually on Patriots Day (the third Monday in April), ends on Boylston Street. A BosTix outlet, the place to score discounted theater tickets, stands at the corner of Boylston Street and Dartmouth Street. The farmers market fills the square Tuesdays and Fridays from 11 am to 6 pm, late May through November. The Friends of Copley Square sponsors its annual Holiday Tree Lighting on the first Thursday after Thanksgiving. Summer months bring folk and swing dancing performances to the square on Tuesday evenings, as well as a bevy of sun-seeking loungers.

Architecture & Sculpture

The Boston Public Library is America's oldest public library. The Renaissance-revival style structure holds within it over seven million books, as well as busts of famous writers and prominent Bostonians. Big bonus: It offers wireless Internet access. Across the square you'll find the neo-Romanesque Trinity Church, designed by notable architect H.H. Richardson. The stained glass windows alone are worth a trip inside.

John Hancock Tower

The John Hancock Mutual Life Insurance Company, which already inhabited buildings on Clarendon Street and Berkeley Street, needed more space to house its employees, so it opted to build a 60-story black glass tower. What better place to put it than next to the Public Library and an old church? Designed by architect I. M. Pei, and completed in 1976, the John Hancock Tower became famous for being the tallest building in New England, and simultaneously infamous for falling apart.

Locals were upset when a foundation collapse in the early stages of construction nearly sucked Trinity Church into the ground. They became outraged when, in January 1973, one of the building's 10,000-plus glass windows "popped off" and shattered on the ground below, followed by dozens more 500-pound window panes. All told, 65 panes fell onto the roped-off area below the building before workers changed the solder used to mount the windows. In the meantime, locals had dubbed the Hancock "The Plywood Palace," in reference to the black plywood sheets put in place to substitute for the fallen panes. Not long after, engineers discovered the building was in danger of being sheared in half by the wind, resulting in another expensive fix. Today, the Hancock Tower stands sturdy, tall, and proud, and locals have even grown to love it. (Classic Boston photo op: Trinity Church is reflected in the mirrored side of the Hancock Tower, a clichéd but perfect example of Boston's mix of old and new.)

The observation deck on the 60th floor, originally opened to the public in response to community feedback, was permanently closed for security reasons after the events of September 11, 2001. Height junkies must now head over to the nearby Prudential Center for a what-a-view fix.

How to Get There—Driving

From the south, take I-93 N to Exit 18 (Massachusetts Avenue/Roxbury). Follow signs to Massachusetts Avenue and turn right. Turn right on Huntington Avenue, then left onto Dartmouth Street. From the north, take I-93 S to Exit 26 (Storrow Drive). Follow Storrow Drive west to the Copley Square exit. Turn right onto Beacon Street and, after two blocks, turn left onto Clarendon Street. After five blocks, turn right onto St. James Avenue. This is one of two examples in the city (the other being the Pru) where the "look up, locate the giant building, and drive towards it" method of navigation works well.

How to Get There—Mass Transit

Take the Green Line to the Copley stop. Alternatively, take the Orange Line to the Back Bay stop, exit, and head to your right along Dartmouth Street. Again, if you're not sure which way to go, look for the giant glass building.

General Information

NFT Map:	6
Address:	700 Boylston St, Boston, MA 02116
Phone:	617-536-5400
Website:	www.bpl.org
Hours:	Mon–Thurs: 9 am–9 pm, Fri–Sat: 9 am–5 pm, Sun: 1 pm–5 pm (Oct–May)

Overview

The Boston Public Library, founded in 1848, was the country's first publicly-supported municipal library. The BPL was also the first public library to lend a book and the first to institute a children's room. All adult Massachusetts residents are entitled to borrowing and research privileges to the 7.5 million books currently house at the BPL. Its circulating collection and the Norman B. Leventhal Map Center (home to a whopping 350,000 maps), Rare Books and Manuscripts Department (M–F 9 am–5 pm), and many other research-oriented nooks and crannies continue to attract scholars and tourists alike. Additionally, the BPL's ever-changing exhibits are always good for a rainy-day, freebie activity, as are the frequent talks by bestselling authors.

The BPL's main branch is the Central Library, composed of two august buildings adjacent to Copley Square that hold a lot more than just books. Facing Dartmouth Street, the McKim Building (the "old wing") was designed by noted 19th-century architect Charles Follen McKim and opened in 1895. The old wing, which houses the Research Library, is built around a delightful Italianate courtyard that offers readers a most un-library-like place to relax with a book. A set of murals painted by John Singer Sargent hangs inside. Sargent, better known for his portraits than for large installations, intended for these mammoth murals to be his masterpiece. There's also a set of allegorical murals by Pierre Puvis de Chavannes and the architecturally significant Bates Hall.

Opened to the public in 1972, the Johnson Building was designed by legendary architect Philip Johnson. The building, which houses the General Library, faces Boylston Street and is still referred to as the "new wing." (Granted, a better nickname might be the "ugly wing.") The Johnson Building has less knock-out art than the McKim Building, but it does have the tiled architectural frieze *The Goose Girl*, which is worth seeking out if you're wandering through the building. The BPL offers guided tours of both the old and new wings.

Internet

If you're ever stuck without Internet access, head over to the Central Library. Both the old and new wings have PCs available for use by the general public. (All computers have Internet connections and Microsoft Office software.) The first floor of the new wing also has "express" PCs that limit use to 15 minutes—handy for a quick e-mail hit. Both buildings are also equipped with Wi-Fi access.

For the Kids

Besides the weekly and seasonal programs it offers for everyone small from infants to teens, the Central Library has an outstanding collection of materials for even the youngest readers. Most of these materials can be found in the Margret and H.A. Rey Children's Room, named for the creators of that beloved, inquisitive simian, Curious George. The Children's Room also offers access to computers with Internet filtering software, which is helpful for protecting fragile little minds. For more information, check the website or call 617-859-2328.

Restaurants

The Central Library now has two restaurants to sate you during long hours of research. Novel, the fancier of the two restaurants, is set in a spacious room overlooking the courtyard in the center of the McKim Building. (Tip: Nip in for afternoon tea, served 2:30 pm to 4 pm on weekdays.) Next door to Novel, Sebastian's Map Room Café serves breakfast, lunch, and snacks. Quickly notice that for reservations at Novel, or for additional information, call 617-385-5660. Note that food and drink are generally prohibited from the public areas of the Central Library, so chug your coffee before entering.

How to Get There—Driving

From the north or the south, take I-93 to Exit 26 (Storrow Drive). From Storrow Drive, take the Copley Square exit. The exit dead-ends at Beacon Street. Turn right on Beacon Street, drive four blocks to Exeter Street, and make a left. Drive along Exeter Street until you reach Boylston Street. The Central Library is on the corner of Boylston Street and Exeter Street.

From the west, take the Mass Pike (I-90 E) to Exit 22 (Prudential Center/Copley Square). Move to the right lane and follow the road in the tunnel toward Copley Square. The tunnel exits onto Stuart Street. Quickly move to the far left lane of Stuart Street and make a left at the next light onto Dartmouth Street. Drive through the next set of lights. The Central Library will be on the left.

Parking

The Central Library's location near Copley Square doesn't offer much in the way of street parking. If you're feeling unlucky, try the parking garage on Stuart Street between Dartmouth Street and Exeter Street.

How to Get There—Mass Transit

Take the T's Green Line to the Copley stop or the Orange Line to the Back Bay stop. From there, it should be pretty obvious: Look for the biggest, oldest, and grayest building around.

Overview

Cambridge Common was the center of rebel activity in the early years of the Revolution and has been a hub of political and social activity ever since. George Washington rallied the 16,000-man Continental Army under an elm tree on the green on July 3, 1775, and the area became the primary training ground for the troops.

William Dawes, along with Paul Revere and Dr. Samuel Prescott, rode his horse across the Common on his way to warn those in Lexington and Concord that "the regulars are coming" (not that "the British are coming"). While Revere inspired a famous poem and became the namesake of many American cities, Dawes was commemorated with some lousy bronze hoof prints in the pavement of the Common.

Three cannon that the colonists seized from the Lobsterbacks still sit by the flagpole. There's also a memorial to victims of the Irish Potato Famine.

Even with the addition of a playground and a softball field, this historical urban oasis remains an important place to voice ideas and protests. Just steps away from Harvard University, the Common's corner on Mass Ave has been used by activists protesting everything from the occupation of Iraq to the existence of SUVs.

Attractions

Relaxing and people-watching are, by far, the two best activities to undertake on the Common. With its prime location next to Harvard Square, you can feel like a Harvard student, without the excessive course fees and mandatory high IQ, though tree-shaded benches are available for reading if you want to play the part.

Cambridge Common is the focal point of the Cambridge Common Historic District, which also includes Christ Church, Old Harvard Yard, Massachusetts Hall, and Gannett House (the oldest surviving building on Harvard University's campus).

The park has a fenced-in playground, located on the corner of Garden and Waterhouse Streets, where kids can frolic safely. The playground was last renovated in 1990 (including the addition of a wooden climbing structure, swings, bridges, slides, and benches/picnic tables) and is recommended for parents with children aged one to ten.

Sports

There's a softball field, soccer fields, and designated areas for other light recreation along with bike paths for cyclists, skaters, joggers, and walkers. Despite the close link between afternoon softball games and booze, the rules forbid alcoholic beverages on the ball field.

General Information

NFT Map: 8
Address: 1st Ave, Charlestown, MA 02129
Phone: 617-242-5601 (Visitor Center);
            617-242-5671 (USS Constitution)
Websites: www.nps.gov/bost/Visiting_Navy_Yard.htm
            www.cityofboston.com/freedomtrail/
            ussconstitution.asp
            www.charlestownonline.net/navyyard.htm
Hours: 10 am–4 pm daily (Winter); 9 am–6 pm
            (Summer); 9 am–5 pm (Fall); free admission

Practicalities

The Charlestown Navy Yard is a must-see for anyone who likes big ships or US naval history. The two main attractions are the *USS Cassin Young* and "Old Ironsides" herself, the *USS Constitution*. The yard was established in 1800 as one of the first naval shipyards in the country, and the *Constitution* is almost as old as the country itself. When the Navy retired the yard in 1974, the yard became part of the Boston National Historic Park.

Attractions

Typical Fourth of July celebrations in Boston range from backyard barbecues to beach sunbathing, but the Navy Yard has its own unique tradition. Independence Day is celebrated with the customary turning of the *Constitution*—an annual practice in which the great vessel is tugged out of the dock and rotated to ensure uniform weathering. The *Cassin Young* has battle scars from its service in both World War II and the Korean War. The nearby Commandant's House, the oldest building in the Navy Yard, is no longer a private home, but an elegant museum, which is open to the public. The Navy Yard

Visitor Center/Bunker Hill Pavillion also serves those visiting the nearby Bunker Hill Monument.

How to Get There—Driving

From the north, take I-93 S to Exit 28 (Sullivan Square/ Charlestown), go under I-93, and follow signs to Sullivan Square. Bear left at the first traffic light and drive into the Sullivan Square rotary; take the second right onto Bunker Hill Street, turn right onto Chelsea Street, and make an immediate left onto Fifth Street. Drive one block (Fifth Street dead-ends) and turn left onto First Avenue.

From the south, take I-93 N to Exit 26 (Storrow Drive) and aim for the "North Station, USS Constitution" signs. Turn left onto Martha Road (which becomes Lomasney Way), left on Causeway Street, then left at N Washington Street, and get into the right lane as quickly as possible. At the end of the bridge, turn right onto Chelsea Street.

From the west, take the Mass Pike (I-90 E) to I-93 N, and follow the directions above.

Parking

Though public transportation is strongly recommended for this area, discounted parking with Boston National Historical Park validation is available from the Nautica Parking Garage across from the park's Visitor Center on Constitution Road.

How to Get There— Mass Transit

Visitors can take the MBTA Water Shuttle to Pier 4 at the Navy Yard from Long Wharf for $1.70. (See page 258 for more information.) Or follow the Freedom Trail from North Station.

General Information

NFT Map: 3
Address: 147 Tremont St (b/w Temple Pl & West St)
Phone: 617-426-3115
Websites: www.bostonusa.com
www.cityofboston.gov/freedomtrail/
bostoncommon.asp
www.cityofboston.gov/parks/streettrees/
inventories.asp

Overview

One of the nation's oldest public parks, Boston Common was purchased by the Commonwealth of Massachusetts in 1634 to serve as livestock grazing ground. The city charged each household six shillings to pay for "the Commonage." (It was Tax-achusetts even back then!) People also used the Common to watch others being hanged at the gallows (like them cursed Quakers), for public meetings, and for military drills. The gallows were removed in 1817 and cow grazing was officially banned in 1830, around the time that urban cow ownership began falling out of fashion. In 1910, the Olmsted brothers oversaw a massive landscape renovation, designating Boston Common as the anchor of the "Emerald Necklace," a system of connected parks that winds through many of Boston's neighborhoods. Boston Common is the beginning of the Freedom Trail and the Black Heritage Trail.

Situated across from the State House, Boston Common embodies the spirit of the city around it. Tourists, students, lunching suits, homeless Bostonians, and strolling older folks all share the park. On the lawn, squirrels and pigeons fight the latest chapter in their centuries-old gang war, while ducks enjoy free bread from park-goers. It is home to America's first and second subway stations (Park St and Boylston St), the Central Burying Ground, and the Robert Gould Shaw Civil War Memorial (a.k.a. the dudes from *Glory*).

Adjacent to the park is the Public Garden, former swampland that was filled in 1837. The nation's first botanical garden, the Public Garden's French style of ornamental beds and paths stand in sharp contrast to the Common's informal, pastoral English layout. This is where you can ride the famous Swan Boats and admire the *Make Way for Ducklings* sculpture.

Activities

The Freedom Trail is a 2.5-mile path through central Boston that passes by 16 of the city's historic landmarks. You'll find detailed route maps and information at the Visitor Center on Boston Common. Many of the sites along the red-painted line offer free admission, others "recommend" a donation, and some actually charge.

Frog Pond serves as a part-time ice-skating rink in winter and a splashing pool for children in summer. The smooth, paved paths that traverse the Common make it ideal for cyclists, rollerbladers, scooters, joggers, and walkers. Throughout the year the park hosts concerts, plays, political rallies, and other formal and informal gatherings.

How to Get There

Tremont, Beacon, Charles, Park, and Boylston Streets bound Boston Common. Parking is available, believe it or not, under the Common on Charles Street. By car, take the Mass Pike (I-90) to the Copley Square exit. Go straight at the off ramp onto Stuart Street. Take a left onto Charles Street by the Radisson Hotel.

By mass transit, take the Green Line or the Silver Line bus to the Boylston T stop at the corner of Boylston Street and Tremont Street. This stop is heavily used by tourists and locals, so expect crowds. Another equally bustling option is to take the Red Line or Green Line to the Park Street T stop at the northeastern edge of the Common.

Freedom Trail & Black Heritage Trail

General Information

NFT Maps: 1, 2, 3, 4, 8
Address: Visitor Center, 147 Tremont St, Boston, MA 02111
Freedom Trail: www.thefreedomtrail.org
Black Heritage Trail: www.afroammuseum.org/trail.htm
Walking Tours: Available daily during spring/summer/fall, from Boston Common to Faneuil Hall, daily: 11 am, 12 pm, 1 pm, & 3:30 pm; Mon–Fri: 10 am, 1:30 pm, & 4:45 pm. From Faneuil Hall to Boston Common, daily: 10:30 am & 1 pm. ($12 adults, $6 children, cash only)
Audio Tours: Available at the Visitor Center $15 rental; 617-357-8300

Freedom Trail Overview

The Freedom Trail conveniently links several important colonial and post-colonial historical sites. Marked by a thick red path on the sidewalks, either painted or made of inlaid brick, the trail leads sightseers from the Visitor Center on Boston Common to the Charlestown Navy Yard on the opposite side of the Charles River. The 2.5-mile trek passes by 16 different sites, including the location of the Boston Massacre, Paul Revere's house, a couple of old cemeteries, and Bunker Hill. Walking tours led by costumed guides leave the Visitor Center or Faneuil Hall, and a complete trail walk usually lasts about 90 minutes. Audio tours are also available.

Trail Head: The Boston Common—America's oldest public park, 44-acre Boston Common is home to well-fed squirrels, pigeons, walkers, joggers, bikers, fat squirrels, pigeons, dogs, ducks, and pigeons.

1. **The State House**—The Massachusetts state government sits here in this gold-domed building, the oldest on Beacon Hill, in fact. Tour Hours: Mon–Fri 10 am–4 pm; 617-727-3676.

2. **Park Street Church**—The Evangelical Church was constructed in 1809 and has since stood as a testament to Bostonian faith. Lucky passersby may even be treated to a tirade being given from the outdoor pulpit. Traditional worship: 8:30 am and 11 am.
Contemporary worship: 4 pm and 6 pm.

3. **Granary Burying Ground**—An epitaph here reads "Revere's Tomb" near the resting places of both John Hancock and Samuel Adams, along with a giant monolith paying tribute to the family of Boston-born Ben Franklin. This is the city's third-oldest burial ground, the resting place of the victims of the Boston Massacre. Open daily 9 am–5 pm; 617-635-4505.

4. **King's Chapel**—The chapel site dates from 1688, and the current chapel was built in 1754 with the objective that it "would be the equal of any in England." The bell was made by Paul Revere. Summer hours: Sun 1:30 pm–4 pm, Mon–Sat 10 am–4 pm; winter hours: Sat 10 am–4 pm, Sun 1:30–4 pm. Entry is free but there's a $2 "suggested" donation. Concerts on Tuesdays at 12:15 pm and Sundays at 5 pm. Services are held Wednesdays 12:15 pm and Sundays 9:45 am and 11 am; 617-227-2155.

King's Chapel Burying Ground—Older than the Granary and the final resting place of some of Boston's first settlers. Open daily, 9 am–5 pm.

5. **Benjamin Franklin's Statue/Site of the First Public School**—Boston Latin School, founded in 1635, is still open (but it's since moved to the Fenway). The old high school is considered the top public school in Boston. A mosaic in the sidewalk marks its original site nearby to a statue of one of its famous students, Ben Franklin. Both are in the courtyard of Old City Hall, also worth a look.

6. **Old Corner Bookstore Building**—Built in 1718, this is one of Boston's oldest surviving structures. Once an apothecary, during the 19th century the building housed the publisher of classic New England titles *Walden* and *The Scarlet Letter*.

7. **Old South Meeting House**—"Voices of Protest," a permanent exhibit in the house, speaks of generations who made history under one roof, including Samuel Adams, William Dawes, Benjamin Franklin (and his parents and grandparents), Phillis Wheatley, and the instigators of the Boston Tea Party. Nov–Mar, 10 am–4 pm. Apr–Oct, 9:30 am–5 pm. Adults $5, students and seniors $4, children (6-18) $1, children under six free; 617-482-6439.

8. **Old State House**—The oldest surviving public building in Boston, its lush exterior will draw you inside where the Bostonian Society houses a library along with its museum of Boston's past.
Library: Tues, Wed, and Thurs 10 am–3:30 pm, closed weekends and holidays. Daily use fee: non-members $10, college students $5.
Museum: 9 am–5 pm, extended hours in summer, closed New Year's Day, Thanksgiving, and Christmas Day. Adults $5, older adults (62+) $4, students (over 18) $4, children (6-18) $1; 617-720-1713.

9. **Site of the Boston Massacre**—Cobblestones now mark this historic site outside the Old State House.

10. **Faneuil Hall**—Shopping mixed with history, with some eateries to boot. If you like touristy knick-knacks, this is the place to shop. The actual hall still holds public meetings and houses an armory museum. Open daily 9 am–9 pm. Historical talks every thirty minutes, 9:30 am–4:30 pm. See page 196.

11. **Paul Revere House**—See how Boston's favorite patriot once lived. Keep in mind that when he lived there, the area wasn't filled with Italian restaurants. Apr 15–Oct 31, 9:30 am–5:15 pm. Nov 1–Apr 14, 9:30 am–4:15 pm. Closed Mondays in Jan–Mar and on Thanksgiving, Christmas Day, and New Year's Day. Adults $3, seniors and college students $2.50, children (5-17) $1; 617-523-2338.

12. **Old North Church**—"One if by land, two if by sea," goes the poem. And so two lanterns were placed in the Old North Church, the oldest church building in Boston, warning that the British were making their way across the Charles towards Lexington and Concord. The church has held services since 1723 and is the most visited historical site in Boston. Winter hours: 9 am–5 pm daily. Summer hours: 9 am–6 pm daily; 617-523-6676.

13. **Copp's Hill Burying Ground**—The site began as a cemetery in the 1660s and was later used by the British as a strategic vantage point in the Battle of Bunker Hill. Open daily 9 am–5 pm.

14. **Bunker Hill Monument**—A 221-foot granite obelisk commemorates the Battle of Bunker Hill—the first major battle of the American Revolution. The monument sits atop Breed's Hill, where the misnamed battle actually took place. Exhibitions at the visitor's center explain how the battle came to be and how it was won. Hours: 9 am–4:30 pm daily; 617-242-5641.

15. **USS Constitution**—a.k.a. "Old Ironsides," America's oldest commissioned warship, with daily flag-raising and lowering ceremonies accompanied by cannon fire. Winter hours: Thurs–Sun, 10 am–4 pm. Summer hours: Tues–Sun: 10 am–6 pm. Tours depart every half hour; 617-242-5670. See Charlestown Navy Yard, page 189.

Freedom Trail & Black Heritage Trail

Freedom Trail
1. State House
2. Park Street Church
3. Granary Burying Ground
4. King's Chapel
5. Ben Franklin Statue
6. Old Corner Bookstore
7. Old South Meeting House
8. Old State House
9. Boston Massacre Site
10. Faneuil Hall
11. Paul Revere House
12. Old North Church
13. Copp's Hill Burial Ground
14. Bunker Hill Monument
15. USS Constitution Museum

Black Heritage Trail
1. Shaw Memorial
2. Middleton House
3. Phillips School
4. Smith House
5. Charles Street Meeting House
6. Hayden House
7. Coburn Gaming House
8. Smith Court Residences
9. African Meeting House
10. Smith School

Black Heritage Trail Overview

Running north from the State House, this trail recognizes the historical significance of Boston's post-Revolution African-American community. Before being forced into the South End and Roxbury in the 20th Century, the first community of free African-Americans actually lived in Beacon Hill after the American Revolution, in what is now known as the North Slope. According to the first federal census in 1790, Massachusetts was the only state in the country without slaves. The Museum of African-American History is housed in two of the buildings on the Trail, the African Meeting House and the Abiel Smith School, which are open to visitors. Most of the historic homes on the Trail are private residences, closed to the public.

1. **Robert Gould Shaw and the 54th Regiment Memorial**— Located on Boston Common across from the State House, this monument was built in 1897 in honor of the first all-black regiment that fought for the Union Army during the Civil War.

2. **George Middleton House**—(5–7 Pinckney St) George Middleton was the commander of an all-black military company during the Revolutionary War called the Bucks of America. His house, erected in 1797, is the oldest standing wooden structure on Beacon Hill. It is a private residence.

3. **The Phillips School**—(Anderson & Pinckney Sts) One of the first Boston public schools to be integrated (in 1855) as a result of the historic court case *Roberts v. The City of Boston*, which opposed the racial segregation of the city's schools.

4. **John J. Smith House**—(86 Pinckney St) John J. Smith was born free in Virginia in 1820 and eventually moved to Boston where he opened a successful barbershop that catered to many wealthy white customers from all over the city. His shop served as a haven for anti-slavery debates, fugitive slaves, and advocates for equal education rights.

5. **Charles Street Meeting House**—(Mt Vernon & Charles Sts) Built in 1807, the Charles Street Meeting House was originally the site of the segregated Third Baptist Church. After a failed attempt to desegregate the church, Timothy Gilbert and several other abolitionist sympathizers left to form Free Baptist Church (now the Tremont Temple), the first integrated church in America. In 1876, the Meeting House was sold to the African Methodist Episcopal Church, which eventually left Beacon Hill for Roxbury in 1939, due to changing economic conditions in the area.

6. **Lewis and Harriet Hayden House**—(66 Phillips St) Lewis and Harriet Hayden ran a boarding house out of their home, which was also a stop on the Underground Railroad. Lewis Hayden was an ardent African-American abolitionist and community leader who served as a delegate for the Republican Convention, fought for women's rights, and helped found the Museum of Fine Arts.

7. **John Coburn Gaming House**—(2 Phillips St) Home to one of Boston's wealthiest African-Americans, clothier James Coburn, the gaming house was built in 1843. Serving Boston's white elite, it became one of the most successful black-owned businesses in the city. Coburn used the profits to finance several abolitionist groups in the community, including the Massasoit Guards. Founded as an all-black military company to support the state's troops in case of war, the Guards also patrolled Beacon Hill to protect African-Americans from slave catchers.

8. **Smith Court Residences**— (3, 5, 7, 7A, & 10 Smith Ct) Five remaining wooden houses located on Beacon Hill's north slope were all purchased by middle-class African-Americans from white landowners in the mid-1800s.

9. **The African Meeting House**—(8 Smith Ct) Founded as a response to racial discrimination in Boston's religious communities, the African Meeting House remains the oldest standing Black church building in the country. The structure was built using labor and donations from the African-American community. It was used for religious services, as a safe haven for political discussion, and as a makeshift school for black children until the Abiel Smith School came into existence. It is currently being restored to its original appearance. With the Abiel Smith School, it houses the Museum of African-American History.

10. **Abiel Smith School**—(46 Joy St) Built in 1834 as the first schoolhouse in America to educate black school children, the Abiel Smith School was consistently overcrowded and neglected by the city. Substandard conditions led to *Roberts v. Massachusetts* and the desegregation of schools in 1855. Hours: 10 am–4 pm, Mon–Sat. Extended summer hours, Thurs 10 am–8 pm. Closed Thanksgiving, Christmas, and New Year's Day. Admission is free. 617-725-0022.

General Information

NFT Maps: 14, 15, 16, 17, 30, & 31
Address: Two Brookline Pl, Brookline, MA 02445
Phone: 617-232-5374
Websites: www.emeraldnecklace.org
www.cityofboston.gov/parks/necklace.asp

Overview

Known primarily for his work designing New York's Central Park, celebrated landscape architect Frederick Law Olmsted also created a beautiful string of Boston parks when he moved to Brookline in 1883. Olmsted's Necklace was designed as an uninterrupted five-mile walkway from Back Bay to Franklin Park, where Bostonians could stroll barefoot and without worry. The Necklace has been broken up over the years, both by the construction of the Casey Overpass near Franklin Park and by the conversion of the Riverway, Jamaicaway, and Arborway from pleasant carriage paths to major roads carrying highway-amounts of traffic. The city and conservation groups are putting together a "master plan" for the severed sections of the Necklace and together are trying to balance path restoration with traffic concerns. With the future construction of the Rose Kennedy Greenway where the Central Artery once stood, the idea is to link all of Boston's parks into an actual necklace.

Franklin Park

Occupying 500 acres, Franklin Park is the Necklace's largest park and was originally designed as a country retreat in the vein of Central Park in New York. Named after Benjamin Franklin, the park encompasses the Zoo (617-541-LION), one of the first public golf courses in the country (617-265-4084), 100 acres of woodland, and the seven-acre Scarboro Pond. The Franklin Park Zoo (not part of Olmsted's original plan), which opened in 1911, is home to the "Butterfly Landing," a butterfly enclosure open seasonally from June through September. The zoo made headlines in 2003 when adolescent gorilla "Little Joe" escaped from his enclosure—twice. The first time, he stayed on site. The second time, he ended up at a bus stop in Roxbury. Zoo entry: Adults $11, children $6, seniors $9.50, half price the first Sat of each month, 10 am–12 pm; winter hours (Oct 1–Mar 31), 10 am–4 pm; summer hours, 10 am–5 pm weekdays, and 6 pm weekends and holidays, admission is free the Friday after Thanksgiving; www.zoonewengland.com.

Arnold Arboretum

The oldest arboretum in the country, Arnold Arboretum is named after its financier, whaling tycoon and horticulturalist James Arnold. Visitors come primarily to stroll amongst the exotic greenery, which includes bonsai and lilac trees. Because Arnold left most of his estate to Harvard and the school uses the arboretum as a nature museum, it seems only fair for the city to allow the grand university to rent the land for just a dollar a year. Open every day until dusk, the visitor center is open 9 am–4pm weekdays, 10 am–4 pm Sat, 12 pm–4 pm Sun, and closed holidays. Entry is free!

Jamaica Park

Wealthy Bostonians of yesteryear built their summer homes in this spot, called "the jewel in the Emerald Necklace" because of the 60-acre sparkling Jamaica Pond. The largest and purest body of water in Boston, the glacier-formed pond is fed by natural springs and is 90 feet deep in some places. The pond is so clean that it serves as a back-up city reservoir. Joggers and dog-walkers share the 1.5 mile paved trail around the pond. Fishing is one of the most popular activities, and every year the City of Boston stocks the pond with trout, salmon, and indigenous pickerel, bass, hornpout, and perch. The boathouse rents canoes, sailboats, and rowboats, and, in winter, has a fireplace going. Around Halloween, the community organization Spontaneous Celebrations sponsors a lantern walk around the pond.

Olmsted Park

A joint project between the City of Boston and the Town of Brookline to tie the two cities together, Olmsted Park showcases the landscape architect's unique design philosophy with a series of ponds and wooded paths that open onto expansive views that help you understand why Olmsted is the Boston Brahmin equivalent of a rock star. (The city boasts at least one Olmsted impersonator.) A great feature of the park is the human-made Muddy River, currently the site of a major dredging project. Leverett, Willow, and Ward's Ponds are more secluded and less crowded than nearby Jamaica Pond. A new bike/pedestrian path system on the Brookline side from Jamaica Pond to Boylston Street (Route 9) was completed in 1997.

Riverway Park

Hidden below the busy street level is the narrowest park in the system and also the only one that is completely human-made. Riverway lies in the valley of the Muddy River (the boundary between Boston and Brookline), and features several small islands, wooded paths, and pretty footbridges. Its steep tree-lined banks protect visitors from the city bustle above. Footbridges connect the Boston and Brookline sides, but these are poorly lit at night.

Back Bay Fens

Olmsted's first phase of the Necklace in 1878, the Back Bay Fens was a sewage-infested saltwater marsh on the verge of extinction when he stepped in, transforming the swampy area into a meandering brackish creek. The creation of the Charles River Dam in 1910 turned the Fens into a freshwater marsh. Today, the Fens has quite a few notable attractions, including recreational facilities, the Kelleher Rose Garden, War Memorials, and the Victory Garden. The Victory Garden was created in 1941, in an effort to grow extra food for troops, and is currently tended to by local green thumbs who shell out $20 per year to maintain personal plots. A former parking lot, the western end of the Fens was recently converted into green space. But it's a notorious local fact that more than mere gardening takes place on the grounds—think George Michael.

General Information

NFT Map: 2
Phone: 617-523-1300
Websites: www.faneuilhallmarketplace.com
www.faneuil.com
www.cityofboston.gov/freedomtrail/
faneuilhall.asp
www.nps.gov/bost/Faneuil_Hall.htm

Faneuil Hall

Faneuil Hall was built as a food and produce market/meeting hall by Boston's wealthiest merchant, Peter Faneuil, in 1742. It's a historically poignant section of commercial property: At this location, Samuel Adams rallied for independence (prior to his interest in brewing beer), the doctrine of "no taxation without representation" was established, and George Washington and company celebrated our country's freedom. In later years it was the site of abolitionist rallies. It's still both a commercial spot and a meeting place used by campaigning politicians, with shops in the basement and the first floor, the Great Hall on the second, and a museum on the third.

Since its inception, the Faneuil Hall Marketplace has been a major shopping arena, and it's now stocked with more than 100 stores and pushcarts and 17 sit-down restaurants as well as a gastronomic orgy of a food hall. The marketplace alone attracts more than 12 million visitors a year and hosts numerous events and festivals. Local talent includes jugglers, mimes (yes, those, too), magicians, bands, and the occasional strolling Ben Franklin. If you're looking to be entertained while you shop, Faneuil Hall is your place.

Four buildings make up the marketplace: Faneuil Hall, Quincy Market, North Market, and South Market. Touristy and crowded at times, it's still one of the best and most visually pleasing places to buy souvenirs, shop in a mall-like environment, and try any number of local dishes. Standard mall stores occupy most of North and South Market, while local vendors and souvenir slingers can be found in the Hall or at pushcarts in Quincy Market. The Hall and all pushcarts are open Monday through Saturday from 10 am to 9 pm, and from noon to 6 pm on Sundays. Shopping hours in the other marketplaces vary by vendor. The Hall and all shops are closed on Christmas.

Quincy Market

Located directly behind Faneuil Hall, Quincy Market is where you go to chow down. The food court runs the length of the building and far exceeds a typical food court in both variety and quality of offerings. Whatever you crave, it's hard to go away disappointed. It is usually crowded at lunch, especially during the field trip and leaf-peeping seasons, so avoid peak hours if you're in a rush. Various sit-down bars and restaurants and pushcarts encircle the food court around the perimeter. The North Market and South Market, which stand on either side

of Quincy Market, have other places to sit for a meal, including the still-there Durgin Park.

Like many places in Boston, Quincy Market is built on landfill in what used to be Boston Harbor. Unlike other sections, when you're in Quincy Market, you're standing on bones. The butchers who used to occupy the wharves behind Faneuil Hall would let their unusable animal parts pile up, creating a sanitation nightmare. Then, someone had the bright idea of throwing the bones in the water, which eventually helped fill the wharf area and allowed for the construction of Quincy Market.

Museum

Ancient and Honorable Artillery Company Museum; 617-227-1638; www.ahacsite.org

Located on Faneuil Hall's third floor, the museum and library showcase the history of the Ancient and Honorable Artillery Company. The oldest military organization in the US (and third-oldest in the world), this august body was established as the Military Company of Boston in 1637 and still holds military drills and participates in various ceremonial events. The museum proudly displays the company's artifacts. It is a unique collection that is well worth a visit for military and history buffs. The museum is open Monday–Friday; 9 am–3:30 pm.

How to Get There—Driving

From the south, take I-93 N to Exit 23 ("Government Center"). Upon exiting, follow the signs to the Aquarium. At Surface Road, turn left. Faneuil Hall will be on the right-hand side.

From the west, take the Mass Pike (I-90) to Exit 24B (I-93 N). From I-93, take Exit 23 ("Government Center") and follow the directions above.

From the north, take I-93 S to Exit 24A toward Government Center. Stay to the right, and follow the signs for Faneuil Hall. Immediately off the exit, turn right. Faneuil Hall will be directly in front of you.

Parking

There are over 10,000 parking spaces within a two-mile radius of Faneuil Hall. The 75 State Street garage near the intersection of State Street and Broad Street offers a $2 discount on weekdays with store validation, and $10 parking after 5 pm daily and on selected holidays with store validation.

How to Get There—Mass Transit

To get to Faneuil Hall Marketplace, take the T's Green Line to Government Center or Haymarket, the Blue Line to State or Aquarium, or the Orange Line to State or Haymarket.

Parks & Places · **Faneuil Hall Marketplace**

Shopping

A Hat for Every Head (pushcart)
Ann Taylor
Bill Rodgers Running Center
Boston Logos (pushcart)
Boxers To Go (pushcart)
Build A Belt (pushcart)
Celtic Weavers
Coach
Cuoio
Fantasy Island (pushcart)
Harvest Fare (pushcart)
Head Games
La Cloche (pushcart)
Life is a Highway (pushcart)
Michal Negrin
Nightshirts To Go (pushcart)
Nine West
Orient Express (pushcart)
Orvis
Sacs (pushcart)
Sea Boston USA (pushcart)
Sock It To Me
Urban Outfitters
Victoria's Secret

Goods & Gifts

African Collections (pushcart)
Air Brush Tattoos (pushcart)
Anytime (pushcart)
Arman Time Company (pushcart)
Art for 'Em (pushcart)
Atmosphere (pushcart)
Best of Boston
Boston Art Work (pushcart)
Boston Campus Gear
Boston Pewter Company
The Boston Sun Spot
Bostonian Society Museum Shop
Build-A-Bear Workshop
Camera Center
Cheers Gift Shop
Christmas In New England
The Christmas Dove
Conversations (pushcart)
Crabtree & Evelyn
Crate & Barrel
Destination Boston
Every Bead of My Heart (pushcart)
Exotic Flowers
Funusual
Gateway News
Geoclassics
Godiva Chocolatier
Happy Hangups (pushcart)
Harley Davidson-Boston (pushcart)
Headlines of America (pushcart)
Henri's Glassworks
Illusions (pushcart)
Irish Eyes (pushcart)
Local Charm

Lokta Paper (pushcart)
Magic Rice (pushcart)
Magnetic Chef (pushcart)
Museum of Fine Arts Store
Musically Yours (pushcart)
Newbury Comics
On the Edge
Origins
Pillow Pets (pushcart)
Sluggers Upper Deck Kiosk (pushcart)
Stuck on Stickpins (pushcart)
Sunglass Hut & Watch Station
Teeny Billboards (pushcart)
Yankee Candle Company
Zip It (pushcart)

Food

A La Carte
Al Mercantino
Ames Plow Tavern
Aris Barbeque
Bangkok Express
Bistany International
Bombay Club
Boston & Maine Fish Co
Boston Chipyard
Boston Chowda
Boston Kitchen
Boston Pretzel
Brown Derby Deli
Carol Ann's Bake Shop
Colleen Bawn Fine Foods (pushcart)
Columbo Frozen Yogurt Shoppe
Dick's Last Resort
The Dog House
Durgin Park
El Paso Enchilada
Fisherman's Net
The Green Organic Bowl
Jen Lai Rice & Noodle Company
Joey's Gelateria
Kilvert & Forbes
Kingfish Hall
La Pastaria
McCormick & Schmick's
Megumi
MMMac & Cheese
The Monkey Bar
North End Bakery
Philadelphia Steak & Hoagie
Piccolo Panini
Pizzeria Regina
Plaza III, the Kansas City Steak House
The Prime Shoppe
Quincy's Place
Roasted Nuts (pushcart)
Salty Dog Seafood Grill & Bar
Sam's Café at Cheers
Slugger's Dugout
Sprinkles Ice Cream
Starbucks

Steve's Greek Cuisine
Ueno Sushi
Wagamama
West End Strollers
Zuma's Tex Mex Café

Bars & Entertainment

Cheers
Comedy Connection
Coogan's
Hard Rock Cafe
Jose MacIntyre's
Ned Devine's Irish Pub
Parris
The Monkey Bar
Trinity

Services

Bean Town Trolley Tours (pushcart)
BosTix Ticket Booth
City View Trolley Tours
Faneuil Hall Marketplace Information
Old Town Trolley Tours (pushcart)
Super Duck Tours (pushcart)

Nearby Bars

The Atrium Lounge
Bell in Hand Tavern
Black Rose
Dockside Restaurant & Bar
Hennessey's
McFadden's
Kitty O'Shea's
The Rack
The Place
Purple Shamrock
Sissy K's
Union Oyster House
Vertigo

Tileston St
Hanover Ave
N Bennet St
Harris St
Margaret St
Prince St
Salem St
Clark St
N Bennet St
Fleet St
Union Wharf
Union Wharf
Hanover St
Garden Ct
Lewis St
Sun Court St
Parmenter St
North St
North Sq
Eastern Ave
MAP 2
Lewis Wharf
Sumner Tunnel
Fulton St
Lewis Wharf
Boston Inner Harbor
North St
Callahan Tunnel
Commercial St
Commercial Wharf N
Commercial Wharf
Commercial Wharf
Boston Charlestown
93
Clinton St
Christopher Columbus Park
(Summer Only)
Harbor Cruises
Faneuil Hall Marketplace
PAGE 194
Atlantic Ave
Chatham St
Long Wharf
Aquarium
State St
Central St
Central Wharf
New England Aquarium
Central St
Old Atlantic Ave
Central Wharf
Milk St
E India Row
Water St
Milk St
India St
India Wharf
Broad St
Well St
Batterymarch St
Water Shuttle
93
Oliver St
Franklin St
Logan Airport Ferry
Rowes Wharf
Hingham Ferry
Rowes Wharf
Foster Wharf
MAP 4
Foster's Wharf
Pearl St
High St
Northern Ave (pedestrian bridge)
Congress St
Purchase St
Seaport Blvd

Overview

Originally named Boston Pier, Long Wharf juts into Boston Harbor at the bottom of State Street, while Rowes Wharf is farther south, near Broad Street. In the 1700s, Long Wharf extended more than one-third of a mile into Boston Harbor, but the dumping of urban landfill has resulted in a significant portion of the pier being surrounded by land rather than water. Purportedly the oldest continually operating wharf in the US, Long Wharf is the site of the Chart House. It has operated as a restaurant since 1961, and is the oldest existing pre-Revolutionary War warehouse in Boston.

Attractions

During the warmer months, stop by the Landing Bar on Long Wharf for a drink in the sunshine. It's the perfect place to hang out and catch a Red Sox game on television after work or when you're waiting to board a ferry.

The New England Aquarium is located at nearby Central Wharf and operates an IMAX Theatre next door. The Aquarium allows scientists and researchers to study marine and aquatic habitats and to educate visitors about conservation issues. One of the most exciting events to participate in is a "release party," when an animal is returned to its natural habitat. Hours: 9 am–5 pm weekdays (6 pm summer), 9 am–6 pm weekends (7 pm summer). Closed Thanksgiving and Christmas Day. Adults $18.95, children (3–11) $10.95. www.neaq.org; 617-973-5200.

There are several whale-watching excursions that leave from the wharves. Whale-watching season starts in April and ends in the fall.

- **Voyager III** • Central Wharf • 617-973- 5281
- **Boston Harbor Cruises** • 1 Long Wharf • 617-227-4321
- **Massachusetts Bay Lines Whale Watch** • 60 Rowes Wharf • 617-542-8000

Long Wharf is also where you catch the Harbor Express boat to the Boston Harbor Islands. There are 34 islands in all, six of which are staffed and serviced by a free boat shuttle from the headquarters on Georges Island. These islands are still underutilized by locals and unfrequented by tourists. They vary in size, but most offer trails, old forts, diverse flora and fauna, camping (on Grape, Lovells, and Bumpkin), and great views of Boston and the harbor. Spectacle Island's past as a former quarantine island, glue factory, and garbage dump has been covered with rubble from the Big Dig and transformed into an eco-friendly recreation spot. The island is now open to the public and features a visitor center and a café. The islands open seasonally, so check the website, www.bostonislands.com, or call 617-223-8666.

If you're prone to seasickness, or if watching whales isn't your bag, the newly-renovated Christopher Columbus Park is a short walk from Long Wharf. The playground for the little ones is top-notch, and its famous rose garden is dedicated to Rose Fitzgerald Kennedy. It's also a good viewing spot for the fireworks on First Night. Next door is Tia's, a popular after-work, meat market bar in the summer.

Architecture

Rowes Wharf features a commanding arch that looks out onto Boston Harbor. The complex is a mixed-use complex that has won numerous design awards, including the Urban Land Institute's "Award for Excellence." The complex is shared by the Boston Harbor Hotel, 100 luxury condominiums, and offices. There is a little-known observation area on the ninth floor named the Forester Rotunda, offering views of both the city and harbor. Though not advertised, you can go through the hotel to gain access. In the summertime, a floating dock hosts outdoor concerts and movies under the stars.

Ferries

Both Long Wharf and Rowes Wharf serve as ferry terminals for the MBTA. F1 transports people to and from Rowes Wharf and Hingham Shipyard. F2 and F2H stop at Long Wharf, Logan Airport, and the Fore River Shipyard in Quincy. F2H also has limited service to Pemberton Point in Hull. F4, which travels to the Charlestown Navy Yard, also uses the Long Wharf terminus. The Harbor Express to Georges Island also leaves from Long Wharf. For more information on ferries, see page 254. For schedules and maps, go to www.mbta.com/schedules_and_maps/boats, or call 617-222-5000. You can also catch the high-speed catamaran ferry to Provincetown from Long Wharf. For schedules, fares, and area information visit www.bostonharborcruises.com/ptown_main.html.

How to Get There—Driving

To Long Wharf from the north, take I-93 S, and get off at Exit 24A (Government Center/Aquarium). Follow signs to the Aquarium. From the south, take Exit 23 (Government Center) and follow signs to the Aquarium.

To Rowes Wharf from the north, take I-93 S and get off at Exit 23 (aim for South Station). Turn left onto Congress Street and immediately left onto Atlantic Avenue. The wharf is on the right, two blocks past the intersection of Congress Street and Atlantic Avenue.

From the south, take I-93 N to Exit 20, and follow signs to South Station. Once you drop onto Atlantic Avenue, proceed through the Congress Street intersection and drive two blocks. The wharf will be on your right.

Parking

There is *very* limited street parking in the area, so if you want to forego driving around to find a free spot, you should try one of the many parking garages that are all within walking distance of the various wharves. Parking fees can cost $25 or more, depending on how long you stay, though there are usually discounted rates on weekends and after 5 pm on weekdays. If you're willing to shell out the cash, here are a few nearby garages:

- **The Rowes Wharf building** features an underground discounted parking garage with an entrance on Atlantic Avenue.
- **Harbor Garage at the Aquarium,** 70 East India Row; 617-367-3847
- **Dock Square Garage,** 200 State St; 617-367-4373
- **Laz Parking,** 290 Commercial St; 617-367-6412
- **Fitz-Inn Parking,** 269 Commercial St; 617-367-1681
- **Central Parking,** 2 Atlantic Ave; 617-854-3365

How to Get There—Mass Transit

To Long Wharf, take the T's Blue Line to the Aquarium stop. To Rowes Wharf, take either the Blue Line to Aquarium or the Red or Silver Line to South Station.

Stores

1	PF Chang's China Bistro
5	US Post Office
11	Ann Taylor Loft
17	Au Bon Pain
17	Tossed
19	Best of Boston
21	St Francis Chapel
23	Dunkin' Donuts
25	Ann Taylor
33	Jasmine Sola
39	Godiva
41	Free People
43	GameStop
45	Florsheim Shoes
46	Travel 2000
47	Truffles Fine Confections
103	Legal Sea Foods
107	Sephora
111	F Carriere
113	Talbots Collection/ Talbots Kids/ Talbots Mens
123	Olympia Sports
125	Chico's
127	The Body Shop
131	Alpha Omega
133	Johnston & Murphy
135	Aldo
139	Sunglass Hut
141	Teavana
143	Papyrus
145	Landau Collections
147	Optical Shop of Aspen
153	L'Occitane
155	California Pizza Kitchen
159	Crane & Co
163	Yankee Candle
165	Swarovski
167	Arden B
171	Levenger
173	J Jill—The Store
175	Club Monaco
175A	Charles David
177	Franklin Covey
179	Barnes & Noble
181	The Sharper Image
183	Sovereign Bank
187	Cold Stone Creamery
189	The Cheesecake Factory
193	Applebee's
197	FitCorp

Food Court

FC1	Qdoba Mexican Grill
FC2	Panda Express
FC3	Pizzeria Regina
FC4	Poulet Rotisserie Chicken
FC5	Boston Chowda
FC6	Flamers
FC7	Gourmet India
FC8	Sakkio Japan
FC9	Ben & Jerry's
FC10	Paradise Bakery & Café
FC11	Louis Barry Florist

General Information

NFT Maps: 5 & 6
Address: 800 Boylston St, Boston, MA 02199
Phone: 1-800-SHOP-PRU or 617-236-3100
Website: www.prudentialcenter.com

Overview

The Prudential Center opened in 1965 and, at 52 stories, reigned as the city's tallest building until the 60-story John Hancock Tower was completed eleven years later. With the exception of the top two floors, which house an observation deck and a restaurant, the Prudential Tower is used mainly as office space. The Prudential Mall (not be confused with the more highbrow Copley Place mall, attached to the Prudential Mall by a natty skywalk) was opened in the 1990s on the lower floors and houses almost 50 shops, including Saks Fifth Avenue and numerous restaurants and services. The "Pru" is also home to several apartment buildings and is connected to the Hynes Convention Center and the Sheraton Boston Hotel. If you're not in the mood for the maddening crowd, avoid the mall, which is always teeming with tourists, hardcore browsers, and convention attendees.

Skywalk and Top of the Hub

The Prudential Tower gives you two options for catching its spectacular: Skywalk Observatory and Top of the Hub restaurant. Both offer breathtaking sights of Boston and its suburbs, as well as the harbor, Blue Hill, and—way off in the distance—Cape Cod. (By default, the Prudential Center became the best place to see Boston from on high after the observatory at the John Hancock Tower closed following September 11.) The Skywalk is open daily from 10 am until 9:30 pm (8 pm in the winter). Skywalk tickets cost $12 adults, $10 seniors and students, and $8 children under 12. As you walk around the Skywalk, focus on the huge windows, which are marked to help you locate some of the more well-known features of the Boston skyline.

Top of the Hub offers a somewhat more cost-effective viewing experience, and one that's two floors above the Skywalk, at that. Entrees are pricey, but juice and cocktails from the bar are fairly priced and served with a spectacular view. And if you're acrophobic, a little nip might be exactly what you need to be able to relax and enjoy the view as you peer down at the city or across at the top of the John Hancock Tower

with beverage in hand. The restaurant and lounge get busy at night, especially when the jazz band is playing. A semi-casual but "anti-slob" dress code is in effect.

How to Get There—Driving

From the north, take I-93 S to Exit 26 (Storrow Drive) and follow it to the Copley Square exit on the left. Take a right onto Beacon Street and follow it to Exeter Street. Make a left onto Exeter Street and the Prudential Center Garage will be four blocks down on the right.

From the west, follow the Mass Pike (I-90 E) into Boston. Get off at Exit 22 (Copley Square/Prudential Center) and follow the signs for Prudential Center. This will take you directly to the Prudential Center Garage entrance on your right.

From the south, take I-93 N to Exit 26 (Storrow Drive) and follow to the Copley Square exit on the left. Take a right onto Beacon Street and follow it to Exeter Street. Take a left onto Exeter Street. The Prudential Center Garage will be four blocks down on the right.

If you get lost, try this: Look up. Find the giant building that says "Prudential" on top. Drive towards it.

How to Get There—Mass Transit

The Green Line will take you to the Prudential T stop on Huntington Avenue (E train only; FYI: Only the doors of the first car open for this stop), the Copley stop on Boylston Street at Dartmouth Street, and the Hynes/ICA stop on Newbury Street at Mass Ave. The Orange Line and the MBTA Commuter Rail both stop at Back Bay Station, just across the street from Copley Place and a short walk away.

Overview

Originally one of the least fashionable streets of Back Bay, Newbury Street has undergone quite a transformation, morphing into Boston's most popular shopping area and an excellent place to hang out and strut your stuff.

A beautiful stretch of real estate featuring late 19th- and early 20th-Century architecture, Newbury Street runs eight blocks from the Public Garden west to Massachusetts Avenue. The cross streets run alphabetically from east to west, starting with Arlington, then Berkeley, Clarendon, etc. Stores pack the buildings along Newbury, which were originally designed for residential use, making for a lot of oddly shaped, quirky boutiques. The good shopping extends to either side of Newbury St with trendy stores and big name designers lining Boylston Street and many of the cross roads. Though the area features shops for all ages and tax brackets, the ambiance of Boston's most famed street may make an indulgence in $300 shoes or a $15 martini seem perfectly sensible.

In the summertime, the cafés spill out onto the sidewalk, providing a perfect spot from which to partake in unparalleled people-watching. The street is a veritable human car crash; the "hippest" elements of every age group, from 80-year-olds to eight-year-olds, interact and fight for space (and attention) on the same small sidewalk.

For an updated list of shops, see www.newbury-st.com.

History

The whole of Back Bay was swampland until about 1870, when workers completed a massive filling project. As a result, Back Bay is the only neighborhood in Boston to benefit from a modern urban planning. Streets actually cross each other at 90-degree angles, and at no point is there a rotary or an eight-way intersection. Fluctuations in the water table, however, are rotting the wooden planks on which most of the area's structures sit. The result: Back Bay is sinking.

The architecture on Newbury Street is fairly uniform, since most of the development occurred during the same half-century. Emmanuel Church, designed by Alexander Estey in 1862, was the first building completed on Newbury Street. The Church of the Covenant, built in 1865, houses some spectacular stained glass windows and was once described by Oliver Wendell Holmes as "absolutely perfect." Its Emmaus Window shines even in the dimmest of lights.

How to Get There—Driving

Newbury Street is easy to get to. From I-93 take Exit 26 to Storrow Drive. Take the exit for Arlington Street, and proceed up Arlington until you hit Newbury Street (right turn only, one-way). Newbury Street lies between Boylston Street and Commonwealth Avenue, so if you get twisted around use these larger streets as landmarks.

How to Get There—Mass Transit

From the T's Green Line you can get off at the Arlington stop, the Copley stop, or the Hynes/ICA stop. Note that the Green Line's E train breaks off the main track at Copley, so use the B, C, or D train to get to Hynes/ICA.

Shopping

Unless you have bionic feet, a shopping day on Newbury Street is going to leave your dogs barking. Luckily, the layout of the veritable brownstone mall that is Newbury Street is laid out in such a way that the most expensive boutiques are found near the Boston Public Garden end of Newbury Street, with shops gradually becoming cheaper and funkier by the time you collapse at Mass Ave.

Newbury Street probably wouldn't have gotten to where it is today without the support of some of the heavy hitter and high end chain stores, so you can't damn them for being there. And, as a result, their presence also gave the nearby little guy a steady stream of patrons. Some of the better (read: less ostentatious) chains here include: **Urban Outfitters** (361), **Patagonia** (346), **Puma** (333), **Johnny Cupcakes** (279), **1154 Lill Studio** (220), **Lush** (166), and **O & Company** (161). Unfortunately, between retail space progression and the down economy, the chains appear to be taking more than their fare share lately, so enjoy the hidden gems while they're still around. Check out **Mastu** (259), **Army Barracks** (173), **Trident Booksellers & Café** (138), **Condom World** (332), **Envi-Eco Fashion Boutique** (164), **Poor Little Rich Girl** (166), **Newbury Yarns** (164), **Queen Bee** (85), **Paperchase** (172), **Too Timid** (297), and **Dress** (221), to name a few.

Restaurants

If you don't stop to eat on Newbury Street, you're missing half the fun. Even if you've dropped most of your cash on shopping, you can still afford to stuff your face with good cheap eats like **Upper Crust** (222), **Steve's Greek** (316), **Snappy Sushi** (144), **Bottega Fiorentina** (264), **Boloco** (247), **JP Licks** (352), and **Kashmir** (279). Or pick up a little piece of prepared food heaven at **DeLuca's Market** (239). But if your coffers still have a little silver left in 'em, splurge at **Stephanie's on Newbury** (190), **Tapeo Restaurant & Tapas Bar** (268), **Capital Grille** (359), or **Bouchee** (159). Either way, you'll never make it on this street without some fuel in your belly.

Nightlife

Even if you only go to one store, a trip to Newbury Street will most certainly merit a nightcap (even if it's still day time). Unfortunately, there seems to be a dearth of boozin' spots specifically on this street. Fortunately a great deal exists on adjacent streets (see Map 5 and 6). In the meantime, the best waterin' holes 'round these parts include **The OtherSide Cosmic Café** (407), the martini bar at **Sonsie** (327), and **Bukowski's** at the end of the line on 50 Dalton Street.

All addresses are on Newbury Street

Clothing

A Pea in the Pod · 10 · maternity wear
AG Adriano Goldschmied · 201 ·
men's and women's clothing
Akris Boutique · 16 · shoe store
Alan Bilzerian · 34 · designer clothes
Alan Rouleau Couture · 73 ·
custom tailoring
Aldo · 180 · shoes and leather goods
Allen Edmonds · 36 ·
shoes and cedar products
American Apparel · 138 ·
men's and women's clothing
American Eagle Outfitters · 201 ·
youth clothes
Ana Hernandez Bridal · 165 ·
bridal boutique
Ann Taylor · 18 · women's clothes
Aria Bridesmaids · 39 ·
custom dresses
Army Barracks · 328 · military duds
Banana Republic · 28 ·
men's and women's clothing
Barbour by Peter Elliot · 134 ·
men's and women's clothing
BCBG Max Azaria · 71 ·
women's designer clothing
Bebe · 349 ·
women's clothing, accessories
Bella Bridesmaid · 163 ·
wedding clothing
Best of Scotland · 115 ·
sweaters at mill prices
Betsey Johnson · 201 ·
designer clothes
Betsy Jenney of Boston · 114 ·
women's unusual designer clothes
Borelli · 73 · high-end fashion
The Boston Baked Bean · 291 ·
keychains and more
Boutique Giorgio Armani · 22 · clothes
Boutique Longchamp · 139A ·
French handbags
Brooks Brothers · 46 ·
classy clothing for men and women
Burberry Limited · 2 ·
clothes for men and women
Calypso · 114 · women's clothing
Camper Shoes · 139 · shoes
Ceri · 31 · women's clothing
Chanel · 5 · clothing and accessories
Classic Tuxedo · 223 · ummm...?
The Closet · 175 · consignment;
men's and women's clothing
Cole-Haan · 109 ·
men's and women's clothing
Cuoio · 115 ·
European shoes for women
Daniela Corte Fashion · 91 ·
women's fashion
Designer Shoes · 125 · designer shoes
Diesel · 339 · clothing
DKNY · 37 · clothing
Dress · 221 · women's clothing
Easter Wings · 244 · women's clothing
Ecco Newbury Shoes · 216 · shoes
Emporio Armani · 210-214 ·
men's and women's clothing

Envi-Eco Fashion Boutique · 164 ·
womens fashion accessories
Fiandaca · 73 · couture clothing
Flair Bridesmaid Boutique · 129 ·
wedding clothing
Footstock · 153 · shoes
French Connection · 208 ·
men's and women's clothing
G-Star Raw · 348 ·
men's and women's clothing
Guess? · 80 · clothing
H&M · 100 ·
men's and women's clothing
Hempest · 207 · hemp clothing
I Boutique · 251 ·
men's and women's clothing
In the Pink · 133 · women's clothing
Intermix · 186 · women's clothing
Jasmine Sola Shoes · 329 · shoes
Jessica McClintock · 201 ·
women's cocktail attire
John Fluevog Shoes · 302 · shoes
Johnny Cupcakes · 279 ·
men's and women's clothing
Juicy Couture · 12 · women's clothing
Karmaloop Boston · 160 ·
men's and women's clothing
Kate Spade Shoes · 117 ·
shoes, purses, etc.
Kenneth Cole Productions · 128 · shoes
Lester Harry's · 115 · bedding,
children's and infant's clothing
Life is Good · 285 ·
men's and women's clothing
Lingerie Studio · 264 · lingerie
LF Stores · 353 · women's clothing
Loro Piana · 43 ·
men's and women's clothing,
accessories, tailoring and alteration
Lucky Brand · 229 · denim
Luna Boston · 286 ·
accessories and handbags
Maha Barson · 127 · women's clothing
Marc Jacobs · 81 · fashion
Matsu · 259 · handbags
Max Mara · 69 · women's clothing
Mudo · 205 · clothing
Nanette Lepore · 119 ·
women's clothing
Niketown · 200 · everything Nike
Oilily · 31 ·
Dutch clothing for women and children
Oilily Women's · 32 · women's clothes
Patagonia · 346 · clothing for the great
outdoors
Pavo Real Boutique · 115 ·
women's clothing and accessories
Petit Bateau · 171 · women's clothing
Players of Newbury · 250 ·
women's clothing
Puma · 333 · wildlife
Queen Bee · 85 · women's clothing
Ralph Lauren · 95 · clothing
Reiss · 132 ·
men's and women's clothing
Relic · 116 ·
men's and women's clothing
Riccardi Boutique · 116 · clothing
Rockport · 83 · shoes
Rugby Ralph Lauren · 342 ·
men's and women's clothing

Sean Store · 154 · men's clothing
**Second Time Around Collections · 176
& 219 ·** new and consignment clothes
Serenella · 134 ·
European women's clothes
Soudee · 293 · fashion
Stel's · 334 · men's and women's
clothing, accessories, and jewelry
Steve Madden · 324A ·
shoes and handbags
Stil · 170 · women's clothing
Technical · 230 · skate style and art
Thom Brown of Boston · 337 & 331 ·
shoes
United Colors of Benetton · 140 ·
women's clothing
Urban Outfitters · 361 · clothing
Valentino · 47 ·
men's and women's clothing
Vera Wang · 253 · wedding clothing
Victoria's Secret · 82 · fig leaves
Whim Boutique · 253 ·
men's and women's clothing

Restaurants

29 Newbury · 29 · new American food
Ben & Jerry's · 174 · ice cream
Boloco Inspired Burritos · 247 ·
burritos
Boston Baked Bean · 291 ·
gourmet gifts
Bouchee · 159 ·
American and French food
Bostone Pizza · 225 · pizza
The Capital Grille · 359 · steak house
**Charley's Eating & Drinking Saloon ·
284 ·** American food
Ciao Bella · 240 · Italian food
Daisy Buchanan's · 240 · bar
Emack & Bolio's Ice Cream · 290 ·
ice cream
Emporio Armani Café · 214 ·
Italian cuisine
Espresso Royale Café · 286 ·
coffee house
The Jewel of Newbury · 254 ·
Italian food
JP Licks Ice Cream · 352 ·
local ice cream shop
Kashmir · 279 · Indian food
L'Aroma Café · 85 · coffee shop
Marcello's Restaurant · 272 ·
Persian, Italian
Pazzo · 268 · Italian food
Piattini Wine Café · 226 · Italian food
Scoozi · 237 · pizza and sandwiches
Shino Express Sushi · 144 ·
Japanese food
Sonsie · 327 · international cuisine
Stephanie's on Newbury · 190 ·
American food
Steve's · 316 · Greek-American food
Tapeo · 268 · Spanish food
Tealuxe · 108 · tea bar
Thai Basil · 132 · Thai food
The Upper Crust · 222 · pizza
Wisteria House · 264 ·
Chinese-American cuisine

Gifts & Miscellaneous

1154 Lill Studio • 220 • handbags
A Touch of France Gallery • 173 • art gallery
Acme Fine Art • 38 • bought and sold modern American art
Aldo Accessories • 184 • accessories, handbags, jewelry
Alfred J. Walker Fine Art • 162 • art gallery
Alpha Gallery Inc • 38 • art gallery
Andrea Marquit Fine Arts • 38 • art gallery
Arden Gallery • 129 • art gallery
Atelier Janiye • 165 • jewelry
Aurum • 293 • jewelry
Axelle Fine Arts • 91 • art gallery
Back Bay Oriental Rugs • 154 • rugs
Barbara Krakow Gallery • 10 • art gallery
Bauer Wines Spirits • 330 • liquor store
Beadworks • 167 • make your own jewelry
Beth Urdang Gallery • 14 • art gallery
Bliss • 121 • home furnishings, cooking and dining
Brodney Antiques & Jewelry • 145 • antiques and jewelry
Cartier • 40 • jewelry
CD Spins • 324 • music and records
Chase Gallery • 129 • art gallery
Childs Gallery • 169 • art gallery
Cohen's Fashion Optical • 179 • sunglasses and glasses
Comenos Fine Arts • 9 • art gallery
Commonwealth Fine Art • 236 • art gallery
CoSo Artist's Gallery • 158 • art gallery
Dajuli Sparkles • 304 • jewelry
Diptyque • 123 • French perfumery
Domain Home Fashions • 7 • furniture
Dona Flor • 246 • home ceramics
Dorfman Jewelers • 24 • jewelry
Down to Basics • 249 • bedding
DTR Modern Galleries • 167 • art gallery
Erwin Pearl • 4 • jewelry
European Watch Co • 232 • watch repair and shop
Fairy Shop • 302 • Fairies, bubbles, incense, jewelry, you name it
Family Treasures Bookstore • books and magazines
Felicia's Cosmetics • 314 • cosmetics
Firefly Jewelry and Gifts • 270 • jewelry and gift shop
Firestone and Parson • 8 • antique jewelry
Fresh • 121 • bath products
Galerie d'Orsay • 33 • art gallery
Gallery NAGA • 67 • art gallery
Guido Frame Studio • 118 • ready-to-frame prints
The Guild of Boston Artists • 162 • art gallery
Hope • 302 • unique gift shop
Howard Yezerski Gallery • 14 • art gallery

International Poster Gallery • 205 • poster art gallery
Inviting Company • 213 • stationery
Judi Rotenberg Gallery • 130 • art gallery
Judy Ann Goldman Fine Art • 14 • art gallery
Kiehl's • 112 • beauty products
Kitchen Arts • 161 • kitchen tools
Kitty World • 279 • Hello Kitty heaven
Knit and Needlepoint • 11 • crafts and sewing supplies
L'Attitude Gallery Sculpture Garden • 218 • art gallery
Lalo Treasures • 255 • jewelry
Lanoue Fine Art • 160 • art gallery
Lavender Home & Table • 173 • home and garden, bedding, antiques
Lush Cosmetics • 166 • beauty products
M-A-C Newbury • 112 • beauty products
Madura Company • 144 • home furnishings, bedding
Marcoz Antiques • 177 • Antiques
Martin Lawrence Gallery • 77 • art gallery
Mayan Weavers • 268 • Native American crafts
Mercury Gallery • 8 • art gallery
Miller Block Gallery • 14 • art gallery
Needlepoint of Back Bay • 125 • crafts and sewing
Newbury Comics • 332 • music and video store
Newbury Fine Arts Gallery • 29 • art gallery
Newbury Visions • 215 • sunglasses and glasses
Newbury Yarns • 164 • crafts and sewing supplies
Nielsen Gallery • 179 • art gallery
O & Company • 161 • olive oil store
O'Brien Stephen B • 268 • art gallery
Pageo • 33 • Jewelry
Pepper Gallery • 38 • art gallery
Pierre Deux • 109 • gourmet gifts and home accessories
Poggenpohl Boston Showroom • 135 • designer kitchens
Pottery Barn • 122 • home décor
Pratesi Linens • 110 • bed and bath linens
Prem-La • 211 • home and garden
Pucker Gallery • 171 • art gallery
Q Optical • 287 • glasses and sunglasses
Richardson-Clarke Gallery • 38 • art gallery
Robert Klein Gallery • 38 • art gallery
Robert Marc Newbury Street • 35 • glasses and sunglasses
Royka's Fine Arts Antiques Gallery • 213 • antiques
SAC Gallery • 175 • art gallery
Sarkis Sajonian • 273 • jewelry
Shu Uemura • 130 • beauty products
Simon Pearce Glass • 115 • glassware
Small Pleasures • 142 • jewelry
So Good Jewelry • 349 • jewelry
Solstice • 168 • glasses and sunglasses
St George Gallery • 245 • art gallery

Sunglass Hut International • 182 & 86 • sunglasses store
Swiss Watch Boston • 217 • timepieces
Teuscher Chocolates of Switzerland • 230 • chocolates
Time & Time Again • 249 • watch store
Timeless Teas • 85 • tea
Trident Booksellers and Café • 338 • bookstore and café
Victoria Munroe Fine Art • 179 • art gallery
VOSE Galleries of Boston Inc. • 238 • art gallery
Waterworks • 103 • bathroom accessories

Boston Convention & Exhibition Center

Exhibit Hall A

Exhibit Hall B1

Exhibit Hall B

Exhibit Hall B2

Exhibit Hall C

MCCA Executive Offices

East Registration

Loading Dock

050
051
052A
052B
053
054

EXHIBIT LEVEL

Entrance Plaza

Summer Street
North Lobby

101
102A
102B
103
104A
104B
104C
105

Open to
Exhibit Hall A
below

105
151A
151B
152
153A
153B
153C
154

Skybridge

Open to
Exhibit Hall B
below

155
156A
156B
156C
157A
157B
158
158

Tastes
of Boston
Food Court

Skybridge

106
107A
107B
107C
108C
109A
109B

Open to
Exhibit Hall C
below

159
160A
160B
160C
161
162A
162B

MEETING LEVEL 1

MAP 10

Plaza Below

Lobby Below

Kitchen

203
204A
204B
205A
205B
205C
206A
206B
207

208
209
210A
210B
210C
211
212
213

Exhibit Hall A (below)

Exhibit Hall B (below)

Exhibit Hall C (below)

251
252A
252B
253A
253B
253C
254A
254B
255

256
257A
257B
258A
258B
258C
259A
259B
260

261

MEETING LEVEL 2

Grand Ballroom

West   East

Exhibit Hall A (below)

Exhibit Hall B (below)

Exhibit Hall C (below)

BALLROOM LEVEL

General Information

NFT Map: 10
Address: 415 Summer St,
                Boston, MA 02210
Phone: 617-954-2000
Fax: 617-954-2299
Websites: www.mccahome.com
                www.advantageboston.com

Overview

It took longer than expected to complete (what doesn't in this town?) and was plagued by cost overruns and contractor squabbling, but the Boston Convention & Exhibition Center finally opened in June 2004. In our humble opinion, it was worth the wait. Designed by noted architect Rafael Viñoly, the BCEC, which stands near Fort Point Channel on Summer Street (about a half-mile from South Station), is a stunning addition to the South Boston waterfront landscape.

Put simply, the BCEC is gargantuan. With 516,000 square feet of contiguous exhibition space, 160,000 square feet of flexible meeting space, more than 80 meeting rooms, and a 40,000-square-foot grand ballroom, the building covers an overall area of 1.7 million square feet. The BCEC now holds the coveted title of New England's Largest Man-Made Space and is big enough to hold 16 football fields.

The new complex is the centerpiece of the city's initiative to attract more convention business to Boston. As the old real estate mantra goes, it's all about "location, location, location," and a prime selling point for the BCEC is its proximity to both South Station and Logan Airport. Only two miles from Logan, the BCEC is closer to its city airport than the convention center of any other American city.

Services

The BCEC is used for large-scale conferences, meetings, and exhibitions. To schedule an event and be assigned a personal coordinator, contact the sales department at 617-954-2411 or sales@masscovention.com.

Catering services at the BCEC are provided by Aramark. If you are planning a catered event, contact Aramark at 617-954-2211.

How to Get There—Driving

The BCEC is easy to reach from the Mass Pike (I-90). From the Pike, take Exit 25 (South Boston). Turn right onto Congress Street, then right onto D Street, then the second right onto Summer Street. The BCEC will be immediately on the left. It's hard to miss.

From the south, take I-93 N, get off at Exit 20, follow the signs to I-90 E and Exit 25. Follow the directions above.

From the north, take I-93 S, get off at Exit 23 (Purchase Street/South Station), proceed straight onto Purchase Street at the end of the exit ramp, and take a left onto Summer Street at South Station. Drive about a mile down the road to D Street and make a right.

Parking

If you must drive, you'll probably be dropping your car in a garage or fenced parking lot. The establishments listed below are the closest to the BCEC.

LAZ Parking · 10 Necco St, 617-426-1556
Fitz-Inn Auto Parks · 30-60 Necco St, 617-426-1556
Farnsworth Parking Garage · 17-31 Farnsworth St, 617-737-8161
Stanhope Garage · 338 Congress St, 617-338-5657
Stanhope Garage · 381 Congress St, 617-426-5326
Fanpier Parking Lots · 28 Northern Ave, 617-737-0910
Transpark · 390 Congress St, 617-737-3363
Transpark · 25 Northern Ave, 617-451-7732

How to Get There—Mass Transit

The Silver Line stops at the BCEC (alight at the World Trade Center stop, escalate to the top entrance, and traverse the bridge). To connect to the Silver Line from points other than Logan Airport, take the T's Red Line to South Station. The BCEC is only a few hundred yards away from South Station, so if you want to stretch your legs take a stroll across Fort Point Channel instead of transferring to the Silver Line.

PLAZA LEVEL

SECOND LEVEL

THIRD LEVEL

General Information

NFT Map: 5
Address: 900 Boylston St, Boston, MA 02115
Phone: 617-954-2000
Websites: www.mccahome.com
              www.advantageboston.com

Overview

The John B. Hynes Veterans Memorial Convention Center is a relatively small center, with just 193,000 square feet of exhibit space, a 25,000-square-foot ballroom, and 41 meeting rooms. The Hynes is conveniently located in Back Bay with many hotels, historical sites, and tourist attractions within close proximity. Only a short walk from the Green Line's Hynes Convention Center/ICA stop, it is easily accessible by public transportation.

Once the big name in town for would-be conventioneers, the Hynes Convention Center now plays second fiddle to the Boston Convention and Exhibition Center (see page 204). Because the Hynes adjoins the Prudential complex and sits in the midst of a few thousand hotel rooms, it continues to attract convention business, focusing on mid-size meetings (think the American Association of Immunologists and the National Council of Teachers of Mathematics) and letting the biggest fish (like the International Boston Seafood Show) swim to the Southie Starship.

Services

The Hynes is used for conferences, meetings, exhibitions, and most other events where groups of people gather. (Word to the wise: Stay far, far away during CollegeFest.) To schedule an event and be assigned a personal coordinator, contact the sales department by phone at 617-954-2411, or by email at sales@massconvention.com.

Like every other big building in the universe, catering services at the Hynes are provided by Aramark. If you are considering planning a catered event, contact Aramark at 617-954-2330.

How to Get There—Driving

The Hynes is only four miles from Logan Airport. Two major roadways, I-93 and the Mass Pike (I-90), will deliver you close to the venue. From I-93, take Exit 26 B (Storrow Drive). Follow Storrow Drive for about two miles to the Fenway/Kenmore exit and head towards Fenway. Continue to the first set of lights and merge left onto Boylston Street.
From the Mass Pike, take Exit 22 (Prudential/Copley Place), stay left as you exit, and turn onto Huntington Avenue. At the next set of lights (Belvidere Street), take a right, follow the curve, and bear right onto Dalton Street. At the lights, turn right onto Boylston Street.

The main entrance to the Hynes is at 900 Boylston Street and is easily accessible to taxis and buses via an access lane, which is set apart from Boylston Street.

Parking

There are numerous parking garages within a three-block walk of the Hynes, totaling more than 4,400 spaces. There is metered parking available around the Hynes and adjacent streets, but these spots are hard to come by.

- **Prudential Center Parking Garage**,
  800 Boylston St, 2–10 hours for $34, and the daily maximum is $39. 617-236-3060.
- **Copley Place Parking Garage**,
  100 Huntington Ave (corner of Huntington Ave & Dartmouth St), $6 for the first half hour with an increase of $4 for every additional half hour, $26 for 3–10 hours, but only $7 for three hours with validation. Maximum day rate is $32. 617-369-5025.
- **Boston Marriott Hotel Copley Place**,
  100 Huntington Ave, self-parking $32 per day, valet parking $42 per day. 617-236-5800.
- **Westin Copley Place Parking Garage**,
  10 Huntington Ave, $21 for up to 2 hours, $27 for 2–4 hours, $32 for 4–6 hours, $35 for 6–8 hours, and $40 per night (with unlimited in-and-out access). 617-262-9600.
- **Colonnade Hotel Parking Garage**,
  120 Huntington Ave, $12 for the first hour, with a $4 increase every additional hour; $24 for 3–12 hours. $36 for overnight parking. 617-424-7000.
- **Back Bay Hilton Hotel Parking Garage**,
  40 Dalton St, $5 for 1/2 hour, $12 for 1 hour, $20 for 1–2 hours. $22 for 2–3 hours, $24 for 3–12 hours, $35 for overnight parking, $39 for overnight parking with valet service. 617-236-1100.

How to Get There—Mass Transit

The subway stops just two blocks away from the Hynes. Take the Green Line (B, C, or D train) to the Hynes Convention Center/ICA stop. Once you get off the subway, exit at any entrance and follow signs to the Hynes.

Bayside Expo & Conference Center

General Information

NFT Map: 32
Address: 200 Mt Vernon St, Columbia Point
Boston, MA 02125
Phone: 617-474-6000
Website: www.baysideexpo.com

Overview

Located three miles from downtown Boston, the Expo Center was once "New England's largest conference center and hotel complex," but has now ceded that crown to the much larger Boston Convention and Exhibition Center in Southie. Built on the site of a bankrupt mall and ringed by parking lots, the stark white, square Expo Center didn't win any design awards, but the building is functional, allowing visitors to focus on the boat, auto, RV, trade, or flower show that attracted them there in the first place.

The center's single-level exhibit space includes 12 meeting rooms, a full-service restaurant, lounge, cafeteria, and concessions. While they are convenient, on-site vendors' price-to-quality ratios are not the best. A small cup of coffee costs more than $2—and that's for the standard stuff, not a chic, unpronounceable foreign blend. An alternative would be to tailgate in the Expo Center's immense parking lot, but that will cost you, too ($12, to be precise), making the T the best choice for thrifty show-goers.

Adjacent to the exhibit space, the Executive Conference Center has everything an executive could wish for (well, almost everything), such as T-1 Internet access, wireless LAN, and wireless phone and video conferencing.

On nice days, be sure to take a drive around the back to the center's "bayside," where there are pleasant views of grassy Old Harbor, South Boston, and planes landing at Logan Airport.

The Doubletree Hotel (240 Mt Vernon St; 617-822-3600) markets itself to business travelers and vacationing tourists alike. This 197-room hotel's loftier rooms offer both city and ocean views. In addition to standard hotel amenities such as a fitness room, lounge, and a tour/recreation desk, the Doubletree Club offers free chocolate chip cookies at check-in.

How to Get There—Driving

From the south, take I-93 N to Exit 14. Stay in the right lane and follow Morrissey Boulevard. At the third set of lights, take a right onto Mt Vernon Street. Follow the signs and take the third left into the Bayside Expo main entrance.

From the north and west, take the Mass Pike (I-90) E to I-93 S. Get off I-93 at Exit 15 (Columbia Road). Stay in the left lane and take a left off the ramp. Go three-quarters of the way around the rotary and bear right onto Day Boulevard. Proceed past the Massachusetts State Police barracks and take the first right into the Bayside Expo north entrance.

Parking

Don't be fooled into off-site parking by the shifty folks at the Sovereign Bank parking lot across the street from the Expo Center. If you do, you'll have to lug your stuff across the street, only to walk by dozens of available spaces in the Expo Center lot. Make sure you follow the signs for on-site parking at Bayside Expo Center. Parking costs $12 on show days.

How to Get There—Mass Transit

Take the Red Line T or MBTA Commuter Rail to the JFK/UMass station. The Expo Center is directly across the street. The red "Beantown Trolley" runs from the T stop to the front entrance of the Expo Center, a distance of about a half-mile.

Bayside Expo & Conference Center

Hampden

Berkshire

Storage

Phones

Coat Room

Stairs to Bayside Conference Center Lobby

Pre-Function Space

Suffolk

Norfolk

Bristol

The Board Room

Phones

Elevators from Lobby

LEVEL 1

Exhibit Hall B

5

2

Exhibit Hall A

6

Exhibit Hall C

8

14
13
12
11
10

Exhibit Hall D

7

9

D
C
B
A

1   3

E   F   G

EXHIBITION AREA

Arlington

Storage

Berkeley

Clarendon

Dartmouth

Exeter

Lobby

Stairs to Level One

LEVEL 2

General Information

NFT Map: 32
Address: Columbia Point
Boston, MA 02125
Phone: 617-514-1600
Website: www.jfklibrary.org
Hours: 9 am–5 pm daily except Thanksgiving,
Christmas, and New Year's Day
Research Library is open M–F 8:30–
4:30 by appointment
Admission: Adults $10, seniors and students
$8, children $7, free for children 12 and
under

Overview

The John F. Kennedy Library and Museum, dedicated to our 35th president on October 20, 1979, houses 25 multimedia exhibits examining the life and work of JFK, his administration, his family, and his legacy. The library is one of eleven presidential libraries administered by the National Archives and Records Administration, a federal government agency. The library draws approximately 200,000 visitors each year.

The library, which overlooks Boston Harbor from windswept Columbia Point, was designed by architect I.M. Pei (who also designed the Christian Science Center next to the Pru and the Hancock Tower). The centerpiece of the complex is a nine-story concrete tower fronted by a glass-enclosed pavilion. The adjacent Stephen E. Smith Center, used for educational programs and conferences, opened in 1991. Outside on the lawn sits *Victura*, JFK's 26-foot sloop.

What's Inside

The JFK Library holds 8.4 million pages of presidential papers, 180,000 still photographs, six million feet of film and videotape, and 15,000 catalogued museum objects. The library also houses the world's most comprehensive collection of the papers and mementos of Ernest Hemingway, but they are available to professional researchers only. If you are a scholar who seeks access to Papa's papers, check the library's website to review the restrictive rules.

The library's Centennial Room displays rotating exhibits showcasing the Kennedy White House's embrace of cultural values and the arts. Visitors can watch a 17-minute film about the Kennedy administration before entering the main exhibit space. On weekends, the 2 pm showing of the introductory film is replaced by a 30-minute film about JFK's brother/attorney general, Robert F. Kennedy. Visitors can also watch a 20-minute film about the Cuban Missile Crisis.

A museum café serves light meals and snacks from 9 am to 5 pm, and the gift shop is open during visiting hours.

How to Get There—Driving

The JFK Library is off Morrissey Boulevard next to the UMass Boston campus. From the north or the south, take I-93 to Exit 14 (Morrissey Boulevard) and follow the signs. From the west, take the Mass Pike (I-90) east to the intersection with I-93. Take the exit toward I-93 S, get off I-93 at Exit 14, and follow the signs. The library provides free on-site parking.

How to Get There–Mass Transit

Take the T's Red Line to the JFK/UMass stop. A free shuttle bus runs between the T stop and the library. Shuttle buses run every 20 minutes between 8 am and 5 pm.

General Information

Cape Cod Chamber of Commerce:
508-362-3225; www.capecodchamber.org
Wellfleet Bay Wildlife Sanctuary:
508-349-2615; www.wellfleetbay.org
Cape Cod National Seashore Salt Pond Visitor Center:
508-349-3785; www.nps.gov/caco

Overview

Thanks to the eternal appeal of picturesque beaches, fried seafood, and miniature golf, Cape Cod is one of New England's most popular getaway destinations. Separated from mainland Massachusetts by the Cape Cod Canal, the Cape is located on the portion of the state that looks like a strong, flexing arm. There are only two roads that cross the canal, both via bridge; those Cape Cod Canal Tunnel stickers on locals' cars are just a mind game played on the out-of-towners.

The Cape is composed of 15 towns, with a permanent population of roughly 230,000 that swells to over 550,000 in the summer months. The islands of Martha's Vineyard and Nantucket are not officially part of Cape Cod, but are generally considered the same destination region. Each town has its own character: Bustling and bawdy Provincetown is home to a large and proud gay community, while Falmouth is a more tranquil, wooded locale.

Highlights and essentials:

• Beaches—With a total of 559.6 miles of coastline, the Cape is perhaps most well-known for its beaches, many of which are open to the public for a modest daily parking fee. The northern ocean water resists warming though, so swimming is generally, let's say, refreshing.

• Seafood—Fried clams, twin lobsters, steamers, baked stuffed quahogs…need we say more?

• Christmas Tree Shops—The merchandise sold at this thriving retail chain can be best described as discount "stuff." The company has expanded beyond its Cape Cod origins, but there is no better place to go when you need picture frames, beach toys, or souvenir tchotchkes.

• Miniature Golf—The Cape has elevated mini-golf landscaping to a fine art. Whether you prefer putting in a serene garden setting or braving darkened caves in a pirate-inspired golf adventure, Cape Cod has something for you.

• Lighthouses—If you have time to visit a lighthouse or two, we recommend the Nobska Point Lighthouse at Woods Hole, an oft-photographed white tower at the southwestern tip of Cape Cod, the Cape Cod (Highland) Lighthouse in North Truro, or the Chatham Lighthouse on the southeastern corner of the Cape.

• Whale Watches—Hop aboard a whale watch voyage out of Wood's Hole, Hyannis, or Provincetown to experience the truly breathtaking phenomenon of cruising alongside some of the world's largest and most powerful creatures.

The Towns

The Cape, about 70 miles in length, is often divided into three regions:

The Upper Cape—The first area you reach after crossing the canal, the Upper Cape includes the towns of Falmouth, Mashpee, Sandwich, and Bourne. For the best views and smoothest journey, avoid the highways and take surface routes, such as 28A, that take you close to the water. Film buffs might consider a visit to Woods Hole, where part of the movie *Jaws* was filmed.

The Mid Cape—Continuing eastward, the next area you will reach includes Dennis, Yarmouth, and Barnstable, a town containing seven villages: Hyannis, Osterville, Centerville, Cotuit, West Barnstable, Barnstable Village, and Marstons Mills. Almost 70% of the Cape's permanent population resides in the Hyannis area, so the downtown remains busy throughout the year, and it is about the only place in the area to find such national chains as Barnes and Noble or Old Navy. If such conventional commercialism isn't on your vacation itinerary, take the Old King's Highway (Route 6A) to stay in the Cape mood.

The Outer Cape—Home of the peaceful Cape Cod National Seashore, Nickerson State Park, and the quiet towns of Brewster, Orleans, Eastham, Wellfleet, Chatham, Harwich, and Truro, it's difficult to imagine the spectacle sitting at the tip of the Outer Cape: Provincetown. At land's end sits one of the most "out" towns, where gay couples are as plentiful as seagulls, and the prevailing aesthetic can best be described as "flamboyant." After a day in the sun, cruise into P-town for a night of revelry. Gay or straight, the town knows how to party. For full effect, visit during Carnival in August. More information is available at www.provincetown.com.

The Islands—Martha's Vineyard and Nantucket each possess a distinct feel. Martha's Vineyard is well known for great beaches, ocean vistas, and the annual (and controversial) Monster Shark Tournament. It's even better known for its well-heeled folk and the Kennedy Compound. Nantucket, only three and a half by fourteen miles, is a quaint New England destination where tourists roam the cobble-stoned streets year-round. In addition to shops and galleries, the downtown is home to the Nantucket Whaling Museum. The best way around the island is by moped or a bicycle but remember to pack a lunch if you head to the beaches because there are no restaurants or snack bars.

The Outdoors

Sculpted dunes, haunting marshlands, and miles of hiking trails make the Cape an ideal area for outdoor exploration. If the water calls, you can splash about at one of the Cape's many bay or ocean beaches, take a boat out to sea, dive or snorkel in the bay, canoe or kayak, parasail, kiteboard, or enjoy one of the whale- or seal-watching excursions offered.

Flora and fauna enthusiasts come here to explore the lush plant and animal life at the Cape's many sanctuaries. The Audubon Society's Wellfleet Bay Wildlife Sanctuary is the only sanctuary with a visitor's center. It boasts 1,000 acres of woodlands, wetlands, and grasslands that

attract an exciting variety of wildlife, including songbirds and shorebirds. Five miles of scenic trails wind through the various habitats, while the newly renovated Nature Center includes "green" elements such as solar heating and composting toilets. Inside the nature center, you'll find two 700-gallon aquariums that feature the underwater worlds of the salt marsh and tidal flats. Other sanctuaries on the Cape include Long Pasture near Barnstable, Skunknett River near Osterville, Sampson's Island (accessible only by private boat from local marinas and town landings), and Ashumet Holly near Falmouth. The Cape Cod National Seashore Salt Pond visitor center in Eastham offers guided tours and nature walks through the salt marshes.

Monomoy Island, established in 1944 as a National Wildlife Refuge, is a barrier island that sits ten miles south of Chatham. It is prime habitat for migratory birds and a seal population that has grown in recent years. It is not uncommon to sit on Nauset beach to the north and see seals swimming regularly along the shoreline, which wasn't the case ten years ago. Monomoy has hiking trails and bird watching opportunities as well as commercial boat tours for seal-watching. Check out www.fws.gov/northeast/monomoy.

Sports

Cape Cod is an ideal location for sport fishing. Charters and tours are available and, for those looking to have a little fun on the water, ships such as the *Yankee* offer party cruises, perfect for those who hate lugging around a heavy cooler. Be warned: Drinking and waves are not always the best combo.

Golf is also popular here. There are a dozen or so courses on the Cape, varying in price, size, and level of difficulty. Dennis Pines and Dennis Highlands are two highly-respected municipal courses where a challenging game can be had for a reasonable price, and Highland Links in Truro is perched atop sheer bluffs that overlook the ocean.

Biking is another favorite pastime in the area, with free trails including the epic 22-mile RailTrail at Cape Cod National Park. The trail runs along the bed of a defunct railroad (hence the name) from Dennis (get on at Route 134 just south of Exit 9 from Route 6) to the South Wellfleet General Store.

Diehard baseball fans shouldn't miss the 104-year-old Cape Cod League, where top college athletes are recruited to play in the summer, many of whom go on to the majors. Thurman Munson, "Nomah" Garciaparra, Jason Varitek, and other stars once played in one of the league's ten teams. Attending one of their early evening games is what summer is all about. Bring your beach chair, grab a hot dog, and watch the little kids scramble for foul balls.

Arts and Culture

Though better-known for its natural splendor, Cape Cod also boasts a thriving arts community. Every summer, the Cape Cod Melody Tent in Hyannis hosts popular music and comedy acts ranging from Willie Nelson to Lewis Black. In Dennis, the Cape Playhouse mounts theatrical productions such as *Guys and Dolls* and *Thoroughly Modern Millie*.

Galleries, studios, specialty museums, and whimsical artisan shops are to be found on almost every corner. For help navigating, drop $9.95 on Amazon.com or at the Cape Cod Chamber of Commerce for a copy of *Arts and Artisans Trails*, a book featuring self-guided tours of the Cape and Islands that highlight the best of the area's arts scene.

Ever since Henry David Thoreau penned *Cape Cod*, the region has also been the full-time or summer home of a number of notable authors. Norman Mailer, the late Kurt Vonnegut, and mystery maven Mary Higgins Clark are among the Cape's more prominent literary names.

If you aspire to join this tradition, check out the Fine Arts Work Center in Provincetown, where summer workshops in painting, drawing, and writing could help you find your hidden muse.

How to Get There

By Car: The only two driving routes onto Cape Cod are via the overburdened Bourne and Sagamore bridges. This limited access has traditionally resulted in multi-mile gridlock on Friday evenings and Saturday mornings. The Sagamore Rotary has recently been replaced with a direct ramp known as the flyover, intended to tame the traffic. Plan to travel outside of the peak times and slowdowns should be minimal. Once on the Cape, most places are easily drivable, though downtown areas such as Hyannis and Provincetown can get a bit tangled up.

By Ferry: Avoid traffic and cut down on gas expenditures by hopping a ferry to Provincetown or the Islands. Bringing along a car or bike generally increases the fare, but the price may be a bargain if you have limited patience for the traffic that driving across the Canal can entail.

Bay State Cruise Company • 617-748-1428 •
www.boston-ptown.com
Boston-Provincetown. May–October.
Round-trip fare: $44 on weekend excursion ferry, $58–$79 on daily fast ferry. $12 for bikes.

Boston Harbor Cruises Provincetown Fast Ferry •
617-227-4321 • www.bostonharborcruises.com
Boston-Provincetown. May–October.
Round-trip fare: $58–$79. $6 for bikes.

Hy-Line Cruises • 800-492-8082 • www.hy-linecruises.com
Hyannis-Martha's Vineyard. High-speed ferry,
April–October. Standard ferry, May–October.
Hyannis-Nantucket, High-speed ferry year-round.
Standard ferry, May–October.
Martha's Vineyard-Nantucket. June–September
Round-trip fare: $25–$71. $12 for bikes.

Island Queen Ferry • 508-548-4800 • www.islandqueen.com
Falmouth Harbor- Martha's Vineyard. June–September.
Round-trip fare: $9–$18. $6 for bikes.

Steamship Authority • 508-693-9130 •
http://steamshipauthority.com
Woods Hole-Martha's Vineyard. Year-round.
Hyannis-Nantucket, Year-round.
Woods Hole-Martha's Vineyard round-trip fare:
$8-$15. $6 for a bike. $85–$155 for a car.
Hyannis-Nantucket round-trip fare:
$17–$65. $12 for a bike. $250–$430 for a car.

Berklee College of Music

1. 130 Massachusetts Avenue
2. Berklee Performance Center
3. 150 Massachusetts Avenue
4. 155 Massachusetts Avenue
5. 171 Massachusetts Avenue
6. The Berklee Bookstore
7. 120 Belvidere Street
8. 19 Belvidere Street
9. 1140 Boylston Street
10. 22 The Fenway
11. 198 Hemingway Street
12. Boston Architectural Center
13. 921 Boylston Street
14. 264-270 Commonwealth Avenue
15. 100 Massachusetts Avenue
16. 168 Massachusetts Avenue
17. 899 Boylston Street
18. 867 Boylan Street
19. 855 Boylan Street

General Information

NFT Map: 5
Address: 1140 Boylston St, Boston, MA 02215
Phone: 617-266-1400
Website: www.berklee.edu

Overview

Berklee is the largest independent music college in the world and calls itself the "premier institution for the study of contemporary music." Founded in 1945 by pianist and MIT-trained engineer Lawrence Berk, the school became accredited in 1973. Berklee offers four-year degrees as well as diploma programs that allow students to forego the liberal arts and focus exclusively on music. Facilities include more than 250 private practice rooms. In addition to performance, students study Music Business/Management, Music Education, and Music Therapy. During the summer, the school offers specialized programs including Berklee in Los Angeles.

The college enrolls close to 4,000 students, with the highest percentage (about 26%) of international students of any college in the United States from more than 70 different countries. The student body is a funky, diverse lot, with many musicians from Japan, Korea, Germany, Switzerland, and Brazil. They tend to congregate on Mass Ave, particularly outside the Berklee Performance Center where bedraggled musical geniuses stand around with their instruments. Tracy Bonham, Melissa Etheridge, Patty Larkin, Branford Marsalis, Howard Shore, and Aimee Mann are among Berklee's notable alumni. Furthermore, Berklee was the first college to recognize the guitar as a principal instrument and develop a curriculum for it back in the '60s.

Tuition

For the 2009–2010 academic year, tuition fees will amount to $33,780 and housing will be an additional $15,080 per year. However, costs vary between degree and diploma programs, and additional fees may apply. Fourteen million dollars in scholarship funds are available to Berklee students each year.

Sports

There are no college-level athletics at Berklee, but student clubs do offer soccer, basketball, softball, and yoga, among others. Nearby fitness facilities, including the YMCA, the Tennis and Racquet Club, and Boston Kung-Fu Tai-Chi Institute offer discounted rates for students. Much more popular than sports are the 350-plus student music ensembles in an impressive range of styles.

Culture on Campus

Housed in the historic Fenway Theater, the 1,220-seat Berklee Performance Center (BPC) stands as one of the finest concert halls on the East Coast. Located at 136 Massachusetts Avenue near the intersection with Boylston Street, the BPC offers numerous performances by major concert promoters as well as faculty and student concerts throughout the year. To attend a performance, check out the Event Calendar at www.berkleebpc.com or call the box office at 617-747-2261.

Departments

Admissions 617-747-2047
Financial Aid . . . . 617-747-2274 or 800-538-3844
Registrar. 617-747-2240
Housing 617-747-2292
Alumni Relations. 617-747-2236
Berklee Performance Center 617-747-2474
Library. 617-747-2258

Newton Campus
1. Alumni House
2. Law Library
3. East Wing
4. Smith Wing
5. Stuart
6. Kenny-Cottle
7. Barat
8. Mary
9. Quonset Hut

Game Field

Rochester

Westchester

Practice Field

Newton Centre

Newton Campus

Centre St

Sumner St

Chase St

Warren St

Glen Ave

Mill St

Commonwealth Ave

Colby St

Mass Pike (Exit 17)

90

Chestnut Hill Campus
1. More
2. 110 St. Thomas More R
3. Southwell Career Cente
4. 90 More Road
5. Corcoran Common
6. Robsham Theater
7. Bapst Art Library
8. Bea House
9. Lawrence
10. Hopkins
11. Heffernan
12. Faber
13. Rahner
14. Donaldson
15. Bourneuf
16. Brock
17. Bowman
18. Botolph
20. Lyons
21. Gasson
22. Devlin
23. Higgins
24. Fulton
25. Cushing
26. Service Building
27. Administrative Office
28. Merkert Chemistry Cent
29. Campion
30. McGuinn
31. Carney
32. McElroy Commons
33. Hovey
34. Daly
35. Roberts
36. Canisus
37. IREPM
38. Connolly Carriage Hous
39. Murray Carriage House
40. Waul House
41. Murray
42. Connolly House
43. Haley
44. Haley Carriage House

Tudor Rd

Crosby Rd

Priscilla Rd

Hammond St

College Rd

Quincy Rd

Mayflower Rd

Old Colony Rd

Waban Hill Rd

Beacon St

Suffolk Rd

Old England Rd

Old Orchard Rd

Lee Rd

Stone Ave

Acacia Ave

Reservoir Ave

O'Neill Library

Campanella Way

Conte Forum

Alumni Stadium

Flynn Rec Complex

Campanella Wy

Visitor Parking Entrance

Shea Field

MDC Park

St Thomas More Rd

Chestnut Hill Dr

Chestnut Hill Campus

Chestnut Hill Rd

Chestnut Hill Reservoir

General Information

Main Campus: 140 Commonwealth Ave,
                 Chestnut Hill, MA 02467
Newton Campus: 885 Centre St,
                 Newton Center, MA 02459
Phone: 617-552-8000
Website: www.bc.edu

Overview

It all began one day in Paris in 1534, when a group of students at the University of Paris got together and decided to combine their devotion to God with their commitment to bettering society. They called themselves the Society of Jesus, or the Jesuits. A few centuries later, in 1863, three Jesuits opened a college in the South End and cleverly named it Boston College. The college began with just 22 students, but even then the Jesuit profs envisioned a grander institution that would integrate intellectual development with religious and ethical growth.

Over the past century-and-a-half, the school has drifted a bit, both geographically and ethically. Once located in Boston proper, the school now sits six miles to the west, sprawling over 117 acres in Chestnut Hill and another 40 in Newton. And while the college is still officially Jesuit through and through, today's BC students aren't known for being particularly pious or devout.

BC's 9,000 undergraduates and 4,700 graduate students have a bit of a bad reputation among locals and students at other area colleges—the stereotype pegs all BC guys as binge-drinking jock wannabes sporting backwards baseball caps, more likely to be looking for a fight than searching for knowledge. It is widely rumored that the girls' appetite for Abercrombie & Fitch is matched only by their thirst for peach schnapps. Overlooked by naysayers is BC's excellent academic reputation. Its 8 colleges and schools offer degree programs in more than fifty fields of study, and *U.S. News & World Report* rated BC the 34th best college in the country. In 2003, two BC students were selected as Rhodes Scholars and a school-record of 14 Fulbright Grants were awarded to graduating seniors.

Tuition

For the 2009–2010 academic year, undergraduate tuition will amount to $45,830 with room, board and fees. However, approximately 65% of students receive financial aid.

Sports

Boston College has been hailed by *U.S. News & World Report* as having one of the top 20 overall college sports programs. Supporting 31 varsity and 38 club and intramural sports, the college boasts a diverse and strong athletic department. The varsity teams all compete at the NCAA Division I level. In 2007, the football team won the Meineke Car Care Bowl, making it BC's seventh consecutive bowl win. The biggest game every year is against Notre Dame. The men's hockey team has been perennially successful, winning the national championship in 2001 and losing in the semifinals of the Frozen Four in 2004. In 2008, however, Boston College won, much to the BU's chagrin. In 2008 Boston College won the Beanpot, which is a hockey tournament amongst Boston colleges.

Culture on Campus

The Robsham Theater Arts Center is Boston College's creative center. Built in 1981, the theater seats 591 people. The building also includes a black box theater that seats 150–200 people. The three main departments housed in the facility are the Department of Theater Arts, the Robsham Dance and Theater Company, and the Boston Liturgical Dance Ensemble. The university presents four faculty-directed and two student-directed productions each year, and 20 musical and dance groups perform throughout the year. BC also has its share of improv and sketch comedy troupes including one that puts on comedic, part-improv murder mysteries once per semester. Worth checking out to get a better sense of the school's culture is the Web site for "The BC" (www.bc.edu/clubs/thebc/) a send-up of "The OC" that is set at the Heights (local-speak for BC's Chestnut Hill campus). Download one of the show's commercials such as "Jon Bon Jesuits" for an hysterical, rocking-good time.

Another source of culture at Boston College is the McMullen Museum of Art. Located on the first floor of Devlin Hall, the museum is housed in one of the many Neo-Gothic buildings on the main campus. Aside from its notable permanent collection, the museum has frequent exhibitions of international and scholarly importance from all periods and cultures. The museum is free and open to the public. Hours: Mon–Fri 11 am–4 pm and Sat–Sun 12 pm–5 pm.

Departments

Undergraduate Admissions 617-552-3100
A&S Graduate Admissions 617-552-3265
Carroll Graduate School of Management . . 617-552-3920
Connell School of Nursing 617-552-4928
Law School Admissions 617-552-4350
Lynch School of Education 617-552-4214
Graduate School of Social Work 617-552-4024
Student Services 617-552-3300
. . . . 800-294-0294
Athletic Departments and Tickets 617-552-GoBC
O'Neill Library 617-552-4470

General Information

NFT Map: 16
Address: One Sherborn St, Boston, MA 02215
Phone: 617-353-2000
Website: www.bu.edu

Overview

If you really want to go to school *in* Boston, BU is the school for you. Consisting of a strip of buildings along Commonwealth Avenue, BU's campus doesn't win any points for style, beauty, or landscape architecture (since that would require having a clearly defined landscape). Aside from several thousand red banners on the lampposts that say "Boston University," and a larger than usual concentration of jaywalking young folk along Comm Ave, there's little indication that you've even entered BU's domain.

The fourth-largest private university in the country, the school's "campus" is the learning center for all students and the residence of many of its 30,000 undergraduates and grad students. The upshot of the ill-defined BU campus is that its students are truly living in the city. BU students make the best of the little green space they have. "The Beach," a strip of greenery on the inbound side of Storrow Drive (which runs along the Charles), is a springtime hotspot for socializing and sunbathing.

When the university was founded in 1839, it was intended to be a theological school for ministers of the Methodist Episcopal Church. As the years went by, the university expanded its curriculum in order to accommodate the needs and interests of its growing student population. Today, there are 11 schools and colleges and over 250 different degree programs. Boston University students represent all 50 states, as well as 140 countries. BU also holds the distinction of having the most property owned by a non-government institution in the City of Boston. The university also boasts a bevy of outspoken alumni including Howard Stern, Bill O'Reilly, and Rosie O'Donnell (who didn't graduate).

Longtime president and infamous curmudgeon John Silber stepped down in 1996 after more than thirty years of leading the school to wherever he pleased. His replacement, former NASA chief Daniel Goldin, was called off the job even before he began his first day due to conflicting ideas about how the university should be run. Goldin said he took the job on the condition that Silber would not occupy a seat on the board of trustees. The Executive Committee balked at this stipulation and, after a little mud was slung, Goldin's termination was signed, thereby embarrassing the university in national headlines. Following the reign of an interim president since the resignation of Jon Westling in 2002, BU's tenth and current president, Robert A. Brown, was inaugurated to the post in April 2006.

Tuition

Undergraduate tuition costs run at about $50,288 per year with room, board, and fees. Graduate student tuition, fees, and expenses vary by college.

Sports

Notwithstanding the termination of the university's football program in 1997, the Terriers have quite an impressive athletics department. With 24 NCAA Division I varsity sports, Boston University provides a rich environment for sports lovers. The department prides itself on its equal emphasis on women's and men's varsity sports. The men's varsity ice hockey team is, by far, the most popular sports team at BU, with the most enthusiastic community support. There is fierce competition every year for the Beanpot—the "New England Invitational" tournament. In the past 53 years, BU has won the Beanpot 28 times, with Boston College being their biggest rival for the title. The university's hockey and basketball teams play in the Agganis Arena, a spiffy new facility that also hosts other sporting and entertainment events.

Culture on Campus

The first university to have a music program, BU remains committed to the arts. The Boston University Art Gallery is located at 855 Commonwealth Avenue. Although the gallery has no permanent collection, the architecture of the building is like an exhibit unto itself. Alluding to both the Classical and the Medieval, the columns that adorn the façade are a rare beauty and have attracted many people on that basis alone. You would never guess that the building is actually a converted Buick dealership. If this piques your interest, you'll be happy to learn that the gallery is open and free to the public, but only during the academic school year: Tues–Fri 10 am–5 pm and Sat–Sun 1 pm–5 pm.

Departments

Undergraduate Admissions	617-353-2300
Graduate Admissions	617-353-2696
Graduate School of Management	617-353-9720
School of Medicine	617-638-4630
School of Law	617-353-3100
School of Education	617-353-4237
School of Public Health	617-638-4640
School of Social Work	617-353-3765
Athletic Department and Ticket Office	617-353-GoBU
Mugar Memorial Library	617-353-3732

Building Legend

1. 1019 Commonwealth Ave (major residence)
2. Case Athletic Center
3. West Campus (major residence)
4. Office of Housing
5. Fitness and Recreation Center
6. 10 Buick St (major residence)
7. Center for English Language and Orientation Programs
8. Comptroller; Financial Assistance; Registrar; Student Health Services
9. College of General Studies
10. College of Fine Arts; University Art Gallery
11. School of Hospitality Administration; Metropolitan College Academic departments and other programs
12. Boston University Academy
13. George Sherman Union; Dean of Students; Student Activities Center; Howard Thurman Center
14. Mugar Memorial Library;University Information Center
15. School of Law
16. Metropolitan College; Summer Term
17. School of Theology; University Professors Program
18. Marsh Chapel
19. Photonics Center
20. College of Arts and Sciences
21. School of Social Work
22. Graduate School of Arts and Sciences
23. The Tsai Performance Art Center
24. The Castle
25. Warren Towers (major residence)
26. Office of Information Technology
27. College of Engineering
28. Sargent College of Health and Rehabilitation Sciences
29. College of Communication
30. School of Education
31. Morse Auditorium
32. Biological and Physics Research Buildings
33. The Towers (major residence)
34. Chancellor's Office; President's Office; Provost's Office; Development and Alumni Relations
35. School of Management
36. 575 Commonwealth Ave (major residence)
37. Metcalf Science Center
38. Admissions Reception Center
39. Kenmore Classroom Building
40. Shelton Hall (major residence)
41. International Students and Scholars Office; Career Services; Disability Services; Judicial Affairs & Student Safety
42. University Computers
43. Barnes & Noble at BU; Asian Archeology & Cultural History
44. Hotel Commonwealth
45. Miles Standish Hall (major residence)
46. Danielsen Hall (major residence) (off map)
47. Agganis Arena

Colleges & Universities · Emerson College

1. Ansin Building
2. Cutler Majestic Theatre
3. Little Building
4. Walker Building
5. Tufte Performance and Production Center
6. Student Campus Center
7. Student Residence
8. Student Union
9. Student Residence
10. Student Residence
11. Piano Row Residence

General Information

NFT Maps: 3 & 6
Address: 120 Boylston St, Boston, MA 02116
Phone: 617-824-8500
Website: www.emerson.edu

Overview

Emerson College is the country's only comprehensive college or university dedicated solely to communication and the arts in a liberal arts context. In close proximity to Boston's Theater District, Emerson is near all of the city's major media interests. Founded as a small oratory school in 1880, Emerson has expanded its curriculum over the years to include other forms of communication. Today, Emerson specializes in communications, marketing, communication sciences and disorders, journalism, the performing arts, the visual and media arts, and writing, literature, and publishing. Emerson also operates semester-study programs in Los Angeles and the Netherlands. There is also a thriving continuing education department, recently renamed the Department of Professional Studies and Special Programs, which offers—besides communications classes—certificate programs in media, publishing, and screenwriting.

The college enrolls about 3,000 full-time undergraduates and 1,000 graduate students, many of whom can be found sporting funky haircuts and smoking outside Emerson buildings between classes. Students take pride in their award-winning radio station, WERS (88.9 FM). Most alumni go on to pursue careers in the communications and entertainment fields. Notable alumni include talk show host Jay Leno, actor Denis Leary, and entrepreneur and make-up artist Bobbi Brown.

Tuition

Undergraduate tuition fees were $29,208. Room and board costs about $12,280. Add on books, service fees, activity fees, and personal expenses. Graduate student tuition, fees, and expenses vary by the number of credits taken.

Sports

Although Emerson does have an athletic department, it has never been one of the school's top priorities. Since most of the students attending Emerson College are interested primarily in the fields of communications and performing arts, sports are considered nothing more than a lighthearted diversion. Still, Emerson College sponsors 13 men's and women's varsity teams that compete in the NCAA's Division III.

Culture on Campus

Because Emerson considers itself an arts school, it takes great pride in its theater. The aptly named Majestic Theatre was built in 1903 as an opera house. In 2001, the college closed the theater temporarily for renovation and reopened its doors in 2003. Today, the historic venue seats 1,200 people and has become an integral part of the campus. Not only does it provide a venue for all types of productions by Emerson students, it also serves the greater New England community. It hosts more operas than any other theater in New England and is the top stop for most touring dance companies. To visit the theater or check out a performance, go to the theater box office located at 219 Tremont Street in Boston or call 617-824-8000.

Departments

Undergraduate Admissions Office 617-824-8600
Graduate Admissions Office 617-824-8610
Majestic Theatre 617-824-8000
                                                       or 800-233-3123
Athletics Department 617-824-8690
Fitness Center. 617-824-8692
Library. 617-824-8668

Dorchester Bay

MAP 32

UMass-Boston

JFK Library PAGE 210

Mt Vernon St

University Dr W

University Dr N

Columbia Pl

To Morrissey Blvd
JFK/UMass
T Stop

Clark Athletic Center

Quinn Admin

Massachusetts State Archives/ Commonwealth Museum

Healey Library

Science Center

Site of Student Center

University Dr S

McCormack

Wheatley (CCDE Office)

University Dr E

General Information

NFT Map:	32
Address:	100 Morrissey Blvd, Boston, MA 02125
Phone:	617-287-5000
Website:	www.umb.edu

Overview

The University of Massachusetts Boston is one of five UMass campuses. The campus opened in 1982 when UMass acquired Boston State College. The university has been described as a sensibly priced, high-quality college that provides excellent academic programs to people from all walks of life. UMass Boston aims "to bring technical, intellectual, and human resources to the community."

The school's most famous alum is Boston Mayor Thomas M. Menino. Not exactly renowned for his oratory skills, he is nevertheless a well respected champion of the low-income neighborhoods. Menino graduated from UMass Boston at the age of 45 in 1988 with a degree in community planning. UMass Boston's campus, which has been described as a "concrete jungle," is only three miles from downtown Boston and is pretty easy to reach by public transportation. (Take the Red Line to JFK/UMass Station, then jump on the shuttle buses, which run almost constantly.)

While on campus, be sure to check out the Campus Center—simply look for the most modern-looking (and attractive) building on campus. A graceful building featuring huge windows that overlook magnificent Boston Harbor, the Center makes it easy to forget that the rest of the campus is pockmarked by bomb-shelteresque architecture. Also, a trip to campus should always include a quick walk or drive over to the JFK Presidential Library, which shares Columbia Point Peninsula with UMASS Boston.

Tuition

Recent controversial tuition hikes have put undergraduate tuition costs at about $22,800 per year for out-of-towners and $10,600 for in-state residents. Graduate tuition costs run at about $22,081 per year for out-of-towners and $11,574 for in-state residents.

Sports

The University of Massachusetts Boston offers 14 varsity sports, including basketball, soccer, lacrosse, and ice hockey. All teams compete in the NCAA's Division III. The Beacon Fitness Center is open to all students and staff free of charge. The UMass teams are called the Beacons, carry the slogan "Follow the Light," and have been named All-Americans 64 times in seven sports. UMass Boston provides a community service program which offers, for free or at very low cost, the use of all athletic facilities and coaches to the general public.

Culture on Campus

Often considered a commuter-centric school, UMass Boston is nonetheless a mini-mecca of culture, offering everything from rampant community-service opportunities to myriad student-run publications. The current Performing Arts Department is actually a conglomerate of three previously separate theater arts, music, and dance departments. Music courses provide grounding in music theory, history, and performance. Private music lessons are also available for one credit. The college Jazz Band, Chamber Orchestra, and Chamber Singers all give public performances at the end of each semester.

Departments

Undergraduate Admissions	617-287-6100
Graduate Admissions	617-287-5700
Graduate College of Education	617-287-7600
College of Nursing & Health Sciences	617-287-7500
Performing Arts Department	617-287-5640
Athletic Department	617-287-7801
Healey Library	617-287-5900
Honors Program	617-287-5520
Campus Center	617-287-4800

1. Quad Athletic Facility
2. Hilles Library
3. Harkness Commons/Child
4. Pound Hall/Administration
5. Maxwell-Dworkin/Pierce
6. Areeda/Langdell Hall/Library
7. Pierce
8. Austin
9. Jefferson Lab
10. Music Building
11. Science Center/Cabot Science Library
12. Hoffman Lab/Mallinckrodt Lab/
    Naito/Gibbs/Converse/Conant Lab
13. 38 Oxford
14. Biological Labs
15. Fairchild Biochemistry Lab
16. Memorial Hall/Sanders Theatre/Annenburg Hall
17. Graduate School of Design/Gund Hall
18. Fogg Art Museum/Busch-Reisinger Museum
19. Carpenter Center
20. Barker Center
21. Loeb Library
22. Lamont Library
23. Widener Library
24. Adams House/Westmorely
25. American Repertory Theatre/
    Loeb Drama Center
26. Brattle Theatre
27. Taubman
28. One Eliot/Littauer/Belfer
29. Malkin Athletic Center
30. Amelia Tataronis Rieman
    Center for the Performing Arts

31. Palmer Dixon Courts
32. Dillon Field House
33. Briggs Cage
34. Blodgett Pool
35. Bright Hockey Center
36. Murr Center
37. Gordon Indoor Track
    & Tennis Facility
38. Cotting
39. Morgan Hall
40. Baker Library
41. Aldrich
42. Dean's House
43. Shad Hall
44. Class of 1959 Chapel
45. Rock Center
46. Cumnock
47. Spangler Center
48. Burden
49. Baker Hall
50. McCollum
51. McArthur
52. Kresge

Radcliffe
Quadrangle

North
Hall

Harvard
Divinity
School

Harvard Law
School

Harvard Yard

Cambridge Common

PAGE 186

Old
Burying
Ground

MAP 20

Radcliffe
Yard

Mason St

Longfellow
Park

Harvard
Yard

Harvard

2A

J F Kennedy
School of
Government

JFK Park

Memorial Dr

Charles River

Anderson Bridge

Harvard Business
School

Harvard
Stadium

Soldiers
Field
Athletic
Area

Soldiers
Field
Park

Soldiers Field Rd

Burns
Playground

General Information

NFT Map: 20
Address: University Hall, Cambridge, MA 02138
Phone: 617-495-1000
Website: www.harvard.edu

Overview

You've probably heard quite a bit about Harvard. Chances are, you associate it with academic excellence, cutting-edge research, red brick, and students with at least two roman numerals after their names.

That stereotype hits the nail at least partly on the head. Founded in 1636, Harvard remains the richest and most revered university in the country (and perhaps even the world). True to myth, its pool of 19,000+ undergrads and grad students include children of royalty, famous actors, heirs, heiresses, and an assortment of other fortunate sons and daughters. But the truth is that these folks are more the exception than the rule. Harvard's deep pockets have allowed it to offer generous scholarships and increase the cultural and financial diversity of its student population (and to allow such great intellectuals like Conan O'Brien to attend). The same loot also helps them net world-class professors in each of its 11 schools and colleges.

With the goal of properly housing and educating "the best of the best" in all fields from arts and humanities to business and technology, Harvard is hungry for more than just talented minds. The university continues to gobble up land in Cambridge and across the river in Allston, disgruntling some locals.

Perhaps Harvard needs more space for its livestock. A phrase coined to mock the local accent states that you cannot "pahk the cah in Havahd Yahd," since automobile traffic is prohibited there. However, an old contract clause allows each full professor to pasture one cow in the Yard. Assistant faculty members are allowed a sheep. Luckily for Harvard, no professor in recent memory has taken advantage of this opportunity.

In early 2007, Harvard made news yet again by naming its first female president, historian Drew G. Faust.

Tuition

Undergraduate tuition, room, board, and college fees amounted to $54,800. Graduate school tuition varies depending on the program.

Sports

Athletics at Harvard began around 1780, when a small group of students began challenging each other to wrestling matches, thereby starting an early version of *Fight Club*. Since then, the spirit of athletic competition has remained integral to the Harvard experience. Harvard introduced its crew team in 1844, and won its first championship just two years later. Since then, the men's heavyweight and lightweight crew teams have won 15 championships between them and the women's lightweight crew team has won five championships. Years ago, Harvard was a football powerhouse, always ranked among the top ten in the nation. Harvard still consistently tops the Ivy League, and games against the likes of Yale continue to fill century-old Harvard Stadium on fall afternoons. The men's tennis team has also been a source of pride in the athletic department, consistently producing top-class players, many of whom have gone on to play professionally. In the fall of 2004, the team captured their second consecutive Eastern College Athletic Conference title.

Not all jocks are dumb: Since 1920, Harvard athletes have netted 45 Rhodes Scholarships.

Not all nerds suck at sports: More than 100 Harvard athletes have participated in the Olympics.

Culture on Campus

Harvard boasts four art museums (free every day after 4:30 pm and from 10 am until noon on Saturdays), each showcasing art from different parts of the world. The university also runs an extensive music and theater program. Music department performances are held in the prestigious Sanders Theater, renowned for its acoustics and design. Aside from hosting most of the orchestral and choral performances by Harvard groups, Sanders Theatre is also a popular venue for professional groups such as the Boston Philharmonic, the Boston Chamber Music Society, and the Boston Baroque.

Harvard's various dance troupes perform at the Amelia Tataronis Rieman Center for the Performing Arts.

The country's only not-for-profit theater company housing a resident acting company and an international training conservatory, the American Repertory Theater (A.R.T.) operates out of the Harvard University campus.

A building shaped suspiciously like "Linguo, the Grammar Robot" of *Simpsons* fame houses the offices of the Harvard Lampoon on Mt Auburn Street. Graduates of this famed humor publication have gone on to work for *Saturday Night Live*, *The Simpsons*, and *The Office*.

Departments

Undergraduate Admissions	617-495-1551
Graduate School of Arts and Sciences	617-495-1814
Graduate School of Education	617-495-0740
Kennedy School of Government	617-495-1100
Harvard Crimson	617-576-6565
Harvard Law School	617-495-3100
Harvard Medical School	617-432-1000
Harvard Business School	617-495-6000
Athletics Department Ticket Office	877-GO-HARVARD or 617-495-2211
Sanders Theatre	617-496-2222

General Information

NFT Maps: 26 & 27
Address: 77 Massachusetts Ave, Cambridge, MA 02139
Phone: 617-253-1000
Website: www.mit.edu

Overview

Just down the Chuck River from Harvard, MIT is one of the top tech schools in the world. The school's 998 faculty and over 10,000 slide-rule-bearing graduate and undergraduate students inhabit a 168-acre "factory of learning" that features both neoclassical domes and some of the most aggressively modernist buildings in Boston (including the Stata Center, designed by world-renowned architect Frank Gehry).

MIT profs are infamous for assigning massive amounts of work, but some students can't seem to get enough of engineering, spending their downtime planning and executing "hacks,"

technically elaborate pranks. A frequent target of hackers is MIT's Great Dome. In 1994, a replica of an MIT police cruiser appeared atop the dome. In 1996, it was adorned with a gigantic beanie cap complete with a fully functioning propeller. Just before the release of *Star Wars Episode One: The Phantom Menace*, students decorated the dome to look like the robot R2-D2. Harvard is another frequent target of hackers. During a 1990 Harvard-Yale football game, players and spectators alike were surprised when an 8.5' x 3.5' rocket-propelled banner with the letters MIT sprang up from under the end zone as Yale lined up to kick a field goal.

Tuition

Undergraduate tuition fees, room, and board total $52,000.

Sports

Whoever said science nerds can't play sports was totally right. Nevertheless, they keep trying, posting moderate success in both Division II and III. Believe it or not, MIT actually boasts the largest

1. Pierce Laboratory
2. Fluid Dynamic Laboratory/ Dept of Mathematics
3. Maclaurin Buildings
4. Maclaurin Buildings
5. Pratt School
6. Eastman Laboratories
6B. Solvent Storage
8. Rogers Building
9. 21 Ames Street
9. Center for Advanced Educational Services
10. Maclaurin Building/Alumni Center
11. Homberg Building
12. 60 Vassar Street
12A. Waste Chemical Storage
13. Bush Building
14. Hayden Memorial Library
16. Dorrance Building
17. Wright Brothers Wind Tunnel
18. Dreyfus Building
24. CANES/Center for Nanofluids Technology ESG/Dept of Nuclear Science and Engineering
26. Compton Laboratories
31. Sloan Laboratories
32. State Center
33. Guggenheim Laboratory
34. EG & G Education Center
35. Sloan Laboratory
36. Fairchild Building

37. McNair Building
38. Fairchild Building
39. Brown Building
41. Lean Aerospace Initiative/ Fuel Cell Lab
42. Power Plant
43. Power Plant Annex
44. Cyclotron
45. Brain and Cognitive Sciences
48. Parsons Laboratory
50. Walker Memorial
51. Wood Sailing Pavilion
54. Green Building
56. Whitaker Building
57. MIT Alumni Pool
62. Alumni Houses: Munroe Hayden Wood
64. Alumni Houses: Walcott Bemis Goodale

66. Landau Building
70. Koch Biology Building
E1. Gray House
E2. Senior House
E15. Wiesner Building
E17. Mudd Building
E18. Ford Building
E19. Ford Building
E23. Health Services
E25. Whitaker College
E28. Publishing Services Bureau (PSB)/Reference Publications Office (RPO)
E33. Rinaldi Tile

E34. Earth Resources L
E38. Suffolk Building
E39. MIT Press
E40. Muckley Building
E48. MIT Investment M Company
E51. Tang Center
E52. Sloan Building
E53. Hermann Building

number of NCAA-sponsored programs in the nation, and the coaches and students have received numerous awards for sports excellence. The heavyweight crew squads and the men's cross-country and track teams have garnered accolades for the university.

Culture on Campus

In a time when art and technology are often indistinguishable, it's not hard to believe that MIT has a happening arts program, too. We highly recommend a visit to the MIT Museum. Holographic images, scientific photographs, and mechanical sculptures with names like "Untitled Fragile Machine" show just how beautiful math-type stuff can be.

The Weisner Building (designed by I.M. Pei and housing the Media Laboratory) opened in 1985 and was used, for much of its first decade, to explore digital video and multimedia. The Media Lab allows for interdisciplinary research, and the developing focus of study is on how electronic information affects our daily lives—how we use it to think, express, and communicate ideas. Many of the Media Lab's research projects are made possible

through corporate sponsorship, and the lab fosters a positive relationship between academia and industry.

According to the MIT website, the Media Lab "houses a gigabit fiber-optic plant that connects a heterogeneous network of computers, ranging from fine-grained, embedded processors to supercomputers." Unfortunately, in its role as an academic research laboratory, the Media Lab is not able to accommodate visits from the general public.

Departments

Undergraduate Admissions	617-253-4791
Graduate Admissions	617-253-2917
School of Humanities, Arts, and Social Sciences	617-253-3450
School of Engineering	617-253-3291
School of Science	617-253-8900
Sloan School of Management	617-253-2659
Office of the Arts	617-253-4003
Athletic Department	617-253-4498

55. Eastgate
60. Arthur D Little Building
70. Badger Building
N4. Albany Garage
N9. Superconducting Test Facility
N10. High Voltage Research Lab
N16. Cooling Tower & Oil Reserve
N16A. 60 Albany Street
N42. Information Services & Technology
N51. Design Fabrication Group
N52. MIT Museum
N57. Library Storage Annex
NE18. 1 Cambridge Center
NE20. 3 Cambridge Center
NE25. 5 Cambridge Center
NE30. Broad Institute
NE46. 400 Technology Square

NE47. 500 Technology Square
NE48. 700 Technology Square
NE49. 600 technology Square
NE80. Hill Building

NW10. Edgerton House
NW12. Nuclear Reactor Laboratory
NW13. 144 Albany Street
NW14. Francis Bitter Magnet Lab
NW15. Francis Bitter Magnet Lab
NW16. Plasma Science & Fusion Center
NW17. Plasma Science & Fusion Center
NW20. Albany St Generator Shelter
NW21. Plasma Science & Fusion Center
NW22. Plasma Science & Fusion Center
NW30. 224 Albany Street
NW61. Random H all
NW62. Volvo Garage
NW86. 70 Pacific Street Dormitory
W1. Ashdown House
W2. 311 Memorial Drive
W4. McCormick Hall
W5. Green Hall
W7. Baker House

W8. Pierce Boathouse
W11. Kosher Kitchen
W13. Bexley Hall
W15. MIT Chapel
W16. Kresge Auditorium
W20. Stratton Student Center
W31. Du Pont Athletic Gymnasium
W32. Du Pont Athletic Gymnasium
W33. Rockwell Cage
W34. Johnson Athletics Center
W35. Zesiger Sports & Fitness Center
W45. West garage
W51. Burton-Conner House
W53. Carr Indoor Tennis Facility
W59. Heinz Building
W61. MacGregor House
W70. New House
W71. Next House
W79. Simmons Hall
W84. Tang Hall
W85. Westgate
W89. Campus Police
W91. Information Services & Technology Operations
WW15. Mail Services (off map)

East Campus

Draper Laboratories

Main St

Broadway

MAP 26

Kendall/MIT

Albany St

Annex Lot

Vassar St

Killian Court

Stata Center

Green Building

Media Lab Extension

Walker Memorial

Amherst St

← Memorial Dr

→ Memorial Dr

Charles River

Northeastern University

1. O'Bryant African-American Institute
2. Meserve Hall/Holmes Hall
3. Lake Hall/Nightingale Hall
4. Knowles Center
5. Stearns Center
6. Dockster Hall
7. Kariotis Hall
8. Cushing Hall
9. Cahners Hall
10. Cullinane Hall
11. Hurtig Hall
12. Dodge Hall
13. Mugar Life Sciences Building
14. Robinson Hall
15. Eli Hall
16. Blackman Auditorium
17. Curry Student Center
18. Richards Hall
19. Hayden Hall
20. Churchill Hall
21. Snell Library
22. Barletta Natatorium
23. Forsyth Building
24. Latino/a Student Cultural Center
25. Dana Research Center/Snell Engineering Center
26. Egan Engineering/Science Research Center
27. Architecture Studio
28. Columbus Place
29. Renaissance Park
30. Cargill Hall
31. Hillel Frager
32. ROTC Office
33. Speare Hall

General Information

NFT Maps: 5, 13, & 15
Address: 360 Huntington Ave, Boston, MA 02115
Phone: 617-373-2000
Website: www.northeastern.edu

Overview

Northeastern University has come a long way from being a commuter school with a fairly unimpressive urban campus. In recent years, the university has emerged as an important national research institution with sparkly new academic, athletic, and residential facilities. NU originally began as a five-year school with an academic model called "Practice-Oriented Education," a program that combines education and internships (co-op) and is alternatively dubbed "real-life learning" by school officials. The school added more four- and five-year options, along with online study for a number of degrees. Northeastern University is ranked 98th among the nation's top 500 universities by *U.S. News & World Report*.

Founded in 1898 as a part-time night school, Northeastern is located on more than 67 acres along Huntington Avenue and served by three Green Line E train stops. The current enrollment at NU is approximately 15,000 full-time undergraduate students and around 4,800 graduate students with a male-to-female ratio that is pretty evenly matched. However, cultural diversity isn't something for which the university is known. The most popular degree programs on offer are in Business, Health, and Engineering/Technology. The now 20-year-old University Honors Program is also a big draw for potential undergrads.

Tuition

Undergraduate tuition costs run at about $33,320 per year with room and board adding up to an additional $11,510. Books, lab fees, and personal expenses are, as always, extra. Graduate student tuition and fees vary by college, as do individual online courses.

Sports

The Northeastern Huskies compete in Division I with varsity teams in nine men's and ten women's sports. The school's various teams had their finest collective performance ever in the 2002-03 season. The Huskies sent four teams to the NCAA playoffs and won a total of seven conference titles—Northeastern's most ever in both categories.

Culture on Campus

While Northeastern University doesn't offer much in the way of the arts, it is located in a prime spot for cultural enrichment. Huntington Avenue, also known as "Avenue of the Arts," runs through the urban campus, making it easy to visit the neighborhood museums. Among the most notable are the Isabella Stewart Gardner Museum, a ten-minute walk from the center of campus, and the Museum of Fine Arts (page 326), a four-minute walk from the main quad. Massachusetts College of Art is also located just a few T stops away and Symphony Hall (Boston Pops, anyone?) is next door. Thai, soul food, and pizza abound—whether you walk or T it, you can hit anywhere from five to infinite restaurants with one stone.

For on-campus entertainment, AfterHOURS, the campus's late-night club, welcomes various musical acts, ranging from local unknowns to bigger names like Gavin DeGraw. Additionally, the Curry Student Center is a magnet for Huskies in search of a bite (the Food Court includes everything from a salad bar to a Taco Bell) or an e-mail fix.

Departments

Admissions	617-373-2200
	(TTY) 617-373-3768
Library	617-373-2350
Registrar	617-373-2300
Athletics Department	617-373-2672
Athletics Ticket Office	617-373-4700

Undergraduate:

Admissions	617-373-2200
College of Arts & Sciences	617-373-3980
Bouvé College of Health Sciences	617-373-3321
College of Business Administration	617-373-3270
College of Computer & Information Science	617-373-2462
College of Criminal Justice	617-373-3327
College of Engineering	617-373-2152
School of Engineering Technology	617-373-7777
School of Nursing	617-373-3649

Graduate:

Bouvé College of Health Sciences	617-373-2708
College of Arts & Sciences	617-373-3982
College of Business Administration	617-373-5992
College of Computer & Information Science	617-373-2464
College of Criminal Justice	617-373-3327
College of Engineering	617-373-2711
Law School	617-373-2395
School of Professional & Continuing Studies	617-373-2400

1. Mugar Hall
2. Dowling Hall
3. Goddard Hall
4. Granhoff Family Hillel Center
5. Dana Lab
6. Barnum Hall
7. Ballou Hall
8. Goddard Chapel
9. Eaton Hall
10. Miner Hall
11. Paige Hall
12. Lincoln-Filene Center
13. Braker Hall
14. East Hall
15. Packard Hall
16. Bendelson Hall
17. Central Heating Plant
18. Lane Hall

19. Dewick-MacPhie Hall
20. Bookstore
21. Elizabeth Van Huyson Mayer Campus Center
22. 55 Talbot Ave
23. Pearson Chemical Laboratory
24. Michael Lab
25. Academic Computing Building
26. Costume Shop
27. Jackson Gym
28. Baltch Arena Theatre
29. Remis Sculpture/ Leir Hall
30. Cohen Auditorium
31. Aidekman Arts Center
32. Baronian Field House
33. Anderson Hall
34. Robinson Hall
35. Bromfield-Pearson

37. Hamilton Pool
38. Halligan Hall
39. 177 College Ave
40. Office Services
41. Curtis Hall
42. Psychology Building
43. Bray Laboratory
44. Central Services
45. Bacon Hall
46. Science and Technology Center
47. Eliot-Pearson Child Development Center
48. Eliot-Pearson Children's School
49. West Hall
50. Olin Center
51. Cabot Center
52. Scene Shop

General Information

NFT Map:	22
Tufts Admin Building:	169 Holland St, Somerville, MA 02144
Medford/Somerville Campus:	Medford, MA 02155
Boston Campus:	136 Harrison Ave, Boston, MA 02111
North Grafton Campus:	200 Westboro Rd, North Grafton, MA 01536
Tufts General Phone:	617-628-5000
Website:	www.tufts.edu

Overview

There's a perception that Tufts is a school for kids who didn't get into Harvard, just two Red Line stops away. This is (mostly) not true. Tufts possesses academic prowess in its own right, especially in its engineering, veterinary, international relations, and science departments. The Fletcher School is the country's oldest graduate school of international affairs, and its prestige and strong curriculum draw students from across the globe. To boot, Tufts boasts a kick-ass study-abroad program (pick a continent, any continent) and a laudable community-service focus.

The university has three campuses. The main Medford/Somerville campus is where approximately 5,500 students, mostly liberal arts undergrads, live and learn. The Medford/Somerville campus also houses the School of Engineering, the Graduate School of Arts and Sciences, and the School of Special Studies. Tufts prides itself on diversity: A whole center is devoted to lesbian, gay, bisexual, and transgender students, and on any given day the "viewpoints" section of *The Tufts Daily*—the school's impressive and professional-looking student newspaper—will have several pieces about the LGBT community. As touchy-feely as campus politics may be, though, academics remain pretty hardcore.

The centrally located Boston campus houses the School of Medicine, School of Dental Medicine, Sackler School of Graduate Biomedical Sciences, Jean Mayer USDA Human Nutrition Research Center on Aging, and The Gerald J. and Dorothy R. Friedman School of Nutrition Science and Policy.

Tuition

Undergraduate tuition fees total $39,432. Room and board cost an additional $10,746. Books, service fees, activity fees, and personal expenses are extra. Graduate student tuition, fees, and expenses vary by college.

Sports

If you ever find yourself at Tufts University and, more specifically, in the office of the Athletic Director, you might notice a peanut butter jar with ashes in it. Don't be frightened; it's only Jumbo. Jumbo is the elephant mascot of Tufts University. P.T. Barnum, of the Barnum and Bailey Circus, was one of the University's original trustees. His prize act was an elephant named Jumbo, who was hit by a train and killed in 1885. His stuffed body was donated to Tufts, where it was stored in a museum on campus that eventually became a student lounge. Sadly, however, the museum burned in 1975 and Jumbo went up with it. The ashes in the jar are said to be those of Jumbo, though university officials say they have no evidence that that is the case. Luckily, they have his tail in a cardboard bucket in their archives. (Extra trivia fun: Jumbo also has the honor of being the only mascot mentioned in *Webster's*. Take that, Ivy Leaguers.)

If that isn't enough to attract you to the sports, then maybe the recent successes of the golf and women's sailing teams will pique your interest.

There's also an old campus joke: "What's Brown and Blue and loses every weekend?" Answer: "The Tufts football team." It's not really funny, but often astute.

Culture on Campus

If sports aren't your thing, cultural activities are plentiful at Tufts. In the Aidekman Arts Center on the Medford/Somerville campus, you'll find the Tufts University Art Gallery. Again, the mantra seems to be diversity, diversity, and more diversity. The Gallery's mission is to explore art through all of its cultural complexities.

Over 70 students make up the Tufts Symphony Orchestra, which performs regularly throughout the school year. A capella groups abound, ranging from all-male to all-Jewish. The Department of Drama and Dance is where all of the performing artists can be found. Its students—a tight-knit, talented group—perform regularly at the Balch Arena Theater. Lately, though, music has been taking center stage on the Medford Campus: In February 2007, the $27-milion, 55,000-square-foot Granoff Music Center opened to campus-wide accolades.

Departments

Undergraduate Admissions	617-627-3170
Graduate and Professional Studies	617-627-3395
The Fletcher School	617-627-3040
School of Medicine	617-636-7000
School of Dental Medicine	617-636-6828
Sackler School of Graduate Biomedical Sciences	617-636-6767
School of Nutrition and Science Policy	617-636-3737
School of Veterinary Medicine	508-839-5302
School of Engineering	617-627-3237
Athletics Department and Ticket Office	617-627-3232
Balch Arena Theater	617-627-3524
Tufts Symphony Orchestra	617-627-4042
Tisch Library	617-627-3460

Continuing Education in Boston

Harvard, MIT, Boston College…the city of Boston has long been associated with academic achievement. But even if you're not ready to matriculate at one of the city's famed institutions of higher learning, Boston is a great place to learn everything and anything from basic Arabic to authentic Italian cooking.

For those looking to change careers—or simply get ahead in a current position—many of the area's renowned schools offer continuing education or professional development classes. Tuition at Harvard Extension School is very reasonable and comes with unbeatable name recognition. Even community colleges like North Shore Community College, Bunker Hill, and Quincy College (Red line accessible) offer credited and non-credited courses from everything like computers to feng shui.

Those who are feeling less cerebral can try gymnastics at Cambridge's Jam'nastics or take a golf lesson at CityGolf. Got an urge to indulge your creative side? Explore painting or sculpture with a studio art class at the MFA or learn the craft of glass-blowing at Diablo Glass and Metal.

Adrenaline junkies can hop the commuter rail and head out to Trapeze School, hidden in the Jordan's Furniture complex in suburban Reading.

Continuing Education and Professional Development

Boston College Woods College of Advancing Studies, www.bc.edu, 617-552-3900, 140 Commonwealth Ave, Chestnut Hill

Boston Language Institute, www.bostonlanguage.com, 617-262-3500, 648 Beacon St, Boston

Boston University Metropolitan College, www.bu.edu/met, 617-353-6000, 755 Commonwealth Ave, Boston

Bunker Hill Community College, www.bhcc.mass.edu/, 617-228-2000, 250 New Rutherford Ave, Boston

Harvard Extension, www.dce.harvard.edu/extension, 617-495-4024, 51 Brattle St, Cambridge

MIT, www.mit.edu/education/professional, 617-253-1000, 77 Massachusetts Ave, Cambridge

North Shore Community College, www.northshore.edu/, 978-762-4000, 1 Ferncroft Rd, Danvers

Northeastern University, www.ace.neu.edu, 617-373-2000, 360 Huntington Ave, Boston

Quincy College, www.quincycollege.edu/, 617-984-1700, 150 Newport Ave, Quincy

Little Bit of Everything

Boston Center for Adult Education, www.bcae.org, 617-267-4430, 5 Commonwealth Ave, Boston

Cambridge Center for Adult Education, www.ccae.org, 617-547-6789, 42 Brattle St, Cambridge

Arts and Lifestyle

Beadworks, www.beadworksboston.com, 617-247-7227, 167 Newbury St, Boston and 617-868-9777, 23 Church St, Cambridge

Boston Wine Tasting Classes, www.invinoveritas.com, 617-784-7150, 1354 Commonwealth Ave, Allston

Cambridge School of Culinary Arts, www.cambridgeculinary.com, 617-354-2020, 2020 Massachusetts Ave, Cambridge

Diablo Glass and Metal, www.diabloglassandmetal.com, 617-442-7444, 123 Terrace St, Boston

Grub Street Writing Center, www.grubstreet.org, 617-695-0075, 160 Boylston St, Boston

Massachusetts College of Art, www.massart.edu, 617-879-7000, 621 Huntington Ave, Boston

Mudville Pottery Classes, www.nanhamilton.com/mudville/mudville/, 617-623-9191, 181 Pearl St, Somerville

Museum of Fine Arts, www.mfa.org, 617-267-9300, 465 Huntington Ave, Boston

Spark Craft Studios, www.sparkcrafts.com, 617-718-9132, 50 Grove St, Somerville

Athletics and Dance

Boston Sailing Center, www.bostonsailingcenter.com, Lewis Wharf, Boston

CityGolf Boston, www.citygolfboston.com, 617-357-4653, 38 Bromfield St, Boston

Fred Astaire Dance Studios, www.fadsboston.com, 617-247-2435, 179 South St, Boston

GottaDance Cambridge, www.gottadance.org, 617-864-8675, 11 Garden St, Cambridge and 7 Temple St, Cambridge

Green Street Studios, www.greenstreetstudios.org, 617-864-3191, 185 Green St, Cambridge

Jam'nastics, www.jamnastics.org, 617-354-5780, 199 Columbia St, Cambridge

Trapeze School, http://boston.trapezeschool.com, 781-942-7800, 50 Walkers Brook Dr, Reading

Sports • Boating / Sailing / Rowing

Overview

Bostonians love that dirty water, but we like clean water even better. This fact is best reflected by the Boston Harbor Project. Thanks to over $3 billion spent cleaning it up, the Hub's harbor is no longer on that shameful list of the country's dirtiest waterways, but it's still a work in progress. So while you may still hear that damn Standells' song coming from every bar on Lansdowne Street, you no longer need to worry about general makeup should you go for a swim in the Charles. However, NFT does not recommend donning your speedos and goggles just yet. Instead, consider more appropriate activities as reflected in the slew of yacht clubs and boating centers that decorate the coastline and upriver all the way to Watertown.

A perfect place to start is at one of Boston Harbor's 34 beautiful islands, which have been collectively designated a National Recreation Area. Nine of the islands are either fully or partially accessible to the public and are a great, affordable getaway within 10-miles of downtown Boston. For the most part, amenities consist of composting toilets, but if you come prepared, the islands are great for a picnic or a camping excursion (www.bostonislands.com). On George's Island (Boston Harbor Cruises) you will find historic Fort Warren, a former Civil War prison replete with ghost—the wife of a Civil War inmate nicknamed "Lady in Black." The trails across 48-acre Lovell's Island pass through dunes, forests, and the ruins of Fort Standish. There's a supervised swimming beach, some picnic areas, and 11 campsites. Little Brewster Island is the home of Boston Light, the oldest continually used lighthouse site in America (1716), While not open to casual visitors, private boaters and tours are welcomed, call for specifics (617-223-8666). If your boss is scheduling a Survivor-style teamwork safari or if your kids are looking for that Kevin Bacon, *White Water Summer* role model, chances are you're heading to privately owned Thompson Island. If you want to venture a bit farther out, consider Buzzards Bay to the south. Touching more than 280 miles of the Massachusetts coastline, the bay stretches from Rhode Island Sound to the Cape Cod Canal. Calmer waters inside the bay make for good sailing conditions.

Back on the Charles (don't even *think* about pronouncing the "r"), crew is a popular sport, particularly among the local colleges and universities. Many of the clubs and organizations offer instruction to the general public. The Head of the Charles Regatta, held every fall, is the world's largest two-day rowing event. The race schedule includes single and team events and draws competitors from around the world. Check out www.hocr.org for more information.

The nonprofit Community Boating Inc. (located between the Charles/MGH Red Line stop and the Hatch Shell) offers summer kayaking, windsurfing, and sailing lessons for kids aged 10–18 for just $1. (Participants must be able to swim 75 yards.) Visit www.community-boating.org for more information.

If you're looking for waves but find the Harbor a bit intimidating, check out the Jamaica Pond Boat House (617-522-5061) for mini-sailboat and rowboat rentals. At around 68-acres, the pond is the purest and largest body of water within city limits and the only date-friendly glacial-kettlehole in town. It's also a great spot to watch kamikaze drivers on the Jamaicaway. As they scream expletives and give each other the finger, you can fish in the liberally stocked pond and gloat. If that isn't relaxing, what is? Visit www.jamaicapond.com for further information.

Boston is also home to the CRASH—B World Indoor Rowing Championships, held annually in February at Agganis Arena at Boston University. More information is available at www.crash-b.org.

Sailing/Boating Centers

	Address	Phone	Website
Boston Harbor Cruises	1 Long Wharf, Boston	617-227-4321	www.bostonharborcruises.com
Boston Harbor Sailing Club	58 Batterymarch St, Boston	617-720-0049	www.bostonharborsailing.com; moorings/hire/lessons racing/clothing
Boston Harbor Shipyard & Marina	256 Marginal St, East Boston	617-561-1400	www.bhsmarina.com; moorings/lessons
Boston Sailing Center	The Riverboat at Lewis Wharf	617-227-4198	www.bostonsailingcenter.com; hire/courses/lessons/racing
Community Boating	21 David Mugar Way, Boston	617-523-1038	www.community-boating.org; sailing lessons
Courageous Sailing Center	One 1st Ave, Charlestown	617-242-3821	www.courageoussailing.org; lessons/racing
Jamaica Pond Boat House	Jamaicaway at Pond St, Jamaica Plain	617-522-5061	www.jamaicapond.com; sailing/rowing
Lincoln Sailing Center	PO Box 492, Hingham	781-741-5225	www.lincolnsailing.com; non-profit/lessons/sailing/racing
MIT Sailing	134 Memorial Dr, Cambridge	617-253-4884	http://sailing.mit.edu; lessons/racing
Piers Park Sailing	95 Marginal St, East Boston	617-561-6677	www.piersparksailing.org; hire/lessons/racing/sale

Yacht Clubs

	Address	Phone	Website
Bass Haven Yacht Club	10 McPherson Dr, Beverly	978-922-9712	www.basshavenyachtclub.com
Boston Yacht Club	1 Front St, Marblehead	781-631-3100	www.bostonyc.com
Braintree Yacht Club	9 Gordon Rd, Braintree	781-843-9730	N/A
Corinthian Yacht Club	1 Nahant St, Marblehead	781-631-0005	www.corinthianyc.org
Danversport Yacht Club	161 Elliott St, Danvers	978-774-8620	www.danversport.com
Eastern Yacht Club	47 Foster St, Marblehead	781-631-1400	www.easternyc.org
Hull Yacht Club	5 Fitzpatrick Wy, Hull	781-925-9739	www.hullyc.org
Jeffries Yacht Club	565 Sumner St, East Boston	617-567-9656	www.jeffriesyachtclub.com
Jubilee Yacht Club	126 Water St, Beverly	978-922-9611	www.jubileeyc.net
Metropolitan Yacht Club	39 Vinedale Rd, Braintree	781-843-9882	www.metyc.com
New Bedford Yacht Club	208 Elm St, South Dartmouth	508-997-0762	www.nbyc.com
Old Colony Yacht Club	235 Victory Rd, Dorchester	617-436-0513	N/A
Peninsula Yacht Club	671 Summer St, Boston	617-464-7901	www.pycboston.org
Plymouth Yacht Club	34 Union St, Plymouth	508-746-7207	www.plymouthyachtclub.org
Sandy Bay Yacht Club	5 T Wharf, Rockport	978-546-9433	www.sandybay.org
South Boston Yacht Club	1849 Columbia Rd, South Boston	617-268-6132	www.southbostonyc.com
Squantum Yacht Club	646 Quincy Shore Dr, Quincy	617-770-4811	www.squantumyc.org
Wianno Yacht Club	101 Bridge St, Osterville	508-428-2232	www.vsb.cape.com/~wianno/
Winthrop Yacht Club	649 Shirley St, Winthrop	617-846-9774	www.win-yc.org

Rowing Clubs

	Address	Phone	Website
Community Rowing (Apr–Oct)	600 Pleasant St, Watertown	617-923-7557	www.communityrowing.org
Whaling City Rowing Club	5 Dover St, New Bedford	508-517-1251	www.whalingcityrowing.org

General Information

City of Boston Bicycling:	www.ci.boston.ma.us/transportation/bike.asp
City of Cambridge Bicycling:	www.ci.cambridge.ma.us/CDD/et/bike/index.html
MassBike:	www.massbike.org
Charles River Wheelmen:	www.crw.org
Rubel BikeMaps:	www.bikemaps.com
Bike to Bridge Boston:	www.hubonwheels.org

Overview

The city's streets are narrow, congested, and short-tempered, bike-hating drivers abound. Make no mistake, Boston is tough for cyclists.

That said, Boston and the surrounding cities are making efforts to increase the accessibility and safety of bike transportation, and it's a great way to explore the city. Relatively flat and compact, it's generally quicker to get around on a bike, and you'll find, even in the middle of winter, hardy cyclists trekking through the city, delivering packages, and heading to class. Bike-only or mixed-use bike/pedestrian paths run through most of the area's parks, paralleling major roads such as the Riverway, Storrow Drive, and Memorial Drive. While getting "doored" is a serious threat in Central Square, a much-needed repaving of Mass Ave has smoothed the bike lane connecting Boston to Harvard.

Danger lurks around every non-perpendicular corner. To avoid catastrophe, have your best cycling wits about you and be especially wary of:

- **Drivers**—Boston drivers reserve some of their most venomous roadrage for cyclists. They're also notoriously self-centered, erratic, prone to underestimate your speed, and quick to double-park to dash in for liquor or donuts.

- **Potholes**—They can sneak up on you, especially at night. The bigger ones will swallow you whole, while bumping over the little ones lead to nasty bruises in the nether regions.

- **Trolley Tracks**—Green Line tracks will flip you over and buckle your wheel, especially in parts of Mission Hill, Jamaica Plain, and in Cleveland Circle. If you're going to cross the tracks, take them at a 90-degree angle.

- **Bridges**—All the bridges across the Charles are narrow and heavily trafficked.

- **Pedestrians**—They jaywalk into your path, they text while doing so, and they can't hear your screams because their iPod is set to volume level "jet engine." Also, keep in mind that even if they can hear you scream "On Your Left," 99% of them will step directly to the left to ensure that you die.

If you plan on biking in Boston and you have a brain that you'd like to keep, invest in a helmet and a battery-powered red light to place below your seat or on your back. Front lights and rear reflectors are the law after dark.

The city offers many options for recreational riding, including the popular 11-mile Minuteman Bikeway through Lexington and the 17-mile Charles River Bikeway growing past Watertown. Shorter but handy for commuting, the Southwest Corridor sends you from Northeastern along the Orange Line to Forest Hills. Recent funding should improve one of the serious flaws of the Boston bike system: a lack of cross-trail connections, crossing lights, or route markings. This makes them less than ideal for outing with small children. Of particular danger to families are the many bridge intersections along the south Charles River Bikeway.

For something a little longer and farther away, the Bay Circuit Trail winds its way 150 miles from Newburyport on the North Shore to Duxbury on the South Shore, creating a "C" shape around Boston. Cycling enthusiasts refer to it as "Boston's outer Emerald Necklace." You'll find the boy racers skipping the summer crowds on the Minuteman for spins around Concord and many of the cycle shops sponsor club teams. The Charles River Wheelmen is one of the nation's oldest bicycle clubs with a year round calendar of rides and site full of cue sheets. For the distance riders, the BMB (Boston-Montreal-Boston) ride draws randonneurs from across the country for the grueling 90 hour, 1,200K ride.

Rubel BikeMaps produces maps of riding paths and trails throughout the Greater Boston area and is well worth five bucks. You'll likely want both the Boston map and the Eastern Mass map. They can be purchased at most bike shops, bookstores, or on the Rubel website. Take it to the State House with MassBike, the primary lobbying and bicycle advocacy group in the state. They maintain an extensive website of all things pedal-powered in Massachusetts. Bike to Bridge Boston is a new addition to the city and organizes free tours to offbeat Boston during the summer. DIY guides to biking Jewish Boston, the Underground Railroad, and other routes are on their web site, and they organize a city bike rally and ride in early October.

Bikes and Mass Transit

Bikes are allowed on the Red, Orange, and Blue Lines, on the MBTA Commuter Rail with some limitations, on all busses equipped with bike racks, and on the MBTA ferries at all times. Bikes (with the exception of folding bikes) are not permitted on the Green Line, the Mattapan Trolley, or the Silver Line. On the subway and commuter rail, bikes are permitted during non-rush hours (roughly 10 am–2 pm and after 7pm). Bikes are allowed at all subway stations except Park Street, Downtown Crossing (except to transfer), and Government Center. Crosstown buses are equipped with bike racks and can be used at any time. Other bus services do not provide racks and bikes are not permitted on board.

If you're traveling on commuter rail, wait for the conductor's instructions before entering or exiting the train. On subways, head for the rear of the train. You're only allowed to enter the last carriage and, even then, there's a two-bikes-per-carriage limit. There is no additional fee for bikes on any public transportation. See the MBTA website for (www.mbta.com) for schedules.

Bike Shops and Makers

Boston's got a great variety of shops. While most will have a low-end city cruiser or two, it's worth getting to know your local shops for their specialties, whether the high-end racing bikes at ATA or fixies at Beacon Street. Oddly enough, Boston's most famous shop and mechanic, Sheldon Brown, are way out in West Newton at Harris Cyclery. However, if you don't mind getting your hands dirty, we applaud the rent-by-the-hour stands and geniuses at Broadway Bicycle School.

· **Ace Wheelworks** ·
145 Elm St, Somerville · 617-776-2100

· **ATA Cycle** ·
1773 Massachusetts Ave, Cambridge · 617-354-0907

· **Back Bay Bicycles** ·
366 Commonwealth Ave, Boston · 617-247-2336

· **Bicycle Bill's** ·
253 North Harvard St, Allston · 617-783-5636

· **Bicycle Exchange** ·
2067 Massachusetts Ave, Cambridge · 617-864-1300

· **Bikes Not Bombs** ·
18 Bartlett Sq, Jamaica Plain · 617-442-0004

· **Broadway Bicycle School** ·
351 Broadway, Cambridge · 617-868-3392

· **Cambridge Bicycle** ·
259 Massachusetts Ave, Cambridge · 617-876-6555

· **Community Bike Supply** ·
496 Tremont St, Boston · 617-542-8623

· **Federico's Bike Shop** ·
126 Emerson St, Boston · 617-269-1309

· **Ferris Wheels Bicycle Shop** ·
66 South St, Jamaica Plain · 617-522-7082

· **Harris Cyclery** ·
1353 Washington St, West Newton · 617-244-1040

· **International Bicycle Center** ·
89 Brighton Ave, Brighton · 617-783-5804

· **Jamaica Cycle** ·
667 Centre St, Jamaica Plain · 617-524-9610

· **Paramount Bicycle Repair** ·
860 Broadway, Somerville · 617-666-6072

· **Park Sales & Service** ·
510 Somerville Ave, Somerville · 617-666-3647

· **Revolution Bicycle Repair** ·
753 Atlantic Ave, Boston · 617-542-4327

· **Ski Market** ·
860 Commonwealth Ave, Boston · 617-731-6100

When out on the road, what's better than showing off some Yankee ingenuity? Boston's been a center of bike fabrication since Columbia popularized the ready-made bike in 1877. Here are some sweet hand-crafted builders welding new traditions:

· **A.N.T.** ·
24 Water St, Holliston · 508-429-3350

· **Independent Fabrication** ·
86 Joy St, Somerville · 617-666-3609

· **Seven Cycles** ·
125 Walnut St, Watertown · 617-923-777

Overview

If you like the idea of lowering your center of gravity and darting around at high speeds on tiny wheels or thin blades, then Boston is the place for you. The city is jam-packed with parks and rinks that accommodate inline skaters in the summer and ice skaters in the winter.

Inline Skating

Boston drivers are no more sympathetic to skaters than they are to bikers. If you're skating for recreation, it is probably best to stick to the numerous places designated for outdoor activities. A favorite haunt of Boston skaters is Harvard's Arnold Arboretum (125 Arborway, Jamaica Plain, 617-524-1718), which offers one of the most scenic (and hilly) skates in the area. The best thing about this place is that skaters are welcome everywhere. There are two or three miles of paved paths and you don't have to worry about cars (although you might find yourself dodging strollers, cyclists, and fellow skaters, particularly on sunny weekends).

Boston Common (see page 188) is another popular skating destination, but the pedestrian traffic on the Common makes skating quite challenging. The Common is usually crowded with meandering tourists and fast-walking business folk who don't take too kindly to being mowed down by skaters. The upside, though, is that you can take in some impressive cityscapes as you zip around. The best way to get there is to take the T to Park Street. Note: Wearing skates on the T is prohibited.

For a great view of the bridges that stretch over the Charles River, try the Charles River Bike Path. The trail runs along both sides of the river between the Galen Street Bridge in Watertown and River Street Bridge in Boston, and from the Science Museum to Watertown Square. The path is about 8.5 miles each way.

Beacon Hill Skate Shop (135 Charles St S, 617-482-7400) rents top-of-the-line inline skates, roller skates, and ice skates. Rentals cost $10/hour, $15/day, and $20 overnight. Beacon Hill Skate Shop accepts cash only and requires you to leave a credit card as deposit. All rentals come with safety equipment.

Ice Skating

Even on crisp winter days, when the cold makes it almost unbearable to be outside, Boston Common's famous Frog Pond entices skaters to bundle up and head out for some good, old-fashioned ice skating—either that or some good, old-fashioned heckling from the sidelines. Skating is free for children 13 and under and $4 for everyone else. Skate rental is $5 for children and $8 for everyone else. Lockers are available for a dollar. Regulars might consider buying individual season passes for children or a family pass for $150. Lunchtime passes are valid Mon-Fri, 11 am to 3 pm (holidays excluded), and cost $60. Frog Pond is open Sun–Thurs 10 am-9 pm (except Mon when the rink closes at 5 pm) and Fri-Sat 10 am–10 pm. For more information, call 617-635-2120.

The Larz Anderson Park in Brookline is a great back-up option when Frog Pond gets too crowded (and it will). Larz Anderson Park is located on a former 64-acre estate and is the largest park in Brookline. In addition to the outdoor skate rink, the park has picnic areas, ball fields, and an incredible view of Boston. The only downside is that the skating rink is only open a few months every year, from December to February. Skating fees cost $4 for adults and $3 for kids ($7

and $4, respectively, for non-residents). The rink is open Tues and Thurs 10 am–12 pm, Fri 7:30 pm–9:30 pm, Sat-Sun 12 pm–5 pm. For more information, call 617-739-7518.

Ice Skating Rinks

If you have your own skates, you might opt for one of the following rinks run by the Department of Conservation and Recreation, where skating in the winter is free. Call rinks for hours of operation:

Bajko Memorial Rink,
75 Turtle Pond Pkwy, Hyde Park, 617-364-9188
Jim Roche Community Ice Arena,
1275 VFW Pkwy, West Roxbury, 617-323-9532
Daly Memorial Rink,
1 Nonantum Rd, Brighton, 617-527-1741
Devine Memorial Rink,
995 Morrissey Blvd, Dorchester, 617-436-4356
Emmons Horrigan O'Neill Memorial Rink,
150 Rutherford Ave, Charlestown, 617-242-9728
Flynn Skating Rink,
2 Woodland Rd, Medford, 781-395-8492
Kelly Outdoor Skating Rink,
1 Marbury Ter, Jamaica Plain, 617-727-7000
LoConte Memorial Rink,
3449 Veterans Pkwy, Medford, 781-395-9594
Murphy Memorial Rink,
1880 William J Day Blvd, South Boston, 617-269-7060
Porazzo Memorial Rink,
20 Coleridge St, East Boston, 617-567-9571
Reilly Skating Rink,
355 Chestnut Hill Ave, Brighton, 617-277-7822
Skating Club of Boston,
1240 Soldiers Field Rd, Brighton, 617-782-5900
Simoni Memorial Rink,
155 Gore St, Cambridge, 781-982-8166
Steriti Memorial Rink,
561 Commercial St, Boston, 617-523-9327
Veterans Memorial Rink,
570 Somerville Ave, Somerville, 617- 623-3523

Skateboarding

The Charles River Skatepark, 40,000 square feet of pipes, ramps, and rails, will be constructed at North Point Park along the Charles River where Cambridge meets Charlestown. As of now, the site is still not under construction due to some minor funding and planning set backs, but the plan is to get it fully underway for a 2009–10 opening to the public. Once finished, it will be one of the largest skateparks in the country, perfect for catching air like Tony Hawk or busting backside lipslides like Ryan Sheckler. For info, go to www.charlesriverskatepark.org. Until then, you can thrash it all year long on the indoor mini ramp at Underground Snowboard (860 Commonwealth Ave, Boston, 617-232-8680).

Gear

Beacon Hill Skate Shop,
135 Charles St S, Boston, 617-482-7400
Coliseum Skateboard,
150 Huntington Ave, Boston, 617-399-9900
True East Skate Shop,
32 Province St, Boston, 617-451-8999
Underground Snowboard,
860 Commonwealth Ave, Boston, 617-232-8680

General Information

Boston Parks and Recreation Office
Phone: 617-635-4505
Hotline: 617-635-PARK
Website: www.cityofboston.gov/parks

Brookline Recreation Department
Phone: 617-730-2083
Website: www.townofbrooklinemass.com/
          recreation/Tennis.html

Cambridge Recreation Department
Phone: 617-349-6200
Website: www.cambridgema.gov

Department of Conservation and Recreation
  (Division of Urban Parks)
Phone: 617-626-1250
Website: www.mass.gov/dcr/recreate/tennis.htm

Outdoor Courts—Open to the Public

These public courts operate on a first-come, first-served basis. Most courts are not equipped with lights, so get there early to get your game in. Although many courts are in good condition, some have pretty major divots, à la the Boston Garden's parquet floor, making the ball spin in unexpected directions. Courts are managed by the city or the town recreation department, or by the Commonwealth's Department of Conservation and Recreation's Division of Urban Parks (DCR). Until recently, the DCR was the Metropolitan District Commission (MDC), so the courts might still be labeled with the wrong acronym. Don't let it affect your game! Many locals also use the well-maintained school courts in the university-rich area. Each school has a different policy regarding outsiders depending on season, location, and the mood of the athletic director on a particular day. Contact the schools or just take your chances.

Tennis Courts	Address	Type	# of Courts	Map
Charlesbank Park (DCR)	Charles St	Public	4	1
North End Park (DCR)	Commercial St	Public	2	2
Boston Common	Boylston St & Charles St	Public	2	3
Pagoda Park	Kneeland St	Public	1	4
Cook Street Play Area	Hill St & Cook St	Public	1	8
Porzio Park	Maverick Sq	Public	2	9
Boston Athletic Club	653 Summer St	Private		11
Marine Park (DCR)	Day Blvd	Public	1	11
Clifford Playground	Norfolk Ave & Proctor St	Public	1	12
Carter Playground	Columbus Ave & Camden St	Public	5	13
Jeep Jones Park	King St	Public	1	13
Malcolm X Park	Dale St & Bainbridge St	Public	2	13
Trotter School Playground	Humboldt St & Waumbeck St	Public	1	13
Mission Hill Deck (DCR)	Southwest Corridor Park	Public	2	14
South Street Mall	South St & Carolina Ave	Public	2	14
Stony Brook Deck (DCR)	Southwest Corridor Park	Public	2	14
Amory Clay Tennis Courts	Amory St	Public		16
Longwood Playground Park	Newall Rd off Kent St	Public	3	16
Waldstein Playground	37 Dean Rd	Public	8	17
Rogers Park	Lake St & Foster St	Public	2	18
Coolidge Playground	Kenwood St b/w Harvard St & Columbia St	Public	1	19
Devotion Playground	Steadman St off Harvard St	Public	3	19
Driscoll School	Washington St	Public	2	19
Ringer Playground	Allston St & Griggs Pl	Public	2	19
Anderson Courts	Pemberton St & Haskell St	Public		22
George Dilboy Field (DCR)	Alewife Brook Pkwy	Public	2	22
Saxton J Foss Park (DCR)	McGrath Hwy & Broadway	Public	2	24
Hoyt Field	Western Ave & Howard St	Public		27
Riverside Press Park	River St & Memorial Dr	Public		27
Harvard Street Park	Harvard St & Clark St	Public		28
Joan Lorentz Park at Cambridge Public Library	Broadway & Ellery St	Public		28

Public Courses

	Address	Phone	Par	Fees (WD/WE)	Map
Franklin Park Golf Course	1 Circuit Dr, Dorchester	617-265-4084	70	$23–26 weekday / $29–34 weekend	n/a
Fresh Pond Golf Course	691 Huron Ave	617-349-6282	35/70	$30 weekday / $36 weekend	n/a
Presidents Golf Course	357 W Squantum St, Quincy	617-328-3444	70	$35 weekday / $44 weekend	n/a
Putterham Meadows Golf Club	1281 W Roxbury Pkwy, Chestnut Hill	617-730-2078	71	$35 weekday / $38 weekend	n/a

Driving Ranges

	Address	Phone		Fees (WD/WE)	Map
Boston Golf Academy	200 Stuart St	617-457-2699		$10/bucket	3
City Golf Boston	38 Bromfield St	617-357-4653		$10/bucket	3

Bowling

First and foremost, if you prefer tenpin over candlepin bowling than you are clearly not from Boston. If you are trying to fit in with the cutters or if want your girlfriend to think you're the real life Will Hunting, then you better learn how to hit those skinny sticks. On the other hand, if you are comfortable admitting that you were born in upstate New York and that you collected Don Mattingly cards when you were a kid, then embrace the tenpin, no one will think less of you for it (yeah, right).

All kidding aside, bowling has become hip and bowling has become expensive. Take **Kings (Map 16)**, for instance. Go there on a Friday night and it's filled with people who wouldn't have been caught dead bowling on a Friday night back in high school. Then there's **Lucky Strike Lanes (Map 16)** with a friggin' dress code. If that's your idea of bowling, by all means, have at it. If you're an old-school bowler, the kind that embraces leagues and finds no kitsch value in a button up short sleeve with your name in cursive on it (your real name), then you must head straight to **Lanes & Games**, order yourself a Bud and some steak tips, and get out your lucky glove. Another similar option is **Sacco's Bowl Haven (Map 22)** in Somerville (candlepin only). And here's one of those moments that remind you why you bought this little awesome book in the first place—**Boston Bowl Family Fun Center (Map 32)** on Morrissey Boulevard is open all night! You read correctly: In the squarest late-night town in America, where your options are your buddy's stained futon or the South Street Diner, Boston Bowl has you covered 24 hours a day.

Bowling Lanes

	Address	Phone	Fees	Map
King's Boston	50 Dalton St	617-266-2695	$5.50/game, $4/shoes	5
Central Park Lanes	10 Saratoga St	617-567-7073	$2.50/game, $1/shoes	9
South Boston Candlepin	543 E Broadway	617-464-4858	$3.50 per person/ per game; $1.50 shoes	11
Lucky Strike Lanes	145 Ipswich St	617-437-0300	$4/game, $3/shoes	16
Sacco's Bowl Haven	45 Day St	617-776-0552	$3/game, $2/shoes	22
Boston Bowl (open 24 hours)	820 Morrissey Blvd,	617-825-3800	$4.95/game, $4.25/shoes	32
Lanes & Games	195 Concord Tpke, Cambridge	617-876-5533	$4.75/game, $2.75/shoes	n/a

Yoga

Yoga	Address	Phone	Website	Map
Dahn Yoga	122 Cambridge St	617-742-9642	www.dahnyoga.com	1
Exhale Mind Body Spa	28 Arlington St	617-532-7000	www.exhalespa.com	3
Bikram Yoga Boston	108 Lincoln St	617-556-9926	www.bikramyogaboston.com	4
Back Bay Yoga Studio	1112 Boylston St	617-375-0785	www.backbayyoga.com	5
Dahn Yoga	551 Boylston St	617-262-9642	www.dahnyoga.com	6
Charlestown Yoga	191 Main St	617-241-0824	www.charlestownyoga.com	8
South Boston Yoga	141 Dorchester Ave	617-548-2694	southbostonyoga.net	12
Blissful Monkey Yoga Studio	663 Centre St	617-522-4411	www.blissfulmonkey.com	14
Dahn Yoga	10B Green St	617-983-9642	www.dahnyoga.com	14
Inner Space	17 Station St	617-730-5757	www.yogainthevillage.com	16
Dahn Yoga	235 Harvard St	617-264-4851	www.dahnyoga.com	17
The Yoga Studio	29 Harvard St, 2nd Fl	617-566-1489	www.yogastudio.org	17
Ayurvedic Rehabilitation Center	103 Bennett St	617-782-1727	www.ayurvedicrehabilitation center.com	18
Rock City Body	14 Harvard Ave	617-782-4410		19
Zen Athletica	1065 Commonwealth Ave	617-789-3733	www.zenathletica.com	19
Baptiste Power Yoga	2000 Massachusetts Ave	617-661-9642	www.baronbaptiste.com	23
Baptiste Power Yoga	25 Harvard St	617-661-9642	www.baronbaptiste.com	23
O2 Yoga	288 Highland Ave	617-625-0267	www.o2yoga.com	23
Cambridge Racquet & Fitness Club	215 First St	617-491-8989	www.cambridgefitness.com	26
Dahn Yoga	1110 Massachusetts Ave	617-576-9642	www.dahnyoga.com	27
Karma Yoga Studio	1120 Massachusetts Ave	617-547-9642	www.karmayogastudio.com	27
Mystic River Yoga	196 Boston Ave	781-396-0808	www.mysticriveryoga.com	n/a

Billiards

Billiards	Address	Phone	Fees	Map
Boston Beer Works	112 Canal St	617-896-2337	$10/hr	2
Felt	533 Washington St	617-350-5555	$14/hr	3
King's Boston	50 Dalton St	617-266-2695	$14/hr	5
4 X 4 Billiards	1260 Boylston St	617-424-6326	$12/hr	15
Lucky Strike Lanes	145 Ipswich St	617-437-0300	$14/hr weekends; $10/hr weekdays	16
Big City	138 Brighton Ave	617-782-2020	$10/hr	19
Sacco's Bowl Haven	45 Day St	617-776-0552	$7.50/hr	22
Good Time Emporium	30 Assembly Square Dr	617-628-5559	$11/hr	25
Flat Top Johnny's	One Kendall Sq, Bldg 200	617-494-9565	$12/hr	26
Boston Bowl (open 24 hours)	820 Morrissey Blvd	617-825-3800	$13/hr	32

Hiking in Boston

While it may not be the greatest city for driving, Boston is a great walking city. Whether you're in the mood for a casual stroll or a major trek, the city offers a surprisingly wide array of hikes and walks from which to choose. The trails closest to the city tend to be more scenic walks than hikes—appropriate for strolling students or families who want to get out and about in the city. If you're hungering for some real hiking, you'll need to be prepared for a drive. Boston's outskirts offer plenty of rigorous hiking trails with breathtaking views of the city and a taste of Massachusetts nature. If none of that is hardcore enough for you, the White Mountains of New Hampshire are just a Zipcar (see page 261) away.

A great source for information about various Boston trails is *Exploring in and Around Boston on Bike and Foot* by Lee Sinai (Appalachian Mountain Club Books).

Boston Harbor Islands

Seven miles from downtown Boston, this cluster of pretty much undiscovered islands is a great day trip to walk around historical forts and bucolic landscapes, birdwatch, or do some beachcombing. The inexpensive ferry from Long Wharf drops you off at Georges Island, where you can explore Fort Warren, a former Civil War prison that supposedly has its own ghost, "The Lady in Black." From there you can take free shuttles to the other islands. Peddocks Island has the longest coastline of all the islands and the most diverse set of trails. Grape Island takes you through forests, orchards, and rocky shoreline. Lovells has nice sand dunes and swimming beaches. Ferry service runs six times a day to Spectacle Island, a former dump site, which has been refurbished with excavated dirt from the Big Dig. It features a renewable energy visitor center, electric cars, a marina, beaches, and five miles of trails. There is camping on Peddocks, Grape, Lovells, and Bumpkin, but you must pack in and pack out everything yourself. Ferries to Spectacle Island and Georges Island operate from 9 am until sunset in the summer. Round-trip tickets cost $10–$12, $7–$9 seniors, and anywhere from free to $7 for children, depending on their age. For more information, go to www.bostonislands.com or call 617-223-8666 for schedules.

HarborWalk

With the cleaning up of Boston Harbor (though we still wouldn't swim in it) and the removal of the Central Artery, the waterfront has become more beautiful and accessible to pedestrian traffic. Finally realizing that people are attracted to a picturesque waterfront, Boston decided to capitalize on its coastal setting and incorporate it into the life of the city. The HarborWalk is a multi-use attraction consisting of walkways, parks, benches, artwork, restaurants, and swimming spots extending from Chelsea to Neponset. Currently 38 miles long, it is 80% complete and meanders through diverse waterfront neighborhoods with views of the Harbor Islands and Boston skyline. A don't-miss highlight is the Institute of Contemporary Art (ICA), which recently relocated here in a glass building perched over the waterfront. It is really quite pleasant on warm summer nights to wander among the boats and the lights of the city and revisit neighborhoods from a whole new perspective. With the Rose Kennedy Greenway complete (and catching flack for not having enough people on it), feel free

to give that a stroll from where it parallels the Harbor Walk on Atlantic Ave. The signs might be the best part—especially the one that speaks directly to your pooch.

Arnold Arboretum

Harvard's Arnold Arboretum, located in Jamaica Plain, occupies 265 acres and boasts a dizzying array of woody plants, more than 700 of which are over 100 years old. You can take a free guided tour of the grounds (call 617-524-1718 for tour schedules) or amble along the three-mile trail at your own pace. The arboretum welcomes dogs as long as they're kept on a leash. The botanical haven is just two blocks away from the Forest Hills T stop (Orange Line) and parking is available outside the main gate. Restrooms are located next to the entrance gate in the Hunnewell Visitor Center. The grounds are open every day of the year during daylight hours. For more information, visit www.arboretum.harvard.edu.

Fresh Pond Reservation

This is a favorite of local residents and Harvard students. Located just one mile from the university and six miles from downtown Boston, the Fresh Pond Reservation offers a rather easy 2.25-mile paved trail around comely Fresh Pond, the 155-acre reservoir. The trail has become a hot spot for joggers, cyclists, and skaters. If you take your dog, be sure to check out the pooper-scooper dispensers! But it's not just the athletic types that reap the benefits of the reservation—the reservoir provides drinking water to many residents and businesses in Cambridge. To reach the reservation by train, take the Red Line to Alewife (last stop). By car, follow Route 2 east or west to Fresh Pond Parkway. The reservation lies on the corner of Huron Avenue and Fresh Pond Parkway. You'll find the best entrance to the reservation directly across from Wheeler Street. Parking in the reservation is reserved for cars with a Cambridge permit. For more information, you can walk to the Tobin School, or take bus #72, #74, #75, or #78. For more information, visit www.friendsoffreshpond.org or call 617-349-6319.

Mount Auburn Cemetery

Hailed as America's first landscaped cemetery and a National Historic Landmark, Mount Auburn provides two miles of leisurely walking, alternating between paved walkways and unpaved footpaths, and is considered one of the best birding spots in the state. Aside from the 86,000 graves, the cemetery is home to over 5,000 native and foreign trees. Located just 1.5 miles west of Harvard Square, the cemetery can be reached via Route 2 or 3 to Route 16 at the Mount Auburn/Brattle Street intersection on Fresh Pond Parkway. If you follow Mount Auburn Street (Rte 16) west for two blocks, you will reach the entrance. Contact the Friends of Mount Auburn Cemetery (617-547-7105) for information about guided tours and lectures or visit their website at www.mountauburn.org. No dogs allowed.

Forest Hills Cemetery

Jamaica Plain's Forest Hills Cemetery is overshadowed in popularity (perhaps unfairly) by Mount Auburn Cemetery. Established in 1848, it's one of the country's oldest burial grounds, featuring 275 acres of beautifully sculpted landscape. The cemetery offers guided tours ($5–$8) or brochures and maps to help visitors create their own (free) tours of the grounds and its famous residents, including Eugene O'Neill and e.e. cummings. One of its most impressive features is Lake Hibiscus, which hosts the Buddhist-inspired lantern lighting festival held annually in the summer season. Another highlight is the Sculpture Path, a revolving exhibit of work by contemporary local and national artists. The cemetery is located conveniently next to the Forest Hills T stop. If you're driving, take the Arborway east over the Casey Overpass and follow signs for the cemetery exit, located on the right on Shea Circle. The grounds are open year-round during daylight hours. For more information, visit www.foresthillscemetery.com or call 617-524-0128.

Hammond Pond Reservation

Hammond Pond is located behind a suburban mall in Chestnut Hill—an unlikely place to find a reservation. You can see the department stores as you hike through the 114 acres of woodlands. It's also one of the few outdoor places in Boston where you can rock climb. The best place to start is at the entrance to the reservation, located on the left of Hammond Pond at the north side of the parking lot. Walk through the metal gate and remain on the wide main path through the woods. If you're interested in rock climbing, you'll see rocks to your left a little way along the path. If climbing rocks is not your thing, continue on for two miles of easy walking or try fishing in the pond. Hammond Pond Reservation can be reached by foot from the Chestnut Hill T stop. Hammond Pond Reservation is open year-round during daylight hours. For more information, call 617-698-1802.

Breakheart Reservation

Hidden amidst strip malls and fast-food joints along Route 1, this 640-acre hardwood forest is a treasure for hikers lucky enough to stumble across it. The reservation offers many miles of scenic views and plenty of strenuous trails to get your heart pumping. Fishing, bird watching, cross-country skiing, swimming, and biking are other attractions that lure nature lovers out to Breakheart. As there's really no way to get to there by mass transit, you'll have to drive. Take Route 1 to the Lynn Fells Parkway exit towards Melrose and Stoneham. Turn right onto Forest Street, and follow the signs to Breakheart Reservation. A good place to begin your hike is on the paved Pine Tops Road, located next to the parking lot adjacent to the headquarters building. For more information, call 781-233-0834.

Skyline Trail

This seven-mile trail is located in Blue Hills Reservation (near Milton), the largest open space within 35 miles of Boston. The Skyline Trail winds through rocky hills and provides superb views of the city. With an elevation gain of 2,500 feet, this hike is not for the faint of heart. This is a strenuous hike that will take at least half a day. But don't fret! If you're not up for a real workout, there are plenty of less challenging trails in the park and the color-coded trail map available at the headquarters building will help you find your way around. To get there, take Route 138 to Exit 3 towards Houghton's Pond. After exiting, turn right at the stop sign onto Hillside Street and travel about a mile until you reach Houghton's Pond. The trail is open year-round from sunrise until sunset. Also in the Reservation is the

Ponkapoag Pond trail, a four-mile loop around the pond, the highlight of which is a boardwalk trail (two miles roundtrip) through a rare Atlantic white cedar swamp. It's fun and different, but be warned: Wear waterproof shoes. Seriously. The boardwalk is made up of half submerged logs.

Middlesex Fells Reservation Eastern Section

Located seven miles north of Boston, Middlesex Fells is a 2,060-acre reservation where you'll find some of the area's most challenging hikes, many of which are considered some of the Boston area's best kept secrets. (If anyone asks, you didn't hear about it from us.) Middlesex Fells is off I-93 past the Stone Zoo. Parking is available on Pond Street. The beginning of the trail is located on the south side of Pond Street and begins behind a Virginia Wood sign near Gate 42. The trail is approximately 5.5 miles long, but can be extended to 16 miles if you connect trails. All of the hikes in this area are fairly strenuous and involve climbing and descending rocky slopes.

Moose Hill Wildlife Sanctuary

This is the oldest and second-largest Massachusetts Audubon Society (MAS) sanctuary. Moose Hill covers 1,984 acres that teem with wildlife and offers more than 25 miles of well-marked trails. One trail in particular, the Warner Trail, provides an exceptional view of the surrounding area from 491 feet. (You have to earn the view by climbing up Bluff Head.) Admission is $4 for adults, $3 for seniors and children aged 3–12. Members enter for free. Trails are open daily from dawn to dusk. The best way to get to Moose Hill is off Route 128/I-95 S. Take Exit 10. At the end of the ramp, make a left towards Sharon Street; then travel a quarter-mile and turn right onto Route 27 towards Walpole. After half a mile, turn left onto Moose Hill Street. Follow the MAS signs to the parking lot on the left. Find your way to the Visitor Center. All of the trails stem from there. For more information call 781-784-5691.

Walden Woods

Henry David Thoreau's account of his two-year stay in Walden is credited with sparking the conservation movement. Though nestled between railroad tracks and busy Route 2, Walden Pond is still a peaceful and pleasant setting for an afternoon walk no matter what season. The 102-foot deep Walden Pond is just one part of the 2680-acre Walden Woods. There is an easy loop trail around the pond, which passes by the site of Thoreau's house (a replica sits in the parking lot). If you get too hot, you can always stop for a quick dip. Easy interconnecting trails link up with the neighboring Walden Woods and Lincoln Conservation Trust. The main parking area is on Route 126 off of Route 2. Parking ($5) is limited to 350 spaces and fills up quickly on hot summer days. If there is no ranger at the gate, you will need exact change for the annoying automated ticket machine, inevitably causing longer delays than dealing with a live person. On crowded days, there are designated times of the day when they let people in. Call ahead at 781-259-4700, and visit www.walden.org for more information.

Sports • Swimming

General Information

City of Boston Swimming:	www.cityofboston.gov/bcyf/facilities.asp
Department of Conservation Resources:	www.mass.gov/dcr/recreate/swimming.htm
MIT Zesiger Center:	http://web.mit.edu/zcenter/aquatics/index.html
YMCA of Greater Boston:	www.ymcaboston.org
New England Masters Swimming:	www.swimnem.org

Overview

With your swimming options including universities, the oldest Y in the country, and few local gyms, it's easier to skip the many poorly maintained pools of the city with their odd hours. While the city's pools are the cheapest option (meaning free), they're only open from mid-June to mid-August. You'll find the city's website little help in locating pools and the only way to get schedules is to call each pool directly. For serious lap swimmers, the largest indoor pool in Boston is at **MIT's Zesiger Center (Map 27)**, running short course all winter and changing lanes to a 50 m for summer. Day passes are available. New England Masters maintains a comprehensive listing on swimming clubs, workout locations, and stroke clinics. There are also YMCAs scattered around the metro area.

In the summer, the DCR operates many outdoor swimming and wading pools and public beaches along the Bay and at local ponds. Their Website lists the hours and locations. The most famous wading pool is the Frog Pond in Boston Common. If fighting for pool space amongst hordes of screaming children is not your thing, favorite alternatives include taking a dip in Walden Pond in Concord (get there early, as the parking lot fills up fast) and strolling the busy beaches at Revere and Wollaston, which can be accessed by the Blue and Red Lines respectively. The Standells might "love that dirty water," but ongoing efforts to improve the once dangerous water quality of the Charles River continue, and the Charles River Swimming Club held its first ever one-mile swim in 2007 to demonstrate its safety (toxic algae postponed it in 2006), but recreational swimming is not encouraged, especially after a heavy rain. For those of you with a little extra cash burning some holes in your designer swim trunks, the **Colonnade Hotel (Map 6)** has a rooftop pool that has a $25 weekday pass for the public. It's like a club scene up there though, so make sure to spray tan on some abs if you're on the flabbier side.

Where to Swim

	Address	Phone	Fees	Map
Boston Harbor Island National Park Beach	ferry leaves from Long Wharf outside Marriott Hotel, 296 State St	617-223-8666	Free (but unavoidable $10–12 ferry ticket)	2
Mirabella Pool	585 Commercial St	617-635-5235	$10 adults, kids under 5 free	2
Central Branch YMCA Pool	316 Huntington Ave	617-536-6950	Membership $55.60 per month. Plus $100 joining fee	5
Colonnade Hotel - Rooftop Pool	120 Huntington Ave	617-424-7000	$25 per day pass (weekdays only)	6
Blackstone Community Center	50 W Brookline St	617-635-5162	$25 per year, children	7
Charlestown Community Center	255 Medford St	617-635-5169	$25 per year adults, $5 children	8
Harborside Community Center	312 Border St	617-635-5114	$25 per year adults, $5 children	9
Paris Street Pool	113 Paris St	617-635-5122	$20 per year adults, $5 children	9
Condon Community Center	200 D St	617-635-5100	$5 adults, $3 youth	10
Curley Community Center	1663 Columbia Rd	617-635-5104	$25 per year	11
Madison Park Community Center	55 New Dudley St	617-635-5206	$10 per year adults, $4 children	13
Curtis Hall Community Center	20 South St	617-635-5193	$25 per year adults, $5 children	14
Hennigan Community Center	200 Heath St	617-635-5198	$25 per year adults, $5 children	15
Cloughterty Pool	Bunker Hill St	617-635-5173	Free	16
Dealtry Memorial Pool	114 Pleasant St	617-923-0073	Free	16
Brookline Swimming Pool	60 Tappan St	617-713-5435	$5 adults, $3 students	17
Brighton/Allston Pool	380 N Beacon St	617-254-2965	Free	18
Oak Square YMCA	615 Washington St	617-782-3535	$58/month	18
McCrehan Memorial	356 Rindge Ave	617-354-9154	Free	22
Cambridge Family YMCA	820 Massachusetts Ave	617-661-9622	$48 per month & $50 joining fee	27
Veterans Memorial Pool	719 Memorial Dr	617-354-9381	Free	27
Zesiger Sports and Fitness Center	120 Vassar St	617-452-3690	$12 per day adults, $7 children	27
Mason Pool	159 Norfolk Ave	617-635-5241	$10 per year (adult), $5 (under 18)	28
Boston Chinatown Neighborhood Center Pool	885 Washington St	617-635-5129	$32 per year adults, $12 children	31
Constitution Beach	Orient Heights, E Boston	617-626-4973	Free	n/a
Crane Beach	Argilla Rd, Ipswich	978-356-4354	$2 per car for members / $7 per car for non-members	n/a
Nantasket Beach	Nantasket Ave, Hull	617-727-8856	Free	n/a
Revere Beach	Revere Beach Blvd, Revere	617-727-8856	Free	n/a

General Information

NFT Map: 16
Address: 4 Yawkey Wy
Boston, MA 02215
Phone: 617-267-9440
Website: www.redsox.com

Overview

It would be only the slightest of exaggerations to say that, in Boston, the Red Sox are a religion and Fenway Park is a house of worship. Situated just outside Kenmore Square, Fenway Park is a place where the reputedly unfriendly locals find fellowship in their deep love of the Sox and an even deeper hatred of the Yankees. In fact, Red Sox Nation is still (and will forever be) gloating over the historic 2004 comeback win against the evil men in pinstripes. Yet, our gloating increased quite a bit in 2007, as the Sox once again brought home the World Series Trophy with a four game sweep of the Colorado Rockies, while the Yankees were at home washing their uniforms. That's two World Series wins in two seasons, after an 86-year drought. Boston is truly in its baseball renaissance.

Despite this devotion, even the most die-hard fan cannot deny two basic truths: Fenway is old and Fenway is small. The first game at Fenway Park, played on April 20, 1912, got bumped off the front page of the newspapers by the breaking news of the Titanic sinking a few days earlier. With only 39,928 seats, it is the smallest park in the majors, though management has recently added a few thousand more seats in some very creative locations to expand capacity.

With age, however, comes a rich sense of history, and the dusty corners of Fenway have more personality than perhaps any other park in the game. The best-known of these character traits is the towering Green Monster, the 37-foot left field wall whose odd location can turn pop flies into homers and homers into singles. Marking the right field foul line is Pesky's Pole, named for Sox legend Johnny Pesky. On the manually operated scoreboard in left field, Morse Code dots and dashes spell out the initials of Red Sox owner Tom Yawkey and his wife.

Truly patriotic citizens of Red Sox Nation should take the Fenway Park tour. A tour leaves from Yawkey Way every hour Mon–Sun 9 am–4 pm. To get more information (recommended), call the Tours Hotline on 617-226-6666 or email tours@redsox.com.

How to Get There—Driving

Ha Ha Ha. Oh man, that's a good one. I guess if you LOVE traffic then you can head on down. Still, street parking locks up about 3 hours before game time, but if you've got no other option, then take the Fenway exit off of Storrow Drive and cross your fingers as you head up Boylston Street. Use your horn and hand gestures wisely.

Parking

If you're one of the brave souls who have decided to drive in for a game, keep in mind the following. First, Fenway does not provide parking unless you play for the Red Sox. Garages will charge triple for game-time parking, so expect to drop $30 bucks to be trapped inside one for hours, as it slowly empties after the Red Sox trounce whatever horrible team dared to face us. Street parking is as easy as winning the Mass Millions, but if you show up early enough, you might just be able to get a 2 hour meter...for a 4 hour game. Take. The. T.

How to Get There—Mass Transit

Take the Green Line to Kenmore and follow the crowd to the ballpark. If you're on the D train of the Green Line, use the Fenway stop. The MBTA Commuter Rail's Worcester/Framingham line also goes to Yawkey, a short walk from Fenway Park. There's also a free game-day-only shuttle that connects Gate B at Fenway Park with the Ruggles stop, served by the T's Orange Line and the MBTA Commuter Rail's Attleboro/Stoughton, Needham, and Franklin lines. Subway fare is $1.70; commuter rail fares range from $1.70 to $7.75.

How to Get Tickets

Always difficult to score, Red Sox tickets have become even more precious commodities since the team's curse-shattering World Series win. The first places to try for individual game and season ticket information, are the Red Sox box office at 877-REDSOX9 and the team's website. Ticket prices range from $12 bleacher seats to $312 dugout box seats. For a unique Fenway experience, try to get tickets on the Green Monster: $30 for standing room only and $140 for actual, you know, seats. If the conventional route fails, you will need a combination of money and luck. Check StubHub.com, eBay, or craigslist, but beware of scams. And there are always scalpers trawling Kenmore Square on game day, usually peddling tickets at a substantial mark-up, especially during the playoffs and games against the hated Yankees.

General Information

Address:	One Patriot Pl Foxborough, MA 02035
Phone:	508-543-8200
Websites:	www.gillettestadium.com www.patriots.com www.revolutionsoccer.net

Overview

As far as NFL franchises go, the New England Patriots were a joke until Bill Parcells took over as head coach in 1993 and Robert Kraft bought the team in 1994. The team continued to play in a mediocre stadium until 2002. Old Schaefer/Sullivan/Foxboro Stadium was an unsightly, obsolete, charmless concrete slab, but the Pats sent it packing in style. The last game at Foxboro Stadium was the hotly debated "Snow Bowl" vs. the Oakland Raiders. Depending on your loyalties, QB Tom Brady either fumbled or "tucked" the ball during a key late-game possession. (It was a tuck.) The Pats won, propelling them to victory in the 2002 Super Bowl.

The 2002 season was ushered in by the opening of Gillette Stadium, where the Patriots proved that their first championship season was no fluke, winning two more Super Bowls over the next three years. Unfortunately the stadium couldn't cap off a perfect season in 2008. The stadium has been accessorized with a 12-story lighthouse and a replica of the Longfellow Bridge at one end of the field. Game attendees who crave a snack may be pleased by the selection of 106 different concession stands, some of which now sell Patriot-brand meat products such as the First Down Beef Frank and the Sack Attack Mild Italian Sausage. A high definition screen, nearly 1,300 square feet in size, hangs over each end zone.

With a seating capacity of over 68,000, Gillette Stadium does triple duty, also acting as the home of Major League Soccer's New England Revolution and a major concert venue. It can be a good place to catch big names like the Rolling Stones or U2, but, given the size of the stadium, make sure to bring a pair of binoculars if you have anything but the best seats.

The first phase of Patriot Place, a one-million-square-foot entertainment, shopping, and commercial complex on land around the stadium opened in 2007. In other words, it will be a wicked huge mall. Look for more shops and attractions to open in the coming years.

How to Get There—Driving

From Boston, take I-93 S to I-95 S; take I-95 S to Exit 9 (Wrentham) onto Route 1 S. Follow Route 1 S approximately three miles to Gillette Stadium (on the left).

■ Upper Level, Corner/End Zone	■ Lower Level, Corner/End Zone
■ Upper Level, Sideline	■ Lower Level, Sideline
■ Mezzanine Level, Corner/End Zone	* N/A=Non-Alcoholic Section

Parking

The lots open four hours before Pats games and three hours before concerts and other events and two hours before Revolution games, leaving plenty of time for tailgating—an opportunity fans use to the fullest. General Seating ticket holders should enter lot P2, P5, or P10 from Route 1. Follow signs for "General Stadium Parking." Disabled parkers and limos should head for P2, buses for P5, and RVs for P10. For Patriots games, car parking costs $35, and limo parking costs $125, and bus parking costs $200. Prices vary for other Gillette events.

How to Get There— Mass Transit

MBTA commuter rail trains leave South Station for Foxboro Station on game days. A round-trip ticket costs $10. The train departs from the stadium 30 minutes after the game.

How to Get Tickets

With the Pats Dynasty status firmly cemented as the team of the Century, and the Greatest Football Team to Ever Exist (fact), you're going to have some ticket troubles, especially after Tom Brady took a season off. To get on the season ticket waiting list, visit the Patriots' website and have $100 a seat on hand for a deposit. For regular tickets (or concert tickets), call Ticketmaster at 617-931-2222. Game tickets range from $59 to $125. The ubiquitous scalpers can be found roaming the parking lots and approaches to the stadium. StubHub.com, eBay, and Craiglist also accommodate folks who are selling and buying tickets, but be careful—season ticket holders have been known to lose their seats after being caught selling extra tickets online.

General Information

NFT Map: 1
Address: 150 Causeway St
             Boston, MA 02114
Phone: 617-624-1805
             Celtics: 617-854-8000
             Bruins: 617-624-1900
Websites: www.tdbanknorthgarden.com
             www.bostonceltics.com
             www.bostonbruins.com

Loge   Club   Balcony

Overview

Greater Boston's long regional sports nightmare is over. Once again Celtics and Bruins fans can accurately say that their teams compete in "the Garden." The original Boston Garden, which opened in 1928, earned the adoration of Bostonians as the arena in which Bird, McHale, and Parish propelled the team to dynasty status. In footage of the team's 1984 NBA finals victory over the Lakers, fans crowd the sidelines and rush the court with time left on the clock. Bruins games could be even less civil and, correspondingly, even more fun.

As the 1980s drew to a close, however, both the Celtics and the Garden lost a bit of their luster. The team began a slow decline from glory and the venue grew more and more decrepit. Finally in 1995, the FleetCenter was constructed next door and both the Celtics and the Bruins said goodbye to their old stomping grounds. The new name took years to catch on among the area's stubborn traditionalists. When Fleet was acquired by Bank of America, the new parent company sold the naming rights—for $6 million a year—to TD Banknorth, who promptly restored the proper name. Then in 2009 TD Northbank became TD so now we have TD Garden. Can we just replace TD with "Boston" and get this over with! The 19,580-seat TD Garden has all that you would expect from a modern arena—rocket-launched t-shirts, overpriced food and beer, luxury box TVs, and airline and casino promotions during timeouts—but still holds on to touches of tradition, including the Celtics' legendary parquet floor. Nonetheless, even with the relative success of the Celtics and Bs in recent years, the new venue just doesn't seem to inspire the same sort of love as did its dilapidated predecessor. Having said that, The Celtics NBA Record 17th Banner now hangs from these new rafters, hopefully ushering in a new dynasty for our boys in Green. Even more fitting was the fact that we won it against those old purple and gold Lakers, at home, proving once again that in NBA history it's Celtics first, Lakers a solid and distant second.

The Bruins are now the only team to have not won a championship in the last decade, so hopefully some of the mojo that the C's brought with them rubs off, and allows Boston to fully cement it's Title-Town moniker.

In addition to sporting events, the TD Garden hosts the circus and concerts by artists ranging from Beyonce to U2.

How to Get There—Driving

Driving to the Garden is no more difficult than getting any place else in Boston by car—which is to say that it is quite difficult. From the north, take I-93 S to Exit 26A (Leverett Circle/Cambridge). Follow the signs (if construction hasn't relocated them) towards North Station/TD Garden. Take a right at the end of the ramp; the arena will be on your left. From the south, take I-93 N to Exit 26 (Storrow Drive). After the exit, keep left and follow the signs (see above warning) for TD Garden. Watch out, it's a left-hand exit. The Garden will be on your left.

Parking

Reason number two not to drive: The TD Garden doesn't have its own parking facilities, but there are several nearby garages ready and willing to gouge you, including a parking facility underneath the arena.

How to Get There— Mass Transit

The TD Garden sits atop the North Station commuter rail station, which services the northern suburbs. Directly underneath is a new "superstation" that finally puts North Station's Green Line and Orange Line T stops in the same location. The Charles/MGH Red Line stop and the Bowdoin Blue Line stop are less than a ten-minute walk away. Commuter rail fares range from $1.70 to $7.75.

How to Get Tickets

To get Celtics season tickets, call 866-4CELTIX or visit the Celtics' website. They offer full-season, half-season, and multi-game packages. Individual ticket prices range from $25 nosebleed seats to $275 courtside seats. The mid-range $55 end-court seats offer an excellent value.

To get Bruins season tickets call 617-624-BEAR or visit the Bruins' website. The Bs offer full-season, half-season, and ten-game packages, with individual ticket prices ranging from $26 to $101, topping out with the mysteriously un-priced Premium Club. (If you have to ask, you can't afford them.)

If you don't have tickets but have cash to burn, scalpers can be found on Causeway Street on game days.

Airline	Terminal	Phone Number
Aer Lingus	E	800-474-7424
Air Canada/ Air Canada Jazz	B	888-247-2262
Air France	E	800-237-2747
AirTran	C	800-247-8726
Alaska Airlines	B	800-252-7522
Alitalia	E	800-223-5730
American (except int'l arrivals)	B	800-433-7300
American (int'l arrivals only)	E	800-433-7300
American Eagle	B	800-433-7300
British Airways	E	800-247-9297
Cape Air	C	800-352-0714
Continental	A	800-525-0280
Delta Air Lines	A	800-221-1212
Delta Connection/Com Air	A	800-354-9822
Delta Shuttle	A	800-221-1212
Finnair	E	800-950-5000
Iberia	E	800-772-4642

Airline	Terminal	Phone Number
Icelandair	E	800-223-5500
JetBlue (except int'l arrivals)	C	800-538-2583
JetBlue (int'l arrivals only)	E	800-538-2583
Lufthansa	E	800-645-3880
Midwest	C	800-452-2022
Northwest/ KLM	E	800-225-2525
SATA	E	800-762-9995
Spirit Airlines	B	800-772-7117
Swiss	E	877-359-7947
TACV	E	866-359-8228
United	C	800-241-6522
United Express	C	800-241-6522
US Airways	B	800-428-4322
US Airways Express	B	800-428-4322
US Airways Shuttle	B	800-428-4322
Virgin Atlantic	E	800-862-8621

General Information

Website: www.massport.com/logan
Customer Service: 617-561-1800
Ground Transportation Info: 800-23-LOGAN
Logan Lost and Found: 617-561-1714
Parking Office: 617-561-1673

Overview

The country's 19th busiest airport (according to Bureau of Transportation Statistics), Logan International Airport features all the serpentine security lines and two-mile gate runs of most major airports and is located in an area of the country where weather can ground planes at any time of the year. Nonetheless, it was ranked seventh in traveler satisfaction in a 2007 survey by J.D. Power and Associates. And, thanks to the completion of the Big Dig and the extension of the Silver Line, getting to Logan is easier now than ever.

Jutting into the harbor from East Boston, Logan opened in 1923 as the "temporary occupant" on landfill originally intended to serve as a port. By 1939, flying contraptions had proven their worth and the site was made permanent. The airport is named after Lt. General Edward Lawrence Logan, a local and a Harvard grad who served in the Spanish-American War, the Massachusetts House of Representatives, and the Senate.

The decade-long Logan Modernization Project, now in its later stages, has yielded new and improved Terminals A and C, a new T station, an extended Silver Line, a new arrivals hall in international-serving Terminal E, standardized and improved signage, and improved access to the Central Parking Garage. And in 2009, Health Magazine ranked Logan as the 8th healthiest airport in the country. Terminal A is the world's first airport terminal certified by the U.S. Green Building Council for using the highest green construction standards, with a heat reflecting roof, low-flow faucets, waterless urinals, self-dimming lights, and recycled construction materials.

If good planning or bad weather leaves you with time to kill before your flight, you can grab a gourmet snack at Todd English's Bonfire or one of the three Legal Seafood locations, relax in one of 50 wooden rocking chairs (16 decorated by local artists), or just spend an hour letting yourself be hypnotized by the rhythmic movements of billiard balls through the kinetic sculpture in Terminal C.

How to Get There—Driving

To get to Logan from the west, take the Mass Pike (I-90) E through the Ted Williams Tunnel until the highway ends. From the south, use I-93 N and take Exit 20 to I-90 E. From the north, take I-93 S and follow the signs to the Callahan Tunnel. Check www.massport.com for traffic and construction updates.

Parking

Hourly and daily parking are available at Central Parking Garage, Terminal B Garage, and Terminal E Parking Lots 1 and 2. Rates range from $3 to $24 during the day and $36 to $48 a day for overnight parking. The Economy Parking lot charges a daily rate of $27 and a weekly rate of $108.

How to Get There—Mass Transit

Seriously, do yourself a favor by taking the T. It's a quick ride on the Blue Line from downtown to the Airport stop. A free shuttle bus (that runs 4am–1am (and prevents 7 tons of emissions from polluting the atmosphere every year by running on compressed natural gas), will take you from the T stop to your terminal. Or take the Red Line to South Station and transfer to the Silver Line bus, which stops at each airport terminal. If you're coming in from the 'burbs, check out the Logan Express buses that service Braintree, Framingham, Peabody, and Woburn. A Park-and-Ride system is in place, and although the prices for parking and buses vary, they will always be cheaper than taking a cab, especially with the proposed—and possibly massive—toll hikes in the works to fill in state budget gaps. If you're downtown near the water, the MBTA's Harbor Express water taxi can get you from Long Wharf to the airport in less than ten minutes.

How to Get There—Taxi

It's hard to get to Logan from anywhere except Eastie for less than $20. Boston Cab: 617-536-5010; Checker Cab: 617-536-7000; City Cab: 617-536-5100; Green Cab (Somerville): 617-623-6000; Cambridge Cab: 617-776-5000.

Rental Cars

Alamo   800-327-9633
Avis   800-831-2847
Budget   800-527-0700
Dollar   800-800-4000
Hertz   800-654-3131
National   800-227-7368
Enterprise   800-325-8007 (off-airport)
Thrifty   800-367-2277 (off-airport)

Hotels

Courtyard Boston Tremont • 275 Tremont St • 617-426-1400
Embassy Suites • 207 Porter St • 617-567-5000
Hampton Inn • 230 Lee Burbank Hwy • 781-286-5665
Hilton • 85 Terminal Rd • 617-568-6700
Holiday Inn • 225 McClellan Hwy • 617-569-5250
Hyatt • 101 Harborside Dr • 617-568-1234 • 800-633-7313
Marriott Long Wharf • 296 State St • 617-227-0800
Omni Parker House • 60 School St • 617-227-8600
Hilton Boston Downtown •
89 Broad St • 617-556-0006

History

The story begins just after World War II. When the good people at the Massachusetts Department of Public Works noticed the increasing popularity of automobiles and the stream of people leaving the city for the suburbs, they decided to make plans to build some major highways. The first highway to be completed was I-93, the Central Artery, hailed at the time as "a futuristic highway in the sky."

It soon became apparent that I-93 totally sucked. It was ugly, disruptive to neighborhoods, and boasted a high accident rate due to the excessive number of entry and exit ramps along the 1.5-mile stretch through the city. Recognizing that the Central Artery was a disaster, community groups fought successfully to stop other major highway projects. Two plans that never came to fruition were the Inner Belt (unbuilt I-695), which would have taken traffic around I-93 via a new, ten-lane BU bridge, and the Southwest Corridor Highway (unbuilt I-95), which would have run from the 93/128 split up through Hyde Park and JP to central Boston.

While averting construction of two new highways was a small victory for city dwellers, I-93 was still operating at triple its capacity, resulting in traffic jams at most hours of the day. The solution to the congestion was to dig a highway under the city—a solution that rather resembled performing open-heart surgery on a fully awake patient. Planning the project took the entirety of the 1980s and construction finally began in September 1991. After fifteen years and almost fifteen billion dollars, the project is officially finished. Hallelujah!

What is the Big Dig?

As most Bostonians know, the substantially completed "Central Artery/Tunnel Project" was, as the Massachusetts Turnpike Authority puts it, "the largest, most complex and technologically challenging highway project ever." The most important element of the Big Dig is the routing of I-93 from the Central Artery to a new (and leaky) tunnel. Other major aspects of the Dig include the extension of the Mass Pike to Logan Airport through the Ted Williams Tunnel, the construction of the beautiful Leonard P. Zakim Bunker Hill Bridge (yeah, it's a ridiculously long name), the erection of the Leverett Circle Connector Bridge, and a complete overhaul of the roads and traffic patterns around Logan Airport. The 2006 opening of the Albany Street off-ramp from I-93 S marked the point when all of the Dig's tunnels and bridges and their connection and ramps to surface roads were open to general traffic.

But when exactly does a civil engineering project of this magnitude "end"? Is it when the last orange pylon is removed from the road, or when the litigation finally wraps up? The I-93 tunnel (O'Neill Tunnel) sprouted a leak in 2004 shortly after opening to traffic. In its design for the tunnel, contractor Bechtel/Parsons Brinckerhoff recommended an approach that had never been used for another highway tunnel in the US, rejecting the more conventional design of lining the huge slurry walls with a concrete "tunnel box" in favor of making the slurry walls the tunnel's *only* walls. When the tunnel construction later necessitated waterproofing, the lack of interior walls caused some major problems. While the leaky walls and the endless construction are causes of concern and ennui for the daily commuters, the faulty bolts that fasten the concrete ceiling tiles are another issue all together. In July 2006, a woman was killed when one such tile falling on her car in the I-90 connector on her way to Logan Airport, a tragic event that lead to comprehensive inspections within the tunnels and the discovery of dangerous structural flaws and evidence of negligence. After extensive closings and traffic rerouting, the tunnel ceiling tiles have all reportedly been reinforced, though, and we are told that travel is once again wet and safe, but the loss of human life has added an unfortunate and serious undertone to Big Dig's already infamous story.

Development Plans

As of December 31, 2007, the Big Dig is officially finished, with the final price tag ringing up at $14.8 billion (ouch), which Bostonians may end up paying for via toll and mass transportation rate hikes. Either way, some has to pay the piper ... or, digger. On a more positive note, the old elevated 93 has finally come down, leading to a great deal more walking traffic from Faneuil Hall to the North End, and requiring facelifts on the sides of the buildings that now face the lovely new Rose Kennedy Greenway, a 15-acre green space extending from Chinatown to the North End. Post-Dig developers also hope to incorporate the construction of parks and other pedestrian-friendly spots along the Fort Point Channel, along the Charles River between the Museum of Science and the North End, and in East Boston.

General Information

Mass Highway Department: www.mhd.state.ma.us
Massport: www.massport.com
Big Dig: www.masspike.com/bigdig

Overview

The first bridge built in the American colonies (a pile bridge, incidentally) was completed in 1662, connecting Cambridge and Brighton. It stood where the Larz Anderson Bridge stands today. Fast-forward 350 years and you'll find no fewer than ten bridges spanning the Charles River from the Inner Harbor to Brighton, including the Boston University Bridge, the Harvard Bridge (a.k.a. the Mass Ave Bridge), and the Longfellow Bridge (with its salt-and-pepper-shaker towers), all of which offer great views of the skyline. (The view from the BU Bridge is our favorite.) Other bridges further upstream cross the river at River Street, Western Avenue, JFK Street/North Harvard Street (the Larz Anderson Bridge), and Gerry's Landing Road/Soldiers Field Road (the Eliot Bridge).

The Hub's new pet landmark is the Leonard P. Zakim Bunker Hill Bridge. No postcard of the Boston skyline seems complete without the Zakim, which connects downtown Boston with Charlestown. Perhaps the only Big Dig undertaking worth its salt, the Zakim is the widest cable-stayed bridge in the world, with soaring towers designed to reflect nearby Bunker Hill Monument. The bridge gives off a luminous glow at night, adding to its impressive appearance. According to the *Portsmouth Herald*, some call it the "Bill Buckner Bridge" as traffic passes through an inverted Y-shaped structure like the ball that passed through the legs of the Red Sox first baseman during the 1986 World Series. Poor Bill Buckner. Unlike the other bridges crossing the Charles, the Zakim is virtually not open to pedestrians. The Charlestown Bridge, now somewhat overshadowed by the Zakim, connects the North End and Charlestown and was once the scene of many Irish/Italian gang fights.

The old green lady crossing the Mystic River and connecting Charlestown with Chelsea is the Tobin Bridge. The three lanes on the lower level of the Tobin run northbound; the three lanes on the upper level run southbound. Drivers heading south on the Tobin must pay a toll (30 cents with a resident commuter permit and $3 for everyone else).

The Evelyn Moakley Bridge, built in the mid-1990s over the Fort Point Channel to divert traffic from the historic-but-decaying Northern Avenue Bridge, is itself decaying at an alarmingly fast pace. Be careful walking across the bridge at high tide.

And remember: The Callahan Tunnel takes you to the airport (no toll) and the Sumner Tunnel takes you from the airport (yes, toll).

Bridge	Engineer (E); Architect (A)	Length	Opened
Boston University Bridge	Desmond and Lord (A)		1928
	John Rablin (E)		
Charlestown (N Washington St) Bridge			1901
Congress Street Bridge			1930
Eliot Bridge	Maurice Witner (A)		1950
	Burns & Kennerson (E)		
Evelyn Moakley Bridge	Ammann & Whitney (A)	800'	1996
	Modern Continental (E)		
Harvard Bridge	William Jackson (E)	364.4 smoots, one ear	1891
Larz Anderson Bridge	Wheelright, Haven, and Hoyt (A)		1915
	John Rablin (E)		
Leverett Circle Connector Bridge	HNTB Corporation (E)	830'	1999
Longfellow Bridge	Edmund M. Wheelwright (A)	1,768'	1906
	William Jackson (E)		
Malden (Alford St) Bridge		2420'	
Northern Avenue Bridge		636'	1908
River Street Bridge	Robert Bellows (A)	330'	1926
	John Rablin (E)		
Summer Street Bridge	John Cheney (A)		1899
	William Jackson (E)		
Tobin Memorial Bridge	JE Grenier Co (A)	1,525'	1950
Weeks Footbridge	McKim, Mead, and White (A)		1924
	John Rablin (E)		
Western Avenue Bridge	John Rablin (E)	328'	1924
Leonard P. Zakim Bunker Hill Bridge	Christian Menn (designer)	1,457'	2002
	Miguel Rosales (A)		
	HNTB Corporation (E)		

Tunnel	Engineer	Length	Opened
Callahan Tunnel			1961
O'Neill Tunnel	Bechtel/Parsons Brinckerhoff (E)		2003
Sumner Tunnel			1934
Ted Williams Tunnel	Jacobs Engineering Group (designer)	8,500'	1995
	Bechtel/Parsons Brinckerhoff (E)		

General Information

Websites:
Boston: www.cityofboston.gov/transportation/parking.asp
Brookline: www.town.brookline.ma.us/transportation
Cambridge: www.cambridgema.gov/traffic
Somerville: www.ci.somerville.ma.us
Mass. RMV: www.state.ma.us/rmv

Phones:
Boston: 617-635-4680
Brookline: 617-730-2177
Cambridge: 617-349-4700
Somerville: 617-666-3311

Overview

Boston drivers have somehow made order out of chaos. We offer very few signs, have roadways simultaneously labeled both North and South (causing you to believe you've found the nexus of the universe), and claim, with pride mind you, the most aggressive road-ragers in the entire Northeast. Driving in the city itself is done more by "feel" than by specific directions, as every trip becomes an adventure in side streets, wrong turns, and clusterf**ks. And don't even ask about the endless civil war between drivers, bikers, and pedestrians.

The road system (if you can call it that) in Boston grew organically as the city expanded, not, as legend has it, out of cow paths (though it's a reasonable misconception). Little, if any, urban planning took place. The result is the chaos of today: an exasperating, exhilarating tangle of streets that are a source of pride to those who master them. The only exception to this pandemonium is Back Bay, which was given the benefit of foresight in its planning when this former marshland was filled and developed in the 1850's. The result: a grid-like pattern and alphabetized street names. But where's the fun in that?

State legislation prohibits the majority of national auto insurance providers from doing business in Massachusetts, though it's easy to just assume that they'd be insane to insure Bostonian drivers in the first place. But as a rule, we are both aggressive and competent. We know precisely how far we can push the envelope on sudden lane changes and risky passing maneuvers.

The novice may find himself reduced to tears on the side of the road, but the initial challenge makes the eventual mastery that much more satisfying.

Learn the Vocabulary

The Boston Turnaround: the act of turning one's car a full 180 degrees in the middle of the street with no regard for oncoming traffic in either direction.

The Boston Creep: the act of executing a turn by slowly creeping one's car into the middle of an intersection, which eventually leads to a complete blockage of both lanes of oncoming traffic. This allows the driver to successfully negotiate the turn—or cause an accident.

Rotary: Known in other parts of the country as a roundabout or traffic circle. Usually, vehicles already in the rotary have right-of-way. But no one in Boston follows this rule. Watch out.

Square: A location at which several feeder streets connect in odd formations and strange angles (see Harvard or Davis). Squares are rarely, if ever, square.

Masshole: From the mouths of out-of-staters, a derogatory term. For a true Boston driver, a label worn with pride.

Registry of Motor Vehicles (RMV): Known in other parts of the country as the DMV. The main RMV is in Chinatown, but other, equally disgruntled branches exist in Watertown, Cambridge, and the suburbs. You will have to pay the RMV $90 to become an officially licensed Masshole if you're changing from out-of-state.

Survival Tips

Be aggressive: You're never gonna make it in this town without a thick skin. Seriously, we will run you off the road.

Pay it forward: If you want people to let you in, you have to let them in—once in a while.

Be wary of cabs and buses: They WILL cut you off if you don't gun it.

Be color blind: A yellow light (and the first ten seconds of a red light) are considered the functional equivalent of a green light. This goes both ways though, so be careful. But the faster you gun it, the less honks you'll hear.

Trust your instincts: If you think that unlabeled street is the one you want, it probably is. If you think that guy is going to cut you off, he probably will. Tailgate the lady in front of you as a preventative measure.

You will get lost: Resistance is futile. A GPS won't save you. Neither will Google Maps. Leave yourself some extra time. We promise, one day it will start making sense. Or you'll have a nervous breakdown and never drive again.

General Information

Websites:

Boston: www.cityofboston.gov/transportation/
parking.asp

Brookline: www.town.brookline.ma.us/
transportation/parking/parking.html

Cambridge: www.cambridgema.gov/Traffic/
index.cfm

Somerville: www.ci.somerville.ma.us

Phones:

Boston: 617-635-4680
Brookline: 617-730-2230
Cambridge: 617-349-4700
Somerville: 617-625-6600

Overview

When parking within the city, you'll need time, patience, and a sixth sense for parking spots that are *about* to open up. With a few notable exceptions (near Fenway during Sox games comes to mind), careful circling of a target area will eventually yield results. If patience fails, a willingness to pay the outrageous fees at a parking garage is also helpful. There are, however, bargains to be found; the rates at the Post Office Square garage are amazing considering its location and the Cambridgeside Galleria charges only $1 per hour.

Depending on where you live, and whether parking in Boston causes you to regularly lose your temper, you might want to reconsider even owning a car. To relinquish driving is to lower your blood pressure considerably. The North End and Allston are crowded neighborhoods with narrow streets jam-packed with parked cars. When it snows (and it will snow), Boston residents become fiercely protective of their parking spots, illegally using traffic cones, lawn chairs, and other assorted paraphernalia to claim their freshly shoveled spots. Fisticuffs over disputed parking spots are not unheard of. Somerville, Cambridge, and Brookline, however, aren't quite as bad for parking, in part due to vast "resident-only parking" zones, plus the fact that there is no overnight parking allowed in Brookline. Remember, if you own a car and live in the city, always lock your doors, tuck in your mirrors, and remove any valuables. The Club ain't a bad investment, either.

Ultimately, if you live in Boston and own a car, you will receive *at least* one ticket a month. Maybe there was street cleaning the night before. Maybe there was a parking ban because of snow. Or maybe you got towed because there's a construction project and you missed the half-hidden "Tow Zone" sign that workers positioned conveniently on the sidewalk under a discarded pizza box. It doesn't matter what you do and how careful you are—*they will get you*—so just add it to the monthly budget.

How to Get Permits

In Somerville, take a current bill or bank statement with your address and your registration to 133 Holland Street. In Boston, take your registration and a current bill with your address to City Hall, Room 224, at Government Center. All Brookline wants is $15 and, apparently, they don't care where you live. Brookline Town Hall is at 333 Washington Street. In the People's Republic of Cambridge, you need your registration saying that either you or your car (it's not clear which) weighs less than 2.5 tons and proof of residency (other than a lease). You can visit the website and download the form and send copies of the above with a check for $8 (bargain!) to Cambridge Traffic, Parking & Transportation, Resident Parking, 238 Broadway, Cambridge, MA 02139.

Towing

Cars get towed for snow emergencies, street cleaning, and other emergency violations, so keep an eye out for Nor'easters, third Thursdays, and massive construction. If your car gets towed, it'll cost you at least $100 to get it back.

The Boston BTD Tow Lot is located at 200 Frontage Road, near the Andrew T stop in Dorchester/Southie. The City of Boston website says that "walking is not encouraged" due, obviously, to the Big Dig. Cabs can be hailed at the Andrew T stop.

Brookline, Somerville, and Cambridge use private, commercial lots to store your newly towed car. Call one of the numbers above, and they'll (hopefully) be able to tell you where your car is.

The Somerville tow lot is, for reasons unknown, Pat's Auto Body on McGrath Highway near Union Square.

Cambridge either has a top-secret tow lot, or it rotates. If your car gets towed, they ask you to call the police (617-349-3300), who will presumably then tell you where your car is.

Brookline has a similarly clandestine car imprisonment system. A call to their transportation/parking office should unearth your car.

Tickets

Because it allows them to take your money immediately, all four places offer online ticket payment. Tickets are dispensed for offenses such as double-parking, expired meters, non-resident parking on a resident-only street, street cleaning violations, and the city/town needing money. Regardless of the city, you're looking at about 50 bucks per infringement.

Transit • MBTA Subway

General Information

Website: www.mbta.com
Phone: 617-222-5000

Overview

Maps of the T show its four subway lines (Red, Orange, Blue, and Green) and the Silver Line (the T's mash-up of a subway line and a bus). All of the T lines except the Green Line's B train move you across the city at a decent clip. But if you need to get from Davis Square (Somerville) to Cleveland Circle (Brighton), well...it's not easy. Despite the proximity of the two places, you have to go downtown on one line (Red) and back out on another (Green)—an 11-mile trip connecting destinations that are 6.5 miles apart. Another T peeve is that the last trains depart from stations between midnight and 1 am, even though last call at Boston bars is between 1 and 2 am. (Some Redcoat traditions live on.) Late-night revelers are left to shell out for cabs.

he Red Line: The T's flagship line, the Red Line runs from Alewife in Cambridge through Davis Square, Harvard Square, MIT, the Esplanade (where you can admire the sparkling new Charles/MGH station,) the Common, Southie, and Dorchester. At the JFK/UMass stop, the line splits in two: The Ashmont train goes to Dorchester (with a connecting trolley to Mattapan), and the Braintree train runs through Quincy. A fun game to play on the Red Line: Bet with your friends about which student riders and professorial-looking types will get off at which university stops.

The Green Line: This is the oldest operational subway in the country, and it shows. Not a grown-up subway like the Red, Orange, and Blue Lines, the Green Line features light-rail "trolleys"—130-foot-long green Twinkies—that shoot you beneath the city of Boston before emerging onto streets and getting stuck in traffic.

The Green Line runs from Lechmere in Cambridge as far as Kenmore in Boston. Stops along the way include the Museum of Science, TD Banknorth Garden, Faneuil Hall, the Common, Back Bay, and Fenway Park. At Kenmore, the B (Boston College), C (Cleveland Circle), and D (Riverside) trains diverge and emerge from the ground as trolleys. The E train parts ways two stops back at Copley. The B is the slowest train because god forbid the Boston University kids walk anywhere. Lots of stops + lots of red lights = long rides. The B takes you through BU, Allston, Brighton, and as far as Boston College. The C runs along Beacon Street through Coolidge Corner (in Brookline) to Cleveland Circle (in Brighton). When getting off the train at Cleveland Circle, note the trolley making a wide circular turn through four-way traffic, which, inexplicably, leads to a lot of accidents. The D runs through Fenway and Brookline Village to Chestnut Hill before hitting several Newton neighborhoods. The E (Heath Street) train splits before Kenmore at Copley and services Symphony Hall, Mission Hill, Northeastern University, the Museum of Fine Arts, and Longwood Medical Area. Don't believe the maps that tell you E trains terminate at Forest Hills. This service was "temporarily" suspended in 1986—meanwhile, the 39 bus will take you from Heath Street to Forest Hills.

Somerville residents have been patiently waiting for the arrival of a long-promised, but controversial, extension of the Green Line. This extension, which would take the Green Line from Lechmere through exhaust-clogged Union Square to West Medford, is now expected to open no sooner than 2011, and even that delayed date could be pushed back.

The Orange Line: The Southwest Corridor Park and the Orange Line follow a path originally designed for the extension of I-95 through Boston. Community groups defeated the proposal in 1979, convincing officials to put a subway and park on the land instead. The Orange Line runs from Oak Grove in Malden to Forest Hills in Jamaica Plain. Stops along the way include Sullivan Square, Bunker Hill Community College, TD Garden, Faneuil Hall, Downtown Crossing, Chinatown, New England Medical Center, Back Bay/South End, as well as a few stops in Roxbury and Jamaica Plain.

The Blue Line: Who rides the Blue Line? MBTA ridership figures show a little over 55,000 daily boardings on the Blue Line, compared to 154,000 on the Orange, 210,500 on the Red, and about 205,000 on the Green. Running from Bowdoin Street downtown to Wonderland in Revere, this is the line you want to ride if you're going fishing, flying, or betting on horses and dogs (though dog racing in Mass is set to end by January 1, 2010). On your way east, you'll pass the Aquarium, Logan Airport, Suffolk Downs, and Revere Beach before winding up at Wonderland and its dog track. The stations at Aquarium and Logan have been renovated and made more accessible; other stations on the Blue Line are due to get the same treatment over the next couple of years.

The Silver Line: Now the most convenient way to the airport, this is actually a high-speed bus line. See page 252 for all the salacious details.

Parking

Your chances of finding parking increase as you move further away from downtown, but generally only end cap stations and suburban stations provide day parking. Garages and lots fill up quickly on weekdays. Prices vary. Parking in resident-only spots will result in a ticket and, in some areas, a keying.

Fares and Passes

In 2007, the MBTA replaced subway tokens with the magnetic-stripe CharlieCard and the paper CharlieTicket. (The "Charlie" moniker was taken from the Kingston Trio's 1959 hit, "Charlie on the MTA.") A subway ride costs $1.70 using the CharlieCard, and $2 using the paper CharlieTicket. The monthly subway/bus "Linkpass" costs $59, and reduced fares are available for seniors, people with disabilities, and junior-high and high school students. Children under 11 ride free when accompanied by an adult. Passes are sold at certain T stops and in some stores, however—the T has stated that it will no longer give away the rechargeable plastic CharlieCard, and will instead charge a fee for new and replacement cards. To find out where to buy a pass or to purchase one online, visit www.mbta.com.

MBTA Buses

Website: www.mbta.com
Phone: 617-222-3200

Every day, intrepid T bus drivers pilot their behemoth vehicles down too-narrow streets filled with angry drivers, errant pedestrians, unfortunate bikers, and, in the winter, ice and snow. (A simple "thank you" to the driver as you get off the bus isn't too much to ask.) MBTA buses run everywhere the subway doesn't, and some places it does. Usually at least one of any bus route's end points is a subway station. The T also runs several popular express buses from outlying neighborhoods to downtown along the Mass Pike and other highways.

The T is in the process of replacing the bulk of its aging diesel fleet with new Compressed Natural Gas (CNG) buses. Identifiable by their blue strip and the low roar of their engines, the new buses reduce emissions by up to 90 percent and, so far, are cleaner on the inside as well (just give them a few years). Some buses on busy routes feature low floors and articulated midsections, such as those used along the Silver Line and JP's 39 bus.

The MBTA has discontinued its popular but unprofitable Night Owl service (is a public service supposed to be profitable, anyway?). The Night Owl used to run buses along the subway routes until 2:30 am on Friday and Saturday nights, helping late-night partiers with a lift home. No word from the MBTA on whether this service will ever re-appear. Although with the state now frantically searching for ways to seal up its ever widening budget gaps, it certainly wouldn't hurt to start Night Owl back up again.

With the fare increase in January 2007 and the updating of the T's fare payment system, buses cost $1.50 if you use the paper Charlie Ticket or $1.25 if you use the plastic Charlie Card. The fares on the express buses are also different depending on if you use the ticket ($3.50 for inner express buses $5 for outer express) or card ($2.80 for inner express and $4 for outer express). Monthly bus passes are $40 and subway/bus combos cost as little as $59 for a subway/ local bus packages, while express bus combos are either $89 or $129. Students, seniors, and disabled persons can purchase monthly passes at reduced rates. Bus passes can be bought at several T stations or online at www.mbta. com. And you should be able to pick up a Charlie Card at customer service booths in T stations or buy a pre-loaded one at the T's Web site.

Silver Line

Website: www.allaboutsilverline.com
Phone: 617-222-3200

Although the Silver Line appears on the MBTA's subway map, it is actually a high-speed bus line (a "state-of-the-art Bus Rapid Transit system," no less) that, according to the MBTA, "combines the quality of rail transit with the flexibility of buses." The MBTA's public relations materials may be as gassy as the CNG used by some of the new buses, but in fact the new system provides much-needed additional public transport options for Roxbury residents, and is proving handy to airport travelers, Moakley Courthouse staff, and people working at construction sites along the waterfront. It's also a convenient way to get to the Bank of America Pavilion for concerts or to one of the many Seaport district restaurants, like the Legal Test Kitchen or Anthony's Pier Four, for dinner and drinks.

The Silver Line is being constructed in three phases. Completed Phase I runs between Downtown Crossing and Dudley Square in Roxbury. Phase II, also completed, runs from South Station to Boston Marine Industrial Park, and City Point. (The MBTA is waffling on its original plan to extend the Silver Line to the Andrew T stop in South Boston/Dorchester.)

Phase III is scheduled to be completed in 2016, but because there hasn't yet been a decision taken on how the buses will actually get into the tunnel, it's anyone's guess when Phase III will go on-line.

The Silver Line Waterfront fare follows the above fare structure for the subway (subway passes are valid) and the Silver Line Washington Street follows that of the bus (bus passes are valid), with Charlie Tickets and Cards in effect for both.

Cambridge EZRide

Website: www.masscommute.com/tmas/crtma/ ezride.html
Phone: 617-839-4636

Cantabridgians who traverse the Charles each morning on their daily commute should check out the EZRide bus service, whose cheery sky-blue coaches run through Cambridge to North Station. The EZRide route begins in Cambridgeport and passes through University Park, Kendall Square, and East Cambridge, making a dozen or so stops along the way.

EZRide operates Monday through Friday only, and does not run on holidays. Service in the morning runs from approximately 6:15 am to 10 am; afternoon service runs from approximately 3:30 pm to 7:30 pm.

A trip on EZRide costs $1. Students, seniors, disabled persons, and children aged 5–11 traveling with an adult pay 50 cents. Flashing an MIT ID lets you ride for free.

Greyhound

NFT Map: 4
Website: www.greyhound.com
Phone: 800-231-2222

Greyhound buses leave from the South Station bus terminal and they'll take you *anywhere*. It ain't the Concorde, but it'll eventually get you to one of its 3,700 stations across North America. Round-trip tickets to New York usually cost $55–$65 round-trip to Washington DC is $132–$142, and Boston to Philadelphia is $92–$118 round-trip.

South Station is on Atlantic Avenue, one block down from Summer Street. The bus terminal is the taller building behind the rail building.

To get to South Station from the Mass Pike (I-90), take Exit 24A. This exit drops you onto Atlantic Avenue—the bus terminal is on the right side. From I-93 N, take Exit 20 and follow signs for Downtown and South Station. At the lights, continue straight onto Atlantic Avenue.

From I-93 S, take Exit 23 onto Purchase Street, make a left on Kneeland Street, continue to the end of the street, and then take a left onto Atlantic Avenue. On-street parking is scarce. If you're pinched, try the bus terminal's parking garage. The entrance is on Kneeland Street.

The Red Line T line has a stop at South Station, also the end point for the southern routes of the commuter rail. Walk through the train station and past the tracks to reach the bus station entrance.

Chinatown Buses

If you want to get to New York City for *really* cheap, take a Chinatown bus. A round-trip ticket will only cost you $30 on Boston Deluxe, Fung Wah, Lucky Star, or Sunshine. Chinatown buses range from small coaches to full-blown buses with stinky bathrooms and non-functional TVs. We strongly recommend using the bathrooms only in emergency situations, and even then we're not so sure. Fung Wah is the best known, most recently because its notoriously speedy drivers have been involved in several accidents and bus fires. The other carriers are likely to be less crowded and chaotic. Watch out—you don't get left behind in Connecticut during the bathroom break at the Roy Rogers or the buffet at the strip mall.

If you take a late Chinatown bus from NYC, you will get into Boston after the T closes, meaning you'll have to pay for a cab that will cost more than the 200-plus-mile journey from New York.

Boston Deluxe

www.gotobus.com/bostondeluxe/; 617-354-2101
Christian Science Plaza, 175 Huntington Ave (Map 5)
Pick up the Boston Deluxe near the Prudential Center for trips to New York City and Hartford. New York-bound buses depart Friday through Sunday at 8:30 am, 11 am, 1 pm, 4:30 pm, 6 pm, and 10:30 pm and drop off at Broadway and 32nd Street as well as E 86th Street and Second Avenue. Buses to Hartford depart Friday to Sunday at 8:30 am, 11 am, 1 pm, 6 pm, and 10:30 pm and drop off at 365 Capitol Avenue (Charter Oak Supermarket). Both routes cost $30 round-trip.

Fung Wah Bus

www.fungwahbus.com; 617-345-8000
South Station, 700 Atlantic Ave (Map 4)
Buses to New York depart every hour on the hour, from 7 am until 10 pm, with an additional trip at 11:30 pm. Round-trip tickets cost $30. Buses leave from Gate 25 at South Station (left side) and drop off at 139 Canal Street in New York's Chinatown.

Lucky Star Bus

www.luckystarbus.com; 617-426-8802
South Station, 700 Atlantic Ave (Map 4)
Buses to New York depart every hour on the hour, from 7 am until 8 pm. There are also departures at 11:30 pm and 2 am. Round-trip tickets cost $30 (add $10 for the 2 am trip). Buses leave from Gate 13 at South Station and drop off at Christie and Hester Streets in New York's Chinatown.

Sunshine Travel

www.sunshineboston.com;
617-328-0862 or 617-695-1989
31 Harrison Ave, Boston (Map 4);
McDonald's Plaza, Fields Corner, Dorchester (Map 32)
Along with buses departing hourly for NYC ($15 each way, $25 for the 2 am bus), Sunshine Travel offers two-, three-, and four-day tours to places like Tennessee (four days, $178), Chicago (four days, $269), Washington DC (three days, $118), Niagara Falls (two days, $105), and destinations in eastern Canada ($128–$278). Buses to the Mohegan Sun casino in Connecticut depart five times daily, picking up in Dorchester, Boston, and Quincy. Round-trip tickets cost $10, and you'll receive a $20 gambling voucher and a $15 dining voucher if you're 21 years of age or older.

Bolt Bus

NFT Map: 4
Website: www.boltbus.com/
Phone: 1-877-BOLTBUS

In 2009, a new joint venture between Greyhound and Peter Pan was launched, called the Bolt Bus. Bolt Bus provides service between Boston and New York City, and connecting service to Philadelphia, Baltimore, Cherry Hill, and Washington DC out of New York. Round-trip tickets to New York run about $30, although the earlier you book your trip, the more the price goes down (it can go as low as $1!). Each bus includes free wireless internet, three extra inches of legroom per seat, and power outlets throughout.

Megabus

NFT Map: 4
Website: www.megabus.com/us/
Phone: 877-GO2-MEGA

The popular UK no-frills bus line called Megabus also began operating out of Boston in 2008. Megabus provides service from Boston to Hartford and New York, and connecting service from New York to Albany, Atlantic City, Baltimore, Buffalo, Niagara Falls, Philadelphia, Rochester, Syracuse, Toronto, and Washington. As with Bolt Bus, the earlier you book, the less you're likely to pay. Round trip tickets to New York round out to about $36 (maximum). Many locations of Megabus stops are on public streets (usually either outside train stations or transportation hubs), college campuses, or at park-and-ride lots. All Megabus buses are equipped with free Wi-Fi.

General Information

Website: www.mbta.com
Phone: 617-222-3200 or 800-392-6100

Overview

The commuter rail is a series of train lines that service the outer limits of Greater Boston, the suburbs, and points as far out as Worcester and Providence, Rhode Island. Northbound routes leave from North Station, and southbound routes depart from South Station. Compared to the commuter rail systems of other East Coast cities, Boston's trains make for a relatively pleasant experience. Massachusetts is working to renovate all of the stations, outfitting them with new platforms, electronic signaling, and new ramps and elevators to make them handicapped accessible. As with any major transit network, there are occasional (read: daily) delays on the commuter rail. Still, a ride on the rails is 1,000 percent less stressful than driving in and out of the city every day.

The commuter rail is also a great option for day-trippers going in either direction. Taking the train allows inbound visitors to enjoy, rather than just get lost in, the city. City-dwellers who want to escape the familiar urban landscape can head up to Gloucester for a day at the beach, venture to Plymouth for a history lesson, or just explore a new city down in Providence.

If you're looking at the commuter rail map for the first time, you might think that the lack of a connection between North Station and South Station is a mistake. Well, it may be a mistake, but not on the part of the mapmakers. To get from one station to another, you'll have to use the T (and transfer to a second T), take a cab, or walk. Seriously. For additional information about North Station and South Station, see the next page.

In the long term, Gov. Deval Patrick has pledged to bring commuter rail service back to the cities of New Bedford and Fall River by 2016.

Parking

Parking is available at every commuter rail station except Back Bay, Belmont Center, Chelsea, JFK/UMass, Morton Street, Porter Square, River Works, Ruggles, Silver Hill, Uphams Corner, Waverley, Windsor Gardens, and Yawkey. Rates vary, with some as low as $1 per day.

Fares and Passes

Commuter rail tickets range in price from $1.70 to $7.75. Each destination is assigned a zone number that determines the price of your ticket. Tickets can be purchased on the train, but depending on how busy the train is and the ticket-taker's mood, a surcharge may be added to the price. Kids 5–11, high school students, seniors, and disabled persons ride for half-price. Children under five and blind people ride free. The cost of monthly passes ranges from $59 to $250, depending on the zone. Some monthly passes offer varying perks like free subway, bus, and ferry use. Passes are sold at certain T stops and other locations (usually a local shop close to the station), as well as online at www.mbta.com. If you're buying your ticket at a T stop, be sure to look up your zone number ahead of time on the MBTA website. And make sure you're boarding a commuter rail train and not an Amtrak train. (This happens more often than you'd think.)

MAP 1

TD Garden

PAGE 243
North Station

93

Auerbach Wy

D Steel Federal Reserve

Causeway St

Lomasney Wy

Staniford St

Canal St

North Station

Thacher St

N Washington St

Cooper St

Commercial St

Prince St

N Margin St

Salem St

Snowhill St

Charter St

Battery St

Merrimack St

Market St

New Chardon St

N Washington St

Richmond St

North St

Hanover St

Endicott St

Cross St

Commercial St

New Sudbury St

Haymarket

Cross St

Bowdoin

Cambridge St

New Sudbury St

Clinton St

Christopher Columbus Park

Somerset St

Bowdoin St

Government Center

City Hall

Faneuil Hall

Quincy Market

Aquarium

Ashburton P.

Congress St

PAGE 194

State St

State

Kilby St

India Row

East

Nassau St

Beacon St

School St

Water St

Broad St

4

PAGE 188

Park Street

Tremont St

Washington St

Province St

Franklin St

Milk St

Oliver St

Pearl St

High St

Devonshire St

Downtown Crossing

Temple Pl

Boston Common

Bromfield St

Winter St

Summer St

Franklin St

Arch St

Federal St

Congress St

Atlantic Ave

Purchase St

Northern

Seaport Blvd

Avery St

West St

Ave de Lafayette

Chauncy St

Kingston St

Bedford St

South Station

MAP 4

Fort Point Channel

Boylston

Tremont St

Essex St

Lincoln St

South Station

Dorchester Ave

Congress St Bridge

Chinatown

Beach St

Atlantic Ave

Lagrange St

General Information

NFT Maps: 1 & 4
Websites: www.amtrak.com (Amtrak)
　　　　　www.mbta.com (MBTA)
Amtrak: 800-872-7245 (800-USA-RAIL)
MBTA: 617-222-5215

Overview

North Station and South Station are the main Amtrak and MBTA Commuter Rail depots in Boston. North Station, near the North End and underneath TD Garden, sits above the T's new "superstation" that (finally) connects the Green Line and Orange Line. South Station, on Atlantic Avenue and Summer Street at the gateway to South Boston, is served by MBTA and Amtrak and also has a bus terminal, a food court in the domed arrival hall, a bar, a newsstand, and a bookstore.

Traveling between Stations

There is a one-mile gap between the two Amtrak stations. The North Station stop is on the Orange and Green Lines of the MBTA subway, and the South Station stop is on the Red Line. Yes, it *is* crazy that the stations aren't on the same line and don't directly connect to each other. No, they're *not* going to do anything to correct the problem in the near future. Yes, they *could* have rolled it into the Big Dig project, since they were digging under the city anyway. No, we *don't* know why they didn't. And yes, it *does* seem odd that they spent billions to improve automobile transportation while ignoring public transportation. As it stands, travelers going from New York to Maine have to get off the train at South Station and either take a cab, take two subway lines, or walk to get to North Station to continue their journey. Where's "Amtrak Joe" Biden when you need him?

How to Get There—Driving

Both stations are located off I-93 in downtown Boston. For North Station, take Exit 26 (Storrow Drive), and for South Station, take Exit 23 (Purchase Street/South Station). To get to South Station from the Mass Pike (I-90), take Exit 24B to Atlantic Avenue.

Parking

The MBTA says there's no parking at either station, but "street or private parking may exist." Helpful, huh? In fact, both North Station and South Station are served by nearby, expensive parking garages, and neither station offers much in the way of street parking. Lovely.

How to Get There—Mass Transit

North Station is on the T's Green and Orange Lines. South Station is on the Red Line.

Amtrak

Amtrak trains leave out of North Station and South Station going north to Portland, Maine and south to NYC and beyond. When you go north, they call it the Downeaster (that's Mainer for "near Canada"). When you go south, they call it a bunch of things, including "the Federal," "the Acela," and the mundanely titled "Regional." The Acela is Amtrak's flagship route, offering "high-speed" service from South Station to NYC, Philly, and DC, with stops along the way. On a good day, the Acela chugs from Boston to New York in 3.5 hours, which is still only slightly faster than a bus and, at $100 a ticket, costs much more than taking one of the Chinatown buses or Greyhound (see page 253).

Baggage Check

Three items of baggage weighing up to 50 lbs each may be checked up to 30 minutes prior to train departure. For an additional fee of $10 per bag, three additional pieces can be checked. Each passenger is allowed two carry-on items on board. No dangerous, fragile, valuable items, animals, or household goods can be checked. Bikes, skis, and other odd-shaped equipment usually count as one checked bag and should not be carried aboard the train. With the exception of service animals, all pets are prohibited on Amtrak trains.

How to Get Tickets

To purchase train tickets, call Amtrak or visit their website. The website sometimes offers discounts for purchasing on-line, so it's worth checking the website before heading to the station.

Going to New York

One-way fares start at $62 and the journey takes about 4.5 hours from South Station. You could cut an hour off your commute by riding express on the Acela, but the comfort and convenience will cost ya ($100 or more).

Going to Philadelphia

One-way fares start at $60 and the ride takes about six hours. Fares on the speedier Acela Express start at $115 and cut about an hour off the journey.

Going to Washington DC

A trip to Washington on the regular Amtrak train will cost you at least $65 and will take you between eight and nine hours. Acela Express tickets start at $124 and the trip takes between six and seven hours.

Transit · MBTA Ferries / Water Taxis

CHARLESTOWN

MAP 8

46

Navy Yard

45

43

F4

22

Charles River

EAST BOSTON

Commercial Wharf

19

18

MAP 9

16

Long Wharf

15

East Boston Piers

Boston Marina

68

Aquarium

14

Boston Inner Harbor

1

BOSTON

MAP 1

Logan International Airport

PAGE 244

Rowes Wharf

Courthouse

7

Logan Airport

MAP 2

9

8

F2/F2H

F1

World Trade Center

5

F2/F2H

4

Fleet Boston Pavilion (summer only)

F1

MAP 10

2

Reserved Channel

Boston Harbor

SOUTH BOSTON

MAP 11

Pleasure Bay

Black Falcon Terminal

F2H only

Pemberton Point (limited service)

HU

Dorchester Bay

F2/F2H

F1

Fore River Shipyard

Hingham Shipyard

QUINCY

HINGHAM

Fort Point Channel

Legend:
- Commuter Boats
- Limited Service
- Inner Harbor Ferries
- ○ Ferry Station
- ● Rowes Wharf Water Taxi
- ❷ City Water Taxi

General Information (Ferries)

MBTA: www.mbta.com/schedules_and_maps/boats/; 617-222-5215

Harbor Express: www.harborexpress.com; 617-222-6999

Overview

The MBTA Commuter and Excursion Boat Service connects Boston to Logan Airport and is one of the best routes in and out of Charlestown and other shore side communities. One thing that makes the T boat better than any other form of Boston transportation is the fun factor. On a nice day, paying a buck and a half for a quick jaunt across the harbor feels like a steal. And on any day, not having to deal with Boston traffic is priceless. The views of the city from the water are gorgeous, and since the routes are in the Inner Harbor, the ride remains relatively smooth even in bad weather. There is also that delicious old-time feeling that comes with ferrying across the harbor. You'll want to keep in mind that boat schedules are more limited than bus schedules (particularly on weekends) and are more susceptible to disruptions due to inclement weather.

Most ferries operated by the MBTA leave from Long Wharf and travel to the Charlestown Navy Yard, the Fore River Shipyard in Quincy (F4), and Pemberton Point in Hull (F2H). The F1 boat travels between Rowes Wharf and Hingham Shipyard.

The F2 and F2H boats, catamarans operated by Harbor Express, stop at Logan Airport, but not at all times of the day—check the MBTA website for timetables. During rush hour (and decent weather) the Harbor Express is a sensible choice for getting to the airport. It takes a mere seven minutes to get to the airport dock from Long Wharf and about 25 minutes from Quincy and Hull. From the airport dock, take the free Water Shuttle bus 66 to the terminals. The 66 bus takes about 15 minutes to visit all terminals and return to the dock.

All ferry stops are accessible to wheelchair users. Bicycles can also be taken on board for free.

Parking

Parking for commuter ferry stops in the Inner Harbor is available only on the street or in a garage. Parking in Quincy costs $1 for a day and $6 overnight. In Hingham, parking costs $1 for a day and $1.75 overnight. Free parking is available at Hull High School.

Fares

A trip on a boat between destinations in the Inner Harbor costs $1.70 (pay a crewmember when boarding the boat). Trips from Hull, Quincy, and Hingham to the Inner Harbor (Rowes Wharf or Long Wharf) cost $6 ($3 for kids, seniors, and disabled persons). Trips from Quincy and Hull to Logan Airport on the Harbor Express are $12 ($10 for seniors, $3 for kids 5–11). Pay a crewmember when boarding the boat.

General Information (Water Taxis)

City Water Taxi: www.citywatertaxi.com; 617-422-0392

Rowes Wharf Water Taxi: www.roweswharfwatertaxi.com/ 617-406-8584

Massport: www.massport.com/logan/getti_typeo_water.html; 800-23-LOGAN

Overview

On the charmed waters of the Inner Harbor, two water taxi companies ply their trade. During the warmer months, water taxis provide an enjoyable way to cross the Inner Harbor. Both water taxi companies stop at the Logan Airport dock.

City Water Taxi

City Water Taxi offers direct service to the entire Boston waterfront, year-round, with enclosed boats that are heated when the weather is bad. (Mon–Sat 7 am–10 pm; Sun 7 am–8 pm. In addition to the airport dock, City Water Taxi serves 16 other points, including Bank of America Pavilion, Fan Pier, Charlestown Navy Yard, Black Falcon Terminal, and all the major wharves in the Inner Harbor. (To get to the Boston Convention and Exhibition Center, aim for the World Trade Center.) To catch a City Water Taxi from the airport, take Massport's 66 bus to the airport dock. Use the call box at the dock to call for a boat if there isn't one already there. From other destinations, call City Water Taxi to arrange a pick-up.

Tickets are sold on board the boat. Fares to downtown points and Logan Airport cost $10 one-way and $17 round-trip. There is a $20 minimum to Charlestown, North Station, and Black Falcon Terminal, but if you have a traveling companion, the fare is $15 each.

Rowes Wharf Water Taxi

Also operating year-round, Rowes Wharf Water Taxi provides on-call service to 31 points in the Inner Harbor (from Nov 2–April 1, service runs 7 am–7 pm; from April 2–Nov 1, service runs from 7 am–10 pm Mon–Sat and 7 am–8 pm on Sun). After-hours service is available upon request. Rowes Wharf Water Taxi serves 17 different docks and now operates a Seaport Express providing weekday service between Rowes Wharf, Central Wharf, and the Seaport World Trade Center for $1.70. For the complete schedule, look online. To hail a boat from the airport dock, use the company's call box; from other destinations, give them a call from your own phone.

Tickets are sold on board. The fare costs $10 one-way and $17 round-trip.

Car Rental

Map 1 · Beacon Hill / West End

Avis	3 Center Plz	617-534-1400
Dollar	209 Cambridge St	617-723-8312

Map 2 · North End / Faneuil Hall

Enterprise	1 Congress St	617-723-8077

Map 3 · Downtown Crossing / Park Square / Bay Village

Budget	28 Park Plz	617-497-3669
Hertz	30 Park Plz	617-338-1500

Map 4 · Financial District / Chinatown

Alamo	270 Atlantic Ave	617-557-7179
Dollar	30 Rowes Wharf	617-367-2654
Hertz	2 International Pl	617-204-1165
Hertz	Summer St & Atlantic Ave	617-338-1503
National	270 Atlantic Ave	617-557-7179

Map 5 · Back Bay (West) / Fenway (East)

Enterprise	800 Boylston St	617-262-8222
Select	39 Dalton St	617-236-6088

Map 6 · Back Bay (East) / South End (Upper)

Avis	100 Clarendon St	617-534-1404
Dollar	110 Huntington Ave	617-578-0025
Hertz	10 Huntington Ave	617-338-1506
Hertz	145 Dartmouth St	617-338-1500

Map 9 · East Boston

Affordable	84 Condor St	617-561-7000
Alamo	2 Tomahawk Dr	617-561-4100

Map 10 · South Boston (West) / Fort Point

Select	1 Seaport Ln	617-345-0203

Map 12 · Newmarket / Andrew Square

Enterprise	230 Dorchester Ave	617-268-1411

Map 13 · Roxbury

Enterprise	17 Melnea Cass Blvd	617-442-7500

Map 16 · Kenmore Square / Brookline (East)

Select	500 Commonwealth Ave	617-532-5060

Map 18 · Brighton

Rent A Wreck	2022 Commonwealth Ave	617-254-9540

Map 19 · Allston (South) / Brookline (North)

Adventure	226 Harvard Ave	617-566-1018
Adventure	27 Harvard Ave	617-783-3000
Budget	95 Brighton Ave	617-497-3608
Enterprise	292 Western Ave	617-783-2240
Enterprise	996 Commonwealth Ave	617-738-6003
Hertz	414 Cambridge St	617-787-2894
U-Save	25 Harvard Ave	617-254-1000

Map 20 · Harvard Square / Allston (North)

Alamo	1663 Massachusetts Ave	617-661-8747
Avis	1 Bennett St	617-534-1430
Hertz	24 Eliot St	617-338-1520
National	1663 Massachusetts Ave	617-661-8747
Thrifty	110 Mt Auburn St	617-876-2758

Map 23 · Central Somerville / Porter Square

Hertz	646 Somerville Av	617-625-7958

Map 24 · Winter Hill / Union Square

Americar	190 Highland Ave	617-776-4640l

Map 25 · East Somerville / Sullivan Square

Enterprise	37 Mystic Ave	617-625-1766

Map 26 · East Cambridge / Kendall Square / MIT

Enterprise	1 Broadway	617-577-0404

Map 27 · Central Square / Cambridgeport

Budget	20 Sidney St	617-577-7606
Enterprise	25 River St	617-547-7400

Map 28 · Inman Square

U-Save	70 Prospect St	617-628-8800

Zipcar General Information

Website: www.zipcar.com
Phone: 617-933-5070

Background

Zipcar rents out cars by the hour. The company, which now runs similar services in DC, New Jersey, New York, and elsewhere, was founded at MIT: "People would achieve transportation nirvana by having a transit pass and a Zipcard in their pockets. The result would be reduced congestion, fewer auto emissions, more green space, and a revolution in urban planning." That's Cantabridgian for "Give us $9/hr, we'll give you a Jetta." This seems like the smartest idea on wheels if you live in congested areas like the North End, Allston, or Harvard Square and you need to get somewhere the T can't take you. For infrequent drivers, the $25 application fee and minimum annual fee of $50 still make Zipcar service cheaper than owning a car.

How It Works

If you're 21 or older, in possession of a valid driver's license, and you've completed the online application, all you need to do is call or go online to reserve one of the hundreds of cars available at zipcar.com. (You get to choose from a fleet of BMWs, Minis, pick-ups, and others.) Your Zipcard unlocks the car that has been reserved for you, which you pick up at the most convenient of their many locations. Cars must be returned to the same spot where they were picked up. The car unlocks when a valid Zipcard is held to the windshield; your card will only open the car during the time you have reserved it.

Costs

The cost of Zipcar varies depending on the pick-up location, but rates start at $9 an hour. A reservation for 24 hours, the maximum amount of time that a car can be reserved, starts at about $68. The first 125 miles are free; each additional mile costs about 35 cents. Membership costs are additional. Make sure to return your car on time, as Zipcar charges exorbitant hourly late fees on unreturned cars. The best part: gas and insurance are included with every reservation.

If you've just moved to Boston and need a crash course on the "sights," you must check out the **Freedom Trail** (see page 189). Yes, it's touristy, but it's the best self-guided tour of Revolution-era Boston and gives you the skinny on aspects of Boston colonial history that every resident should know. To gain a better appreciation of just where it is you live, hit the top of the **Prudential Tower (Map 5)** for a bird's eye view, which will show you that Boston has a lot more hills and water than you might have suspected. For a more human perspective, get familiar with the Charles River with a stroll along the **Esplanade (Map 6)**, or, for a walk with an impressive view of Beacon Hill and Back Bay, cross the **Harvard Bridge (Map 26)** and take a stroll along Memorial Drive in Cambridge. For a nice rest, grab a snack in Harvard Square, and find a tree in **Harvard Yard (Map 20)** under which to chill.

If winter keeps you from strolls outside, there's plenty to see indoors. The **Museum of Fine Arts (Map 15)** (see page 326) is world-class. Across the street, the **Isabella Stewart Gardner Museum (Map 15)** has a first-rate collection, and the setting (inspired by a 15th-century Venetian palace) is stunning. The ornate interior of **Trinity Church (Map 6)** and the Sargent Murals of the **Boston Public Library (Map 6)** (see page 185) are also impressive. Boston's best concert halls are in the neighborhood,

so why not catch a show at internationally acclaimed **Boston Symphony Hall (Map 5)** or one of the many free shows at the New England Conservatory's **Jordan Hall (Map 5)**. You'll also not want to overlook the many museums of Harvard, notably the **Fogg Art Museum (Map 20)** (focusing on Western art) and the **Natural History Museum (Map 20)** (with its brilliant glass flowers).

If you've already checked out Boston's big hits, there are plenty of quirky spots to fill your time. See the skull of Phineas Gage, the 19th century medical oddity who survived a thirteen-pound rod of steel shot through his brain at the **Warren Anatomical Museum (Map 15)**. The **Boston Athenaeum (Map 1)** has a true crime account bound with the skin of its author. If that's not to your sense of everlasting life, you could sip coffee in the North End and wander over to see if Peter Baldassari is home and his folksy **All Saints Way (Map 2)** is open. Roxbury has the only scale Nubian tomb at the **Museum of the National Center for Afro-American Artists (Map 13)**. The Mapparium at the **Christian Science Center (Map 5)** highlights the ambitions of Mary Baker Eddy and her clean-living movement. Those with a more criminal bent can find mobster haunts like "Whitey" Bulger's old Southie **liquor store (Map 10)** or the garage of the **Brink's Job (Map 2)** in the North End.

Map 1 • Beacon Hill / West End

Abiel Smith School	46 Joy St	Center of 19th-century African-American Boston.
Acorn Street	b/w West Cedar St & Willow St, running parallel to Chestnut St	The most photographed street in America.
Boston Athenaeum	10 1/2 Beacon St • 617-227-0270	Old books, including one true crime account bound in the author's skin.
Leonard P Zakim Bunker Hill Bridge	100 Beverly St	World's widest cable-stayed bridge. Boston's newest landmark.
Longfellow Bridge	Cambridge St & Charles St	The "salt and pepper shaker bridge."
Louisburg Square	b/w Mt Vernon St & Pinckney St	Charming square with elegant homes, including John Kerry's.
Make Way for Ducklings	Beacon St & Charles St	Inspired by the Robert McCloskey children's book.
Massachusetts General Hospital	55 Fruit St • 617-726-2000	The Ether dome, site of first the use of ether; contains an antique surgical museum.
TD Banknorth Garden	150 Causeway St • 617-624-1050	Looking for the FleetCenter? This is it. Used to be historic Boston Garden.
Vilna Shul	18 Phillips St • 617-523-2324	Recently revived Beacon Hill synagogue.

Map 2 • North End / Faneuil Hall

All Saints Way	Battery St & Hanover St	Peter Baldassari's folksy, handcrafted devotional alley.
The Boston Stone	Marshall St	Centre of ye olde city.
Boston Tea Kettle	63 Court St	Long before Starbucks, this gigantic 1873 copper kettle was steaming.
The Brink's Job	165 Prince St	Where Brink's gang robbery occurred in 1950; now used for TD Banknorth Center parking.
Christopher Columbus Park	Atlantic Ave at Richmond St	Destruction of the Artery gives this park new breath.
City Hall	1 City Hall Plz • 617-635-4000	The box Faneuil Hall came in.
Faneuil Hall	Congress St & North St • 617-523-1779	Faneuil Hall (that is, the building) dates from 1742.
Holocaust Memorial	Congress St & Union St • 617-457-8755	Six glass towers, with victims' numbers representing six camps.
New England Aquarium	Central Wharf • 617-973-5200	Check out penguin snack-time.
North End Playground	Commercial St & Foster St	Site of the famous Great Molasses Flood.
Old North Church	193 Salem St • 617-523-6676	One if by land, two if by sea.
Paul Revere House	19 North Sq • 617-523-2338	Where Paul was born and raised.
Union Oyster House	41 Union St • 617-227-2750	Oldest restaurant in America, saddle up to oyster bar.

Map 3 • Downtown Crossing / Park Square / Bay Village

Arlington Street Church	351 Boylston St • 617-536-7050	Congregation dates from 1729, building from 1861.
Boston Irish Famine Memorial	School St & Washington St	Statue commemorating the Great Hunger of the 1840s.
Boston Opera House	539 Washington St • 617-259-3400	Beaux-Arts landmark open again after many years.
Colonial Theatre	106 Boylston St • 617-426-9366	Boston's oldest continuously operating theater, since 1900.
Four Seasons Hotel	200 Boylston St • 617-338-4400	The preferred local home of the Rolling Stones.
Frog Pond	Boston Common	Cool statues. Ribbit.
Granary Burying Ground	Tremont St & Park St • 617-635-4505	Featuring John Hancock, Mother Goose, and many others.
Harpoon Brewery	306 Northern Ave • 617-574-9551	Brewery tours, seasonal special events.

Hub of the Universe Bronze Marker	Washington St & Summer St	Um, located in the floor of a fruit and vegetable stand.
John Hancock's Phallic Gravestone	Tremont St & Park St	Size matters.
Old South Meeting House	310 Washington St • 617-482-6439	Where Sam Adams gave the order for the Boston Tea Party.
Old State House	206 Washington St • 617-720-1713	Oldest surviving public building in Boston.
Omni Parker House	60 School St • 617-227-8600	One-time employees included Ho Chi Minh and Malcolm X.
State House	Beacon St & Park St • 617-727-3679	Finished in 1797. Gold dome added later.
Swan Boats	Arlington & Boylston St • 617-522-1966	Since 1877. Ideal for wee ones.
Wang Theatre	270 Tremont St • 617-482-9393	Eye-popping, opulent interior. A must see.

Map 4 • Financial District / Chinatown

Boston Harbor Hotel	70 Rowes Wharf • 617-439-7000	The "building with a hole in the middle."
Chinatown Gate	Beach St & Hudson St	Everything under the sky is for the people.
Custom House Tower	3 McKinley Sq	Boston's first "skyscraper," completed in 1915.
Federal Reserve	600 Atlantic Ave • 617-973-3463	Easy-to-spot concrete monolith, built in 1983.
South Station	Atlantic Ave & Summer St	Busier train station, with the new Silver Line and bus terminal.

Map 5 • Back Bay (West) / Fenway (East)

Burrage House	314 Commonwealth Ave	19th-century French-Renaissance mansion. Private.
Christian Science Center	175 Huntington Ave • 617-450-3790	Mother Church, Mapparium, reflecting pool. Quite nice.
Hynes Convention Center	900 Boylston St • 617-954-2000	Still a convention center, for now.
Jordan Hall	30 Gainsborough St	Hundred-year-old theater seats over 1,000 and has remarkable acoustics.
Prudential Tower	800 Boylston St • 617-236-3100	The other tall building. Equally loved and reviled.
Symphony Hall	301 Massachusetts Ave • 617-266-1492	Home of the Boston Symphony Orchestra.

Map 6 • Back Bay (East) / South End (Upper)

Boston Public Library	700 Boylston St • 617-536-5400	Impressive. Enjoy a respite in the beautiful courtyard.
Charles River Esplanade	Storrow Drive	Great place to run or read a book.
Church of the Covenant	67 Newbury St	Gothic revival church called "absolutely perfect" by Oliver Wendell Holmes.
Commonwealth Ave	Arlington St to Mass Ave	Boston's most distinguished promenade with oddest collection of statues.
Copley Square	Boylston St & Dartmouth St	Back Bay's living room.
First Church in Boston	66 Marlborough St • 617-267-6730	Founded 375 years ago.
French Library and Cultural Center	53 Marlborough St • 617-912-0400	Classes, food, and movies, tous en francais.
Harriet Tubman Square	Columbus Square	Statue, park, and timeline tablet honoring Tubman and her work.
Hatch Shell	Esplanade	Where the Pops play each July 4.
John Hancock Tower	200 Clarendon St	New England's tallest building, designed by I.M. Pei.
New England Historic Genealogical Library	101 Newbury St • 617-536-5740	Trace your roots back to the Mayflower.
Old South Church	645 Boylston St • 617-536-1970	Northern Italian Gothic, finished in 1875.
Trinity Church	206 Clarendon St • 617-536-0944	Romanesque, with massive open interior. Completed in 1877.

Map 7 • South End (Lower)

| Cathedral of the Holy Cross | 1400 Washington St • 617-542-5682 | Mother church of the Archdiocese of Boston. |
| SoWa Building | 450 Harrison Ave | A converted warehouse, now home to several galleries. |

Map 8 • Charlestown

Bunker Hill Monument	Monument Ave • 617-242-5641	Battle actually took place on nearby Breed's Hill.
Charlestown Navy Yard	Constitution Rd & Warren St • 617-242-5601	Home of the USS Constitution ("Old Ironsides").
Tobin Memorial Bridge	US-1	Lovingly photographed in Mystic River.
Warren Tavern	2 Pleasant St • 617-241-8142	One of Paul Revere's favorite watering holes.

Map 9 • East Boston

| LoPresti Park | Summer St | Best view of the Boston skyline and harbor for landlubbers. |

Map 10 • South Boston (West) / Fort Point

Boston Children's Museum	300 Congress St • 617-426-8855	Featuring the giant Hood milk bottle.
Boston Convention & Exhibition Center	415 Summer St • 617-954-2100	The Southie Starship.
Boston Sailing Center	54 Lewis Wharf • 617-227-4198	Ahoy, matey! Learn to sail the high seas.
Institute of Contemporary Art	100 Northern Ave • 617-478-3100	Stunning new building. Oh, and the art's pretty good too.
South Boston Liquor Mart	295 Old Colony Ave • 617-269-3600	Whitey Bulger's HQ.

General Information · **Landmarks**

Map 11 · South Boston (East)

Bank of America Pavilion	290 Northern Ave · 617-728-1690	Music venue.
Black Falcon Terminal	1 Black Falcon Ave · 617-330-1500	Heavily trafficked cruise boat terminal.
Boston Design Center	1 Design Center Pl · 617-338-6610	For interior design junkies; several dozen showrooms.
Boston Fish Pier	P Street	Opened in 1914, the oldest working fish port.
Giant Unholy Rat of Disease	212 Northern Ave	OMG! Kill it. It's dead? KILL IT AGAIN!
L Street Bathhouse	William J Day Blvd & L St	Old-timey bathhouse, home of the L Street Brownies.
L Street Tavern	658 E 8th St · 617-268-4335	Matt & Ben's pub in that movie.
World Trade Center Boston	200 Seaport Blvd · 617-385-5090	Event space that's part of "The Seaport Experience."

Map 12 · Newmarket / Andrew Square

Suffolk County House of Correction	20 Bradston St · 617-635-1000	Just so you know.

Map 13 · Roxbury

Highland Park	Fort Ave & Beech Glen St	Little visited Fort Hill monument with great views
Islamic Cultural Center	1 Malcolm X Blvd	Largest mosque in the Northeast.
Malcolm X and Ella Little-Collins House	72 Dale St	Malcolm X lived here with his sister during formative years.
National Center for Afro-American Artists	300 Walnut Ave · 617-442-8614	Puddingstone mansion holds Nubian tomb model.
Roxbury Center for Arts	182 Dudley St · 617-541-3900	Located in the recently renovated Hibernia Hall.
Shirley-Eustis House	33 Shirley St · 617-442-2275	18th-century royal governor's country estate.

Map 14 · Jamaica Plain

Arnold Arboretum	125 Arborway · 617-524-1718	The most famous collection of trees in America, an oasis.
Doyle's Café	3484 Washington St · 617-524-2345	A century's worth of pols have slapped backs here.
First Church, Unitarian Universalist	6 Eliot St · 617-524-1634	The first church in Jamaica Plain, ca. 1853. Impressive stone façade, creepy graveyard.
The Footlight Club	7A Eliot St · 617-524-3200	Oldest running theater in the US.
The Loring-Greenough House	12 South St · 617-524-3158	Built as a country estate in 1760. Open for tours.
Samuel Adams Brewery	30 Germania St · 617-368-5080	Love the product, but not much of an experience.
Spontaneous Celebrations	75 Danforth St · 617-524-6373	JP community arts organization.

Map 15 · Fenway (West) / Mission Hill

Isabella Stewart Gardner Museum	280 The Fenway · 617-278-5180	Eccentric collection highlighting the Renaissance and the pleasures of having money. A gem.
Mission Church Basilica	1545 Tremont St · 617-445-2600	Mission Hill landmark. Recently renovated.
Museum of Fine Arts	465 Huntington Ave · 617-267-9300	Arguably one of the top museums in the country. Go for the Copleys.
Warren Anatomical Museum	10 Shattuck St · 617-432-6196	Phineas Gage's skull and other medical oddities.

Map 16 · Kenmore Square / Brookline (East)

BU Bridge	Essex St & Mountfort St	Arguably Boston's best river/skyline view.
Citgo Sign	Commonwealth Ave & Beacon St	Beloved Kenmore Square landmark.
Fenway Park	4 Yawkey Wy · 617-267-9440	Home to the Sox since 1912.

Map 17 · Coolidge Corner / Brookline Hills

Frederick Olmstead Home	99 Warren St	Genius of American landscapes, the ultimate home office.

Map 19 · Allston (South) / Brookline (North)

JFK National Historic Site	83 Beals St · 617-566-7937	Understated residential home, open only in summer.
The Publick Theatre	1400 Soldiers Field Rd · 617-782-5425	Outdoor theater along the Charles.

Map 20 · Harvard Square / Allston (North)

Brattle Theatre	40 Brattle St · 617-876-6837	Oldest repertory cinema in Boston, since 1953 and still projecting.
Fogg Art Museum	32 Quincy St · 617-495-9400	Fine collection, more humane scale than the MFA.
Harvard Museum of Natural History	26 Oxford St · 617-495-3045	The public face of the botanical, zoological, and geological museums.
Harvard Stadium	N Harvard St & Soldiers Field Rd	The nation's oldest stadium.
Harvard Yard	Kirkland St, b/w Broadway, Quincy St, Peabody St, & Massachusetts Ave	The core of the campus–full of historical landmarks.
John Harvard Statue	Massachusetts Ave	The "statue of the three lies."
Memorial Hall	45 Quincy St · 617-496-4595	Gorgeous architecture and interior. Try to see a show there.
Out of Town News	Harvard Sq · 617-354-7777	The sensible Harvard Square rendezvous spot.
The Pit	Harvard Sq	Favorite hang-out for the counter-culture kids.
Weeks Footbridge	Memorial Dr & DeWolfe St	Most beautiful bridge on the Charles, hosts full moon tangos.

Map 22 · North Cambridge / West Somerville

Somerville Theatre	55 Davis Sq · 617-625-5700	Movies, concerts, and more.

Map 23 · Central Somerville / Porter Square

Art at Porter Square	Somerville Ave & Massachusetts Ave	The T's best public art display.
Milk Row Cemetery	439 Somerville Ave	Historic 1804 boneyard. Next to a supermarket.
Powderhouse	College Ave & Broadway	Revolutionary War-era gunpowder store, park centerpiece.
Random British Soldier Grave	145 Elm St	
The Round House	36 Atherton St	Round since 1856. Not open to the public.
Somerville Museum	1 Westwood Rd · 617-666-9810	Great exhibits of Somerville history.

Map 24 · Winter Hill / Union Square

Prospect Hill Monument	Munroe St b/w Prospect Hill Ave & Walnut St	Excellent view of Boston from Somerville.
Somerville City Hall	93 Highland Ave · 617-625-6600	A classic New England municipal building.

Map 25 · East Somerville / Sullivan Square

Schrafft's Building	529 Main St	Once the country's largest candy factory.

Map 26 · East Cambridge / Kendall Square / MIT

Harvard Bridge	Massachusetts Ave	364 smoots and an ear, the Harvard Bridge leads to MIT.
Kendall / MIT T Station	Main St	Every T-Stop should have musical instruments by MIT students.
Stata Center	32 Vassar St	Frank Gehry's curvy and colorful MIT building.

Map 27 · Central Square / Cambridgeport

Cambridge City Hall	795 Massachusetts Ave · 617-349-4000	Recently got a needed facelift.
Edgerton Center & Strobe Alley	77 Massachusetts Ave · 617-253-4629	4th floor of Building 4 displays of slow-mo destructive photography and tech.
Necco Building/Novartis	250 Massachusetts Ave	Yet another candy company leaves Cambridge.
Polaroid Bldg	784 Memorial Dr	Distinctive Art Deco ex-headquarters of Polaroid.
Shell Oil Sign	187 Magazine St	Can't miss it. Logo designed by Raymond Loewy.
Simmons Hall	229 Vassar St · 617-253-5107	Aggresively modernist MIT dorm by Stephen Holl.
University Park	Massachusetts Ave & Sidney St	Complex of cool structural and landscape architecture.

Map 28 · Inman Square

Julia Child's Home	103 Irving St	The kitchen was dismantled and moved to the Smithsonian.

Map 29 · West Roxbury

Millennium Park	VFW Pkwy & Gardner St	Clear your head by flying a kite.

Map 30 · Roslindale

Forest Hills Cemetery	95 Forest Hills Ave · 617-524-0128	This 250-acre beautiful cemetery is not only home to such literary greats as e.e. cummings but is also great spot to picnic and bike ride.
Roslindale Square	Washington St	Or, Roslindale Village.

Map 31 · Mattapan / Dorchester (West)

Franklin Park Zoo Bear Cages	1 Franklin Park Rd	The abandoned bear cages outside the zoo's fences make for a creepy outing.
United House of Prayer	206 Seaver St · 617-445-3246	Impressive Mishkan Tefila synagogue, now church and soul food kitchen.

Map 32 · Dorchester (East)

All Saints' Church	209 Ashmont St · 617-436-6370	Founded in 1867. Beautiful stained glass.
Commonwealth Museum	220 Morrissey Blvd · 617-727-9268	Operated by the Massachusetts Historical Society.
Dorchester North Burying Ground	Columbia Rd & Stoughton St	Interesting and eerie gravestones spanning 4 centuries.
The James Blake House	735 Columbia Rd	Built in 1648, Boston's oldest house.
John F Kennedy Library and Museum	Morrissey Blvd & Columbia Pt · 617-514-1600	Houses 21 permanent exhibits examining JFK's life and work.
Strand Theatre	543 Columbia Rd	Vaudeville, movie house time capsule. Under renovation.

Map 33 · Hyde Park

Stony Brook Reservation	Washington St	Great option for biking and hiking.

Hospitals

Boston's medical facilities rank among the best in the world. Many medical firsts happened in Boston, including the:

- First public demonstration of anesthesia during surgery, at Massachusetts General Hospital (1846).
- First identification and analysis of appendicitis, at Massachusetts General Hospital (1886).
- First surgical procedure to correct a congenital cardiovascular defect, performed by Dr. Robert Gross (1938).
- First successful fertilization of a human ovum in a test tube, by researchers at Peter Bent Brigham Hospital (1944).
- First successful pediatric remission of acute leukemia, achieved by Dr. Sidney Farber (1947).
- First isolation of the polio virus, at Children's Hospital (1948).
- First successful kidney transplant, at Peter Bent Brigham Hospital (1954).
- First demonstration of the effectiveness of an oral contraceptive, by Dr. John C. Rock (1959).

The Longwood Medical Area (see map on the facing page) compresses a dozen medical institutions into a handful of blocks below Mission Hill. These institutions, including **Brigham and Women's Hospital (Map 15)**, **Beth Israel Deaconess Medical Center (Map 16)**, **Children's Hospital (Map 15)**, **Dana-Farber Cancer Institute (Map 15)**, **Joslin Diabetes Center (Map 16)**, the **CBR Institute for Biomedical Research (Map 16)**, and Harvard's medical, dental, and public health schools, comprise what is probably the world's leading center for health care and medicine.

Massachusetts General Hospital (Map 1), which opened in 1811, is the oldest and largest hospital in New England. Each year MGH admits over 45,000 in-patients, processes over 76,000 emergency visits, and, at its West End main campus and four satellite facilities, handles more than 1.5 million outpatient visits.

Mount Auburn Hospital (Map 21) is a Harvard Medical School teaching hospital and the most prominent hospital in Cambridge.

Emergency Rooms	Address	Phone	Map
Massachusetts Eye and Ear Infirmary	243 Charles St	617-523-7900	1
Massachusetts General Hospital	55 Fruit St	617-726-2000	1
Tufts-New England Medical Center	750 Washington St	617-636-5000	3
Boston Medical Center	1 Boston Medical Ctr Pl	617-638-8000	7
Brigham and Women's Hospital	75 Francis St	617-732-5500	15
Children's Hospital	300 Longwood Ave	617-355-6000	15
Beth Israel Deaconess Medical Center	330 Brookline Ave	617-667-7000	16
Mount Auburn	330 Mt Auburn St	617-492-3500	21
Somerville Hospital	230 Highland Ave	617-591-4500	23
The Cambridge Hospital	1493 Cambridge St	617-665-1000	28

Other Hospitals	Address	Phone	Map
Boston Shriners Hospital	51 Blossom St	617-722-3000	1
Spaulding Rehabilitation Hospital	125 Nashua St	617-573-7000	1
Jewish Memorial Hospital & Rehabilitation Center	59 Townsend St	617-989-8315	13
Arbour Hospital	49 Robinwood Ave	617-522-4400	14
CBR Institute for Biomedical Research	220 Longwood Ave	617-734-9500	15
Dana-Farber Cancer Institute	44 Binney St	866-408-3324	15
New England Baptist Hospital	125 Parker Hill Ave	617-754-5800	15
VA Boston-Jamaica Plain Campus	150 S Huntington Ave	617-232-9500	15
Joslin Diabetes Center	1 Joslin Pl	617-732-2400	16
Franciscan Hospital for Children	30 Warren St	617-254-3800	18
St Elizabeth's Medical Center	736 Cambridge St	617-789-3000	18
The Boston Center	14 Fordham Rd	617-783-9676	19
Youville Hospital & Rehabilitation Center	1575 Cambridge St	617-876-4344	28

Post Offices & Zip Codes

Post Offices	Address	Phone	Zip Code	Map
Charles Street Station	136 Charles St	617-723-7434	02114	1
John F Kennedy Station	25 New Chardon St	617-523-6566	02114	1
State House Station	24 Beacon St	617-742-0012	02133	1
Hanover Street Station	217 Hanover St	617-723-6397	02113	2
Post Offices	1 Faneuil Hall Sq	800-275-8777	02109	2
Fort Point Station	25 Dorchester Ave	617-654-5302	02205	4
Lafayette Station	7 Ave de Lafayette	617-423-7822	02111	4
Milk Street	31 Milk St	617-482-1956	02109	4
Astor Station	207 Massachusetts Ave	617-247-2429	02115	5
Prudential Center Post Office	800 Boylston St	617-267-4164	02199	5
Back Bay Annex Station	390 Stuart St	617-236-7800	02117	6
Post Offices	31 St James Ave	800-275-8777	02116	6
Cathedral Station	59 W Dedham St	617-266-0989	02118	7
Charlestown	23 Austin St	617-241-5322	02129	8
East Boston Station	50 Meridian St	617-561-3900	02128	9
South Boston Station	444 E 3rd St	617-269-9948	02127	10
Roxbury Station	55 Roxbury St	617-427-4898	02119	13
Jamaica Plain Station	655 Centre St	617-524-3620	02130	14
Mission Hill Station	1575 Tremont St	617-566-2040	02120	15
Boston University	775 Commonwealth Ave	617-266-0665	02215	16
Kenmore Station	11 Deerfield St	617-437-1113	02215	16
Brookline Branch	1295 Beacon St	617-738-1649	02446	17
Brookline Village Branch	207 Washington St	617-566-1557	02445	17
Brighton	424 Washington St	617-254-5026	02135	18
Allston Station	47 Harvard Ave	617-789-3769	02134	19
Soldiers Field Station	117 Western Ave	617-354-0131	02163	19
Harvard Square Station	125 Mt Auburn St	617-876-3883	02138	20
West Somerville	58 Day St	617-666-2255	02144	22
Porter Square	1953 Massachusetts Ave	617-876-5599	02140	23
Somerville Branch	237 Washington St	617-666-2332	02143	24
Winter Hill Branch	320 Broadway	617-666-5225	02145	24
East Cambridge Station	303 Cambridge St	617-876-8558	02141	26
Kendall Square Station	250 Main St	617-876-5155	02142	26
MIT	84 Massachusetts Ave	617-494-5511	02139	26
Cambridge	770 Massachusetts Ave	617-575-8700	02139	27
Inman Square Station	1311 Cambridge St	617-864-4344	02139	28

General Information

All Emergencies: 911
Crime Stoppers: 800-494-TIPS
Boston Area Rape Crisis Center (BARCC): 617-492-RAPE
State Police: 617-727-7775
Boston: www.ci.boston.ma.us/police
Brookline: www.brooklinepolice.com
Cambridge: www.ci.cambridge.ma.us/~CPD/
Somerville: www.ci.somerville.ma.us

Statistics

	Jan–July 2008	2007	2006	2005	2004	2003
Murder	36	53	55	75	73	61
Rape & Attempted	128	216	234	297	268	269
Robbery & Attempted	1,179	1,712	2,071	2,678	2,649	2,428
Aggravated Assault	2,120	3,379	3,510	4,358	4,113	4,159
Burglary & Attempted	1,682	2,892	3,041	4,007	4,531	4,545
Larceny & Attempted	8,126	13,235	12,824	16,372	15,957	17,526
Vehicle Theft & Attempted	1,279	2,740	3,199	4,076	4,717	5,545

Police Stations

	Address	Phone	Map
District A-1	40 New Sudbury St	617-343-4240	1
Temporarily relocated to 152 North End St			
District D-4	650 Harrison Ave	617-343-4250	7
District A-7	69 Paris St	617-343-4220	9
District C-6	101 W Broadway	617-343-4730	10
District B-2	135 Dudley St	617-343-4270	13
District E-13	3345 Washington St	617-343-5630	14
Brookline Police Department	350 Washington St	617-730-2222	17
District D-14	301 Washington St	617-343-4260	18
Somerville Police Department	220 Washington St	617-625-1600	24
Cambridge Police Department	5 Western Ave	617-349-3300	27

Map 1 · Beacon Hill / West End

		last pick-up
Self-Service	170 Canal St	7:45 pm
Self-Service	55 Fruit St	7 pm
Self-Service	7 Bulfinch Pl	6:30 pm
Self-Service	25 New Chardon St	6:30 pm
Self-Service	165 Cambridge St	6:30 pm
Self-Service	101 Merrimac St	6:30 pm
Self-Service	50 Staniford St	6 pm
Self-Service	185 Cambridge St	6 pm
Self-Service	1 Bowdoin Sq	4:30 pm
FedEx Kinko's	2 Center Plz	4:30 pm
Self-Service	15 New Sudbury St	4 pm

Map 2 · North End / Faneuil Hall

Self-Service	200 State St	7:45 pm
Self-Service	343 Commercial St	7:30 pm
Self-Service	28 State St	7:30 pm
Self-Service	240 Commercial St	7:30 pm
Self-Service	98 N Washington St	7 pm
Self-Service	77 N Washington St	7 pm
Self-Service	1 Boston Pl	7 pm
Self-Service	66 Long Wharf	6:30 pm
Prince Postale	71 Prince St	6 pm
FedEx Kinko's	60 State St	6 pm
Self-Service	1 Congress St	5:30 pm

Map 3 · Downtown Crossing / Park Square / Bay Village

Jewelers Bldg	333 Washington St	8 pm
Self-Service	75 Arlington St	7:45 pm
Self-Service	821 Washington St	7:30 pm
Self-Service	750 Washington St	7 pm
Self-Service	73 Tremont St	7 pm
Self-Service	80 Boylston St	6:30 pm
Self-Service	1 Beacon St	6:30 pm
Self-Service	252 Washington St	6 pm
Self-Service	141 Tremont St	6 pm
Self-Service	10 Park Plz	6 pm
FedEx Kinko's	252 Washington St	6 pm
FedEx Kinko's	125 Tremont St	6 pm
Self-Service	260 Tremont St	5 pm
Mail Boxes Etc	276 Washington St	5 pm
Self-Service	45 School St	4:30 pm

Map 4 · Financial District / Chinatown

Self-Service	75 Federal St	8 pm
Self-Service	225 Franklin St	8 pm
Self-Service	150 Federal St	8 pm
Self-Service	101 Arch St	8 pm
Self-Service	100 Summer St	8 pm
Self-Service	1 International Pl	8 pm
Self-Service	1 Financial Ctr	8 pm
Self-Service	745 Atlantic Ave	7:30 pm
Self-Service	600 Atlantic Ave	7:30 pm
Self-Service	45 Batterymarch St	7:30 pm
Self-Service	25 Dorchester Ave	7:30 pm
Self-Service	155 Federal St	7:30 pm
Self-Service	125 Summer St	7:30 pm
Self-Service	265 Franklin St	7:15 pm
Self-Service	1 Federal St	7:15 pm
Self-Service	99 High St	7 pm
Self-Service	33 Arch St	7 pm
Self-Service	260 Franklin St	7 pm
Self-Service	21 Custom House St	7 pm
Self-Service	136 Harrison Ave	7 pm
Self-Service	100 Federal St	7 pm
Penfield's	250 Franklin St	7 pm
Self-Service	99 Summer St	6:30 pm
Self-Service	88 Broad St	6:30 pm
Self-Service	470 Atlantic Ave	6:30 pm
Self-Service	31 Milk St	6:30 pm
Self-Service	50 Milk St	6 pm
Self-Service	211 Congress St	6 pm
Self-Service	175 Federal St	6 pm
FedEx Kinko's	211 Congress St	6 pm
FedEx Kinko's	10 Post Office Sq	6 pm
Self-Service	1 Lincoln St	5:30 pm
Self-Service	35 Kneeland St	4:30 pm
Self-Service	7 Ave De Lafayette	4 pm

Map 5 · Back Bay (West) / Fenway (East)

Self-Service	800 Boylston St	8 pm
Self-Service	346 Washington Ave	6 pm
Penfields	39 Dalton St	6 pm
Self-Service	900 Boylston St	4 pm
Self-Service	800 Boylston St	4 pm
Self-Service	380 Massachusetts Ave	4 pm

Map 6 · Back Bay (East) / South End (Upper)

Self-Service	500 Boylston St	8 pm
Self-Service	197 Clarendon St	8 pm
Self-Service	699 Boylston St	7:30 pm
Self-Service	399 Boylston St	7:30 pm
Self-Service	31 St James Ave	7:30 pm
Self-Service	187 Dartmouth St	7:30 pm
Self-Service	142 Berkeley St	7:30 pm
Self-Service	162 Columbus Ave	7:15 pm
Self-Service	116 Huntington Ave	7:15 pm
Self-Service	200 Clarendon St	7 pm
Self-Service	101 Huntington Ave	7 pm
Self-Service	380 Stuart St	6 pm
Self-Service	100 Huntington Ave	6 pm
Self-Service	10 St James Ave	6 pm
Penfields	10 Huntington Ave	6 pm
FedEx Kinko's	575 Boylston St	6 pm
FedEx Kinko's	187 Dartmouth St	6 pm
Self-Service	95 Berkeley St	5 pm
Self-Service	745 Boylston St	5 pm
Self-Service	200 Berkeley St	5 pm

Map 7 · South End (Lower)

Self-Service	88 E Newton St	8:15 pm
Self-Service	80 E Concord St	8 pm
Self-Service	818 Harrison Ave	7:45 pm
Self-Service	715 Albany St	6 pm
FedEx Kinko's	715 Albany St	6 pm
Self-Service	700 Albany St	5 pm
Self-Service	85 E Concord St	4 pm

Map 8 · Charlestown

Self-Service	Charlestown Navy Yard	7 pm
Self-Service	20 City Sq	7 pm
Self-Service	149 13th St	7 pm
Self-Service	1 Thompson Sq	6:30 pm
Self-Service	1 Constitution Plz	6:30 pm
Self-Service	23 Austin St	6 pm

Map 9 · East Boston

Self-Service	50 Meridian St	6:30 pm
Self-Service	256 Marginal St	6:30 pm
Self-Service	580 Chelsea St	6 pm

Map 10 · South Boston (West) / Fort Point

Self-Service	68 Fargo St	8 pm
Self-Service	313 Congress St	7:30 pm
Self-Service	25 Thomson Pl	7:30 pm
Self-Service	2 Seaport Ln	7:30 pm
Self-Service	430 W Broadway	7 pm
Self-Service	280 Summer St	7 pm
Self-Service	1 Gillette Park	7 pm
Self-Service	415 Summer St	4 pm
FedEx Kinko's	415 Summer St	4 pm

Map 11 · South Boston (East)

Self-Service	775 Summer St	9 pm
Federal Express	775 Summer St	9 pm
Self-Service	212 Northern Ave	7:15 pm
Self-Service	88 Black Falcon Ave	7 pm
Self-Service	1 Design Center Pl	7 pm
Self-Service	1 Harbor St	5 pm

Map 12 · Newmarket / Andrew Square

Self-Service	8c Allstate Rd	6 pm
Self-Service	1 Widett Cir	6 pm
Self-Service	1010 Massachusetts Ave	5 pm
Self-Service	100 Newmarket Sq	5 pm

Map 13 · Roxbury

Self-Service	716 Columbus Ave	7 pm
Self-Service	1135 Tremont St	6 pm
Self-Service	55 Roxbury St	4 pm

Map 14 · Jamaica Plain

Self-Service	670 Centre St	6 pm
Self-Service	64 South St	4 pm

Map 15 · Fenway (West) / Mission Hill

Self-Service	44 Binney St	8 pm
Self-Service	300 Longwood Ave	8 pm
Self-Service	4 Blackfan Cir	7:30 pm
Self-Service	75 Francis St	7 pm
Self-Service	370 Huntington Ave	7 pm
Self-Service	300 Fenway	7 pm
Self-Service	200 Longwood Ave	7 pm
Self-Service	188 Longwood Ave	7 pm
Self-Service	180 Longwood Ave	7 pm
Mobile Unit	44 Binney St	7 pm
Self-Service	677 Huntington Ave	6:30 pm
Self-Service	150 S Huntington Ave	6:30 pm

Self-Service	125 Parker Hill Ave	6:30 pm
Self-Service	550 Huntington Ave	6 pm
Self-Service	43 Leon St	6 pm
Self-Service	11 Leon St	6 pm
Self-Service	1 Blackfan Cir	6 pm
Self-Service	20 Shattuck St	5:30 pm
UPS Store	360 Huntington Ave	5 pm
Self-Service	221 Longwood Ave	5 pm
Self-Service	1620 Tremont St	5 pm

Map 16 • Kenmore Square / Brookline (East)

Self-Service	375 Longwood Ave	7:30 pm
Self-Service	890 Commonwealth Ave	7 pm
Self-Service	771 Commonwealth Ave	7 pm
Self-Service	675 Commonwealth Ave	7 pm
Self-Service	330 Brookline Ave	7 pm
Self-Service	364 Brookline Ave	6:45 pm
Self-Service	590 Commonwealth Ave	6:30 pm
Self-Service	44 Cummington St	6:30 pm
Self-Service	110 Francis St	6:30 pm
Self-Service	1 Overland St	6:30 pm
Self-Service	1 Deaconess Rd	6:30 pm
Self-Service	1 Brookline Pl	6:30 pm
Self-Service	1 Joslin Pl	6:15 pm
Self-Service	401 Park Dr	6 pm
Self-Service	330 Brookline Ave	6 pm
Self-Service	1 Autumn St	6 pm
FedEx Kinko's	115 Cummington St	6 pm
Self-Service	15 Deerfield St	5 pm

Map 17 • Coolidge Corner / Brookline Hills

Self-Service	235 Cypress St	6 pm
Self-Service	207 Washington St	6 pm
Self-Service	138 Harvard St	6 pm
Self-Service	1295 Beacon St	6 pm
Mail Boxes Etc	258 Harvard St	6 pm
FedEx Kinko's	1370 Beacon St	6 pm
Self-Service	1295 Beacon St	4 pm

Map 18 • Brighton

Self-Service	736 Cambridge St	7 pm
elf-Service	736 Cambridge St	7 pm
Self-Service	20 Guest St	7 pm
Self-Service	424 Washington St	6:45 pm
Self-Service	1660 Soldiers Field Rd	6:30 pm

Map 19 • Allston (South) / Brookline (North)

Self-Service	214 Lincoln St	7:30 pm
Self-Service	881 Commonwealth Ave	7 pm
Self-Service	1505 Commonwealth Ave	7 pm
Self-Service	119 Braintree St	6:45 pm
Self-Service	300 Western Ave	6 pm
Signal Graphics	450 Cambridge St	3 pm

Map 20 • Harvard Square / Allston (North)

Self-Service	1 Mifflin St	8 pm
Self-Service	79 JFK St	7 pm
Self-Service	50 Church St	7 pm
Self-Service	48 Quincy St	7 pm
Self-Service	33 Kirkland St	7 pm
Self-Service	20 University Rd	7 pm
Self-Service	1563 Massachusetts Ave	7 pm
Self-Service	124 Mt Auburn St	7 pm
Self-Service	35 Oxford St	6:30 pm
Self-Service	12 Oxford St	6:30 pm
Self-Service	60 Garden St	6 pm
Self-Service	230 Western Ave	6 pm
Self-Service	1350 Massachusetts Ave	6 pm
FedEx Kinko's	1 Mifflin Pl	6 pm

Map 21 • West Cambridge

Self-Service	36 Bay State Rd	6:30 pm

Map 22 • North Cambridge / West Somerville

Self-Service	62 Whittemore Ave	7 pm
Self-Service	5 Cameron Ave	7 pm
Self-Service	199 Alewife Brook Pkwy	7 pm
Self-Service	2067 Massachusetts Ave	6:30 pm
Self-Service	167 Holland St	6:30 pm
Self-Service	406 Highland Ave	6 pm
Self-Service	186 Alewife Brook Pkwy	6 pm
Self-Service	147 Sherman St	5:30 pm
Self-Service	90 Sherman St	5 pm

Map 23 • Central Somerville / Porter Square

Self-Service	48 Grove St	7 pm
Self-Service	1972 Massachusetts Ave	7 pm
Self-Service	1815 Massachusetts Ave	7 pm
Self-Service	815 Somerville Ave	6 pm

Map 24 • Winter Hill / Union Square

Self-Service	100 Fellsway W	7 pm
Self-Service	237 Washington St	6 pm

Map 25 • East Somerville / Sullivan Square

Self-Service	529 Main St	7 pm
Self-Service	500 Rutherford Ave	7 pm
Self-Service	52 Roland St	5:45 pm

Map 26 • East Cambridge / Kendall Square / MIT

Self-Service	1 Broadway	M-Th 6 pm
Self-Service	400 Technology Square	7:30 pm
Self-Service	600 Technology Sq	7 pm
Self-Service	5 Cambridge Ctr	7 pm
Self-Service	43 Thorndike St	7 pm
Self-Service	25 1st St	7 pm
Self-Service	101 Main St	7 pm
Self-Service	1 Memorial Dr	7 pm
Self-Service	1 Main St	7 pm
Self-Service	1 Kendall Sq	7 pm
Self-Service	4 Cambridge Ctr	6:30 pm
Self-Service	245 1st St	6:30 pm
Self-Service	55 Cambridge Pkwy	6 pm
Self-Service	31 Ames St	6 pm
FedEx Kinko's	600 Technology Sq	6 pm
Self-Service	300 3rd St	5:30 pm
Self-Service	223 3rd St	5 pm

Map 27 • Central Square / Cambridgeport

Self-Service	350 Massachusetts Ave	7:15 pm
Self-Service	675 Massachusetts Ave	7 pm
Self-Service	64 Sidney St	7 pm
Self-Service	38 Sidney St	7 pm
Self-Service	359 Green St	7 pm
Self-Service	26 Landsdowne St	7 pm
Self-Service	21 Erie St	7 pm
Self-Service	1033 Massachusetts Ave	7 pm
Self-Service	875 Massachusetts Ave	6 pm
Self-Service	840 Memorial Dr	6 pm
Self-Service	790 Memorial Dr	6 pm
Self-Service	2 Central Sq	6 pm
Self-Service	955 Massachusetts Ave	4:30 pm

Map 28 • Inman Square

Self-Service	950 Cambridge St	6:30 pm
Self-Service	432 Columbia St	6:30 pm
Self-Service	120 Beacon St	6:30 pm
Self-Service	201 Broadway	6 pm
Self-Service	141 Portland St	6 pm

Though Boston is chiefly known for its college-town feel, there is plenty for the younger set to enjoy. You're bound to find something to hold the attention of your little ones among the many, MANY museums and parks.

The Best of the Best

- **Best Kid-Friendly Restaurant:** Full Moon (344 Huron Ave, Cambridge, 617-354-6699). Full Moon is the brainchild of two restaurateurs who also happen to be moms. The result is a restaurant that features a sophisticated menu with an extensive wine list for adults and a tasty assortment of kids' tried-and-true favorites. With sippy cups, toy buckets at every table, and a play area stocked with pretty much every toy imaginable, Full Moon gives you "grown-up dining with a kid-friendly twist."
- **Quaintest Activity:** Swan Boats in the Public Garden (Public Garden, Boston, 617-522-1966). Owned and operated by the same family for over 120 years, the swan boats have directly inspired two children's classics: Robert McCloskey's *Make Way for Ducklings* and E.B. White's *The Trumpet of the Swan*. The people-paddled boats can hold up to 20 passengers during the 15-minute cruise around the lagoon and under the world's smallest suspension bridge. An inexpensive and adorable treat for all. Open April–Sept.
- **Funnest Park:** Rafferty Park (799 Concord Ave, Cambridge). One of the area's best-hidden playgrounds, this wooded park provides tons of fun stuff for older children, including a new metal climbing structure with a twisty slide, wobbly bridge, boat-shaped sand box, and a mini schoolhouse with a chalkboard roof. Basketball hoops, tennis courts, and a baseball field reside next door.
- **Coolest Bookstore:** Curious George Goes to Wordsworth (1 JFK St, Harvard Square, Cambridge, 617-498-0062). With floor-to-ceiling shelves packed with books for children of all ages, there's something for everyone in this charming jungle-themed bookstore. And if you're tired of reading, they've got TOYS.
- **Best Rainy Day Activity:** Children's Museum (300 Congress St, Boston, 617-426-8855). This world-renowned museum—reopened in spring 2007 after a pricey and well-received renovation and expansion—has designed early learning experiences for kids of all ages with its inventive hands-on exhibits. Permanent exhibits include the Japanese House, where children experience the culture of Kyoto, Japan through a replica of a silk merchant's house, as well as a Hall of Toys, in which children can look at toys of the past, but not touch.
- **Cutest Event:** The Annual Ducklings Day Parade (Boston Common). Held every year on Mother's Day, the parade commemorates Robert McCloskey's children's book *Make Way for Ducklings* set on Boston Common. Children come dressed as their favorite duckling character and ready to parade.
- **Neatest Store:** Irving's Toy and Card Shop (371 Harvard St, Brookline, 617-566-9327). Since 1939, Irving's has been a favorite neighborhood source for ice cream, candy, and little nostalgic toys galore. This small store is packed with everything you never knew you needed from kazoos, to jacks, to tiny plastic farm animals.

Shopping Essentials

- **Nine Months Maternity and Infant Wear** (mom & baby clothes) 272 Newbury St, Boston, 617-236-5523
- **Barefoot Books Store** (kids' books) 1771 Massachusetts Ave, Cambridge, 617-349-1610
- **Barnes & Noble:**
  325 Harvard St, Brookline, 617-232-0594
  660 Beacon St, Boston University, 617-638-5496
  800 Boylston St, Prudential Center, 617-247-6959
- **Black Ink** (stamps):
  101 Charles St, Boston, 617-723-3883
  5 Brattle St, Cambridge, 617-497-1221

- **Boing!** (toys) 729 Centre St, Jamaica Plain, 617-522-7800
- **Borders Books & Music:**
  100 Cambridgeside Pl, Cambridgeside Galleria, Cambridge, 617-679-0887
- **Calliope** (toys & kids' clothes) 33 Brattle St, Cambridge, 617-876-4149
- **The Children's Book Shop** (kids' books) 237 Washington St, Brookline, 617-734-7323
- **Co-op for Kids at the Harvard Co-op** (kids' books) 1400 Massachusetts Ave, Harvard Square, Cambridge, 617-499-2000
- **Curious George Goes to Wordsworth** (kids' books & toys) 1 JFK St, Harvard Square, Cambridge, 617-498-0062
- **Discovery Channel Store** (educational gifts) 40 South Market Building, Faneuil Hall, 617-227-5005
- **Fish Kids** (kids' clothes) 1378A Beacon St, Coolidge Corner, Brookline, 617-738-1006
- **Henry Bear's Park** (kids' books & toys) 361 Huron Ave, Cambridge, 617-547-8424
- **KB Toys** (toys) 100 Cambridgeside Pl, Cambridgeside Galleria, Cambridge, 617-494-8519
- **Oilily** (up-scale kids' clothes) 32 Newbury St, Boston, 617-247-9299
- **The Red Wagon** (kids' toys & clothes) 69 Charles St, Boston, 617-523-9402
- **Sloane's Children's Shoes** (kids' shoes) 1349 Beacon St, Coolidge Corner, Brookline, 617-739-0582
- **Stellabella Toys** (toys)
  1360 Cambridge St, Inman Square, Cambridge, 617-491-6290
  1967 Massachusetts Ave, Porter Square, Cambridge, 617-864-6290

Parks for Playing

Kids need fresh air. And singing into the rotating fan doesn't count. Take them out for a swing. In addition to the roomy Boston Common and Cambridge Common, Boston boasts many smaller neighborhood parks:

- **Alden Playground** (Oxford St and Sacramento St, Cambridge). A great neighborhood playground located in the shadow of Baldwin School and Lesley University, this toddler and big-kid-friendly park includes a mini-track, jaw-dropping climbing equipment, and what may be the World's Coolest Slide.
- **Charlesbank/Esplanade Playground** (Charles St at Longfellow Bridge). This large play area features several climbing structures, slides, and swings for all ages with a nearby snack bar, open during the summer months.
- **Christopher Columbus Park** (Atlantic Ave & Commercial Wharf, Boston). One large climbing structure dominates this playground that is mostly geared towards the six-and-under set.
- **Clarendon Street Playground** (Clarendon St & Commonwealth Ave, Boston). This fenced and gated area provides ample scope for the imagination of children of all ages. The park features several climbing structures, slides, swings, and a sand area, along with a larger, open area for games of tag and soccer.
- **Constitution Beach** (Orient Heights, East Boston). Lifeguarded swimming areas, a bathhouse with a snack bar, tennis courts, and a playground with lots of climbing and sliding prospects make this a great destination to take the kids.
- **Emerson Park** (Davis Ave & Emerson St, Brookline). The Park boasts one of the town's oldest spray pools, with lots of trees for shade and a casual open space for tag.
- **Green Street Playground** (Green St, Jamaica Plain). On summer days, the city turns on the water, and kids in bathing suits splash around in the fountains. Families set up picnics around the periphery, and there is a sandy jungle gym and swingset area nearby.
- **Huron Avenue Playground** (Huron Ave, Cambridge). This newly renovated play area has two climbing structures for

children of all ages, as well as a play train and spray fountain for the summer months. The lack of tree shade may bother some parents.

- **Langone Park** (Commercial St, Boston). The park features a brand-new playground with multi-age, multi-level climbing structures, and a swing set hovering on the edge of the harbor, great for that flying-across-water feeling. There are also three bocce courts and a baseball field.
- **Larz Anderson Park** (Newton, Avon, & Goddard Sts, Brookline). The largest park in Brookline holds an enclosed playground, picnic areas, ball fields, and an outdoor skating rink open December though February.
- **Millennium Park** (VFW Pkwy & Gardner St, West Roxbury). This park is larger than the Boston Common and TD Banknorth Garden combined and located on the site of the former Gardner Street landfill. The park provides picnic areas, play structures, and hiking and walking trails, as well as access to the river for boating and fishing.
- **Myrtle Street Playground** (Myrtle St & Irving St, Boston). Situated at the top of Beacon Hill, this playground features several climbing structures, a glider, a fire pole, swings, and a crazy daisy.
- **Public Garden** (Between Arlington St & Charles St, Boston). The first public botanical garden in the US, the Public Garden has 24 acres of flowers and green in the middle of the bustling city. Among the park's winding pathways and tranquil lagoon are the prized bronze statues of a mama duck and her brood commemorating Robert McClosky's famous children's book, *Make Way for Ducklings*.
- **Rafferty Park** (799 Concord Ave, Cambridge). One of the area's best-hidden playgrounds, this wooded park provides tons of fun activities for older children, including a new metal climbing structure with a twisty slide, wobbly bridge, boat-shaped sand box, and a mini-schoolhouse with a chalkboard roof. Basketball hoops, tennis courts, and a baseball field reside next door.
- **Raymond Street Park** (Walden St & Raymond St, Cambridge). Located on the shady side of the field, this playground is split up into two sections: one sandy, sunken area for the younger toddlers and one area for older children, equipped with a large climbing structure. Play gear ranges from a bridge to swing sets, including one handicapped swing seat.
- **Stoneman Playground** (Fairfield Ave & Massachusetts Ave, Cambridge). This playground is divided into a toddler area and an older children's space, with entertaining activities for both groups. Supervised model sailboat racing and fishing takes place on Sundays in the summer months.

Rainy Day Activities

It rains in Boston. A lot. It's also one of the windiest cities in the country. Foul weather can drench even the highest aspirations for outdoor fun. Here are some dry alternatives:

Museums with Kid Appeal

- **Museum of Afro-American History** (46 Joy St, Boston, 617-725-0022). The first publicly-funded grammar school built for African-Americans now has interactive exhibits for kids. www.afroammuseum.org
- **Children's Museum** (300 Congress St, Boston, 617-426-8855). This world-renowned museum, freshly renovated, has designed early learning experiences for children of all ages with its inventive hands-on exhibits. Permanent exhibits include the Japanese House, where children get to experience the culture of Kyoto, Japan through a replica of a silk merchant's house, as well as a Hall of Toys where children can look at toys of the past,

but not touch. www.bostonkids.org

- **New England Aquarium** (Central Wharf, 617-973-5200). Among the many exhibits you'll find here are the sea lion show and a supervised hands-on demonstration that allows children to touch sea stars, snails, and mussels. Whale-watching trips and summer classes are also offered through the aquarium. www.neaq.org
- **Larz Anderson Auto Museum** (Larz Anderson Park, 15 Newton St, Brookline, 617-522-6547). Located in the grand Carriage House, the museum features an extensive exhibit on the history of the automobile, as well as America's oldest car collection. www.mot.org
- **Museum of Science** (Science Park, 617-723-2500). This award-winning interactive science museum features permanent and changing exhibits, including a Virtual Fish Tank, where children see life through the eyes of a fish. The museum also houses the Charles Hayden Planetarium, featuring sky and laser shows, and the five-story IMAX Mugar Omni Theater. Various science classes are also available. www.mos.org.
- **Harvard Museum of Natural History** (26 Oxford St, Cambridge, 617-495-3045). This museum has great educational programs and exhibits for little explorers interested in botany, zoology, and geology. The Sunday afternoon programs and lectures are highly recommended for families with middle school children. www.hmnh.harvard.edu

Other Indoor Distractions

- **The Clayroom** (1408 Beacon St, Brookline, 617-566-7575). Paint your own pottery place. Great for parties. www.clayroom.com
- **Lanes and Games** (195 Concord Tpke, Rte 2, Cambridge, 617-876-5533). Candlepin bowling and ten-pin lanes for the whole family. www.lanesgames.com
- **Puppet Showplace Theater** (32 Station St, Brookline, 617-731-6400). This 100-seat theater has staging shows for Boston's young brood for over 30 years. The company stages classic puppet shows, as well as many original productions. Shows are recommended for children five and older. Great for parties. www.puppetshowplace.org

Outdoor *and* Educational

For when you've come to realize your children are a little too pale from sitting inside and playing video games all day.

- **Boston Duck Tours** (departure points: Prudential Center and Museum of Science, information: 617-267-DUCK). The Boston Duck is an original WWII amphibious landing vehicle that takes guests on an 80-minute tour (rain or shine) around the city by land and by sea. Kids are encouraged to quack at passersby. Tickets go fast inside the Prudential Center and Museum of Science beginning at 8:30 am. An additional ticketing location is at Faneuil Hall. Operating season: March 27th–Nov 26th. www.bostonducktours.com
- **Zoo New England** (1 Franklin Park Rd, Boston, 617-541-LION). The zoo holds all the standard zoo fare, plus the Butterfly Landing exhibit, a tented outdoor area where you can walk among more than 1,000 butterflies in free flight. (Smaller but still fun is the other Zoo New England site, Stone Zoo, in suburban Stoneham.) Adults: $9.50, seniors: $8, children (2–12): $5.50, under 2: free, and half-price tickets the first Sat of each month 10 am–12 pm. www.zoonewengland.com

General Information · **For the Kids**

Classes

Boston kids can participate in any number of structured activities that could help to mold and shape them like the blobs of clay that they are.

- **Boston Ballet School** (19 Clarendon St, Boston, 617-695-6950). Ballet classes for kids ages three and up. www.bostonballet.org
- **Boston Casting** (129 Braintree St, Suite 107, Allston, 617-254-1001). Acting classes for kids ages five and up. www.bostoncasting.com
- **Boston Children's Theatre** (321 Columbus Ave (Studio/Office), Boston, 617-424-6634). "Theatre for children by children," this theatre group has children involved in all phases of production. The theatre also offers acting classes and a summer creative arts program, in which kids learn stage combat, clowning, and juggling. www.bostonchildrenstheatre.org
- **Brookline Arts Center** (86 Monmouth St, Brookline, 617-566-5715). A non-degree school for the visual arts, the Brookline Arts Center offers classes for children ages two to teen in subjects ranging from jewelry-making to sculpture. www.brooklineartscenter.com
- **Cambridge Multicultural Arts Center** (41 Second St, Cambridge, 617-577-1400). A program designed for Cambridge residents to promote cross-cultural interchange using dance, music, writing, theater, and the visual arts. www.cmacusa.org
- **Community Music Center of Boston** (34 Warren St, 617-482-7494). A music program designed to promote musical development through experiential learning for kids of all ages. The center also offers visual arts classes, summer programs, and individual instruction. www.cmcb.org
- **French Library and Cultural Center** (53 Marlborough St, Boston, 617-912-0400). French classes for children ages three to ten. www.frenchlib.org
- **Full Moon** (344 Huron Ave, Cambridge, 617-354-6699). This kid-friendly restaurant offers cooking classes for parents and children ages three and up. www.fullmoonrestaurant.com
- **Grace Arts Project** (Grace United Methodist Church, 56 Magazine St, Cambridge, 617-864-1123). The program offers non-sectarian classes in music.
- **Grub Street Writers, Inc.** (160 Boylston St, Boston, 617-695-0075). Boston's only private writing school offers workshops and summer courses for young adults. www.grubstreet.org
- **Happily Ever After** (799 Concord Ave, Cambridge, 617-492-0090). The classes use fitness with creative stories and games for children ages three to six. Great for birthday parties. www.evergreendayschool.org
- **Hill House** (127 Mt. Vernon St, Boston). A non-profit community center that offers activities such as inline skating, karate, and youth soccer teams to downtown residents. www.hillhouseboston.org
- **Isis Maternity** (Two Brookline Pl, Brookline, 781-429-1599; 397 Massachusetts Ave, Arlington, 781-429-1598; 110 2nd Ave, Needham, 781-429-1597). The brainchild of Boston-area moms and health professionals, each Isis Center offers classes to stimulate everyone from the newly born to those about to bop into kindergarten. Infant massage, anyone? www.isismaternity.com
- **Jeanette Neill Children's Dance Studio** (261 Friend St, Boston, 617-523-1355). Since 1979, the program has offered children ages three to 12 an "intelligent dance alternative" with its focus on education, not preparation. www.jndance.com

- **Jose Mateo's Ballet Theatre** (Old Cambridge Baptist Church, 400 Harvard St, Cambridge, 617-354-7467). A professional performance company that provides ballet instruction for children ages three through 18. www.ballettheatre.org
- **Longy School of Music** (1 Follen St, Cambridge, 617-876-0956). Music instruction for children ages 1 to 18. www.longy.edu
- **Made By Me in Harvard Square** (1685 Massachusetts Ave, Cambridge, 617-354-8111). A paint-your-own-pottery studio. Great for birthday parties. www.made-by-me.com
- **Make Art Studio** (44 N Bennett St, Boston, 617-227-0775). Children ages four to 13 are encouraged to "choose their own medium" with guidance and instruction in small, age-appropriate classes.
- **Mudflat Studio** (149 Broadway, Somerville, 617-628-0589). For the past 30 years, the studio has offered hand-building, pot throwing, and individual workshops for children ages four and up. www.mudflat.org
- **Museum of Fine Arts** (465 Huntington Ave, Boston, 617-267-9300). The museum offers weekday and Saturday instruction that combines gallery study and creative expression for children. www.mfa.org/learn/index.asp?key=3117
- **New School of Music** (25 Lowell St, Cambridge, 617-492-8105). Newborns and up are provided with musical instruction for all levels of interest and skill, as well as musical theater classes for the older kids. www.cambridgemusic.org
- **North Cambridge Family Opera** (23 North St, Cambridge, 617-492-4095). Adults and children ages seven to 14 can participate in theatrical and operatic production. www.familyopera.org
- **North End Music and Performing Arts Center** (Paul Revere Mall, between Hanover St and Unity St, Boston, 617-227-2270). The center offers classes in music, language, and the performing arts to North End residents. www.nempac.org
- **New England Conservatory** (290 Huntington Ave, Boston, 617-585-1130). Music lessons for kids ages four and up at the oldest independent school of music in the US. www.newenglandconservatory.org
- **Oak Square YMCA** (615 Washington St, Brighton, 617-782-3535). The center offers instruction in swimming, gymnastics, basketball, and art as well as after school programs for kids of all ages. www.ymcaboston.org
- **The Skating Club of Boston** (1240 Soldiers Field Rd, Brighton, 617-782-5900). Classes for skaters and hockey players of all levels. www.scboston.org
- **Topf Center for Dance Education** (551 Tremont St, Boston, 617-482-0351). The center provides underserved youth access to classes in jazz, tap, ballet, hip hop, and African dancing. www.topfcenter.org
- **Upon a Star** (441 Stuart St, Studio 4, Boston, 617-797-5562). Music and movement classes for children ages 14 months to three. www.uponastar.net
- **Wang YMCA of Chinatown** (8 Oak St W, Boston, 617-426-2237). Activities ranging from swimming instruction to music and art classes for children of all ages. www.ymcaboston.org
- **Wheelock Family Theatre** (180 The Riverway, Boston, 617-879-2147). The Theatre offers classes for kids ages four to 17. www.wheelock.edu/wft

For more information, visit www.gocitykids.com

Overview

The Boston Public Library, founded in 1848, was the first publicly supported municipal library in the United States, and is the only public library in the United States that is also a Presidential library, that of John Adams. It is also the first library to open and operate neighborhood branches. By far the coolest looking branch, the **Honan-Allston (Map 19),** was designed by Machado & Silvetti Associates, Inc. and features tree guards and bike racks created by artist Rich Duca. The BPL now operates 27 branch libraries, each of which offers free wireless Internet access. Check out the details on the BPL's website. If you're looking for a getaway in Copley Square, the Italian courtyard is the perfect place to sit down with a book or a bagged lunch. For more information on the BPL's main branch and just how much cultural heat it's packing **(see page 185).**

Brookline, Cambridge, and Somerville have their own public libraries, which are part of the Minuteman System. The Brookline Public Library houses government documents, Russian and Chinese materials, Brookline high school yearbooks and newspapers, DVDs, videos, new books, and local newspapers. The **Cambridge Public Library's Main Library (Map 28)** has occupied the same building since 1889, and is currently undergoing renovations and expansion slated for completion in 2008. It is temporarily located in the old Longfellow School at 359 Broadway. The Cambridge History and Local History Collections will be available to the general public within the next two years, when the Main Library renovations are complete. The 93-year-old **Somerville Public Library (Map 24)** is also considering new construction in the future. Both Cambridge and Somerville libraries offer residents free passes to visit the Children's Museum, Harvard University Museum of Natural History, the JFK Library and Museum, the Museum of Fine Arts, the New England Aquarium, the Roger Williams Park Zoo, and others. To reserve FREE tickets, call 617-623-5000 (Somerville) or 617-349-4040 (Cambridge). For more information about hours, collections, and special events, check the library websites.

Library	Address	Phone	Map
West End	151 Cambridge St	617-523-3957	1
North End	25 Parmenter St	617-227-8135	2
Kirstein Business	20 City Hall Ave	617-523-0860	3
The Mary Baker Eddy Library	200 Massachusetts Ave	617-450-7000	5
Boston Public Library	700 Boylston St	617-536-5400	6
South End	685 Tremont St	617-536-8241	7
Charlestown	179 Main St	617-242-1248	8
East Boston	276 Meridian St	617-569-0271	9
Washington Village	1226 Columbia Rd	617-269-7239	10
South Boston	646 E Broadway	617-268-0180	11
Dudley	65 Warren St	617-442-6186	13
Connolly	433 Centre St	617-522-1960	14
Jamaica Plain	12 Sedgwick St	617-524-2053	14
Parker Hill	1497 Tremont St	617-427-3820	15
Brookline Main Library	361 Washington St	617-730-2370	17
Brighton	40 Academy Hill Rd	617-782-6032	18
Faneuil	419 Faneuil St	617-782-6705	18
Coolidge Corner	31 Pleasant St	617-730-2380	19
Honan-Allston	300 N Harvard St	617-787-6313	19
Boudreau Public Library	245 Concord Ave	617-349-4017	21
O'Neill Public Library	70 Rindge Ave	617-349-4023	22
Somerville West	40 College Ave	617-623-5000	22
Somerville East	115 Broadway	617-623-5000	24
Somerville Main Library	79 Highland Ave	617-623-5000	24
O'Connell Public Library	48 Sixth St	617-349-4019	26
Central Square Public Library	45 Pearl St	617-349-4010	27
Cambridge Main Library	359 Broadway	617-349-4030	28
Valente Public Library	826 Cambridge St	617-349-4015	28

General Information • **LGBT**

Websites

Boston Gay Men's Chorus • www.bgmc.org
Now in its 24th year, the BGMC, through its collaboration with The Boston Pops, was the first gay chorus in the world to be recorded with a major orchestra on a major label.

craigslist • http://boston.craigslist.org
General community site (for straights, gays, and everyone else) that offers heavily trafficked "men seeking men" and "women seeking women" sections, as well as other community-related listings and information.

EDGE Boston • www.edgeboston.com
Gay Boston news and entertainment.

Gay & Lesbian Advocates & Defenders (GLAD) • www.glad.org
New England's leading legal rights organization dedicated to ending discrimination based on sexual orientation.

Greater Boston Business Council • www.gbbc.org
Promotes the vitality of Boston's LGBT business and professional community.

Out In Boston • www.outinboston.com
Local news and events, personal ads, business ads, chat, and community message boards.

PinkWeb • www.pinkweb.com
The LGBT yellow pages for New England and beyond.

Provincetown Business Guild • www.ptown.org
A gay and lesbian guide to P'town.

Publications

BayWindows—New England's largest gay and lesbian newspaper is a weekly publication that prints local, national, and international news as well as community events and guides. www.baywindows.com.

In Newsweekly—News and entertainment weekly, including a calendar of events and a club guide. www.innewsweekly.com.

Bookstores

Calamus Bookstore • 92B South St, Boston • 617-338-1931 • www.calamusbooks.com

Sports

Beantown Softball League • www.beantownsoftball.com
LGBT softball since 1978.

Boston Bay Blades • www.bayblades.org/boston
For rowers and scullers.

Boston Boasts Squash League • www.bostonboasts.com
The country's oldest and largest gay and lesbian squash league.

Boston Gay Basketball League • www.bgbl.com
The country's largest LGBT basketball league.

Boston Strikers • www.bostonstrikers.com
Indoor and outdoor soccer league for gay and straight players of all levels.

Cambridge-Boston Volleyball Association • www.gayvolleyball.net
Indoor league with three levels of play.

Chiltern Mountain Club • www.chiltern.org
New England's largest LGBT outdoor recreation club.

East Coast Wrestling Club • www.eastcoastwrestlingclub.org
Gay men's wrestling group for athletes of all abilities.

FLAG Flag Football • http://flagflagfootball.tripod.com/flagflagfootballonline
Plays a full fall season and an abbreviated spring season.

FrontRunners Boston • www.mindspring.com/~frontrunners/index.htm
Welcomes joggers, walkers, and runners of all experience levels.

PrideSports Boston • 617-937-5858 • www.geocities.com/pridesportsboston
Gay & lesbian athletic alliance with more than 20 sports clubs.

Health Centers & Support Organizations

Boston Alliance of Gay Lesbian Bisexual and Transgender Youth · 617-227-4313 · www.bagly.org
For young people 22 and under.

Dignity Boston · 617-421-1915 ·
www.dignityboston.org
An inclusive community of LGBT Catholics.

Fenway Community Health · 7 Haviland St, Boston ·
617-267-0900 · www.fenwayhealth.org
Provides high-quality medical and mental health care to Boston's gay and lesbian community; also a leader in HIV care.

Gay Men's Domestic Violence Project ·
800-832-1901 · www.gmdvp.org
Offers shelter, guidance, and resources to allow gay, bisexual, and transgender men in crisis to remove themselves from violent situations and relationships; also operates a 24-hour free-of-charge crisis center.

MassEquality · 617-878-2300 ·
www.massequality.org
Grassroots advocacy group defending equal marriage rights for same-sex couples.

The Network · 617-423-SAFE ·
www.thenetworklared.org
Provides information and resources for battered lesbian, bisexual, and transgendered women.

Annual Events

Boston Pride Week · 617-262-9405 ·
www.bostonpride.org
Begins on a Friday in June with a flag raising at City Hall; the parade and festival usually take place on the Saturday of the following weekend.

Boston Gay/Lesbian Film/Video Festival ·
617-267-9300 · www.mfa.org
Usually held in May at the MFA.

Mass Red Ribbon Ride · 617-450-1100 ·
www.massredribbonride.org
This bike ride across the state raises money for AIDS organizations. Takes place annually in August.

Venues – Lesbian

- **Aria** (Saturdays) · 246 Tremont St, Boston · 617-417-0186
- **Dyke Night Productions** · www.dykenight.com
- **Midway Cafe** (Sundays) · 3496 Washington St, Jamaica Plain · www.midwaycafe.com
- **Milky Way Lounge** (Sundays) · 401 Centre St, Jamaica Plain · 617-524-3740 · www.milkywayjp.com
- **The Modern** (Thursdays) · 36 Lansdowne St, Boston · www.lesbiannightlife.com
- **Toast** (Fridays) · 70 Union Sq, Somerville · 617-623-9211 · www.toastlounge.com
- **Tribe** (at Felt) · 533 Washington St, Boston · 617-350-5555 · www.tribenightclub.com

Venues – Gay

- **The Alley** · 14 Pi Aly, Boston · 617-263-1449 · www.thealleybar.com
- **Avalon** (Sundays) · 15 Lansdowne St, Boston · 617-262-2424 · www.avalonboston.com
- **Club Cafe** · 209 Columbus Ave, Boston · 617-536-0966 · www.clubcafe.com
- **Eagle** · 520 Tremont St, Boston · 617-542-4494
- **Flaunt** (Saint Nightclub) · 90 Exeter St, Boston · 617-236-1134
- **Fritz** · 26 Chandler St, Boston · 617-482-4428 · www.fritzboston.com
- **Heroes** (Saturdays at **Toast**) · 70 Union Sq, Somerville · 617-623-9211 · www.toastlounge.com
- **Jacques Cabaret** · 79 Broadway St, Boston · 617-426-8902 · www.jacquescabaret.com
- **Machine** (Thurs–Sat) · 1256 Boylston St, Boston · 617-226-2986 · www.ramrodmachine.com
- **Paradise** · 180 Massachusetts Ave, Cambridge · 617-868-3000 · www.paradisecambridge.com
- **Ramrod** · 1254 Boylston St, Boston · 617-226-2986 · www.ramrodmachine.com
- **Rise** (members only, after-hours) · 306 Stuart St, Boston · 617-423-7473 · www.riseclub.us
- **Shine Restaurant & Lounge** · 1 Kendall Sq, Cambridge · 617-621-9500 · www.shinecambridge.com
- **Venu** (Wednesdays) · 101 Warrenton St, Boston · 617-695-9500

General Information · **Hotels**

After years of suffering from a shortage of hotel accommodations, Boston's hotel market has finally warmed up. Developers, encouraged by an improving economic climate and continued high demand for rooms, have moved forward with several large projects, most of which are located on or near the waterfront, where developers hope to leverage locations close to the Boston Convention & Exhibition Center. But it's not all just about harbor views and cafeteria-sized restaurants—boutique hotels are also popping up in various locations around town. Newcomers in the boutique market include **Hotel 140 (Map 6)** (a historic building in the shadow of the Hancock Tower), sleek **Nine Zero (Map 3)** (on Tremont Street), the **Bulfinch Hotel (Map 1)** (near North Station), and the **Beacon Hill Hotel (Map 1)** (on Charles Street, near the Common). **Jurys' (Map 6)** first Boston location has opened in the fully renovated former headquarters of the Boston Police Department. Another recently-opened property, the **Hampton Inn & Suites (Map 12)** (near Newmarket Square), may not be as luxurious as Jurys, but its suites are a decent option for long-term stays, and its proximity to I-93 and the Mass Pike make it easy to get to other locations. For visitors largely confined to happenings at the Boston Convention Center, the newly opened **Westin Boston Waterfront (Map 4)** and the **Seaport Hotel (Map 11)** are safe, convenient bets.

But Boston residents shouldn't let tourists have all the fun. Even if you're not staying the night, it's worth popping into one of Boston's classic hotels to soak up the atmosphere. The lobby of the **Fairmont Copley Plaza (Map 6)** exudes luxuriousness, as does its acclaimed restaurant, the Oak Room. For those looking for a respite from retail therapy on nearby Newbury Street, the **Eliot Hotel (Map 5)** on Commonwealth Avenue can rejuvenate even the weariest shopper. Genteel rivals the **Four Seasons (Map 3)** and

the **Taj Boston (Map 3)** (formerly home to the oldest Ritz Carlton in the country) both overlook the Public Garden. (The Bristol Lounge at the Four Seasons serves what many argue is the city's best-known high tea.) Across the Common, towards the financial district, the **Omni Parker House (Map 3)** stands as a Boston institution and a literary landmark (and has been known to flaunt its claim to fame as the birthplace of Parker rolls and Boston Cream Pies). The **Langham Hotel (Map 4)**, located smack dab in the middle of Boston's high-finance hub, offers a chocolate buffet on Saturdays that is To Die For. If you're killing time in Back Bay, check out the charming and cozy lobby of the **Lenox Hotel (Map 6)**. Playing up its proximity to techie heaven is the **University Park Hotel @ MIT (Map 20)**, decorated with tributes to the art of engineering. In Harvard Square, the **Charles Hotel (Map 20)** offers nightly jazz at the Regattabar as well as organic fine dining at Henrietta's Table. And if you're suffering from wanderlust of the spirit, ask about the weekend retreats at the **Monastery of the Society of St. John the Evangelist (Map 20)**.

Marriott's Custom House (Map 2) is located in one of Boston's most prominent historic landmarks, the Custom House Tower. The original Custom House building, completed in 1847, was described by Walt Whitman as "the noblest form of architecture in the world." The tower was added in 1915. The open-air observation deck on the 26th floor is open to the public and offers prime views of the harbor and the open spaces created by the demolition of the Central Artery.

See the average room rates listed below? Pretty expensive, huh? Whether you're booking for yourself or the in-laws, call the hotels to ask about specials and check websites such as hotels.com, Orbitz, Hotwire, Travelocity, and All-Hotels for discounts. Maybe you'll get lucky.

Map 1 · Beacon Hill / West End

Beacon Hill Hotel	25 Charles St	617-723-7575	$245
Bulfinch Hotel	107 Merrimac St	617-624-0202	$169
Charles Street Inn (B&B)	94 Charles St	617-314-8900	$250
Holiday Inn	5 Blossom St	617-742-7630	$200
John Jeffries House (B&B)	14 David G Mugar Wy	617-367-1866	$105
Onyx Hotel	155 Portland St	617-557-9955	$209
Shawmut Inn	280 Friend St	617-720-5544	$109
XV Beacon Hotel	15 Beacon St	617-670-1500	$375

Map 2 · North End / Faneuil Hall

Boston Marriott Long Wharf	296 State St	617-227-0800	$349
Golden Slipper (floating B&B)	Lewis Wharf	781-545-2845	$175
Harborside Inn	185 State St	617-723-7500	$129
Marriott's Custom House	3 McKinley Sq	617-310-6300	$429
Millennium Bostonian Hotel	26 North St	617-523-3600	$269

Map 3 · Downtown Crossing / Park Square / Bay Village

Boston Park Plaza Hotel	64 Arlington St	617-426-2000	$125
Courtyard Boston Tremont	275 Tremont St	617-426-1400	$179

Doubletree Boston	821 Washington St	617-956-7900	$189
Four Seasons Hotel	200 Boylston St	617-338-4400	$475
Hyatt Regency Boston	1 Ave de Lafayette	617-912-1234	$189
Milner Hotel	78 Charles St S	617-426-6220	$89
Nine Zero Hotel	90 Tremont St	617-772-5800	$206
Omni Parker House	60 School St	617-227-8600	$279
Radisson Hotel Boston	200 Stuart St	617-482-1800	$249
Ritz-Carlton Boston Common	10 Avery St	617-574-7100	$295
Taj Boston	15 Arlington St	617-536-5700	$275

Map 4 · Financial District / Chinatown

Boston Harbor Hotel	70 Rowes Wharf	617-439-7000	$275
Hilton Boston	89 Broad St	617-556-0006	$171
InterContinental Boston	510 Atlantic Ave	617-747-1000	$526
The Langham Hotel	250 Franklin St	617-451-1900	$185
Westin Boston Waterfront	245 Summer St	617-532-4600	$199

Map 5 · Back Bay (West) / Fenway (East)

436 Beacon Street	436 Beacon St	617-536-1302	$79
Central YMCA	316 Huntington Ave	617-536-7800	$46
Commonwealth Court Guest House	284 Commonwealth Ave	617-424-1230	$79
Eliot Hotel	370 Commonwealth Ave	617-267-1607	$275
Hilton Boston Back Bay	40 Dalton St	617-236-1100	$179
Hosteling International	12 Hemenway St	617-536-9455	$28 (dorm)
			$70 (private room)
Midtown Hotel	220 Huntington Ave	617-262-1000	$99
Newbury Guest House (B&B)	261 Newbury St	617-437-7666	$99
Oasis Guest House	22 Edgerly Rd	617-267-2262	$79
Sheraton Boston Hotel	39 Dalton St	617-236-2000	$249

Map 6 · Back Bay (East) / South End (Upper)

Boston Marriott Copley Place	110 Huntington Ave	617-236-5800	$199
Charlesmark Hotel	655 Boylston St	617-247-1212	$159
The College Club	44 Commonwealth Ave	617-536-9510	$90
Colonnade Hotel	120 Huntington Ave	617-424-7000	$234
Copley House	239 W Newton St	617-236-8300	$85
Copley Inn	19 Garrison St	617-236-0300	$105
Copley Square Hotel	47 Huntington Ave	617-536-9000	$168
Courtyard by Marriott Copley Place	88 Exeter St	617-437-9300	$179
Fairmont Copley Plaza Hotel	138 St James Ave	617-267-5300	$479
Hotel 140	140 Clarendon St	617-585-5600	$129
International Guest House	237 Beacon St	617-437-1975	$120 (single)
			$95 (dorm)
Jewel of Newbury	254 Newbury St	617-536-5523	$200
John Hancock Hotel & Conference	40 Trinity Pl	617-933-7700	$115
Jurys Boston Hotel	350 Stuart St	617-266-7200	$295
Lenox Hotel	61 Exeter St	617-536-5300	$179
Westin Copley Place	10 Huntington Ave	617-262-9600	$209

Map 7 · South End (Lower)

Chandler Inn	26 Chandler St	617-482-3450	$129
Clarendon Square Inn (B&B)	198 W Brookline St	617-536-2229	$155
Encore Bed & Breakfast	116 W Newton St	617-247-3425	$140
Hampton Inn & Suites Boston Crosstown Center	811 Massachusetts Ave	617-445-6400	$125
Rutland Square House	56 Rutland Sq	617-247-0018	$165
YWCA/Berkeley Residence	40 Berkeley St	617-375-2524	$60 (men & women)

Map 8 · Charlestown

Bunker Hill Bed & Breakfast	80 Elm St	617-241-8067	$135
Constitution Inn	150 2nd Ave	617-241-8400	$129
Marriott Residence Inn Boston Harbor	34 Charles River Ave	617-242-9000	$229

Map 9 · East Boston

Embassy Suites Boston at Logan	207 Porter St	617-567-5000	$206

Map 10 · South Boston (West) / Fort Point

Nolan House (B&B)	10 G St	617-269-1550	$95

Map 11 · South Boston (East)

Seaport Hotel	1 Seaport Ln	617-385-4000	$469

Map 12 · Newmarket / Andrew Square

Best Western Inn Roundhouse Suites	891 Massachusetts Ave	617-989-1000	$135
Holiday Inn Express	69 Boston St	617-288-3030	$104

Map 15 · Fenway (West) / Mission Hill

Best Western Longwood Medical	342 Longwood Ave	617-731-4700	$149
Brigham Guest House	698 Huntington Ave	617-566-8947	$48
Howard Johnson	1271 Boylston St	617-267-8300	$135

Map 16 · Kenmore Square / Brookline (East)

Anthony's Town House	1085 Beacon St	617-566-3972	$90
Beacon Inn	1087 Beacon St	617-566-0088	$80
Buckminster Hotel	645 Beacon St	617-236-7050	$104
Gryphon House (B&B)	9 Bay State Rd	617-375-9003	$149
Holiday Inn Boston at Brookline	1200 Beacon St	617-277-1200	$155
Hotel Commonwealth	500 Commonwealth Ave	617-933-5000	$293
Longwood Inn (B&B)	123 Longwood Ave	617-566-8615	$79

Map 17 · Coolidge Corner / Brookline Hills

Beacon-Plaza	1459 Beacon St	617-232-6550	$65
Bertram Inn (B&B)	92 Sewall Ave	617-566-2234	$99
Coolidge Corner Guest House	17 Littell Rd	617-734-4041	$69
Courtyard by Marriott Brookline	40 Webster St	617-734-1393	$179
Samuel Sewall Inn (B&B)	143 St Paul St	617-713-0123	$139

Map 18 · Brighton

Best Western Terrace Inn	1650 Commonwealth Ave	617-566-6260	$143
Days Inn	1800 Soldiers Field Rd	617-254-0200	$88

Map 19 · Allston (South) / Brookline (North)

Abercrombie's Farrington Inn	23 Farrington Ave	617-787-1860	$27.50
Days Hotel	1234 Soldiers Field Rd	617-254-1234	$116
Doubletree Guest Suites	400 Soldiers Field Rd	617-783-0090	$279

Map 20 · Harvard Square / Allston (North)

Charles Hotel	1 Bennett St	617-864-1200	$219
Harvard Square Hotel	110 Mt Auburn St	617-864-5200	$199
The Inn at Harvard	1201 Massachusetts Ave	617-491-2222	$259
Mary Prentiss Inn (B&B)	6 Prentiss St	617-661-2929	$184
Monastery of the Society of St John the Evangelist	980 Memorial Dr	617-876-3037	$50
Sheraton Commander Hotel	16 Garden St	617-547-4800	$219

Map 21 · West Cambridge

Best Western Hotel Tria	220 Alewife Brook Pkwy	617-491-8000	$189

Map 22 · North Cambridge / West Somerville

A Cambridge House, B&B Hotel Inn	2218 Massachusetts Ave	617-491-6300	$109
Meacham Manor	52 Meacham Rd	617-623-3985	$75
Morrison House (B&B)	221 Morrison Ave	617-627-9670	$65

Map 24 · Winter Hill / Union Square

Holiday Inn Boston/Somerville	30 Washington St	617-628-1000	$143
La Quinta Inn & Suites	23 Cummings St	617-625-5300	$119

Map 25 · East Somerville / Sullivan Square

Hampton Inn Boston/Cambridge	191 Monsignor O'Brien Hwy	617-494-5300	$152

Map 26 · East Cambridge / Kendall Square / MIT

Holiday Inn Express Hotel & Suites	250 Monsignor O'Brien Hwy	617-577-7600	$152
Hotel Marlowe	25 Land Blvd	617-868-8000	$224
Kendall Hotel	350 Main St	617-577-1300	$275
Marriott Cambridge	2 Cambridge Ctr	617-494-6600	$229
Residence Inn by Marriott - Cambridge	6 Cambridge Ctr	617-349-0700	$249
Royal Sonesta Hotel Boston	40 Edwin H Land Blvd	617-806-4200	$259

Map 27 · Central Square / Cambridgeport

Cambridge Bed & Muffin	267 Putnam Ave	617-576-3166	$75
Hyatt Regency Cambridge	575 Memorial Dr	617-492-1234	$179
University Park Hotel at MIT	20 Sidney St	617-577-0200	$259

Map 28 · Inman Square

A Bed & Breakfast in Cambridge	1657 Cambridge St	617-868-7082	$75
A Friendly Inn at Harvard (B&B)	1673 Cambridge St	617-547-7851	$97
Amory Guest House (B&B)	62 Amory St	617-308-4237	$70
Harding House (B&B)	288 Harvard St	617-876-2888	$85
Irving House at Harvard (B&B)	24 Irving St	617-547-4600	$75
Prospect Place (B&B)	112 Prospect St	617-864-7500	$85

And this is good old Boston.
The home of the bean and the cod.
Where the Lowells talk to the Cabots,
And the Cabots talk only to God.
                    —John Collins Bossidy (a toast given
                    at a Harvard alumni dinner in 1910)

Useful Phone Numbers

General Info	411
Emergencies	911
Boston Globe	617-929-2000
Boston Herald	617-426-3000
Boston Public Library	617-536-5400
Boston City Hall	617-635-4000
Brookline Town Hall	617-730-2000
Cambridge City Hall	617-349-4000
Somerville City Hall	617-625-6600
Boston Board of Elections	617-635-4635
Brookline Town Clerk	617-730-2010
Cambridge Board of Elections	617-349-4361
Somerville Board of Elections	617-625-6600, ext. 4200
Boston Police Headquarters	617-343-4200
Keyspan Energy Delivery	617-469-2300
NStar	617-424-2000
Comcast	888-633-4266
Verizon	800-256-4646
Red Sox Ticket Line	877-733-7699

Websites

www.notfortourists.com/boston.aspx—
    The Boston site written by the people, for the people.
www.beantownbloggery.com—
    Anything and everything beantown.
www.boston.com—Website of the *Boston Globe*.
www.boston.craigslist.org—
    Classifieds in almost every area, with personals, apartments
    for rent, musicians, job listings, and more.
www.boston.citysearch.com—
    Portal channeling the Yellow Pages.
www.boston-online.com—
    Forums and fun facts; guide to Boston English.
www.bostonist.com—
    About Boston and everything that happens in it.
www.cambridgema.gov—
    Cambridge government resources.
http://cheapthrillsboston.blogspot.com—
    Perfect for those on an NFT salary.
www.cityofboston.gov—Boston government resources.
www.ci.somerville.ma.us—
    Somerville government resources.
www.eatanddestroy.com—Amazing Boston food blog.
www.town.brookline.ma.us—
    Brookline government resources.
www.universalhub.com—Info hub for the Hub.

We're the First!!!

- America's first public park (Boston Common, 1634)
- America's first public college (Harvard, founded in 1636)
- America's first public school (Boston Latin, 1645)
- America's first public library (Boston Public Library, 1653)
- America's first post office (Richard Fairbanks' Tavern, 1639)
- America's first regularly issued newspaper (*Boston News-Letter*, 1704)
- America's first lighthouse (Boston Harbor, 1716)
- First flag of the American colonies raised on Prospect Hill (January 1, 1776)

- America's first published novel (*The Power of Sympathy* by William Hill Brown, 1789)
- First demonstration of surgical anesthesia (1845)
- First telephone call (Alexander Graham Bell, 1876)
- America's first subway (1897)
- First person-to-person network email (BBN Technologies, 1971)
- First "First Night" New Year's celebration (1976)

Boston Timeline

A timeline of significant Boston events (by no means complete)

1620	Mayflower arrives in Plymouth.
1630	Dorchester founded by Gov. John Winthrop.
1630	City of Boston chartered.
1634	Boston Common, first public park in America, opens.
1636	Harvard College opens.
1643	America's first canal cut near Dedham.
1645	Boston Latin School, first public school in America, opens.
1692	Witchcraft trials begin in Salem.
1693	Society of Negroes founded.
1704	First regularly issued American newspaper, the *Boston News-Letter*.
1706	Benjamin Franklin born.
1716	First American lighthouse built (Boston Harbor).
1770	Boston Massacre.
1773	Boston Tea Party.
1775	Revolutionary War begins at Lexington and Concord.
1775	Battle of Bunker Hill.
1776	First flag of the American colonies raised on Prospect Hill in Somerville.
1776	British evacuate Boston.
1780	John Hancock becomes first elected Governor of Massachusetts.
1788	Massachusetts ratifies Constitution.
1795	The "new" State House built.
1796	John Adams, of Quincy, elected second president.
1806	African Meeting House, first church built by free African-Americans, opens.
1820	Maine separates from Massachusetts.
1824	John Quincy Adams elected sixth president.
1826	Union Oyster House opens.
1831	William Lloyd Garrison publishes first abolitionist newspaper, the *Liberator*.
1837	Samuel Morse invents electric telegraph machine.
1845	Sewing machine invented by Elias Howe.
1846	Boston dentist William T.G. Morton publicly demonstrates the use of anesthesia in surgery.
1846	From 1846 to 1849, 37,000 Irish people flee the Potato Famine for Boston.
1860	From 1860 to 1870, the Back Bay is filled in, greatly increasing the landmass of Boston.
1863	University of Massachusetts at Amherst chartered.
1868	From 1868 to 1874, Boston annexes Charlestown, Brighton, Roxbury, West Roxbury, and Dorchester.
1872	*Boston Globe* prints its first newspaper.
1872	Great Fire.
1876	First telephone call by Alexander Graham Bell.
1877	Helen Magill becomes first woman Ph.D. in US (at BU).
1882	John L. Sullivan becomes bare-knuckle boxing champ.
1886	*Irish Echo* newspaper founded.
1888	Construction begins on new building for Boston Public Library.
1892	JFK grandfather John F. "Honey Fitz" Fitzgerald elected to state senate.
1894	Honey Fitz elected to US Congress.
1896	First US public beach opens in Revere.
1897	First American subway opens.
1900	Symphony Hall opens.
1901	Boston Red Sox play first game against New York Yankees.
1903	Red Sox (then the Americans) win first World Series.
1906	Honey Fitz becomes first Boston-born Irish-American mayor.

1912 Fenway Park opens.
1914 James Michael Curley elected mayor for the first time.
1915 Custom House Tower completed, tallest building in Boston at time.
1919 Great Molasses Flood kills 21 in the North End.
1920 Red Sox owner Harry Frazee sells Babe Ruth to Yankees for $100,000.
1920 Irish-Italian gang fights begin.
1924 Boston Bruins play first game.
1924 World's first mutual fund established.
1927 Sacco and Vanzetti wrongly executed for robbery shootings.
1928 Boston Garden opens.
1928 First computer invented at MIT.
1929 Bruins win their first Stanley Cup trophy.
1934 JFK's father, "Old Joe" Kennedy, named SEC chairman.
1941 Ted Williams hits .406, last player to hit over .400.
1942 Fire at Cocoanut Grove nightclub kills 491 people.
1946 JFK elected to Congress.
1946 Boston Celtics play first game.
1946 Red Sox lose World Series after tragic player error.
1947 Microwave oven invented at Raytheon.
1947 Polaroid camera invented.
1947 Dr. Sidney Farber introduces chemotherapy.
1950 Red Auerbach becomes Celtics coach.
1952 Boston Braves play final game in Boston, move to Milwaukee.
1956 Celtics draft Bill Russell.
1957 Massachusetts Turnpike opens.
1958 Celtics win first of 16 championships.
1958 Demolition of the West End neighborhood begins.
1959 Central Artery opens.
1960 Boston Patriots play first game.
1960 John F. Kennedy elected 35th president.
1960 Ted Williams homers in last at-bat for Red Sox.
1962 From 1962 to 1964, Boston Strangler kills 13 women. Albert DeSalvo is convicted and killed in prison.
1963 JFK assassinated in Dallas.
1964 Prudential Tower built.
1965 Havlicek steals the ball! Celtics win championship.
1966 Bobby Orr plays first game as a Bruin.
1966 Edward W. Brooke becomes first African-American elected to US Senate since Reconstruction.
1967 Red Sox's Impossible Dream" season ends in defeat.
1971 First e-mail sent by BBN Technologies.
1973 John Hancock building, tallest in Boston, nears completion—giant windows start falling out.
1974 Federal court declares "de facto segregation" of Boston public schools; orders desegregation by busing. Demonstrations and violence ensue.
1975 Carlton Fisk hits 12th inning Game 6 homer, does baseline foul pole dance. Sox go on to lose Game 7.
1975 Gangster Whitey Bulger begins relationship with FBI agents, reign as Boston's biggest crime lord.
1976 Boston "First Night" New Year's celebration.
1978 Blizzard of '78 paralyzes Southern New England.
1978 Bucky Dent! Sox lose to Yanks.
1986 Celtics draft pick Len Bias dies of a drug overdose.
1986 Red Sox lose World Series Game 6 to Mets after excruciating 10th inning error, go on to lose Game 7.
1987 Big Dig construction begins in Charlestown.
1988 Cleanup of Boston Harbor begins.
1988 Governor Michael Dukakis runs for president, rides tank, loses to Bush the First.
1993 Celtics captain Reggie Lewis dies.
1993 Former Mayor Ray Flynn named ambassador to Vatican.
1993 Thomas M. "Mumbles" Menino elected Boston's first Italian-American mayor.
1995 Boston Garden closes; FleetCenter opens.
1995 Whitey Bulger goes on the lam after his FBI handlers are indicted.
1998 *Boston Globe* columnists Patricia Smith and Mike Barnicle fired over fabrications and plagiarism, respectively.

2001 Jane Swift becomes first female governor of Massachusetts.
2001 Planes that destroy NYC World Trade Center leave Logan Airport.
2002 After a 0-2 start, New England Patriots win their first Super Bowl.
2002 Ted Williams dies, cryogenically frozen in two pieces.
2002 Catholic clergy sexual abuse scandal explodes; Cardinal Bernard Law resigns amid controversy.
2003 Billy Bulger forced to resign as UMass president due to controversy about his gangster brother, Whitey.
2004 Supreme Judicial Court rules that gay couples have the right to marry.
2004 Demolition of Central Artery.
2004 Sox win World Series for first time since 1918.
2005 New England Patriots win their third Super Bowl in four years.
2006 Boston elects Deval Patrick, first Black Governor of Massachusetts
2007 Sox end three year drought by winning the World Series (again!).
2008 Boston Celtics beats LA Lakers for record 17th NBA championship

15 Essential Boston Movies

The Boston Strangler (1968)	*Far and Away* (1992)
The Thomas Crown Affair (1968)	*Good Will Hunting* (1997)
Love Story (1970)	*A Civil Action* (1998)
The Paper Chase (1973)	*Monument Ave* (1998)
Between the Lines (1977)	*Next Stop, Wonderland* (1998)
The Verdict (1982)	*Mystic River* (2003)
The Bostonians (1984)	*The Departed* (2006)
Glory (1989)	*Gone Baby Gone* (2007)

15 Essential Boston Songs

"Boston" — The Byrds
"Charlie on the MTA" — The Kingston Trio
"Dirty Water" — The Standells
"Down at the Cantab" — Little Joe Cook & the Thrillers
"Government Center" — Jonathan Richman
"Highlands" — Bob Dylan
"I Want My City Back" — The Mighty Mighty Bosstones
"Massachusetts" — The Bee Gees
"Roadrunner" — Jonathan Richman
"Rock and Roll Band" — Boston
"Sweet Baby James" — James Taylor
"Tessie" — Dropkick Murphys
"The Ballad of Sacco & Vanzetti" — Joan Baez
"Twilight in Boston" — Jonathan Richman
"UMass" — The Pixies

15 Essential Boston Books

All Souls, Michael Patrick McDonald
The Autobiography of Benjamin Franklin
Black Mass, David Lehrer and Gerard O'Neill
The Bostonians, Henry James
Dark Tide: The Great Boston Molasses Flood of 1919, Stephen Puleo
Faithful, Stewart O'Nan and Stephen King
The Handmaid's Tale, Margaret Atwood
The House of the Seven Gables, Nathaniel Hawthorne
Infinite Jest, David Foster Wallace
John Adams, David McCullough
Johnny Tremain, Esther Forbes
Little Women, Louisa May Alcott
Make Way for Ducklings, Robert McCloskey
The Trumpet of the Swan, E.B. White
Walden, Henry David Thoreau

Overview

There's always something going on in Boston—the list below is just a smattering of the hundreds of annual parades, festivals, and wing-dings. Note that the dates indicated below for September through December reflect schedules for 2008, and the dates indicated for January through August reflect schedules for 2009. As always, it's a good idea to check an event's website when making plans. Now get out and enjoy!

- **First Night** · Dec 31/Jan 1 · www.firstnight.org · Family-oriented First Night got its start in Boston. Celebrate the new year with live performances, interactive events, and in most years, bitter cold. The purchase of a First Night Button gains you admission to participating performance centers.

- **Boston Wine Expo** · Late Jan/Early Feb · www.wine-expos.com/boston · Largest consumer wine event in the country, with a long bill of celebrity chefs to boot.

- **Chinese New Year** · Late Jan–Early Feb · Fireworks, parades, and special banquets in Chinatown.

- **Black History Month Music Celebration** · Feb · www.berkleebpc.com · A series of concerts at the Berklee Performance Center.

- **Winter Restaurant Week** · Early March · www.restaurantweekboston.com · Local eateries offer specially priced lunches and dinners. A chance to sample meals you could never otherwise afford!

- **New England Spring Flower Show** · Early March · www.masshort.org · Flower and craft exhibition at the Bayside Expo Center.

- **Evacuation Day** · Mar 17 · British troop withdrawal from Boston was the perfect excuse for infamous Mayor Curley to make St. Paddy's Day an official holiday for all Suffolk County municipal workers. Gotta love the Irish.

- **St. Patrick's Day Parade** · March· www.saintpatricksdayparade.com/boston · Marching through Southie since 1737.

- **Red Sox Opening Day** · Early Apr · www.redsox.com · Unofficial holiday.

- **Anime Boston** · Apr 2–4 · www.animeboston.com · Japanese animation convention at the Hynes Convention Center.

- **Boston Marathon/Patriots Day** · Apr 20 · www.baa.org · Pseudo local holiday with the 111th running of the marathon and an early Red Sox game.

- **Wake Up the Earth Festival** · Early May · spontaneouscelebrations.org · Hippies and children alike enjoy stilt walking, puppets, live bands, and community bonding in Jamaica Plain.

- **Lilac Sunday at the Arnold Arboretum** · Early May · www.arboretum.harvard.edu · Follow the perfume of the lilac and the hippie in a Morris dancing outfit. Fun atmosphere at the Arnold Arboretum for families and friends.

- **MayFair 2008** · First Sunday in May · www.harvardsquare.com/mayfair/ · Harvard Square festival featuring everything from Literary tours to indie rock to Morris dancers.

- **Walk for Hunger** · Early May · www.projectbread.org · 20-mile walk whose proceeds fund over 400 emergency food programs **each year.**

- **Street Performers Festival** · Late May · Faneuil Hall carnival that's especially fun for kids. Magicians, sword swallowers, and lil' one activities like the Kid's Kazoo Parade.

- **Feast of the Madonna di Anzano** · Early June · www.anzanoboston.com · Procession and gala feast in the North End Italian community.

- **Scooper Bowl** · Early June · www.jimmyfund.org · World's biggest all-you-can-eat ice cream festival. Proceeds go to the Jimmy Fund.

- **Boston Gay Pride Parade** · Early/Mid June · www.bostonpride.org · New England's largest, capping a week of pride events.

- **Cambridge River Festival** · Mid June · Summer-starting festival along Memorial Drive between JFK Street and Western Ave, featuring music, food, art, kid-stuff.

- **Dragon Boat Festival** · Early/Mid June · www.bostondragonboat.org · Celebration of Chinese Dragon Boat racing at the Weeks footbridge, on Memorial Drive. Races, food, activities all day long.

- **Bloomsday** · Jun 16 · www.artsandsociety.org · Celebration of James Joyce's *Ulysses* at BU.

- **Bunker Hill Parade** · Around June 17 · www.charlestownonline.net · Celebration of Bunker Hill Day in Charlestown.

- **Boston Globe Blues and Jazz Festival** · Late Jun · Jazz and blues on the waterfront.

- **Boston Harborfest** · Early July ·
www.bostonharborfest.com · Over 200 events
celebrating Boston's colonial and maritime history
through reenactments, concerts, and historical
tours.

- **Boston's Fourth of July** · Guess · www.july4th.org
Ridiculously crowded Boston Pops concert and
fireworks on the Esplanade.

- **Puerto Rican Festival** · Late July ·
Franklin Park goes loco for 5 days with amusement
rides, food, and general fun in the name of Puerto
Rico. Lots of live music.

- **Feast of St. Agrippina** · Early Aug · Featuring a
procession, block party, and a giant tug-of-war.

- **August Moon Festival** · Mid Aug ·
At the Chinatown Gateway arch on Harrison Ave,
celebrating Chinese culture and marked by tasty
flaky pastries with an interesting history,

- **Feast of the Madonna del Soccorso** · Mid Aug ·
www.fishermansfeast.com · Boston's longest-
running Italian festival.

- **St. Anthony's Feast** · Late Aug ·
www.saintanthonysfeast.com · With Italian-
American festivals in the North End every
weekend throughout late July and August, this is
the one to get off your coolie for. True
combination of kitsch and classic.

- **Summer Restaurant Week** · August ·
www.bostonusa.com · Discounted *prix-fixe* meals
at scores of area restaurants—a terrific bargain.

- **Boston Carnival** · Late Aug ·
www.bostoncarnival.com · Celebration of
Caribbean culture in Dorchester.

- **Khoury's State Spa Big Man Run** · Late Summer ·
www.clydesdale.com · A 4.8-mile race through
Somerville during which runners stop three times
to consume a hot dog and a beer.

- **Central Square World's Fair** · September ·
September is evidentially carnival month in
Cambridge.

- **Boston Film Festival** · Mid/Late Sep ·
www.bostonfilmfestival.org · Plenty to please the
most finicky cinephile.

- **Boston Freedom Rally** · Mid/Late Sep ·
www.masscann.org · That ain't freedom they're
smoking.

- **Boston Folk Festival** · Mid Sep ·
www.wumb.org/folkfest · Pickin' and grinnin'.

- **Phantom Gourmet Food Festival** · Late Sep ·
www.phantomgourmetfoodfestival.com · $40 for
the Landsdowne St Grand Bouffe that's unlike any
other in Boston, featuring booths hand picked by
the Phantom himself.

- **Boston Tattoo Convention** · Early Oct ·
www.bostontattooconvention.com · Celebrating
the newly legal (in Mass) art form.

- **Opening Night at the Symphony** · Early Oct ·
www.bso.org · Kicks off Maestro Levine's second
season at the BSO.

- **Harvard Square Oktoberfest** · Early Oct ·
www.harvardsquare.com · Don't expect liters of
free beer.

- **Head of the Charles** · Oct 23–24 · www.hocr.org ·
The world's largest two-day rowing event.

- **Belgian Beer Fest** · Late Oct ·
www.beeradvocate.com/fests · *Sluit je aan bij de
Bierrevolutie!*

- **Boston Jewish Film Festival** · Nov · www.bjff.org ·
Now in its 17th season.

- **Boston International Antiquarian Book Fair** ·
Mid Nov · www.bostonbookfair.com · The
country's longest running antiquarian book fair
features autographs, photographs, maps, and
more.

- **Black Nativity** · Weekends in Dec ·
www.blacknativity.org · One part Harlem
Renaissance, one part folk music, dance, and verse
celebration of the birth of Jesus Christ. Held at the
Tremont Temple.

- **Prudential Center Christmas Tree Lighting** ·
Early Dec · www.prudentialcenter.com · Each year
Nova Scotia thanks Boston for helping Halifax
recover from a 1917 disaster by sending down a
huge tree.

- **Boston Tea Party Reenactment** · Mid Dec ·
www.oldsouthmeetinghouse.org · A fine excuse to
don your tri-cornered hat.

- **Boston Common Menorah Lighting** · Late Dec ·
www.cityofboston.gov/arts · Celebrating the first
night of Hanukkah.

Television

2	WGBH	(PBS)	www.wgbh.org
4	WBZ	(CBS)	www.wbz4.com
5	WCVB	(ABC)	www.thebostonchannel.com
7	WHDH	(NBC)	www1.whdh.com
25	WFXT	(FOX)	www.fox25.com
27	WUNI	(Univision)	www.wunitv.com
38	WSBK	(UPN)	www.upn38.com
44	WGBH	(PBS)	www.wgbh.com
56	WLVI	(WB)	www.wb56.trb.com
66	WUTF	(Telefutura)	www.univision.com
68	WBPX	(PAX)	www.paxboston.tv

AM Radio

590	WEZE	Christian radio	www.wezeradio.com
680	WRKO	Talk	www.wrko.com
740	WJIB	Instrumental Pop/Light Oldies	
850	WEEI	Sports	www.weei.com
950	WROL	Religious	
1030	WBZ	News/Talk/Sports	www.wbz.com
1060	WBIX	Business Talk	
1090	WILD	Urban	
1120	WBNW	Financial Talk	www.moneymattersradio.net
1150	WJTK	Religious	
1260	WMKI	Radio Disney	www.radio.disney.go.com/mystation/Boston/
1510	WWZN	Sports	www.1510thezone.com
1600	WUNR	Leased-time/ethnic	
1670	Allston-Brighton Free Radio		www.abfreeradio.org

FM Radio

88.1	WMBR	MIT	wmbr.mit.edu
88.9	WERS	Emerson College	www.wers.org
89.7	WGBH	NPR News/Classical	www.wgbh.org
90.3	WZBC	Boston College	www.wzbc.org
90.9	WBUR	NPR/BU	www.wbur.org
91.5	WMFO	Tufts University	www.wmfo.org
91.9	WUMB	Folk/Jazz	www.wumb.org
92.9	WBOS	Modern AC	www.wbos.com
94.5	WJMN	R&B/R&B	www.jamn.com
95.3	WHRB	Harvard University	www.whrb.org
96.9	WTKK	Talk	www.wtkk.com
98.5	WBMX	Modern AC	www.mix985.com
99.5	WCRB	Classical	www.wcrb.com
100.1	WBRS	Brandeis University	www.wbrs.org
100.7	WZLX	Classic Rock	www.wzlx.com
101.7	WFNX	Modern Rock	www.wfnx.com
102.5	WKLB	Country	www.wklb.com
102.9	WCFM	Caribbean Music	www.choice1029.com
103.3	WODS	Oldies	oldies1033.com
104.1	WBCN	Modern Rock	www.wbcn.com
104.9	WBOQ	Soft Rock	www.northshore1049.com
105.7	WROR	Classic Rock	www.wror.com
106.7	WMJX	Soft Rock	www.magic1067.com
107.3	WAAF	Active Rock	www.waaf.com
107.9	WXKS	Pop	www.kissfm.com

Print Media

Bay Windows	www.baywindows.com	617-266-6670	LGBT newsweekly.
Beacon Hill Times	www.beaconhilltimes.com	617-523-9490	Newsweekly serving Beacon Hill.
Boston Business Journal	www.bizjournals.com/boston	617-330-1000	Business weekly.
Boston Globe	www.boston.com	617-929-2000	Daily broadsheet.
Boston Haitian Reporter	www.bostonhaitian.com	617-436-1222	Free monthly for Haitian-American community.
Boston Herald	www.bostonherald.com	617-426-3000	Daily tabloid.
Boston Irish Reporter	www.bostonirish.com	617-436-1222	News from and about the Irish in Boston.
Boston Metro	www.metropoint.com	617-338-7985	Weekday tabloid aimed at commuters.
Boston Magazine	www.bostonmagazine.com	617-262-9700	Glossy monthly.
Boston Phoenix	www.bostonphoenix.com	617-536-5390	Progressive news and entertainment listings.
Boston Review	www.bostonreview.net	617-258-0805	Leftish politics and culture magazine.
Boston Russian Bulletin	www.russianmass.com	617-277-5398	Russian community news, in Russian.
Brookline TAB	www.townonline.com/brookline	617-566-3585	Brookline newsweekly.
Cambridge Chronicle	www.townonline.com/cambridge	617-577-7149	Cambridge newsweekly.
Cambridge TAB	www.townonline.com/cambridge	617-497-1241	Cambridge newsweekly.
Charlestown Patriot-Bridge	www.charlestownbridge.com	617-241-8500	Charlestown newsweekly.
Dorchester Reporter	www.dotnews.com	617-436-1222	Dorchester news.
Improper Bostonian	www.improper.com	617-859-1400	Free entertainment and lifestyle magazine.
In Newsweekly	www.innewsweekly.com	617-426-8246	LGBT news and entertainment.
Jamaica Plain Gazette	www.jamaicaplaingazette.com	617-524-2626	JP news.
The Jewish Advocate	www.thejewishadvocate.com	617-367-9100	News about Boston's Jewish community.
Mass High Tech	www.masshightech.com	617-242-1224	Technology news.
Mattapan Reporter	www.bostonneighborhoodnews.com	617-436-1222	Mattapan neighborhood news.
Patriot Ledger	www.patriotledger.com	617-786-7000	Daily south shore news.
Pilot	www.thebostonpilot.com	617-746-5889	Catholic newsweekly.
Sampan	www.sampan.org	617-426-9492	Chinese/English bimonthly.
Somerville Journal	www.townonline.com/somerville	617-625-6300	Weekly Somerville news.
South Boston Tribune	www.southbostoninfo.com	617-268-3440	Weekly South Boston news.
Stuff@Night	www.stuffatnight.com	617-859-3333	Entertainment listings and "what's hot."
Weekly Dig	www.weeklydig.com	617-426-8942	Humor, news and nightlife.

WiFi

Starbucks	1 Charles St	617-742-2664	1
Starbucks	222 Cambridge St	617-227-2959	1
Starbucks	97 Charles St	617-227-3812	1
Boston Bean Stock Coffee	97 Salem St	617-725-0040	2
Starbucks	2 Atlantic Ave	617-723-7819	2
Starbucks	63 Court St	617-227-2284	2
Starbucks	84 State St	617-523-3053	2
Rachel's Kitchen	12 Church St	617-423-3447	3
Starbucks	12 Winter St	617-542-1313	3
Starbucks	143 Stuart St	617-227-7332	3
Starbucks	240 Washington St	617-720-2220	3
Starbucks	27 School St	617-227-7731	3
Starbucks	62 Boylston St	617-338-0067	3
Starbucks	1 Financial Ctr	617-428-0080	4
Starbucks	1 International Pl	617-737-4688	4
Starbucks	101 Federal St	617-946-0535	4
Starbucks	125 Summer St	617-737-0250	4
Starbucks	211 Congress St	617-542-4439	4
Espresso Royale	286 Newbury St	617-859-9515	5
Espresso Royale	44 Gainsborough St	617-859-7080	5
Starbucks	151 Massachusetts Ave	617-236-4335	5
Starbucks	273 Huntington Ave	617-536-6501	5
Starbucks	346 Huntington Ave	617-373-8860	5
Starbucks	350 Newbury St	617-859-5751	5
Starbucks	10 Huntington Ave	617-867-0491	6
Starbucks	165 Newbury St	617-536-5282	6
Surreal Image Café	300 Boylston St	617-244-3030	6
Starbucks	441 Stuart St	617-859-0703	6
Starbucks	443 Boylston St	617-536-7177	6
Starbucks	755 Boylston St	617-450-0310	6
Tealuxe	108 Newbury St	617-927-0400	6
Francesca's	564 Tremont St	617-482-9026	7
Starbucks	627 Tremont St	617-236-7879	7
Sorelle	100 City Sq	617-242-5980	8
Emack & Bolio's	736 Centre St	617-524-5107	14
Fiore's Bakery	55 South St	617-524-9200	14
June Bug Café	403A Centre St	617-522-2393	14
Sweet Finnish	761 Centre St	617-522-5200	14
Starbucks	283 Longwood Ave	617-277-5202	15
Espresso Royale	736 Commonwealth Ave	617-277-8737	16
Starbucks	148 Brookline Ave	617-867-6545	16
Starbucks	874 Commonwealth Ave	617-734-3691	16
Starbucks	15 Harvard St	617-232-5063	17
Starbucks	1655 Beacon St	617-232-5940	17
Starbucks	1660 Soldiers Field Rd	617-782-1325	18
Starbucks	277 Harvard St	617-739-3453	19
Starbucks	473 Harvard St	617-738-8005	19
Upper Crust	286 Harvard St	617-739-8518	19
Peet's Coffee & Tea	100 Mt Auburn St	617-492-1844	20
Simon's Coffee House	1736 Massachusetts Ave	617-497-7766	20
Starbucks	1662 Massachusetts Ave	617-491-0442	20
Starbucks	31 Church St	617-492-7870	20
Starbucks	36 JFK St	617-492-4881	20
Tealuxe	0 Brattle St	617-441-0077	20
Starbucks	220 Alewife Brook Pkwy	617-876-1070	21
Diesel Café	257 Elm St	617-629-8717	22
Starbucks	260 Elm St	617-623-4497	22
Starbucks	711 Somerville Ave	617-776-6783	23
Beantowne Coffee House	One Kendall Sq	617-621-7900	26
Starbucks	100 Cambridgeside Pl	617-621-9507	26
Starbucks	6 Cambridge Ctr	617-577-7511	26
1369 Coffee House	757 Massachusetts Ave	617-576-4600	27
Clear Conscience Café	581 Massachusetts Ave	617-661-1580	27
Starbucks	655 Massachusetts Ave	617-354-5471	27
1369 Coffee House	1369 Cambridge St	617-576-1369	28
Starbucks	468 Broadway	617-491-9911	28

Internet

FedEx Kinko's	2 Center Plz	617-973-9000	1
FedEx Kinko's	60 State St	617-523-8174	2
FedEx Kinko's	125 Tremont St	617-423-0234	3
FedEx Kinko's	10 Post Office Sq	617-482-4400	4
FedEx Kinko's	211 Congress St	617-482-0701	4
FedEx Kinko's	900 Boylston St	617-954-2725	5
FedEx Kinko's	187 Dartmouth St	617-262-6188	6
FedEx Kinko's	575 Boylston St	617-536-2536	6
FedEx Kinko's	715 Albany St	617-414-2679	7
FedEx Kinko's	415 Summer St	617-954-2203	10
FedEx Kinko's	115 Cummington St	617-358-2679	16
FedEx Kinko's	1370 Beacon St	617-731-3100	17
FedEx Kinko's	252 Washington St	617-723-7263	18
FedEx Kinko's	1 Mifflin Pl	617-497-0125	20
FedEx Kinko's	600 Technology Sq	617-494-5905	26

Self Storage / Van & Truck Rental

Self Storage

Self Storage	Address	Phone	Map
Planet Self Storage	33 Traveler St	617-426-7229	7
Town & Country Moving & Storage	9 Appleton St	617-350-6683	7
William Lowe & Sons Moving & Storage	50 Terminal St	617-242-6800	8
A-Plus Moving & Storage	44 Border St	857-540-9531	9
Planet Self Storage	135 Old Colony Ave	617-268-8282	10
Castle Self Storage	39 Old Colony Ave	617-268-5056	12
Gentle Movers Moving & Storage Centers	25 Boston St	617-268-0500	12
Patriot Self Storage	968 Massachusetts Ave	617-541-5600	12
Planet Self Storage	100 Southampton St	617-445-6776	12
Public Storage	290 Southampton St	617-445-6287	12
U-Haul	985 Massachuetts Ave	617-442-5600	12
Extra Space Storage	3175 Washington St	617-323-1110	14
Extra Space Storage	235 North Beacon St	617-782-1177	18
EZ Storage	145 N Beacon St	617-779-0005	18
Road Warrior Moving & Storage	86 Lincoln Street	617-782-5400	18
Brighton Self Storage	1360 Commonwealth Ave	617-739-4401	19
Simply Self Storage	130 Lincoln St	617-787-4325	19
Yellow Brick Self Storage	138 Harvard Ave	617-254-5007	19
O B Gray Moving & Storage	200 Harvard Way	617-825-4416	20
Cambridge Self Storage	445 Concord Ave	617-876-5060	21
Extra Space Storage	460 Somerville Ave	617-625-1000	23
Extra Space Storage	14 McGrath Hwy	617-623-7690	25
Storage Bunker	420 Rutherford Ave	617-242-6400	25
Planet Self Storage	39 Medford St	617-497-4800	28
U-haul Center Of Somerville	151 Linwood St	617-625-2789	28

Van & Truck Rental

Van & Truck Rental	Address	Phone	Map
Budget	33 Traveler St	617-426-7886	7
Budget	95 Brighton Ave	617-497-3608	19
Budget	420 Rutherford Ave	617-242-8044	25
Ryder	280 W 1st St	617-269-8000	10
U-Haul	985 Massachusetts Ave	617-442-5600	12
U-Haul	1579 Columbus Ave	617-445-0405	14
U-Haul	240 N Beacon St	617-782-0355	18
U-Haul	844 Main St	617-354-0500	27
U-Haul	151 Linwood St	617-625-2789	28

Locksmiths

	Phone
ABC Lock & Keys Services	617-522-2646
Boston Lock & Safe	617-787-3400
Champion Locks	617-723-7000
Flying Locksmiths	617-720-4571
Greater Boston 24 Hour Lock Smith	617-254-8674
Mass Ave Lock	617-247-9779
MegaLockSmith	617-723-5433

Plumbers

	Phone
Beacon Hill Plumbing	617-723-3296
Drain Doctor	617-547-6969
Drain King	617-439-3929
John's (Brookline)	617-277-1447
Metro Sewer & Drain	617-426-8939
Plumbing Express	617-288-0777
Roto-Rooter	617-267-1489
Sudden Service	617-367-8300

Bowling (yes, bowling)

	Address	Phone	Map
Boston Bowl	820 Morrissey Blvd, Dorchester	617-825-3800	32

Convenience Stores

	Address	Phone	Map
Store 24	177 State St	617-367-0034	2
Store 24	141 Massachusetts Ave	617-353-1897	5
Store 24	717 Boylston St	617-424-6888	6
Store 24	140 Main St	617-241-7865	8
Store 24	684 Centre St	617-524-9893	14
Store 24	542 Commonwealth Ave	617-424-8856	16
Store 24	1912 Beacon St	617-738-4874	18
White Hen Pantry	462 Washington St	617-787-3719	18
Store 24	509 Cambridge St	617-782-3900	19
Store 24	957 Commonwealth Ave	617-783-5466	19
White Hen Pantry	1868 Massachusetts Ave	617-547-7255	23

Copy Shops

	Address	Phone	Map
FedEx Kinko's	2 Center Plz	617-973-9000	1
FedEx Kinko's	187 Dartmouth St	617-262-6188	6
Copy Cop	601 Boylston St	617-267-9267	6
FedEx Kinko's	1 Miffin Pl	617-497-0125	20

Pharmacies

	Address	Phone	Map
Walgreens	841 Boylston St	617-236-1692	5
CVS	587 Boylston St	617-437-8414	6
CVS	210 Border St	617-567-5147	9
Walgreens	1 Central Sq	617-569-5278	9
CVS	1426 Massachusetts Ave	617-354-4420	20
CVS	211 Alewife Brook Pkwy	617-661-6422	21
CVS	36 White St	617-876-5519	23
Rite Aid	14 McGrath Hwy	617-776-3003	25

Restaurants

	Address	Phone	Map
Bova's Bakery	134 Salem St	617-523-5601	2
IHOP	1850 Soldiers Field Rd	617-787-0533	18

Veterinary

	Address	Phone	Map
MSPCA Angell Memorial Animal Hospital	350 S Huntington Ave	617-522-7282	14

Hungry?

Seafood

Legal Sea Foods (Map 3, 6, 26) has the highest profile among local fishmongers and deserves its good reputation, despite its high prices. For the best New England clam chowder, it's an even toss up between **Warren Tavern (Map 8)** and **Union Oyster House (Map 2)**. Worth the trip to Inman Square is **East Coast Grill & Raw Bar (Map 28)**, which also excels at barbecue. For something upscale in Cambridge, try **Dolphin Seafood (Map 27)**; in Somerville, **Out of the Blue (Map 22)**. For lovers of Chinese food, some of the best seafood dishes can be found at **Peach Farm (Map 4)**. In the summer, get out of the city and eat your seafood by the seashore.

Italian

Boston is blessed with numerous outstanding Italian restaurants. In the North End, **Mamma Maria (Map 2)** and **Bricco (Map 2)** are two among many standouts. Or, if you're tight on cash and can make it to the North End on a weekday afternoon, check out **Galleria Umberto (Map 2)**. For a fine Italian meal elsewhere in Central Boston, reserve a table at **Domani (Map 6)**, **Teatro (Map 3)**, or **Grotto (Map 1)**. Brookliners should look into **La Morra (Map 17)**. On the other side of the river, Vinny's at **Night (Map 25)** dishes out Southern Italian to a loyal following who swear the food is better than anything in the North End. And Roslindale's **Delfino (Map 30)** has legions of local fans.

Pizza

Few foods inspire as much passion (and contentiousness) as pizza; as such, identifying Boston's best pizza is a filling but thankless task. Our favorites? In no particular order: **Penguin Pizza (Map 15)**, **Pizzeria Regina (Map 2)**, **Santarpio's (Map 9)**, **Emma's (Map 28)**, **Upper Crust (Map 1, 5, 6, 7, 15, 17, 19, 20)**, **Cambridge, 1 (Map 20)**, **Stone Hearth Pizza Co. (Map 22)**, and **Leone's (Map 24)**.

East Asian

As with the North End and its Italian food, Chinatown has scads of high-quality restaurants. If you're looking for full-on dim-sum craziness, try **China Pearl (Map 4)** or **Hei La Moon (Map 4)** for weekend brunch. If you want more sedate surroundings in Chinatown, try **King Fung Garden (Map 4)**, **Hong Kong Eatery (Map 4)**, or **Peach Farm (Map 4)**. Want Thai? Try **Ronnarong Thai Tapas (Map 24)** or **Dok Bua (Map

17)**. Korean? Try **Koreana (Map 27)**. Sushi? Try **Oishii (Map 7)** or **O Ya (Map 4)**. Cambodian? Try **Elephant Walk (Map 16, 22)**. Vietnamese? Try **Pho 2000 (Map 32)** or **Ba-Le (Map 32)**. If you can't decide, go for fusion, like **Myers + Chang (Map 7)** or **Pho Republique (Map 7)**.

South Asian

Central Square (home to reliable standby **India Pavilion (Map 27)**) is no longer the only place to get good Indian food. Consider trying Brookline's **Rani Indian Bistro (Map 17)**, Harvard Square's **Tamarind Bay (Map 20)**, Jamaica Plain's **Bukhara (Map 14)**, Dorchester's Shanti: **Taste of Indian (Map 32)**, or Kenmore Square's **India Quality (Map 16)**. If you want top notch Indian food for dirt cheap, check out **Punjabi Dhaba (Map 28)**. For something different (and pleasant), try the Afghan cuisine at East Cambridge's **Helmand (Map 26)**.

Bars

Better known as drinking and meeting spots, but also serving damn good grub, are **The Asgard (Map 27)**, **Bukowski's (Map 5, 28)**, **Blarney Stone (Map 32)**, **Grendel's Den (Map 20)**, **James's Gate (Map 14)**, **PJ Ryan's (Map 22)**, **Miracle of Science (Map 27)**, The **Paradise (Map 19)**, **Other Side Cosmic Café (Map 5)**, and **Silvertone Bar & Grill (Map 3)**.

Grease

Diner enthusiasts should try **Mike's City Diner (Map 7)**, **Breakfast Club Diner (Map 19)**, or **Rosebud Diner (Map 22)**. For a big breakfast, consider **Sound Bites (Map 23)**, **Broken Yolk (Map 23)**, **Neighborhood Restaurant & Bakery (Map 24)**, or the slightly more civilized **Trident Bookstore & Café (Map 5)**.

Top-End

Want to celebrate a special occasion? Have your concierge reserve a table downtown at **The Federalist (Map 1)**, **Mantra (Map 3)**, **No. 9 Park (Map 3)**, or **Radius (Map 4)**, in the South End at **Hamersley's Bistro (Map 7)**, around Back Bay at **Mistral (Map 6)**, **Grill 23 (Map 6)**, or **Clio (Map 5)**, or over the river at **Harvest (Map 20)**, **Craigie On Main (Map 27)**, **Oleana (Map 28)**, or **Henrietta's Table (Map 20)**.

Key: $: Under $10 / $$: $10–$20 / $$$: $20–$30 / $$$$: $30–$40 / $$$$$: $40+
* : Does not accept credit cards / † : Accepts only American Express / ‡ : Accepts only Visa and Mastercard
Time listed refers to kitchen closing time on weekend nights

Map 1 · Beacon Hill / West End

75 Chestnut	75 Chestnut St	617-227-2175	$$$$	10 pm	Featuring a Sunday jazz brunch.
Artu	89 Charles St	617-227-9023	$$$	11 pm	Affordable Italian. Fresh ingredients. Take-out panini.
Beacon Hill Bistro	25 Charles St	617-723-1133	$$$$	11 pm	Elegant cooking in a cozy space.
BoYo	175 Cambridge St	617-227-2696	$$*	10 pm	Tasty froyo and other chilly treats.
Click	215 Charles St	617-224-4004	$$$	11 pm	The former Charles St. Jail is now a restaurant. Get locked up! Yuk Yuk...
The Federal	204 Cambridge St	617-391-0025	$$	2 am	Great pressed sandwiches and so-so pizza.
The Federalist	15 Beacon St	617-670-2515	$$$$$	10 pm	A thoroughly top-end experience with an old Boston atmosphere.
Figs	42 Charles St	617-742-3447	$$$	10 pm	Beacon Hill branch of upscale pizza chain.
Grotto	37 Bowdoin St	617-227-3434	$$$	10 pm	Good value Italian in a Beacon Hill basement.
Harvard Gardens	316 Cambridge St	617-523-2727	$$$	11 pm	More for meeting and drinking than eating.
Hungry I	71 1/2 Charles St	617-227-3524	$$$$	10 pm	French. Cozy spot for intimate meals.
King & I	145 Charles St	617-227-3320	$$	10:30 pm	No-brainer for decent, inexpensive Thai.
Lala Rokh	97 Mt Vernon St	617-720-5511	$$$	11 pm	Alluring Persian in a pleasant Beacon Hill townhouse.
Ma Soba	156 Cambridge St	617-973-6680	$$$	11 pm	Sleek Asian fusion.
Panificio	144 Charles St	617-227-4340	$	9 pm	Paninis, pastries. Try the formaggio.
The Paramount	44 Charles St	617-720-1152	$$	11 pm	Popular local spot for all three meals. Fantastic brunch.
Phoenicia	240 Cambridge St	617-523-4606	$$	10 pm	Excellent grape leaves.
Pierrot	272 Cambridge St	617-725-8855	$$$$	11 pm	Authentic French bistro.
Upper Crust	49 Brattle Way	617-497-4111	$$	11 pm	Fancy schmancy, crisp-crust pizza.
Upper Crust	20 Charles St	617-723-9600	$$	10:30 pm	Fancy schmancy, crisp-crust pizza.
Villa Mexico Cafe	2996 Cambridge St	617-957-0725	$*		Amazing Mexican street food in Grampy's Gas Station. Yes.

Map 2 · North End / Faneuil Hall

Al's State Street Café	110 State St	617-720-5555	$††	2 am	Good sandwiches on the cheap, but order fast. You have been warned!
Antico Forno	93 Salem St	617-723-6733	$$$	10:30 pm	A home-style North End stand-out. Great pizza.
Billy Tse	240 Commercial St	617-227-9990	$$$	11 pm	Pan-Asian near the waterfront.
Boston Sail Loft	80 Atlantic Ave	617-227-7280	$$	11 pm	Good seafood with a great view.
Bova's Bakery	134 Salem St	617-523-5601	$*	24-hrs	Baked goods available 24/7!
Bricco	241 Hanover St	617-248-6800	$$$$	2 am	Boutique Italian cuisine. Rather popular.
Caffe Paradiso	255 Hanover St	617-742-1768	$	2 am	Coffee and cannoli. Local landmark.
The Daily Catch	323 Hanover St	617-523-8567	$$$*	11 pm	For those who can stand the heat in the kitchen.
Ernesto's	69 Salem St	617-523-1373	$	11 pm	One of the best slices in town.
Galleria Umberto	289 Hanover St	617-227-5709	$*	3 pm	Tasty, dirt cheap, greasy Italian lunch.
Green Dragon Tavern	11 Marshall St	617-367-0055	$$	11 pm	Pretend you're Sam Adams while having the same.
Haymarket Pizza	106 Blackstone St	617-723-8585	$*	7 pm	Enjoy a great slice in the company of pigeons.
Il Panino Express	11 Parmenter St	617-720-1336	$$	11 pm	Grab a quick bite of decent Italian.
L'Osteria	104 Salem St	617-723-7847	$$	11 pm	Family-style red sauce joint.
La Famiglia Giorgio's	112 Salem St	617-367-6711	$$	10:30 pm	Cheap family style Italian without any fancy pants.
La Summa	30 Fleet St	617-523-9503	$$	11 pm	More low-key than most North End places, and it will leave your belly satisfied.
Lucca	226 Hanover St	617-742-9200	$$$$	12:15 am	Stylish Northern Italian.
Lulu's Bake Shoppe	227 Hanover St	617-720-2200	$	11 pm	The cupcakes cost more than a package of Twinkies, but they are worth it.
Mamma Maria	3 North Sq	617-523-0077	$$$$	11 pm	High-end Italian in a charming townhouse.
Massimino's Cucina Italiana	207 Endicott St	617-523-5959	$$	11 pm	Out-of-the-way Italian, largely tourist-free
Maurizio's	364 Hanover St	617-367-1123	$$$$	10:30 pm	Tiny, yet amazing, Italian restaurant on the main drag
McCormick & Schmick's	1 Faneuil Hall Marketplace	617-720-5522	$$$$	12 am	Enormous fresh seafood selection in steak-house atmosphere.
Nebo Pizzeria	90 N Washington St	617-723-6326	$$	12 am	Decent North Endish spot. Perfect for a pizza and a carafe of vino.
Neptune Oyster	63 Salem St	617-742-3474	$$$$	12 am	Great oysters, of course, and the most amazing lobster roll –worth every penny.
Pizzeria Regina	11 1/2 Thacher St	617-227-0765	$$*	12 am	Local landmark. Worth the wait.
Prezza	24 Fleet St	617-227-1577	$$$$$	10 pm	High-end Italian. Don't forget to try the Key Lime Martini.
Sel de la Terre	255 State St	617-720-1300	$$$$	10 pm	A taste of Provence.

Arts & Entertainment · **Restaurants**

Map 2 · North End / Faneuil Hall—*continued*

Sensing	5 Battery St	617-994-9001	$$$$	10 pm	Asian and French fusion at the Fairmont Battery Wharf.
Taranta	210 Hanover St	617-720-0052	$$$$	10 pm	Delicious Italian food with a Peruvian twist.
Theo's Cozy Corner	162 Salem St	617-241-0202	$*	3 pm	Cozy diner. Killer hash browns.
Trani	111 Salem St	617-624-0222	$*	12 am	Stunt pastries.
Trattoria Il Panino	11 Parmenter St	617-720-1336	$$	11pm	In a sea of Italian restaurants Il Panino is a pearl!
Union Oyster House	41 Union St	617-227-2750	$$$	10 pm	Oldest restaurant in America, saddle up to oyster bar.
Wagamama Faneuil Hall	Quincy Market Building	617-742-9242	$	10 pm	Wag the noodle. Fast food style Japanese noodle house.

Map 3 · Downtown Crossing / Park Square / Bay Village

Bonfire	50 Park Plaza	617-262-3473	$$$$$	11 pm	More than a steakhouse. Go for gourmet tacos.
Buddha's Delight	5 Beach St	617-451-2395	$$	9 pm	All-vegetarian Asian.
Chacarero	426 Washington St	617-542-0392	$*	5 pm	Unique Chilean sandwich. Lunch, take-away only.
Dedo	69 Church St	617-338-9999	$$$$	1 am	Rib-eye for the queer guy.
Emperor's Garden	690 Washington St	617-482-8898	$$	10 pm	Dim sum for the masses.
Herrera's Mexican Grille	11 Temple Pl	617-426-2350	$*	4 pm	Good and cheap Cali-Mex.
Intermission Tavern	228 Tremont St	617-451-5997	$$	1 am	Drinks and burgers until 1 am.
Ivy	49 Temple Pl	617-963-1534	$$	11:30 pm	Small plate Italian with a kick-ass wine list.
Jacob Wirth	31 Stuart St	617-338-8586	$$	12 am	Germany. Local institution since 1868 with barroom sing-a-long on Friday nights.
Know Fat!	530 Washington St	617-451-0043	$	9 pm	Healthy-ish burgers and sandwiches.
Legal Sea Foods	26 Park Plz	617-426-4444	$$$	12 am	Fresh fish, famous chowder. Legal's sleekest space.
Locke-Ober	3 Winter Pl	617-542-1340	$$$$	10 pm	Worth it just for the ambiance and history although the food should be better.
Lu's Sandwich Shop	2 Knapp St	626-292-1453	$	7 pm	Delicious Banh Mi made fresh in back of a jewelry store!
Mantra	52 Temple Pl	617-542-8111	$$$$	10 pm	Frenchy/Indian in a stylish former bank.
Marliave	10 Bosworth St	617-422-0004	$$	10 pm	Cozy, old-time dead end street eats.
McCormick & Schmick's	34 Columbus Ave	617-482-3999	$$$$	11 pm	$2 "social hour" bar menu is a great deal.
Mike and Patty's	12 Church St	617-423-3447	$	3 pm	Eponymous owners whip up the sammies.
Montien	63 Stuart St	617-338-5600	$$$	10 pm	If you don't like raw fish, you can always order a Pad Thai.
New Saigon Sandwich	696 Washington St	617-542-6296	$*	6:30 pm	Cheap sandwiches, boxed lunches. Delicious!
New York Pizza	224 Tremont St	617-482-3459	$$	3 am	Perfect for late night noshing.
No 9 Park	9 Park St	617-742-9991	$$$$$	11 pm	Consistently rated among Boston's best.
Penang	685 Washington St	617-451-6373	$$	11 pm	Well-established Malaysian out of NYC.
Pigalle	75 Charles St S	617-423-4944	$$$$	10 pm	Modern French cuisine in an intimate setting.
Sam LaGrassa's	44 Province St	617-357-6861	$$	3:30 pm	Monster sandwiches. Try the pastrami.
Silvertone Bar & Grill	69 Bromfield St	617-338-7887	$$*	11 pm	Great after-work lounge with tasty home cooking.
Smith & Wollensky	101 Arlington St	617-423-1112	$$$$$	11 pm	The castle has been taken.
Teatro	177 Tremont St	617-778-6841	$$$	12 am	Sleek Italian next to Loews Cinema.
Tequila Mexican Grill	55 Bromfield St	617-482-8822	$*	4 pm	Muy sabroso hole-in-the-wall.
Via Matta	79 Park Plz	617-422-0008	$$$$	11 pm	Stylish Italian, stylish crowd.
Viga	304 Stuart St	617-542-7200	$	4 pm	Cheap and tasty take out.

Map 4 · Financial District / Chinatown

Chau Chow City	83 Essex St	617-338-8158	$$	4 am	Best known for their Dim Sum. Open late.
China Pearl	9 Tyler St	617-426-4338	$$	11 pm	Dim sum for beginners and experts.
Ginza	16 Hudson St	617-338-2261	$$	3:30 am	Waitresses in kimonos, great sushi, Japanese people actually eat here.
Hei La Moon	88 Beach St	617-338-8813	$*	11 pm	Best Dim Sum in Boston!
The Hong Kong Eatery	79 Harrison Ave	617-423-0838	$*	10:30 pm	Mountains of pork and rice for just a few bucks.
J Pace & Son	1 Federal St	617-227-4949	$	5 pm	Hot and cold Italian for take-away.
Julien	250 Franklin St	617-451-1900	$$$	10 pm	Elegant French in the Langham Hotel.
King Fung Garden	74 Kneeland St	617-357-5262	$*	10 pm	Serving the best peking raviolis, scallion pancakes, and noodle dishes.
Les Zygomates	129 South St	617-542-5108	$$	11 pm	French bistro. Comprehensive wine list, pleasant bar.
Mei Sum Inc	40 Beach St	617-357-4050	$	7 pm	Another tasty option for Bahn Mi and baked goods in the heart of Chinatown.
Meritage	70 Rowes Wharf	617-439-3995	$$$$$	11 pm	Serious about pairing food with wine.
Milk Street Cafe	50 Milk St	617-542-3663	$	3 pm	Dependable lunch option.
New Shanghai	21 Hudson St	617-338-6688	$$	11 pm	Critically acclaimed Shanghainese.

Noodle Alcove	10 Tyler St	617-542-5857	$$	11 pm	Fresh, fresh noodles, knife-cut, and hand-pulled.
Ocean Wealth	8 Tyler St	617-423-1338	$$	3 am	Cantonese seafood specialists open late…very late…
Osushi	101 Arch St	617-330-1777	$$$	11 pm	Copley fave now open in the Financial District.
Peach Farm	4 Tyler St	617-482-1116	$$	3 am	Family-style Cantonese. Cool seafood tanks.
Pho Hoa	17 Beach St	617-423-3934	$	11 pm	Phat pho.
Pizza Oggi	131 Broad St	617-345-0022	$	9 pm	Creative Pizzas and outdoor tables.
Pressed Sandwiches	2 Oliver St	617-482-9700	$	3 pm	Potential ironic indie band name.
Radius	8 High St	617-426-1234	$$$$$	11 pm	A Financial District jewel. Expensive, worth it.
Rowes Wharf Sea Grille	70 Rowes Wharf	617-856-7744			Waterfront dining in the Harbor Hotel.
Sakurabana	57 Broad St	617-542-4311	$$$	9 pm	Good bet for low-key sushi.
Shabu-Zen	16 Tyler St	617-292-8828	$$	12 am	Pay to cook your own food in a delicious broth? Yeah, it is worth it!
Sophia's Green Cafe	14 Dorchester Ave	617-426-1115	$$	7:30 pm	A "green" cafe in Boston's Green Building with decent chow.
South Street Diner	178 Kneeland St	617-350-0028	$	24-hrs	Night shift dining excellence with a liquor license.
Sultan's Kitchen	116 State St	617-570-9009	$	4 pm	Terrific Turkish. A great lunch choice.
Taiwan Café	34 Oxford St	617-426-8181	$$*	1 am	For opponents of the PRC's "one China" policy.
Umbria	295 Franklin St	617-338-1000	$$$	12 am	Good food, but doubles as a dance club. Be ready to pay a cover charge.
Umbria Prime	295 Franklin St	617-338-1000	$$$		An Italian steakhouse during the week, and a nightclub on the weekends.
Upper Crust	245 Summer St	617-367-0066	$$	3 pm	Fancy schmancy, crisp-crust pizza.
Xinh Xinh	7 Beach St	617-422-0501	$$	10 pm	Exceptional Vietnamese. Not much ambiance.

Map 5 • Back Bay (West) / Fenway (East)

Bangkok City	167 Massachusetts Ave	617-266-8884	$$$	10 pm	Solid Thai served in a large, blue room.
Bhindi Bazaar	95 Massachusetts Ave	617-450-0660	$$		Go for the dinner, not the mediocre buffet.
Bukowski's	50 Dalton St	617-437-9999	$$*	1:30 am	Watering hole also has great chili, p.b.j. sandwiches, late hours.
Café Jaffa	48 Gloucester St	617-536-0230	$	11 pm	Affordable, delicious Middle Eastern.
Capital Grille	359 Newbury St	617-262-8900	$$$$$	11 pm	Arise, Sir Loin!
Casa Romero	30 Gloucester St	617-536-4341	$$$	11 pm	Mexican. Decent food, good atmosphere.
Chilli Duck	829 Boylston St	617-236-5208	$$	11 pm	Thai eatery with modern decor, slightly-elevated prices, and expectedly-tangy sauces.
Clio	370A Commonwealth Ave	617-536-7200	$$$$	11 pm	Sublime spot in the Eliot Hotel.
India Samraat Restaurant	51 Massachusetts Ave	617-247-0718	$$	10:15 pm	Good Indian food. Pretty good value. Great delivery!
Island Hopper	91 Massachusetts Ave	617-266-1618	$$	12 am	How can you not want to eat at a place with a name like this?
Kashmir	279 Newbury St	617-536-1695	$$	11 pm	Excellent mug saagwala.
Other Side Cosmic Café	407 Newbury St	617-536-9477	$	12 pm	Good for a bite and beer on their outdoor patio. Cheap PBR!
Pour House	907 Boylston St	617-236-1767	$	10 pm	Wonderful, cheap bar food. Opens at 8 am.
Sonsie	327 Newbury St	617-351-2500	$$$$	1 am	People-watching mainstay. Nice French-doors street exposure.
Spike's Junkyard Dogs	1076 Boylston St	617-266-0909	$*	2 am	Perfect summer eats.
Tapeo	266 Newbury St	617-267-4799	$$$	11 pm	Tasty tapas. Sip sangria outside on warm days.
Top of the Hub	800 Boylston St	617-536-1775	$$$$	11 pm	Almost worth the price for the amazing view atop the Pru.
Trident Booksellers & Café	338 Newbury St	617-267-8688	$	11 pm	All-day breakfast in a cool bookstore.

Map 6 • Back Bay (East) / South End (Upper)

33	33 Stanhope St	617-572-3311	$$$$	11 pm	Enticing menu, snazzy digs. Patio too.
Abe & Louie's	793 Boylston St	617-536-6300	$$$$	12 am	Popular local steakhouse.
b.good	131 Dartmouth St	617-424-5252	$	10 pm	Healthy, quick lunches.
Bouchee	159 Newbury St	617-450-4343	$$$	11 pm	Two-story French bistro, killer crème brulee.
Brasserie Jo	120 Huntington Ave	617-425-3240	$$$$	11 pm	French brasserie near Symphony Hall. Usually very busy.
Charlie's Sandwich Shoppe	429 Columbus Ave	617-536-7669	$*	2:30 pm	A local institution with an old Boston feel. A good lunch choice.
Claremont Café	535 Columbus Ave	617-247-9001	$$$	12 am	(Too) popular for weekend brunch. Good scones, though. Delicious dinners!
Davio's	75 Arlington St	617-661-4810	$$$$	11 pm	Good food, but it's about the river view.
Domani	51 Huntington Ave	617-424-8500	$$$$	11 pm	Eat like there's no, er, "tomorrow."
Flash's	310 Stuart St	617-574-8888	$$$	1 am	Friendly service, mean cocktails. Good lunch specials.
Grill 23 & Bar	161 Berkeley St	617-542-2255	$$$$$	11 pm	Classic steakhouse. Ideal for business dinners.
House of Siam	542 Columbus Ave	617-267-1755	$$	11 pm	If you are off to the symphony, this is a good bet.
L'Aroma Café	85 Newbury St	617-412-4001	$	10 pm	We're so glad that there is an alternative to Starbucks!

293

Arts & Entertainment · **Restaurants**

Key: $: Under $10 / $$: $10–$20 / $$$: $20–$30 / $$$$: $30–$40 / $$$$$: $40+
* : Does not accept credit cards / † : Accepts only American Express / †† : Accepts only Visa and Mastercard
Time listed refers to kitchen closing time on weekend nights

Map 6 · Back Bay (East) / South End (Upper)—*continued*

Laurel	142 Berkeley St	617-424-6664	$$$	10 pm	Five-star meals at two-star prices.
Legal Sea Foods	800 Boylston St	617-266-6800	$$$	11 pm	At the Pru, sporting a new look.
Mistral	223 Columbus Ave	617-867-9300	$$$$	11 pm	Superb. Great bar, too. Look sharp.
The Oak Room	138 Saint James Ave	617-267-5300	$$$	11 pm	Go for the old school Boston vibe, not the overpriced menu and mediocre martinis.
Osushi	10 Huntington Ave	617-266-2788	$$$	11 pm	Good sushi in the Westin? You better believe it!
Parish Café	361 Boylston St	617-247-7777	$$	1 am	Inventive sandwiches. Full bar too.
Petsi Pies	285 Beacon St	617-661-7437	$	6 pm	Name a dinner or dessert pie…any pie…and they probably make it.
Shino Express Sushi	144 Newbury St	617-262-4530	$$††	9:45 pm	Cheap sushi (for Newbury Street). Great lunch specials.
Upper Crust	222 Newbury St	617-262-0090	$$	11 pm	Fancy schmancy, crisp-crust pizza.

Map 7 · South End (Lower)

Addis Red Sea	544 Tremont St	617-426-8727	$$	11 pm	Ethiopian. Get jiggy with some injera.
Appleton Bakery & Café	123 Appleton St	617-859-8222	$	5 pm	Melt-in-your-mouth muffins meet sandwiches with a twist.
Aquitaine	569 Tremont St	617-424-8577	$$$$	11 pm	A solid French bistro.
B&G Oysters	550 Tremont St	617-423-0550	$$$$	11 pm	Stylish oyster shop. Good wine list. Best lobster rolls in town!
BanQ	1375 Washington St	617-451-0077	$$$$	11 pm	Sleek and tasty pan-Asian.
DaVinci Ristorante	162 Columbus Ave	617-350 0007	$$$	11 pm	South End's answer to the North End hegemony on Italian food.
Delux Café	100 Chandler St	617-338-5258	$$*	10 pm	Small, hip spot with good eats, music.
El Triunfo	147 E Berkeley St	617-542-8499	$*	11 pm	Cheap tacos. Good tongue!
flour bakery + café	1595 Washington St	617-267-4300	$	9 pm	Beyond exceptional bakery. Also serves dinners for take-away.
Franklin Café	278 Shawmut Ave	617-350-0010	$$$	12 am	Delicious late-night option.
Garden of Eden	571 Tremont St	617-247-8377	$$	11 pm	Popular brunchonette. Excellent veggie sandwiches.
Gaslight 560	560 Harrison Ave	617-422-0224	$$	12 am	Good French food. Stainless steel bar is a nice touch.
Hamersley's Bistro	553 Tremont St	617-423-2700	$$$$	10 pm	Outstanding. Deserves its reputation.
Joe V's	315 Shawmut Ave	617-426-0862	$$$	10 pm	Relatively unknown, people like their pizza, pleasant room.
Masa	439 Tremont St	617-338-8884	$$$	11 pm	Tiniest $1 tapas specials that we've ever seen.
Mela	578 Tremont St	617-859-4805	$$	11 pm	Two thumbs: lunch buffet.
Metropolis Café	584 Tremont St	617-247-2931	$$$	11 pm	Try the cranberry pancakes for brunch.
Mike's City Diner	1714 Washington St	617-267-9393	$*	3 pm	A trusty not-too-greasy spoon.
Morse Fish	1401 Washington St	617-262-9375	$$	9 pm	The neighborhood's only fish shack.
Myers + Chang	1145 Washington St	617-542-5200	$$	11 pm	Fun Asian fusion.
Oishii	1166 Washington St	617-482-8868	$$$$$	12 am	The only place with better sushi is their other location.
Orinoco	477 Shawmut Ave	617-369-7075	$$	11 pm	The South End puts a twist on Venezuelan food and it's delicious!
Pho Republique	1415 Washington St	617-262-0005	$$$††	12 am	Vietnamese gets the South End treatment.
Picco	513 Tremont St	617-927-0066	$$	11 pm	The gated community of ice cream. Serves pizza, too.
Red Fez	1222 Washington St	617-338-6060	$$$	12 am	Open late. Red fez not required for entry.
Rocca	500 Harrison Ave	617-451-5151	$$$	11 pm	People flock here for the Sunday Supper specials.
Sage	1395 Washington St	617-248-8814	$$$$	10 pm	Tasty Italian/American. Might trouble claustrophobics.
Sibling Rivalry	525 Tremont St	617-338-5338	$$$$	11 pm	Fighting brothers serve up great food, outdoor dining when warm.
South End Plta	473 Albany St	617-556-2600	$	11 pm	South End Shwarma that will hook you for life.
Stella	1525 Washington St	617-247-7747	$$$	11 pm	Too Stylish, whitish spot. Mostly Italian menu.
Tremont 647	647 Tremont St	617-266-4600	$$$$	10 pm	One of the South End's best.
Union Bar and Grille	1357 Washington St	617-423-0555	$$$	12 am	Expensive and tasty!
Upper Crust	683 Tremont St	617-927-0090	$$	11 pm	Fancy schmancy, crisp-crust pizza.

Map 8 · Charlestown

Figs	67 Main St	617-242-2229	$$$	10 pm	Charlestown branch of upscale pizza chain.
Ironside Grill	25 Park St	617-242-1384	$$	11 pm	Formerly managed by Raymond Burr.
Jenny's Pizza	320 Medford St	617-242-9474	$*	9 pm	Subs, too. Nice view of the, erm, Autoport.
Navy Yard Bistro & Wine Bar	One 1st Ave	617-242-0036	$$	10 pm	Mid-priced bistro fare near the ships.

Ninety Nine	29 Austin St	617-242-8999	$$	12 am	Take your step-kids.
Olives	10 City Sq	617-242-1999	$$$$	10 pm	Mediterranean mecca.
Paolo's Trattoria	251 Main St	617-242-7229	$$$	10 pm	Italian, including wood-oven-cooked pizzas.
Sorelle	1 Monument Ave	617-242-2125	$*	3 pm	Tasty sandwiches, baked goods, alcohol, too.
Sorelle	100 City Sq	617-242-5980	$	9 pm	Tasty sandwiches, baked goods, alcohol, too.
Tangierino	83 Main St	617-242-6009	$$$	11 pm	Rockin' Moroccan.
Warren Tavern	2 Pleasant St	617-241-8142	$$	10 pm	One of Paul Revere's favorite watering holes.

Map 9 · East Boston

Angela's Café	131 Lexington St	617-567-4972	$	9 pm	By far the best Mexican food in town prepared by someone else's Grandma...
Café Belo	254 Bennington St	617-561-0833	$	10 pm	One of the many Café Belo's serving up Brazilian food around Boston.
Café Italia	150 Meridian St	617-561-6480	$$	12 am	
Café Meridian	271 Meridian St	617-561-6622	$$	11 pm	For enjoying jazz with coffee and dessert.
El Buen Gusto	295 Bennington St	617-561-6333	$$	11 pm	Relaxing Colombian restaurant
El Chalan	405 Chelsea St	617-567-9452	$	11 pm	Upscale Salvadoran taqueria.
Jeveli's	387 Chelsea St	617-567-9539	$	10 pm	Finest pollo in Eastie.
La Frontera	290 Bennington St	617-569-8600	$*	10 pm	Italian. Has a bar.
La Terraza	19 Bennington St	617-561-5200	$	11 pm	Mexican/Salvadoran hole in the wall. Straight-forward Colombian cooking. Try the flan.
Rincon Limeno	409 Chelsea St	617-569-4942	$	11 pm	Specializing in Peruvian rotisserie chicken.
Santarpio's Pizza	111 Chelsea St	617-567-9871	$*	12 am	Thin and crispy. A side of lamb and homemade sausage from the grill.
TacoMex	65 Maverick Sq	617-569-2838	$	11 pm	Tongue taco, a sign of real Mexican.
Taqueria Cancun	192 Sumner St	617-567-4449	$	11 pm	Don't count on tequila slammers.

Map 10 · South Boston (West) / Fort Point

6 House	28 W Broadway	617-268-6697	$$	10 pm	Open air, long bar.
Amrheins	80 W Broadway	617-268-6189	$$	11 pm	Has been here since Southie was mostly German.
Anthony's Pier 4	140 Northern Ave	617-482-6262	$$$$	3 pm	A Boston institution that has passed its glory days.
Barking Crab	88 Sleeper St	617-426-2722	$$	11 pm	Make a mess while viewing the harbor skyline.
The Daily Catch	2 Northern Ave	617-772-4400	$$$*	11 pm	Italian seafood specialists' Moakley Court-house spot.
Fresh Tortillas	475 W Broadway	617-269-0061	$	11 pm	Mexican take-out.
Kingston Station	25 Kingston St	617-482-6224	$$	2 am	Unusually tasty and reasonable grub down-town.
Lucky's	355 Congress St	617-357-5825	$$	12 am	Well-liked retro cocktail lounge. Music most nights.
Mul's Diner	80 W Broadway	617-268-5748	$	3 pm	Three words. Grilled Blueberry Muffins.
R&L Delicatessen	313 Old Colony Ave	617-269-3354	$	10 pm	For large sandwiches.
Salsa's Mexican Grill	118 Dorchester St	617-269-7878	$$	10 pm	Legit Mexican.
Stadium	232 Old Colony Ave	617-269-5100	$$	1 am	Not into sports? Don't eat here.
Teriyaki House	32 W Broadway	617-269-2000	$	1 am	Japanese, some other Asian. Good value.

Map 11 · South Boston (East)

Aura	1 Seaport Ln	617-385-4300	$$$$	10 pm	Seafood for doing deals over.
Boston Beer Garden	732 E Broadway	617-269-0990	$$	11 pm	If you are looking for a place right by the game, this is it.
Café Porto Bello	672 E Broadway	617-269-7680	$$*	11 pm	Straight-forward, honest Italian.
Kelly's Landing	81 L St	617-268-8900	$$	10 pm	"The original" is back, specializing in seafood.
L Street Diner	108 L St	617-268-1155	$	10 pm	Southie standby.
LTK (Legal Test Kitchen)	225 Northern Ave	617-330-7430	$$$	12 am	Hip cousin to Legal chain has attentive service, i-Pod docks.
No Name Restaurant	15 Fish Pier St E	617-338-7539	$$	10 pm	Attracts tourists and waterfront workers alike.
Playwright	658 E Broadway	617-269-2537	$$	11 pm	For socializing and television watching.
Summer Street Grille	653 Summer St	617-269-2200	$$	11 pm	Undemanding American at the BAC.
Terrie's Place	676 E Broadway	617-268-3119	$*	1 pm	Home of the meatloaf omelet.

Map 12 · Newmarket / Andrew Square

224 Boston Street	224 Boston St	617-265-1217	$$$	11 pm	Big portions, good prices! Oh crap!
Alex's Pizza	580 Dorchester Ave	617-464-3663	$	12 am	Steak subs and pizza, late nights near the T.
Avenue Grille	856 Dorchester Ave	617-288-8000	$$	9 pm	Always something tasty here. A good choice.
Baltic Deli & Café	632 Dorchester Ave	617-268-2435	$	8 pm	Foods from the old country.
Café Polonia	611 Dorchester Ave	617-269-0110	$	10 pm	Polish. Small, inviting, authentic. Have a Zywiec.
Franklin Café	152 Dorchester Ave	617-269-1003	$$$	2 am	Newest Franklin Cafe location at the edge of Southie. Cocktails. Mm-hmm.

Key: $: Under $10 / $$: $10–$20 / $$$: $20–$30 / $$$$: $30–$40 / $$$$$: $40+
* : Does not accept credit cards / † : Accepts only American Express. / †† : Accepts only Visa and Mastercard
Time listed refers to kitchen closing time on weekend nights

Map 12 · Newmarket / Andrew Square—continued

The Hen House	1033 Massachusetts Ave	617-442-WING	$	2 am	I reckon this"ll be the place ya"ll wanna eat some waffles at ya"ll.
Restaurante Laura	688 Columbia Rd	617-825-9004	$$	10 pm	Scary outside, lovely Cabo Verde inside. Live music.
Singh's Roti Shop	692 Columbia Rd	617-282-7977	$	10 pm	Huge roti. Also try the channa doubles.
Taqueria Casa Real	860A Dorchester Ave	617-282-3135	$	8 pm	Mexican; good hot sauce options.
Venetian Garden	1269 Massachusetts Ave	617-288-9262	$$	1 am	A '60s time warp for Rat Pack Mexican food.
Victoria's Diner	1024 Massachusetts Ave	617-442-5965	$	12 am	Great diner chow, loads of sausage, and open 24 hours on weekends!
World Seafood Restaurant	400 Dorchester Ave	617-269-1456	$$	8 pm	Fishmonger with fish, chips, and decent crab cakes.

Map 13 · Roxbury

Breezeway Bar and Grill	153 Blue Hill Ave	617-541-5400	$$	2 am	Decent American. Tasty wings. Occasional live music.
Ideal Sub Shop	522 Dudley St	617-442-1560	$*	3 pm	The freshest, largest, best-deal-ever subs.
Merengue	156 Blue Hill Ave	617-445-5403	$$	10 pm	Dominican. Tropical vibe. Gets props from the Sox.
Pepper Pot	208 Dudley St	617-445-4409	$	12 am	Jerk and ginger beer for dem belly a yawn.
Stash's Grille	150 Dudley St	617-989-0200	$	12 am	With a name like that, you expect more than pizza and subs.

Map 14 · Jamaica Plain

Alchemist Lounge	435 S Huntington Ave	617-477-5741	$$	10:30 pm	Go for the ambiance and the music. A little more effort would make the food better.
Alex's Chimis	358 Centre St	617-522-5201	$*	9 pm	How can you complain about a giant plate full of chicken and chicharrones?
Bukhara	701 Centre St	617-522-2195	$$	11 pm	Well-liked Indian bistro. Level of tastiness is like a mystery wheel.
Café D	711 Centre St	617-522-9500	$$$	11 pm	Dressed-up comfort food. Cool newspapered walls.
Centre Street Café	699 Centre St	617-524-9217	$$	10 pm	Groovy, particularly for brunch.
Cha Fahn	763 Centre St	617-983-3575	$$	10 pm	An unexpected spot for delicious tea sandwiches and sake martinis.
Dogwood Café	3712 Washington St	617-522-7997	$$	12 am	Enjoy your wood-fired pizzas while listening to an actual human playing an actual piano.
Doyle's Café	3484 Washington St	617-524-2345	$$*	12 am	The history and great atmosphere make up for the mediocre food.
El Oriental de Cuba	416 Centre St	617-524-6464	$$	10 pm	Always packed. So, be ready to wait for your cubano.
Fredy's Pastelito	3381 Washington St	617-524-4079	$	8 pm	A newcomer to Washington Street in JP does not disappoint. Delicious and inexpensive!
The Galway House	720 Centre St	617-524-9677	$	10 pm	Resisting the onion rings is futile.
Great Wall	779 Centre St	617-522-0277	$	11 pm	Cheap and tasty take-out featuring the Irish-influenced curry fries?
James's Gate	5 McBride St	617-983-2000	$$	11 pm	Enjoy the fireplace while getting busy on your Sheppard's & your Guinnes
J.P. Licks	659 Centre St	617-524-2020	$	12 am	Popular ice cream shop..
JP Seafood Café	730 Centre St	617-983-5177	$$	10 pm	Some like it. Some don't. I don't.
La Pupusa Guanaca	378 Centre St	617-524-4900	$	9 pm	Little-known Salvadoran kitchen serving up some mighty fine food for cheap.
Miami Restaurant	381 Centre St	617-522-4644	$	11 pm	Go for the cubano … don't leave without a beef patty.
Sorella's	388 Centre St	617-524-2016	$*	2 pm	Worth waiting for famous, diner-style breakfasts.
Tacos El Charro	349 Centre St	617-983-9275	$$	11 pm	Actual Mexican food enjoyed well getting down with some mariachi!
Ten Tables	597 Centre St	617-524-8810	$$$	10 pm	Short, precise, inspired menu. Delicious.
Vee Vee	763 Centre St	617-522-0145	$$	10 pm	One of JP's newest restaurants that not only cares about your eating experience but also where the food comes from. Menu changes with the seasons.
Wonder Spice Café	697 Centre St	617-522-0200	$$	10 pm	Tasty Cambodian/Thai. Well named. Get their Crispy Fish!
Yely's Coffee Shop	284 Centre St	617-524-2204	$*	10 pm	Coffee? The counter is stacked full of pork, chicken, sausages, and plantains.
Zon's	2 Perkins St	617-524-9667	$$	11 pm	Home-cooking done right for hipsters and their families.

Map 15 • Fenway (West) / Mission Hill

Name	Address	Phone	$	Hours	Notes
Bravo	465 Huntington Ave	617-369-3474	$$$$	8:30 pm	At the MFA. Stick with the art.
Brigham Circle Chinese Food	728 Huntington Ave	617-278-2000	$	1 am	TWo words- Wonton Soup. Or is that three? Won Ton Soup? Eh. Get it.
Brigham Circle Diner	737 Huntington Ave	617-277-2730	$*	2 pm	Dirty & tasty. Good hash browns.
Brown Sugar Café	129 Jersey St	617-266-2928	$$	11 pm	Sometimes it is good, but too often it is mediocre.
Chacho's	1502 Tremont St	617-445-6738	$	9 pm	Pizza and subs.
Halal Indian Cuisine	736 Huntington St	617-232-5000	$	11 pm	Decent and different for this part of town.
Huntington Pizza & Café	764 Huntington Ave	617-566-1177	$	11 pm	Pretty clear, huh?
Longwood Grille & Bar	342 Longwood Ave	617-232-9770	$$$	10 pm	Hotel restaurant serving the medical community; designed like a chain restaurant.
Mississippi's	103 Terrace St	617-541-4411	$	5 pm	Good for a hot lunch.
Penguin Café	735 Huntington St	617-277-9200	$	1 am	Recommended, and not just for the name.
Solstice Café	1625 Tremont St	617-566-5958	$$	10 pm	Tasty, sort of hip, and friendly.
Squealing Pig	134 Smith St	617-566-6651	$	1 am	Toasties served by indifferent staff.
Upper Crust	1330 Boylston St	617-266-9210	$$	11pm	Fancy schmancy, crisp-crust pizza.

Map 16 • Kenmore Square / Brookline (East)

Name	Address	Phone	$	Hours	Notes
Ankara Café	472 Commonwealth Ave	617-437-0404	$	12 am	Turkish place popular with student snackers.
Audubon Circle	838 Beacon St	617-421-1910	$$	11 pm	Chill out with tasty bar food.
Boston Beer Works	61 Brookline Ave	617-536-2337	$$	12 am	Cavernous suds shop across from Fenway Park.
Café Belo	636 Beacon St	617-236-8666	$	10 pm	Another Café Belo featuring great Brazilian food.
Cornwall's	654 Beacon St	617-262-3749	$$		Eat only to soak up pints.
Eastern Standard	528 Commonwealth Ave	617-532-9100	$$$	12 am	At the Hotel Commonwealth with lip-smackingly good drinks.
Elephant Walk	900 Beacon St	617-247-1500	$$$	11 pm	French-Cambodian local legend.
Ginza	1002 Beacon St	617-566-9688	$$$	1:30 am	Sushi/Japanese. Pompous, overpriced.
India Quality	484 Commonwealth Ave	617-267-4499	$$	11 pm	Quality Indian. The name says it all.
La Verdad	1 Lansdowne St	617-351-25800	$$	2 am	Good, overpriced Mexican.
New England Soup Factory	2 Brookline Pl	617-739-1899	$	9 pm	Creative, home-style soups. Recommended.
Noodle Street	627 Commonwealth Ave	617-536-3100	$	11 pm	Unexpected spices transcend everyday Asian fare.
O'Leary's Pub	1010 Beacon St	617-734-0049	$$	1 am	Try the Guinness stew.
Petit Robert Bistro	468 Commonwealth Ave	617-375-0699	$$$	11 pm	Traditional bistro fare. Try the skate wing.
Taberno de Haro	999 Beacon St	617-277-8272	$$$	11 pm	Solid tapas spot with a great Sherry menu.
Uburger	636 Beacon St	617-536-0448	$††	11 pm	Burgers and frappes right by BU.

Map 17 • Coolidge Corner / Brookline Hills

Name	Address	Phone	$	Hours	Notes
Boca Grande	1294 Beacon St	617-739-3900	$	11 pm	Lots of good taqueria fare. Consider ordering carnitas.
Bottega Fiorentina	41 Harvard St	617-738-5333	$	8 pm	Tuscan sandwiches to go.
Brookline Family Restaurant	305 Washington St	617-277-4466	$$	11 pm	Top notch Turkish food.
Chef Chow's House	230 Harvard St	617-739-2469	$$	10 pm	Decent Chinese food outside of Chinatown.
Dok Bua	411 Harvard St	617-277-7087	$	11 pm	Tastiest Thai around! Their best dishes are not the noodle dishes.
Fireplace	1634 Beacon St	617-975-1900	$$$	11 pm	Warning: food also capable of inducing nap.
Fugakyu	1280 Beacon St	617-738-1268	$$$	1 am	Sushi, very popular. Be prepared to wait.
Gourmet India	1335 Beacon St	617-734-3971	$	10 pm	Fast food Indian.
Khao Sarn	250 Harvard St	617-566-7200	$$	11 pm	Relax and enjoy excellent Thai.
La Morra	48 Boylston St	617-739-0007	$$$$	10:30 pm	Popular Northern Italian.
Martin's Coffee Shop	35 Harvard St	617-566-0005	$	3 pm	Brookline Village's own greasy spoon features breakfast, heavenly home fries.
Matt Murphy's Pub	14 Harvard St	617-232-0188	$	11 pm	Stylish Irish pub with good food and occasional live music.
Michael's Deli	256 Harvard St	617-738-3354	$	2:30 pm	Deli authenticity in stylish Coolidge Corner.
Orinoco	22 Harvard St		$$$	11 pm	Make sure to make a reservation for their Saturday tasting table.
Pho Lemongrass	239 Harvard St	617-731-8600	$$	12 am	Pho, Brookline-style.
Rani Indian Bistro	1353 Beacon St	617-734-0400	$$	11 pm	Serving all your Indian favorites alongside some Hyderabadi specialties.
Rod Dee	1430 Beacon St	617-738-4977	$*	11 pm	So tasty that we wish it was more than just a small take-out joint.
Shawarma King	1383 Beacon St	617-731-6035	$*	11 pm	Excellent Middle-Eastern—informative service, fresh-fruit beverages, traditional desserts.
Village Fish	22 Harvard St	617-566-3474	$$	11 pm	Neighborhood standby.
Virgina's Fine Foods	8 Cypress St	617-566-7775	$	5 pm	Slightly pricey shop with multiple breads for sandwiches, including veggie-friendly fare.
Washington Square Tavern	714 Washington St	617-232-8989	$$$	11 pm	Good American food, but not as cheap as the name might suggest.

297

Key: $: Under $10 / $$: $10–$20 / $$$: $20–$30 / $$$$: $30–$40 / $$$$$: $40+
*: Does not accept credit cards / † : Accepts only American Express / †† : Accepts only Visa and Mastercard
Time listed refers to kitchen closing time on weekend nights

Map 18 · Brighton

Bamboo	1616 Commonwealth Ave	617-734-8192	$$	11 pm	Very good Thai at Washington Street.
Bangkok Bistro	1952 Beacon St	617-739-7270	$$	11 pm	Thai for the BC crowd.
Bluestone Bistro	1799 Commonwealth Ave	617-254-8309	$$	12 am	Pizza and pasta, small and hopping.
Café Mirror	362 Washington St	617-779-9662	$	5 pm	Sandwiches and small bites.
Cityside Bar & Grill	1960 Beacon St	617-566-1002	$$	10 pm	More for watching television than dining.
Devlin's	332 Washington St	617-779-8822	$$$	11 pm	A little better than other places around here.
Green Briar	304 Washington St	617-789-4100	$$	11 pm	Generic pub food. Stick with beer.
IHOP	1850 Soldiers Field Rd	617-787-0533	$	24-hrs	Pancakes anytime.
Jasmine Bistro	412 Market St	617-789-4676	$$$	11 pm	Hungarian-French-Lebanese. Somehow this works.
Moogy's	154 Chestnut Hill Ave	617-254-8114	$	11 pm	Enjoy a cheese omelette while playing Connect Four.
Roggie's	356 Chestnut Hill Ave	617-566-1880	$$	3 am	Hang out with BC kids, drink beer, and eat greasy food.
Soho	386 Market St	617-562-6000	$$	12 am	Sleek, fine dining spot-cum-nightclub.
Tasca	1612 Commonwealth Ave	617-730-8002	$$	12 am	Good (but not great) tapas for all budgets!

Map 19 · Allston (South) / Brookline (North)

Aneka Rasa	122 Harvard Ave	617-562-8989	$	11 pm	Top notch Malaysian food that is easy on the wallet.
Angora Café	1024 Commonwealth Ave	617-232-1757	$	12 am	Great wraps and not-to-miss fro-yo with exhaustive and surprising toppings.
Anna's Taqueria	446 Harvard St	617-227-7111	$*	11 pm	It doesn't mean much, but they roll up one of the best burritos in town.
Bagel Rising	1243 Commonwealth Ave	617-789-4000	$*	6 pm	Funky bagel joint.
Big City	138 Brighton Ave	617-782-2020	$$	1 am	For the beer and pool, not food and service.
Bottega Fiorentina	313B Harvard St	617-232-2661	$	8 pm	Tuscan sandwiches to go.
Breakfast Club Diner	270 Western Ave	617-783-1212	$$	2 pm	The shiniest diner found outside New Jersey.
Buk Kyung II	151 Brighton Ave	617-254-2775	$	11 pm	Top-notch Korean food. Good luck finding a parking space on weekends.
Café Brazil	421 Cambridge St	617-789-5980	$$	11 pm	Authentic, home-style Brazilian.
Camino Real	48 Harvard Ave	617-254-5088	$$	10 pm	Good-value Colombian.
Charlie's Pizza & Café	177 Allston St	617-277-3737	$	1 am	Best hummos around. Delicious kabobs too.
Coolidge Corner Clubhouse	307 Harvard St	617-566-4948	$$	1:15 am	Home of the Big Papi Burger.
El Cafétal	479 Cambridge St	617-789-4009	$$	10 pm	Co-yum-bian.
Gitlo's	164 Brighton Ave	617-782-2253	$	10:30 am	Dim Sum for Dinner? It doesn't get any better than this!
Grasshopper	1 N Beacon St	617-254-8883	$$	11 pm	Hip Asian vegan.
Grecian Yearning	174 Harvard Ave	617-254-8587	$*	3:30 pm	Classic diner with a good variety of sausages.
Habanero Mexican Grill	166 Brighton Ave	617-254-0299	$	11 pm	El Salvadoran chow. Hell yes to the fried plantains.
Indian Dhaba Roadside Diner	180 Brighton Ave	617-787-5155	$	11 pm	Curried goodness. Not actually a diner.
La Mamma Pizza	190 Brighton Ave	617-783-1661	$	1 am	Stick with the empanadas and Chilean specialties.
Mr Sushi Japanese Restaurant	329 Harvard St	617-731-1122	$$	11 pm	Good basic sushi with no frills.
Nori Sushi	398 Harvard St	617-277-3100	$$	11 pm	Among multitude of Brookline sushi options, this one's intimate and spot-on.
Paradise Rock Club & Lounge	967 Commonwealth Ave	617-562-8814	$$*	1 am	Major rock acts. Tasty food and smaller bands in Lounge.
Paris Creperie	278 Harvard St	617-232-1770	$	11 pm	A variety of sweet and savory crepes.
Pho Viets	1095 Commonwealth Ave	617-562-8828	$	10 pm	Best Vietnamese subs (Bahn Mi) in town for just a few bucks.
Quan's Kitchen	1026 Commonwealth Ave	617-232-76175	$	2 am	Fast, cheap Chinese—open late, good lemon chicken, flat-screen TV.
Rangoli	129 Brighton Ave	617-562-0200	$$	11 pm	Emphasizes South Indian. Delicious!
Redneck's Roast Beef	140 Brighton Ave	617-782-9444	$††	3 am	Open til 3 am; great drunk food. Not sure how it tastes when sober.
Reef Café	170 Brighton Ave	617-202-6366	$	12 am	One of the best Lebanese joints in Boston.
Saigon	431 Cambridge St	617-254-3373	$$*	10 pm	Pleasant Vietnamese, good value. Try the catfish.
Saray	1098 Commonwealth Ave	617-383-6651	$$	11 pm	Just the thought of their kabobs and eggplant dishes is making me drool.
Spike's Junkyard Dogs	108 Brighton Ave	617-254-7700	$*	1 am	Quick sausage fix.
Steve's Kitchen	120 Harvard Ave	617-254-9457	$*	6 pm	The best diner in Allston even though Lisa no longer works there.
Sumi	182 Brighton Ave	617-254-7010	$$††	10 pm	Tasty meats and fish on a stick for dirt cheap.

Sunset Grill & Tap	130 Brighton Ave	617-254-1331	$$	1 am	Huge Mexican platters and tons of great beer.
Super 88 Food Court	1095 Commonwealth Ave	617-787-2288	$*	8 pm	Boston's largest Asian food court.
Upper Crust	286 Harvard St	617-739-8518	$	11 pm	Fancy schmancy pizza with wifi.
Victoria Seafood	1029 Commonwealth Ave	617-783-5111	$††	1 am	Good food and dirt cheap prices! Great Chinese seafood options.
Wisteria	1095 Commonwealth Ave	617-787-8288	$	11 pm	Gourmet Chinese food court cuisine.
YoMa	5 N Beacon St	617-783-1372	$*	10 pm	Fantastic Burmese food finally arrives to Boston!
Zaftigs Delicatessen	335 Harvard St	617-975-0075	$$	10 pm	Comfort food for breeders who brunch.

Map 20 · Harvard Square / Allston (North)

Algiers	40 Brattle St	617-492-1557	$	11 pm	An excellent, and oddly tourist-free, lunch and coffee spot.
b. good	24 Dunster St	617-354-6500	$	11 pm	Healthier fast food.
Border Café	32 Church St	617-864-6100	$$	12 am	Feeding students sub-par Tex-Mex for years.
Café Pamplona	12 Bow St	617-492-0352	$*	12 am	Mellow Cuban hangout with outdoor patio.
Caffe Paradiso	1 Eliot Sq	617-868-3240	$	11 pm	For students getting their just desserts.
Cambridge, 1	27 Church St	617-576-1111	$$	12 am	Tasty innovative pizzas and salads. Relaxed, stripped-down space.
Casablanca	40 Brattle St	617-876-0999	$$$	11 pm	Still popular with the Harvard crowd.
Charlie's Kitchen	10 Eliot St	617-492-9646	$	1 am	Old School at the old school. Best jukebox around.
Crazy Doughs	36 JFK St	617-492-4848	$	10 pm	Pizza in The Garage.
Darwin's Ltd	148 Mt Auburn St	617-354-5233	$*	9 am	Hidden Harvard Square refuge.
Flat Patties	81 Mt Auburn St	617-871-6871	$	11 pm	Try their shredded pork sandwich and an order of fries.
Grafton Street	1230 Massachusetts Ave	617-497-0400	$$$	12 am	High-volume, high-end Irish restaurant offering an eclectic menu.
Grendel's Den	89 Winthrop St	617-491-1050	$	1 am	For the laid-back academic. Reasonable prices. Excellent after work specials.
Harvest	44 Brattle St	617-868-2255	$$$$	11 pm	Excellent. Nice garden terrace.
John Harvard's Brew House	33 Dunster St	617-868-3585	$$	12 am	Large and loud, good for crowds.
Mr & Mrs Bartley's Burger Cottage	1246 Massachusetts Ave	617-354-6559	$*	9 pm	Classic burger joint across from the Yard. .
My Thai Vegetarian Café	404 Harvard St	617-739-8830	$	11 pm	If you are looking for beef, chicken, or pork, you have come to the wrong place.
OM	92 Winthrop St	617-576-2800	$$$$$	10 pm	Super expensive.
Pho Pasteur	35 Dunster St	617-864-4100	$$	11 pm	Reliable Vietnamese. You can't go wrong here.
The Red House	98 Winthrop St	617-576-0605	$$$	11 pm	Seasonal menus served in an old red house.
Rialto	1 Bennett St	617-661-5050	$$$$$	11 pm	Probably Harvard's finest restaurant.
Sabra Grill	20 Eliot Sq	617-868-5777	$*	10 pm	Tasty, cheap Greek food.
Sandrine's	8 Holyoke St	617-497-5300	$$$$	10:30 pm	Have a flammekueche—hard to say, easy to eat.
Shilla	57 JFK St	617-547-7971	$$	12 pm	Quiet, subterranean Japanese/Korean.
Takemura Japanese Restaurant	18 Eliot St	617-492-6700	$$	11 pm	Creative sushi on a budget.
Tamarind Bay	75 Winthrop St	617-491-4552	$$	10 pm	One of the best Indian restaurants in town. Try the bhuna paneer.
Tory Row	3 Brattle St	617-876-8769	$$	11 pm	"Euro American food."
UpStairs on the Square	91 Winthrop St	617-864-1933	$$$$	11 pm	Neoclassical food in an expressionist room.
Wagamama	57 JKF St	617-499-0930	$$	11 pm	Like everything they touch, even fast food is better in Japan
Veggie Planet	47 Palmer St	617-661-1513	$$*	10 pm	At Club Passim. Mostly for pizzas, some vegan.

Map 21 · West Cambridge

Armando's	163 Huron Ave	617-354-8275	$*	11 pm	Cheap and delicious pizza.
Cheddars	201 Alewife Brook Pkwy	617-661-3366	$	8 pm	Fresh-from-the-oven pizza and sandwiches, complete with a local cult following.
Full Moon	344 Huron Ave	617-354-6699	$$	9 pm	For a night out with the children.
Hi-Rise Bread Company	208 Concord Ave	617-876-8766	$*	5 pm	Every neighborhood should have a place this good.
Il Buongustaio	369 Huron Ave	617-491-3133	$*	10 pm	Very good pizzas, calzones, paninis.
Trattoria Pulcinella	147 Huron Ave	617-491-6336	$$$$	11 pm	For those not going to the North End.

Map 22 · North Cambridge / West Somerville

Anna's Taqueria	236 Elm St	617-666-3900	$*	11 pm	Fastest burritos in town.
Antonia's Italian Bistro	37 Davis Sq	617-623-6700	$$	11 pm	Solid choice for the carb-starved.
Bue Shirt Cafe	424 Highland Ave	617-629-7641	$	11 pm	Feel the force of vitamin B12.
Café Barada	2269 Massachusetts Ave	617-354-2112	$	9 pm	Relaxed Middle Eastern.
Dave's Fresh Pasta	81 Holland St	617-623-0867	$††	7:30 pm	Homemade pasta and sauces.

Arts & Entertainment · **Restaurants**

Map 22 · North Cambridge / West Somerville—*continued*

Diesel Café	257 Elm St	617-629-8717	$	1 am	Coffee and sandwich shop with an attitude.
Diva Indian Bistro	246 Elm St	617-629-4963	$$	1 am	Flashy and tasty, but pricey.
Elephant Walk	2067 Massachusetts Ave	617-492-6900	$$$	11 pm	French-Cambodian local legend.
Gargoyles on the Square	219 Elm St	617-776-5300	$$$$	10 pm	Deservedly popular Davis Square haunt with amazing apps and top-notch drinks.
House of Tibet	235 Holland St	617-629-7567	$$	9 pm	Delicious, but where's the yak butter?
Jasper White's Summer Shack	149 Alewife Brook Pkwy	617-520-9500	$$$	11 pm	Seafood. More a hangar than a shack.
Jose's	131 Sherman St	617-354-0335	$$	12 am	It's all about the Margaritas.
Joshua Tree	256 Elm St	617-623-9910	$$	10 am	Achtung, baby.
Martsa on Elm	233A Elm St	617-666-0660	$$	11 pm	Your meal is best accompanied by a Tibetan server.
Namaskar	236 Elm St	617-623-9911	$$$	11 pm	Above-average Indian with good variety.
Orleans	65 Holand St	617-591-2100	$$$	10 pm	People-watching, food. Don't look so expectant.
Out of the Blue	215 Elm St	617-776-5020	$$$††	10 pm	Good value for seafood, Italian. Colorful room.
Qingdao Garden	2382 Massachusetts Ave	617-492-7540	$	11 pm	Casual, delicious. Sells dumplings-to-go in bulk.
Redbones	55 Chester St	617-628-2200	$$*	12 am	Don't dig on swine? Then come for the beers.
Renee's Cafe	198 Holland St	617-623-2727	$*	1:30 pm	No-cash, early-closing pancake heaven. Try the specials.
Richardson's Ice Cream	55 Davis Sq	978-774-5450	$		A delicious New England institution.
Rosebud Diner	381 Summer St	617-666-6015	$$	12 am	Wise choice for a comfort food fix.
Rudy's Café	248 Holland St	617-623-9201	$$	12 pm	Serving up generous Tex-Mex portions with a taco selection of tequila.
Sabur	212 Holland St	617-776-7890	$$$	10:30 pm	Food from Greece, North Africa, and the Balkans in a casbah-like atmosphere.
Sangra	400 Highland Ave	617-625-0200	$$$	10 pm	Rustic, eastern region Italian cuisine, great menu, small portions.
Snappy Sushi	420 Highland Ave	617-625-0400	$$$	11pm	Yummy brown rice sushi.
Spike's Junkyard Dogs	217 Elm St	617-440-1010	$*	1 am	Awsome veggie dogs and real ones too!
Teele Square Café	1153 Broadway	617-625-0082	$*	8 pm	Sandwiches with heart (not literally).
Tip Top Noodle Shop	1153 Broadway	617-627-9333			Italian noodles! Asian flavors!

Map 23 · Central Somerville / Porter Square

Anna's Taqueria	822 Somerville Ave	617-661-8500	$*	11 pm	Fastest burritos in town.
Blue Fin	1815 Massachusetts Ave	617-497-8022	$$	10 pm	Not the best sushi, but close to the cheapest.
Broken Yolk	136 College Ave	617-628-6621	$	3 pm	Mmm, pancakes.
Café Mami	1815 Massachusetts Ave	617-547-9130	$	9 pm	It's amazing what they can do with a little ground beef and an egg.
Café Rustica	356 Beacon St	617-491-8300	$*	4 pm	Friendly neighborhood café.
Caffé Rossini	278 Highland Ave	617-625-5240	$*	10 pm	Comfy Italian.
Christopher's	1920 Massachusetts Ave	617-876-9180	$$	12 am	Good for relaxing on a wet day.
Kelly's Diner	674 Broadway	617-623-8102	$*	3 pm	Old-school greasy spoon known for its "Kiss My Grits!" service.
Lemon Thai	215 Highland Ave	617-591-1772	$††	11 pm	Quality on the cheap like crispy bean beef.
Lil Vinny's	525 Medford St	617-628-8466	$$	11 pm	Spin-off of East Somerville's Vinny's at Night.
Lyndell's Bakery	720 Broadway	617-625-1793	$	6 pm	Old-fashioned bakery.
Passage to India	1900 Massachusetts Ave	617-497-6113	$$	11 pm	Good Indian, served late. Try the curries.
RF O'Sullivan's	282 Beacon St	617-492-7773	$††	1 am	Quite possibly the best burgers in Boston.
Stone Hearth Pizza Col.	1782 Mass Ave	617-492-1111	$$	10 pm	Pizza chain using organic, sustainable ingredients.
True Grounds	717 Broadway	617-591-9559	$*	7 pm	Low key hangout with the laptop crowd.
Sound Bites	708 Broadway	617-623-8338	$*	3 pm	For filling breakfasts.
Sugar & Spice	1933 Massachusetts Ave	617-868-4200	$$$	11 pm	Thai food when you're not in the mood for the Japanese.
Tacos Lupita	13 Elm St	617-666-0677	$*	11 pm	Cozy Mexican and El Salvadorian hybrid is 100% authentic.
Tu y Yo	858 Broadway	617-623-5411	$$	10 pm	Authentic Mexican—no burritos here.
Wang's Fast Food	509 Broadway	617-623-2982	$	1 am	Best Mandarin hole-in-the-wall on this side of the river. Try the dumplings.

Map 24 · Winter Hill / Union Square

Café Belo	120 Washington St	617-623-3696	$	10 pm	Brazilian cafeteria.
Fasika Ethiopian Restaurant	145 Broadway	617-628-9300	$$*	1 am	Best Ethiopian in town in the oddest setting.
Great Thai Chef	255 Washington St	617-625-9296	$$††	10 pm	It's Thai, it's great, there's a chef.

Leone's	292 Broadway	617-776-2511	$*	11 pm	Meatball subs that are To-Die-For.
Machu Picchu	25 Union Sq	617-623-7972	$	10 pm	Peruvian. Definitely worth trying.
Neighborhood Restaurant & Bakery	25 Bow St	617-623-9710	$*	4 pm	Big, good breakfasts + patio = summer morning bliss.
Ronnarong Thai Tapas Bar	255 Washington St	617-615-9296	$$††	10 pm	It's Thai, it's great, there's a chef.
Sherman	257 Washington St	617-776-4944	$	7 pm	Good lunch spot; comes recommended by Mr. Peabody.
Sweet Ginger	22 Bow St	617-625-5015	$$	10 pm	Typical, tasty Thai.
Taqueria la Mexicana	247 Washington St	617-776-5232	$$	10 pm	The real deal. Terrific flautas.

Map 25 · East Somerville / Sullivan Square

Beijing Taste	99A Cambridge St	617-241-5077	$	12 am	For emergencies only.
Mount Vernon	14 Broadway	617-666-3830	$$	1 am	Sleepy spot with occasional lobster specials.
Vinny's at Night	76 Broadway	617-628-1921	$$$	10 pm	Quality home-style Italian tucked behind a deli.

Map 26 · East Cambridge / Kendall Square / MIT

Aceituna	605 W Kendall St	617-252-0707	$$	8 pm	Mediterranean for lunch at the Genzyme building.
Bambara	25 Land Blvd	617-868-4444	$$$	11 pm	Hit-or-miss at Hotel Marlowe.
Black Sheep Café	350 Main St	617-577-1300	$$	10 pm	In the Kendall Hotel. Go for breakfast.
The Blue Room	One Kendall Sq	617-494-9034	$$$$	11 pm	Terrific food, popular. Somehow elegant and casual.
Court House Seafood	498 Cambridge St	617-491-1213	$$	8 pm	One step removed from bookstore for fish.
Desfina	202 Third St	617-868-9098	$$	1 am	Greek for geeks.
Helmand Restaurant	143 First St	617-492-4646	$$$	11 pm	Delightful, authentic. Family ties with Afghanistan's president.
Legal Sea Foods	5 Cambridge Center	617-864-3400	$$	11 pm	Another Legal Seafoods for your fishy pleasure.
Second Street Café	89 Second St	617-661-1311	$$*	3:30 pm	Plenty of fresh, inexpensive choices.
Technique	215 1st St	617-218-8088	$$	1:30 pm	The student run restaurant at Le Cordon Bleu.

Map 27 · Central Square / Cambridgeport

Asgard	350 Massachusetts Ave	617-577-9100	$$	2 am	Enormous "Celtic" gastropub.
Asmara	739 Massachusetts Ave	617-864-7447	$$	11 pm	Once was the only Ethiopian restaurant in Cambridge.
Brookline Lunch	9 Brookline St	617-354-2983	$*	4 pm	Popular diner. For food, not service.
Café Baraka	80 1/2 Pearl St	617-868-3951	$$*	10 pm	A tiny restaurant serving up some good Moroccan cuisine.
Carberry's Bakery & Coffee House	74 Prospect St	617-576-3530	$	8 pm	Bakery items and good sandwiches.
Central Kitchen	567 Massachusetts Ave	617-491-5599	$$$	11 pm	Simple Mediterranean menu featuring incredibly flavorful dishes with great wines to match.
Coast Cafe	233 River St	617-354-7644	$	9 pm	Breadcrumb-laden fried chicken, mac 'n cheese 'n collard greens.
Cuchi Cuchi	795 Main St	617-864-2929	$$$	11 pm	You either love this place or hate it. Find out for yourself!
Dolphin Seafood	1105 Massachusetts Ave	617-661-2937	$$	10 pm	Unpretentious fish house.
Four Burgers	704 Massachusetts Ave	617-441-5444	$	11 pm	Truth in advertising. The menu? Four burgers.
Green Street Grill	280 Green St	617-876-1655	$$$	10 pm	New American, seasonal, local-based menu.
Hi-Fi Pizza & Subs	496 Massachusetts Ave	617-492-4600	$	3 am	Soak up the beer you drank at T.T.'s.
India Pavilion	17 Central Sq	617-547-7463	$$	11 pm	Reliable Indian that's been a part of Central Square forever. A decent value.
Olive Tree Cafe	245 Massachusetts Ave	617-441-8689	$	11 pm	Cheap, excellent Jordanian + pipes + Confederate artifacts.
Mary Chung	464 Massachusetts Ave	617-864-1991	$$*	11 pm	This Central Square institution is still going strong.
The Middle East	472 Massachusetts Ave	617-864-3278	$$	12 am	Cheap and tasty food before going to see a show.
Miracle of Science	321 Massachusetts Ave	617-868-2866	$$	1 am	Energetic neighborhood mainstay. Great burgers, quesadillas.
Moody's Falafel Palace	25 Central Sq	617-864-0827	$*	3 am	Located in what was once a White Castle.
Picante Mexican Grill	735 Massachusetts Ave	617-576-6394	$	11 pm	Cali-Mex. Pretty good salsas.
Pu Pu Hot Pot	907 Main St	617-491-6616	$	10 pm	Chinese. Much better than it sounds.
Rangzen Tibetan Restaurant	24 Pearl St	617-354-8881	$$	10 pm	For a feast fit for a monk try the Gyakor Tibetan Hot Pot.
Rendezvous	502 Massachusetts Ave	617-576-1900	$$$$	11 pm	Fancy restaurant pops up in what was once a Burger King. No dollar menu anymore.
Salts	798 Main St	617-876-8444	$$$$	10 pm	New ownership, higher prices. Tasty.
Zoe's	1105 Massachusetts Ave	617-495-0055	$	10 pm	Retro-ish diner food, breakfast of the day.
ZuZu!	474 Massachusetts Ave	617-492-9181	$$	1 am	Funky, colorful. Make a meal of maza.

Key: $: Under $10 / $$: $10–$20 / $$$: $20–$30 / $$$$: $30–$40 / $$$$$: $40+
* : Does not accept credit cards / † : Accepts American Express / †† : Accepts only Visa and Mastercard
Time listed refers to kitchen closing time on weekend nights.

Map 28 · Inman Square

All-Star Sandwich Bar	1245 Cambridge St	617-868-3065	$*	10 pm	Old-fashioned favorites like Mom used to make.
Amelia's Trattoria	111 Harvard St	617-868-7600	$$$	10 pm	The best Italian in this area.
Atasca	50 Hampshire St	617-621-6991	$$$	11 pm	Nothing better than bacalhau with a Portuguese red.
Café Kiraz	119 Hampshire St	617-868-2233	$	11 pm	Subs and shwarma.
City Girl Café	204 Hampshire St	617-864-2809	$$	9 pm	Comfy and cool. Try the lasagna.
Dali	415 Washington St	617-661-3254	$$$	11 pm	Fun taparia. Worth the wait. Usually worth the price.
East Coast Grill & Raw Bar	1271 Cambridge St	617-491-6568	$$$$	10 pm	Awesome seafood, barbecue. Try the Hell Sausage.
Emma's Pizzeria	40 Hampshire St	617-864-8534	$$	10 pm	Design your own gourmet pie. Worth waiting.
EVOO	118 Beacon St	617-661-3866	$$$$	11 pm	Creative cuisine. One of Somerville's best.
The Friendly Toast	1 Kendall Sq	617-621-1200	$$	10 pm	Late-night spot for the domestic American hipster.
Hungry Mother	233 Cardinal Medeiros Ave	617-499-0090	$$$	1 am	As Southern as boiled peanuts and the steady presence of sorghum.
Koreana	154 Prospect St	617-576-8661	$$	12 am	Cooking tasty Bulgogi right at your table.
Midwest Grill	1124 Cambridge St	617-354-7536	$$$	12 am	Brazilian sword-play.
Montien	1287 Cambridge St	617-868-1240	$$	11 pm	Thai in the Theater District with giant yummy sushi.
Muqueca	1093 Cambridge St	617-354-3296	$$	9 pm	Their specialty is a Brazilian-style seafood stew.
O Cantinho	1128 Cambridge St	617-354-3443	$$	11 pm	NFT approved Portuguese spot. Easy on the wallet.
Ole Mexican Grill	11 Springfield St	617-492-4495	$$	11 pm	Delicious guacamole made right at your table.
Oleana	134 Hampshire St	617-661-0505	$$$$	11 pm	Top-notch Mediterranean. Patio seating in warm weather.
Pho Lemon	228 Broadway	617-441-8813	$	10 pm	Vietnamese. Not fancy, but good value.
Punjabi Dhaba	225 Hampshire St	617-547-8272	$*	12 am	Some of the best Indian food for dirt cheap.
S&S Restaurant	1334 Cambridge St	617-354-0777	$$	12 am	Serving deli, comfort food for eighty years.
Toscanini and Sons	406 Washington St	617-868-0014	$*	7 pm	Scrumptious café food and, of course, great ice cream.
Tupelo	1193 Cambridge St	617-868-0004	$$	10 pm	Food for the southerner in ya'll.

Map 29 · West Roxbury

Himalayan Bistro	1735 Centre St	617-325-3500	$$$	11 pm	Nepali for your inner sherpa.
MaSoNa Grill	4 Corey St	617-323-3331	$$$$	10:30 pm	Euro-Peruvian eclectic grill, West Roxbury's best
Real Deal	1882 Centre St	617-325-0754	$	9 pm	Imagine a typical sub shop with creative fixin's.
Samia Bakery	1894 Centre St	617-323-5181	$	8 pm	Absolutely delicious kabobs.
Skara Grill	1985 Centre St	617-327-1114	$$	10 pm	Greek chow in an old Friendly's building in the middle of West Rox.
Vintage	1430 VFW Pkwy	617-469-2600	$$$	11 pm	Pricey steakhouse for locals unwilling to drive downtown for a better deal.
Upper Crust	1727 Centre St	617-323-6400	$$	10 pm	Fancy schmancy, crisp-crust pizza.
West on Centre	1732 Centre St	617-323-4199	$$$	11 pm	Casual American; plenty of brick and mahogany.

Map 30 · Roslindale

Birch Street Bistro	14 Birch St	617-323-2184	$$	10 pm	Inviting place to kick back for dinner.
Delfino	754 South St	617-327-8359	$$$	10 pm	Tiny, popular spot serving good-quality Italian.
Diane's Bakery	9 Poplar St	617-323-1877	$*	1 pm	Croissant sandwiches, snack cakes.
Geoffrey's Café	4257 Washington St	617-325-1000	$$$	12 am	South End, Back Bay transplant, brunch rocks.
John's Bakery	31 Poplar St	617-323-9465	$	2 pm	Famous hideaway for pizza. Arbitrarily open.
Pleasant Cafe	4515 Washington St	617-323-2111	$$	11 pm	Pizza and other basics. Don't be scared of the sketchy exterior..
Primavera	289 Walk Hill St	617-522-1186	$$††	9 pm	Cheap Italian that occasionally hits the spot..
Romanos Pizzeria & Taqueria	4249 Washington St	617-325-2885	$	11 pm	Two great foods under one roof.
Roslindale House of Pizza	4168 Washington St	617-327-9170	$	11 pm	Pizza. Ya know, pizza.
Sophia's Grotto	22 Birch St	617-323-4595	$$	10:30 pm	Cozy family trattoria. Enjoy the mussels in the courtyard.
Village Sushi & Grill	14 Corinth St	617-363-7874	$$	10 pm	Japanese and Korean.
Yucatan Tacos	1417 Centre St	617-323-7555	$	8 pm	Authentic Mexican food, apparently.

Map 31 · Mattapan / Dorchester (West)

Ali's Roti	1188 Blue Hill Ave	617-298-9850	$	10 pm	You have not experienced life until you dive into a delicious roti.
Bon Appetit	1138 Blue Hill Ave	617-825-5544	$$	10:30 pm	Haitian food supposedly makes you a better lover.
Brothers	1638 Blue Hill Ave	617-298-5224	$	5 pm	Southern. Huge side portions.
Flames	461 Blue Hill Ave	617-989-0000	$$	11 pm	Unusually stylish for this neighborhood.
Flames	663 Morton St	617-296-4972	$$	11 pm	Jamaican. Serves ackee!
Lenny's Tropical Bakery	1195 Blue Hill Ave	617-296-2587	$*	9 pm	Double parking for the patties.
P&R Ice Cream	1284 Blue Hill Ave	617-296-0922	$	2 am	Nothing beats a beef patty followed by a scoop of Grape Nut ice cream.
Picasso Creole Cuisine	1296 Blue Hill Ave	617-296-1300	$	10 pm	Haitian home-style cooking.
Pit Stop Bar-B-Q	888A Morton St	617-436-0485	$	12 am	A rib shack, literally. Stick to the ribs.
R&S Jamaican Restaurant	770 Blue Hill Ave	617-287-8600	$	11 pm	Mmore Goat Curry than you can eat in two sittings for $12.
Simco's on the Bridge	1509 Blue Hill Ave	617-296-3800	$*	1:30 am	Boston's best hotdogs since the 1930s.
Tastee Jamaican Restaurant	522 River St	617-296-1935	$*	10 pm	Pretend you're not in Boston with tasty jerk chicken and a ginger beer.
United House of Prayer	206 Seaver St	617-445-3246	$*	6 pm	Friendly soul food in basement of Boston's old stadt shul.

Map 32 · Dorchester (East)

Antojitos y Panaderia Chapinas	299 Hancock St	617-288-3201	$	11 pm	Good Guatemalan.
Ashmont Grill	555 Talbot Ave	617-825-4300	$$$		Bringing flair to Peabody Square.
Ba-Le Restaurant	1052 Dorchester Ave	617-265-7171	$*	10 pm	Wonderful crisp Vietnamese sandwiches.
Blarney Stone	1505 Dorchester Ave	617-436-8223	$$	11 pm	Hodgepodge of good pub-type food.
Blasi's Café and Fat Belly Deli	762 Adams St	617-825-4566	$$	10 pm	Sit down or take out. Big, fat portions.
CF Donovan's	112 Savin Hill Ave	617-436-6690	$$	1 am	Friendly neighborhood restaurant/bar.
Charlie's Place	1740 Dorchester Ave	617-265-3111	$	10:30 p m	Pizza and steak sandwiches.
Chef Lee's	554 Columbia Rd	617-436-6634	$$	8 pm	Second location of Boston soul food institution.
dBar	1236 Dorchester Ave	617-265-4490	$$$		So chic, you could be in Downtown Crossing.
Irie Jamaican Style Restaurant	310 Bowdoin St	617-929-3866	$$		One love for the jerk chicken and ice-cream, Praise Jah!
Ka' Carlos	33 Hancock St	617-282-4616	$$*	10 pm	Cape Verdean and Portuguese food under the same roof!
Lucky Café	1107 Dorchester Ave	617-822-9888	$*	9 pm	Chinese BBQ. Meat-elicious.
Phillips Old Colony House	780 Morrissey Blvd	617-282-7700	$$$$	10 pm	Brunch to impress your grandmother visiting from Iowa.
Pho 2000	198 Adams St	617-436-1908	$$	10 pm	Serving a delicious 7 course beef dinner.
Pho Hoa	1356 Dorchester Ave	617-287-9746	$$	11 pm	Phat pho.
Restaurante Cesaria	266 Bowdoin St	617-282-1998	$$	11 pm	Something for everyone—grilled octopus to chicken parmesean.
Shanti: Taste of India	1111 Dorchester Ave	617-929-3900	$$	11 pm	Go for the goat.
Sunrise	1157 Dorchester Ave	617-288-7314	$	10 pm	Pho and other ethereal delights.

Map 33 · Hyde Park

African Cuisine	1248 Hyde Park Ave	617-364-9999	$	11 pm	Sketchy from the outside, but step inside for great food.
Dottie's Deli	5 Fairmount Ave	617-364-9814	$*	3 pm	An old fashioned breakfast joint with its original charm.
Rincon Caribeno	18 Fairmount Ave	617-361-3210	$	10:30 pm	A new addition to Fairmont that serves predominately Puerto Rican food.
Townsend's Restaurant	81 Fairmount Ave	617-333-0306	$$	12 am	One of them gastropubs. Fancy food, tasty drinks.

It's not quite the city that never sleeps, but Boston's nightlife is vast and varied, catering not only to teeming masses of college students and eager yuppies and disaffected hipsters alike. Since this is a city founded by people that were so uptight the British annoyed them (Pot paging kettle...), we are still stuck with the blue-law mentality that anything that might be fun has to be completely controlled at all times. Thus, all of our bars shutter for the evening at 1 or 2 am. This would be fine for most people if the MBTA, you know, the way the majority of people get around in a city with little parking, didn't manage to close BY TWELVE F*@KING THIRTY. After-hours joints do exist, but are for members-only, so when those lights come up and you are doing your best Last Call Shuffle to get a number—keep in mind cabs are as easy to get after closing time as Red Sox Yan-kee ticks are on opening day. Despite these best efforts, though, the variety of bars, dance clubs, and live music venues keep growing, so you'll be able to find just the right spot to be seen, be picked up, dance, throw some Red Sox-Yankee darts, or sit and share a pint with a friend while you catch a Sox game. Remember that clubs are always in flux, so it makes sense to call ahead and confirm what's up before rounding up your crew and hitting town.

Beer

Like Dunkin' Donuts shops, you can't throw a shillelagh in this town without hitting an Irish pub. Some of the best Guinness this side of the Atlantic can be found (usually poured by authentic Irish hands) at many of these fine establishments. Try **The Junction (Map 10)** or **The Blackthorn Pub (Map 10)**, both in the Irish stronghold of Southie. If stout is not your thing, there are several good microbreweries around town including **Boston Beer Works (Map 2)**, **Cambridge Brewing Company (Map 26)**, and **John Harvard's Brew House (Map 20)**. Large (we mean large) beer selections can be found at **Sunset Grill & Tap (Map 19)**, **Bukowski's (Map 5, 28)**, **Roggie's (Map 5, 18)**, and, to a smaller degree, **Christopher's (Map 23)**, **Pour House (Map 8)**, **Cambridge Common (Map 20)**, and **Doyle's (Map 14)**. **Redbones (Map 22)** has a beer wheel you can spin if you're having trouble making up your mind. If you insist on going straight to the source, take a tour and quaff some samples at the **Harpoon (Map 11)** and **Sam Adams (Map 14)** breweries.

Sports

Almost every bar in Boston becomes a sports bar when the Sox, Pats, and C's are playing (and if the B's ever get good again, we'll add them to that list). It's a good thing, too, since tickets to actual games are prohibitively expensive and the Sox decided to broadcast their games only on cable. If you're desperate to see your (non-Boston) team or follow every March Madness game, try **Sports Depot (Map 19)**, **The Four's (Map 1)**, **Stadium (Map 10)**, **Champions (Map 6)**, **Game On! (Map 16)**, **Tequila Rain (Map 16)**, or **Lir (Map 5)**.

Elegant and Nice

Sometimes you just need to dress up and treat yourself to see how the other half lives. For a change of pace from drunken sports fans and bottles of Bud, or for a good way to impress a date, sip a cocktail in the refined elegance of **Parker's Bar (Map 3)**, **City Bar (Map 6)**, or **Rowes Wharf Bar (Map 4)**. Have a nice romantic evening taking in the view of the Boston skyline at **Top of the Hub (Map 5)** in the Prudential Center. Or don your coolest duds for some cocktails and peoplewatching at **Whiskey Park (Map 3)** or **Sonsie (Map 5)**. For exotic drinks in a far-out futuristic setting, don't miss **Diva Lounge (Map 22)** in Davis Square. The newest nightlife destinations that usually have lines out the door at **Clink (Map 1)** located in the old Charles Street Jail and **Bond (Map 4)** in the Langham Boston Hotel. Bring someone awesome and loads of cash.

Dive

The smoking ban threatened the livelihoods of many a beloved Boston dive, and while some have revamped their image to draw in different crowds, the few hardy stalwarts are still alive and still dives. Go get lost at **Sullivan's Tap (Map 1)**, **Pete's Pub (Map 2)**, **Silhouette Lounge (Map 19)**, **Punter's Pub (Map 15)**, or **T.C. Lounge (Map 5)**, or more upscale dives that feature live bands like the **Midway Café (Map 14)** and **Abbey Lounge (Map 28)**. While not quite dives, good local color can be absorbed at the **Sligo Pub (Map 22)**, **Beacon Hill Pub (Map 1)**, and the **People's Republik (Map 27)**.

Live Music

For such a small city, Boston has a thriving live music scene, its local community of musicians nurturing each other and able to get lots of exposure in a wide array of venues. The Cars, The Pixies, Jonathan Richman, J. Geils, Guster, and Aerosmith are just a few decent names to come out of this town. On the flip side you can thank Beantown for torturing us with New Kids on the Block in the '80s and on behalf of all Bostonians we apologize for their recent reunion tour. Whether you're in the mood for rock, blues, roots, punk, folk, rockabilly, jazz, or yes, even bluegrass, some-body in Boston is playing in. If you're looking for country music—Rhode Island is south of here. Go find it.

While huge national acts play at the Garden and Comcast Center, many also opt for smaller venues like the 2,800-seat Orpheum Theater for its great acoustics. Berklee College has graduated the likes of Branford Mar-salis, Quincy Jones, and Diana Krall, and at its Berklee Performance Center (www.berkleebpc.com, 617-747-2261) you can catch performances by big names and famous alumni or cheap concerts by teachers and students. Who knows? You may be watching the next John Mayer. Other places to catch national acts in a club atmosphere are the spacious **Roxy (Map 3)**, and the brand new and incredibly awesome **House of Blues (Map 16)** that has eaten the club corpses of Axis and Avalon. If it's summer, the best venue in all of Beantown is the **Bank of America Pavillion (Map 11)** right on the waterfront.

For jazz, you can grab dinner and a show at the classy **Regattabar (Map 20)** or **Scullers (Map 19)**. Both in Cambridge, they host world-class performers. If you're on a budget, there are cheaper venues like **Ryles (Map 28)** in Inman Square, **Good Life (Map 4)** in Downtown Crossing, and **Wally's (Map 5)** in the South End, a tiny neighborhood bar where you'll sometimes find Berklee students sitting in with the evening's combo.

Rock 'n rollers head to **Paradise Rock Club (Map 19)**. If the downstairs is packed, go upstairs for a bird's-eye view of the band. If you get tired of moshing, the adjoining Paradise **Lounge (Map 19)** features smaller bands and food in a more relaxed setting. In Central Square, watch out for the door for **T.T. the Bear's Place (Map 27)**. At next door's **Middle East (Map 27)**, one of the coolest clubs on the planet, you can grab some grape leaves before heading to one of its three rooms of music. **Harper's Ferry (Map 19)** gets a good mix of rock, blues, and New Orleans funk. And if you're pining for some old school blues and rock, head to the **Cantab (Map 27)** on the weekend for the still-rocking Little Joe Cook and the Thrillers. Smaller bars to catch a good groove include **Sky Bar (Map 23)**, **O'Briens (Map 19)**, **Midway Café (Map 14)**, **PA's Lounge (Map 24)**, **Great Scott (Map 19)**, and **Abbey Lounge (Map 28)**.

Folkies and singer-songwriters worship at the altar that is **Club Passim (Map 20)**. A 40-plus-year-old land-mark dedicated to promoting independent musicians. Joan Baez, Bob Dylan, and Muddy Waters have all graced its stage. Be warned that they do not sell drinks, just coffee, tea, and vegetarian meals. And if you're dying to dust off that old banjo of yours, re-turn to the **Cantab (Map 27)** on Tuesday nights for its bluegrass pickin' party.

You can find reggae, hip-hop, and Afrobeat at **Western Front (Map 27)**. Latin music and salsa dancing heat up **Green Street Grill (Map 27)**, **Mojito's Lounge (Map 3)**, and **Milky Way Lounge (Map 14)**, which also hosts a popular karaoke night and skee ball.

Can't decide what mood you're in? For every kind of musical act, both local faves and national legends, **Johnny D's (Map 22)** in Somerville reigns supreme. The **Lizard Lounge (Map 20)**, a laid-back neighborhood hang in Cambridge, hosts an eclectic mix of music and performances seven nights a week, ranging from punk to acoustic, rock and roll, experimental, and poetry slams.

Many pubs and bars feature local bands or musicians, often for free or a minimal surcharge. It's a great way to get to know the scene. Check weekly listings for schedules. Some worth paying a visit to are **The Plough and Stars (Map 27)**, **Sally O'Brien's (Map 24)** and **Atwood's Tavern (Map 28)**. Probably the best of these is **Toad (Map 23)**. The room is small, and you usually have to sneak past the bass player to get to the bathroom, but the wide variety and high quality of bands make this a popular gathering place.

Clubs

That sound of hundreds of club kids crying out in frustration and pain is because the once proud Landsdowne Street club Avalon is no more. **Tequila Rain (Map 16)** (maybe the worst new business name in Boston), tries to pick up the slack but you're now better off heading towards downtown. Central Boston has a smaller clusters of clubs in the Theater District (such as the **Roxy (Map 3)**, **Aria (Map 3)**, or **Venu (Map 3)**, around Faneuil Hall (such as **Boston Rocks (Map 2)**, **Vertigo (Map 2)**, and **Parris (Map 2)**), and in Downtown Crossing (the self-important **Felt (Map 3)** or the salsa heaven **Mojito's Lounge (Map 3)**). Even the Leather District is join-ing the fray with **District (Map 4)**. If you're in Cambridge, check out **Phoenix Landing (Map 27)**, on Saturday for a hilarious '80s night. **Jacque's (Map 3)** is Boston's oldest drag club, with shows on most nights. Many clubs have 18+ nights and gay nights, so check their schedules.

Karaoke

Everyone's got that one friend who cannot get enough of singing in front of complete strangers, and Boston provides quite well for them and their entourages. For the truly diehard fanatics, there are a few notable venues for you to prove your vocal met-tle. **Limelight Stage and Studio (Map 3)** applies pitch correction technology so you can finally nail that high note from *Don't Stop Believing* in front of a large crowd or in a private studio. **Do Re Mi (Map 19)** also rents private rooms for hilariously loud birthday parties, but you'll have to sneak your booze past the front desk. Other worthy spots include the college-oriented **An Nua Tua (Map 16)**, after-work **Elephant & Castle (Map 4)**, Harvard Square's **Tommy Doyle's (Map 20)**, and the touristy **Purple Shamrock (Map 2)**.

Map 1 • Beacon Hill / West End

21st Amendment	150 Bowdoin St	617-227-7100	Favorite of the State House crowd.
6B	6 Beacon St #B	617-742-0306	Martinis and snacks for the after-work crowd.
Alibi Lounge	215 Charles St	857-241-1144	How many restaurants/bars are IN the Liberty Hotel? Sweet lord.
Beacon Hill Pub	149 Charles St	617-625-7100	Dive popular with young Hill residents.
Cheers	84 Beacon St	617-227-9605	If you must.
The Four's	166 Canal St	617-720-4455	Sports tavern across from the Garden.
Greatest Bar	262 Friend St	617-367-0544	Big deal.
The Harp	85 Causeway St	617-742-1010	Pack in after an evening at the Garden.
Hill Tavern	228 Cambridge St	617-742-6192	Middling Beacon Hill hangout.
Seven's	77 Charles St	617-523-9074	Sturdy Beacon Hill local.
Sullivan's Tap	168 Canal St	n/a	Dive. Proper before Celtics and Bruins games.

Arts & Entertainment · **Nightlife**

Map 2 · North End / Faneuil Hall

Bell in Hand Tavern	45 Union St	617-227-2098	Welcoming thirsty travelers since the 18th century.
Black Rose	160 State St	617-742-2286	Tourist-crowded, unremarkable. Try somewhere else first.
Boston Beer Works	112 Canal St	617-896-2337	Cavernous suds shop near the Garden.
Boston Rocks	245 Quincy Market	617-726-1110	Generic nightclub.
Boston Sail Loft	80 Atlantic Ave	617-227-7280	Big outside deck on the water, good crowds.
Green Dragon Tavern	11 Marshall St	617-367-0055	Pretend you're Sam Adams while having the same.
The Hong Kong	65 Chatham St	617-227-2226	Scorpion bowl anyone?
McFadden's	148 State St	617-227-5100	Eek!
Paddy O's	33 Union St	617-263-7771	The name tells you it's Oirish, you know.
Parris	Quincy Market	617-248-8800	Tucked inside the less impressive Ned Devine's.
Purple Shamrock	1 Union St	617-227-2060	Giggly and bland.
Sanctuary	189 State St	617-573-9333	For the young and fashion-aware.
Tia's on the Waterfront	200 Atlantic Ave	617-227-0828	Warm-weather party house.
Vertigo	126 State St	617-723-7277	Downtown hot spot.

Map 3 · Downtown Crossing / Park Square / Bay Village

Aria	246 Tremont St	617-338-7080	DJs Tuesday through Saturday.
Felt	533 Washington St	617-350-5555	Club/upscale pool hall. DJ most nights.
Jacque's	79 Broadway	617-426-8902	Drag, but all welcome. Nightly cabaret.
Limelight Stage and Studios	204 Tremont St	617-423-0785	Karaoke on a grand scale; private studios available.
Matrix	275 Tremont St	617-542-4077	Large dance club.
MJ O'Connor's	27 Columbus Ave	617-482-2255	Large Irish pub. Outdoor seating when warm.
Mojitos Lounge	48 Winter St	617-817-2533	For those who like their salsa hot.
Parker's Bar	60 School St	617-227-8600	Elegant. Try the Boston Creme martini.
Roxy	279 Tremont St	617-338-7699	Large, popular dance club. Matrix is downstairs.
Rumor	100 Warrenton St	617-442-0045	Tuesday's the big night here.
The Tam	222 Tremont St	No phone	Local dive.
Venu	100 Warrenton St	617-338-8061	Always changing; check before you go.
Whiskey Park	64 Arlington St	617-542-1483	Swank, popular. Dress up.

Map 4 · Financial District / Chinatown

An Tain	31 India St	617-426-1870	For after work; DJs on Thursday, Friday.
Aqua	120 Water St	617-720-4900	Nice glass walls, anyway.
Bond	250 Franklin St	617-956-8765	One of Boston's newest trendy spots. Prepare yourself for the line.
Elephant & Castle	161 Devonshire St	617-350-9977	Large pub handy for groups. Skip the food.
Good Life	28 Kingston St	617-451-2622	Martinis and jazz.
The International	184 High St	617-542-4747	An empty bar with cocktails and chicken wings. An experiment in isolation.
JJ Foley's	21 Kingston St	617-338-7713	Attracts a big after-work crowd.
Jose McIntyre's	160 Milk St	617-451-9460	Casual DJ and dance spot. Popular and simple.
Les Zygomates	129 South St	617-542-5108	Comprehensive wine list, pleasant bar.
Mr Dooley's Boston Tavern	77 Broad St	617-338-5656	Irish. Popular after-work drinking spot.
Revolution Rock Bar	200 High St	617-261-4200	It's a rock bar in the Financial District. Do suits rock out?
Rowes Wharf Bar	70 Rowes Wharf	617-439-7000	Relax with scotch and an armchair.
Times Restaurant and Bar	112 Broad St	617-357-8463	Irish. Live music and DJs.
Umbria	295 Franklin St	617-338-1000	Italian restaurant goes club at night.

Map 5 · Back Bay (West) / Fenway (East)

Bukowski's	50 Dalton St	617-437-9999	100+ beers served with loud, eclectic music.
Crossroads	495 Beacon St	617-262-7371	Dive popular for its late last call.
Dillon's	955 Boylston St	617-421-1818	Revisiting the Roaring '20s.
Kings	10 Scotia St	617-266-2695	Bowling, pool, TV sports. Goofy fun fun.
The Last Drop	421 Marlborough St	617-262-5555	Supposed latest last call in Boston.
Lir	903 Boylston St	617-778-0089	Upscale Irish. Large, handy for sports watchers.
Match	94 Massachusetts Ave	617-247-9922	More for cocktails than food. Stylish, DJ.
McGreevy's	911 Boylston St	617-262-0911	They remade the Foggy Goggle? Oh it's still an overpriced meat market. eh.
Our House East	52 Gainsborough St	617-236-1890	Branch of Allston college-kid hangout.
Pour House	907 Boylston St	617-236-1767	Wide beer selection, cool bartenders.
Sonsie	327 Newbury St	617-351-2500	People-watching mainstay. Nice French-doors street exposure.
TC's Lounge	1 Haviland St	617-247-8109	Dive for Berklee people and locals.
Top of the Hub	800 Boylston St	617-536-1775	Great view from the top of the Pru.
Wally's Café	427 Massachusetts Ave	617-828-1754	Cramped jazz landmark. For everyone at least once.

Arts & Entertainment · **Nightlife**

Map 6 · Back Bay (East) / South End (Upper)

Anchovies	433 Columbus Ave	617-266-5088	Easy-going neighborhood joint.
Champions	110 Huntington Ave	617-937-5658	Sports. Food wins no trophies.
City Bar	61 Exeter St	617-933-4800	At the Lenox Hotel.
Clery's	113 Dartmouth St	617-262-9874	Bar with food. Location is its best attribute.
Club Café	209 Columbus Ave	617-536-0966	Gay: restaurant in front, scoping in back.
Flashs	310 Stuart St	617-574-8888	Casual South End eatery and cocktail spot
Rattlesnake	384 Boylston St	617-859-8555	Hit the roof deck in the summer.
Rise	306 Stuart St	617-423-7473	For clubbing after 2 am. Arrive with a member.
Saint	90 Exeter St	617-236-1134	Nitery for aspiring Paris Hiltons.
Vox Populi	755 Boylston St	617-424-8300	Strangely soulless.

Map 7 · South End (Lower)

Beehive	541 Tremont St	617-423-0069	There's an old-timey, speakeasy feel to this place.
Delux Café	100 Chandler St	617-338-5258	Small, hip spot with good eats, music.
Eagle	520 Tremont St	617-542-4494	Casual gay local, mostly denim and leather.
Franklin Café	278 Shawmut Ave	617-350-0010	Mainly a restaurant, but a good bar choice too.
Pho Republique	1415 Washington St	617-262-0005	Fave of South End drinking set.

Map 8 · Charlestown

Goody Glovers	50 Salem St	617-367-6444	Irish drinks in a seas of Italian.
Sullivan's Pub	85 Main St	617-242-9515	Relaxed pub off of Thompson Square.
Tavern on the Water	1 Pier 6 at E 8th St	617-242-8040	Good on a warm afternoon. Skyline view.
Warren Tavern	2 Pleasant St	617-241-8142	One of Paul Revere's favorite watering holes.

Map 9 · East Boston

Kelly Square Pub	84 Bennington St	617-567-4627	Neighborhood local, try the ribs.
Trainor's Café	127 Maverick St	617-567-6995	Neighborhood local.

Map 10 · South Boston (West) / Fort Point

Atlantic Beer Garden	146 Seaport Blvd	617-357-8000	Financial District Happy Hour spot and weekend sports bar.
Blackthorn Pub	471 W Broadway	617-269-5510	Real Irish. Pours a mean Guinness.
The Cornerstone	16 W Broadway	617-269-9553	Broadway Square, erm, cornerstone. Parking in rear.
The Junction	110 Dorchester St	617-268-6429	Low-key neighborhood spot.
Lucky's	355 Congress St	617-357-5825	Well-liked retro cocktail lounge. Music most nights.
The Quiet Man	11 W Broadway	617-269-9878	Pub. Try the steak tips.
Shenanigans	332 W Broadway	617-269-9509	Popular watering hole.
Stadium	232 Old Colony Ave	617-269-5100	Two parts sports bar, one part dance club.

Map 11 · South Boston (East)

Boston Beer Garden	732 E Broadway	617-269-0990	Had a makeover recently. Long wine list, too.
Corner Tavern	645 E 2nd St	617-269-9891	Locals only.
Harpoon Brewery	306 Northern Ave	617-574-9551	Brewery tours, seasonal special events.
L Street Tavern	658 E 8th St	617-268-4335	No nonsense local. Appeared in Good Will Hunting.
Murphy's Law	837 Summer St	617-269-6667	Occasional live acoustic acts.
Playwright	658 E Broadway	617-269-2537	For socializing and television watching.

Map 12 · Newmarket / Andrew Square

Aces High	551 Dorchester Ave	617-269-7637	Check out their "new drinks and decor."
Dot Tavern	840 Dorchester Ave	617-288-6288	Neighborhood local.
Sports Connection Bar	560 Dorchester Ave	617-268-4119	Featuring "a big screen TV."

Map 13 · Roxbury

C&S Tavern	380 Warren St	617-442-7023	Neighborhood local.
El Mondonguito	221 Dudley St	617-522-3672	A decent dive bar.
Slade's	958 Tremont St	617-442-4600	Dancing, mostly R&B and hip-hop.

Map 14 · Jamaica Plain

Brendan Behan Pub	378 Centre St	617-522-5386	Well-liked Irish local. Relaxed atmosphere.
Costello's Tavern	723 Centre St	617-522-9263	Friendly JP tavern; decent food and darts.
Doyle's Café	3484 Washington St	617-524-2345	Trusty Irish landmark. Good grub and a mean Bloody Mary.
Drinking Fountain	3520 Washington St	617-522-3424	Locals bar. Cheap beer, pool in the back.
James's Gate	5 McBride St	617-983-2000	Order the mussels, drink the best Guinness, and sit by the fire on winter nights.
Jeanie Johnston Pub	144 South St	617-983-9432	Darts, karaoke, live music, local flavor.
Midway Café	3496 Washington St	617-524-9038	Local watering hole featuring a variety of live bands.
The Milky Way	284 Amory St	617-524-3740	Dance club-Chuck E Cheese hybrid.
Samuel Adams Brewery	30 Germania St	617-368-5080	Tours and samples.

Map 15 · Fenway (West) / Mission Hill

Baseball Tavern	1270 Boylston St	617-867-6526	Sports tavern with a focus on Fenway.
Church	69 Kilmarnock St	617-236-7600	Music, beer, and food—all in the shadow of Fenway.
Flann O'Brien's	1619 Tremont St	617-566-7744	Spirited Brigham Circle local.
Machine	1256 Boylston St	617-536-1950	Large gay club.
Punter's Pub	450 Huntington Ave	n/a	Student dive.
Ramrod	1254 Bolyston St	617-266-2986	Gay denim-and-leather crowd; various theme nights.

Map 16 · Kenmore Square / Brookline (East)

An Tua Nua	835 Beacon St	617-262-2121	Pub and dance club popular with twenty-somethings.
Audubon Circle	838 Beacon St	617-421-1910	Chill out with tasty bar food.
Bill's Bar and Lounge	5 1/2 Lansdowne St	617-421-9678	Predominantly student crowd. Mostly rock.
Cask 'n' Flagon	62 Brookline Ave	617-536-4840	Just behind the Green Monster. Nothing special.
The Dugout	722 Commonwealth Ave	617-247-8656	Babe Ruth's basement dive bar of choice.
Embassy	36 Lansdowne St	617-536-2100	Dress to impress. Mostly hip-hop.
Foundation Lounge	500 Commonwealth Ave	617-859-9900	For sake connoisseurs.
Game On!	82 Lansdowne St	617-351-7001	Yet another sports bar near Fenway.
Lucky Strike Lanes	145 Ipswich St	617-437-0300	Über gaming and lounge establishment.
The Modern	36 Lansdowne St	617-536-2100	Dress to impress.
PJ Kilroy's Pub	822 Beacon St	617-266-3986	Load up on cheap beer before a Sox game.
Tequila Rain	3 Lansdowne St	617-437-0300	Woooo! Woooo!
Who's on First?	19 Yawkey Wy	617-247-3353	Fun Fenway dive.

Map 17 · Coolidge Corner / Brookline Hills

Matt Murphy's Pub	14 Harvard St	617-232-0188	Popular Irish pub. Good food and music.
The Publick House	1648 Beacon St	617-277-2880	Focus here is on the beers.
Washington Square Tavern	714 Washington St	617-232-8989	Pub/restaurant with slightly overpriced food.

Map 18 · Brighton

Cityside Bar & Grill	1960 Beacon St	617-566-1002	Hit the patio if it's nice outside.
Green Briar	304 Washington St	617-789-4100	Pub with frequent live rock.
Irish Village	224 Market St	617-787-5427	Popular, relaxed local.
Joey's	416 Market St	617-254-9381	Don't ask for Joey.
The Last Drop	596 Washington St	617-787-1111	Sibling of Marlborough Street bar.
Mary Ann's	1937 Beacon St	n/a	BC standout dump.
Roggie's	356 Chestnut Hill Ave	617-566-1880	52 beers, televised soccer.
Soho	386 Market St	617-562-6000	Sleek, large dining spot-cum-nightclub.

Map 19 · Allston (South) / Brookline (North)

Avenue Bar & Grille	1249 Commonwealth Ave	617-782-9508	Cheap drafts and college kids.
Big City	138 Brighton Ave	617-782-2020	For beer and pool, not food and service.
Bus Stop Pub	252 Western Ave	617-254-4086	Townie bar with sports.
Common Ground	85 Harvard Ave	617-783-2071	Defending Allston.
District Restaurant & Lounge	180 Lincoln St	617-426-0180	Dance, drink, and be seen at this trendy spot.
Great Scott	1222 Commonwealth Ave	617-566-9014	Loud, live music in a small, dark place.
Harper's Ferry	156 Brighton Ave	617-254-9743	Good place for live, unthreatening rock and blues.
Harry's Bar & Grill	1430 Commonwealth Ave	617-738-9990	Casual and roomy, with a mostly neighborhood crowd.
Joshua Tree	1316 Commonwealth Ave	617-566-6699	Red lights, leather seats…yawn.
The Kells	161 Brighton Ave	617-782-9082	Now with revamped Asia-by-way-of-Ikea theme.
Model Café	7 N Beacon St	617-254-9365	Allston staple, with all the usual suspects.
O'Brien's	3 Harvard Ave	617-782-6245	Live rock, mostly local acts.

Our House	1277 Commonwealth Ave	617-782-3228	So mellow that patrons fall asleep on the couches.
Paradise Rock Club & Lounge	967 Commonwealth Ave	617-562-8814	Major rock acts. Tasty food and smaller bands in Lounge.
Scullers Jazz Club	400 Soldiers Field Rd	617-562-4111	Live jazz most nights. In the Doubletree.
Silhouette Lounge	200 Brighton Ave	617-254-9306	A room full of darts and drunks.
Sports Depot	353 Cambridge St	617-783-2300	Good choice for March Madness drinking.
Sunset Grill & Tap	130 Brighton Ave	617-254-1331	Hundreds of beers to choose from, food until 1 am.
T's Pub	973 Commonwealth Ave	617-254-0807	An institution; free champagne on your birthday.
White Horse Tavern	116 Brighton Ave	617-254-6633	Always hopping, great for sports.
Wonder Bar	186 Harvard Ave	617-351-2665	Wannabe Soho, patronized by wannabe yups.

Map 20 · Harvard Square / Allston (North)

Cambridge Common	1667 Massachusetts Ave	617-547-1228	Local restaurant hang above the Lizard.
Charlie's Kitchen	10 Eliot St	617-492-9646	Old School by the old school. Great jukebox.
Club Passim	47 Palmer St	617-492-7679	Folk singer-songwriter landmark and vegetarian restaurant.
The Comedy Studio	1238 Massachusetts Ave	617-661-6507	A few scorpion bowls and you'll laugh at anything.
Grendel's Den	89 Winthrop St	617-491-1050	Harvard Square mainstay.
Hong Kong Lounge	1238 Massachusetts Ave	617-864-5311	The Scorpion Bowls are a Harvard Square tradition.
John Harvard's Brew House	33 Dunster St	617-868-3585	Large and loud, good for crowds.
Lizard Lounge	1667 Massachusetts Ave	617-547-0759	Great spot to kick back to live music.
Noir	1 Bennett St	617-661-8010	More pretentious than sophisticated.
Redline	59 JFK St	617-491-9851	A decent spot, but too often cramped.
Regattabar	1 Bennett St	617-661-5000	Serious jazz club.
Shay's Lounge	58 JFK St	617-864-9161	Lo-fi wine bar and pub with outdoor seating.
Temple Bar	1688 Massachusetts Ave	617-547-5055	Popular and impressed with itself.
Tommy Doyle's	96 Winthrop St	617-864-0655	Two-story Harvard hangout.
West Side Lounge	1680 Massachusetts Ave	617-441-5566	For those who find Temple Bar too pretentious.

Map 22 · North Cambridge / West Somerville

The Burren	247 Elm St	617-776-6896	Well-known Irish; live music.
Diva Lounge	246 Elm St	617-629-4963	Sprung from the loins of adjacent Diva Restaurant.
Johnny D's Uptown	17 Holland St	617-776-2004	Music nightly, wide variety.
PJ Ryan's	239 Holland St	617-625-8200	Brick and beer bar.
Redbones	55 Chester St	617-628-2200	Don't dig on swine? Then come spin the beer wheel.
Sligo Pub	237A Elm St	617-625-4477	A landmark of sorts.
Somerville Theatre	55 Davis Sq	617-625-5700	Occasional live music.

Map 23 · Central Somerville / Porter Square

Christopher's	1920 Massachusetts Ave	617-876-9180	Large selection of drafts, friendly staff, warm food.
Newtowne Grille	1945 Massachusetts Ave	617-661-0706	Divey, but lively.
Olde Magoun Saloon	518 Medford St	617-776-2600	Nicer than it looks neighborhood favorite with good beer and Sox games
On the Hill Tavern	499 Broadway	617-629-5302	DJs Thursday through Saturdays.
Samba Bar & Grill	608 Somerville Ave	617-718-9177	Brazilian vibe.
Toad	1912 Massachusetts Ave	617-497-4950	Cramped but fun. Live music nightly.

Map 24 · Winter Hill / Union Square

11th Chapter Saloon	366 Somerville Ave	n/a	Hard to find, tiny corner bar.
The Independent	75 Union Sq	617-440-6022	Irish pub on one side, upscale bar on the other.
Khoury's State Spa	118 Broadway	617-776-0571	Large, easy-going joint. Pool, darts.
PA's Lounge	345 Somerville Ave	617-776-1557	Cool spot for live, modern rock.
Sally O'Brien's	335 Somerville Ave	617-666-3589	Local bands, local sports, decent pub food.
Toast	70 Union Sq	617-623-9211	Basement lounge. DJs most nights.

Map 25 · East Somerville / Sullivan Square

Good Time Emporium	30 Assembly Square Dr	617-628-5559	Enormous. TVs, arcade games, batting cage, etc.
Night Games	30 Washington St	617-628-1000	Party at the Holiday Inn, yo!

Map 26 · East Cambridge / Kendall Square / MIT

Cambridge Brewing Company	One Kendall Sq, Bldg 100	617-494-1994	Decent microbrews. Some outdoor seating.
Flat Top Johnny's	One Kendall Sq, Bldg 200	617-494-9565	Cambridge's best large pool hall.
Pugliese's	635 Cambridge St	617-491-9616	Cambridge's oldest family-owned bar.

Map 27 • Central Square / Cambridgeport

All Asia	334 Massachusetts Ave	617-497-1544	Restaurant squeezes in live bands most nights.
Cantab Lounge	738 Massachusetts Ave	617-354-2685	Legendary quasi-dive. Little Joe Cook still plays.
The Cellar	991 Massachusetts Ave	617-876-2580	Stuck between Central and Harvard? Here you go.
Enormous Room	567 Massachusetts Ave	617-491-5550	Trendy couch lounge with tasty bar food.
The Field	20 Prospect St	617-354-7345	Dark and gritty Irish pub.
The Middle East	472 Massachusetts Ave	617-864-3278	Venerable venue that gets high-profile music bookings.
Middlesex	315 Massachusetts Ave	617-868-6739	Rotating DJ line-up, fun modular seating.
Miracle of Science	321 Massachusetts Ave	617-868-2866	Energetic mainstay, always playing cool music.
People's Republik	880 Massachusetts Ave	617-492-8632	Toast 'til 2:00.
Phoenix Landing	512 Massachusetts Ave	617-576-6260	Irish pub with club music every night.
Plough & Stars	912 Massachusetts Ave	617-441-3455	Well-loved local. Frequent live music.
River Gods	125 River St	617-576-1881	Hipster house. DJs spin frequently.
TT the Bear's Place	10 Brookline St	617-492-2327	Live rock nightly. Showcases local bands.
Western Front	343 Western Ave	617-492-7772	Mostly reggae and world, occasional hip-hop.

Map 28 • Inman Square

Abbey Lounge	3 Beacon St		Boston's "best dive bar"? You decide. Music nightly.
Atwood's Tavern	877 Cambridge St	617-864-2792	Food 'til late and live local music.
Bukowski's	1281 Cambridge St	617-497-7077	100+ beers. More chill than its Boston brother.
The Druid	1357 Cambridge St	617-497-0965	Well-liked Irish pub.
Ryles Jazz Club	212 Hampshire St	617-876-9330	Two-level club with jazz, world, Latin.
Thirsty Scholar Pub	70 Beacon St	617-497-2294	Laid-back neighborhood local. Good food, too.

Map 30 • Roslindale

JJ Foley's Fireside Tavern	30 Hyde Park Ave	617-338-7713	A great old man bar that is slowly being taken over by the young'uns

Map 32 • Dorchester (East)

Banshee	934 Dorchester Ave	617-436-9747	Irish pub.
Boston Bowl	820 Morrissey Blvd	617-825-3800	Open 24 Hours. Family fun all night long.
dBar	1236 Dorchester Ave	617-265-4490	Hip, gay bar. Food till 10pm, then the dancing starts.
Eire Pub	795 Adams St	617-436-8974	Politicians and sports fans welcome.
Harp & Bard	1099 Dorchester Ave	617-265-2893	Patio makes this a summertime Irish standout.

Map 32 • Dorchester (East)

Townsend's Restaurant	81 Fairmount Ave	617-333-0306	Draft beer to write home about.

It's difficult to typecast Boston shoppers. This is due in part to the varied levels of crazy inhabiting this place—ranging from the Burberry-sporting, Beacon Hill-dwelling elite to the thrift shop-shopping Cambridge funksters in paint splattered Chuck Taylors. The city's climate (eleven months of Winter and 4 weeks of Spring, Summer, and Fall) compel most Bostonians to spend their weekends popping into climate controlled shops that range from uncomfortably exclusive to quietly quaint to downright weird. In addition to the extreme consumerist lifestyle of many of its dwellers, the city also has its fair share of psychotic, year-round outdoor athletes, for whom purveyors of gear appear throughout the city. The fleet of moving trucks clogging this college town on the first of every month from March through October keeps the furniture-and-houseware hawkers in business. Despite the few malls that have weaseled their way onto the scene, the dependable disparity and constant movement of the city results in a throbbing, colorful, and some-times shocking mass of consumers.

Clothing: New, Used & Vintage

For the label checking, what-do-you-drive-yuppies in our midst, the Boston shopping scene certainly delivers. Start in the Back Bay on Newbury Street at **Louis Boston (Map 6)** then head across the street to **Brooks Brothers (Map 6)** and similar venues. More reasonably priced but still plenty preppy is **Eddie Bauer (Map 3)** downtown. On the other side of the coin, Boston has a ton to offer those seeking funkier duds—you just need to know where to look. The **Garment District (Map 28)** in Cambridge is a gargantuan thrift/vintage store with every-thing from '60s sweaters to contemporary second-hand treasures—contrary to New York, it's a store, not a neighborhood. Poke around the North End's tiny shops and you'll eventually stumble onto the treasures to be found in **Karma (Map 2)**. **Poor Little Rich Girl (Map 2)** in Davis Square has a great selection of vintage duds. Even upscale Newbury Street has its share of vintage chic—the **Army Barracks (Map 5)** is an old fave. And Boston is really a walking city (you know, when it's not hailing), so outfit your feet with shoes from **Berks (Map 20)**, **The Tannery (Map 20)** in Back Bay and Harvard Square, or **DSW (Map 2)** in Downtown Crossing.

For the Home/Apartment/Dorm

Though driving through Brookline and Beacon Hill on September 2—after most apartments have been vacated, their perfectly usable furniture left on the curb—is a fabulous way to outfit your own digs, you may wish to take a gander at the furniture 'n' stuff offered throughout a city that's constantly turning over. If nothing else, you won't have to worry about that greenish blue stain on the free chair from the corner. Despite the terrific selection and prices offered by the obvious **Crate and Barrel (Map 6, 20)**, beware the slalom of newly-engaged couples registering for gifts. **Bowl and Board (Map 17)** is similar, but more diverse as far as neat little trinkets for every room in the home. Crowded, annoying, one-stop house shopping can be achieved at the wicked huge **Bed Bath & Beyond (Map 16)** in Kenmore. **Economy Hardware (Map 5, 16, 19, 20)** is always a safe—albeit pricey—bet for furniture, gadgets, even paint (oh, and hardware). Check out counter-intuitive spots like **Urban Outfitters (Map 20, 5)** and **Absolutely Fabulous (Map 28)** for finishing touches like pretty pillows, cool lamps, and funky artwork. Antique hunters will be kept happy at **Cambridge Antique Market's (Map 26)** five floors of yesteryear.

Sports

As the city that's most associated with a certain 26.2 mile race, Boston is well equipped to provide you with whatever you need to get your heart rate pumping. **Marathon Sports (Map 17)** in Brookline lets you test drive their sneakers on the sidewalk and makes sure you leave with exactly the right pair. For those runners who'd like to get advice (and maybe a pair of kicks) from a four time Marathon winner—check out Faneuil Hall for **Bill Rodgers Running Center (Map 2)**. What-ever the season, you can find what you're looking for at **City Sports (Map 3, 6, 19, 20, 23)**. Boston's also a biker city (think pedals, not crotchrockets). Riders can get tune-ups, gear, and honest advice at **International Bicycle Center (Map 19)**. **REI (Map 16)** is also good for bikes along with anything you might need for a cliff-hangin' good time.

Computing Machines

Thanks to its many universities, hospitals, and research facilities, Boston is awash with computer-loving dweebs. **Micro Center (Map 27)** is swarmed on the weekends. Two centrally located **Best Buys (Map 16, 26)** feature their usual merchandise and crowds. The PC-user-repellant **Apple Store (Map 26)** in the Cambridgeside Galleria is one stylin' geek boutique only matched by the three-story **Apple Store (Map 6)** that sits like a see through shrine to Geekdom on Boylston Street.

Music Maniacs

The rise of the iPod has given Bostonians yet another excuse to keep eyes forward and not interact with fellow human beings that dare cross their path. But there are still plenty of options for those in search of disks and vinyl. **Newbury Comics (Map 2, 5, 20, 21)** delivers on their offer of "a wicked good time" with not only music, but movies, novelties, and general craziness. For those in search of vinyl, vintage, and generally hard-to-find tunes, stroll along Mass Ave in Cambridge to find **Cheapo Records (Map 27)**, **Massive Records (Map 27)**, **Stereo Jack's (Map 20)**, and a number of others. Comm Ave near BU and Harvard Square are also places to troll for rare stuff with stores like **In Your Ear (Map 19)**, **Nuggets (Map 16)**, and **Planet Records (Map 20)**. If you're one of the real out there cats, looking for the most random of random discs, try **Weirdo Records (Map 27)** in Central Square for 100% truth in advertising.

Foodie Fanatics

You literally cannot go wrong once you set foot in the North End. **Mike's Pastry (Map 2)**, **Modern Pastry (Map 2)**, and the 24-7 **Bova's Bakery (Map 2)** are just three of about a dozen places to try for sweet goodies. For savory Italian treats try **Salumeria Italiana (Map 2)** or **Salumeria Toscana (Map 2)**. Equally tempting treats can be found at **Athan's Bakery (Map 17)** in Brookline **or Cremaldi's (Map 27)** and **Central Bakery (Map 28)** in Cambridge. If ever you lived abroad and are feeling nostalgic, **Cardullo's (Map 20)** in Harvard Square is a fun place to grab imported anything, from Branston Pickles to real Italian gelato. For ice cream, **Christina's Homemade (Map 28)** in Inman Square is a favorite. For a hot fudge sundae you can't beat **Herrell's (Map 20)**. Other popular spots also include **JP Licks (Maps 5, 14)**, **Toscanini's (Map 27)**, and **Emack & Bolio's (Maps 5, 17, 30)**, all with lines out the door in warmer months. **Lionette's (Map 7)** in the South End, well known for their local, grass-fed meats, also carries a mix of specialty and standard items, sandwiches, prepared foods, and fresh bread. For the gourmet addicts, there's nothing like the cheese counter at **Formaggio (Map 7)** to give you the artisan deliciousness you've been craving.

Malls and 'hoods

Boston has seemingly avoided the typical suburban oasis of a Mall more than other cities, but it does it one better by providing several neighborhood locations where you can store hop, grab a bite to chow on, and maybe people watch simultaneously, with real food, not food court swill. Downtown Cross-ing is a high-energy center of rabid consumerism, very convenient to the T, and boasting the gigantic department store **Macy's (Maps 3, 19)** (which has recently gobbled up the beloved Filene's), discount stores (**Marshall's (Maps 3, 6, 12), TJ Maxx (Map 3)**) and other joints like **H&M (Map 3)** where you can get lost for hours. Clothes aren't the only thing for which to shop here—there are jewelers, shoe stores, and street vendors and performers. It's also within walking distance of **Faneuil Hall Market Place (Map 2)**. One could easily spend a solid afternoon wandering around Harvard Square. **Newbury Comics (Map 20)** and **Little Tibet (Map 20)** are great for gift shopping (for yourself or anyone else), and **Urban Outfitters (Map 20)** always has the latest in hipster apparel and

home decor. Stop for a snack at **Cardullo's (Map 20)**, or recharge at **Tealuxe (Map 20)**, and while you're sipping or munching, flip through a book at the **Coop (Map 20)** or **Harvard Book Store (Map 20)**. Walk the length of **Newbury Street (Map 5)**, and you'll find everything from bookstores (**Tri-dent Booksellers and Café (Map 5)** is a must) to house stuff (**Kitchen Arts (Map 6)**) to ice cream (**Emack & Bolio's (Map 5)**) to art (**International Poster Gallery (Map 6)**), plus clothes and clothes and clothes. Though most of what's found on Newbury is decidedly pricey, things do get more reasonable as you get closer to Mass Ave. Boylston Street (Map 6) runs parallel to Newbury with offerings like **Anthropologie (Map 6), City Sports (Maps 3, 6, 19, 20, 23), Louis Boston (Map 6)**, and **Shreve, Crump & Low (Map 6)**. And yes, as much as we hate to admit it, Boston does have a few "malls"—though they are well camouflaged and the word "mall" does not actually appear in their titles. **The Shops at Prudential Center (Map 5)** in-clude **Sephora (Map 5), Lord & Taylor (Map 6)**, and several others and also cuts through to the even higher-end **Copley Place (Map 6)** where those of you that have the cash can drop quite a load of it at **Barneys New York (Map 6)**. **The Cambridge Side Galleria (Map 26)** is a multi-leveled mecca where MIT kids, Biotech execs, and European tourists flock to the **Apple Store (Map 26)** to satisfy their Mac addictions.

Map 1 • Beacon Hill / West End

Black Ink	101 Charles St	617-723-3883	Amusing tchotches, quirky gifts, purty paper.
DeLuca's Market	11 Charles St	617-523-4343	Good deli, pricey fruit, wine, and beer downstairs.
Eugene Galleries	76 Charles St	617-227-3062	A treasure chest of old maps, prints, books.
The Flat of the Hill	60 Charles St	617-619-9977	Quirky gifts. Lots of pink.
Good	88 Charles St	617-722-9200	Lovely gifts.
Hilton's Tent City	272 Friend St	617-227-9242	Four floors of outdoors needs since 1947.
Moxie	51 Charles St	617-557-9991	Shoes, bags, accessories.
The Red Wagon	69 Charles St	617-523-9402	Pricey kids' clothes and toys.
Savenor's Market	160 Charles St	617-723-6328	For a variety of gourmet goodies.
Wish	49 Charles St	617-227-4441	Trendy, upscale women's clothing and accessories.

Map 2 • North End / Faneuil Hall

Boston Halal Meat Market	114 Blackstone St	617-722-9969	Butcher. Good quality.
Bova's Bakery	134 Salem St	617-523-5601	Pastries, also deli and pizza. Open 24 hours.
Brooks Brothers	75 State St	617-261-9990	Branch of venerable Back Bay clothier.
Dairy Fresh Candies	57 Salem St	617-742-2639	Big selection of candy imported from Italy.
De Pasquale Homemade Pasta Shoppe	66 Cross St	617-248-9269	It's a homemade a pasta from a da North End!
Fresh Cheese	81 Endicott St	617-570-0007	Also sells dozens of oils and vinegars.
Green Cross Pharmacy	393 Hanover St	617-227-3728	Old-world pharmacy. Also sells Italian sundries.
Holbrows Flowers	100 City Hall Plz	617-227-8057	Convenient to Government Center T stop.
Karma	26 Prince St	617-723-8338	Upscale consignment shop.
Maria's Pastry Shop	46 Cross St	617-523-1196	Sweet tooth heaven.
Mike's Pastry	300 Hanover St	617-742-3050	The most famous of the North End Italian bakeries.
Modern Pastry	257 Hanover St	617-523-3783	Boston's best cannoli? You decide.
Monica's Salumeria	130 Salem St	617-742-4101	Homemade takeout and Italian groceries.
Newbury Comics	1 Washington Mall	617-248-9992	Downtown location of successful music/novelties chain.
Salumeria Italiana	151 Richmond St	617-523-8743	Well-regarded Italian specialties store.
Salumeria Toscana	272 Hanover St	617-720-4243	Imported Italian specialties, heat-and-serve meals.
Stanza dei Sigari	292 Hanover St	617-227-0295	17-year-olds take note: hookahs available.
Staples	25 Court St	617-367-1147	Printer ink and other more reasonably priced supplies.
Twilight	12 Fleet St	617-523-8008	This place to have every undergarment a woman needs.

Map 3 • Downtown Crossing / Park Square / Bay Village

Beacon Hill Skate Shop	135 Charles St S	617-482-7400	Rentals available. Also has hockey gear.
Borders	10 School St	617-557-7188	All you've come to expect, plus sidewalk sales.
Bromfield Camera & Video	10 Bromfield St	617-426-5230	Decent selection of new and used cameras.
City Antiques	362 Tremont St	617-423-7600	Used furniture and furnishings.
City Sports	11 Bromfield St	617-423-2015	Covers all the basics in apparel and equipment.
DSW	385 Washington St	617-556-0052	Oodles and oodles of sho[odl]es.
Eddie Bauer Outlet	500 Washington St	617-423-4722	Good deals on quality clothes.
H&M	350 Washington St	617-482-7001	Disposable chic from Swedish mega-merchant.
Lambert's	Washington St & Summer St	N/A	Fruit and veggie stand in the heart of Downtown Crossing.

LJ Peretti	2 1/2 Park Sq	617-482-0218	Oldest family-run tobacconist in the country.
Macy's	450 Washington St	617-357-3000	Once Jordan Marsh. Big outdoor "holiday" tree in December.
Marshall's	350 Washington St	617-338-6205	Discount clothing and other stuff.
Roche-Bobois	2 Avery St	617-742-9611	Très trendy interior design and furnishings.
Staples	25 Winter St	617-426-2290	Smaller than the Court Street branch.
TJ Maxx	350 Washington St	617-695-2424	Put on your bargain-hunting hat. Off-price apparel and housewares.
Windsor Buttons	35 Temple Pl	617-482-4969	A crafter's delight. And buttons for every mood.

Map 4 • Financial District / Chinatown

| Anna's Dessert House | 66 Harrison Ave | 617-542-7903 | One of Chinatown's newer bakery/dessert shops. |

Map 5 • Back Bay (West) / Fenway (East)

Army Barracks	328 Newbury St	617-437-1657	Surplus store. Knives, canteens, T-shirts, and all things cammo.
Back Bay Bicycle	366 Commonwealth Ave	617-247-2336	Accurately monikered.
Bôn Bôn	197 Massachusetts Ave	617-904-0770	Gorge yourself on amazing gelato and other sweet treats.
The Compleat Strategist	201 Massachusetts Ave	617-267-2451	Gaming paraphernalia.
Daddy's Junky Music	159 Massachusetts Ave	617-247-0909	Comprehensive store serving the Berklee community.
Deluca's Market	239 Newbury St	617-262-5990	Good deli, pricey fruit, wine, and beer downstairs.
Economy Hardware	219 Massachusetts Ave	617-536-4280	Hardware, household needs, cheap furniture. Very popular.
Emack & Bolio's	290 Newbury St	617-536-7127	Innovative ice cream flavors.
Firefly Jewelry & Gifts	270 Newbury St	617-375-5885	Unique jewelry, friendly service.
John Fluevog	302 Newbury St	617-266-1079	Indulge the hipster in you with these funky shoes.
Johnny Cupcakes	279 Newbury St	617-375-0100	Trendy T-shirts. Not cupcakes.
Johnson Artist Materials	355 Newbury St	617-536-4065	Tony. Also a selection of stationery.
J.P. Licks	352 Newbury St	617-236-1666	Local ice cream chain. Try the warm peanut butter topping.
Luna Boston	286 Newbury St	866-910-3902	Lotsa handbags.
Matsu	259 Newbury St	617-266-9707	Inviting boutique, unusual clothing and accessories.
Newbury Comics	332 Newbury St	617-236-4930	Now featuring a large DVD section.
Orpheus	362 Commonwealth Ave	617-247-7200	Focusing on classical music.
Sephora	800 Boylston St	617-262-4200	A makeup wonderland—play before you buy.
Snow-N-Nasty	90 Massachusetts Ave	617-266-7171	Saucy cakes for all (adult) occasions.
Trident Booksellers & Café	338 Newbury St	617-267-8688	Busy, independent bookstore/cafe with tons of magazines.
Urban Outfitters	361 Newbury St	617-236-0088	Funky clothes, apartment stuff and novelties.
Utrecht Art Supply Center	333 Massachusetts Ave	617-262-4948	Serious art store near Symphony Hall.

Map 6 • Back Bay (East) / South End (Upper)

All Things Chocolate	31 St James Ave	617-423-9400	For that funny valentine of yours.
Amazing Express	57 Stuart St	617-338-1252	Sex; a vestige of the erstwhile Combat Zone.
Anthropologie	799 Boylston St	617-262-0545	Clothes, accessories and colorful objets d'home.
Barneys New York	100 Huntington Ave	617-385-3300	For those of you with lots of disposable income.
Best of Scotland	115 Newbury St Ste 202	617-536-3048	Cashmere outlet from the olde country.
Brooks Brothers	46 Newbury St	617-267-2600	Flagship store of company operating since 1818.
City Sports	480 Boylston St	617-267-3900	Covers all the basics in apparel and equipment.
Crate & Barrel	777 Boylston St	617-262-8700	Back Bay location of Chicago behemoth.
First Act Guitar Studio	745 Boylston St	617-226-7899	Guitars made, guitars played, in-store concerts.
Hempest	207 Newbury St	617-421-9944	Don't ask if they sell screens.
International Poster Gallery	205 Newbury St	617-375-0076	Prints and posters from around the world.
Kitchen Arts	161 Newbury St	617-266-8701	Broad range of kitchen needs for the serious cook, and the dabbler.
Lindt Master Chocolatier	704 Boylston St	617-236-0571	Nifty gifts for your Swiss miss.
Lord & Taylor	760 Boylston St	617-262-6000	Featuring new façade.
Louis Boston	234 Berkeley St	617-262-6100	High-end men's and women's designer clothing.
Luna Boston	205 Newbury St	866-910-3900	Lotsa handbags.
Lush	166 Newbury St	617-375-5874	British cosmetics merchant.
Marc Jacobs	81 Newbury St	617-425-0707	Will he make it in fashion-challenged Boston?
Marshall's	500 Newbury St	617-262-6066	Discount clothing and other stuff.
Neiman Marcus	5 Copley Pl	617-536-3660	Needless Markup?
O & Co.	161 Newbury St	617-859-8841	Worship at the wall of oil.
Paper Source	338 Boylston St	617-536-3444	DIY paper crafts and quirky gifts.
Saks Fifth Avenue	1 Ring Rd	617-262-8500	A shopping experience.
Second Time Around	176 Newbury St	617-247-3504	Pre-owned chic.
Shreve, Crump & Low	440 Boylston St	617-267-9100	Boston jewelers since 1796.
Stil	170 Newbury St	617-859-7845	Au courant clothes and accessories.
Teuscher Chocolates	230 Newbury St	617-536-1922	For the Swiss chocoholic in you.

Map 7 • South End (Lower)

Aunt Sadie's	18 Union Park St	617-357-7117	Fabulous candles, other gifts.
Bobby from Boston	19 Thayer St	617-423-9299	Vintage clothing.
Brix Wine Shop	1284 Washington St	617-542-2749	Upscale wine shop.
The Butcher Shop	552 Tremont St	617-423-4800	Neighborhood meat shop. Also a wine bar serving specialties.
Community Bicycle Supply	496 Tremont St	617-542-8623	South End bike shop.
Ilex	73 Berkeley St	617-422-0300	Florist.
Lekker	1317 Washington St	617-542-6464	Unique, modern home furnishings.

Arts & Entertainment · **Shopping**

Map 7 · South End (Lower)—*continued*

Lionette's	577 Tremont St	617-778-0360	Food shop associated with Garden of Eden.
Motley	623 Tremont St	617-247-6969	Clothes and weird stuff you didn't know you couldn't live without.
Picco	513 Tremont St	617-927-0066	Ice cream handy to the BCA.
Posh	557 Tremont St	617-437-1970	Gifts, home furnishings and accessories.
South End Buttery	314 Shawmut Ave	617-482-1015	Churning out the treats.
South End Formaggio	268 Shawmut Ave	617-350-6996	Cheese, cured meats, dry goods, and wine.
Uniform	511 Tremont St	617-247-2360	Top clothes for lads.
Urban Living Studio	58 Clarendon St	617-247-8150	Cheery home accessories store.

Map 8 · Charlestown

A Wild Flower	73 Main St	617-242-4214	Florist.
Bunker Hill Florist	1 Thompson Sq	617-242-2124	Florist.
Doherty's Flowers	223 Main St	617-242-1300	Main Street florist.
The Joy of Old	85A Warren St	617-242-6066	Coming soon: "The Joy of Gay Old."
Serenade Chocolates	5 Harvard Sq	617-739-0795	Tastes of Vienna.

Map 9 · East Boston

Brazilian Soccer House	110 Meridian St	617-569-1164	The place to get your soccer kit.
Globos y Fiesta	52A Bennington St	617-569-4908	Order your piñatas here.
Lilly's Flower Shop	512 Saratoga St	617-567-5177	Day Square florist.
Lolly's Bakery	158 Bennington St	617-567-9461	Quality pañeria.
Studium Spanish Bookstore	268 Bennington St	617-569-1253	Los libros en Español.

Map 10 · South Boston (West) / Fort Point

Bob's Your Uncle	25 Channel Center St	617-670-3782	A hipster's wet dream for apartment and apartment decoration.
Machine Age	645 Summer St	617-464-0099	Modern furniture in a huge space.
Scooters Go Green	220 Old Colony Ave	617-269-0050	Want to save the earth and don't mind looking like a dork? Buy a scooter!

Map 11 · South Boston (East)

EP Levine	23 Drydock Ave	617-951-1499	High-end photo shop.
Ku De Ta	663 E Broadway	617-269-0008	A slice of Newbury St prices, in Southie.
Miller's Market	336 K St	617-268-2526	Apparently, the coldest beer in town.
Stapleton Floral	635 E Broadway	617-269-7271	Florist.

Map 12 · Newmarket / Andrew Square

Home Depot	5 Allstate Rd	617-442-6110	Got wood?
Marshall's	8D Allstate Rd	617-442-5050	Discount clothing and other stuff.

Map 13 · Roxbury

Bikes Not Bombs	18 Bartlett St	617-522-0226	Shop for bikes and be socially responsible.

Map 14 · Jamaica Plain

Boing! JP's Toy Shop	729 Centre St	877-264-6400	Friendly toy shop.
Boomerangs	716 Centre St	617-524-5120	Used clothing and housewares.
Canto 6	3346 Washington St	617-983-8688	Baked goodies and a good cup of joe.
City Feed and Supply	66 Boylston St	617-524-1657	Popular neighborhood grocery, meeting spot.
Eye Q Optical	7 Pond St	617-983-3937	Designer eyeglasses.
Fat Ram's Pumpkin Tattoo	380 Centre St	617-522-6444	Skilled ink artists with degrees in fine art.
Ferris Wheels Bicycle Shop	66 South St	617-522-7082	JP bike shop.
Fire Opal	683 Centre St	617-524-0262	Upscale craft gallery.
Gadgets	671 Centre St	617-524-6800	Kitchen stuff, mostly.
Hatched Boston	5 Green St	617-524-5402	Small boutique specializing in organic clothing for little ones.
Honeyspot	48 South St	617-524-2444	Shop for mom, your hipster cousin, and yourself.
J.P. Licks	659 Centre St	617-524-2020	Popular ice cream shop.
Petal & Leaf	48 South St	617-524-2227	Friendly staff, fun gifts, and fresh flowers.
Salmagundi	765 Centre St	617-522-5047	Check out the coolest selection in the city.

Map 16 · Kenmore Square / Brookline (East)

Bed Bath & Beyond	401 Park Dr	617-536-1090	For when holes are growing in your towels.
Best Buy	401 Park Dr	617-424-7900	Awful, annoying electronics retailer.
Blick Art Materials	401 Park Dr	617-247-3322	Art-supply megashop.
Boston Bicycle	842 Beacon St	617-236-0752	Selection geared toward messengers, plenty of fixies.
Economy Hardware	1012 Beacon St	617-277-8811	Hardware, household needs, cheap furniture. Very popular.

Guitar Center	750 Commonwealth Ave	617-738-5958	Also has drums, keys, etc.
Hunt's Photo and Video	520 Commonwealth Ave	617-778-2222	Good selection of used cameras.
Japonaise Bakery	1020 Beacon St	617-566-7730	Mmm...curry donut.
Jean Therapy	524 Commonwealth St	617-266-6555	One stop shopping for designer jeans.
Nantucket Natural Oils	508 Commonwealth Ave	617-437-9800	Aromatherapy and perfumes.
Nuggets	486 Commonwealth Ave	617-536-0679	Sells only used recordings. Quite fun to browse.
REI	401 Park Dr	617-236-0746	Seattle co-op for the gearhead.
Ski Market	860 Commonwealth Ave	617-731-6100	Skis or bicycles depending on the season.
University Computers	533 Commonwealth Ave	617-353-1800	BU store; ask about student discounts.

Map 17 • Coolidge Corner / Brookline Hills

Athan's Bakery	1621 Beacon St	617-734-7028	Exquisite baked goods, chocolates, gelato, and espresso.
EC Florist & Gifts	224 Washington St	617-232-3693	Florist.
Emack & Bolio's	1663 Beacon St	617-731-6256	Innovative ice cream flavors.
Eureka Puzzles	1349 Beacon St	617-738-7352	Old-timey gamers' heaven.
Madras Masala	191 Harvard St	617-566-9943	Indian Grocery store with a good selection of chutneys and prepared food.
Marathon Sports	1638 Beacon St	617-735-9373	Run! Run! Run!
Paper Source	1361 Beacon St	617-264-2800	DIY paper crafts and quirky gifts.
Party Favors	1356 Beacon St	617-566-3330	Satisfies your sweet tooth and your inner party animal.
Petropol	1428 Beacon St	617-232-8820	Russian books and cds.
Pier 1 Imports	1351 Beacon St	617-232-9627	Brought to you by Fat Actress Kirstie Alley.
Russian Village	1659 Beacon St	617-731-2023	Foodstuffs, deli, CDs/videos.
Ten Thousand Villages	226 Harvard St	617-277-7700	Free-trade, handmade crafts from around the world.
Wild Goose Chase	1431 Beacon St	617-738-8020	Crafts, gifts. A flea market, Brookline-style.

Map 18 • Brighton

Amanda's Flowers	347 Washington St	617-782-0686	Florist.
CompUSA	205 Market St	617-783-1900	Has the basics, but service could be sharper.
New Balance Factory Store	40 Life St	877-623-7867	Running gear for cheap runners.
Staples	1660 Soldiers Field Rd	617-254-4822	Printer ink and other more reasonably priced supplies.

Map 19 • Allston (South) / Brookline (North)

Berezka International Food Store	1215 Commonwealth Ave	617-787-2837	Russian goods for the slavophile.
Bicycle Bill's	253 N Harvard St	617-783-5636	Quality, no-attitude, neighborhood bike shop.
Bob Smith's Wilderness House	1048 Commonwealth Ave	617-277-5858	Everything for your outdoor adventures.
Brookline News and Gifts	313 Harvard St	617-566-9634	Since 1963, chances are they have what you're looking for.
Catering by Andrew	402 Harvard St	617-731-6585	Shabbat dinners, Thursdays and Fridays only.
City Housewares	434 Harvard St	617-278-6333	Inexpensive yet stylish kitchen goods.
City Sports	1035 Commonwealth Ave	617-782-5121	Covers all the basics in apparel and equipment.
Clear Flour	178 Thorndike St	617-739-0060	Lines out the door for Boston's honest bread.
Coco Cosmetics	192 Harvard Ave	617-782-1547	Trendy bright shop seems out of place. The future of Allston?
Eastern Mountain Sports	1041 Commonwealth Ave	617-254-4250	Gear for the New England outdoor enthusiast.
Economy Hardware	144 Harvard Ave	617-789-5552	Hardware, household needs, cheap furniture. Very popular.
Herrell's Ice Cream	155 Brighton Ave	617-782-9599	Attracts a loyal following.
In Your Ear	957 Commonwealth Ave	617-787-9755	Good selection of independent, experimental music.
International Bicycle Center	89 Brighton Ave	617-783-5804	Two floors of bikes, one of Boston's largest.
Israel Bookshop	410 Harvard St	617-566-7113	Books in Hebrew.
J.P. Licks	311 Harvard St	617-738-8252	Popular Boston ice cream institution.
Kolbo Fine Judaica	437 Harvard St	617-731-8743	Good place for Jewish gifts.
Kupel's Bake & Bagel	421 Harvard St	617-566-9528	Old school bagel joint.
New England Comics	131 Harvard Ave	617-783-1848	Study break reading material, some independent comics.
Re: Generation Records and Tattoo	155 Harvard Ave	617-782-1313	Good addition to the Allston punk scene.
Richman's Zipper Hospital	318 Harvard St	617-277-0039	The place to go for fixing zippers and tailoring.
Staples	214 Harvard St	617-566-8605	Printer ink and other more reasonably priced supplies.
Stingray Body Art	1 Harvard Ave	617-254-0666	Huge tattoo parlor with sassy boutique.
TJ Maxx	525 Harvard St	617-232-5420	Off-price apparel and housewares.
Urban Renewals	122 Brighton Ave	617-783-8387	Thrift shop with clothes, gifts, and kitsch.
Vespa Boston	22 Brighton Ave	617-254-4000	Imagine you are in Italy with its better drivers.
Wulf's Fish Market	407 Harvard St	617-277-2506	Respected fishmonger.

Map 20 • Harvard Square / Allston (North)

Abodeon	1731 Massachusetts Ave	617-497-0137	Retro housewares.
Adidas Originals	1270 Massachusetts Ave	617-864-0700	When your shell toes are looking beat, renew them here.
Alpha Omega	1380 Massachusetts Ave	617-864-1227	Jewelry, large selection of watches.
Berk's Shoes	50 JFK St	888-462-3757	Arm yourself with the right kicks for the neighborhood.
Black Ink	5 Brattle St	617-497-1221	A blend of quirky and handy gifts.
Bob Slate	1288 Massachusetts Ave	617-547-1230	Popular stationery store. Art supplies, too.
Brattle Square Florist	31 Brattle St	617-547-7089	Delphinium paradise.
Cardullo's Gourmet Shoppe	6 Brattle St	617-491-8888	Craving Swedish ginger cookies? International, gourmet goodies.

Arts & Entertainment • Shopping

Colonial Drug	49 Brattle St	617-864-2222	Unbeatable old-school, family run shop.
City Sports	44 Brattle St	617-492-6000	Moved from Dunster Street.
Crate & Barrel	48 Brattle St	617-876-6300	Harvard Square location of Chicago behemoth.
Harvard Bookstore	1256 Massachusetts Ave	617-661-1515	An independent bookstore selling new, used, and remainders.
Harvard Coop	1400 Massachusetts Ave	617-499-2000	Good for books, maps, and school stuff.
Herrell's Ice Cream	15 Dunster St	617-497-2179	Try the hot fudge.
Hidden Sweets	25 Brattle St	617-497-2600	Bulk candy and other crap.
In Your Ear	72 Mt Auburn St	617-491-5035	Good selection of independent, experiment music.
LA Burdick Homemade Chocolates	52D Brattle St	617-491-4340	Sublime confections and some killer hot chocolate.
Leavitt & Pierce	1316 Massachusetts Ave	617-547-0576	Best tobacconist in Cambridge. Chess sets too.
Little Tibet	1174 Massachusetts Ave	617-868-1030	Far-eastern clothing, jewelry, incense, and more.
Lizzy's Ice Cream	29 Church St	617-354-2911	Homemade.
Lush	30 JFK St	617-497-5874	British cosmetics merchant.
Mint Julep	6 Church St	617-576-6468	Boutique for the ladies or for the men looking for a gift for the ladies.
Museum of Useful Things	49 Brattle St	617-576-3322	Museum shop celebrates the Beauty of Function.
Newbury Comics	36 JFK St	617-491-0337	A zoo on weekends.
Nomad	1741 Massachusetts Ave	617-497-6677	An eclectic mix with a Mexican bent.
On Church Street	54 Church St	617-497-7070	Replaced CD Spins here.
Oona's	1210 Massachusetts Ave	617-491-2654	Nifty little vintage shop.
Out of Town News	0 Harvard Sq	617-354-7777	The sensible Harvard Square rendezvous spot.
Planet Records	54B JFK St	617-492-0693	CDs, some vinyl. Grab a $1 "mystery bag."
Proletariat	36 JFK St	617-661-3865	Cool clothes and other fun nonsense.
Staples	57 JFK St	617-491-1166	Printer ink and other more reasonably priced supplies.
Stereo Jack's	1686 Massachusetts Ave	617-497-9447	Specializing in jazz, blues, and the like.
Tannery	11A Brattle St	617-491-0810	Known for huge selection. Hit-or-miss service.
Tealuxe	9 Brattle St	617-441-0077	Good spot to hide from Harvard Square crowds.
Tennis and Squash Shop	67 Mt Auburn St	617-864-8800	Serious gear for those who like to wear white.
Tess and Carlos	20 Brattle St	617-864-8377	Well-chosen selection of pricey designer clothing and accessories.
Twisted Village	12B Eliot St	617-354-6898	Focusing on experimental, modern psychedelic music.
Urban Outfitters	11 JFK St	617-864-0070	Funky clothes and apartment stuff. Great bargain basement.
ZIPA Jewelry	1316 Massachusetts Ave	617-491-6991	Some tobacco with your jewels?

Map 21 • West Cambridge

Formaggio Kitchen	244 Huron Ave	617-354-4750	Cheese and other gourmet imports.
Henry Bear's Park	361 Huron Ave	617-547-8424	Chi-chi toy store.
Newbury Comics	211 Alewife Brook Pkwy	617-491-7711	Fresh Pond location of successful music/novelties chain.

Map 22 • North Cambridge / West Somerville

Bicycle Exchange	2067 Massachusetts Ave	617-864-1300	Porter Square bike shop.
Black & Blues	89 Holland St	617-628-0046	Laid back duds, friendly shopkeepers.
CD Spins	235 Elm St	617-666-8080	A good choice for selling back CDs.
China Fair	2100 Massachusetts Ave	617-864-3050	Inexpensive kitchen gear and housewares.
Chinook Outdoor Adventure	93 Holland St	617-776-8616	Sporty, stylish. Clothes for him and her.
Cibeline	85 Holland St	617-625-2229	Party clothes, whatever your mood.
Magpie	416 Highland Ave	617-623-3330	Featuring over 350 indie crafters and artists.
McKinnon's Choice Meat Market	239A Elm St	617-666-0888	Smart choice before a barbecue.
Modern Brewer	2304 Massachusetts Ave	617-498-0400	Everything for your home-brewing needs.
Nellie's Wildflowers	72 Holland St	617-625-9453	Florist.
Poor Little Rich Girl	255 Elm St	617-684-0157	Good spot to shop for fun clothes.
Staples	186 Alewife Brook Pkwy	617-547-3948	Printer ink and other more reasonably priced supplies.

Map 23 • Central Somerville / Porter Square

Ace Wheelworks	145 Elm St	617-776-2100	Davis Square bike shop.
Big Fish, Little Fish	55 Elm St	617-666-2444	Pet store with more than just fish.
Bob Slate	1975 Massachusetts Ave	617-547-8624	Popular stationery store. Art supplies too.
Cambridge Music Center	1906 Massachusetts Ave	617-547-8263	Sells instruments and hard-to-find sheet music.
Cambridge Naturals	23 White St	617-492-4452	Quality selection of all things yogi.
City Sports	1815 Massachusetts Ave	617-661-1666	Covers all the basics in apparel and equipment.
Greenward	1776 Massachusetts Ave	617-395-1338	Unique, eco-friendly somethings.
Joie de Vivre	1792 Massachusetts Ave	617-864-8188	Silly gifts, nostalgic toys, good stocking stuffers.
Lyndell's Bakery	720 Broadway	617-625-1793	Tasty pastries.
Paper Source	1810 Massachusetts Ave	617-497-1077	DIY paper crafts and quirky gifts.
Porter Square Books	25 White St	617-491-2220	Fiercely independent!
Roach's Sporting Goods	1957 Massachusetts Ave	617-876-5816	100 years of sporting goods, camp supplies, and guns.

Map 24 • Winter Hill / Union Square

Bombay Market	359 Somerville Ave	617-623-6614	Good Indian grocery, Bollywood movies.
Bostonian Florist	92 Highland Ave	617-629-9300	Florist.
Christmas Tree Shops	177 Middlesex Ave	617-623-3428	Everything including the kitchen sink.
Mudflat Studio	149 Broadway	617-628-0589	Pottery classes and studios.

| Reliable Market | 45 Union Sq | 617-623-9620 | Overflowing East Asian grocer. |
| Ricky's Flower Market | 9 Union Sq | 617-628-7569 | Great outdoor market. Mind the traffic, though. |

Map 25 · East Somerville / Sullivan Square

| Home Depot | 75 Mystic Ave | 617-623-0001 | Got wood? |
| Vinny's Superette | 76 Broadway | 617-628-1921 | Damn good Italian cold-cuts. |

Map 26 · East Cambridge / Kendall Square / MIT

Apple Store	100 Cambridgeside Pl	617-225-0442	Mac heaven in the Galleria.
Best Buy	100 Cambridgeside Pl	617-577-8866	Awful, annoying electronics retailer.
Calumet Photographic	65 Bent St	617-576-2600	High-end photo shop.
Cambridge Antique Market	201 Monsignor O'Brien Hwy	617-868-9655	Five floors to keep you busy.
Mayflower Poultry	621 Cambridge St	617-547-9191	Live poultry, fresh killed.

Map 27 · Central Square / Cambridgeport

Buckaroo's Mercantile	5 Brookline St	617-492-4792	Kitsch niche.
Cambridge Bicycle	259 Massachusetts Ave	617-876-6555	Bike shop near MIT.
Cheapo Records	538 Massachusetts Ave	617-354-4455	A treasure trove of older tunes.
Cremaldi's	31 Putnam Ave	617-354-7969	Gourmet shop.
Economy Hardware	438 Massachusetts Ave	617-864-3300	Hardware, household needs, cheap furniture. Very popular.
Great Eastern Trading Company	49 River St	617-354-5279	Like the Garment District's little sister on crack
Hubba Hubba	534 Massachusetts Ave	617-492-9082	Focusing on the naughty bits.
Looney Tunes	1001 Massachusetts Ave	617-876-5624	Records covered with the finest dust.
Micro Center	730 Memorial Dr	617-234-6400	Computer have-it-all. Avoid going on Saturdays.
Pandemonium Books	4 Pleasant St	617-547-3721	Books, Role-Playing Supplies, and tables for all your D&D needs.
Pearl Art & Craft Supplies	579 Massachusetts Ave	617-547-6600	Arts and crafts, Central Square style.
Shalimar	571 Massachusetts Ave	617-868-8311	Huge selection of spices.
Ten Thousand Villages	694 Massachusetts Ave	617-876-2414	Free-trade, handmade crafts from around the world.
Toscanini's	899 Main St	617-491-5877	In our opinion, Boston's best ice cream.
University Stationery	311 Massachusetts Ave	617-547-6650	A friendly little shop near MIT.
Weirdo Records	844 Massachusetts Ave	857-413-0154	Bizarre and rare vinyl - this aint easy listening.

Map 28 · Inman Square

Boston Costume Company	200 Broadway	617-482-1632	Rentals and sales.
Boutique Fabulous	1309 Cambridge St	617-864-0656	Inman Square maxi-boutique.
Central Bakery	732 Cambridge St	617-547-2237	Unembellished interior and a menu with nothing over $3.
Christina's Homemade Ice Cream	1255 Cambridge St	617-492-7021	Clever flavors; good spice shop next door.
The Garment District	200 Broadway	617-876-5230	Vintage threads, costumes, clothing by-the-pound.
Inman Square Market	1343 Cambridge St	617-354-8697	Independent quickie mart.
Royal Pastry	738 Cambridge St	617-547-2053	Caters to a devoted clientele.
Sadye & Company	121 Hampshire St	617-547-4424	Good antiques store.
Target	180 Somerville Ave	617-776-4919	Oh, you know.
Urban Oasis	243 Hampshire St	617-491-0176	Get hydrated in the community hot tubs.
Wine Cask	407 Washington St	617-623-8656	Wine, cheese, specialties.

Map 29 · West Roxbury

| Irish Cottage | 1898 Centre St | 617-323-4644 | Food, kitsch. Gag us with a shamrock. |
| Jack Davis Florist | 2097 Centre St | 617-323-6006 | Florist. |

Map 30 · Roslindale

Atlas Liquors	591 Hyde Park Ave	617-323-8202	Sousing the locals since 1933.
Boston Cheese Cellar	18 Birch St	617-325-2500	Free samples. European stinkies for $12.99/lb.
Droubi Bakery	748 South St	617-325-1585	Cheap veggies and fruit along with delicious Middle Eastern baked goods.
Emack & Bolio's	2 Belgrade Ave	617-323-3323	Innovative ice cream flavors.
Exotic Flowers	609 American Legion Hwy	617-247-2000	Florist.
Fornax Bread Baking Company	27 Corinth St	617-325-8852	Sandwiches, too.
Joanne Rossman: Purveyor of the Unnecessary & the Irresistible	6 Birch St	617-323-4301	Curios for the rich. Cool stuff, nice lady.
Pazzo Books	4268 Washington St	617-323-2919	Used and rare books with skeeball in the basement.
Roslindale Fish Market	38-39 Poplar St	617-327-9487	Come early for fresh fish.
Solera	12 Corinth St	617-469-4005	Wine.
Thrift Shop of Boston	17 Corinth St	617-325-5300	A small thrift store packed with tons of possible treasures and the friendliest staff!
Village Books	751 South St	617-325-1994	Beloved community bookstore.

Map 31 • Mattapan / Dorchester (West)

Dark Horse	2297 Dorchester Ave	617-298-1031	Antiques. Friendly.
Le Foyer Bakery	132 Babson St	617-298-0535	Long lines for patties at this Haitian bakery.
Taurus Records	1282 Blue Hill Ave	617-298-2655	Small shop is best source for reggae, tons of singles.

Map 32 • Dorchester (East)

Asian Bookstore	1392 Dorchester Ave	617-822-9996	Tidy bookstore specializing in Vietnamese books.
Boston Winery	26 Ericson St	617-265-9463	Make your own wine, own your own barrel.
Coleen's Flowershop	912 Dorchester Ave	617-282-0468	Cute florist on Dot Ave.
Greenhill's Irish Bakery	780 Adams St	617-825-8187	Soda bread, scones and sandwiches with blood pudding.
Open Boxes	1080 Dorchester Ave	617-288-5588	Creepiest store in Boston.

Map 33 • Hyde Park

Capone Foods	14 Bow St	617-629-2296	All your specialty food shop needs.
Marascio's Market	1758 River St	617-361-6847	Italian specialties.
Ron's Gourmet Ice Cream	1231 Hyde Park Ave	617-364-5274	Candlepins too!
Tutto Italiano	1893 River St	617-361-4700	Deli. A mayoral favorite.

With all the students and schools that Boston manages to cram into it's small borders, we suffer from a distinct lack of places to catch a film. Currently we're down to two locations—the **AMC Loews Boston Common (Map 3)** and **Regal Fenway 13 (Map 16)**. Be forewarned as these joints are the only players in the game, the ticket and food prices reflect the lack of competition. Also, for those of you that actually want to WATCH the movie, these locations draw a large number of teenagers who can't shut off their cell phones for 90 minutes. Still, if it's a new release that's a must see, they both deliver. If you can wait until the movie of your desire is a bit older, **The Somerville Theater (Map 22)** does a good chunk of second run business, and it also has hooch.

To watch a movie with 90% less teenager text message ringtone, then you'll have to venture to **Landmark Kendall Square Cinema (Map 26)**, the **Brattle Theatre (Map 20)**, the **Harvard Film Archive (Map 20)**, the **Museum of Fine Arts (Map 15)**, or the best damn joint to see a flick in greater Boston—the **Coolidge Corner Theatre (Map 17)**.

From the end of June through the end of August, check out Free Friday Flicks at the **Hatch Shell (Map 6)** on the Esplanade. Movies start at sundown, but arrive early to get your spot on the grass. And for heaven's sake, don't forget to bring some wine and cheese.

Huge-screen freaks should hit the **Mugar Omni Theater (Map 1)** at the Museum of Science and the **Simons IMAX Theatre (Map 2)** at the New England Aquarium. If you just have to shop for furniture before seeing a movie in IMAX or 3-D, you owe yourself a trip to **Jordan's Furniture** (1-866-8JORDANS) in either Natick (ext. 2860) or Reading (ext. 6800). It might be worth the trip alone if the Red Sox are doing well in the standings, and you feel like taking them up on whatever World Series promo they running.

Movie Theater

Movie Theater	Address	Phone		Map
AMC Loews Boston Common	175 Tremont St	617-423-3499	Blockbusters.	3
AMC Loews Harvard Square	10 Church St	617-864-4580	Get your *Rocky Horror* fix here.	20
Brattle Theatre	40 Brattle St	617-876-6837	*Casablanca*. Every year.	20
Coolidge Corner Theatre	290 Harvard St	617-734-2500	Theme nights and film festivals.	17
Entertainment Cinemas Fresh Pond	168 Alewife Brook Pkwy	617-661-2900	A bit sticky.	22
Harvard Film Archive	24 Quincy St	617-495-4700	Films you won't see at Boston Common.	20
Institute of Contemporary Art	100 Northern Ave	617-266-5152	Arty flicks, no Milk Duds.	10
Landmark Kendall Square Cinema	One Kendall Sq	617-499-1996	Movies for smart grown-ups.	26
Mugar Omni Theatre	1 Science Park	617-723-2500	Don't move your head, you'll puke.	1
Museum of Fine Arts	465 Huntington Ave	617-369-3770	Ever changing array, filmmaker Q&A.	15
National Amusements Circle Cinemas	399 Chestnut Hill Ave	617-566-2170	Numbinus buminus.	18
Regal Fenway Stadium 13	201 Brookline Ave	617-424-6266	On-site parking. Video games in the lobby.	16
Simons IMAX Theatre	Central Wharf	866-815-4629	Wicked big screen.	2
Somerville Theatre	55 Davis Sq	617-625-5700	Now serving beer and wine.	22

Arts & Entertainment • Art Galleries

Newbury Street has Boston's largest and densest concentration of art galleries. You've probably passed by the several dozen galleries on Newbury Street many times without taking a look at what's inside, but popping into just a few of them will give you some idea of the broad scope of what's on offer (even if your budget means you're more likely to be striking deals at the MFA's gift shop). Commercial art fans should check out **International Poster Gallery's (Map 6)** expansive collection of Italian, travel, and Soviet-era posters. The gallery of the **Copley Society of Boston (Map 6)**, also on Newbury Street, hosts several competitions over the course of the year, including showcases of student work.

While Newbury Street galleries may have the city's most established spots, the interesting developments are happening in the South End, where a number of galleries have opened or relocated. The center of the action is the converted warehouse at 450 Harrison Avenue between Thayer Street and Randolph Street. (Take the Silver Line to East Berkeley Street, walk one block to Harrison Avenue, and hang a right.) Big names at the "SoWa Building" include **Bernard Toale Gallery (Map 7)**, **Kingston Gallery (Map 7)**, and **Genovese/Sullivan (Map 7)**. If you're interested in what's emerging in Boston's contemporary art scene, head to SoWa on the first Friday of the month to see the new exhibits. (At the very least, it's an excuse to get dressed up and consume some free wine.) Elsewhere in Boston, consider seeing what's on display at **Axiom Gallery (Map 14)** in Jamaica Plain's Green Street T Station, the **Fort Point Arts Community Gallery (Map 10)**, Roxbury's **Hamill Gallery of African Art (Map 13)**, and Kenmore Square's **Panopticon Gallery of Photography (Map 15)**. Cheaper rents continue to attract artists to East Boston, where the newly reopened **Atlantic Works Gallery (Map 9)** holds regular exhibitions and potluck get-togethers.

In addition to stocked galleries, many of the city's neighborhoods put on "open studio" events where you can satisfy your nosy streak by poking around the studios of artists willing to open them up to the public. Go to www.cityofboston.gov/arts.

Map 1 • Beacon Hill / West End

Gurari Collections	91 Charles St	617-367-9800
Judith Dowling Asian Art	133 Charles St	617-523-5211
Keiko Limited	121 Charles St	617-725-2888

Map 2 • North End / Faneuil Hall

Mayor's Art Gallery	1 City Hall Plaza, 3rd floor	617-635-3245
Scollay Square Gallery	1 City Hall Plaza, 3rd floor	617-635-3245

Map 3 • Downtown Crossing / Park Square / Bay Village

Barbara Krakow Gallery	10 Newbury St	617-262-4490
Comenos Fine Arts	9 Newbury St	617-262-9365
Howard Yezerski Gallery	14 Newbury St	617-262-0550
Miller Block Gallery	14 Newbury St	617-536-4650
Tepper Takayama Fine Arts	20 Park Plz	617-542-0557

Map 4 • Financial District / Chinatown

Gallery Anthony Curtis	186 South St	617-988-8119
JMW Gallery	144 Lincoln St	617-338-9097

Map 5 • Back Bay (West) / Fenway (East)

Kaji Aso Gallery	40 St Stephen St	617-247-1719
St George Gallery	245 Newbury St	617-450-0321

Map 6 • Back Bay (East) / South End (Upper)

Acme Fine Art	38 Newbury St	617-585-9551
Alfred J Walker Fine Art	162 Newbury St	617-247-1319
Alpha Gallery	38 Newbury St	617-536-4465
Arden Gallery	129 Newbury St	617-247-0610
Artful Hand Gallery	100 Huntington Ave	617-262-9601
Axelle Fine Arts Galerie Newbury	91 Newbury St	617-450-0710
Beth Urdang Gallery	129 Newbury St	617-424-5550
Chase Gallery	129 Newbury St	617-859-7222
Childs Gallery	169 Newbury St	617-266-1108
Copley Society	158 Newbury St	617-536-5049
DTR Modern Galleries	167 Newbury St	617-424-9700
Eclipse Gallery	164 Newbury St	617-247-6730
French Library and Cultural Center	53 Marlborough St	617-912-0400
Galerie d'Orsay	33 Newbury St	617-266-8001
Gallery NAGA	67 Newbury St	617-267-9060
Guild of Boston Artists	162 Newbury St	617-536-7660
International Poster Gallery	205 Newbury St	617-375-0076
Judi Rotenberg Gallery	130 Newbury St	617-437-1518
Judy Ann Goldman Fine Art	14 Newbury St	617-424-8468
Kidder Smith Gallery	131 Newbury St	617-424-6900
L'Attitude Gallery and Sculpture Garden	218 Newbury St	617-927-4400
Lanoue Fine Art	160 Newbury St	617-262-4400
Martha Richardson Fine Art	38 Newbury St	617-266-3321
Martin Lawrence Galleries	77 Newbury St	617-369-4800
Mercury Gallery	8 Newbury St	617-859-0054
Newbury Fine Arts	29 Newbury St	617-536-0210
Nielsen Gallery	179 Newbury St	617-266-4835
Pepper Gallery	38 Newbury St	617-236-4497
Pucker Gallery	171 Newbury St	617-267-9473
Robert Klein Gallery	38 Newbury St	617-267-7997
Rolly-Michaux Gallery	290 Dartmouth St	617-536-9898
Royka's Gallery	213 Newbury St	978-582-8207
The Society of Arts and Crafts	175 Newbury St	617-266-1810
Victoria Munroe Fine Art	179 Newbury St	617-523-0661
Vose Galleries	238 Newbury St	617-536-6176

Map 7 • South End (Lower)

Allston Skirt Gallery	65 Thayer St	617-482-3652
Ars Libri	500 Harrison Ave	617-357-5212
BCA Mills Gallery	539 Tremont St	617-426-5000
Berenberg Gallery	4 Clarendon St	617-536-0800
Bernard Toale Gallery	450 Harrison Ave	617-482-2477

Boston Sculptors Gallery	486 Harrison Ave	617-482-7781
Bromfield Art Gallery	450 Harrison Ave	617-451-3605
Gallery AA/B	535 Albany St	617-574-0022
Gallery Kayafas	450 Harrison Ave	617-482-0411
Genovese/Sullivan Gallery	450 Harrison Ave	617-426-9738
Jules Place	1200 Washington St	617-542-0644
Kingston Gallery	450 Harrison Ave	617-423-4113
Laconia Gallery	433 Harrison Ave	617-426-5303
MPG Contemporary	450 Harrison Ave	617-357-8881
OHT Gallery	450 Harrison Ave	617-423-1677
OSP Gallery	450 Harrison Ave	617-778-5265
Qingping Gallery Teahouse	231 Shawmut Ave	617-482-9988
Samson Projects	450 Harrison Ave	617-357-7177
Soprafina	450 Harrison Ave	617-728-0770
Space Other	63 Wareham St	617-451-3500

Map 9 · East Boston

Atlantic Works	80 Border St	n/a

Map 10 · South Boston (West) / Fort Point

Fort Point Arts Community Gallery	300 Summer St	617-423-4299
Studio Soto	63 Melcher St	617-426-7686

Map 11 · South Boston (East)

Artists Foundation	516 E 2nd St	617-464-3559
Crump McCole Gallery	200 Seaport Blvd	617-330-1133
Diana Levine Art Gallery	1 Design Ctr Pl	617-338-9060

Map 12 · Newmarket / Andrew Square

Cambridge Mulitcultural Art Center	41 Second St	617-577-1400

Map 13 · Roxbury

Hamill Gallery of African Art	2164 Washington St	617-442-8204

Map 14 · Jamaica Plain

Axiom	141 Green St	n/a
JP Art Market	36 South St	617-522-1729

Map 15 · Fenway (West) / Mission Hill

Grossman Gallery at School of the Museum of Fine Arts	230 Fenway	617-369-3718

Map 16 · Kenmore Square / Brookline (East)

Boston University Art Gallery	855 Commonwealth Ave	617-353-3329
Boston University Sherman Gallery	775 Commonwealth Ave	617-358-0295

Brookline Arts Center	86 Monmouth St	617-566-5715
Panopticon Gallery of Photography	502 Commonwealth Ave	617-267-8929

Map 17 · Coolidge Corner / Brookline Hills

Artana	1378 Beacon St	617-879-3111
Gateway Gallery	62 Harvard St	617-734-1577

Map 20 · Harvard Square / Allston (North)

Baak Gallery	35 Brattle St	617-354-0407
Cambridge Artists Cooperative	59A Church St	617-868-4434
Hurst Gallery	53 Mt Auburn St	617-491-6888
University Place Gallery	124 Mt Auburn St	617-876-0246

Map 21 · West Cambridge

Kathryn Schultz Gallery	25 Lowell St	617-876-0246
Mobilia Gallery	358 Huron Ave	617-876-2109

Map 22 · North Cambridge / West Somerville

38 Cameron	38 Cameron Ave	617-492-2848
Nave Gallery	155 Powderhouse Blvd	617-625-4823

Map 24 · Winter Hill / Union Square

Scat Gallery	90 Union Sq	617-628-8826

Map 25 · East Somerville/ Sullivan Square

Brickbottom Gallery	1 Fitchburg St	617-776-3410

Map 26 · East Cambridge / Kendall Square / MIT

MIT List Visual Arts Center	20 Ames St	617-253-4680

Map 27 · Central Square / Cambridgeport

Art Interactive	130 Bishop Richard Allen Dr	617-498-0100
Gallery 263	263 Pearl St	781-393-0000

Map 28 · Inman Square

Cambridge Arts Council Gallery	344 Broadway	617-349-4380
Out of the Blue Gallery	106 Prospect St	617-354-5287
Zeitgeist Gallery	186 Hampshire St	617-876-6060

Outside of a dog, a book is man's best friend. Inside of a dog it's too dark to read. —Groucho Marx

Big

As in so many other US cities, **Barnes & Noble (Map 5, 16, 19)** and **Borders (Map 3, 26)** are the big dogs on the Boston bookstore scene. If you're shopping for a book, but not also for a low-fat latte or a high-fat chocolate croissant, get familiar with the large independents **Brookline Booksmith (Map 19)** and the 75-year-old **Harvard Book Store (Map 20)** (unaffiliated with the university). Both focus on new titles but have cellars that handle used books.

Used

Davis Square's **McIntyre & Moore Books (Map 22)** sells an array of used books, with a bent toward school textbooks. When in Roslindale, stop by **Pazzo Books** (4268 Washington St, 617-323-2919, Map 30) for used and rare books and a round of skee-ball on the old machine in the basement. Some people think **Raven Used Books (Map 20)** in Harvard Square delivers the best bang for your buck. A good place to find used guidebooks and fiction is **Rodney's Bookstore (Map 17, 27)**, with locations in both Central Square and Brookline. Downtown Crossing's **Brattle Book Shop (Map 3)** is a well-known used book specialist—check out the outdoor book racks on dry days. Also in Central Boston, and worth checking out for antiquarian books, are **Lame Duck Books (Map 20)** and **Commonwealth Books (Map 3, 16)**. There's also the **Boston Book Annex (Map 16)**, sloppy but well stocked, a fun place for cat lovers and long-term browsing.

Specialty

Quantum Books (Map 26) is the best computer bookstore in the city. The **MIT Press Bookstore (Map 26)** is the best for social sciences, philosophy, economics, and sciences—pretty much everything MIT is best for. For little kids, take a look at Brookline's **Children's Book Shop (Map 17)**. Slightly older kids who dig gaming will enjoy **Pandemonium (Map 27)**. **Ars Libri (Map 7)** has an exemplary collection of rare and out-of-print fine art books. The only remaining LGBT bookstore in Boston is **Calamus (Map 4)**, near South Station. A big tip of the chapeau is due to **Schoenhof's Foreign Books (Map 20)** for its broad selection. **James & Devon Grey Booksellers (Map 20)** specializes in books printed before 1700. **Lucy Parsons Center (Map 6)**, in the South End, stocks many progressive titles. **Trident Booksellers & Café (Map 5)** stocks books and a good variety of mainstream and alternative magazine titles, in addition to serving a mean breakfast.

Cambridge

Several years ago there were more than 25 bookstores in Harvard Square, the greatest concentration of bookstores in the city (and perhaps the country). No longer. Blame high rents, online retail, large chains dominating the market, or a general waning interest in the printed arts, but the sad fact is that many fine shops have packed it in. That being said, there are still a lot of friggin' bookstores and they range from the nuanced to the Coop. Headlining the niche category is NFT's favorite travel bookshop, **Globe Corner Travel (Map 20)**—it fits into the "glad it exists" category (note the new location). **Grolier Poetry Book Shop (Map 20)**, a national poetry landmark, is nothing less than a beacon of art in its tiny space on Plympton Street. Another Harvard Square stalwart is **Revolution Books (Map 20)**, a bookstore particularly conducive to raging against the machine. **The Harvard Coop (Map 20)** is managed by Barnes & Noble and unaffiliated with the school. The previously mentioned Raven, Schoenhof's, James & Devon Grey's, and probably three or four others round out a full day of page flipping. If the clogged walkways and impossible parking makes Harvard Square more trouble than it's worth, there's always **Porter Square Books (Map 23)** and Inman Square's **Lorem Ipsum (Map 28)**, the latter being one of the best resources for used fiction and literature in the area. Now get going, you bookworm.

Map 1 · Beacon Hill / West End

Commonwealth Books	2 Milk St	617-292-0065	Scholarly, used, antiquarian.
Suffolk University Bookstore	148 Cambridge St	617-227-4085	Schoolbooks and campus merchandise.

Map 2 · North End / Faneuil Hall

Newbury Comics	Faneuil Hall	617-248-9992	Comics.

Map 3 · Downtown Crossing / Park Square / Bay Village

Black Library Booksellers	Washington St & Summer St	617-442-2400	African-American literature.
Borders	10 School St	617-557-7188	General.
Brattle Book Shop	9 West St	617-542-0210	Used; outdoor racks when warm.
Commonwealth Books	134 Bolyston St	617-338-6328	Scholarly, used, antiquarian.
Emerson College Bookstore	114 Bolyston St	617-824-8696	Schoolbooks and campus merchandise.
Peter L Stern & Co	55 Temple Pl	617-542-2376	Antiquarian, especially first editions.
Suffolk Law School Book Store	110 Tremont St	617-227-8874	Schoolbooks and campus merchandise.

Map 4 · Financial District / Chinatown

Barbara's Best Sellers	2 S Station	617-443-0060	In South Station.
Calamus Bookstore	92 South St	617-338-1931	Gay & lesbian.
Central China Book Co	44 Kneeland St	617-426-0888	Chinese.
FA Bernett	144 Lincoln St	617-350-7778	Rare and scholarly art and architecture.
Tufts Medical Bookstore	116 Harrison Ave	617-636-6628	Schoolbooks and campus merchandise.
World Journal	216 Lincoln St	617-542-1230	Chinese.

Map 5 · Back Bay (West) / Fenway (East)

Barnes & Noble	800 Boylston St	617-247-6959	General.
Berklee College of Music Bookstore	1080 Boylston St	617-267-0023	Schoolbooks and campus merchandise.
Newbury Comics	332 Newbury St	617-236-4930	Now featuring a large DVD section.
Trident Booksellers & Café	338 Newbury St	617-267-8688	Independent; eclectic.

Map 6 · Back Bay (East) / South End (Upper)

Borders	511 Boylston St	617-236-1444	General.
Brentano's at Copley Place	100 Huntington Ave	617-859-9511	General.
Bromer Booksellers	607 Boylston St	617-247-2818	Fine, rare, and unusual.
Buddenbrooks Fine & Rare Books	31 Newbury St	617-536-4433	Fine, rare.
Lucy Parsons Center	549 Columbus Ave	617-267-6272	Progressive.

Map 7 · South End (Lower)

Ars Libri	500 Harrison Ave	617-357-5212	Rare and out-of-print books on art.
Boston University Medical Center Bookstore	700 Albany St	617-638-5496	Schoolbooks and campus merchandise.

Map 9 · East Boston

Avila's Christian Book Store	112 Chelsea St	617-569-2252	Religious.

Map 13 · Roxbury

Roxbury Community College Bookstore	1234 Columbus Ave	617-442-8150	Schoolbooks and campus merchandise.

Map 14 · Jamaica Plain

Boston Book Co	705 Centre St	617-522-2100	Antiquarian.
Jamaicaway Books & Gifts	676 Centre St	617-983-3204	Multicultural.
Rhythm & Muse	470 Centre St	617-524-6622	Independent.

Map 15 · Fenway (West) / Mission Hill

Emmanuel College Bookstore	400 The Fenway	617-264-7697	Schoolbooks and campus merchandise.
Mass College of Pharmacy & Art Bookstore	625 Huntington Ave	617-739-4772	Textbooks.
Medical Center Coop	333 Longwood Ave	617-499-3300	Schoolbooks and campus merchandise.
Northeastern University Bookstore	360 Huntington Ave	617-373-2286	Schoolbooks and campus merchandise.
Simmons College Book Store	300 The Fenway	617-521-2054	Schoolbooks and campus merchandise.
Wentworth Book Store	103 Ward St	617-445-8814	Textbooks.

Map 16 · Kenmore Square / Brookline (East)

Barnes & Noble at Boston University	660 Beacon St	617-267-8484	General/schoolbooks and campus merchandise.
Boston Book Annex	906 Beacon St	617-266-1090	Used.
Comicopia	464 Commonwealth Ave	617-266-4266	Comics.

Map 17 · Coolidge Corner / Brookline Hills

Book World	77 Harvard St	617-739-5768	Russian.
Children's Book Shop	237 Washington St	617-734-7323	Children's.
Horai-san	242 Washington St	617-277-4321	New age/spiritual.
New England Comics	316 Harvard St	617-566-0115	Comics.
Petropol	1428 Beacon St	617-232-8820	Russian.
Rodney's Bookstore	1362 Beacon St	617-232-0185	General.

Map 19 · Allston (South) / Brookline (North)

Barnes & Noble	325 Harvard St	617-232-0594	General.
Brookline Booksmith	279 Harvard St	617-566-6660	Independent; used book cellar.
Cheetah Trading	214 Lincoln St	617-451-1309	Chinese.
Harvard Business School Co-op	117 Western Ave	617-499-3245	Business.
Israel Bookshop	410 Harvard St	617-566-7113	Judaica.
The Kabbalah Center	14 Green St	617-566-0808	Religious.
Kolbo Fine Judaica	437 Harvard St	617-731-8743	Judaica.
Korean Book & Video (Korean & Japanese)	156 Harvard Ave	617-782-8874	Korean.
New England Comics	131 Harvard Ave	617-783-1848	Comics.

Map 20 · Harvard Square / Allston (North)

Ahab Rare Books	5 JFK St	617-547-5602	Antiquarian, rare books.
Atherton Antiquarian	5 JFK St, 4th Floor	617-547-2664	Old, rare books.
Curious George Goes to Wordsworth	1 JFK St	617-498-0062	Children's.
Globe Corner Book Stores	90 Mt Auburn St	617-497-6277	Travel.
Grolier Poetry Book Shop	6 Plympton St	617-547-4648	Poetry books.
Harvard Book Store	1256 Massachusetts Ave	617-661-1515	Independent, with an academic bent.

Harvard Coop	1400 Massachusetts Ave	617-499-2000	General/schoolbooks and campus merchandise.
Harvard Law School Coop	14 Everett St	617-499-3255	Law.
James & Devon Gray Booksellers	12 Arrow St	617-868-0752	Pre-18th-century.
Lame Duck Books	12 Arrow St	617-868-2022	Rare books, manuscripts, art.
Million Year Picnic	99 Mt Auburn St	617-492-6763	Comics.
New England Comics	14A Eliot St	617-354-5352	Comics.
Raven Used Books	52-B JFK St	617-441-6999	Scholarly used.
Revolution Books	1158 Massachusetts Ave	617-492-5443	Revolution.
Robin Bledsoe Books	1640 Massachusetts Ave	617-576-3634	Out-of-print books on horses and art.
Schoenhof's Foreign Books	76A Mt Auburn St	617-547-8855	Foreign languages.

Map 21 • West Cambridge

| Bryn Mawr Book Store | 373 Huron Ave | 617-661-1770 | Used and rare, stocked by donations. |
| Newbury Comics | 211 Alewife Brook Pkwy | 617-491-7711 | Comics. |

Map 22 • North Cambridge / West Somerville

| Kate's Mystery Books | 2211 Massachusetts Ave | 617-491-2660 | New and used mysteries. |
| McIntyre & Moore Books | 255 Elm St | 617-629-4840 | Scholarly used. |

Map 23 • Central Somerville / Porter Square

Barefoot Books	1771 Massachusetts Ave	617-349-1610	Picture books for the wee.
Barefoot Books	2067 Massachusetts Ave	617-576-0660	Picture books for the wee.
Comicazi	380 Highland Ave	617-623-2664	Comics.
Porter Square Books	25 White St	617-491-2220	Fiercely independent!

Map 24 • Winter Hill / Union Square

| CPAD Bookstore | 100 Washington St | 617-625-1234 | Brazilian. |

Map 25 • East Somerville / Sullivan Square

| Bunker Hill Community College Book Store | 250 Rutherford Ave | 617-241-5161 | Textbooks. |

Map 26 • East Cambridge / Kendall Square / MIT

Borders	100 Cambridgeside Pl	617-679-0887	General.
MIT Co-op	3 Cambridge Ctr	617-499-3200	Schoolbooks and campus merchandise.
MIT Press Bookstore	292 Main St	617-253-5249	MIT Press authors and quality trade.
Quantum Books	4 Cambridge Center	617-494-5042	Computer, technical.

Map 27 • Central Square / Cambridgeport

Bookmarx	550 Massachusetts Ave	617-354-2876	At the Center for Marxist Education.
Pandemonium	4 Pleasant St	617-547-3721	Sci-fi, fantasy, and gaming.
Rodney's Bookstore	698 Massachusetts Ave	617-876-6467	Used, out-of-print, remainders.
Seven Stars	731 Massachusetts Ave	617-547-1317	New Age.
Stratton Center Co-op	84 Massachusetts Ave	617-499-3240	Schoolbooks and campus merchandise.

Map 28 • Inman Square

| Lorem Ipsum | 157 Hampshire St | 617-497-7669 | Used. |

If you're familiar with every painting at the **Gardner (Map 15)**, every print in the **MFA (Map 15)**, every fish in the **Aquarium (Map 2)**, and every cobblestone on the **Freedom Trail** (pg 189), then it's time to take it to the next level by ferreting out some of the city's hidden treasures and discovering something new about some old favorites.

The new facility of the **Institute of Contemporary Art (Map 10)**, whose design evokes a laptop, opened in the winter of 2006. If you're looking for a reason to make your way over to Fan Pier, here it is.

Release your inner child on a Friday night at the (newly expanded and renovated) **Boston Children's Museum (Map 4)**—from 5 pm to 9 pm, admission is just $1. Or, engage your inner adult at the **Museum of Science (Map 1)** with a cocktail (yes, a real cocktail), a movie in the Mugar Omni Theater, or free stargazing at the Gilliland Observatory.

If you want to take in some art during a drive out of town, check out the **DeCordova Museum and Sculpture Park** in Lincoln (not far from Route 2 and Route 128). The DeCordova's 35 acres of woodlands is the largest sculpture garden in New England. The contemporary American outdoor sculpture park changes its exhibitions on a regular basis. Admission to the sculpture park is $9 for adults, $6 for students, seniors, and children ages 6–12. Children five and under, as well as active duty military personnel, are admitted free. For more information, visit www.decordova.org.

And for all of those museums are just too good to be true, check out the **Museum of Bad Art (MOBA)** way out in Dedham (580 High St, 781-444-6757). Contemplate art so bad, it can't be ignored.

Museum	Address	Phone	Map
Ancient and Honorable Artillery Company	Faneuil Hall, 4th Fl	617-227-1638	2
Arthur M Sackler Museum	485 Broadway	617-495-9400	20
Boston Athenaeum	10 1/2 Beacon St	617-227-0270	1
Boston Children's Museum	300 Congress St	617-426-8855	10
Boston Tea Party Ship & Museum	Congress St Bridge	617-269-7150	10
(closed for renovations, scheduled to re-open fall 2008)			
Busch-Reisinger Museum	32 Quincy St	617-495-9400	20
Carpenter Center for Visual Arts	24 Quincy St	617-495-3251	20
Commonwealth Museum	220 Morrissey Blvd	617-727-9268	32
Fogg Art Museum	32 Quincy St	617-495-9400	20
Gibson House Museum	137 Beacon St	617-267-6338	6
Harrison Gray Otis House	141 Cambridge St	617-227-3956	1
Harvard Mineralogical & Geological Museum	24 Oxford St	617-495-3045	20
Harvard Museum of Comparative Zoology	26 Oxford St	617-495-3045	20
Harvard Museum of Natural History	26 Oxford St	617-495-3045	20
Institute of Contemporary Art	100 Northern Ave	617-473-3100	10
JFK National Historic Site	83 Beals St	617-566-7937	19
John F Kennedy Library and Museum	Morrissey Blvd & Columbia St	617-514-1600	32
Larz Anderson Auto Museum	15 Newton St, Brookline	617-522-6547	n/a
The Loring-Greenough House	12 South St	617-524-3158	14
Mapparium/Christian Science Museum	200 Massachusetts Ave	617-450-7000	5
MIT List Visual Arts Center	20 Ames St	617-253-4680	26
MIT Museum	265 Massachusetts Ave	617-253-4444	27
Museum of Afro-American History	46 Joy St	617-725-0022	1
Museum of Bad Art (MOBA)	580 High St, Dedham	781-444-6757	n/a
Museum of Fine Arts	465 Huntington Ave	617-267-9300	15
Museum of Science	Science Park	617-723-2500	1
National Center for Afro-American Artists	300 Walnut Ave	617-442-8614	13
New England Aquarium	Central Wharf	617-973-5200	2
Nichols House Museum	55 Mt Vernon St	617-227-6993	1
Old South Meeting House	310 Washington St	617-482-6439	3
Old State House	206 Washington St	617-720-1713	3
Paul Revere House	19 North Sq	617-523-2338	2
Peabody Museum of Archaeology and Ethnology	11 Divinity Ave	617-496-1027	20
Pierre Menard Gallery	10 Arrow St	617-868-2033	20
The Semitic Museum at Harvard University	6 Divinity Ave	617-495-4631	20
Somerville Museum	1 Westwood Rd	617-666-9810	23
The Sports Museum	150 Causeway St	617-624-1234	1
USS Constitution Museum	Charlestown Navy Yard	617-426-1812	8
Warren Anatomical Museum	10 Shattuck St	617-432-6196	15

General Information

NFT Map: 10
Address: 100 Northern Ave
Phone: 617-478-3100
Website: www.icaboston.org
Hours: Tues, Wed, Sat, Sun: 10 am–5 pm;
                Thurs, Fri 10 am–9 pm; closed Mon,
                except on Martin Luther King, Jr. Day,
                Presidents' Day, Memorial Day, Labor
                Day, Columbus Day, and Veterans' Day.
                Closed Thanksgiving, Christmas, New
                Year's Day, and July 4.
Admission: $15 for Adults - $10 for students
                and seniors. Free for Members and
                children under 17. Free from 5 to 9pm
                every Thursday night.

Overview

In 2006, the city's stodgy art scene got a royal kick in the rear when the Institute of Contemporary Art unveiled its new digs on South Boston's waterfront. The building's architecture by itself—an awe-inspiring modern masterpiece that offers a spectacular view of the harbor, an outdoor grandstand, and open gallery spaces—is well worth the museum's pricey $12 cover charge. Founded in 1936 as The Boston Museum of Modern Art, the original space was a cramped laboratory where artists were encouraged to create works that both inspired and provoked. Renamed in 1948, the ICA continued to push the envelope with a cavalcade of media, ranging from visual arts, film, video, performance, and literature. While many viewed video and digital media as the art scene's bastard stepchild in the '90s, the ICA embraced the marriage of visual design and technology.

The **Institute of Contemporary Art (Map 10)**, at just four years old, is still Boston's newest and most dynamic museum, bringing in huge shows like Shepard Fairey's Obey exhibit, and even hosting indie rock concerts. It's a museum that's cooler than the hipsters it's attracting!

The MoMA-ized new space continues the site-specific tradition with its Art Wall, located along the eastern interior of the museum's glass-enclosed lobby. Recent exhibitor Chiho Aoshima unleashed her digitally manipulated monster mural, "The Divine Gas," on the wall. Illustrated on a Macintosh G4 and printed on adhesive vinyl, the installation is a brazen statement with a Gothic sensibility. With Aoshima's mixed-media piece, it's almost like the ICA is shooting a metaphorical middle finger at those who doubted the impact digital media would eventually have on our cultural landscape.

What to See

A quick stroll from South Station or directly on the Silver Line, the ICA sits right in the middle of the newly constructed Fan Pier at the top of South Boston. You'll want to take them up on their offer of an audio tour narrated by the exhibiting artists and ICA curators that you can download to your Ipod if you brought it, or if not, the front desk will let you borrow one of theirs. They've recently started offering a phone number for people to dial into the audio tours as well, but you might get some dirty looks from the art purists strolling with you. It's interesting to be able to listen to the inspiration behind something as vexing as Misaki Kawai's "Momentum 7," a free-floating home of the future inhabited by puppets juxtaposed with the views from the ICA's permanent collection, with luminaries like Nan Goldin, Cornelia Parker, Thomas Hirschhorn, and Paul Chan.

Nestled beneath the museum's larger-than-life cantilever is the Poss Family Mediatheque where you have access to one of the museum's 18 computer stations. Here's where you can download clips with the art and artists featured at the ICA and check out the museum's footage-archive collection which offers a glimpse of exhibitions from the museum's past. Also, the Mediatheque is where you can experience the dramatic, horizontless view of the Boston Harbor.

Amenities

The museum is handicapped accessible. All bags (including your laptop) will be checked and stored in the lobby. The ICA has limited space to hang coats and it does not have its own parking garage. However, there's a paid lot immediately adjacent to the museum. Both the men's and women's restrooms are located on the first floor.

As far as food, Wolfgang Puck's Water Café offers another stellar view—not to mention some great French-bistro cuisine—where you can open the restaurant's glass doors for outdoor dining. For those who want to skip the art and head straight for the yummy pastries, museum admission is not required to dine.

SECOND FLOOR

FIRST FLOOR

Closed to the Public

West Wing Entrance

Huntington Entrance

MAP 15

1. Japanese Art
2. Islamic Art
3. Brown Gallery
4. Indian Art
5. Egyptian Mummies
6. Graphics
7. Musical Instruments
8. Nubian Art
9. Etruscan Art
10. Greek Art
11. Near-Eastern Art
12. 18th-Century American Furniture
13. 18th-Century French Art
14. 18th-Century Boston
15. English-Silver
16. 19th-Century American
17. American Federal
18. Copley & Contemporary
19. American Neoclassical & Romantic
20. American Folk Painting
21. 19th-Century Landscape
22. American Modern
23. American Masters
24. Early 20th-Century American & European
25. Chinese Art
26. Egyptian Art
27. Roman Art
28. Medieval Art
29. Euro Decorative Arts
30. Impresses
31. 19th-Century French & English
32. Post-Impressionism
33. Coolidge Collection
34. 18th-Century Italian
35. Dutch & Flemish Art
36. Renaissance
37. Spanish Chapel
38. Baroque Art
39. Himalayan Art
40. Tapestries
41. Special Exhibitions

General Information

NFT Map: 15
Address: 465 Huntington Ave
Boston, MA 02115
Phone: 617-267-9300
Website: www.mfa.org

Overview

The Museum of Fine Arts is Boston's largest and most famous art institution. The extensive permanent collection of paintings and sculpture, as well as the various lectures, films, concerts, and special traveling exhibitions, offer something for one-time sightseers and regular visitors alike. While you're there soaking up a little sophistication, enjoy a meal at one of the museum's three restaurants, and buy an artifact from the gift shop or some of their little postcards with the pretty paintings on them. Why? Because the museum needs the money. Though it's one of the largest art museums in the country, it receives little public funding. This, in part, accounts for the high admission fee. But don't worry: You get what you pay for.

The MFA is in the middle of a mammoth project that will increase the size of the museum by 28%, with an expected finish date sometime in 2010. To replace the old east wing of the museum, the MFA is building a new, 60,000-square-foot four floor addition featuring the massive Art of the Americas collection. The new wing will focus heavily on the museum's peerless colonial art of New England collection, and will feature a gallery devoted entirely to John Singer Sargeant. Check the MFA's website for project details including the exciting-sounding Ruth and Carl J Shapiro Family Courtyard.

Hours

The museum is open Mon, Tues, Sat, and Sun 10 am–4:45 pm, and Wed–Fri 10 am–9:45 pm. Special exhibitions close 15 minutes before the museum closes. The gift shop is open until 5:30 pm on Saturdays and Sundays.

Admission Fees

Admission to the MFA costs $17 for adults, $15 for seniors and college students, and $6.50 for kids 7–17 on school days until 3 pm (free at all other times). School group visits are discounted but must be scheduled in advanced.

Paid admission entitles visitors to one free visit within ten days of ticket purchase. On Wednesday evenings 4 pm–9:45 pm, admission is by voluntary contribution.

Tickets for entry can be purchased at the museum. Tickets for concerts, films, lectures, or special exhibitions can be purchased at the museum or online at www.mfa.org.

How to Get There—Driving

From the north, take I-93 S to Exit 26 (Storrow Drive). From Storrow Drive, take the Fenway/Kenmore exit. From the exit, take a left at the first traffic light, heading toward Boylston Street inbound. At the second traffic light, bear right onto The Fenway and proceed to the next set of lights. After passing through two stone gates, take the first right onto Hemenway Street and proceed to the end of the street. Take a left onto Forsythe Way and then a right onto Huntington Avenue. The museum is located a few lights down and on your right. Go past the museum and turn right onto Museum Road to reach the museum's parking lots.

From the south, take I-93 N to Exit 18 and follow the signs for Massachusetts Avenue. Turn right on Massachusetts Avenue, go past Columbus Avenue, and then turn left onto St. Botolph Street. Drive one block and turn right onto Gainsborough Street. Drive one block and turn left onto Huntington Avenue. The museum will be a couple of blocks down on your right. Go past the museum and turn right onto Museum Road to reach the museum's parking lots.

From the west, take the Mass Pike (I-90) E. Upon approaching the Boston city limits, look for Exit 22 (Prudential Center/Copley Square), the first exit after the Cambridge/Brighton toll plaza. You will enter a tunnel and Exit 22 will be on your right. Once on the exit ramp, get into the left lane (Prudential Center) and follow the exit to Huntington Avenue. Follow Huntington Avenue past the Christian Science Center (go through the underpass) and Northeastern University. The museum is located a few lights down on the right. Drive past the museum and turn right onto Museum Road to reach the museum's parking lots.

Parking

There is limited parking available at the museum, including two parking lots on Museum Road. Museum members pay $3.00 for each half-hour, $12 maximum. Non-members pay $4.00 for each half-hour with a $22 maximum for the day. A far cheaper option is public transportation.

How to Get There— Mass Transit

The museum is close to the Green Line's Museum stop (E train only) or the Orange Line's Ruggles stop. You can also take the 39 bus to the Museum stop or the 8 bus, 47 bus, or CT2 bus to the Ruggles stop.

Children's Museum of Boston

General Information

Address: 300 Congress Street
Boston, MA 02210

Phone: 617-426-6500

Website: www.bostonchildrensmuseum.org

Hours: Daily 10 am–5 pm; Fridays 10 am–9 pm.
Closed Thanksgiving and Christmas

Admission: General Admission $10, Seniors $8,
Children (Aged 2–15) $8,
Children (Under 2) $2;
Members are free.
Friday nights 5 pm–9 pm, $1 for everybody.

Overview

A word of advice to adults visiting the Boston Children's Museum: Bring earplugs. The sound of children delighting in scientific wonder can be deafening, and this interactive hands-on museum tends to be very crowded, even on weekdays. The exhibits are fun even for adults, who most likely have forgotten everything they learned in middle school science classes, but if you've ever driven the mean streets of Boston you'll appreciate how difficult it is to fight for space at many of the activities.

Created by a group of teachers in Jamaica Plain in 1913, the Boston Children's Museum moved to its current location near Fort Point Channel on the waterfront in 1979. The goal of the original museum was to teach kids about nature, cultural diversity, and science through hands-on experiences. In the 1960s, the museum expanded and became an innovator in the concept of interactive exhibits, and today there are over 16 permanent learning areas.

Now occupying a former wool factory on the prized Boston waterfront, the small and crowded Children's Museum went through a much needed renovation and expansion in 2007. A new glass-paneled addition borders the newly expanded Harborwalk, with open spaces for additional outdoor exhibits, summer concerts, and special events. More space means more exhibits, including a 3-story climbing maze (New Balance Climb), a health and fitness area with bikes, basketballs, and interactive dance activities in Kid Power, and a brand new 160-seat theater at the Kid Stage. Popular areas include the Science Playground, where kids can engage in scientific exploration, the Japanese silk merchant's house, which is an actual house transported to the museum, the Arthur exhibit, where kids can become a part of the famous children's book and TV series, and the PlaySpace for kids under three.

The outdoor area is still being developed, but there is a Nature trail, boulders to climb on, and a waterfront park to eat lunch, escape the kids, or just sit by the water with

a view of the Boston skyline. Disconcertingly, a museum promoting kids' education and healthy development once housed a McDonald's, but since the renovation, it has been replaced by the somewhat healthier Au Bon Pain. The museum is a nonprofit institution which also offers workshops, seminars, and classroom kits for teachers in their Teacher Leadership Center. Check its Website or call about special events and concerts during the summer.

How to Get There—Driving

From the north: Take I-93 South to Exit 23 "Purchase Street." At the first set of lights, take a left onto Seaport Boulevard. At the next light, take a right onto Sleeper Street. The museum is on your right.

From the south: Take I-93 North to Exit 20 "South Station/I-90." Follow signs for I-90 East, and once in the tunnel, take the first exit, labeled "South Boston." At the end of the ramp, go straight onto East Service Road. At the next intersection, turn left onto Seaport Boulevard. At the first set of lights, turn left onto Sleeper Street. The museum is on the right.

From the east: Take I-90 West to Exit 25 "South Boston." At the end of the ramp, go straight onto B Street. At the next light, take a left onto Seaport Boulevard. At the third set of lights, turn left onto Sleeper Street. The museum is on your right.

From the west: Take I-90 East towards Logan Airport. Once in the tunnel, take Exit 25 "South Boston." At the top of the ramp, bear left towards "Seaport Boulevard." At the next set of lights, stay straight onto East Service Road all the way to the end. At the next light, turn left onto Seaport Boulevard. At the second set of lights, turn left onto Sleeper Street. The museum is on your right.

Parking

The museum doesn't have its own lot or garage, but there are discounted prices for nearby lots. Both the Farnsworth Street Garage (two blocks away) and the Stillings Street Garage (four blocks away) are $9 on weekdays and $6 on weekends with museum validation. Farther away is the Moakley Courthouse Parking Lot. Street parking is hard to find and not recommended.

How to Get There— Mass Transit

Commuter rail and the MBTA Red Line and Silver Line drop you off at South Station, which is about a five minute walk away. The MBTA Silver Line stop at Courthouse Station is only a block away. Bus #4, 6, 7, and #11 all stop at South Station.

Arts & Entertainment · **Theaters**

Boston may not have the Great White Way, but the theater scene—including musical venues—is alive and vibrant; you just might have to look a little harder for it. Where to start looking? Well, the most enthused patron of theatre in the region is Larry Stark of www.theatermirror.com. If there's a production taking place anywhere within 100 miles, Larry and his cast of writers are all over it. The *Boston Phoenix* and *Dig* will also point you to good productions.

Broadway in Boston runs popular mainstream shows (e.g. *Wicked*, *Swan Lake*, *Les Miserables*) at Boston's flagship theaters such as the **Wang Theatre (Map 3)**, neighboring **Shubert Theater (Map 3)**, and the newly-restored **Opera House (Map 3)**. These theaters also produce readings, dance, and a wide variety of performances. Also of note in the Theater District: **Tribe Theatre (Map 6)** which hosts a mix of improv and irreverent performances, Emerson's **Cutler Majestic Theatre (Map 3)**, and the **Charles Playhouse (Map 3)**, with long-running favorites *Blue Man Group* and *Shear Madness*.

Away from the clamor of the Theater District down Tremont Street, you'll find the newly expanded **Boston Center for the Arts (Map 7)**, containing four performance spaces that accommodate everything from *Forbidden Broadway* to one-man shows. **The Lyric Stage Company (Map 6)** nearby on Clarendon Street stages wide-ranging seasons. The **Huntington Theatre (Map 5)** attracts top-name actors in local productions, while the **American Repertory Theater (ART) (Map 20)** in Cambridge features renowned innovative stagings.

For something a little different, check out the **Puppet Showplace Theater (Map 17)** in Brookline. For laughs, try Inman Square's **ImprovBoston (Map 28)** or the North End's **ImprovAsylum (Map 2)** (both, despite the names, do more than just improv). Scattered, smaller theaters worth a look include **Boston Playwrights' Theatre (Map 19)**, associated with BU, and the **Publick Theatre (Map 19)**, which stages open-air Shakespeare productions by the Charles River. If you like a real local flavor in your theater, check out a performance at **Jimmy Tingle's Off-Broadway Theater (Map 22)**, especially if the man himself is performing.

If you're more of a choir and orchestra person, keep your eye on what's playing at the **Sanders Theatre (Map 20)**, which also hosts the occasional jazz, folk, or roots concert. Located in Harvard's Memorial Hall, Sanders Theatre offers terrific acoustics in a classic interior. Built to offer a 180-degree perspective for the audience, the theater was inspired by a Christopher Wren design. And of course, the Boston Symphony Orchestra at **Symphony Hall (Map 5)** has a thing or two to offer as far as classical music goes. The acoustics just can't be beat.

You can pick up half-price, same-day tickets at the BosTix booth in Copley Square or at Faneuil Hall Marketplace (both accept cash only). You can find out performances for which tickets are available at www.bostix.org.

Theater	Address	Phone	Map
BCA Plaza Black Box	539 Tremont St	617-426-5000	7
Berklee Performance Center	136 Massachusetts Ave	617-747-2261	5
Blackman Auditorium/Studio Theater	360 Huntington Ave	617-373-2247	15
Boston Center for the Arts	527 Tremont St	617-426-5000	7
Boston Children's Theater	321 Columbus Ave	617-424-6634	6
Boston Opera House	539 Washington St	617-259-3400	3
Boston Playwrights'Theatre	949 Commonwealth Ave	617-353-5443	5
Charles Playhouse	74 Warrenton St	617-426-6912	3
Colonial Theatre	106 Boylston St	617-426-9366	3
Devanaughn Theatre at The Piano Factory	791 Tremont St	617-247-9777	13
Footlight Club	7A Eliot St	617-524-3200	14
Huntington Theatre Company	264 Huntington Ave	617-266-0800	5
ImprovAsylum	216 Hanover St	617-263-6887	2
ImprovBoston	40 Prospect St	617-576-1253	27
Jorge Hernandez Cultural Center	85 W Newton St	866-811-4111	7
Kresge Little Theatre	48 Massachusetts Ave	617-253-6294	27
Loeb Drama Center	64 Brattle St	617-547-8300	20
Lyric Stage Company	140 Clarendon St	617-437-7172	6
McCormack Theatre	100 Morrissey Blvd		32
Nancy and Edward Roberts Studio Theater	539 Tremont St	617-426-5000	7
Orpheum Theatre	1 Hamilton Pl	617-679-0810	3
The Publick Theatre	1400 Soldiers Field Rd	617-782-5425	19
Puppet Showplace Theatre	32 Station St	617-731-6400	17
Remis Auditorium	465 Huntington Ave	617-369-3770	15
Sanders Theatre	45 Quincy St	617-496-2222	13
Semel Theatre at Emerson College	10 Boylston Pl	617-824-8364	3
Shubert Theatre	265 Tremont St	617-482-9393	3
Stuart Street Playhouse	200 Stuart St	617-426-4499	3
Symphony Hall	301 Massachusetts Ave	617-266-1492	5
Theater at Zero Arrow Street	0 Arrow St	617-547-8300	20
Theatre Cooperative	277 Broadway	n/a	24
Tower Auditorium	621 Huntington Ave	617-879-7000	15
Tribe Theater	67 Stuart St	617-510-4447	6
Virginia Wimberley Theatre	539 Tremont St	617-266-0800	7
Wang Center for Performing Arts	265 Tremont St	617-482-9393	3
Wang Theatre	270 Tremont St	617-482-9393	3
Wheelock Family Theatre	180 The Riverway	617-879-2000	16
Wilbur Theatre	106 Boylston St	617-423-4008	3

General Information

NFT Map:	5
Address:	301 Massachusetts Ave, Boston, MA 02115
Website:	www.bostonsymphonyhall.org
Phone:	617-266-1492
Tickets:	617-266-1200; www.bso.org

Overview

Boston Symphony Hall, home of the Boston Symphony Orchestra and Boston Pops, is regarded as one of the finest concert halls in the world. Modeled after the German Leipzig Gewandhaus and the old Boston Music Hall, Symphony Hall was the first American hall designed to maximize acoustics, thanks to Harvard physics professor Wallace Clement Sabine (and to think you slept through your physics class!). Classical music connoisseurs recognize the hall as a space that produces a near-perfect sound experience, thanks to the sloping walls and floor of the stage and the alignment of the recessed Greek and Roman statues. The Hall, designed by New York architects McKim, Mead, & White, opened in 1900, replacing the Boston Music Hall, which was in the way of the burgeoning subway system. The hall seats 2,625 people in the Boston Symphony Orchestra (BSO) season and 2,371 in the Boston Pops Orchestra season (in the original leather seats from 1900). Don't leave without checking out the Aeolian-Skinner organ with 67 stops and 5,130 pipes. Free tours offer an insight into the history and features of Symphony Hall.

Symphony Hall contains dozens of museum-like items documenting notable events in its history. You can learn just what was so revolutionary about the acoustics and famous composers. Excitement and pride leaps from a reprinted *Boston Globe* article documenting the first performance. A 2006 renovation of the concert floor rebuilt it using the original processes, equipment manufacturers, and the exact same materials, in order to retain its premium acoustic properties.

In the past the Hall has hosted auto shows, mayoral inaugurations, meetings of the Communist Party, and a performance by Harry Houdini. You can also celebrate New Year's in style here as the orchestra performs in the background. (Bring your tux.) The tradition of hosting non-traditional events looks set to continue. In recent years, the US Open Squash Tournament has been held at Symphony Hall, using portable glass courts placed just below the stage.

If you're looking to throw your own Diddy-like party, function rooms and hall spaces can be rented for your own private shindig.

But unless you're making Manny Ramirez-style money, you probably can't afford it. Renting out Symphony Hall for a night costs between $4,700 and $6,200. Five different function spaces are available for rent and cost between $700 and $2,700 per night.

How to Get Tickets

You can purchase tickets to any of the Symphony Hall performances online at www.bso.org, in person at the Symphony Hall box office, or by phone on 617-266-1200 or 617-638-9283 (TDD/TTY).

How to Get There—Driving

From the north, take I-93 to Storrow Drive (Exit 26). Once you're on Storrow Drive, bear left towards Copley Square/Back Bay. Turn right onto Beacon Street. Turn left onto Clarendon Street. Turn right onto St. James Avenue. Bear left onto Huntington Avenue. Symphony Hall is on the corner of Huntington Avenue and Massachusetts Avenue.

From the south, take I-93 to Exit 18 and follow signs toward Massachusetts Avenue. Turn right onto Massachusetts Avenue.

From the west, take the Mass Pike (I-90) to the Prudential Center/Copley Square (Exit 27) and merge onto Huntington Avenue. Symphony Hall is on the corner of Huntington Avenue and Massachusetts Avenue.

Parking

There are two pay parking garages on Westland Avenue, another parking garage on Gainsborough Street next to Jordan Hall at the New England Conservatory, and very limited street parking. The Prudential Center Garage offers discount parking with the presentation of a performance ticket stub from the same day if you enter the garage after 5 pm.

How to Get There—Mass Transit

The Green Line's E train stops at Symphony Hall. Other Green Line trains that stop at the Hynes Convention Center will get you close. Another option is to take the Orange Line to the Massachusetts Avenue stop.

The #1 bus, which runs down Massachusetts Avenue from Harvard Square to Dudley Square, stops mere feet from Symphony Hall.

General Information

NFT Map: 3
Address: One Hamilton Pl, Boston, MA 02108
Website: www.ticketmaster.com/venue/8318
Phone: 617-679-0810
Ticketmaster: www.ticketmaster.com

Overview

The Orpheum has been around since 1852, and despite renovations, it can still feel like its age, which many consider part of the charm. (Apparently, they have not heard of this thing called The Internet either...) The Orpheum originally had an eye on high-brow stuff: Tchaikovsky along with the Boston Symphony Orchestra made debuts there. Now, it packs in close to 3,000 people to witness an eclectic lineup of acts ranging from Larry the Cable Guy to Norah Jones to Nine Inch Nails, and tickets often sell out quickly. Bands love the Orpheum for its premium acoustics (several live albums have been recorded here), and view-wise there isn't a bad seat in the house, though leg room is notably sparse.

How to Get Tickets

Tickets can be purchased from the Orpheum Theater Box Office Mon–Sat, 10 am–5 pm. Tickets can also be purchased online at www.ticketmaster.com or by calling 617-679-0810.

How to Get There—Driving

From the north, take I-93 S to Exit 24A (Government Center). At the bottom of the ramp, bear right onto New Chardon Street. At the second set of lights, take a left onto Cambridge Street. Stay on the right-hand side of Cambridge Street, which will become Tremont Street as soon as you pass City Hall Plaza (on your left). Drive two blocks down on Tremont Street. The Orpheum will be on your left on Hamilton Place.

From the south, take I-93 N to Exit 23 (Government Center). At the end of the ramp, follow signs for Government Center/Faneuil Hall. At the set of lights, make a left onto North Street. Drive a quarter-mile to the end of North Street, then make a left onto Congress Street. Take your first right onto State Street, which turns into Court Street after a few feet. Follow Court Street to the end, then make a left at the fork onto Tremont Street. Drive two blocks farther on Tremont Street. The Orpheum will be on your left on Hamilton Place.

From the west, take the Mass Pike (I-90) E to Exit 24B, which will dump you onto I-93 N. From there follow the directions above for driving from the south.

Parking

Street parking will be scarce, especially during event hours. The closest parking lots are on Tremont Street, under Boston Common, and on Washington Street.

How to Get There—Mass Transit

Take the Red or Green Line to the Park Street stop or the Orange Line to Downtown Crossing. The theater is just a short walk from both stops. It's directly across from the Park Street Church.

General Information

NFT Map: 3
Address: 270 Tremont St, Boston, MA 02116
Website: www.citicenter.org
Phone: 617-482-9393
Tele-charge: www.telecharge.com, 800-447-7400

Overview

The Shubert Theatre is the "Little Princess" to the Wang Theatre's "Grand Dame." The 1,600-seat venue opened in 1910 and has since undergone two major renovations. The theater's elaborate entranceway was destroyed during the widening of Tremont Street in 1925, and in 1996, $6 million was spent restoring and improving the theater's original ornate French Renaissance architecture. The intimacy within the Shubert remained intact, and the theater is now the home of the Boston Lyric Opera, many Boston arts organizations, as well as several touring companies. Broadway shows, including such classics as The King and I and South Pacific, debuted at the Shubert before making their way to New York. Once part of the not-for-profit Wang Center for the Performing Arts, both theaters have sadly had to sell off naming rights in an attempt to stay solvent. The Wang and Shubert are now owned by the Citigroup umbrella and carry the Citi moniker in front of their traditional names.

How to Get Tickets

You can purchase tickets for the Shubert Theatre online at www.telecharge.com or by calling Tele-charge at 800-447-7400.

How to Get There—Driving

From the north, take I-93 S to Exit 23 (South Station), which dumps you onto Purchase Street. Immediately after the Chinatown Gate (on your right), take a right onto Kneeland Street. Go straight for several blocks and then turn left onto Tremont Street. The Shubert Theatre is on your right.

From the south, take I-93 N to Exit 20 (South Station) and immediately get into the left-hand lane. The sign overhead will read "Detour South Station via Frontage Road." Take this left exit off the ramp and follow Frontage Road north to South Station. Turn left onto Kneeland Street. Go straight for several blocks, and then turn left onto Tremont Street. The Shubert Theatre is on your right.

From the west, take the Mass Pike (I-90) to Exit 24A. Turn left onto Kneeland Street. Go straight for several blocks and then turn left onto Tremont Street. The Shubert Theatre is on your right.

Parking

Your best bets are the parking lot on the corner of Tremont and Stuart Streets, the lot at the Radisson Hotel on Stuart Street, the Kinney Motor Mart on Stuart Street, or the Fitz-Inn lot on Kneeland Street.

How to Get There—Mass Transit

The Orange Line's New England Medical Center stop and the Green Line's Boylston Street stop are both one block away from the theater. The Red Line's Park Street stop on Tremont Street is three or so blocks from the theater.

General Information

NFT Map: 3
Address: 270 Tremont St, Boston, MA 02116
Website: www.citicenter.org
Phone: 617-482-9393
Tele-charge: www.telecharge.com,
                800-447-7400

Overview

Surviving several name changes and heavy renovation over the years, the Wang Theatre has remained a prominent feature of the Boston theater scene. With 3,600 seats, it is the larger of the two performance spaces once operated by the Wang Center for the Performing Arts and now owned by Citigroup (the other is the famous Shubert Theatre) across the street). Though the Wang and Shubert keep their names, the complex is now known as the Citi Performing Arts Center.

Opened in the "Roaring Twenties" (1925) as the Metropolitan Theatre, the venue was considered to be a "magnificent movie cathedral" with its ornate interior resembling something from Louis XIV's palace. Renamed the Music Hall in 1962, the theater became home to the then-fledgling Boston Ballet. As the years passed, the shiny gem began to lose some of its luster and relevance. Some minor renovations were made, but it wasn't until 1983, when Dr. An Wang stepped in to resuscitate the theater, that things took a turn for the better. Since the restoration, the theater has played host to such classics as *Les Miserables*, *The Phantom of the Opera* , and *Spamalot*, and still houses one of New England's largest movie screens. Still home to the Boston Ballet, the Wang has expanded its repertoire to include pop concerts and comedians. The *Nutcracker at the Wang* (snicker...) holiday tradition is no more (it moved to The Opera House), replaced by the very un-Boston "Radio City Christmas Spectacular" featuring high-kicking Rockettes wearing reindeer antlers.

How to Get Tickets

You can purchase tickets for the Wang Theatre online at www.telecharge.com or by calling Tele-charge at 800-447-7400. The Wang Theatre Box Office, open Monday through Saturday from 10 am until 6 pm, sells tickets without the nasty service charges levied by external vendors.

How to Get There—Driving

From the north, take I-93 to Exit 20A (South Station), which dumps you onto Purchase Street. Immediately after the Chinatown Gate (on your right) take a right onto Kneeland Street. Go straight for several blocks and then turn left onto Tremont Street. The Wang Theatre is on your left.

From the south, take I-93 N to Exit 20 (South Station) and immediately get into the left-hand lane. Follow signs for South Station and take the left exit for South Station/Chinatown. At the second light, turn left onto Kneeland Street. Go straight for several blocks, turn left onto Tremont Street. The Wang Theatre is on your left.

From the west, take the Mass Pike (I-90) E to Exit 24A. Turn left onto Kneeland Street. Go straight for several blocks and then turn left onto Tremont Street. The Wang Theatre is on your left.

Parking

Your best bets are the parking lot on the corner of Tremont and Stuart Streets, the lot at the Radisson Hotel on Stuart Street, the Kinney Motor Mart on Stuart Street, or the Fitz-Inn lot on Kneeland Street.

How to Get There—Mass Transit

The Orange Line's New England Medical Center stop and the Green Line's Boylston Street stop are both one block away from the theater. The Red Line's Park Street stop on Tremont Street is about three blocks from the theater.

Join us for
lunch, dinner,
and late night drinks.

Hong Kong Restaurant

Harvard Square
1238 Mass Ave, Cambridge
617-864-5311
hongkongharvard.com

Call us for delivery and catering.

Key to Boston neighborhoods	
AL	Allston
BR	Brighton
DO	Dorchester
EB	East Boston
HP	Hyde Park
JP	Jamaica Plain
MT	Mattapan
RS	Roslindale
RX	Roxbury
SB	South Boston
WR	West Roxbury

Boston

1st St	29	B1
E 1st St		
(1-480)	10	B2
(482-999)	11	B1/B2
W 1st St	10	A1/B2
2nd St	29	B1
E 2nd St		
(34-539)	10	B2
(540-948)	11	B1/B2
W 2nd St		
(1-28)	12	A2
(29-475)	10	A1/B2
2nd New Way	33	B2
3rd Pl	10	B2
E 3rd St		
(400-458)	10	B2
(459-898)	11	B1/B2
W 3rd St	10	A1/B1/B2
3rd New Way	33	B2
W 3rd Street Pl	10	B1
E 4th St		
(465-595)	10	B2
(596-999)	11	B2
W 4th St		
(1-15)	7	A2
(16-87)	12	A2
(88-464)	10	A1/B1
4th Street Pl	10	B2
E 5th St		
(388-475)	10	B2
(476-899)	11	B1/B2
W 5th St		
(1-18)	12	A2
(19-308)	10	A1/B1
E 6th St		
(400-484)	10	B2
(485-899)	11	B1/B2
W 6th St		
(1-49)	12	A2
(50-268)	10	B1
E 7th St		
(397-480)	10	B2
(481-810)	11	B1/B2
W 7th St	10	B1
E 8th St		
(223-481)	10	B1/B2
(482-799)	11	B1
W 8th St	10	B1
E 9th St	10	B1
W 9th St	10	B1
A St [HP]	33	B2
A St [SB]	10	A1
A St [WR]	29	B1
Abandoned Railroad	29	B2
Abbey Rd	18	A2
Abbot St	31	A1

Abbotsford St	13	B1
Aberdeen St	16	A2
Acacia Rd	29	B2
Academy Ct	13	B1
Academy Rd	13	B1
Academy Ter	13	B1
Academy Hill Rd	18	B2
Acadia St	11	B2
Accolyn Way	1	A2
Achorn Cir	14	B1
Ackley Pl	14	B2
Acorn St	1	B1
Acton St	33	B1
Ada St	30	B2
Adair Rd	18	A1
Adams Pl	1	B1
Adams St [DO]		
(1-1135)	32	A2/B1
(1136-1299)	31	B2
Adams St [HP]	33	B1
Adams St [RX]	13	A2
Adams Ter	32	B1
Adamson St	19	A1
Adanac Ter	32	B1
Addington Rd	29	A1/A2
Adelaide St	14	A2
Adelaide Ter	14	A2
Adella Pl	19	A1
Adirondack Pl	31	B2
Adrain St	13	B2
Agassiz Rd	15	A2
Agassiz Park	14	B1
Agawam St	32	B1
Agnes Ave	31	B1
Aguadilla St	7	A1
Ainsley St	32	B1
Ainsworth St	30	B1
Akron Pl	13	B1
Akron St	13	B1
Alabama St	31	B1
Alameda Rd	29	A2
Alaric St	29	B2
Alaric Ter	29	B2
Alaska St	13	B2
Alban St	32	B1
Albano St	30	B1
Albany St		
(165-168)	4	B1
(169-790)	7	A2/B1/B2
(791-999)	13	A2
Albemarle Ct	5	B2
Albemarle Ct [HP]	33	B1
Albemarle St	5	B2
Albemarle Ter	5	B2
Alberta St	29	A2
Albion St [HP]	33	B2
Albion St [RX]	12	B1
Albright St	29	A1
Alcorn St	19	A2
W Alcorn St	19	A2
Alcott St	19	A1
Alder St	30	B1
Aldie St	19	A1
Aldine St	4	A2
Aldo Ter	33	B2
Aldrich St		
(1-90)	30	B1
(91-199)	29	A2
Aldwin Rd	30	B2
Aldworth St	14	B1
Alexander St	32	A1
Alfred St	14	B2
Alfred Ter	23	A2

Alger St		
(1-51)	12	A2
(52-99)	10	B1
Algonquin St	31	A2
Alhambra Rd	29	A2
Alicia Rd	32	B2
Alkyris Rd	29	B2
Allandale St	30	A1
Alleghany St	15	B1/B2
Allen Rd	18	B1
Allen St [HP]	33	B1
Allen St [RS]	30	B1
Allenwood St	29	A2
Allerton St		
(1-19)	13	A2
(20-99)	12	B1
Alley 516	7	A1
Alleyne St	29	B2
Allstate Rd	12	B1
Allston St [AL]	19	A1/B1
Allston St [DO]	32	B1
Almont St	31	B1
Alna Pl	9	B1
Alpha Rd	32	B1
Alpheus Rd	33	A1
Alpine Ct	31	B1
Alpine Pl	13	B1
Alpine St [MT]	31	B1
Alpine St [RX]	13	A1/B1
Alpine Way	32	A2
Alta Crest Rd	29	B2
Altair Rd	29	B2
Althea St	32	B1
Alther St	13	A2
Alton Ct	15	B2
Alvah Kittredge Park	13	A1
Alvan Ter	32	A1
Alvarado Ave	33	B1
Alveston St	14	B1/B2
Alveston Ter	14	B2
Alward Rd	29	A2
Alwyn St	33	B1
Amboy St	19	A2
Ambrose St	13	A2
American Legion Hwy		
(1-568)	31	A1
(569-864)	30	B2
(867-1099)	33	A2
Ames St	31	A1/B2
Amesbury St	29	A1
Amherst St	30	B1
Amory Ave	14	A2
Amory St	14	A2/B2
Amory Ter	14	A2
Amy Ct	1	A2
Anawan Ave	29	A2
Anawan Ter	29	A2
Anchor Way	11	A2
Anderer Ln	29	A1
Anderson St	1	B1
N Anderson St	1	B1
Andover Rd	30	A1
Andrew McArdle Brg	9	A1
Andrews Pl	7	B2
W Andrews Pl	7	B2
Andrews St	7	B2
Andria Rd	33	A2
Angell St	31	A1
Anita Ter	13	A1
Ann St	32	B2
Annabel St	32	A1
Annafran St	33	A2

Street Index

Street	Page	Grid
Annapolis St	32	A1
Annunciation Rd	15	A2
Ansel Rd	31	B1
Anselm Ter	18	B1
Anson St	14	B1
Ansonia Rd	29	B2
Anthony Pl	2	B1
Anthony J Grieco Ter	19	A1
Antwerp St	9	A1
Appian Pl	19	A1
Appian Way	19	A1
Appleton St		
(1-129)	7	A1/A2
(130-399)	6	B1
Aquadilla St	7	A1
Aramon St	9	B2
Arbella Rd	31	B2
Arborcrest Ter	31	B1
Arboretum Rd	30	A2
Arborfield Rd	33	A2
Arborough Rd	30	B1
Arborview Rd	30	A1
Arborway	31	A1
(1-502)	14	B1/B2
Arborway Ter	14	B1
Arbroth St	32	B2
Arbutus St	31	B1
Arcadia St [DO]	32	B1
Arcadia St [RX]	14	A2
Arcadia Ter	32	B1
Arcadia Park	32	B1
Arch St	4	A1
Arch Way	2	B2
Archdale Rd	30	B2
Archer St	13	A1
Arcola St	14	A2
Ardale St	30	B1
Ardee St	9	B2
Arden St	19	A1
Ardent St	30	B1
Ardmore Rd	29	A2
Argus Pl	18	B2
Argyle St	32	B1
Argyle Ter	32	B1
Arion St	14	A2
Arklow St	18	A1
Arlington Ct		
Arlington St		
(1-7)	1	B1
(9-176)	3	A1/B1
(181-199)	7	B1
Arlington St [BR]	18	A1/A2
Arlington St [HP]	33	A2
Armandine St	31	B2
Armington St	19	A1
Armstrong St	14	A2
N Arsenal St	18	A2
Arthur St	16	A2
Arundel St	14	A2
Arvale Rd	31	A2
Ascot St	18	A2
Ash St	4	B1
Ashburton Pl	1	B2
Ashcroft St	14	A1
Asheville Rd	33	A1
Ashfield St	30	B1
Ashford Ct	19	A2
Ashford St	19	A1
Ashford St	19	A1/A2
Ashford Ter	29	B2
Ashland Ave	31	B2
Ashland St	31	B2
Ashley St	14	A2
Ashmont Ct	32	B1
Ashmont St	32	B1/B2
Ashmont Park	32	B1
Ashmore Rd	30	B2
Ashton St	31	B1
Ashwood Ter	30	B2
Ashworth Park	13	B1
Aspen St	13	B2
Aspinwall Rd	31	A2
Asticou Rd	30	A2
Astoria St	31	B1
Astral St	31	A2
Athelwold St	10	A1/B1/B2
Athens St	32	B1
Atherstone St	30	B1
Atherton Ave	14	A2
Atherton Pl	14	A2
Atherton St	14	A2
Athol St	19	A1
Atkinson St	12	B1
Atlantic Ave		
(1-248)	2	A2/B2
(252-799)	4	A2/B1/B2
Atlantic St	10	B2
Atlantis St	29	A1
Atwill Rd	29	A2
Atwood Rd	18	B2
Atwood Sq	14	B1
Auckland St	32	A1
Augustus Ave	30	B1
Auriga St	32	B1
Austin St [DO]	31	A1
Austin St [JP]	33	A2
Autumn St	16	B1
Autumn St [WR]	29	B2
Avalon Rd	29	A2
Avander Ct	31	B1
Avenue de Lafayette		
(1-8)	3	A2
(9-99)	4	A1
Avenue Louis Pasteur	15	A1
Averton St	30	B1
Avery Pl	3	A2
Avery St	3	A2
Avila Rd	33	B1
Avon St	3	A2
Avon St [JP]	30	A1
Avondale St	33	B2
Ayles Rd	18	B2
Ayr Rd	33	B2
B St [HP]	10	A1/A2
B St [SB]	16	A1
Babbitt St	31	B1
Babson St	31	B1
Back St	1	B1
Badger Rd	33	B2
Bagnal St	19	A1
Bailey St	32	B1
Baird St	31	B1
Baker Ave	32	A1
Baker Ct	12	B1
Baker Pl	29	A1
Baker St	29	A1/B1/B2
Bakers Aly	2	B1
Bakersfield St	32	A1
Balch St	2	A1
Baldwin Pl	18	B2
Baldwin Pl [BR]	10	A1
Baldwin St	13	B2
Balfour St	31	B2
Balina Pl	13	A2
Ball St	14	B1
Ballard St	14	B1
Ballard Way [JP]	14	B1
Ballard Way [SB]	11	A2
Balliol St	19	A1
Ballou Ave	31	B1/B2
Ballou Pl	31	B2
Balmoral Park	11	B1
Balsam St	31	B1
Bancroft St	14	A2
Banfield Ave	31	B1
Bangor Rd	29	A2
Banks St	29	A1
Banton St	32	B1
Bantry Way	11	B1
Barbara St	14	A2
Barclay Rd	29	A2
Bard Ave	13	A2
Bardwell St	14	B1
Barker St	18	A2
Barlow St	30	A2
Barna Rd	32	B1
Barnard Pl	11	B1
Barrett Ave	11	B1
Barrington Rd	32	B1
Barrows St	19	A1
Barry St [DO]	32	A1
Barry St [HP]	33	B1/B2
Barry Park	32	A1
Barstow St	18	A2
Bartlett Ave	29	B1
Bartlett Pl	2	A1
Bartlett Sq	14	B2
Bartlett St	13	A1
Basile St	30	B1
Basto Ter	30	B1
Batchelder St	12	B1
Bateman St	33	A1
Bateswell Rd	32	B1
Battery St	2	A2
Battery Wharf	2	A2
Batterymarch St	4	A2
Batterymarch Arm	4	A2
Baxter St	10	B1
S Bay Ave	12	A1
Bay St	3	B1
Bay St [DO]	32	A1
Bay State Pl	11	B1
Bay State Road	16	A1/A2
Bay View Pl	11	B1
Bayard St	19	A1
Bayside St	32	A2
Beach St		
(1-15)	3	B2
(16-199)	4	B1
Beach St [DO]	32	B1
Beach Point Pl	32	A2
Beacon St		
(1-105)	1	B1/B2
(106-297)	6	A1/A2
(298-588)	5	A1/A2
(589-1230)	16	A1/A2
Beacon St [HP]	33	B2
N Beacon St		
(1-58)	19	A1
(59-381)	18	A1/A2
Beal Pl	33	B1
Beale St	32	B1
Bearse Ave	32	B1
Beaufield St	32	B1
Beauford Ln	13	B2
Beaufort Rd	14	A1
Beaumont St	32	B1
Beaver Pl	1	B1
Beaver St	1	B1
Beaver St [HP]	33	A1/B1
Beck St	9	A2
Becket St	32	B1
Beckler Ave	11	B1
Beckwith St	32	A1
Bedford St		
(1-15)	3	A2
(19-199)	4	B1
Beech St		

Street	Pg	Grid
(1-218)	29	A2
(219-402)	30	B1
(403-799)	33	A1
Beech Glen St	13	B1
Beechcroft St	18	A1
Beecher St	14	A2
Beechland St	30	B1
Beechmont St	33	A1/A2
Beechmont Ter	33	A2
Beechwood St	31	A2
Beethoven St	14	A2
Belden Sq	32	A1
Belden St	32	A1
Belfort St	32	A1
Belgrade Ave		
(1-257)	30	B1
(258-499)	29	B2
Belgrade Ter	29	A2
Belgravia Pl	2	A2
Bell Ct	10	B1
Bellaire Rd	29	A2
Belle Ave	29	B1
Bellevue St [DO]	32	A1
Bellevue St [WR]		
(1-307)	29	A2/B2
(308-399)	33	A1
Bellevue Ter	23	A2
Bellevue Hill Rd		
(1-54)	29	A2
(55-199)	33	A1
Bellflower St	33	A1
W Bellflower St	12	B2
Bellingham Pl	1	B1
Bellvista Rd	19	B1
Belmore Ter	14	A2
Belnap Rd	33	B1
Belnel Rd	31	B1
Belton St	32	B2
Belvidere St	5	B2
Bennet Pl	9	A1
N Bennet Pl	2	A1
Bennet St	4	B1
N Bennet St	2	A1
N Bennett Ct	2	A1
Bennett St	18	A1/A2
Bennington St	9	A1/A2
Benson St	18	A2
Bent Ct	10	B2
Bentham Rd	32	B1
Bentley St	18	A2
Benton St	13	A1
Beram St	33	A1
Berkeley St		
(1-83)	7	A1/A2
(84-399)	6	B2/B2
E Berkeley St	7	A2
Berkshire St	32	B1
Bernard Pl	11	B1
Bernard St	31	A2
Bernice St	32	B2
Berry St	32	B2
Bertram St	19	A1
Bertson Ave	29	A1
Berwick St	29	A1
Beryl St	30	B1
Bethune Way	13	A2
Beverly St		
(1-125)	2	A1
(126-299)	30	A2
Bexley Rd	30	B1/B2
Bickford Ave	15	B1
Bickford St	14	A2
Bicknell St	31	A2
Bigelow Cir	18	A1
Bigelow St	18	A1
Billings Ln	30	A1
Billings St	29	B1
Bills Ct	15	A2
Bilodeau Rd	31	A2
Biltmore St	14	B2
Binford St	10	A1
Binney St	15	A1
Birch Rd	29	B2
Birch St	30	B1
Birchcroft Rd	33	A2
Birchland Ave	29	B2
Birchland Ter	29	B2
Birchwood St	29	B2
Bird St		
(1-153)	32	A1
(154-199)	13	B2
Bishop St	14	B2
Bismarck St [JP]	14	A2
Bismarck St [MT]	31	B1
Bispham St	32	B1
Black Falcon Ave	11	A1
Blackfan St	15	A1
Blackstone St	2	B1
Blackwell St	32	B2
Blackwood St	5	B2
Blagden St	6	A1
Blaine St	19	A1
Blake St		
(1-63)	33	A2
(64-199)	31	B1
Blakemore St	30	B2
Blakeville St	32	A1
Blanchard St	13	A1
Blanche St	32	B2
Blandford St	16	A2
Blanvon Rd	30	B2
Blenford Rd	18	B2
Bloomfield St	32	B1
Bloomington St	32	B2
Blossom Ct	1	A1
Blossom St	1	A1
Blue Hill Ave		
(1-358)	13	B2
(359-1699)	31	A1/A2
Blue Hills Pky	31	B1
Blue Ledge Dr	33	A1
Blue Ledge Ter	33	A1
Bluefield Ter	31	B1
Blueview Cir	29	B2
Blueview Rd	29	B2
Board Aly	2	B1
Boates Ct	4	A2
Bobolink St	33	A1
Bodwell St	32	A1
Bogandale Rd	29	B2
Bolster St	14	A2
Bolton St	10	A1/B1
Bonad Rd	29	A2
Bonair St	29	A1/A2
Bond St	7	A2
Bonnel Ter	13	A1
Bonner Ter	13	A1
Boradal St	2	A2
Border St	9	A1/B1
Boriken St	7	A1
Boston Pl	2	B1
Boston St	12	B2
Boston Fish Pier	11	A1
Boston Medical Center Pl	7	B1
Bostonia Ave	18	B1
Bosworth St	3	A2
Bothwell Rd	18	A1
Boulevard Ter	19	B1
W Boundary Rd	29	B2
Bourne St	30	B2
Bournedale Rd	30	B2
Bourneside St	32	B1
Boutwell St	32	B2
Bow St		
(1-26)	33	B2
(27-199)	23	A2
Bowditch Rd	30	A1
Bowdoin Ave	31	A2
Bowdoin St [DO]		
(1-92)	31	A2
(93-499)	32	A1/B1
Bowdoin Park	32	A1
Bowen St	10	B1
Bower St	13	B1
Bower Ter	14	B1
Bowker St	1	A2
Bowman St	32	B2
Boxford Ter	29	A2
Boyd St	32	B1
Boyden St	31	B2
Boylston St	3	B1
Boylston Pl [JP]	14	A2
Boylston Sq	3	B2
Boylston St		
(1-440)	3	B1/B2
(442-699)	6	A1/A2
(700-1155)	5	A2/B1/B2
(1156-1499)	15	A1/A2
Boylston St [JP]	14	A2/B2
Boynton St	14	B1/B2
Brackett St	18	A1
Bradbury St	19	A1
Braddock Park	6	B1
Bradeen St	30	B2
Bradfield Ave	30	B1
Bradford Cir	30	B1
Bradford Rd	31	B2
Bradford St	7	A2
Bradlee Ct	33	A2
Bradlee Ln	33	A2
Bradlee St [DO]	31	A2
Bradlee St [HP]	33	A2
Bradlee Park	33	A2
Bradshaw St	31	A2
Bradston St	12	A1
Bradstreet Ave	30	B2
Bradwood St	29	A2
Braeburn Rd	33	A1
Braemore Rd	18	B2
Braewood St	33	A1/A2
Bragdon St		
(1-40)	13	B1
(41-109)	14	B1
Brahms St	30	B1
Brainard Rd	33	B1
Brainerd Rd	19	B1
Braintree St	19	A1
Branch St	1	B1
Branchfield St	31	B1
Branton St	32	B2
Branwin Harris Way	13	A2
Brattle Way	1	A2/B2
Bray St	13	B1
Bremen Pl	9	B1
Bremen St	9	A1/A2/B1
S Bremen St	9	B1
Bremen Ter	30	B1
Brenen St	9	A2
Brent St	32	B1
Brenton St	31	A2
Brentwood St	19	A1
Brewer St	14	B1
Brewster St	11	B1
Bridge Ct	1	B1

Street Index

Street Index

Street	Map	Grid
Bridge St		
(1-199)	31	B1
(340-399)	29	B1
Brier Rd	29	B2
Briercliff Ter	31	B1
Briggs Pl	7	A2
Brigham St	9	B1
Brighton Ave	19	A1/A2
Brimmer St	1	B1
Brinsley St	31	A2
Brinton St	13	B1
Bro Joseph A Herran Way	29	B1
Broad St		
(1-49)	2	B1
(50-199)	4	A2
Broadlawn Park	29	A1
Broadway	3	B1
E Broadway		
(481-567)	10	B2
(568-999)	11	B1/B2
W Broadway	10	A1/B1/B2
Brock St	18	A1/B1
Brockton St	31	B1
Bromfield St	3	A2
Bromley St	15	B2
Bronsdon St	18	A2
Bronx Rd	29	B2
Brook Ave	13	B2
Brook Farm Rd	29	A1/A2
Brook Marshall Rd	13	A1
Brookdale St	30	B2
Brookfield St	30	B1
Brookford St	13	B2
Brookledge St	31	A1
Brookley Rd		
(1-17)	14	B2
(18-56)	30	A2
(57-118)	31	A1
Brookline Ave	16	A2/B1
Brookline Pl	16	B1
E Brookline St	7	B1/B2
W Brookline St	7	A1/B1
Brooks St	9	A1
Brooks St [BR]	18	A1
Brooksdale Rd	18	A1
Brookside Ave	14	B2
Brookvale St	31	B1
Brookview St	31	B1
Brookway Rd	30	A2/B2
Brookway Ter	30	B2
Brookwood Ter	30	B1/B2
Brown Ave	31	A2
Brown Ter	14	B1
Browning Ave	31	A2
Brownson Ter	30	A1
Bruce St	32	B1
Brucewood St	29	A2
Brunswick St	31	A2
Brush Hill Ter	33	B2
Brushwood Cir	33	B2
Bryant Rd	29	B2
Bryon Rd	29	A1
Buchanan St	30	A1/B1
Buckingham St	33	B1
Buckley Ave	15	B1
Bucknam St	19	A2
Buick St	19	A2
Bulfinch Pl	1	A2/B2
Bullard St	31	A2
Bullock St	10	A1/A2
Bumstead Ct	3	B1
Bungalow Rd	29	B2
Bunker St	33	B1
Burard St	29	A1
Burbank St	5	B1
Burgess St	32	A1
Burgoyne St	32	B1
Burke St [RX]	13	A1
Burke St [SB]	10	B1
Burley St	33	A2
Burlington Ave	16	A2
Burmah St	31	B1
Burnett St	14	B2
Burney St	15	B2
Burnham Pl	11	B1
Burnside Ave	29	A2
Burr St	14	A2
Burrage St	14	A1
Burrell St	12	B1
Burrill Pl	11	B1
Burroughs Pl	14	B1
Burroughs St	14	B1
Burwood Rd	29	A2
Burt St	32	B1
Burton Ave	13	B2
Burwell Rd	29	A2
Bush St	7	B2
Bushnell St	32	B1
Business St	33	B1/B2
Business Ter	33	B1
Bussey St	30	B2
Buswell St	16	A1
Butland Ct	11	B2
Butler Pl	2	A1
Butler Row	2	B1
Butler Sq	2	B1
Butler St	10	A2
Butler St [DO]	31	B2
Buttonwood Ct	12	B2
Buttonwood St		
(1-21)	32	A1
(22-199)	12	B2
Bynner St	14	A1/A2
Byrd Ave	30	B2
Byron St	1	B1
C St		
(1-24)	11	A1
(59-550)	10	A1/A2/B1
Cabot St	13	A1
Caddy Rd	31	B2
Cahners Pl	13	A1
Calder St	31	A1
Caledonian Ave	29	B1
Call St	14	B2
Callahan Pl	20	B1
Callahan Tunl	2	B1
Callender St	31	B1/B2
Calumet St	15	B1
Calvin Pl	10	A2
Calvin Rd	30	A1
Cambria St	5	B2
Cambridge St	1	B1
Cambridge St [AL]		
(1-567)	19	A1/A2
(568-799)	18	A2/B2
Cambridge Ter	19	A1
Cambridge Street Ave	1	B1
Camden St	13	A1/A2
Camelia Rd	33	A2
Camelot Ct	18	B2
Cameron St	32	A1
Camp Rd	29	B2
E Campbell Pl	13	A2
Canaan St	31	B1
Canal St		
(1-103)	2	A1/B1
(104-199)	1	B2
Candor Pl	14	B2
Canterbury St	30	B2
Canton Pl	7	A1
E Canton St	7	B2
W Canton St		
(1-173)	7	A1
(174-299)	6	B1
Capen Pl	31	B2
Capen St	29	A1
Capital St	11	A2
Capstan Way	13	B1
Cardington St	6	B1
Carleton St	30	B2
Carlford Rd	13	B2
Carlisle St	31	B1
Carlos St	32	B1
Carlotta St	29	A2
Carlson Cir	33	B2
Carlson Rd	15	B2
Carmel St	32	B1
Carmela Ln	31	A2
Carmen St	10	B1
Carmody St	19	B1
Carol Ave	29	B2
Carol Cir	14	B1/B2
Carolina Ave	14	B2
Carolina Pl	10	B1
Carpenter St	29	A1
Carroll St	29	B2
Carrolton Rd	32	B1
Carruth St	32	A1
Carson St	31	A1
Cary St	31	B2
Caryll St	29	A1
Caspar St	32	A2
Caspian Way	29	B2
Cass St	32	B1
Cassnet St	9	B1
Castle Ct [EB]	7	B1
Castle Ct [RX]	31	A2
Castlegate Rd	32	A1
Castlerock St	14	A1
Castleton St	14	B1
Cataumet St	13	B1
Catawba St	30	A2
Catenaccia Way	30	B2
Catherine St	31	B1
Caton St	1	A2
Causeway St		
(1-159)	1	A2
(160-299)	32	A1
Cawfield St	6	B2
Cazenove St	32	A1
Cedar Pl	3	B1
S Cedar Pl	29	B2
Cedar Rd	13	B1
Cedar Sq	31	A2/B2
Cedar St [MT]	31	A1/B1
Cedar St [RX]	1	B1
W Cedar St	32	B2
Cedar Grove St	13	B1
Cedar Lane Way	1	B1
Cedar Park	13	A1
Cedarcrest Cir	29	B2
Cedarcrest Ln	29	B2
Cedarcrest Rd	29	B2
Cedarwood Rd	30	A1
Cedric St	12	B1
Cedrus Ave	29	A2
Cefalo Rd	29	B2
Celia Rd	31	A1
Cemetery Rd	18	B1
Cenacle Rd	29	B2
Centervale Park	32	B1
Centola St	18	A2
Central Ave [HP]	33	A2/B2
Central Ave [MT]	31	B2

Street Index

Street	Page	Grid
Central Sq	9	A1
Central St	2	B1/B2
Central Wharf	2	B2
Centre Ave	32	B1
Centre Ct	32	B1
Centre Ln	29	B2
Centre Pl [DO]	32	B1
Centre Pl [RX]	13	A1
Centre St		
(1-178)	13	A1/B1
(189-891)	14	A1/A2/B1
(892-1569)	30	A1/B1
(1570-2699)	29	A2/B2
Centre St [DO]	32	B1
Centre Ter	29	B1
Centre Street Ter	13	B1
Cerdan Ave		
(1-41)	30	B1
(42-99)	29	A2
Cerina Rd	14	B2
Ceylon St	13	B2
Chadwick St	13	A2
Chamberlain St	31	A2
Chambers Pl	6	B2
Chamblet St	13	B2
Champlain Cir	31	A2
Champney Pl	1	B1
Chandler Rd	18	B1
Chandler St		
(1-99)	7	A1
(100-199)	6	B2
Channel St	11	A1
Chapel Pl	2	B1
Chapel Rd	33	A2
Chapin Ave	29	A2
Chapman Pl	3	A2
N Charlame Ct	13	B1
S Charlame Ct	13	B1
Charlame Pl	13	B2
Charlame St	13	B1/B2
N Charlame Ter	13	B2
S Charlame Ter	13	B2
Charlemont St	32	B2
Charles Rd	31	B2
Charles St	1	A1/B1
Charles St [DO]	32	B1
Charles St [HP]	33	B1
Charles St S	3	B1
Charles Park Rd	29	B1
Charles River Sq	1	B1
Charlesgate E	5	A1/B1
Charlesgate W	16	A2
Charlesview St	18	A1
Charlotte St	31	A1
Charme Ave	30	B2
Charter St	2	A1/A2
Chase St	32	A1
Chatham Row	2	B1
Chatham St	2	B1
Chaucer St	9	A2
Chauncy St	4	A1
Cheever Ct	9	B1
Chellman St	29	A1/A2
Chelmsford St	32	B1
Chelsea St	9	A1/A2/B1
Chelsea Ter	9	A1
Cheney St	31	A1/A2
Cheriton Rd	29	B2
Cherokee St	15	B1
Cherry Rd	29	B2
Cheryl Ln	33	B1
Chesbrough Rd	29	A1
Cheshire St	14	B2
Chester Pl	29	A2
Chester St	19	A1
Chester Park	31	B1
Chesterfield St	33	B1
Chesterton St	12	B1
Chestnut Ave	14	A2/B2
Chestnut Pl [BR]	18	B2
Chestnut Pl [JP]	14	A2
Chestnut Rd	29	B2
Chestnut Sq	14	A2
Chestnut St	1	B1
Chestnut St [HP]	33	A1/A2
Chestnut Ter	14	A2
Chestnut Hill Ave	18	B2
Chestnut Hill Drwy	18	B1
Cheverus Rd	32	B1
Chicamauga Park	13	B1
Chickatawbut St	32	B2
Chickering Pl	3	B2
Chilcott Pl	14	B2
Child St [HP]	33	A1/B1
Child St [JP]	14	B1/B2
Children's Rd	15	A1
Chilton Rd	29	A2
Chipman St	31	B2
Chisholm Rd	33	A1
Chisholm Ter	33	A1
Chiswick Rd	18	B1/B2
Chiswick Ter	18	B1
Chittick Rd	33	B1
Christopher St	32	B1
Church Ave	10	B1
Church St	3	B1
Church St [DO]	32	A1
Church St [HP]	33	B1
Church St [WR]	29	A2
Churchill Rd	29	B2
Circuit Sq	13	B1
Circuit St	13	B1/B2
City Hall Ave	3	A2
City Point Ct	11	B2
Claflin St	10	A2
Clancy Rd	31	B2
Clapp St	12	B1
Clare Ave		
(1-49)	30	B2
(50-299)	33	A2
Claremont St		
(2-49)	6	B1
(50-99)	5	B2
Claremont Park	6	B1
Clarence St	13	B2
Clarendon St		
(1-58)	7	A1
(59-299)	6	A1/A2
Clarendon Park	30	B1
Claridge Ter	31	B2
Clark St	2	A2
Clarkson St	32	A1
Clarkwood St	31	B1
Claron St	33	A1
Claxton St	30	B2
Clay St	33	A2
Claybourne St	32	B1
Claymont Ter	32	B2
Claymoss Rd	18	B2
Clayton Ave	23	A2
Clayton Pl	32	B1
Clayton St	32	B1
Clearwater Dr	31	B2
Clearway St	5	B2
Cleaves St	31	A1
Clematis St	32	A1
Clement Ave	29	A2
Clementine Park	32	B1
Clermont St	32	B1
Cleveland Pl	2	A1
Cleveland St [HP]	33	B1
Cleveland St [RX]	13	B2
Cleveland Park	13	B2
Clevemont Ave	19	A1
Cliffmont St	30	B2
Clifford St	13	B1
Clifford St [HP]	33	B1
Clifford St [RX]	13	B1
Clifton St		
(1-62)	12	B1
(63-199)	32	B1
Cliftondale St	30	B1
Clinton St	2	B1
Clipper Ship Ln	9	B1
Clive St	14	A2
Clout St	13	A2
Clover St	32	B2
Clyde St	9	B1
Cobden St	13	B1
Coburn Ct	1	B1
Codman St	31	B2
Codman Hill Ave	31	B2
Codman Park	13	B1
Coffey St	32	B2
Cohasset St	30	B1
Colberg Ave		
(1-46)	30	B1
(47-199)	29	A2
Colbert St	29	A2
Colborne Path	18	B2
Colborne Rd	18	B2
Colburn St [DO]	29	B2
Colburn St [JP]	15	B1
Colby St	30	B1
Colchester St	33	B1
Colebrook St	10	B2
Coleman St	32	A1
Colerain St	19	A1
Coleus Park	31	A2
Colgate Rd	30	B2
Collidge Ave	1	B2
Collins St	33	A2
Colliston Rd	18	B2
Colonial Ave	31	A2/B2
Colorado St	31	B1
Columbia Pl	32	A1
Columbia Rd		
(1-370)	31	A1/A2
(371-1149)	32	A1
(1150-1470)	10	B1/B2
(1471-1899)	11	B1/B2
Columbia St	4	A1
Columbia Ter	31	A2
Columbus Ave		
(1-100)	3	B1
(101-587)	6	A2/B1/B2
(588-879)	13	A1/A2/B1
(880-1499)	15	B2
(1500-1990)	14	A2
(1991-2071)	31	A1
Colwell Ave	18	B1
Comet St	13	A2
Commercial St	2	A1/A2/B2
Commercial Wharf	2	B2
Commercial Wharf W	2	B2
N Commercial Ter	2	B2
Commodore Ter	33	B1
Common St	3	B2
Commonwealth Ave		
(1-46)	3	A1
(48-192)	6	A1
(193-443)	5	A1/A2
(444-898)	16	A1/A2
(899-1520)	19	A2/B1/B2
(1521-2204)	18	B1/B2
Commonwealth Ct	19	B1

Street Index

Street	Pg	Grid
Commonwealth Ter	19	B1
Como Rd	33	B1
Conant St	15	B1
Concord Pl	7	A1
Concord Sq		
(1-65)	7	A1
(66-99)	6	B1
E Concord St	7	B1
W Concord St	7	A1/B1
Condor St	9	A1/A2
Congress St		
(2-40)	2	B1
(42-301)	4	A1/A2
(302-399)	10	A1/A2
Congreve St	30	B1
Coniston Rd	33	B1
Connolly St	13	A2
Conrad St	32	A1
Conry Cres	30	A1
Constance Rd	29	B1
Constitution Rd	31	B1
Constitution Wharf	2	A2
Converse St	18	A1
Conway St	30	B1
S Conway St	30	B1
Cookson Ter	31	B1
Coolidge Rd [AL]	19	A1
Coolidge Rd [DO]	32	B1
Cooper St	2	A1
Copeland Pl	13	B2
Copeland St	13	B2
Copeland Park	13	B2
Copenger St	15	B1
Copley St	14	A2
Coppersmith Way	9	B1
Copps Hill Ter	2	A1
Corbet St	31	B2
Corcoran Cir	33	B2
Corcoran Dr	33	B2
Corey Ave	4	B1
Corey Rd	19	B1
Corey St	29	A1/A2
Corey Ter	29	A2
Corinne Rd	18	A1
Corinth St	30	B1
Corman Rd	31	B1
Cornauba St	30	B1/B2
Cornelia Ct	15	B2
Cornell St		
(1-17)	33	A1
(18-385)	30	B1
(386-399)	29	A2
Cornhill St	2	B1
Cornwall St	14	B2
Corona St		
(1-42)	31	A2
(43-99)	32	B1
Coronado Rd	31	B1
Cortes St	3	B1
Corwin St	32	B1
Cottage Ct	13	B2
Cottage Pl [EB]	9	B1
Cottage Pl [HP]	33	B1
Cottage Rd	29	B2
Cottage St [EB]	9	B1
Cottage St [SB]	10	B1
E Cottage St		
(1-233)	12	B1/B2
(234-282)	32	A1
W Cottage St	13	B2
Cotton St	30	B1
Cottrell St	12	B2
Cotuit St	29	A1
Countryside Dr	31	B2
Court Sq	2	B1
Court St	2	B1
Courtland Rd	31	B1
Courtney Rd	29	A1
Coventry St	13	A1
Covington St	10	B2
Cowing St		
(1-42)	33	A1
(43-199)	29	B2
Cowper St	9	A2
Craft Pl	30	A2
Craftsman St	15	A1
Craftson Way	31	B1
Cragmere Ter	30	B1
Crandall St	33	A2
Crane St	33	B2
Cranmore Rd	14	A2
Cranston St		
(1-106)	31	A1
(107-199)	13	B1
Creek Sq	2	B1
Crehore Rd	29	A2
Creighton St	14	A2
Crescent Ave	32	A1
N Crescent Circuit	18	B1
S Crescent Circuit	18	B1
Crest St	29	A2
Cresthill Rd	18	A1
Creston St		
(1-63)	31	A2
(64-99)	13	B2
Creston Park	13	B2
Crestwood Park	13	B1
Cricket Ln	29	A2
Crispus Attucks Pl	13	B1
Crockers Ln	29	B2
Crockett Ave	32	B2
Croftland Ave	32	B1
Cromwell Rd	33	A2
Crosby Sq	13	A2
Cross Rd	29	B2
Cross St	2	B1/B2
Cross St [HP]	33	B1
Crossland St	18	B2
Crossman St	31	B1
Crosstown Ave	31	B2
Crowell St	31	B2
Crowley Rogers Way	10	A1/B1
Crown Path	31	A2
Crown Point Dr	29	B2
Croydon St		
(1-77)	31	B1
(78-99)	33	A2
Culbert St	31	B1
Cumberland St	5	B2
Cummings Rd	18	B2
Cummings St	12	A1
Cummington St	16	A1/A2
Cummins Hwy		
(1-411)	30	B1/B2
(412-614)	33	A2
(615-964)	31	B1
Cumston Pl	7	B1
Cumston St	7	B1
Cunard St	13	A1
Cunningham St	13	B2
Curlew St	29	B2
Curley St	30	B2
Currier St	31	B1
Curtis St	9	A2
Curve St	4	B1
Cushing Ave	32	A1
Cushman Rd	18	A2
Custer St	14	B1
Custom House St	4	A2
Cuthbert Rd	29	B2
Cutler Ct	11	B1
Cutter Rd	29	A1
Cygnet St	19	A1
Cypher St	10	A1/A2
Cypress Rd	18	A2
Cypress St	29	B1
Cypress Ter	29	B1
D St	10	A1/A2/B1
Dabney St	13	B1
Dacia St	13	B2
Dacy St	33	B1
Dade St	13	A2
Dakota St		
(1-34)	31	A2
(35-199)	32	A1/A2
Dale St [RS]	33	A1/A2
Dale St [RX]	13	B1/B2
Dalessio Ct	13	B2
Dalin Pl	13	B2
Dalkeith St	14	A2
Dalrymple St	5	A2/B2
Dalton St	32	B1
Daly St	32	B1
Damon Pl	33	B1
Damon St	33	B1
Damrell St	10	B1
Dana Ave	33	B2
Dana Rd	29	B2
Danbury Rd	33	A2
Dane St	14	B1
Danforth Pl	13	A1
Danforth St	14	A2
Dania St	31	B1
Dania Ter	31	B1
Daniel Ct	33	B1
Danny Rd	33	B1
Danube St	13	B2
Danville St	29	A2
Darius Ct	10	B1
Darling St	15	B1
Darlington St	31	B2
Dartmouth Pl	7	A1
Dartmouth St		
(1-83)	7	A1
(84-399)	6	A1/B1/B2
Davenport St	13	A1
Davern Ave	32	A1
David Rd	30	A1
Davidson Ave	32	A1
Davis Ct	9	A1
Davison St	33	A2/B2
Davitt St	32	A2
Dawes St	12	B2
Dawes Ter	32	A1
Dawson St	32	B1
Day St	14	A2
Dayton St	32	B1
Deacon St	7	B1
Deaconess Rd		
(1-44)	16	B1
(45-99)	15	A1
Deady Ln	11	B1
Dean St	13	B2
Dean Way	11	B1
Dearborn St	13	A2
Deblois St	7	B1
Decatur Ave	15	B2
Decatur St	9	B1
Deckard St	13	B1
Dedham Blvd	33	B1
Dedham Pky	33	A1/B1

Street	Page	Grid
Dedham St [HP]	33	B1
Dedham St [WR]	29	A1/B1
E Dedham St	7	B2
W Dedham St	7	A1
Deer St	32	A1
Deerfield St	16	A2
Deering Rd	31	B1
Deforest St	33	A1
Degautier Way	13	A2
Delaney Ct	18	B2
Delano Ct	30	B1
Delano St	32	B1
Delano Park	30	B1
Delaware Pl	18	A2
Delford St	30	B2
Delhi St	31	B1
Dell Ave	33	A2
Dell Ter	33	A2
Delle Ave	15	B2
Dellmore Rd	30	B2
Delmont St	32	B1
Delnore Pl	31	B1
Delore Cir	30	B2
Denby Rd	19	A1
Dennis St	13	B2
Dennison St	13	B1
Denny St	32	A2
Dent St	29	A1/A2
Denton Ter	30	B1
Denvir St	32	B1
Derne St	1	B2
Deroma Rd	29	B2
Derry Rd	33	A2
Design Center Pl	11	A1
Desmond Rd	31	B2
Desoto Rd	29	B2
Destefano Rd	30	B2
Dever St	32	B1
Devine Way	10	B1
Devon St	31	A2
Devonshire St		
(1-95)	2	B1
(96-299)	4	A1
Dewar St	32	A1
Dewey St	13	B2
Dewey Ter	13	B2
Dewitt Dr	13	A1/A2
Dewolf St	32	A1
Dexter St	12	B2
Dickens St	32	B1
Dickinson Rd	18	B1
Dietz Ct	33	B1
Dietz Rd	33	B1
Dighton St	18	B1/B2
Dilworth St	13	A2
Dimock Pl	13	B1
Dimock St		
(1-37)	13	B1
(38-99)	14	A2
Dingley Pl	3	B1
Ditmus Ct	13	A2
Ditson St	32	B1
Dix St	32	B1
Dixfield St	10	B2
Dixwell St	13	B1
Dodge Rd	33	B1
Dolans Ct	14	B2
Dolphin Way	11	A2
Don St	31	B1
Donald Rd	31	A1
Doncaster St	33	A2
Donna Ter	33	B1
Donnybrook Rd	18	A1
Donwood Ter	31	B1
Doolin Pl	10	B1
Doone Ave	31	B2
Dorchester Ave		
(1-48)	4	A2/B2
(49-910)	12	A2/B2
(911-2080)	32	A1/B1
(2081-2299)	31	B2
W Dorchester Ave	12	A2
Dorchester St		
(1-383)	10	B1/B2
(384-669)	12	B2
Dore St	3	B1
Doris St	32	A1
Dorr St	13	A1
Dorset St	12	B2
Douglas Ct	2	A1
Douglas St	10	B2
Douglas Park	13	A2
Dove Ct	13	B2
Dove St	13	B2
Dow Rd	29	A1
Downer Ave	32	A1
Downer Ct	32	A1
Downey Ct	13	B2
Dracut St	32	B1
Drake Pl	9	B1
Draper St	32	A1/B1
Draper's Ln	7	A1
Drapper Rd	33	B2
Drayton Ave	32	A1
Dresden St	14	A2
Dresser St	10	B2
Driftwood Rd	30	A1
Driscoll Dr	31	B2
Dromey St	13	B2
Druce Ct	32	A1
Druid St	31	B2
Drummond St	13	B2
Drury Rd	33	B1
Dry Dock Ave	11	A1
Dudley St		
(1-616)	13	A1/A2/B2
(617-899)	32	A1
Dudley Ter	32	A1
Duke St	31	B1
Dumas St	31	B1
Dunbar Ave	32	A1
Dunbarton Rd	29	B2
Dunboy St	18	A1
Duncan Pl	32	B1
Duncan St	32	B1
Duncan Ter	32	B1
Duncklee St	18	A1
Dunford St	13	B1
Dungarven Rd	31	A1
Dunkeld St	13	B2
Dunlap St	31	A2
Dunmore St	13	B2
Dunn St	32	A1
Dunning Way	30	A2
Dunns Ter	32	B2
Dunreath St	13	B2
Dunreath Ter	13	B2
Dunster Rd	14	B1
Dunwell St	29	B1
Durant St	29	A1
Durham St	6	B1
Durland St	18	A1
Durnell Ave	30	B1
Dustin St	18	A2
Duval St		
(1-20)	19	A1
(21-99)	18	A2
Duxbury Rd	31	B2
Dwight St	7	A2
Dwinell St	29	A1/A2
Dyer Ave	10	B2
Dyer Ct	31	B2
Dyer St	31	B2
E St		
(1-27)	29	B1
(145-599)	10	A2/B1/B2
(600-675)	11	A1
Eagle Sq	9	B2
Eagle St	29	B2
E Eagle St	9	A1/A2
W Eagle St	9	A1
Earhardt Rd	30	B1
Earl St	10	B1
Earnshaw St	29	B2
East Pl	4	B2
East St		
(1-99)	4	B1/B2
(354-361)	10	B2
East St [DO]	32	A1
Eastbourne St		
(1-16)	29	A2
(17-99)	30	B1
Eastburn Pl	18	B1
Eastburn St	18	B1
Eastern Ave	2	A2
Eastland Rd	30	B2
Eastman St	32	A1
Eastmont Rd	33	B1
Easton Ave	33	B2
Easton St	19	A1
Eastwood Ct	29	B1
Eastwood Circuit	29	B1
Eatonia St	19	A1/A2
Edgar Allan Poe Way	3	B1
Edge Hill St	14	A2
Edgebrook Rd	29	A2
Edgemere Rd	29	A2
Edgemont St	30	B1
Edgerly Pl	3	B1
Edgerly Rd	5	B1/B2
Edgewater Dr	31	B2
Edgewood St	13	B2
Edgewood Park	13	B2
Edinboro St	4	A1
Edison Green	32	A1
Edith St	33	B2
Edna Rd	32	B1
Edson St [DO]	31	B2
Edson St [HP]	33	B1
Edson Ter	33	B1
Edwardson St	33	A2
Edwin St	32	B1
Egan Way	18	B1
Egleston St	14	A2/B2
Egremont Rd	18	B2
Eileen Cir	15	B1
Elba Ter	32	A1
Elbert St	13	B1
Elbow St	9	B1
Elder St	32	A1
Eldon St [DO]	31	B2
Eldon St [RS]	31	A2
Eldora St	15	B1
Eldridge Rd	30	B2
Eleanor St	18	A2
Electric Ave	18	A1
Elene St	31	B1
Elgin St	29	A2
Elinor Rd	29	B2
Eliot Pl	3	B2
Eliot Pl [JP]	14	B1
Eliot St	3	B2
Eliot St [JP]	14	B1
Eliot Ter	13	A1
Elizabeth St	31	B1

Street Index

Street	No.	Grid
Elkins St	11	B1
Elko St	18	A2
Eliard Rd	33	A2
Ellerton Rd	29	B2
Ellery St	12	B2
Ellery Ter	12	B2
Ellet St	32	B1
Ellington St	31	A1/A2
Ellingwood St	15	B1
Ellis St [HP]	33	B1
Ellis St [RX]	13	B1
Ellison Ave	31	B2
Ellswood St	29	A1
Ellsworth St	32	A1
Elm St [DO]	32	B1
Elm St [HP]	33	A2
Elm St [JP]	14	B2
Elm Hill Ave		
(1-28)	13	B2
(29-199)	31	A1
Elm Hill Park	13	B2
Elm Lawn St	32	B1
Elmdale St	32	B1
Elmer Rd	32	B1
Elmhurst St	31	B2
Elmira St	18	A2
Elmont St	31	A2
Elmore St	13	B1
Elmore Park	13	B1
Elmwood St	13	A1
Elton St	32	A1
Elven Rd	30	B2
Elwell Rd	30	A1
Elwyn Rd	31	A2
Ely Rd	32	B1
Embankment Rd	1	B2
Embassy Rd	18	B1
Emelia Ter	29	A2
Emerald Ct	7	A2
Emerson Pl	1	A1
Emerson St		
(1-65)	10	B2
(66-326)	11	B1
Emery Rd	19	A1
Emmet Pl	9	B1
Emmet St	11	B1
Emmett St	33	A1
Emmons St	9	B1
Emmonsdale Rd	29	B2
Empire St	19	A1/A2
Emrose Ter	13	B2
Emsella Ter	14	A2
Endicott St	2	A1
Endicott Ct	2	A1/B1
Endicott Ter	32	B1
Enfield St	14	A2
Enneking Pky	33	A1/B1
Ennis Rd	31	A1
Enterprise St	12	B1
Epping St	31	B2
Eric Rd	19	A1
Ericsson St	32	B2
Erie Pl	14	B2
Erie St	31	A2
Ernest Ave	33	B1
Ernst St	14	A2
Errol St	31	B1
Eskridge St	31	B2
Esmond St	31	A1/A2
Essex St		
(2-22)	3	B2
(24-298)	4	A1
Estabrook Rd	33	A1
Estella St	31	B1
Estes Ave	31	A2
Estes Pl	4	A2
Estey St	15	B1
Esther Rd	29	A2
Estrella St	14	A2
Ethel St	30	B1
Etna St	18	A2
Euclid St	31	B2
Eugene Cir	15	B1
Eugenia Rd	30	B1
Eulita Ter	18	B2
Eunice St	32	B1
Eustis St	13	A2
Euston Rd	18	B2
Eutaw St	9	A1
Evandale Ter	32	A2
Evans Rd	18	B2
Evans St	31	B2
Evans Way	15	A2
Evelyn St	31	B1
Everdean St	32	B2
Everett Ave	32	A1
Everett Ct	9	B2
Everett Pl	9	B2
Everett Sq	19	A1
Everett St [AL]	19	A1
Everett St [DO]	32	B1/B2
Everett St [EB]	9	B1/B2
Everett St [HP]	33	B2
Everett St [JP]	14	B2
Evergreen St	14	A2
Everton St	31	A2
Ewer St	10	B1
Exchange St	2	B1
Exeter Pl	4	A1
Exeter St	6	A1
F St	10	B1/B2
Fabyan St	31	B1
Factory St	33	B2
Fairbanks St	18	A1
Fairbury St	13	B2
Fairfax St	32	B1
Fairfield Pl	2	A2
Fairfield St	5	A2
Fairland St	13	B2
Fairlane Rd	29	B1/B2
Fairlawn Ave	31	B1
Fairlawn Apartment	31	B1
Fairmount Ave	33	B2
Fairmount Ct	33	B2
Fairmount St	31	B2
Fairview Ave	33	B1
Fairview St	30	B1
S Fairview St	30	B1
Fairway St	31	B1
Faith Hill	33	B1
Falcon St	9	A1
Falkland St	18	A1
Fall Rd	29	B2
Faneuil St	18	A1/A2
Faraday St	33	B2
Fargo St		
(1-86)	10	A2
(87-199)	11	A1
Farmington Rd	29	A2
Farnham St		
(1-65)	13	A2
(66-199)	12	B1
Farnsworth St	10	A1
Farquhar St	30	B1
Farragut Rd	11	B2
Farragut St	29	A1
Farrar Ave	33	A2
Farrin St	33	B1
Farrington Ave	19	A1
Farwell Ave	33	B2
Father Francis Gilday St	7	B1
Father Songin Way	12	B2
Faulkner Cir	32	B1
Faulkner St	32	B1
Faunce Rd	31	B1
Favre St	31	B1
Fawndale Rd	30	B2
Faxon St	15	B2
Fay St	7	A2
Fayette Ct	3	A2
Fayette St	3	B1
Fayston St	13	B2
Federal Ct	4	A1
Federal St	4	A1/A2
Fellows St	13	A2
Fellsway St	32	B1
Fencourt Rd	15	A2
Fendale Ave	31	B2
Fenelon St	32	B1
Feneno Ter	19	B1
Fenno St	13	B1
Fensmere Rd	29	B2
Fenton St	32	B1
Fenway		
(2-54)	15	A1/A2
(60-402)	16	A2
(404-498)	16	A2
Fenway Plz	16	A2
Fenwick St	13	B1
Fenwood Rd	15	A1/B1
Fermoy Heights Ave	31	A1
Fern St	19	A1
Fernald Ter	32	A1
Fernboro St	31	A2
Ferncroft Rd	29	A2
Ferndale St	31	B2
Fernwood Rd	29	A2
Ferry St	2	B1
Fessenden St	31	B1
Fid Kennedy Ave	11	A1/A2
Fidelis Way	18	A2
Field Ln	33	A2
Field St	15	A2
Fieldmont St	33	A2
Fields Ct	12	B1
Fields St	32	A1
Fifield St	30	B1
Filomena Rd	30	B1
Firth Rd	30	B1/B2
Fish Ln	11	B1
Fish Pier Rd	11	A1
Fish Pier St W	11	A1
Fisher Ave	15	B1
Fiske Ter	19	B1
Flaherty Way	10	B1
Flavia St	32	B2
Fleet St	2	B1
Fleet St [HP]	33	B1
Fletcher St	30	B1
Flint Pl	11	B1
Flint St	31	B1
Floral Pl	33	B2
Florence St	30	B1/B2
Florian St	30	B2
Florian Way	30	B2
Florida St	32	B1
Floyd St	31	B1
Follen St	6	B1
Folsom Ave	15	B2
Folsom St [DO]		
(1-14)	32	A1
(15-99)	13	B2
Folsom St [HP]	33	B2
Folsom St [RS]	30	B2
Foodmart St	12	A1
Forbes St	14	A2

Street Index

Street	Grid	Ref		Street	Grid	Ref		Street	Grid	Ref
Fordham Rd	19	A1		(120-399)	31	B2		Gilmer St	31	B1
Forest Pl	13	B2		Fullerton St	16	A2		Gilmore Ter	29	A2
Forest St	13	A2/B2		Fulton Pl	2	B1		Ginita St	32	B1
Forest Hills Ave	31	B1		Fulton St	2	B2		Glade Ave	31	A1
N Forest Hills Ave	31	A1		Fulton St [HP]	33	B2		Gladeside Ave	31	B1
Forest Hills St				Furbush Rd	29	A1		Gladeside Ter	31	B1
(1-57)	14	B2		Furnival Rd	30	A1		Gleason St	31	A2
(58-399)	31	A1		G St	10	B2		Glen Rd		
Forestvale Rd	33	B1		Gaffney St	19	A2		(1-36)	14	B2
Forsyth	15	A2		Gage St	13	A2		(37-99)	31	A1
Forsyth St	15	A2		Gainsborough St				Glen St	32	A1
Forsyth Way	15	A2		(1-32)	13	A1		Glenarm St	31	A1
Fort Ave	13	A1/B1		(33-199)	5	B1/B2		Glenburnie St	13	B2
Fort Avenue Ter	13	B1		Gallivan Blvd				Glenburnie Rd	29	A2
Fossdale Rd	32	B1		(1-255)	31	B2		Glencliff Rd	33	A1
Foster Ct	2	A1		(256-899)	32	B1/B2		Glencoe St	18	A2
Foster St	2	A1		Galty Ave	32	B1		Glendale St	32	A1
Foster St [BR]	18	A1/B1		Gannett St	13	B2		Glendon Pl	9	A2
Foster Ter	18	B1		Garden St	1	B1		Glendon St	9	A2
Foster Wharf	4	A2		Garden Arch	1	B1		Glendower Rd	33	A1
Fottler Rd	31	B1		Garden Ct St	2	A2		Glenellen Rd	29	B2
Foundry St	12	A2		Gardena St	18	A2		Glenham St	29	A1
Fountain Pl	2	A2		Gardenside St	30	B2		Glenhaven Rd	29	B1/B2
Fountain St	13	B1		Gardner Pl [SB]	10	A1		Glenhill Rd	31	B2
Fowle St	30	B2		Gardner Pl [WR]	29	B1		Glenmont Rd	18	B1
Fowler St	31	A2		Gardner St [AL]	19	A1/A2		Glenmore St	31	B2
Fox St	32	A1		Gardner St [WR]				Glenrose Rd	31	B1
Fox Point Rd	32	A2		(1-28)	13	A1		Glenside Ave	31	A1
Francesca St	29	A1		(29-399)	29	A1/B1		Glenvale Ter	14	A2
Francis St	15	A1/B1		Gardner Ter	19	A2		Glenville Ave	19	B1
Francis Parkman Dr	14	A1		Garfield Ave	33	B2		Glenville Ter	19	B1
Franciaire Dr	29	B2		Garfield Rd	33	B1		Glenway St	31	A1/A2
Franconia St	32	B1		Garner Rd	32	B1		Glenwood Ave	33	B1/B2
Frankfort St	9	A2/B1		Garnet Rd	29	A2		Glide St	32	B2
Franklin Ave	2	B1		Garrison St	6	B1		Glines Ave	31	A1
Franklin Ct	12	B1		Garth Rd	29	A2		Gloria Rd	29	A2
Franklin Pl	30	A2		Gartland St				Gloucester St	5	A2
Franklin St	2	B2		(1-19)	14	B2		Glover Ct	10	B1
(1-39)	3	A2		(20-99)	31	A1		Glover Pl	32	A1
(40-299)	4	A1/A2		Gary St	13	A2		Goethe St	29	B2
Franklin St [AL]	19	A1		Gaston St	13	B2		Goff St	33	A1
Franklin St [DO]	32	B2		Gates St	10	B2		Gold St	10	A1
Franklin St [HP]	33	B1		Gavin Way	32	A1/A2		Golding St	31	B2
Franklin Ter	33	B2		Gay St	13	A1		Goldsmith Pl	14	A1
Franklin Hill Ave	31	A1		Gay Head St	14	A2		Goldsmith St	14	B1
Frawley St	15	B1		Gayland St	13	B2		Goodale Rd	31	B1
Frazer St [DO]	32	B2		Gaylord St	31	A2		Goodenough St	18	A2
Frazer St [HP]	33	A2		Gem Ave	18	B1		Goodrich Rd	14	A1
Frederick St	10	B1		Gene St	32	A1		Goodridge Ct	2	A1
Frederika St	32	B1		Geneva Ave				Goodway Rd	30	B2
Fredonia St	32	B1		(1-302)	31	A2		Goodwin Ct	10	B1
Freeland St	31	B2		(303-600)	32	B1		Goodwin Pl	1	B1
Freeman Ave	29	B2		Geneva St	9	B1		Gordon Ave	33	A1/B2
Freeman Pl	1	B2		George St [MT]	33	A2		Gordon Pl	32	B1
Freeman St	32	B1		George St [RX]				Gordon St [AL]	19	A1/B1
Freeport St	32	A1/B1/B2		(1-124)	13	A2/B2		Gordon St [JP]	14	B2
Freeport Way	32	A1		(125-199)	12	B1		Gore St	15	B2
Fremont St	31	B1		Georgetown Rd	29	B2		Gorham St	19	B1
French St	31	B1		Georgetowne Dr				E Gould Ct	9	B1
French Ter	15	B2		(1-398)	29	B2		Gould St [AL]	19	A1
Fresno St	30	B1		(399-799)	33	A1/B1		Gould St [WR]	29	B1
Friend St				Georgetowne Pl	33	B1		Gouldville Ter	13	B2
(1-200)	2	B1		Georgia St	31	A1/A2		Gove St	9	B1
(201-299)	1	A2		Geraghty Ter	33	A2		Grace Ct	11	B2
Friendship Rd	31	B1		Gerald Rd	18	B1		Grace St	32	B1
Frontage Rd				Gerard St	13	A2		Grady Ct	9	B1
(1-225)	12	A1/A2/B2		Germania St	14	B2		Grafton St	32	A1
(226-499)	7	A2		Gerrish St	18	A1		Graham Ct	12	B1
Frontenac St	31	B1		Gertrude Rd	29	A2		Graham St	29	A2
Frost Ave	32	B2		Gibson St	32	B1		Graham Ter	29	A2
Fruean Pl	32	A1		Gifford Pl	10	B1		Grampian Way	32	A2
Fruit St	1	A1		Gilbert Pl	4	A2		Granada Ave	30	B1
Fulda St	13	B1		Gillespies Ln	31	B1		Granada Park	31	A1
Fuller St				Gillette Park	10	A1		Granby St	16	A2
(1-119)	32	B1		Gilman St	30	B2		Grandee St	18	B2
								Grandview St	33	A1

Street Index

Street	Page	Grid
Granfield Ave	30	B2
Granger St	32	B1
Granite Ave	32	B1
Granite St	10	A1
Grant Rd	31	B2
Grant Pl	31	A2
Grant St	32	A1
Grantley St	33	B2
Granville Ave	23	A1
Granville St	32	B1
Grassmere Rd	33	A1
Gray St	7	A1
Grayfield Ave	29	A2
Grayson St	32	B2
Greaton Rd	29	A2
Green St	14	B1/B2
Green Hill St	32	B2
Greenbaum St	12	A1
Greenbrier St		
(1-28)	31	A2
(29-199)	32	B1
Greenbrook St	33	A2
Greendale Rd	31	B1
Greenfield Rd	31	B1
Greenhalge St	12	B1
Greenheys St	31	A2
Greenleaf St	15	A2
Greenley Pl	14	B2
Greenmount St	32	A1
Greenock St	14	B1
Greenough Ave	2	A2
Greenough Ln	14	B1
Greenough Park	14	B1
Greenview Ave	14	B1
Greenville St	13	A2
Greenville Park	13	A2
Greenwich Ct	13	A2
Greenwich St [DO]	32	B1
Greenwich St [RX]	13	A2
Greenwich Park	6	B1
Greenwood Ave	33	A2
Greenwood Sq	33	A2
Greenwood St	31	A2
Greenwood Park	32	B1
Gretter Rd	29	A2
Grew Ave		
(1-99)	30	B2
(100-149)	33	A2
Grew Hill Rd	33	A1
Greycliff Rd	18	B1
Greylock Rd	19	B1
Greymere Rd	18	B1
Gridley St	32	B1
Griffin St	32	B1
Griggs Pl	19	B1
Griggs St	19	B1
Grimes St	10	B1
Groom St	32	A1
Groton St	7	A2
Grotto Glen Rd	14	A2
Grouse St	29	B2
Grove Pl	1	B1
Grove Rd	29	B2
Grove Sq	1	B1
Grove St	1	B1
Grove St [WR]	29	B2
Grove Ter	29	B2
Groveland St	31	B2
Grovenor Rd	14	A1
Grover Ave	30	B2
Guernsey St	29	A2
Guest St	18	A2
Guild Row	13	A1
Guild St	13	A1
Guilford St	18	A2
Gurney St	15	B2
Gustin St	10	B1
Gwinnett St	33	A2
H Ave	29	B1
H St	11	B1
H Street Pl	10	B2
Hackensack Cir	30	A1
Hackensack St	30	A1
Hackensack Rd		
(1-82)	30	A1
(83-199)	29	A2
Hackensack Ter	29	A2
Hadassah Way	3	B1
Hadwin Way	30	B2
Hagar St	14	B1
Hague St	19	A2
Halborn St	31	B1
Hale Ave	23	A2
Hale St	33	A1
Haley St	13	B1
Half Moon St	13	B2
Halford Rd	29	A2
Halifax St	14	A1
Hall Ave	31	A2
Hall Pl	11	B1
Hall St	14	B1/B2
Hallam St	32	A1
Halleck St	15	B2
Hallet Sq	32	B2
Hallet St	32	B2
Hallet Davis St	32	B2
Halliday St	30	B2
Hallowell St	31	B1
Hallron St	33	A1
Halsey Rd	33	B2
Halwood Rd	33	B1
Hamilton Pl	3	A2
Hamilton St [DO]	32	A1/B1
Hamilton St [HP]	33	B1
Hamlet St	32	A1
Hamlin St	10	B2
Hammond St	2	A2
Hammond Ter	13	A2
Hampden St	13	A2
Hampstead Ln	14	B1
Hampstead Rd	14	B1
Hancock St	1	B2
Hancock St [DO]	32	A1
Hannon St	31	B1
Hano St	19	A1
Hanover Ave	2	A2
N Hanover Ct	2	B1
Hanover Pl	2	B1
Hanover St	2	A1/A2/B1
Hansborough St	31	B1
Hansford Pl	13	B2
Hanson St	7	A1/A2
Harbell Ter	32	B1
Harbor St	11	A1
Harbor Crest Ct	32	A2
Harbor Point Blvd	32	A2
Harbor View St	32	A1
Harcourt St	6	B1
Harding Ct	10	B1
Harding Rd	30	B2
Hardwick St	18	A1
Hardwick Ter	18	A1
Hardy St	11	B1
Harem Pl	3	A2
Harlem St	31	A2
Harleston St	13	B1
Harley St	32	B1
Harlow St	13	B2
Harmon St	31	B1
Harmony St	9	A2
Harold Pl	11	B1
Harold St		
(1-219)	13	B1
(220-295)	31	A1
Harold Park	13	B1
Harriet St	18	A1/A2
Harrington Ave	13	A1
Harris Ave	14	B1
Harris St	2	A2
Harrishof St	13	B1
Harrison Ave		
(1-295)	4	A1/B1
(296-856)	7	A2/B1/B2
(857-1199)	13	A2
Harrison St	30	B2
Harrison Archway	7	B1
Harrison Park	32	B1
Harrow St	32	A1
Hart Pl	11	B1
Hartford Ct	13	B2
Hartford St	13	B2
Hartford Ter	13	B2
Hartland St	32	A1
Hartlawn Rd	29	B1
Hartley Ter	19	A2
Hartwell St	31	A1/A2
Harvard Ave [AL]	19	A1/B1
Harvard Ave [DO]	31	A2
Harvard Ave [HP]	33	A2/B2
Harvard Pl	3	A2
Harvard St	4	B1
Harvard St [MT]		
(1-698)	31	A1/A2/B1
(699-1080)	30	B1
(1081-1099)	33	A2
N Harvard St		
(1-203)	19	A1/A2
(204-399)	19	A1
Harvard Ter	19	A1
Harvard Way	20	B1
Harvard Park	31	A2
Harvest St	12	B2
Harvest Ter	12	B2
Harvester St	19	A1
Harvey Steel Rd	19	A1
Harwood St	31	B1
Haskell St	19	A1
Haslet St	30	B1
Hastings St	29	A2
Hatch St	11	B1
Hathaway St	4	A2
Hathaway St [JP]	14	B1
Hatherly Rd	18	B1
Hautvale St	33	A1
Havana St	30	B1
Havelock St	31	B1
Haven St	7	B1
W Haven St	7	A1
Haverford St	14	B2
Havey St	30	B1
Haviland St	5	B1/B2
Haviland Ter	5	B1
Havre St	9	A1/B1
Hawkins St	1	A2
Hawley Pl	4	A1
Hawley St	4	A1
Hawthorne Pl	1	B2
Hawthorne St [RS]	30	B1
Hawthorne St [RX]	13	B1
Hawthorne Ter	30	B1
Hayden St	15	B1
Haydn St	30	B1
Hayes St	30	B1
Haymarket Pl	3	B1

Street Index

Street	Page	Grid
Haynes St	9	B1
Hayward Pl		
(1-43)	3	A2
(45-99)	4	A1
Hazel Park	13	B2
Hazelmere Rd	30	B1
Hazelton St	31	B1
Hazelwood Ct	13	B1
Hazelwood St	13	B1/B2
Head Pl	3	A2/B2
Head Island Cswy	11	B2
Heath St	15	B1/B2
Heathcote St	30	B1
Hebron St		
(2-164)	31	B1
(165-299)	33	A2
Hecla St	32	A1
Hefferan St	20	B1
Heldun St	29	B1
Helen St	31	A2
Helena Rd	32	B1
Hemenway St		
(1-125)	5	B1
(126-299)	15	A2
Hemlock Rd	29	B1
Hemman St	30	B1
Henchman St	2	A1
Henderson Ave	11	B1
Hendry St	32	A1
Henrici St	31	B1
Henry St	9	B1
Henshaw St	18	B2
Henshaw Ter	29	A2
Herald St	7	A2
Herbert St	31	A2
Herbertson Rd	30	B2
Hereford St	5	A2
Herman St	13	B1
Heron St	29	B2
Herrick St	18	A2
Hersey Pl	4	A1
Hesston Ter	32	A1
Hester St	18	A1
Hestia Park	13	B1
Hewes St	13	B1
Hewins St	31	A2
Hewlett St	30	B1
Heyer Ct	30	B2
Hiawatha Rd	31	B1
Hichborn St	18	A2
Higgins Ave	23	A2
Higgins St	19	A1
High Ct	4	A2
High Rd	29	B2
High St	4	A1/A2
High St [DO]	32	A1
High Rock Ave	33	B1
High Rock Way	19	B1
High Street Pl	4	A2
High View Ave	29	B2
Highcrest Rd	33	A1
Highcrest Ter	33	A1
Highfield Rd		
(1-10)	30	B1
(11-99)	33	A1
Highfield Ter	30	B1
Highgate St	19	A1
Highland Ave	13	A1
Highland St	13	A1
Highland St [HP]	33	B2
Highland St [RX]	13	A1/B1
Highland Ter	13	A1
Highland Park Ave	13	B1
Highland Park St	13	A1/B1
Hilburn Pl	30	B2
Hilburn St	30	B1
Hildreth St	31	B1
W Hill Pl	1	B1
Hill Top St	32	B2
Hillcrest St	29	A2
Hillcroft Rd		
(1-10)	14	B1
(11-99)	30	A2
Hillis Rd	33	B1
Hillock St	30	B1
Hillsboro Rd	31	B1
Hillsboro St	32	A1
Hillsdale St	32	B1
Hillside Ave	30	A2
Hillside St	15	B1/B2
Hillview Ave	30	B1
Hilton St	33	A2
Hilton Ter	13	B1
Hinckley St	32	A1
Hobart St	18	A1
S Hobart St	18	A1
Hobson St [BR]	18	A1
Hobson St [RS]	29	A2
Hodgdon Ter	29	A2
Hoffman St	14	A2
Holborn St	13	B2
Holborn Ter	13	B2
Holborn Park	13	B2
Holbrook Ave	32	B2
Holbrook St	14	B1
Holden Ct	2	A2
Holden St	32	A1
Holiday St	32	B1
Holland Pl	4	B1
Hollander St	13	B1
Hollingsworth St	31	B1
Hollis Pl	19	B1
Holly Rd	30	B2
Hollywood Rd	29	A2
Holman St	19	A1
Holmes St	19	A1
Holmfield Ave	31	B1
Holton St	19	A1
Holworthy St	13	B1
Holyoke St	6	B1
Homer St	9	A2
Homes Ave	32	B1
Homestead St	31	A1
Homewood Rd	29	B2
Hommagen Ct	13	B1
Hooker St	19	A1/A2
Hooper St	32	B1
Hooten Ct	9	B1
Hopedale St	19	A1/A2
Hopestill St	31	B1
Hopewell Rd	31	B1
Hopkins Pl	31	B1
Hopkins Rd	30	A1
Hopkins St	30	B2
Horace St	9	A2
Horadan Way	15	B2
Horan Way	14	A2
Horne St	33	B1
Hosmer St	31	B1
Hospital Rd	18	B2
Houghton St	32	B1/B2
Houston St	29	A2
Howard Ave	13	B2
Howard Pl	13	B2
Howard St	13	A2
Howard Johnson Plz	12	B2
Howe St	32	A1
Howe Ter	32	A1
Howell St	12	B2
W Howell St	12	B2
Howes St	32	A1
Howitt Rd	29	B2
Howland St		
(1-25)	31	A1/A2
(26-133)	13	B1
Hoyt St	32	A1
Huban St	15	B2
Hubbard St	14	A2
Hubbard Ter	13	A2
Hubbardston Rd	32	A2
Huckins St	13	B2
Hudson St	4	B1
N Hudson St	2	A1
Hulbert St	13	B1
Hull St	2	A1
Hull Street Ct	2	A1
Hull Street Pl	2	A1
Humarock Way	33	A2
Humboldt Ave		
(1-195)	13	B1
(196-299)	31	A1
Humboldt Ct	13	B1
Humboldt Pl	12	B2
Humes Rd	32	B2
Humphreys Pl	32	A1
Humphreys St		
(1-8)	12	B1
(9-99)	32	A1
Hunneman St	13	A2
Hunter St	30	B2
Huntington Ave		
(1-145)	6	A1/B1
(146-344)	5	B1/B2
(345-998)	15	A2/B1
Huntington Ave [HP]	33	A2
S Huntington Ave		
(1-141)	15	B1
(142-450)	14	A2
Huntoon St	31	B2
Hurlcroft Ave	32	B1
Huron Cir	32	B1
Hutchings St	31	A1
Hutchinson St		
(1-36)	32	B1
(37-99)	31	B1
Hyde Park Ave		
(2-686)	30	A2/B2
(687-1915)	33	A2/B1/B2
I St	11	B1
Ida St	9	B1
Idaho St	31	B2
Iffley Rd	14	B2
Imbaro Rd	19	A1/B1
Imrie Rd	19	A1/B1
Independence Dr	29	A2
E India Row	4	A2
(91-91)	2	B2
India St		
(1-32)	2	B1/B2
(33-66)	4	A2
India Wharf	4	A2
Industrial Dr	33	B1
Ingleside St	13	B2
Inman St	10	A2
Intervale St	31	A2
Intervale Ter	31	A2
Inwood St	32	A1
Iola St	31	A2
Iona St	29	A2
Iowa St	32	B1
Ipswich St	9	B1/B2
Ipswich St		
(1-51)	5	B1
(52-299)	16	A2
Iris Rd	18	A1
Irma St	31	B1

Street Index

Street	Map	Grid
Iroquois St	15	B1
Irving St	1	B2
Irwin Ave	13	B1
Isabella St	3	B1
Island St		
(1-64)	13	A2
(65-99)	12	B1
Island View Pl	32	A2
Islington St	19	A1
Islington Ter	19	A1
Itasca St	31	B1
Ivanhoe St	7	A1
Ives St	31	B1
Ivory St	29	A2
Jackson Ave	2	A1
Jackson Pl	13	B1
Jackson St	33	B2
Jacob St	31	B2
Jacqueline Rd	29	B2
Jaeger Ter	30	A1
Jalleison St	33	A2
Jamaica Pl	14	B1
Jamaica St	14	B1
Jamaicaway		
(2-98)	15	B1
(100-598)	14	A1
Jamaicaway Ct	14	A1
James St	7	B1
James St [HP]	33	A2
Jamestown Ter	31	B1
Jarvis Pl	13	B2
Jason Ter	10	B2
Jay St	11	B1
Jayjay Dr	31	B2
Jeffers St	33	A1
Jefferson St	3	B1
Jeffries St	9	B2
Jenkins St	10	B1
Jennett Ave	29	A2
Jenton Way	4	A2
Jerome St	32	A1
Jersey St	15	A2
Jeshurun St	29	B2
Jess St	14	A2
Jette Ct	18	B2
Jewett St	30	B2
Jimmy Fund Way	15	A1
Jo Anne Ter	32	B1
Joan Rd	33	B1
John A Andrew St	14	B2
John Alden Rd	29	B2
John Eliot Sq	13	A1
Johnny Ct	4	B1
Johnray Rd	31	B1
Johnson Ave	14	A2
Johnson St	29	B1/B2
Johnson Ter	31	B2
Johnston Rd	31	B1
Johnswood Rd	30	B2
Jones Ave	30	B1
Jones Way	31	B2
Joseph St	32	B1
Josephine St	32	B1
Joslin Pl	16	B1
Joy Ct	1	B2
Joy Pl	1	B2
Joy St	1	B2
Joyce Rd	33	A2
Joyce Hayes Way	10	A1/B1
Joyce Kilmer Rd	29	B1
Judge St	15	B1
Judson St	13	B2
Julian St	13	B2
Juliette St	32	A1/B1
June Ln	33	A1
June St	33	A1
Juniper St	13	B1
K St	11	B1
K Street Pl	11	B1
Kalada Park	13	B2
Kane St	32	A1
Kardon Rd	33	B1
Keane Rd	29	A2
Kearsarge Ave	13	A2
Kearsarge Ter	13	A2
Keenan Rd	18	A2
Keith St	29	A1
Kelley St	18	A2
Kelton St	19	B1
Kemble Pl	11	B2
Kemble St		
(1-61)	13	A2
(62-199)	12	B1
Kemp St		
(1-49)	12	B2
(50-99)	32	A1
Kempton St	15	B1
Kenberma Rd	31	A2
Kendall St	13	A2
Kenilworth St	13	A1
Kenmere Rd	32	B1
Kenmore St	16	A2
Kennebec St		
(1-209)	31	B1
(210-299)	33	A2
Kenneth St	29	A2
Kenney St	14	A2
Kenrick St	18	B1
Kensington St	13	B1
Kensington Park	13	B1
Kenton Rd		
(1-30)	14	B2
(31-99)	31	A1
Kenwood St	32	B1
Kerna Rd	29	B2
Kerr Pl	13	A1
Kerr Way	13	A1
Kershaw Rd	29	B2
Kerwin St	31	A2
Keswick St	16	A1
Kevin Rd	32	A1
Keyes Pl	30	A2
Keystone St	29	B1
Kiernan Rd	29	A1
Kilby Pl	4	B1
Kilby St		
(1-35)	2	B1
(36-98)	4	A2
Kilmarnock St	15	A2
Kilsyth Rd	23	A2
Kilsyth Ter	18	B2
Kimball St	32	B1
Kimball St	13	B2
King St	13	A1
King St		
(1-199)	32	B1/B2
Kingsboro Park	14	A1
Kingsdale St	31	A2
Kingsland Rd	29	A1
Kingsley St	19	A1
Kingston St	4	A1/B1
Kinross Rd	18	B2
Kirk St	29	A2
Kirkwood St	18	B1
Kittredge St	30	B1
Kittredge St		
(1-313)	30	B1
(314-398)	33	A1
Kittredge Ter	30	B1
Knapp St	4	B1
Kneeland St		
(1-23)	3	B2
(24-199)	4	B1
Knight St	33	B1
Knights Ct	14	B2
Knoll	30	B1
Knowles St	18	B1
Knowlton St	10	B1
Knox St	3	B1
Kovey Ct	33	B1
Kovey Rd	33	B1
Kristin Ct	33	B1
L St	11	B1
La Grange St	13	B2
Laban Pratt Rd	32	B2
Laconia St	7	A2
Lafayette Ave	2	A1
Lafield St	32	B1
Lagrange St	3	B1/B2
Lagrange St (WR)		
(1-85)	33	A1
(86-1408)	29	A1/A2/B2
Lake St	18	B1
Lake Shore Rd	18	B1
Lakeville Rd	14	A1
Lamartine Pl	14	B2
Lamartine St	14	A2/B2
Lamartine Ter	14	B2
Lambert Ave	13	A1
Lambert St	13	A1
Lamson St	9	B1
Lamson St	9	B1
Lancaster St	1	A2
Landor Rd	31	B1
Landseer St	29	A2
Landseer Ter	29	A2
Lane Pl	4	A2
Lane Park	18	B1
Lanesville Ter	30	A2
Langdon Pl	2	B2
Langdon St		
(1-45)	13	B2
(46-99)	12	B1
Langdon Ter	12	B1
Langdon Park	31	A2
Langford Park	13	B2
Langley Rd	18	B1
Lansdowne St	16	A2
Lantern Ln	29	A2
Larch Pl	30	B2
Larch St	18	B1
Larchmont	32	B1
Laredo St	31	A2
Lark St	10	B1
Larkhill Rd	29	B2
Larose Pl	18	B2
Lasalle Park	32	A2
Lasell St	29	A1/A2
Lathrop Pl	1	B2
Latin Rd	29	B2
Lattimore Ct	13	A2
Laurel Ave	33	A2
Laurel St	13	B1
Lauriat St	31	B2
Laurie Ave	29	B1
Lauten Pl	11	B2
Laval St	33	A2
Lawley St	32	B2
Lawn St	15	B1
Lawn Park	23	A2
Lawndale Ter	14	B2
Lawrence Ave		
(1-45)	13	B2
(46-154)	31	A2
Lawrence Ct	10	A1

Street Index

Street	Page	Grid		Street	Page	Grid		Street	Page	Grid
Lawrence Pl	18	A2		Linda Ln	32	A2		Louis Ter	32	B1
Lawrence St	7	A1		Lindall Ct	1	B1		Louis D Brown Way	32	B1
Lawrence St [BR]	18	A2		Lindall Pl	1	B1		Louis Prang St	15	A2
Lawson Pl	9	A2		Lindall St	30	B1		Louisburg Sq	1	B1
Lawton St	33	B1		Linden Ave	31	B1		Lourdes Ave	31	B1
Lawton Ter	33	B1		Linden Ct	32	A1		Lovejoy Pl	2	A1
Le Fevre St	33	A2		Linden Rd	29	B2		Lovell St	9	A2
Leahaven Rd	31	B2		Linden St [AL]	19	A1		Lovis St	10	B1
Leamington Rd	18	B2		Linden St [DO]	32	A1/B1		Lowell St	3	B2
Lebanon St	32	A1		Linden St [SB]	10	B2		Lower Campus Rd	18	B2
Ledge Hill Rd	29	B1		Lindsey St	32	B1		Loyola Cir	29	B2
Ledgebrook Rd	31	B2		Lingard St	13	B2		Loyola St	13	B2
Ledgedale Rd	30	B1		Linley Ter	11	B1		Lubec St	9	B1
Ledgemere Rd	18	B2		Linnet St	29	A2/B2		Lucerne St	31	B1
Ledgewood Rd	29	A1/A2		Linsky Barry Ct	10	B1		Lyall St	29	A1/A2
Lee St	14	B2		Linvale Ter	31	B1		Lyall Ter	31	A2
Lee Hill Rd	30	B1		Linwood Sq	13	A1		Lyford St	31	B2
Leeds St	10	B1		Linwood St [HP]	33	B1		Lynde St	1	B2
Leedsville St	32	B1		Linwood St [RX]	13	A1		Lyndeboro Pl	3	B2
Legion Pl	30	B2		List Pl	30	B1		Lyndhurst St	31	A2
Leicester St	18	A2/B2		Liszt St	33	A1		Lyne Rd	18	B2
Leighton Rd	33	B1		Litchfield Ct	9	B1		Lynn St	2	A1
Leland Pl	7	A2		Litchfield St				Lynnville Ter	31	B1
Leland Rd	29	A2		(1-68)	18	A2		Lyon St	32	A1
Leland St	30	A2		(69-199)	19	A1		M Ave	29	B1
Leman Pl	4	A2		Lithgow St	32	B1		M St	11	B1
Lena Ter	31	B1/B2		Littledale St	33	A2		M Street Pl	11	B1
Leniston St	30	B1		Livermore St				MacNeil Way	32	A1
Lennoco Rd	30	A2		(1-56)	31	B1		Macdonald St	33	A1
Lennon Ct	11	B2		(57-121)	33	A2		Machester St	29	A1
Lenox St	13	A2		Liverpool St	9	A1/B1		Mackin St	18	A2
E Lenox St	13	A2		Livingstone St	31	B1		Macullar Rd	29	B2
Lenoxdale Ave	32	B1		Lochdale Rd	30	B2		Madeline St	18	A1
Leo M Birmingham Pky	18	A1/A2		Lochland Rd	33	B2		Madison St	33	B1
Leon St	15	A2		Lochstead Ave	14	A1		Madison Park Ct	13	A1
Leonard Ct	32	B1		Locke Pl	11	B1		Magazine St		
Leonard Pl	11	B1		Locksley St	14	A2		(1-62)	13	A2/B2
Leonard St	32	B1		Lockwood St	33	A2		(63-150)	12	B1
Leroy St	32	B1		Locust St	12	B2		Magdala St	32	B1
Leseur Rd	33	B2		Lodgehill Rd	33	A1		Magee St	33	A1/A2
Lesher St	30	B2		Logan St	13	A1		Magnolia Sq	13	B2
Leslie St	32	B1		Logan Way				Magnolia St		
Leslie Park	13	B1		(1-45)	32	A1		(1-135)	32	A1
Lester Pl	14	B1		(46-99)	10	B1		(136-216)	13	A2
Lester St	12	B1		Logan Airport Service Dr	9	A2		(217-299)	31	A2
Leston St	31	B1		Lomasney Way	1	A2		Mahler St	30	B2
Letterfine Ter	13	B2		Lombard Pl	2	A1		Mahnis St	14	A2
Levant St	32	B1		Lombard St	32	B1		Mahoney Pl	30	B2
Leverett Cir	1	A1		London Ct	9	A1		Maida Ter	33	A2
Lewis Pl	13	B2		London St	9	A1/B1		W Main St	31	B1
Lewis St	2	A2/B2		Long Ave	19	B1		Maitland St	16	A2
Lewis St [EB]	9	B1		Long Ter	29	B1		Malbert Rd	18	B1
Lewis Wharf	2	B2		Long Wharf	2	B2		Malcolm Rd	30	A1
Lewiston St	33	A2		Longfellow Pl	1	A2		Malden St	7	B2
Lexington Ave	33	A2		Longfellow St	32	B1		W Malden St	7	B2
Lexington Sq	9	A2		Longmeadow St	12	B1		Mall St	13	A2
Lexington St	9	A1/A2		Longwood Ave	15	A1/A2		Mallard Ave	31	A2
Leyland St	12	B1		Lonsdale St	32	B1		Mallet St	32	B1
Libbey St	29	A1		Lorenzo St	32	B2		Mallon Rd	31	A2
Liberty Pl	10	B1		Lorette St	29	A2		Malta St	31	B1
Life St	18	A2		Loring Pl	33	B2		Malvern St	19	A2
Lila Rd	30	A1		Loring St [HP]	33	B2		Malvern Rd	30	B1
Lilac Ter	30	B1		Loring St [SB]	10	B1		Malverna Rd	30	B1
Lillie Way	29	A2		Lorna Rd	31	B1/B2		Mamelon Cir	31	A2
Lilly St	10	B1		Lorne St	31	A1		Manchester St	31	B2
Lime St	1	B1		Lorraine St	29	A2		Manila Ave	33	B1
Lincoln Pl	7	B1		Lorraine Ter	19	B1		Manion Rd	33	A2
Lincoln Pl [BR]	18	A2		Lothian Rd	18	B2		Manley St	32	B1
Lincoln St	4	A1/B1		Lothrop St	18	A2		Mann St	29	B2
Lincoln St [BR]				Lotus Ave	31	A1		Manning St	30	B2
(1-130)	18	A2		Lotus St				Manor Ct	32	B1
(131-598)	19	A1		(1-48)	31	A1		Mansen Ct	33	B1
Lincoln St [DO]	32	B1		(49-98)	30	A2		Mansen Rd	33	B1
Lincoln St [HP]	33	A2		Louders Ln	33	A1		Mansfield St	19	A1
Lincoln Wharf	2	A2		Louis St	10	A1		Mansur St	33	A2

Street Index

Street	Page	Grid
Manthorne Rd	29	A2
Manton Ter	19	B1
Mapes St	32	B1
Maple Ct	31	A1
Maple Ln	29	A2
Maple Pl	4	B1
Maple St [JP]	14	B1
Maple Rd	29	A2
Maple St [DO]	31	A1
Maple St [HP]	33	B1
Maple St [WR]	29	A2
Maple Ter	29	A2
Mapleton St	18	A2
Maplewood St	29	B2
Marbury Ter	14	A2
Marcella St	13	B1
March Ave	29	A2
March Ter	29	A2
March Way	29	A2
Marcy Rd	31	B1
Marden Ave	31	B1
Margaret St	2	A1
Margaretta Dr	33	B1
Margin St	33	B2
N Margin St	2	A1
Marginal Rd	3	B2
Marginal St	9	B1/B2
Maria Ln	30	B1
Marie St	32	A1
Marine Rd	11	B1
Marion Ct	9	A1
Marion Pl	9	A1
Marion St [EB]	9	A1
Marion St [HP]	33	B1
Marion St [RS]	30	B2
Mariposa St	33	A2
Mark St	14	A2
Market St	2	B1
Market St [BR]	18	A2/B2
N Market St	2	B1
S Market St	2	B1
Marksdale St	13	B1
Marlborough St		
(2-52)	3	A1
(53-208)	6	A1
(209-499)	5	A1/A2
Marlin Rd	29	A1
Marlin Way	32	B1
Marlowe St	32	B1
Marlou Ter	14	B2
Marmion St	2	B1
Marsh Ln	30	B1
Marsh St	32	B2
Marshall St	2	B1
Marshall St [WR]	29	B1
Marshfield St	12	B1
Marston St	33	A2
Martha Rd	1	A1/A2
Martin Rd	32	B2
Martin St	29	B2
Martin Luther King Blvd	13	B1/B2
Martinwood Rd	30	A2
Marvin St	13	A1
Mary Anna Rd	33	A2
Mary Moore Beatty Cir	31	B2
Maryknoll St	31	B2
Maryknoll Ter	31	B2
Maryland St	32	A1
Mascoma St		
(1-16)	13	B2
(17-99)	31	A2
Mascot St	31	B1/B2
Mason St	3	A1
Mason St [HP]	33	B2
Mason St Pl	3	A2
Massachusetts Ave		
(1-445)	5	A1/B2
(446-487)	6	B1
(488-826)	7	B1
(827-849)	13	A2
(850-1299)	12	B1
Massasoit St	31	B1
Mather Ct	32	B1
Mather St	32	B1
Matigon Rd	32	B1
Mattakeeset St	31	B1
Mattapan St	31	B1
Matthew St	31	B2
Matthews St	4	A2
Maverick Sq	9	B1
Maverick St	9	B1/B2
Maxfield St	29	A2
Maxwell St	31	B2
May Pl	4	B1
May St	14	B1
Maybrook St	31	A2
Maybury St	13	B2
Mayfair St	13	B1
Mayfield St	32	A1
Mayhew St	12	B2
Maynard St	13	B2
Maywood St	13	B2
Maywood Ter	13	B2
Maywood Park	13	B2
McBride St	14	B1/B2
McCormack St	9	B2
McCraw St	29	A2
McDonald Ave	20	B1
McDonough Ct	33	B1
McDonough Way	10	B1
McGreevey Way	15	B2
McKay Pl	9	B1
McKenna Ter	29	A2
McKinley Sq	2	B2
McKone St	32	B2
McLellan St	31	A1/A2
Mead St	19	A1
Meadow Rd	33	B2
Meadowbank Ave	31	B2
Mechanic Ct	2	B1
Mechanic St	2	B1
Medfield St	16	A1
Medford St		
(1-49)	2	B1
(50-599)	23	A2
Medway St	31	B2
Meehan Pl	14	B2
Meehan St	14	B2
Melba Way	33	A2
Melbourne St	32	B1
Melcher St	10	A1
Mellen St	32	B1
Melrose St	3	B1
Melton Rd	18	B2
Melville Ave		
(1-6)	31	A2
(7-199)	32	B1
Melville Ln	32	B1
Melvin Ave	18	B2
Melvinside Ter	32	A1
Mendell Way	14	A2
Mendelssohn St	30	B1
Mendum St	30	B1
Menlo St	18	A2
Menton St	31	B2
Mercer St [MT]	31	B1
Mercer St [SB]	10	B1
Merchants Row	2	B1
Mercier Ave	32	B1
Meredith St	29	A2
Meridian Pl	9	A1
Meridian St	9	A1/B1
Merlin St	31	A2
Merola Park	31	B1
Merriam St	14	B2
Merrill St	31	A2
Merrimac St	1	A2
Merton Pl	13	A1
Meshaka St	29	B2
Messinger St	31	B1
Metcalf Ct	14	B1
Metcalf St	30	B1
Metropolitan Ave		
(1-235)	30	B1
(236-1099)	33	A2/B2
Metropolitan Cir	33	A2
Meyer St	30	B2
Miami Ave	29	B2
Miami Ter	29	B2
Michael Rd	18	B1
Michelangelo St	2	A1
Michigan Ave	31	A2
Middle St	10	B1
Middleton St	31	B1
Midland St	32	A1
Midvale Rd	29	A2
Midway St	10	A1
Mildred Ave	31	B1
Miles St	14	A2
Milford St	7	A2
Milhender Pl	12	A2
Milk St		
(1-145)	4	A1/A2
(146-299)	2	B2
Mill St	32	B2
Miller Park	13	B2
Millers Ln	31	B2
Millet St	31	A2/B2
Millicent Way	7	B2
Millmont St	13	A1
Mills St	13	B2
Milton Ave [DO]	31	B2
Milton Ave [HP]	33	B2
Milton Pl	4	A1
Milton St [DO]	32	B1/B2
Milton St [HP]	33	B1
W Milton St	33	B1
Milton Ter	33	B2
Milwood St	32	B1
Milwood Ter	32	B1
Minden St	14	A2
Mindoro St	15	B2
Miner St	16	A2
Minnie Ct	14	B1
Minot St	32	B1/B2
Minot Park	32	B1
Minton St	14	A2/B2
Mission St	15	B1
Mission Park Dr	15	B1
Mitchell St	31	B1
Mohawk St	10	B1
Moloney St	29	B1
Monadnock St	32	A1
Monastery Rd	18	B2
Monks St	11	B1
Monmouth St	9	A1
Monponset St	31	B1
Monsignor Reynolds Way	7	A2
Monson St	31	B2
Montague St	32	B1
Montana St	31	A1
Montcalm Ave	18	A2

Street	Page	Grid
Montclair Ave		
(1-110)	29	A2
(111-199)	30	B1
Montebello Rd	14	B2
Montello St	32	B1
Monterey Ave	31	B1
Montfern Ave	18	A1
Montgomery St	7	A1
Montrose St	13	B2
Montvale Ave	29	A2
Montview St	29	A2
Monument Ct	11	B1
Moody St	31	B2
Moon St	2	A2
Moore St [EB]	9	A2
Moore St [RX]	12	A1
Mora St	31	B2
Moraine St	14	A1
Moreland St	13	B2
Morey Rd	30	B1
Morley St	13	A1
Morrell St	29	B1
Morrill St	32	A1
Morris St	9	A1
Morrow Rd	18	A2
Morse St	31	A2
Morton Ave	23	A1/A2
N Morton Ln	31	A1
Morton Pl	9	A1
Morton St	2	B1
Morton St [JP]		
(1-104)	30	B1
(105-1299)	31	A1/B1/B2
Moseley St	32	A1
Mosgrove Ave	30	B2
Moss Hill Rd	30	A1
Mossdale Rd	30	A1
Mother Julian Rd	31	B2
Moultrie St	32	B1
Mount Bowdoin Ter	31	B1
Mount Bowdoin Green	31	A2
Mount Calvary Rd	30	B2
Mount Cushing Ter	32	A1
Mount Everett St	32	A1
Mount Hood Rd	18	B2
Mount Hope St	30	B2
Mount Ida Rd	32	A1/B1
Mount Pleasant Ave	13	A2/B2
Mount Pleasant Pl	13	A2
Mount Pleasant St	33	B2
Mount Pleasant Ter	13	A2
Mount Vernon Pl	1	B2
Mount Vernon Sq	1	B1
Mount Vernon St	1	B1/B2
Mount Vernon St [BR]	18	B1/B2
Mount Vernon St [DO]		
(1-153)	12	A2
(154-499)	32	A2
Mount Vernon St [WR]	29	A2
Mount Washington Ave	10	A1
Mount Washington Pl	10	A2
Mountain Ave	31	B1
Mountfair Ter	33	B2
Mountfort St	16	A1/A2
Moville St	29	B1
Mozart St	14	A2
Msgr Albert A Jacobbe Rd	9	B1
Msgr O'Callaghan Way	32	A1
Msgr Patrick J Lydon Way	32	B1
Msgr William Casey Hwy	30	A2
Msn Park Dr	15	B1
Mt Ash Rd	33	B1
Mt Washington Ave	10	A1
Mulberry Pl	13	A2
Mulvey St	31	B1
Mulvey Ter	13	B1
Munroe St	13	B1
N Munroe Ter	32	B1
S Munroe Ter	32	B1/B2
Munson St	16	A2
Murdock St	18	A2/B2
Murdock Ter	18	A2
Murphy Ct	2	A2
Murray Ave	13	B2
Murray Ct	9	B1
Murray Way	32	A1
Murray Hill Rd	30	B1
Museum Rd	15	A2
Music Hall Pl	3	A2
Myles Standish Rd	29	B2
Myopia Rd	33	A2
Myrick St	19	A1
Myrtle St	1	B1/B2
Myrtle St [JP]	14	A1/B1
Myrtlebank Ave	32	B1/B2
Mystic St	7	A1/B1
N St	11	B1
Nahant Ave	32	B1/B2
Nantasket Ave	18	B2
Napa St	12	B1
Napier Park	32	A2
Narragansett St	32	B2
Nashua St	1	A1/A2
Nassau St	4	B1
Nathan St	13	A2
National St	10	B2
Navarre St		
(1-55)	30	B2
(56-199)	33	A2
Navillus Ter	32	A1
Nay St	9	A1
Nazing St	31	A1
Nazing Ct	31	A1
Necco St	10	A1
Necco Pl	10	A1
Necco Ct	10	A1
Needham Rd	33	B2
Neillian Cres	30	A1
Nelson Ct	4	A2
Nelson St	31	B2
Neponset Ave [DO]	32	B1/B2
Neponset Ave [HP]	33	B2
Neponset Ave [RS]	30	B2
Neponset Ct	30	B2
Neponset Valley Pky	33	B1/B2
Neptune Cir	9	A2
Neptune Ct	9	A2
Neptune Rd	9	A2
Neptune Ter	9	A2
Nevada St	31	B1
Nevins St	18	B2
New St	9	B1
New Acre Rd	33	B2
New Bedford St	33	B2
New Chardon St		
(1-80)	1	A2
(81-99)	2	A1/B1
New Congress St	2	B2
New Dudley St	13	A1
New Edgerly Rd	5	B2
New England Ave	31	A2/B2
New Haven St	29	B1
New Heath St		
(1-25)	13	B1
(32-99)	15	B2
New Minton St	14	B2
New Northern Ave	4	A2
New Park Ave	29	A2
New Sudbury St		
(1-16)	1	B2
(17-79)	2	B1
New Whitney St	15	B1
Newark St	13	A1
Newbern Ave	23	A2
Newbern St	14	B2
Newburg St		
(1-108)	30	B1
(109-199)	29	A2
Newbury St		
(1-53)	3	B1
(54-192)	6	A1
(193-449)	5	A1/A2
(473-699)	16	A2
Newcastle Ct	13	A2
Newcastle Rd	18	A1
Newcastle St	31	B1
Newcomb St	13	A2
Newcroft Cir	31	B2
Newfield St	29	A1
Newhall Pl	32	B2
Newhall St	32	B2
Newhill Pl	11	B1
Newkirk St	32	B1
Newland Pl	7	A1
Newland St	7	A1/A1
Newman St	13	A2
Newmarket Sq	12	B1
Newport St	32	A1
Newsome Park	14	B1
Newton St	18	A1
E Newton St	7	B1/B2
W Newton St		
(1-109)	7	A1/B1
(110-279)	6	B1
Nightingale St	31	A1/A2
Nikisch Ave	30	B1
Niles St	18	A1
Nira Ave	14	A2
Nixon St	32	B1
Noah St	33	A2
Noble Ct	9	B1
Nonantum Rd	18	A1
Nonquit St	32	A1
Norcross Pl	11	B1
Norfolk Ave		
(1-85)	13	A2
(86-399)	12	B1
Norfolk Ct	31	B1
Norfolk St [DO]	31	B1/B2
Norfolk St [RX]	13	A1
Norfolk Ter	31	B2
Normandy St	31	A2
Norris Rd	33	B2
North Ave	13	B2
North Sq	2	B1
North St	2	A2/B1/B2
North St [SB]	11	B1
N North Grove St	1	A1
North Point Dr	32	A2
Northampton Pl	13	A2
Northampton St	13	A2
Northbourne Rd	30	B1
Northdale Rd	29	B1/B2
Northdale Ter	29	B1
Northern Ave		
(1-17)	4	A2
(18-212)	10	A1/A2
(213-399)	11	A1
Northfield St	13	A2
Norton St [DO]	32	A1/B1
Norton St [HP]	33	B1
Norway St	5	B1/B2
Norway Park	33	B2

Street	Map	Grid	Street	Map	Grid	Street	Map	Grid
Norwell St	31	A2	Orchardfield St	32	B1	Parklawn Rd	29	A2
Norwood St	32	B2	Orchardhill Rd			Parkman Pl	32	B1
Notre Dame St	13	B1	(1-64)	14	B2	Parkman St	1	A1
Nott St	33	B2	(65-99)	30	A2	Parkman St [DO]	32	B1
Nottingham Path	18	B2	Ordway Pl	3	A2	Parkside Dr	30	A1
Nottingham St	31	A2	Oregon Ct	15	B2	Parkson St	33	B1
Nottinghill Rd	18	B2	Organ Park	30	B2	Parkton Rd	14	A1
Noyes Pl	2	A1	Oriole St	29	A2	Parkvale Ave	19	A1
O St	11	B2	Orkney Rd	18	B2	Parkway St	31	A1
O Donnell Sq	32	B2	Orlando St	31	B1	Parkwood Ter	14	A1
O Donnell Ter	32	B1	Orleans St	31	B1	Parley St	14	A1/B2
O Street Pl	11	B2	Ormond St	32	B1	Parley Vale	14	A1/A2
O'Neil Pl	4	B1	Orne St	10	B1	Parmelee St		
Oak Pl [HP]	33	B1	Orton Marotta Way	10	B1	(1-49)	7	B1
Oak Rd	29	B2	Oscar St	15	B2	(50-99)	13	A2
Oak St			Osceola St	31	B1	Parmenter St	2	A1/B1
(1-13)	3	B2	Osgood Ct	13	B1	Parrott St	33	A2
(14-99)	4	B1	Oswald St	15	B1	Parsons St	18	A1/A2
Oak St [HP]	33	B1	Otis Pl	1	B1	Partridge Pl	13	B2
Oak St W	3	B1	Otis Pl [RS]	30	B1	Partridge St	29	B2
Oak Hill Ave	31	B1	Otis St	4	A1	Pasadena Rd	31	A2
Oak Square Ave	18	A1	Otisfield St	13	B2	Patten St	30	B2
Oakcrest Rd	31	B1	Outlook Rd	31	B1	Patterson St	31	B2
Oakdale Pl	14	B2	Overland St	16	A2	Patterson Way	10	B1
Oakdale St	14	B2	Overlook Rd	29	B2	Paul Pl	7	A2
Oakdale Ter	14	B2	Owen St	31	B1	Paul Gore St	14	A2
Oakhurst St	31	B2	Owencroft Rd	32	B1	Paul Gore Ter	14	A2
Oakland Ct	31	B1	Oxford Pl	4	A1	Paul Sullivan Way	7	A2
Oakland Pl	18	A1	Oxford St	4	A1	Paula Rd	31	B2
Oakland St [BR]	18	A1/B1	Oxford St [AL]	19	A1	Paulding St	13	B2
Oakland St [RX]	13	B1	Oyster Bay Rd	32	A2	Paulman Cir	29	A2
Oakley St	31	A2	P St	11	B2	Paxton St	31	A1
Oakman St	32	B2	Pacific St	10	B2	Payne St	32	B2
Oakmere St	29	B1	Packard Ave	31	B2	Payson Ave	32	A1
Oakridge St	31	B2	Page St	31	B2	Payson Ct	10	B1
Oakton Ave	32	B1/B2	Page Ter	31	A2	Payson Rd		
Oakview Ter	13	B1	Pages Ct	10	B1	(1-37)	30	A1
Oakview Ave	14	A2	Paige Ave	11	B1	(90-199)	29	A2
Oakville Ave	13	A1	Paine St	30	B2	Peabody Pl	14	A2
Oakwood St [DO]	31	B2	Paisley Park	32	B1	Peabody Sq	32	B1
Oakwood St [MT]	33	A2	Palace Rd	15	A1/A2	Peaceable St	18	B2
Obierne Pl	13	B1	Palfrey St	30	B2	Peacevale Rd	31	B2
Ocean St	32	B1	Palmer St	13	A2	Peacock Ln	29	A2
Ocean View Dr	32	A2	Pama Gardens	18	B1	Peak Hill Rd	29	A2
O'Connell Rd	31	B2	Paragon Rd	29	B2	Pearl Pl	9	B1
O'Connor Way	12	B2	Paris Ct	9	B1	Pearl St	4	A2
Ogden St	32	B1	Paris Pl	9	B1	Pearl St [DO]	32	A1
Old Rd	31	A1	Paris St	9	A1/B1	Peirson St	12	B1
Old Centre St	29	B2	Parish St	32	A1	Pelham St	7	A1
Old Colony Ave			Park Dr			Pelham Ter	7	A1
(1-388)	10	B1	(1-341)	15	A1/A2	Pelton St	29	A2
(389-599)	32	A2	(343-599)	16	A1/A2	Pemberton Sq	1	B2
Old Colony Ter	32	A2	Park Ln	31	A1	Pembroke St		
Old Harbor St	10	B2	Park Pl	14	B1	(1-160)	7	A1/B1
Old Morton St	31	B2	Park Plz	3	B1	(161-199)	6	B1
Oldfields Rd	31	A2	Park Sq	3	B1	Pender St	29	A2
Oleander St	32	A1	Park St	3	A2	Pendergast Ave	18	B2
Oleary Way	30	A2	Park St [DO]			Penfield St	30	B1
Oliva Rd	18	A1	(1-448)	32	B1	Penhallow St	32	B1
Olive St	18	B1	(449-621)	31	A2	Peninsula Pl	32	A1
Oliver St	4	B1	Park St [HP]	33	A2	Penniman Rd	19	A1
Olmstead St	14	B2	Park St [WR]	29	A2/B2	Pequot St	15	B1
Olney St			W Park St	31	A2	Perabo Ter	29	B2
(1-55)	32	A1/B1	Park Ter	29	A2	Percival Pl	9	B2
(56-199)	31	A2	Park Front Rd	29	A2	Percival St	32	A1
Onslow Ter	11	B1	Park Lane Dr	29	A1	Perham St	29	A1/A2
Opera St	15	A2	Park Street Pl	3	A2	Perkins Ave	33	B1
Ophir St	14	B2	Park View St	31	A1	Perkins Pl	13	A1
Orange Ct	13	A2	Parker St			Perkins Sq	14	A1
Orange St	30	B1	(1-99)	33	A2	Perkins St	14	A1/A2
Orchard St [JP]	14	B1	(400-943)	15	A2/B2	Perkins Ter	13	B2
Orchard St [MT]	33	A2	(944-999)	14	A2	Perrin St	7	A2
Orchard Park St	13	A2	Parker Hill Ave	15	B1/B2	Perry St	14	A1
Orchardale St	32	B1	Parker Hill Pl	15	B1	Pershing Rd	14	A1
			Parker Hill Ter	15	B1	Perth St	13	B2
						Perthshire Rd	18	A1

Street	Page	Grid
Peter Parley Rd		
(1-44)	14	B2
(45-99)	31	B1
Peterborough St	15	A1/A2
Peters St	11	B1
Petrel St	29	B1
Peverell St	32	A1
Pheasant St	33	A1
Philbrick St	30	B2
Philip St	32	B2
Philips Pl	32	A1
Phillips Pl	1	B1
Phillips St	1	B1
Phipps Pl	2	A1
Pickering Ave	13	B1
Pie Aly	3	A2
Piedmont St	3	B1
Pierce Ave	32	B1/B2
Pierce St	33	A2/B2
Pierpont Rd	29	A2
Pike St	13	A2
Pilgrim Pl	32	A1
Pilgrim Rd	16	B1
Pilsudski Way	10	B1
Pinckney St	1	B1
Pine Ave	33	B2
Pine St	4	B1
Pine St [HP]	33	B2
Pine Ter	33	B2
Pine Grove Ter	15	B1
Pine Lodge Rd	29	B2
Pine Ridge Rd	31	B2
Pinecliff Rd	29	B2
Pinedale Rd	30	B2
Pinefield Rd	33	B1
Pinehurst St	30	B1
Pinewood St	33	A2
Ping on St	4	A1
Pingree St	33	B2
Pitsmoor Rd	30	B2
Pittsburgh St	10	A2
Plain St	32	B2
Plainfield St		
(1-27)	31	A1
(28-99)	30	A2
Planet St	33	A2
Plant Ct	14	A2
Platt Rd	18	B1
Playstead Rd [DO]	32	A2
Pleasant Ave	29	A2
Pleasant St [DO]	32	A1
Pleasant St [HP]	33	B2
Pleasant Hill Ave	31	B1
Pleasant Hill Ter	31	B2
Pleasant Valley Cir	29	A2
Pleasantdale Rd	29	B2
Pleasanton St	31	A1
Pleasantview St	33	A2
Plover St	29	B2
Plummer Pl	10	B1
Plymouth St	16	B1
Plympton St	7	B2
Pomeroy St		
(1-3)	19	A1
(4-99)	18	A2
Pomfret St	29	A2
Pomona Ave	29	A1
Pompeii St	12	B1
Pond Cir	14	B1
Pond Rd	29	B2
Pond St [DO]		
(1-11)	12	B2
(12-99)	32	A1
Pond St [HP]	33	B2

Street	Page	Grid
Pond St [JP]		
(1-233)	14	A1/B1
(234-499)	30	A1
Pond Street Pl	2	A1
Pondview Ave	14	A1
Pontiac St	15	B1/B2
Popes Hill St	32	B2
Poplar St		
(1-387)	30	B1/B2
(388-699)	33	A1/A2
Port Norfolk St	32	B2
Porter Pl	9	A1
Porter St [EB]	9	A1/B1
Porter St [JP]	14	A2
Porter Ter	29	A2
Portina Rd	18	B1
Portland St	1	A2
Portsmouth St	18	A2
Post Office Sq	4	A2
Potomac St	29	A2
Potosi St	32	A1
Powell St	29	B2
Powellton Rd	31	A2
Power St	12	B2
Power House St	11	B1
Powers Ct	2	A2
Poydras St	31	B1
Prairie St	31	B1
Pratt St	19	A1/A2
Preble St	10	B1
Prentiss St		
(1-28)	13	A1
(29-99)	15	B2
Presby Pl	13	B2
Prescott Ct	9	A2
Prescott Pl	19	A1
Prescott St [EB]	9	A1/A2
Prescott St [HP]	33	B1
Prescott St [RX]	13	A2
President Rd	30	B1
President Ter	19	A1
Presley Rd	32	B1
Preston Rd	29	A2
Price Rd	19	B1
Priesing St	14	A2
Primrose St	30	B1
Primus Ave	1	B1
Prince St	2	A1
Prince St [JP]	14	A1/B1
Princeton Pl	9	A2
Princeton St	9	A1/A2
Priscilla Rd	18	B2
Proctor St	12	B1
Prospect Ave	30	B2
Prospect Cir	33	B2
Prospect St	33	B2
Prospect Park	33	B2
Providence St		
(101-219)	3	B1
(220-299)	6	B1
Providence St [HP]	33	A2
Province Ct	3	A2
Province St	3	A2
Pt Rd	32	B2
Pulaski Ave	10	B2
Purchase St	4	A2
Puritan Ave	31	A2
Putnam Ave	1	B1
Putnam Pl	13	A1
Putnam St [EB]	9	A1/A2
Putnam St [RX]	13	A1
Quail St	29	B2
Quaker Ln	2	B2
Quarley Rd	30	B2
Queen St	32	B1

Street	Page	Grid
Queensberry St	15	A2
Quincefield St	32	A1
Quincefield St	32	A1
Quincy Ct	2	B2
Quincy St	13	B2
Quincy St		
(1-283)	13	B2
(285-510)	32	A1
Quincy Ter	13	B2
Quincy Shore Dr	32	B2
Quinn Way	29	A2
Quint Ave	19	A1/B1
Radcliffe Rd [AL]	19	B1
Radcliffe Rd [MT]	31	B1
Radcliffe St	31	A2
Radford Ln	32	B1
Radford Pl	33	B1
Radnor Rd	18	B1
Railroad St	29	A2
Rainier Rd	31	B1
Raldne Rd	33	B1
Raleigh St	16	A2
Ralston St	31	B1
Ralwood Rd	31	B1
Rambler Rd	30	A1
Ramsdell Ave	33	A2
Ramsey St	32	A1
Rand Pl	13	B2
Rand St	13	B2
Randall St	13	A2
Randlett Pl	13	B2
Randolph St	7	A2
Ranelegh Rd	18	A1
Range Rd	32	B1
Rangeley St	32	B1
Ranley Rd	31	B1
Ransom Rd	18	B2
Raven St	32	A1
Ravenna Rd	29	A2
Rawson St	12	B2
Rawston Rd	30	B1
Raymond St	19	A1
Raynes Rd	33	B2
Raynor Cir	13	A1
Readfield Pl	13	B2
Reading St	13	A2
Readville St	33	B1
Realton Rd	29	A2
Reardon St	27	A2
Rector Rd	31	B1
Red Pine Rd	33	B2
Reddy Ave	33	A2
Redfield St	32	B2
Redford St	19	B1
Redgate Rd	29	B2
Redlands Rd	29	A2
Redwood St	32	B1
Reed St	13	A2
Reedsdale St	19	A1
Regal St	18	B1
Regan Rd	32	B1
Regent Cir	14	B2
Regent Pl	13	B2
Regent Sq	13	B1
Regent St [HP]	33	B1
Regent St [RX]	13	B1/B2
Regina Rd	31	A2
Regis Rd	31	B1
Remington St	32	B1
Rena St	19	A1
Rendall Rd	29	A2
Renfrew Ct	13	A2
Renfrew St	13	A2
Reservation Rd	33	B1
Rev Robert M Costello Pl	32	B2

Street Index

Street	Map	Grid
Revere Pl	2	A2
Revere St	1	B1
Revere St [JP]	14	B2
Rexford St	31	B1
Rexhame St	29	B1
Reynold Rd	33	B1
Rhoades St	31	B1
Rhoda St	29	A2
Rice St	32	B2
Rich St	31	B1
Rich Hood Ave	33	B2
Richard Ter	31	B2
Richards St	10	A1
Richardson St	18	A2
Richfield St		
(1-20)	31	A2
(21-99)	32	A1
Richfield Park	31	B1
Richmere Rd	2	A1
Richmond Pl	2	B1/B2
Richmond St	2	B1/B2
Richmond St [DO]	31	B2
Richwood St	29	A2
Rickerhill Rd	29	A2
Ridge St	30	B2
Ridgecrest Dr	29	B2
Ridgecrest Ter	29	B2
Ridgemont St	18	A2
Ridgeview Ave	31	B1/B2
Ridgeway Ln	1	B2
Ridgewood St	32	B1
Ridlon Rd	31	B1
Riley Rd	33	B1
Rill St	32	A1
Ring Rd	5	A2
Ringgold St	7	A2
Ripley Rd	31	A2
Risley Rd	29	A2
Rita Rd	32	B2
Ritchie St	13	B1
River Rd	15	B1
River St	1	B1
River St [MT/HP]		
(1-813)	31	B1/B2
(814-1999)	33	A2/B1/B2
River Street Pl	1	B1
River Street Ter	33	B1
Riverbank Pl	31	B1
Riverdale Rd	31	B2
Riverdale St	19	A1
Rivermoor St	29	B2
Riverside Sq	33	A2
Riverview Rd	18	A1
Riverway		
(1-330)	16	A1/B1
(332-398)	15	B1
Riverway St	29	B1
Roach St	32	A1
Roanoke Ave	14	B2
Roanoke Rd	33	A2
Robbart Ln	33	B2
Robert St	30	B1
Roberts Pl	33	B1
Robeson St	31	A1
Robey St	12	B1
Robin St	29	B2
Robin Hood St	13	B2
Robinson St	32	B1
Robinwood Ave	14	A1/A2
Robken Rd	30	B1
Rock Ave	31	B1
Rock Rd	31	B1
Rock St	13	B1
Rock Ter	31	A2
Rock Hill Rd	14	B2
Rockdale St	31	B1
Rockford St	12	B1
Rockingham Ave	29	B2
Rockingham Rd	31	B1
Rockland Ave	13	B2
Rockland St [RX]	13	B1/B2
Rockland St [WR]	29	B2
Rockledge St	13	A1
Rockmere St	32	A2
Rockmount St	31	A2
Rockne Ave	32	B2
Rockvale Cir	14	B2
Rockview St	14	A2
Rockview St	14	A2/B2
Rockville Park	13	B2
Rockway St	31	B1
Rockwell St	31	B2
Rockwood St	30	A1
Rockwood Ter	30	A1
Rocky Nook Ter	31	A1
Rodman St	30	B2
Rodney St	18	A2
Rogers St	10	B1
Rogers Park Ave	18	B1
Rollins Ct	13	B2
Rollins Pl	1	B2
Rollins St	7	A2
Romar Ter	13	A1
Romsey Cir	32	A1
Romsey St	32	A1
Ronald St	31	A2
Ronan St	32	A1
Rosa St	33	A2
Rosaria St	32	B2
Rose Garden Cir	18	B1
Roseberry Rd	31	B1
Roseclair St	12	B2
Rosecliff St	30	B1
Rosecliff Ter	30	B1
Rosedale St	31	A2
Roseglen Rd	33	A2
Roseland St	32	B1
Rosemary St	14	B1
Rosemere Ct	30	B1
Rosemont St [DO]	32	B1
Rosemont St [MT]	31	B1
Roseway St	14	A2
Rosewood St	31	B1
Roslin St	32	B1
Roslindale Ave	14	A2
Roslyn Pl	11	A2
Ross Pl	32	B2
Ross Rd	30	B1
Rosselerin Rd	32	B1
Rosseter St	14	A2
Rossmore Rd		
(1-31)	14	B2
(32-34)	30	A2
(36-119)	31	A1
Roswell St	12	B1
Roucemont St	14	A2
Round Hill St	14	A2
Rowe Ct	30	B2
Rowe St	30	B2
Rowell St	32	A1
Rowena Ct	14	B2
Rowena St	32	B1
Rowes Wharf	4	A2
Rowley St	32	B2
Roxana St	33	B1
W Roxbury Pky	29	A2
Roxbury St	13	A1
Roxton St	31	A1
Royal St	19	A1
Royce Rd	19	B1
Roys St	14	A2
Rozella St	32	B1
Ruffing St	33	A1
Rugby Rd	31	B1
Rugdale Rd	31	B2
Rugg Rd	19	A1
Ruggles Ct	13	A2
Ruggles St		
(1-239)	13	A1/A2
(240-399)	15	A2
Rumford St	29	A1
Rundel Park	32	B1
Running Brook Rd	29	B2
Rupert St	31	A2
Rusfield St	12	B1
Rushmore St	18	B1
Ruskin Rd	33	A2
Ruskin St	29	A2
Ruskindale Rd		
(1-133)	33	A2
(134-299)	31	B1
S Russell St	1	B2
Russett Rd	29	B1
Rustic Rd	29	B2
Rustlewood Rd	29	A2
Ruth St	9	B1
Ruthven St		
(1-25)	13	B1
(26-199)	31	A1
Ruthven Park	31	A1
Rutland St	6	B1
W Rutland Sq	6	B1
Rutland St	7	A1/B1
Rutledge St	29	A2
Ruxton Rd	31	B1
Ryan Rd	18	A2
Sachem St	15	B1
Saco St	32	B1
Safford St	33	A2
Sagamore St	32	A1
Saint Alphonsus St	15	A2/B1/B2
Saint Marys St	16	A1
Saint Richard St	13	B2
Salcombe St	32	A1
Salem Ct	2	A1
Salem St	2	A1/B1
Salina Rd	32	B2
Salisbury Park	32	B1
Salman St	29	B1
Salt Ln	2	B1
Salutation St	2	A2
Sammett Ave	30	B1
Samoset St	32	B1
San Juan St	7	A1
San Juan Way	15	B2
Sanborn Ave	29	A2
Sanderson St	18	A2
Sanford St [HP]	33	B1
Sanford St [MT]	31	B2
Sanger St	10	B2
Santuit St	32	B1
Saranac St	32	B1
Saratoga Pl	9	A1
Saratoga St	9	A1/A2
Sargent St	13	B2
Sargent Crossway	14	A1
Saunders St	18	A2
Savannah Ave	31	B1
Saville St	29	B2
Savin St	13	B2
Savin Hill Ave	32	A1/A2
Savin Hill Ct	32	A2
Savin Hill Ln	32	A2
Savin Hill Ter	32	A2
Savoy Pl	7	A2

Street			Street			Street			Street		
Savoy St	7	A2	Shelby St	9	A2	Southwood St	13	B2
Sawyer Ave	32	A1	Sheldon St	30	B2	Spalding St	14	B1
Sawyer Ter	19	A1	Shenandoah St	32	B1	Sparhawk St	18	A2/B2
Saxton St	32	A1	Shepard Ct	33	B1	Sparrow St	29	B2
Saybrook St	18	A2	Shepard Pl	18	B2	Spaulding St	29	B2
Saybrook Ter	18	A2	Shepard St	18	B2	Speare Pl	15	A2
Sayward Pl	10	B1	Shepard Way	18	B2	Speedway Ave	20	B1
Sayward St	32	A1	Shepherd Ave	15	B1	Speedwell St	32	B1
Schiller Rd	29	B2	Shepton St	32	B1	Spencer St	31	A2
Schiller St	14	A2	Shepton Ter	11	B1	Spinney St	29	B1
Schirmer Rd	29	A2	Sherborn St	16	A2	Spofford St	19	B1
School St	3	A2	Sherbrook St	29	A1/A2	Sprague Pl	33	B1
School St [BR]	18	A2	Sheridan Pl	14	A2	Sprague St	33	B1
School St [RX]			Sheridan St	14	A2	Spring Ln	3	A2
(1-59)	31	A1/A2	Sherman Ct	10	B1	Spring Rd	29	B2
(60-199)	14	A2/B2	Sherman Rd	29	A2	Spring St	29	B1/B2
School Street Pl	31	A1	Sherman St [RS]	30	B1	Spring Garden St	32	A1
Schortmanns Ter	29	B2	Sherman St [RX]	13	B2	Spring Hill Rd	32	A1
Schrepel Pl	11	B1	Sherrin St	33	A2	Spring Park	14	A2
Schubert St	33	A1	Sherwood Ct	12	B1	Spring Park Ave	14	A1/A2
Schuyler St	31	A1	Sherwood St	30	B2	Spring Valley Rd	29	B1
Science Park	1	A1	Shetland St	12	B1	Springdale St	32	A1
Scotia St	5	B2	Shirley St	12	B1	Springer St	11	B1
Scott Aly	2	B1	Short St	16	A1/B1	E Springfield St	7	B1
Scott Pl	11	B1	Shrewsbury Rd	30	A1	W Springfield St		
Scottfield Rd	19	B1	Shurland St	31	A1	(1-230)	7	A1/B1
Scribner Rd	33	B1	Sidlaw Rd	18	B2	(231-240)	6	B1
Sea View Ter	32	A2	Sidley Rd	29	A2	Springvale Ave	29	B2
Seaborn St	32	B1	Sierra Rd	33	B2	Spruce Ct	1	B1
Seager Ct	18	A2	Sigourney St	31	A1	Spruce Pl	1	B1
Seaport Blvd	10	A2	Silloway St	32	B1	Spruce St	1	B1
Searle Rd	29	B2	Silva Pl	13	B2	Spurr St	19	A1
Seattle St	19	A2	Silver Pl	1	B1	St Albans Rd	15	B1
Seaver Pl	3	B1	Silver St	10	A1/B1/B2	St Ann St	14	B1
Seaver St [DO]	31	A1/A2	Silvia Ct	33	B1	St Botolph St		
Seaver St [EB]	9	B1	Simbroco St	29	B1	(1-117)	6	B1
Seaverns Ave	14	B1/B2	Sinclair Rd	19	A1	(118-277)	5	B2
Sedalia Rd	32	B1	Skyline Rd	33	B2	(278-299)	13	A1
Sedgwick St	14	B1/B2	Slayton Way	13	B1	St Brendan Rd	32	B2
Sefton St	33	A2	Sleeper St	10	A1	St Cecilia St	5	B2
Segal St	31	A2	Slocum Rd	30	A1	St Charles St	6	B2
Segel St	14	B2	Smith Ct	1	B2	St Clare Rd	32	B2
Selden St	31	B2	Smith St	15	B1/B2	St Cyprians Pl	13	A1
W Selden St	31	B1/B2	W Smithfield St	33	A1/B1	St Germain St	5	B2
Selkirk Rd	18	B2	Snelling Pl	2	A1	St Gregory St	31	B2
Selwyn St	30	B1	Snow Pl	4	A1	St James Ave		
Seminole St	33	A2	Snow St	18	B2	(1-73)	3	B1
Semont Rd	32	B1	Snow Hill St	2	A1	(74-158)	6	A1/A2
Senders Ct	33	B1	Sobin Park	10	A1	St James Pl	13	A1
Sentry Hill Pl	1	B1	Sojourner Truth Ct	13	A1/A2	St James St	13	A1/B2
Service Pl	12	B1	Solaris Rd	33	B1	St James Ter	13	A1
Service Rd	9	B1	Soldiers Field Pl	18	A2	St John St	14	B1
Seven Pine Rd	19	A1	Soldiers Field Rd			St Joseph St	14	B1
Sewall Pl	4	A1	(1-110)	16	A1	St Jude Ter	32	B2
Sewall St	15	B2	(111-550)	19	A2	St Lukes Rd	19	B2
Sexton Ct	12	B2	(549-1350)	20	B1/B2	St Margaret St	12	B2
Seymour St	30	B2	(1351-1999)	18	A1/A2	St Mark St	14	B1
Shabazz Way	13	A2	Somerset St	1	B2	St Marks Rd	32	B1
Shafter St	31	A2	Sonoma St	31	A1	St Peter St	14	A2
Shandon Rd	31	A1	Sorrento St	19	A2	St Rose St	14	B1
Shanley St	18	B1	W Sorrento St	19	A2	St Stephen St	5	B1/B2
Shannon St	18	B2	South St	4	A1/B1	St Theresa Ave	29	B2
Shapley Ave	23	A2	South St [BR]	18	B2	St Thomas More Rd	18	B1
Sharon Ct	9	A1	South St [JP]			St William St	32	A1
Sharon St	7	B1/B2	(1-292)	14	B1	Stadium Way	20	B1
Sharp St	32	B1	(301-1026)	30	A2/B1	Stafford St	13	B2
Shattuck St	15	A1	South Cedar Pl	3	B1	Stanbro St	33	B1
Shaw St	29	B2	South Point Dr	32	A2	Stanbro St	33	B1
Shawmut Ave			Southampton St	12	A1/B2	Standard St	31	B2
(1-99)	3	B1	Southbourne Rd	30	B2	Standish St	31	A2
(100-539)	7	A1/A2/B1	Souther Rd	32	B1	Stanhope St	6	A2/B2
(540-899)	13	A1/A2	Southern Ave	31	A2/B2	Staniford St	1	A2
Shawmut St	3	B1	Southmere Rd	31	B1	Stanley St	32	A1
Sheafe St	2	A1	Southview St	32	A2	Stanton St	31	B2
Sheffield Rd	30	B1	Southwick St	32	B2	Stanwood St	31	A2
						Stanwood Ter	31	A2

Street Index

Street	Page	Grid
Star St	33	A2
Starbird Ave	30	B2
Stark St	25	B1
Starr Ln	14	B1
State St	2	B1/B2
Station St	15	B2
Stearns Rd	29	B2
Stedman St		
(1-22)	31	A1
(23-99)	30	A2
Stella Rd	30	B2
Stellman Rd	30	B1/B2
Sterling Sq	32	A1
Stillman Pl	2	A1/B1
Stillman St	2	B1
Stimson Rd	29	B2
Stimson St	29	B1/B2
Stock St	32	B2
Stockton St	31	B2
Stockwell St	15	B1
Stone Ter	31	B2
Stonecrest Rd	33	A2
Stonehill Rd	33	B1
Stonehill Ter	33	B1
Stoneholm St	5	B1
Stonehurst St	32	A1/B1
Stonley Rd	30	A2
Storey Pl	14	B1
Story St	10	B2
Stoughton Ave	33	B1
Stoughton St [DO]	32	A1
Stoughton St [RX]	7	B1
Stoughton Ter	32	A1
Stoughton Street Pl	32	A1
Stow Rd	31	B2
Stratford St	29	A2
Strathcona Rd	31	A2
Strathmore Rd	23	A2
Stratton St	31	A1/B1/B2
Strong Pl	1	B1
Stuart St		
(1-340)	3	B1/B2
(341-599)	6	A2/B1
Sturbridge St	31	B2
Sturges Rd	29	A2
Sturtevant St	32	B1
Sudan St	32	A1
Sudbury St	2	B1
Sullivan Pl	4	A1
Summer St		
(1-25)	3	A2
(26-249)	4	A1/A2/B2
(250-567)	10	A1/A2
(568-899)	11	A1/B1
Summer St [HP]	33	A2
Summer St [WR]	29	B2
Summer Street Pl	33	A2
Summit Cir	33	B2
Summit St	33	B2
Sumner Ave	30	B1
Sumner Pl	9	B1
Sumner Sq	32	A1
Sumner St [DO]		
(1-23)	12	B2
(24-99)	32	A1
Sumner St [EB]	9	B1/B2
Sumner Ter	2	B1
Sumner Tunl	2	B1
Sumner Park	32	A1
Sun Court St	2	B1
Suncrest Rd	31	B1
Sunderland St	31	A2
Sunny Ct	14	A2
Sunnybank Rd	29	B2
Sunnyside St [HP]	33	B1
Sunnyside St [JP]	14	A2
Sunnyside Ter	23	A2
Sunset Ave	30	A2
Sunset Ln	32	B1
Sunset St	15	B1
Sunset Hill Path	29	A2
Sunset Hill Rd	29	A2
Supple Rd	31	B2
Surface Artery	2	B1/B2
Surrey St	18	A1/A2/B2
Surrey Hill Ln	30	A1
Susanna Ct	33	B1
Sussex St	13	A2
Sutherland Rd	18	B2
Sutton St	31	B1
Swallow St	11	B1
Swan St	31	B2
Swan St	33	A1
Sweetfern Ter	13	B2
Swift St	9	A2
Swift Ter	9	A2
Sycamore St	30	B1/B2
Sydney St	32	A1/A2
S Sydney St	32	A1
Sylvan St	29	A1
Sylvester Rd	32	B2
Sylvia St	14	B2
Symmes St	30	B1
Symphony Rd	5	B1
T St	29	B1
Taber St	14	A2
Tacoma St	33	A2
Taft Ct	30	B1
Taft St	32	A1
Taft Hill Ter	30	B1
Taft Hill Park	30	B1
Tai-Tung St	4	B1
Talbot Ave		
(1-357)	31	A1/A2/B2
(358-599)	32	B1
Tampa St	33	A2
Tamworth St	3	B2
Tanglewood Rd	31	B2
Tappan St	30	B1
Tarleton Rd	29	A2
Taunton Ave		
(1-70)	33	A2
(71-199)	31	B1
Tavern Rd	15	A2
Taylor St [DO]	32	B2
Taylor St [RX]	7	A2
Taylor Ter	31	B2
Tchapitoulas St	31	B1
Tebroc St	32	B1
Teevals Aly	10	B1
Telegraph St	31	B2
Telford St	19	A1
Temple Pl	3	A2
Temple St	1	B2
Temple St [MT]	31	B2
Temple St [WR]	29	A1/A2
Temple Ter	29	A1
Templeton Way	32	B1
Tenean St	32	B2
Tennis Rd	31	B1
Tennyson St	29	B2
Teresa Ter	33	B2
Termine Ave	14	A2
Terrace Pl	15	B2
Terrace St	15	B2
Tesla St	31	B1
Tetlow St	15	A2
Thacher Ct	2	A1
Thacher St	2	A1
Thane St	31	A2
Thatcher St	33	A2
Thayer St	7	A2
Thelma Rd	32	B1
Theodore St	31	B1
Theodore Glynn Way	12	B1
Theodore Parker Rd	29	A2
Thetford Ave	31	B2
Thomas St	14	B1
Thomas Park	10	B2
Thompson Ct	1	B1
Thompson St	33	B1
Thomson Pl	10	A2
Thor Ter	19	A1
Thorn St [MT]	31	B1
Thorn St [RX]	7	B1/B2
Thorndike St	13	A2
Thornley St	32	A1
Thornton Pl	13	B1
Thornton Rd	29	A2
Thornton St	13	A1/B1
Thornton Ter	13	B1
Thrush St	29	B2
Thurlow St	29	A1
Thwing St	13	B1
Ticknor St	11	B1
Tide St	11	A2
Tilesboro St	32	B2
Tileston Pl	2	A2
Tileston St	2	A1/A2
Tileston St [MT]	31	B1
Tilman St	32	B1
Tina Ave	33	A2
Tiverton Rd	31	B2
Tobin Ct	15	B2
Tobin Rd	29	B2
Toland Ct	32	B1
Toledo Ter	32	B1
Toll Gate Way	30	A2
Tolman St	32	B2
Tonawanda St	31	A2
Tonset St	31	A2
Topalian St	31	B1
Topeka St	12	A1
Topliff St	32	B1
Toppan Ave	30	B2
Torpie St	15	B1
Torrey St	31	B2
Tovar St	32	A1
Tower St	30	A2
Town St	33	B1
Townsend St	13	B1
Tracton Ave	31	B1
Train St	32	B1/B2
Transit St	12	B2
Trapelo St	18	B2
Trask St	13	A2
Traveler St	7	A2
Traverse St		
(1-27)	1	A2
(28-99)	2	A1
Travis St	19	A1
Treadway Rd	32	A1
Trelawney Rd	33	A2
Tremlett St		
(1-28)	31	A2
(29-99)	31	B1
W Tremlett St	31	A2
Tremont Pl	1	B2
Tremont St		
(1)	1	B2
(58-58)	3	A2/B1/B2
(59-386)	7	A1/A2/B1
(387-790)	13	A1/A2
(791-1327)	15	B1/B2
(1328-1699)	15	A1
Trent St	32	A1

Trenton St	9	A1/A2	(100-1999)	29	A1/A2/B1	
Trescott St	32	A1	Vicksburg St	11	B1	
Trevore Ave	29	B2	Victor St	13	B2	
Trilling Rd	11	A1	Victoria St	32	A1	
Trilling Way	11	A1	Victoria Heights Al	33	A2	
Trimount Pl	10	B1	Victory Rd	32	B1/B2	
Trinity St	6	A1/B2	Vienna St	9	A2	
Trotter Ct	13	A2	View South Ave	14	B1	
Trull St	32	A1	Viking St	11	B1	
Truman Hwy	33	A2/B2	Viking Ter	31	B1	
Truman Pky	33	A2/B2	Village Ct	7	A2	
Tucker St	31	B2	Vinal St	19	B1	
Tuckerman St	10	B1	Vincent Rd	29	A2	
Tudor St	10	B1	Vine Ave	13	B2	
Tufts St	4	B1	Vine St	13	A2/B2	
Tupelo St	13	B2	Vineland St	18	A2	
Turner St	18	A1	Vining St	15	B1	
Turquoise Way	15	B2	Vinson St	32	B1	
Turtle Pond Pky	33	A1/B1	Vinton St	10	B1	
Tuttle St	32	A1	Violante St	31	B1	
Twombley Pl	15	B2	Violet St	31	B1	
Twomey Ct	11	B2	Virgil Rd	29	A2	
Tyler St	4	B1	Virginia St	32	A1	
Tyler St [HP]	33	B2	Vista St	30	B1	
Tyndale St			Vitale Pl	15	B2	
(1-62)	30	B1	Vogel St	29	B1	
(63-199)	29	A2	Von Hillern St	12	B2	
Ufford St	31	B2	Vose Ave	33	B2	
Undine Rd	18	B1	Wabash St	31	B1	
Union Ave	14	B2	Wabeno St	13	B1	
Union St	2	B1	Wabon St	13	B1	
Union St [BR]	18	B2	Wachusett St [JP]	30	A2/B2	
Union Park	7	A1	Wachusett St [MT]	31	B1	
Union Park St	7	A2/B2	Wade St	18	B1	
Union Wharf	2	A1	Wadleigh Pl	12	B2	
Unity Ct	2	A1	Wadsworth Pl	1	B2	
Unity St	2	A1	Wadsworth St	19	A2	
Upcrest Rd	18	A1	Wainwright St	32	A1	
Upham Ave	32	A1	Wait St	15	B1	
Uphams Ct	32	A1	Wakefield Ave	33	B2	
Upland Ave	32	B1	Wakullah St	13	B1	
Upton St [HP]	33	B1	Walbridge St	19	B1	
Upton St [RX]	7	A1	Waldeck St	32	B1	
Utica Pl	4	B1	Walden St	14	A2	
Utica St	4	B1	Waldo Ter	18	B2	
Vale St	13	B1	Waldorf St	32	B1	
Valencia Rd	33	B1	Waldren Rd	13	B1	
Valentine St	13	B1	Wales St	31	B1	
Vallaro Rd	33	B1	Walk Hill St			
Valley Rd	31	B2	(1-290)	30	A2/B2	
Van Brunt	33	B2	(291-799)	31	B1	
Van Brunt St	33	B2	Wallace Park	18	B2	
Van Ness St	16	A2	Wallingford Rd	18	B2	
Van Rensselaer Pl	3	B1	Walnut Ave			
Van Winkle St	32	B1	(1-357)	13	B1/B2	
Vancouver St	15	A2	(358-499)	31	A1	
Vanderbilt Ave	33	A2	Walnut Ct [DO]	32	B2	
Varick Rd	29	A1	Walnut Ct [RX]	13	B2	
Varney St	30	A2	Walnut Pl	33	B2	
Vassar St	31	A2	Walnut Rd	29	B2	
Vaughan Ave	31	A2	Walnut St	1	B2	
Ventura St	31	B2	Walnut St [DO]	32	B2	
Vera St	31	B2	Walnut St [HP]	33	B2	
Verdun St	32	B1	Walnut Ave	13	B1	
Vermont St	29	A1/A2	W Walnut Park			
Verndale St	31	B2	(1-8)	13	B1	
Vernon St [HP]	33	B1	(9-199)	14	A2	
Vernon St [RX]	13	A1	Walsh Pl	2	A2	
Verona St	14	B1	Walter St [HP]	33	B2	
Verrill St	31	B1	Walter St [RS]	30	A1/B1	
Vershine St	29	B2	S Walter St	30	B1	
Vesper St	29	A2	Waltham St	7	A1/A2	
Vesta Rd	31	A1	Walton St	32	B1	
Vfw Pky			Walworth St	30	B1	
(1-99)	30	A1	Ward Ct	10	B1	

Ward St [RX]	15	A2/B2
Ward St [SB]	10	B1
Wardman Rd	13	B1
Ware St	32	A1
Wareham St	7	B2
Warner St	31	A2
Warren Ave	7	A1
Warren Ave [HP]	33	B2
W Warren Ave	6	B1
Warren Pl	13	A2
Warren Sq	14	B1
Warren St		
(1-559)	13	A2/B2
(560-699)	31	B2
Warren St [BR]	18	B2
Warren Park	33	B2
Warrenton Pl	3	B1
Warrenton St	3	B1
Warwick St	13	A1/A2
Washburn St	12	B2
Washington Ave	9	A1
Washington Pl	10	A1
Washington St		
(1-99)	2	B1
(101-956)	3	A2/B2
(959-1793)	7	A1/A2/B1
(1794-3061)	13	A1/A2/B1
(3062-3775)	14	A2/B1/B2
(3776-4582)	30	A2/B1/B2
(4583-5350)	29	A2/B2
Washington St [BR]	18	B1/B2
Washington St [DO]	31	A2/B2
Washington St [HP]	33	A1/B2
N Washington St	2	A1
Washington Street Pl	33	B2
Water St		
(1-18)	3	A2
(19-199)	4	A1/A2
Water St [DO]	32	B2
Waterford St	7	A2
Waterloo St	33	B1
Waterlow St	31	A2
Waterman Rd	30	B2
Watson St	13	A1
Waumbeck St	13	B1/B2
Wave Ave	32	A2
Waverly Pl	4	A1
Waverly St	13	B2
Waverly St [BR]	18	A2
S Waverly St	18	A2
Way St	33	B2
Wayburn Rd	30	B2
Wayland St	13	B2
Waymount St	15	B1
Wayne St	31	A1
Weaver Ct	13	B1
Weaver Way	13	B1
Webb Park	11	B1
Webber St	13	A2
Webley St	19	A1
Webster Ave	9	B1
Webster Pl	9	B1
Webster St	9	A1/B1/B2
Webster St [HP]	33	B1
Webster St [WR]	29	B1
Wedgemere Rd	29	B2
Wedgewood Rd	30	B1
Wedmore St	32	A2
Weeks Ave	33	A1
Weitz St	19	A1
Weld Ave	13	B1
Weld St		
(10-208)	30	B1
(209-699)	29	A2
Weld Hill St	30	A2

Street	Grid	Code
Weldon St	13	B2
Well St	4	A2
Welland Rd	29	A1
Welles Ave	32	B1
Wellesley Park	32	B1
Wellington Ct	13	B2
Wellington Pl	9	B1
Wellington Rd	5	B2
Wellington St	31	B1
Wellington Hill St	31	B1
Wellsmere Rd	30	B1
Wellsmere Ter	30	B1
Wellsmere Park	30	B1
Welton Rd	29	A2
Wendell Pl	10	B1
Wendell St	4	A2
Wendeller St	10	B1
Wendover St	32	A1
Wenham St	30	A2
Wenlock Rd	32	B2
Wenonah St	13	B1
Wensley St	15	B1
Wentworth St	31	B2
Wentworth Ter	31	B1
Wesley Pl	2	A1
Wesleyan Pl	3	A2
Wessex St	32	B1
West St	3	A2
West St [HP]	33	A1/A2
Westbourne St	29	A1
Westchester Rd	30	A1
Westcott St	31	A2
Westerly St	14	A2
Western Ave		
(1-312)	20	B1
(313-435)	19	A1
(436-599)	18	A2
Western Pl	19	A2
Westford Pl	19	A1
Westford St	19	A1
Westglow St	32	B1/B2
Westinghouse Plz	33	B1
Westland Ave	5	B1/B2
Westminster Ave	13	B1
Westminster Ct	13	B1
Westminster St [HP]	33	A2
Westminster St [RX]	13	A2
Westminster Ter	13	B1
Westminster Ter [BR]	18	B2
Westmoor Cir	29	B2
Westmoor Rd	29	B2
Westmoor Ter	29	B2
Westmore Rd	31	B1
Westmoreland St	32	B1
Westmount Ave	29	A2
Weston St	33	B1
Westover St	29	A2
Westview St	31	A1/A2
Westview Way	31	A1
Westville St		
(1-63)	31	A2
(64-299)	32	B1
Westville Ter	32	B1
Westwind Rd	32	A2
Westwood St	31	A2
Wexford St	18	A2
Weyanoke St	32	B1
Weybosset St	33	A2
Weymouth Ave	29	B2
Wharf St		
(1-99)	4	A2
Wharton Ct	33	B1
Wheatland Ave	31	A2
Wheatley Way	13	A2
Wheeler Ave	23	A2
Wheelock Ave	32	A1
Whipple Ave	30	B2
Whipple St	5	B1
Whitby Ter	32	A1
Whitcomb Ave	30	A1
White St	9	A1
White Oak Rd	29	B2
White Street Pl	9	A1
Whitfield St	31	A2/B2
Whitford St	30	B1
Whiting St	13	B2
Whitten St	3	A2
Whitlers Aly	2	A2
Whitman St	31	B2
S Whitney St	15	B1
Whitridge St	13	B2
Whittemore St	29	A2
Whittemore Ter	32	A1
Whittier St	32	B1
Whittier Pl	1	A1
Whittier St	13	A1
Wichita Ter	31	B2
Widett Cir	12	A1
Wiget St	2	A1/B1
Wiggin St	2	A1
Wigglesworth St	15	B1
Wilbert Cir	31	A1
Wilbert Rd	31	A1
Wilbur Ct	9	B1
Wilbur St	32	A1
Wilcock St	31	B1
Wilcox Rd	32	B1
Wilcutt Rd	31	A2
Wilder St	31	A2
Wildwood St	31	B1
Wilkins Pl	30	B1
Wilkinson Park	32	A1
Willers St	29	B2
Willet St	29	B2
William Pl	23	A2
William St	23	A1/A2
William Cardinal O'Connell Way	1	A1/A2
William E Mullins Way	7	A2
William F McClellan Hwy	9	A2
William J Day Blvd		
(1-25)	32	A2
(100-1410)	10	B2
(1412-1971)	11	B1/B2
William Jackson Ave	18	B2
William T Morrissey Blvd	32	A2/B2
Williams Ave	33	B2
Williams St [JP]		
(1-79)	14	B2
(80-199)	31	A1
Williams St [RX]	13	A2
Willis St	32	A1
Willis Ter	13	A1
Willoughby Pl	13	A1
Willoughby St	18	B1
Willow Ave	33	A2
Willow Ct	12	B1
Willow St	1	B1
Willow St [WR]	29	A2
Willow Ter	29	A2
Willow Pond Rd	14	A1
Willowdean Ave	29	A2
Willowwood St	31	B1
Wilmington Ave	31	B2
Wilmore St	31	B1
Wilmot St	33	A2
Wilna Ct	29	A2
Wilrose St	31	A2
Wilson St	31	A1
Wilson Park	18	B2
Wilton St [AL]	19	A1
Wilton St [HP]	33	B2
Wilton Ter	19	A1
Wiltshire Rd	18	B1
Winborough St	31	B1
Winchester St	23	A1
Winchester Pl	23	A1
Winchester St	3	B1
Winchester Ter	30	B1
Windermere Rd	32	A1
Windham Rd	33	A2
Windom St	19	A2
Windsor St	13	A1/A2
Winfield St	10	B2
Wingate Rd	33	B1
Winship Pl	18	B2
Winship St	18	B2
Winslow St [HP]	33	B1
Winslow St [RX]	13	A2
Winston Rd	31	B1
Winter Pl	3	A2
Winter St	3	A2
Winter St [DO]	32	A1
Winter St [HP]	33	B1
Winter Hill Rd	23	A2
Winthrop Sq	4	A1
Winthrop St [EB]	9	B1
Winthrop St [HP]	33	B2
Winthrop St [RX]	13	A2/B2
Winton St	33	A1
Wirt St	18	B2
Wise St	14	A2
Withington St	31	B2
Wm E Doucette Sq	32	B2
Wolcott Ct	33	B1
Wolcott Rd	33	B2
Wolcott Sq	33	B1
Wolcott St [DO]	31	A2
Wolcott St [HP]	33	B1
Wolfe St	29	A1
Wollaston Ter	31	B2
Wood Ave	33	A2
Woodale Ave	31	A2
Woodard Rd	29	A2/B2
Woodbine St	13	B2
Woodbole Ave	31	B2
Woodbourne Rd	30	B2
Woodbrier Rd	29	B2
Woodcliff St	13	B2
Woodfield St	32	B2
Woodford St	31	B2
Woodgate St	33	B2
Woodglen Rd	33	B2
Woodhaven St	31	B1
Woodland Pl	33	B2
Woodland Rd	30	A1
Woodlawn St	30	A2
Woodledge St	13	B2
Woodley Ave	29	B2
Woodman St	14	B1
Woodmere St	31	B2
Woodmont St	18	A1
Woodrow Ave	31	B1/B2
Woodrow Wilson Ct	13	A2
Woodruff Way	31	B2
Woodside Ave	14	B2
Woodstock Ave	19	B1
Woodville St	13	B1
Woodville Ter	13	B2
Woodville Park	13	B1
Woodward Ave	13	B2
Woodward Pl	12	B2
Woodward Rd	29	A2
Woodward St		
(1-11)	12	B2
(12-99)	10	B1
Woodward Park St	13	B2
Woodworth St	32	A1

Street Index

Woolsey Sq	14	B2
Woolson St	31	B1
Worcester Sq	7	B1
Worcester St		
(1-158)	7	A1/B1
(159-169)	6	B1
Worley St	29	A2
Wormwood St	10	A1
Worrell St	32	B2
Worthington St	15	B1
Wren St	29	A2/B2
Wrentham St	32	B1
Wright St	30	B1
Wrights Ct	10	B1
Wycliff Ave	29	B1
Wyman Pl	14	A2
Wyman St	14	A2
Wyola Pl	31	A2
Wyoming St	13	B1
Wyvern St	30	B2
Yale Ter	31	A1
Yard Way	10	A1
Yarmouth Pl	6	B1
Yarmouth St	6	B1
Yawkey Way		
(1-40)	16	A2
(41-69)	15	A2
Yeoman Pl	13	A2
Yeoman St	13	A2
York St	31	A2
Yorktown St	29	A2
Youngs Rd	31	B1
Yuill Cir	33	B1
Yuletide Rd	33	A2
Zamora Ct	14	A1
Zamora St	14	A1
Zeller St	30	B1
Ziegler St	13	A1/A2

Brookline

Abbottsford Rd	19	B2
Acron Rd	17	B2
Adams St	19	B2
Addington Path	17	A1
Addington Rd	17	A1
Allerton St	17	A1
Alton Ct	17	A2
Alton Pl	17	A2
Amory St	16	A1
Andem Pl	16	A1
Aspinwall Ave	16	A1/B1
Atherton Rd	19	B1
Auburn Ct	17	A2
Auburn Pl	17	A2
Auburn St	17	A2
Babcock St	19	A2/B2
Bartlett Cres	19	B1
Bartlett St	19	B1
Beacon St		
(1443-1793)	17	A1
(1794-2502)	18	B2
Beaconsfield Path	17	A1
Beaconsfield Rd	17	A1
Beals St	19	B2
Beech Rd	16	A1
Beecher Rd	17	A1
Berkeley Ct	17	A2
Blake Rd	17	A1
Borland St	17	A2
Bowker St	16	B1
Boylston Pl	17	B2
Boylston St	17	B1/B2
Bradford Ter	17	B2
Brington Rd	17	B2

Brook St	16	A1/B1
Browne St		
(1-35)	16	A1
(36-136)	19	B2
Buckminster Rd	17	A1/B1
Cameron St	17	B2
Carlton St	16	A1
Catlin Rd	17	B1
Centre St		
(1-51)	16	A1
(52-199)	19	B1/B2
Channing Rd	17	B1
Chapel St	16	B1
Charles St	17	A2
Chatham Cir	16	A1
Chatham St	16	A1
Chesham Rd	17	A1
Chestnut Pl	17	B2
Chestnut St		
(1-221)	17	B2
(228-399)	14	A1
Chestnut Hill Ave	17	B1
Chilton St	16	A1
Churchill St	16	A1
City View Rd	19	B1
Claflin Path	17	A1
Claflin Rd	17	A1
Clarence St	19	B2
Clark Ct	17	B2
Clark Rd	17	A1
Clearwater Rd	29	A2
Clinton Path	18	B2
Clinton Rd	17	A1
Codman Rd	17	B1
Colbourne Cres	17	A1
Colbourne Path	17	A1
Colchester St	16	A1/B1
Columbia St	19	B1
Columbia Ter	19	B1
Coolidge St	19	B1/B2
Copley St	19	B2
Corey Rd		
(1-26)	17	A1
(27-89)	18	B2
Cotswold Rd	17	A1
Cottage St	17	B1
Cottage Farm Rd	16	A1
Craig Pl	19	B2
Crowninshield Rd	19	B2
Cumberland Ave	17	A2
Cushing Rd	17	B2
Cypress St	17	A2/B2
Dana St	17	A2
Davis Ave	17	A2
Davis Ct	17	A2
Davis Path	17	A2
Dean Rd	17	A1
Devotion St	19	B2
Downing Rd	19	B1
Druce St	17	A1
Dudley St	17	B1
Dudley Way	17	B1
Dummer St		
(1-97)	16	A1
(98-145)	19	B2
Dwight St	19	B2
Edge Hill Rd	17	B2
Edwin St	17	B2
Egmont St		
(1-46)	16	A1
(47-99)	19	B2
Elba St	19	B2
Elm St	17	A2
Emerson St	17	A2
Englewood Ave	18	B2

Essex St	16	A1
Euston St	16	A1
Evans Rd	19	B1
Ewe St	16	A1
Fairbanks St	17	A1
Fairmount St	17	B1
Fisher Ave	17	B1
Fisher Rd	17	B1
Foster St	17	B1
Francis St	16	A1/B1
Franklin Ct	17	B2
Franklin St	17	B2
Freeman St		
(1-173)	16	A1
(174-245)	19	B2
Fuller St	19	B1/B2
Gardner Rd	17	A1
Garrison Rd	17	B1
George Ln	17	B1
Gibbs St	19	B2
Glen Rd	17	B2
Goddard Ave	17	B1
Goodwin Pl	17	A2
Gorham Ave	17	A2
Green St	19	B2
Green Hill Rd	17	B1
Greenough Cir	17	A2
Greenough St	17	A1/A2
Greenway Ct	19	B2
Griggs Rd	17	A1/A2
Griggs Ter	17	A2
Hall Rd	17	B2
Hamilton Rd	19	B2
Hancock Rd	17	A2
Harris St	17	A2
Harrison St	16	B1
Hart St	17	B2
Harvard Ave	17	A2
Harvard Ct	17	A2
Harvard Pl	17	A2
Harvard Sq	17	A2
Harvard St	19	B1/B2
Hawes Pl	16	A1
Hawes St	16	A1/B1
Hawthorn Rd	17	B2
Hayden Rd	17	B1
Heath Hill	17	B1
Hedge Rd	17	B1
Henry St	17	B2
High St		
(1-37)	16	B1
(38-299)	17	B2
High Street Pl	17	B2
Highland Rd	17	B2
Hillside Rd	17	B1
Holden St	17	A2
Holland Rd	17	A1
Homer St	17	A1
Hurd Rd	17	A2
Hyslop Rd	17	A1
Irving St	17	B2
Ivy St	16	A1
Jamaica Rd	17	B2
James St	16	A1
Jenness Rd	19	B1
John St	19	B2
Jordan Rd	19	B1
Juniper St	16	B1
Kendall St	17	B1
Kennard Rd	17	B1
Kent Sq	16	B1
Kent St	16	A1/B1
Kenwood St	19	B1
Kerrigan Pl	17	A2
Kilsyth Rd	18	B2

Street Index

Street		
Lanark Rd	18	B2
Lancaster Ter		
(1-22)	17	A1
(23-299)	19	B1
Lawrence Rd	16	B1
Lawton St	19	B1
Lee St	17	B1
Leicester St	17	B1
Lenox St	16	A1
Leverett St	17	A2/B2
Lincoln Rd	17	A2
Linden Ct	16	B1
Linden Pl	16	A1/B1
Linden St	16	A1/B1
Littell Rd	17	A2
Longwood Ave	16	A1/B1
Lowell Rd	17	A1
Manchester Rd	19	B2
Maple St	17	B2
Marion Path	17	A2
Marion St	17	A2
Marion Ter	17	A2
Marshall St	16	A1/B1
Mason Path	19	B1
Mason St	16	A1
Mason Ter	19	B1
Milton Rd	17	B2
E Milton Rd	17	B2
Monmouth Ct	16	A1
Monmouth St	16	A1
Mulford St	17	B2
Naples Rd	19	B2
Netherlands Rd	16	B1
New Terrace Rd	17	B2
Newell Rd	16	B1
Oakland Rd	17	B2
Orchard Rd	19	B1
Osborne Rd	19	B2
Park St	17	A2
Park Vale	17	A2
Parkman St		
(1-40)	16	A1
(41-99)	19	B2
Parkway Rd	16	B1
Pearl St	16	B1
Perrin Rd	17	B1
Perry St	16	A1/B1
Philbrick Rd	17	B1
Pierce St	17	A2
Pleasant St	19	B2
Pond Ave		
(1-34)	16	B1
(35-399)	17	B2
Powell St	16	A1
Prescott St	16	A1
Prince St	17	A1
Rawson Path	17	A1
Rawson Rd	17	A1
Regent Cir	17	A1
Reservoir Ct	18	B2
Rice St	17	B2
River Rd	16	B1
Roberts St	17	B2
Royal Rd	17	A1
Russell St	19	B1
Saint Marys Ct	16	A1
Salisbury Rd		
(1-94)	19	B1
(95-199)	18	B2
Sargent Rd	17	B1/B2
Sargent Beechwood	17	B2
Sargent Crossway	17	B2
School St	17	A2
Searle Ave	17	A2
Seaver St	17	A1

Street		
Sewall Ave	16	A1/B1
Shailer St	19	B2
Smyth St	17	B2
Somerset Rd	17	A1/A2
South St	29	A2
St Paul St		
(161-202)	16	A1
(203-399)	19	B2
Stanton Rd	17	A2
Station St	16	A1/B1
Stearns Rd	16	A1/B1
Stedman St	19	B2
Stetson St	19	B2
Still St	19	B2
Strathmore Rd	19	B1/B2
Summit Ave	17	A1
Summit Path	17	A1
Sumner Rd	17	A1/B1
Tabor Pl	16	A1
Tappan St	17	A1
Thatcher St		
(1-53)	16	A1
(54-99)	19	B2
Thayer Pl	17	A2
Thayer St	17	A2
Thorndike St	19	B1
Toxteth St	16	B1
University Path	17	A1
University Rd	17	A1
Upland Rd	17	B2
Verndale St	19	B1
Vernon St	17	A2
Village Way	16	B1
Vogel Ter	17	B2
Waldo St	16	A1
Walnut Path	17	B2
Walnut Pl	17	A1
Walnut St		
(1-129)	16	A1/B1
(130-499)	17	B1/B2
Warren St	17	B1
Warwick Rd	18	B2
Washburn Pl	17	A2
Washburn Ter	17	A2
Washington St		
(1-200)	16	A1/B1
(201-736)	17	A1/A2
(737-825)	19	B1
Waverly St	17	A2
Webster Pl	16	A1
Webster St	17	A2
Welch Rd	17	B1
Welland Rd	17	A1/A2
Wellington Ter	17	B2
Wellman St	19	B2
Wentworth Pl	17	B2
Westbourne Ter		
(1-66)	17	A1
(67-134)	19	B1
Weybridge Ln	17	A2
Weybridge Rd	17	A2
White Pl	16	A1
Williams St	19	B2
Williston Rd	19	B1
Winchester Path	17	B2
Winchester St		
(1-32)	16	A1
(33-267)	19	B1/B2
Windsor Rd	18	B2
Winslow Rd	19	B2
Winthrop Rd	17	A1
Woodcliff Rd	29	A1
Worthington Rd	16	A1
York Ter	19	B1

Cambridge

Street		
1st St	26	A2/B2
2nd St	26	A2/B2
3rd St	26	A2/B1
4th Street Pl	26	A2
5th St	26	A1/A2/B1
6th St	26	A1
7th St	26	A1
8th St	26	A1
Acacia St	20	B1
Acorn St	27	B1
Adams Ter	28	A1
Agassiz St	20	A1
Akron St	27	A1
Albany St		
(1-40)	26	B1
(41-308)	27	B2
Alberta Ter	22	A1
Alewife Ctr	22	A1
Alewife Brook Pky		
(2-195)	22	A1/B1
(196-299)	21	A1
Allen St	23	B1
Allston Ct	27	B1
Allston St	27	B1
Alpine St	21	A1
Ames St	26	B1
Amesbury St	27	B1
Amherst St		
(1-131)	26	B1
(133-199)	27	B2
Amory Pl	28	B1
Amory St	28	B1
Andrew St	27	B1
Anglim St	27	B2
Antrim St	28	B1
Appian Way	20	A2
Appleton Rd	21	A2
Appleton St	21	A2/B2
Appleton Ter	21	A2
Arcadia St	23	B1
Arlington St		
(1-30)	23	B1
(31-99)	20	A1
Arnold Cir	27	A1
Arrow St	20	B2
Arsenal Sq	20	A1
Ash St	20	A1/B1
Ash Street Pl	20	B1
Ashburton Pl	27	A2
Ashton St	28	A1
Athenaeum St	26	B1
Athens St	20	B2
Athens Ter	20	B2
Auburn St	27	A1/A2/B2
Auburn Park	27	A2
Audrey St	27	B1
Austin St	27	A1
Austin Park	27	A1
Avon Pl	20	A1
Avon St	20	A1
Avon Hill St	20	A1
Bacon St	26	A1
Bailey Pl	27	B1
Baldwin Street Ct	28	A1
Ballord Pl	27	A1
Bancroft St	27	A1
Banks St		
(1-35)	20	B2
(36-299)	27	A1
Bates St	20	A1
Bay St	27	A1
Bay State Road	21	A1

Street Index

Street	Map	Grid
Beech St	23	B1/B2
Bell Ct	27	B1
Bellevue Ave	20	A1
W Bellevue Ave	20	A1
Bellis Cir	22	B1
Bellis Ct	22	B1
Belmont Ct	22	B1
Belvidere Pl	27	A1
Bennett St	20	B1
Bent St	26	A1/A2/B1
Berkeley Pl	20	A1
Berkeley St	20	A1
Berkshire Pl	28	B2
Berkshire St	28	B2
Bigelow St	27	A1
Binney St	26	A1/A2/B1
Birch St	21	A1
Bishop Richard Allen Dr	27	A1/A2
Blackstone St	27	A1
Blair Pl	22	B1
Blake St	23	A1
Blakeslee St	21	A2/B2
Blanche St	27	A2/B2
Boardman Pl	28	B2
Boardman St	28	B2
Bolton St	22	B1
Bond St	20	A1
Bow St	20	B2
Bowdoin St	20	A1/A2
Boyle Ter	21	A2
Bradbury St	20	B1
Brattle Sq	20	B1
Brattle St		
(1-147)	20	A1/B1/B2
(148-227)	21	B1/B2
Brewer St	20	B1
Brewster St	21	B1
Bristol St	28	B2
Broadway		
(1-189)	26	B1
(190-472)	28	A1/B1/B2
(473-501)	20	B2
Broadway Ct	28	B2
Broadway Ter	28	B1
Brookford St	22	A1
Brookline St	27	A2/B1/B2
Brown St	20	A1
Bryant St	20	A2
Buckingham Pl	20	A1
Buckingham St	20	A1
Buena Vista Park	22	B2
Burns Ct	20	A1
Cadbury Rd	21	A2
Callender St	27	A1
Cambridge Ctr	26	B1
Cambridge Pky	26	A2
Cambridge St		
(1-703)	26	A1/A2/B1
(704-1724)	28	A1/B1/B2
(1725-1899)	20	A2/B2
Cambridge Ter	22	B2
Cambridge Park Dr	22	B1
Cambridgeside Pl	26	A2
Camden Pl	20	B1
Camelia Ave	28	A1
Camp St	22	A2
Canal Park	26	A2
Cardinal Medeiros Ave	28	B2
Carleton St	26	B1
Carlisle St	28	B2
Carver St	20	A2
Cedar Sq	22	A1
Cedar St	22	A1/B1
Central Sq	27	A2
Centre St	27	A1
Chalk St	27	A1/B1
Channing Cir	21	B2
Channing Pl	21	B2
Channing St	21	B2
Chapman St	20	B1
Charles St	26	A1/A2/B1
Chatham St	28	B1
Chauncy Ln	20	A1
Chauncy St	20	A1
Chauncy Ter	20	A1
Cherry Ct	27	A2
Cherry St		
(1-94)	27	A2
(95-199)	26	B1
Chester St	22	B2
Chestnut St	27	B1
Chetwynd Rd	21	A2
Chilton St	21	A1/A2
Church St	20	B1/B2
Churchill Ave	22	A1
Citizens Pl	28	B2
Clary St	28	A2
Clay St	22	A1
Clement Cir	21	A2
Cleveland St	28	B1
Clifton St	22	A1
Clinton St	27	A1
Cogswell Ave	22	B2
Cogswell Pl	22	B2
Columbia St		
(1-124)	27	A2
(125-152)	26	B1
(153-599)	28	A2/B2
Columbia Ter	27	A2
Columbus Ave	22	A1
Concord Ave		
(1-103)	20	A1
(139-578)	21	A1/A2
Concord Ln	21	A1
Coolidge Hill	21	B2
Coolidge Hill Rd	21	B1
Copley St	21	A2
Corliss Pl	28	B1
Cornelius Way	26	B1
Corporal Burns Rd	21	A1
Cottage St	27	A1
Cottage Row	27	A1
Cottage St	27	A1
Cottage Park Ave	22	A1
Cowperthwaite St	20	B2
Craigie Cir	20	A1
Craigie St	20	A1
Crawford St	28	B1
Creighton St	22	B2
Crescent St	20	A2
Cresto Ter	26	A2
Cross St	27	B2
Crossland St	28	B2
Cutler Ave	20	A1
Cypress St	22	B2
Dana Pl	27	A1
Dana St		
(1-21)	27	A1
(22-99)	28	A1/B1
Davenport St	23	B1
Davis St	28	B2
Day St	22	A2/B2
Deacon St	26	B1
Decatur St	27	B1
Dewolfe St	20	B2
Dinsmore Ct	20	B1
Divinity Ave	20	A2
Doane St	20	A1
Dock St	26	B1
Dodge St	20	A1
Donnell St	21	A2
Douglas St	27	A2
Dover St	22	A2
Drummond Pl	22	B2
Dudley Ct	22	A1
Dudley St	22	A1
Dunstable Rd	21	B2
Dunster St	20	B2
East St	26	A2
Eaton St	27	A2
Edmunds St	22	A1
Education St	26	A2
Eliot St	20	B1
Ellery Pl	28	B1
Ellery Sq	28	B1
Ellery St		
(1-27)	27	A1
(28-199)	28	A1/B1
Ellsworth Ave	28	A1/B1
Ellsworth Park	28	A1/B1
Elm St	28	B2
Elmer St	27	A1
Elmwood Ave	21	B1
Emily St	27	B1
Emmet Pl	26	A1
Emmons Pl	28	A1
Endicott St	27	B2
Erie St	27	B1/B2
Essex St	27	A2
Eustis St	23	B1
Everetteze Way	28	B2
Everett St	20	A2/B1
Exeter Park	23	B1
Fainwood Cir	28	B1
Fair Oaks St	22	A2
Fairfield St	22	B2
Fairmont Ave	27	A1
Fairmont St	27	A1/B1
Fallon Pl	27	A1
Farrar St	28	A1
Farwell Pl	20	B1
Fayerweather St	21	A1/A2/B1
Fayette St	28	A1/B1
Fayette Park	28	B1
Felton St	28	A1
Fenno St	21	A2
Fern St	21	A1
Fernald Dr	20	A1
Field St	21	A1/A2
Fisk Pl	27	A2
Flagg St		
(1-77)	27	A1
(78-99)	20	B2
Florence St	27	B1
Foch St	22	A1
Follen St	20	A1
Forest St	23	B1
Fort Washington Pl	27	B1
Foster Pl	20	A1
Foster St		
(1-121)	20	A1/B1
(122-199)	21	B2
Frances Pl	22	B1
Francis Ave	20	A2
Franklin	27	A1
Franklin St	27	A1/A2/B2
Fresh Pond Ln	21	B1
Fresh Pond Pky	21	A1/B1
Frisbie Pl	20	A2
Front St	27	A2
Frost St		
(1-65)	23	B1
(66-99)	20	A2
Frost Ter	23	B1
Fulkerson St	26	A1

Street Index

Street	Page	Grid
Fuller Pl	20	B1
Galileo Galilei Way	26	A1
Garden Ct	21	A2
Garden Ln	20	A1
Garden St		
(1-111)	20	A1/A2
(112-300)	21	A2
Garden Ter	20	A1
Gardner Rd	28	B1/B2
Garfield St	20	A2
George St	22	A1
Gerry St	20	B1
Gerrys Landing Rd	21	B1
Gibson St	21	B2
Gilmore St	27	A1
Gladstone St	22	A1
Glenn Ter	27	B1
Glenwood Ave	27	B1
Gold Star Rd	22	A1/A2
Gold Star Road Ct	22	A2
Gold Star Road Pl	22	A1
Goodman Rd	28	B1
Gordon Pl	27	B1
Gore St	26 A1/A2/B1
Gore Street Pl	26	A1
Gorham St	20	A2
Gracewood Park	21	B1
Granite St	27	B1
Grant St	20	B1
Granville Rd	21	A2
Gray St	20	A1
Gray Gardens E	20	A1
Gray Gardens W	20	A1
Green St	27 A1/A2
Greenmalge St	27	B2
Greenough Ave	28	B1
Greenough Blvd	21	B2
Grove Ave	27	B1
Grozier Rd	21	A1/B1
Gurney St	21	A1
Hadley St	22	B2
Hamilton St	27	B1
Hamlin St	28	B2
Hammond St	20	A2
Hampshire Ct	28	B1
Hampshire Pl	28	B1
Hampshire St		
(1-30)	26	B1
(31-298)	28 A1/B1/B2
Hancock Pl	28	B1
Hancock St		
(1-127)	27	A1
(128-199)	28	B1
Hancock Park	28	B1
Harding St	28	A2/B2
Hardwick St	28	B2
Harold Pl	27	A2
Harrington Rd	22	A1
Harrington Ter	28	B2
Harris St	23	B1
Harrison Ave	22	A1
Harvard St		
(0-44)	23	A1
(100-383)	28	B1/B2
(384-499)	20	B2
Harvey St	22	A1
Harwell Dr	28	B2
Haskell St	22	B2
Hasting Ave	20	A1
Hastings Ave	20	A1
Hastings Sq	27	B1
Hawthorn St	20	A1/B1
Hawthorne Park	21	A1
Hayes St	21	A1
Hayward St	26	B1
Hazel St	21	A2
Healey St	20	A1
Hemlock Rd	21	B2
Henry St	27	B1
Hews St	27	A1
Highland Ave	28	A1/B1
Highland St	21	B1
Highland Park	21	B1
Hilliard Pl	20	B1
Hilliard St	20	B1
Hillside Ave	20	A1
Hillside Pl	20	A1
Hingham St	27	A1
Holden St	28	A1
Holden Green	28	A1
Hollis St	22	B2
Hollis Park	22	B2
Holly Ave	20	A1
Holyoke Pl	20	B2
Holyoke St	20	B2
Hooper Pl	22	B2
Houston Park	22	B2
Hovey Ave	28	A1
Howard St	27	A1
Howland St	20	A2
Hubbard Ave	22	B2
Hubbard Park Rd		
(1-25)	20	B1
(26-99)	21	B2
Hudson Pl	20	A1
Hudson St	20	A1/A2
Humboldt St	20	A2
Hunting St	28	A2
Hurley St	26 A1/A2/B1
Huron Ave		
(1-93)	20	A1
(94-560)	21 A1/A2/B1
Hutchinson St	21	A2
Industrial Park Rd	26	A2
Inman Ct	28	B1
Inman Pl	28	B1
Inman St		
(1-41)	27	A1
(42-199)	28	B1
Irving St		
(1-95)	28	A1
(96-199)	20	A2
Irving Ter		
(1-9)	28	A1
(10-99)	20	A2
Ivy St	21	A2
Jackson Cir	22	B1
Jackson Pl	22	B1
Jackson St	22	A1
Jackson Gardens	28	B1
James St	20	A1
James Way	26	B1
Jarvis St	20	A2
Jay St	27	A1
Jay Street Pl	27	A1
Jefferson St	28	B2
Jefferson Park	22	B1
JFK St	20	B1
Kassul Park	22	A1
Kelley St	21	A2
Kelly Rd	27	A1
Kennedy Rd	21	B2
Kenway St	27	A1
Kenwood St	27	B1
Kimball Ln	22	A1
Kimball St	22	A1
King Pl	28	B1
King St	22	B2
Kinnaird St	27	A1
Kirkland Pl	20	A2
Kirkland Rd	28	A1
Kirkland St		
(1-48)	20	A2
(50-100)	28	A1
Lake View Ave	21	A1/B1
Lambert St	26	A1
Lamont Ave	28	A1
Lamson Pl	27	A2
Lancaster St		
(1-19)	23	B1
(20-99)	20	A1
Land Blvd	26	A2
Landsdowne St	27	B2
Langdon Sq	20	A1
Langdon St	20	A1/A2
Larch Rd	21	A1/B1
Larchwood Dr	21	B1
Laurel St	27	A1
Lawrence St	27	B1
Lee St		
(1-40)	27	A1
(41-99)	28	B1
Leonard Ave	28	A1
Lexington Ave	21	A1/B1
Lilac Ct	28	B2
Lincoln Ln	21	B1
Lincoln Pl	28	B2
Lincoln St	28	B2
Lincoln Way	22	B2
Linden St	20	B2
Line St	28	A1
Linehan St	26	A2
Linnaean St	20	A1/A2
Linskey Way	26 A2/B1/B2
Linwood Pl	28	B2
Livermore Pl	28	B2
Locke St	22	A2
Longfellow Rd	21	B2
Longfellow Park	20	A1
Lopez Ave	26	A2
Lopez St	27	B1
Lowell St	21	B2
Madison Ave	22	A1
Madison St	20	A1
Magazine Ct	27	B1
Magazine St	27 A1/A2/B1
Magee St	27	A1
Magnolia Ave	28	A1
Magoun St	22	A1
Main St		
(1-632)	26	B1/B2
(633-999)	27	A2
Malcolm Rd	21	A1
Manassas Ave	21	A2
Maple Ave	28	A1/B1
Marcella St	28	B2
Marie Ave	28	B1
Market St	28	B2
Marney St	28	B1
Martin St	20	A1/A2
Marvin Pl	27	A2
Mason St	20	A1
Massachusetts Ave		
(1-128)	26	B1
(129-1145)	27 A1/A2/B2
(1146-1737)	20	A2/B2
(1750-2028)	23	B1
(2041-2574)	22 A1/A2/B2
Matignon Rd	22	A1
Max Ave	26	A1
Maynard St	21	B2
McLean Pl	22	A1
McTernan St	27	B1
Meacham Rd	22	A1

Street	Page	Grid
Mellen St	20	A2
Memorial Dr		
(17-372)	26	B1/B2
(374-900)	27	A1/B1/B2
(901-1000)	20	B1/B2
(1016-1098)	21	B2
Mercer Cir	20	A1
Merriam St	27	B2
Merrill St	28	B1
Michael Way	26	B1
Middlesex St	22	B1/B2
Mifflin Pl	20	B1
Mildred Hamilton Pl	27	A1
Mill St	20	B2
Miller Ave	23	A1
Milton St	22	B2
Monsignor Obrien Hwy	26	A2/B1
Montague	27	A1
Montague St	27	A1
Montgomery St	22	A1/B1
Moore St	28	B2
Morrison Ct	22	A1
Mount Auburn St		
(1-7)	27	A1
(8-259)	20	B1/B2
(260-426)	21	B1/B2
Mount Pleasant St	22	B2
Mount Vernon St	23	B1
Msgr O'Brien Hwy		
(1-7)	1	A1
(8-11)	26	A2
Muller Ave	22	A1
Mullins Ct	26	A2
Murdock St	28	B2
Murray Hill Rd	22	A1
Museum St	20	A2
Museum Way	26	A2
Myrtle Ave	28	A1
New St	21	A2
Newell St	21	A2
Newell Ter	20	A1
Newman St	22	A1
Newport Rd	23	B1
Newton St	27	B1
Nichols Pl	28	A1
Norfolk Ct	28	B2
Norfolk St		
(1-145)	27	A2
(151-499)	28	A2/B2
Norfolk Ter	27	A2
Norris St	22	A1
Norton Pl	20	A1
Notre Dame Ave	22	B1
Nutting Rd	20	B1
Oak St	28	A1/A2
Oakland St	28	A2
Olive Pl	22	B1
Orchard St	23	A1/B1
Orrin St	21	A2
Osborne St	21	A2
Otis St	26	A1/A2/B1
Oxford St	20	A2
Pacific St	27	A2
Palermo St	28	B2
Palmer St	20	B2
Parker St	20	A1
Parkway Ter	21	B1
Peabody St	20	B2
Peabody Ter	27	A1
Pearl St	27	A1/A2/B1
Pearl Street Pl	27	B1
Pemberton Ct	22	B2
Pemberton St	22	B1/B2
Pemberton Ter	22	B2
Percy Pl	27	A2
Perry St	27	A1/B1
Peters St	27	B1
Phillips St	20	A1
Pilgrim St	27	B2
Pine St		
(1-66)	27	A2
(67-199)	26	B1
Pleasant Pl	27	A1
Pleasant St	27	A1/B1
Plymouth St	28	B2
Plympton St	20	B2
Pond Pl	27	A1
Poplar Rd	21	A1
Porrington St	27	B2
Porter Cir	23	B1
Porter Rd	23	B1
Porter Sq	23	B1
Porter St	28	B2
Porter Park	23	B1
Portland St		
(1-74)	27	A2
(75-115)	26	B1
(116-169)	28	B2
Portsmouth St	28	B2
Potter St	26	B1
Potter Park	20	A2
Prentiss St		
(1-22)	20	A2
(23-49)	23	B1
Prescott St	20	B2
Prince St	27	B1
Princeton Ave	26	B1
Prospect St		
(1-109)	27	A2
(110-398)	28	A2/B1/B2
Putnam Ave	27	A1/B1
Putnam Ct	27	B1
Putnam Gdns	27	A1
Quincy St	20	A2/B2
Raymond St		
(1-139)	20	A1
(140-298)	22	B2
Reed St	22	A1
Reed Steet Ct	22	A1
Reed Street Ter	22	A1
Regent St	22	B2
Remington St	27	A1
Reservoir St	21	A2/B1/B2
Revere St	20	B1
Rice Cir	22	B2
Rice St	22	A2/B1/B2
Richard Ave	22	A1
Richardson St	28	B2
Richdale Ave		
(1-33)	23	B1
(34-299)	22	B1
Ridgely Ct	20	B2
Riedesel Ave	21	B2
Rindge Ave	22	B1/B2
Rindge Ter	22	B2
Ringefield St	22	B2
River St	27	A1/B1
Riverside Pl	27	A1
Riverside Rd	27	B1
Riverview Ave	20	B2
Roberts Rd	28	A1
Robinson St	20	A1
Rockingham Pl	27	B1
Rockingham St	27	B1
Rockwell St	27	B1
Rogers St	26	A1/A2/B1
Rollins Ct	27	B1
Roseland St	23	B1
Ross St	20	B1
Royal Ave	21	A2
Rufo Rd	26	B1
Rumeal Robinson Pl	27	A2
Russell St		
(1-36)	22	B2
(37-56)	23	A1
Rutland St	20	A2
Sacramento St	20	A2
Sacramento Pl		
(1-70)	20	A2
(71-199)	23	B1
Saginaw Ave	23	B1
Salem St	27	A1
Sargent St	22	B1
Saville St	21	A2
School St	27	A2
Sciarappa St	26	A2
Scott St	28	A1
Scouting Way	28	B1
Seagrave Rd	22	A1
Seckle St	28	B2
Sedgewick Rd	28	A1
Sellers St	27	A1
Shady Hill Sq	28	A1
Shaler Ln	20	B1
Shea Rd	22	A2
Shepard St	20	A1/A2
Sheridan St	22	B2
Sherman St		
(1-83)	21	A2
(85-299)	22	B1
Sibley Ct	20	B1
Sidney St	27	A2/B1/B2
Smart St	27	A2
Soden Pl	27	A1
Soden St	27	A1
South St	20	B2
Sparks Pl	20	B1
Sparks St		
(1-62)	20	A1/B1
(63-199)	21	A2/B2
Speridakis Ter	27	B1
Spring Pl	26	A1/A2/B1
Spring St	28	A1
Springfield St	22	B2
St Gerard Ter	20	A1
St Johns Rd	28	B1
St Mary Rd	27	A2
St Paul St	21	A1
Standish St	27	A2
State St	21	A2
Stearns St	27	A2
Stinson Ct	20	B1
Story St	27	B1
Suffolk St	27	A2
Sullivan Pl	27	A1
Sumner Rd	20	A2
Surrey St	27	A1
Sycamore St	22	B2
Talbot St	27	B1
Technology Sq	26	B1
Temple St	27	A1
Tenney St	23	A1
Terminal Rd	22	B1
Theriault Ct	22	A1
Thorndike St	26	A1/A2/B1
Tierney St	21	A2
Traill St	21	B1
Traymore St	23	B1
Tremont St	28	A2/B2
Trowbridge Pl	28	B1
Trowbridge St		
(1-27)	27	A1
(28-199)	28	A1/B1
Trowbridge Ter	28	B1
Tudor St	27	B1

Street Index

Street	Page	Grid
Tufts St	27	B1
Tyler Ct	22	A1
Union Pl	28	B2
Union St	28	B2
Union Ter	28	B2
University Rd	20	B1
Upland Rd		
(1-60)	23	B1
(61-174)	22	B2
(175-299)	20	A1
Upton St	27	A1
Vail Ct	27	A2
Valentine St	27	B1
Van Norden St	22	B1
Vandine St	28	B2
Vassal Ln	21	A1/A2
Vassar St		
(1-89)	26	B1
(90-499)	27	B1
Verdun St	22	B1
Village St	27	A2
Vincent St	22	B2
Wadsworth St	26	B1
Walbro St	27	A1
Walden St		
(1-190)	22	B2
(191-499)	21	A2
Walden Mews	22	B2
Walden Square Rd	22	B1
Walker Ct	27	A1
Walker St	20	A1
Walker Ter	20	A1
Walker Street Pl	20	A1
Walnut Ave	22	B2
Ware St	28	B1
Warren Pl	20	B1
Warren St	28	B2
Warwick Park	22	B2
Washburn Ave	22	A1
Washburn Ter	22	A1/A2
Washington Ave	20	A1
Washington Ct	27	A1
Washington St	27	A2
Water St	20	A1/A2
Waterhouse St	21	A1
Waterman Rd	26	A2
Watson St	27	A1/B2
Waverly St	27	B1/B2
Wellesley St	26	B1
Wellington St	28	B2
Wendell St	20	A1
West Pl	28	B1
West St	28	B1
Westacott Ct	27	B1
Western Ave	27	A1/A2
Westley Ave	22	A1
White St	23	B1
Whitney Ave	27	B1
Whitney Ct	27	A2
Whittemore Ave	22	A1
Whittier St	20	A1
Willard St	20	A1/B1
Willard Street Ct	20	A1
William St	27	A1
Willow St	28	A2/B2
Wilson Ave	22	B1
Windsor St		
(1-172)	27	A2/B2
(173-599)	28	B2/B2
Winslow St	21	A2
Winter St	26	A2
Winthrop St	20	B1/B2
Wood St	21	A2
Woodbridge St	22	A2
Woodrow Wilson Ct	27	B1
Worcester St	27	A2
Worthington St	21	A1
Wright St	20	A1
Wyman Rd	21	A2
Wyman St	20	A1
Yerxa Rd	22	B2
York Pl	28	B2
York St	28	B2

Charlestown

Street	Page	Grid
13th St	8	A2
16th St	8	A2
1st Ave	8	B2
2nd Ave	8	A2/B2
3rd Ave	8	B2
3rd St	8	B2
5th Ave	8	B2
5th St	8	B2
6th St	8	B2
8th St	8	B2
9th St	8	B2
A St	25	B2
Adams St	8	A1
Albion Pl	25	B2
Alford St	25	A2
Allen Pl	25	B2
Allston St	25	A2
Arlington Ave	25	A2
Armory St	25	B2
Arrow St	8	B1
Auburn Ct	25	B2
Auburn Sq	25	B2
Auburn St		
(1-32)	25	B2
(33-99)	8	A1
Auburn Ter	8	B1
Austin St	8	A1
Avon St	8	A1
Avory Pl	8	A1
B St	25	B2
Badger Pl	8	A1
Baldwin St	25	A2/B2
Bartlett St	8	A1/B1
Beacham St	25	B2
Belmont St	8	A1
Biscoe Pl	8	A1
Blaban Pl	8	A1
Bolton Pl	8	A1
Boswell Ln	8	B1
Boyle St	8	A1
Brighton St	25	A1/A2
Bunker Hill Ct	8	A1
Bunker Hill St		
(1-392)	8	A1/B2
(393-499)	25	A2/B2
Bunker Hill Industrial Park	25	B2
C St	25	A1/A2
Caldwell St	25	A1/A2
Cambridge St	25	A2/B1/B2
Carney Ct	8	A1
Carter St	25	B2
Cary Pl	8	A1
Cedar St	8	B1
Central Pl	8	A1
Chappie St	25	B2
Charles St	8	B1
Charles River Ave	8	B1
Charles Street Pl	25	B2
Chelsea St	8	A2/B1/B2
Chestnut St	8	B1
Church Ct	8	B1
City Sq	8	B1
Clarken Ct	8	A1
Clinton Pl	25	A2
Common St	8	B1
Concord Ave	8	A1/B2
Concord St	8	A1
Constitution Rd	8	B1
Cook St	8	A1
Cook Street Ct	8	A1
Cook Street Pl	8	A1
Coral Pl	8	A1
Cordis St	8	B1
Cordis Street Ave	8	A2
Corey St	26	B1
Crafts St	25	A1/B1
Crescent St	8	B1
Cross St	8	B1
Crystal Pl	8	A1
Decatur St	8	A2/B2
Devens St	8	B1
Dexter Ct	8	B1
Dexter Row	8	B1
Dorrance St	25	A2
Dunstable St	8	A1/B1
East St	25	B2
Eden St	8	B1
Edgeworth	8	A1
Edwards St	25	A2
Ellwood St	8	B1
Elm St	8	A1/B1
Essex St		
(1-11)	8	A1
(12-99)	25	B1
Exeter Ct	8	A1
Exeter Pl	8	A1
Ferrin St	8	B1/B2
Forest Pl	8	A1
Franklin St	25	A2
Gardner St	25	B2
Gibbs Ct	8	A1
Grants Ct	8	A1
Green St	8	A1/B1
Gurnet Ct	25	B2
Hadley St	25	B1
Hamblen St	25	A1
Hancock St	8	B1
Harrison Pl	8	A1
Harvard Pl	8	B1
Harvard Sq	8	B1
Harvard St	8	B1
Hathon Sq	8	B1
Haverhill St	25	A2
Henley St	8	B1
Hickory Ln	8	B1
High St	8	A1/B1
Hilary St	8	B1
Hill St	8	A1
Hillside Pl	25	A2
Holden Row	8	B1
Holston St	8	A1
Howard St	8	B1
Hunter St	8	B2
Jefferson Ave	8	A1
Kingston St	25	A2
Kingston Pl	25	A2
Laurel St	8	B1
Lawnwood Pl	8	B1
Lawrence St	8	B1
Lexington Ave	8	A1
Lexington St	8	A1/B1
Lincoln Pl	8	A1
Ludlow St	8	A1
Lynde St	8	B1
Lyndeboro St	25	B2
Maffa Way	25	A2
Main St		
(1-368)	8	A1/B1
(369-699)	25	A2/B2

Street	Page	Grid
Marshall Pl	8	A1
Marshall Block	8	A1
Mason Ct	8	A1
McNulty Ct	8	A2
Mead St	8	A1
N Mead St	8	A1
Mead Street Ct	8	A1
Mead Street Ter	8	A1
Medford St		
(15-521)	8	A1/A2
(522-598)	25	A2
Middlesex St	25	A2
Mishawum St	25	B2
Monument Ave	8	B1
Monument Ct	8	B1
Monument Sq	8	B1
Monument St	8	A1/B1
Moosal Pl	25	A2
Moulton St	8	B2
Moulton Way	8	A2/B2
Mount Vernon Ave	8	B1
Mount Vernon St	8	B1
Mystic Ave	25	A1/A2
Mystic Pl	8	A1
Mystic St	8	A1
Neal Ct	25	A2
Nearen Row	8	A1
O'Brien Ct	8	A2
O'Meara Ct	8	A1
O'Reilly Way	8	A1/A2
Oak St	8	A2
Old Ironsides Way	8	A2
Old Landing Way	8	A2
Park St	8	B1
Parker St	25	A1/B1
Payson Pl	8	A1
Pearl St	8	A1
Pearl Street Pl	8	A1
Perkins St	25	A1/A2
Phipps St	8	B1
Pleasant St	8	B1
Pleasant Street Ct	8	B1
Polk St	8	A1
Prescott St	8	B1
Prospect Ave	8	B2
Prospect St	8	B1/B2
Putnam St	8	B1
N Quincy Pl	8	A1
S Quincy Pl	8	A1
Roland St	25	B1/B2
Russell St	8	A1
Rutherford Ave		
(1-341)	8	A1
(343-699)	25	A2/B2
Sackville St	8	A1
Saint Martin St	8	A1
Salem St	8	A1
Salem Hill Ct	8	A1
Salem Street Ave	8	A1
Samuel Morse Way	8	A2
School St	8	A1/B1
School House Ct	25	B2
School Street Pl	8	A1
Seminary St	8	B1
Sever St	25	A2
Sheafe St	8	A1
Sherman Sq	25	A2
Sherman St	25	A2
Shipway Pl	8	A2
Short St	25	A2
Short St Pl	25	A2
Short Street Pl	25	A2
Simpson Ct	8	A1
Soley St	8	B1
Spice St	25	A2

Street	Page	Grid
Stacey St	8	B1
Starr King Ct	8	A2
Sullivan St	8	A1
Summer St	8	A1
Temple St	25	A2
Terminal St	8	A1/A2
Thompson St	8	B1
Thorndike St	25	B2
Tibbetts Town Way		
(1-44)	8	A1
(45-99)	25	B2
Tremont St	8	B1/B2
Trenton St	8	A1
Tufts St	8	A2/B2
Union St	8	B1
Vendon Pl	8	B1
Vine St	8	B2
Walford Way	8	A1/A2
Walker St	8	A1
Wall St	8	A1
Wallace Ct	8	B1
Warren St	8	B1
Washington Pl	8	B1
Washington St	8	B1
Webster Ct	8	A1
Wellington Pl	8	A1
Wesley St	8	B1
West St	25	A2
West School St	8	B1
Winthrop St	8	B1
Wistar Pl	8	A1
Wood St	8	B1
Woods Pl	8	A1

Somerville

Street	Page	Grid
1st Ave	25	B1
3rd Ave	25	B1
A Alfred Lombardi St	25	A1/A2
Aberdeen Rd	23	A1
Acadia Park	23	B1
Adams St	23	A2
Adelaide Rd	23	B1
Adrian St	28	A1
Albion Ct	23	A2
Albion Pl	23	A2
Albion St	23	A1/A2/B2
E Albion St	24	A1
Albion Ter	23	A2
Aldersey St	24	B1
Aldrich St	24	B1/B2
Allen Ct	23	B2
Allen St	28	A2
Alpine St	23	A1/A2
Alston St	24	B2
Ames St	23	A2
Appleton St	23	A1
Arlington St	25	A1
Arnold Ave	23	B1
Arnold Ct	23	B2
Ash Ave	24	A1
Ashland St	23	B1
Assembly Square Dr	24	A2
Atherton St	23	B2
Auburn Ave	24	B2
Austin St	25	A1
Autumn St	24	B2
Avon Pl	24	B2
Avon St	23	B2
Bailey Rd	24	A2
Ball Sq	23	A1
Banks St	23	A1
Bartlett St	23	A2
Bay State Ave	23	A1
Beach Ave	28	A2

Street	Page	Grid
Beacon Pl	28	A1
Beacon St		
(1-212)	28	A1
(213-399)	23	B1/B2
Beacon Ter	23	B1
Beckwith Cir	23	B1
Bedford St	28	A2/B2
Belknap St	22	A2
Belmont Pl	23	B2
Belmont Sq	23	B2
Belmont St	23	B1/B2
Belmont Ter	23	B2
Benedict Ave	25	A1
Benedict St	25	A1
Bennett Ct	28	A2
Bennett St	28	A2
Benton Rd	23	B2
Berkeley St	23	B2
Berwick St	23	A2
Bigelow St	24	B1
Billingham St	23	A1
Bishops Pl	24	B2
Blakeley Ave	23	A2
Bleachery Ct	23	B2
Bolton St	28	A2
Bonair St	24	B1/B2
Bond St	24	A1
Bonner Ave	24	B1
Boston Ave	23	A1/A2
Boston St	24	B1/B2
Bow St	24	B1
Bow Street Pl	24	B1
Bowdoin St	24	B1
Bowers Ave	22	B2
Bradford Ave	24	A1
Bradley St	24	B1
Braemore Rd	23	A2
Brastow Ave	23	B1
Bristol Rd	23	A1
Broadway		
(1-101)	25	A1
(102-413)	24	A1/A2/B2
(414-990)	23	A1/A2
(991-1292)	22	A2
Broadway Pl	25	A1
Bromfield Rd	23	A1
Brook St	24	B2
Browning Rd	24	A1
Buckingham St	28	A1
Buena Vista Rd	22	A2
Burnham St	23	A1
Burnside Ave	23	A1
Butler Dr	24	A2
Cady Ave	22	A2
Caldwell Ave	28	A1
Calvin St	28	A1
Cambria St	23	B2
Cameron Ave	22	A2
Campbell Park	22	A2
Campbell Park Pl	22	A2
Canal Ln	24	A1
Carlton St	24	B1
Carter Ter	23	B2
Carver St	23	B1
Cedar Ave	23	B1
Cedar Pl	23	B1
Cedar St	23	A1/A2/B2
Cedar Street Pl	23	B1
Central Av	23	B2
Central St		
(1-164)	23	A2/B2
(165-299)	24	A1
Centre St	23	B2
Century St	24	A1

Street Index

Street	Page	Grid
Chandler St		
(1-51)	22	A2
(52-99)	23	A1
Chapel St	23	A1
Charles E Ryan Rd	23	A2
Charlestown St	28	A2
Charnwood Rd	23	A1
Cherry St	23	A1/B1
Chester Ave	24	B2
Chester Pl	22	B2
Chestnut St	25	B1
Church St	24	B1
Claremon St	22	A2
Clarendon Ave	22	A1/A2
Clark St	28	A2
Cleveland St	23	B2
Clifton St	23	A1
Clyde St	23	A2
Cobble Hill Rd	24	B2
College Ave	23	A1
Colon Ct	28	A2
Columbia Ct	28	A2
Columbus Ave	24	B1
Concord Ave	28	A1/A2
Connecticut Ave	24	A2
Conwell St	23	B1
Cooney St	28	A1
Corinthian Rd	22	A2
Cottage Ave		
(1-8)	23	A1
(9-99)	22	B2
Cottage Cir	23	A1
Craigie St	23	B1
Craigie Ter	23	B1
Cresthill Rd	24	A2
Crocker St	23	B2
Cross Pl	24	B2
Cross St	24	B2
Cross St E	24	A2/B2
Crown St	23	B1/B2
Cummings St	24	A2
Curtis St	22	A2
Cutler St	23	A2
Cutter Ave	24	B2
Cutter St	23	A1
Cutter Park	23	B2
Cypress St	24	B2
Dana St	24	B2
Dane Ave	23	B2
Dane St	23	B2
Dante Ter	23	B1
Dartmouth St	24	A1
Davis Sq	22	A2
Delaware St	24	B2
Dell St	24	B2
Derby St	24	A2
Dickinson St	28	A1/B2
Dickson St	22	A2
Dimick St	28	A1
Direnzo Ter	23	B2
Douglas Ave	24	A1
Dow St	22	A2
Dresden Cir	23	A1
Durham St	28	A1
Earle St	28	A2
Eastman Rd	23	A1
Edgar Ave	23	A1
Edgar Ct	24	A1
Edgar Ter	24	A1
Edmands St	22	A2
Electric Ave	23	B2
Eliot St	23	A2
Ellington Rd	23	A1
Ellsworth St	24	B2
Elm Ct	23	A1
Elm Pl	23	B2
Elm St		
(1-263)	23	A1/B1
(264-299)	22	A2
Elmwood St	22	A2
Elmwood Ter	22	A2
Elston St	23	A1
Emerson St	28	A2
Endicott Ave	22	A1
Essex St	24	B1
Everett Ave	24	B2
Everett St	28	A2
Evergreen Ave	24	A1
Evergreen Sq	23	B1
Fairlee St	23	A2
Fairmount Ave	22	A2
Fairview Ter	24	A1
Farragut Ave	22	A1
Fellsway	24	B2
Fellsway W	24	A2
Fennell St	23	A2
Fenwick St	24	A1
Fisk Ave	23	A2
Fitchburg St	25	B1
Flint Ave	24	B2
Flint St	24	B2
Florence St	25	A1/B1
Florence Ter	24	A1
Foley St	24	A1
Forster St	23	A1
Foskett St	23	A1
Fountain Ave	24	B2
Francesca Ave	23	A1
Francis St	23	B1
Franey Rd	23	A2
Franklin Ave	24	B2
Franklin Pl	24	B2
Franklin St		
(1-24)	25	A1
(25-199)	24	B2
Fremont Ave	24	B1
Fremont St	24	A1
Garden Ct	23	B2
Garfield Ave	24	A2
Garrison Ave	22	A1
George St	25	A1
Gibbens St	23	B2
Giles Park	24	B1
Gilman St	24	B1/B2
Gilman Ter	24	B1
Gilson Ter	23	B1
Glen St	23	B2
Glendale Ave	22	A2
Glenwood Rd	23	A2
Glover Ct	22	A2
Gorham St	23	B1
Gould Ave	24	A2
Governor Winthrop Rd	24	A2
Grandview Ave	24	B1
Granite St	23	B2
Grant St	24	A2
Greene St	23	B2
Greenville Ct	24	B1
Greenville St	24	B1
Greenville Ter	23	B1
Greenwood Ter	23	A1
Grove St	23	B1
Gussie Ter	24	B2
Hadley Ct	23	A1
Hall Ave	23	A1
Hall St	24	B1
Hamlet St	23	A1
Hammond St	28	A1
Hancock St	23	A1
Hanson Ave	23	B2
Hanson St		
(1-45)	23	B2
(46-99)	28	A1
Hardan Rd	22	A2
Harold St	28	A1
Harrison Rd	22	A2
Harrison St	23	B2
Harvard Pl	23	B2
Hathorn St	25	A1
Hawkins St	24	B1
Hawthorne St	23	A1
Hayden Ter	23	B1
Heath St	24	A1
Henderson St	23	A2
Henry Ave	23	A1
Herbert St	22	A2/B2
Hersey St	23	B2
Higgins Ct	25	B1
Highland Ave		
(1-95)	24	B1
(96-499)	23	A1/B1/B2
Highland Rd	23	A1
Hill St	22	A2
Hillside Ave	24	B2
Hillside Cir	23	B1
Hillside Park	24	B1
Hinckley St	23	A2
Hodgdon Pl	23	B2
Holland St	22	A2
Holts Ave	28	A2
Holyoke St	23	B1
Homer Sq	24	B1
Hooker Ave	22	A1
Horace St	28	A2
Houghton St	28	A1/A2
Howard St	22	A2
Howe St	24	A1
Hudson St	23	A1/A2/B2
Ibbetson St	23	B1
Illinois Ave	24	B2
Indiana Ave	25	A1
Inner Belt Rd	25	B1
Irving St	22	A2
Ivaloo St	23	B2
Jackson Rd	24	B1
James St	24	B1
Jaques St	24	A1/A2
Jasper St	24	B1
Jay St	22	A2
Jerome Ct	24	B1
Jerome St	24	B1
Joseph St	28	A2
Josephine Ave	23	A1
Joy St	24	B2
Kenneson Rd	24	A2
Kensington Ave	24	A1
Kent Ct	23	B1
Kent St	23	B1/B2
Kenwood St	23	A1
Kidder Ave	23	A1
Kilby St	23	B1
Kimball St	24	B1
Kingman Rd	23	A1
Kingston St	22	A2
Knapp St	23	B2
Knowlton St	24	B2
Lake St	24	B2
Landers St	23	B2
Langmaid Ave	24	A1
Laurel Ave	23	B2
Laurel St	23	B2
Laurel Ter	23	B2
Lawson Ter	24	B1
Lee St	24	A1
Leland St	23	B2

Street Index

Street	Page	Grid
Leon St	28	A1
Leonard St	23	A1
Lesley Ave	23	A1
Lester Ter	22	A2
Lewis St	28	A1
Lexington Ave	23	A1
Liberty Ave	23	A1
Lincoln Ave	25	A1
Lincoln Pky	28	A1/A2
Lincoln Pl	25	A1
Lincoln St	25	A1
Linden Ave	23	B1
Linden Cir	23	B1
Linden Pl	23	B1
Linden St	28	A2
Linwood St		
(1-99)	25	B1
(100-199)	28	A2
Loring St	23	B2
Louisburg Pl	24	B2
Lovell St	22	A2
Lowden Ave	23	A1
Lowell Cir	23	B2
Lowell St	23	A2/B1/B2
Lowell Ter	23	A2
MacArthur St	24	B2
Madison St	23	B2
Magnus Ave		
(1-40)	23	B2
(41-99)	28	A1
Main St		
(23-50)	24	A1
(51-699)	23	A2
Maine Ave	25	A1
Maine Ter	25	A1
Mallet St	23	A1
Malloy Ct	28	A2
Malvern Ave	22	A2
Mansfield St	24	B2
Maple Ave	24	A1
Mardell Cir	23	B2
Marion St	28	A1/B2
Marshall St	24	A1/B1
Marshall St Cir	24	A1
Mason St		
(1-17)	22	A2
(18-99)	23	A1
May Pl	24	B1
McGrath Hwy		
(1-181)	25	B1
(182-324)	28	A2
(325-899)	24	A2/A2/B2
Meacham St	24	A1
Mead St	22	A2/B2
Medford St		
(1-99)	28	B2/B2
(249-421)	24	A1/B1
Melville Rd	24	A2
Melvin St	24	B2
Memorial Rd	24	A1
Merriam Ave	28	A2
Merriam St		
(1-54)	28	A2
(55-99)	24	B1
Michigan Ave	24	B2
Middlesex Ave	24	A2
Milk Pl	28	A2
Miller St	23	B1
Miner St	23	A2
Minnesota Ave	24	B2
Mondamin St	23	B2
Monmouth St	23	B2
Montgomery Ave	24	A2
Montrose Ct	24	B1
Montrose St		
(1-45)	24	B1
(46-59)	23	B2
Moore St	22	A2
Moreland St	24	A1
Morgan St	23	B2
Morrison Ave	23	A1
Morrison Pl	23	A1
Mortimer Pl	24	A1
Morton St	24	B2
Mossland St	23	B1
Mount Pleasant Ct	25	A1
Mount Pleasant St	25	A1
Mount Vernon St	25	A1/B1
Mountain Ave	23	B1
Munroe St	24	B1
Murdock St	23	A2
Museum St	23	B1
Myrtle Ct	25	B1
Myrtle St	25	A1/B1
Mystic Ave	24	A1/A2
Nashua St	23	A2
Nevada Ave	23	B2
New Rd	25	A1
New Hampshire Ave	25	A1
New Washington St		
(1-37)	24	B2
(38-99)	25	B1
Newberne St	23	A1
Newbury St	22	A2
Newman St	23	A2
Newton Pl	28	A2
Newton St	28	A2
Norwood Ave	23	A2
Oak Ter	23	B1
Oak Street Pl	28	A2
Oakland Ave	24	A1
Olive Ave	23	B1
Olive Sq	24	B1
Oliver St	24	B2
Orchard St	22	A2/B2
Osgood St	23	B2
Ossipee Rd	22	A2
Otis St	24	B2
Oxford St	23	B1/B2
Packard Ave	22	A2
Palmer Ave	24	B2
Park Ave	22	A2
Park Pl	23	B2
Park St	23	B2
Parkdale St	24	B1
Parker Pl	23	B1
Parker St	24	B1
Partridge Ave	23	A2
Pattern Ct	24	B2
Paulina St	22	A2
Pearl St		
(1-60)	25	A1
(61-267)	24	B1/B2
Pearl Ter	24	B2
Pearl Street Pl	24	B2
Pearson Ave	23	A1
Pearson Rd	23	A1
Pembroke Ct	23	B2
Pembroke St	23	B2
Pennsylvania Ave		
(1-72)	25	A1
(73-199)	24	B2
Perry St	24	B1
Peterson Ter	23	B1
Phillips Pl	23	B2
Pinckney St	25	A1/B1
Pitman St	23	B1
Pleasant Ave	24	B1
Poplar St	28	A2
Porter Ave	23	B1
Porter St	23	B1
Powder House Blvd	23	A1
Powder House Sq	23	A1
Powder House Ter	23	A1
Prescott St	24	B1
Preston Rd	23	A1
Prichard Ave	23	A1
Princeton St	23	A2
Properzi Way	23	B2
Prospect St	28	A2
Prospect Hill Ave	24	B1/B2
Prospect Hill Pky	24	B1
Puritan Rd	24	A2
Putnam Rd	24	A2
Putnam St	24	B1
Quincy St	24	B1
Radcliffe Rd	24	B2
Randolph St	24	A1
Record Ct	24	A1
Reeds Ct	24	B2
Remick Ct	24	B2
Rhode Island Ave	24	A2
Richardson St	23	A2
Richardson Ter	23	A2
Richdale Ave	24	A1/B1
River Rd	24	A1
Roberts St	23	A2
Robinson St	23	A2
Rogers Ave	23	A1
Rose St	23	B2
Rossmore St	24	B2
Royce Pl	24	B2
Rush St	24	B2
Russell Rd	22	A2
Sanborn Ave	24	B1
Sanborn Ct	24	B1
Sargent Ave	24	A1
Sartwell Ave	23	B1
School St	24	A1/B1
Sellon Pl	24	B1
Seven Hills Park	22	A2
Seven Pines Ave	22	A2
Sewall Ct	24	A1
Sewall St	24	A1/A2
Shawmut St	24	B2
Shedd St	28	A2
Sherborn St	23	A2
Sherman St	24	A1
Shore Dr	24	A2
Sibley Ct	24	B2
Sibley Pl	24	B2
Silvey Pl	23	B1
Simpson Ave	22	A2
Skehan St	23	B2
Skilton Ave	24	B1
Smith Ave	28	A1
Snow Ter	24	A1
Somerville Ave		
(101-274)	28	A2
(275-438)	24	B1
(439-899)	23	B1/B2
South St	28	A2
Spencer Ave	23	A1
Spring St	23	B2
Spring Hill Ter	23	B2
St Clements Rd	23	A1
St James Ave	23	A1
Stanford Ter	23	B1
Steeves Cir	23	B1
Stickney Ave	24	B1
Stone Ave	23	B1
Stone Pl	24	B1
Sturtevant St	25	A1/A2

Street Index

Street	Page	Grid
Summer St		
(1-67)	24	B1
(68-399)	23	A1/B1/B2
Summit Ave	24	B1
Summit St	23	A1
Sunnyside Ave	24	B1
Sycamore St		
(1-44)	23	B2
(45-199)	24	A1/B1
Sycamore Ter	24	A1
Sydney St	24	A2
Taunton St	28	A1
Taylor St	24	A2
Temple Rd	24	A2
Temple St	24	A1/A2
Ten Hills Rd	24	A2
Tennyson St		
(1-22)	23	B2
(23-99)	24	A1
Thorndike St	24	B1
Thorpe St	24	A1
Thurston St	24	A1
Tower Ct	23	B2
Tower St	23	B2
Tremont Pl	28	A2
Trull Ln	23	B2
Trull St	23	A2
Tufts St	24	B2
Turner Ct	24	B2
Tyler Ct	23	B2
Tyler St	23	B2
Union Sq	24	B1
N Union St	25	A1/A2
Upland Park	23	A2
Vermont Ave	24	B2
Vernon St	23	A2/B2
Victoria St	22	A1
Village St	23	B2
Village Ter	23	B2
Vinal Ave	24	B1
Vinal St	23	A2
Vine Ct	23	B2
Virginia St	24	B1
Wade Ct	23	B1
Waldo Ave	28	A1
Waldo St	23	B2
Walker St	23	A1
Wallace St	22	A2
Walnut Rd	24	A1
Walnut St	24	A2/B1
Walter Ter	24	B1
Ward St	28	A2
Ware St	22	A2
Warner St	23	A1
Warren Ave	24	B1
Warwick St	23	A1
Washington Ave	25	B1
Washington St		
(1-80)	25	B1
(81-339)	24	B1/B2
(340-375)	23	B2
(376-441)	28	A1
Washington Ter	24	B1
Water St	28	A2
Watson St	22	A2
Webster Ave	28	A2/B2
Webster St	24	B2
Wellington Ave	24	A2/B2
Wesley St	24	B2
Wesley Park	24	B1
West St	23	A1
Westminster St	22	A2
Weston Ave	22	A2
Westwood Rd	23	B2
Wheatland St	24	A2
Wheeler St	25	A1
Whipple St	23	B1
White Street Pl	23	B1
Whitman St	22	A2
Wigglesworth St	24	B1/B2
Williams Ct	23	B1
Willoughby St	23	B2
Willow Ave	23	A1
Wilson Ave	23	A2
Wilton St	23	A2
Windom St	23	A1
Windsor Pl	28	A2
Windsor Rd	23	A1
Winslow Ave	23	A1
Winter St	22	A2
Winter Hill Cir	24	A1
Wisconsin Ave	24	B2
Woodbine St	23	A2
Woodstock St	22	A1
Wyatt Cir	28	A1
Wyatt St	28	A1
Yorktown St	22	A2